Human Rights from a Third World Perspective: Critique, History and International Law

Human Rights from a Third World Perspective: Critique, History and International Law

Edited by

José-Manuel Barreto

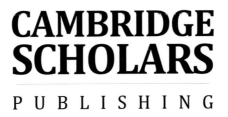

CAMBRIDGE
SCHOLARS
PUBLISHING

Human Rights from a Third World Perspective:
Critique, History and International Law
Edited by José-Manuel Barreto

This book first published 2013

Cambridge Scholars Publishing

12 Back Chapman Street, Newcastle upon Tyne, NE6 2XX, UK

British Library Cataloguing in Publication Data
A catalogue record for this book is available from the British Library

ISBN (10): 1-4438-4058-0, ISBN (13): 978-1-4438-4058-3

[let's imagine a universe—or a human rights field as] 'a sphere whose center is everywhere and the circumference nowhere'
—Jorge Luis Borges, or Pascal

'The future demands thinking beyond the Greeks and Eurocentrism' and 'a radical reconceptualisation of the human rights paradigm'
—Walter Mignolo

TABLE OF CONTENTS

Part III: Decolonizing Constitutional and International Human Rights Law

ACKNOWLEDGEMENTS

The editor and the publishers would like to thank the following for permission to reprint their material:

Fernando Botero and Marlborough Gallery for permission to reproduce the work entitled *Abu Ghraib 75*: © Fernando Botero, courtesy Marlborough Gallery, New York.

Review of Constitutional Studies for permission to reprint a shortened version of William Twining, "Human Rights, Southern Voices: Francis Deng, Abdullahi An-Na'im, Yash Ghai and Upendra Baxi,," *Review of Constitutional Studies* 11 (2006): 203-279.

Hispanic Issues On Line for permission to reprint Walter Mignolo, 2009: "Who Speaks for the 'Human' in Human Rights?" *Human Rights in Latin American and Iberian Cultures*. Ed. Ana Forcinito, Raúl Marrero-Fente, and Kelly McDonough. *Hispanic Issues On Line* 5:1, (Fall) 7–24.

Sur – International Journal of Human Rights for permission to reprint Upendra Baxi, 2007: "The Rule of Law in India," *Sur – International Journal of Human Rights*, 4:6, 6-27. Under Creative Commons 2.5 license.

Sur – International Journal of Human Rights for permission to reprint Nico Horn, 2005: "Eddie Mabo and Namibia: Land Reform and Precolonial Land Rights," *Sur – International Journal of Human Rights*, 2:3, 81-93. Under Creative Commons 2.5 license.

The Johns Hopkins University Press for permission to reprint Susan Eileen Waltz, 2001: "Universalizing Human Rights: The Role of Small States in the Construction of the Universal Declaration of Human Rights." *Human Rights Quarterly* 23:1, 44-72. © 2001 The Johns Hopkins University Press.

The Johns Hopkins University Press for permission to reprint Zehra F. Kabasakal Arat, 2006: "Forging a Global Culture of Human Rights: Origins and Prospects of the International Bill of Rights." *Human Rights Quarterly* 28:2, 416-437. © 2006 The Johns Hopkins University Press.

Introduction

Decolonial Strategies and Dialogue in the Human Rights Field

José-Manuel Barreto

Some Christians encountered an Indian woman, who was carrying in her arms a child at suck; and since the dog they had with them was hungry, they tore the child from the mother's arms and flung it still living to the dog, which proceeded to devour him before the mother's eyes.
—Bartolomé de las Casas

A dog trained to attack the flesh, and torture, kill, and gorge a man and a child in front of the mother connects Fernando Botero's *Abu Grahib* with Bartolomé de las Casas' *Short Account of the Destruction of the Indies*. In this scenario of colonial wars a dog is turned into a beast—a torture dog or a war dog—by the inhumanity of conquistadors and invaders. The dog becomes a powerful machine for terrorizing and destroying the body, and for dehumanizing the colonized—and the colonizer. Five hundred years apart these two images or stories are bind together by their origin: the history of the advance of modern imperialism, and the sensibility of their authors for the suffering of the victims. The violence and dread of these events resonates in the global consciousness and moral sentiment of our times. It is the drive for survival and dignity, the consciousness about the imperative for independence and justice, and the sympathy for the victims what has brought natural or human rights to bear the force of such a capacity for destruction.

Botero's *Abu Grahib* paintings are placed in the collision-point where the current wave of imperial mobilization meets the world-wide urge and stand for human dignity, and are taken to the forefront of human rights discussion by Eduardo Mendieta (Chapter 4). Setting the scenario for this collection of essays, Mendieta's interpretation of Botero's work relies on the notion of "empathic vision"—"a conjunction of affective and critical ways of looking".[1] A door is opened here towards a marriage of intellection and emotion, suggesting perhaps one of those "lost paths for thinking". Where does the power of representation in Botero's *Abu Grahib* reside? The series makes visible the humanity denied to the vanquished—it reveals "the humanity of those who are not allowed to be represented as humans". By the power of unflinching vision Botero rescues from old newspapers, and for moral and political history, images that depict the human/bodily dignity being trashed by the "physicality of torture", and brings to light some of the deliberate—not collateral—effects of contemporary imperialism.

The body of the victims is trapped within the logic of war—the imperial logic—and torture and suffering are placed in front of everybody to be recognized as blatant "embodiments" of neo-colonialism. For Mendieta, Botero's *Abu Grahib* poses a set of questions for the analysis of biopolitical power beyond the conventional understanding of biopolitics and the biopolitical state, namely the biopolitical empire or the biopolitics of imperialism. In addition, Botero's Abu Grahib enables the spectators "to feel morally while seeing". The power of these paintings resides in a capacity for eliciting moral emotions like outrage and sympathy from the public in its different instantiations—the national public opinions and civil societies, the international community, the citizens or the peoples of the world, the global sentiment or the structure of feeling of our epoch. By teaching how to be witness of human suffering and enabling present and future viewers to be moral subjects, Mendieta says, Botero constructs a morality out of "ways of seeing and feeling"—a truthful "moral optics".

But what do we mean when we decide to embrace the quest to decolonize human rights? We have here in mind a particular form of critique, Decolonial Theory, which has been developed by Latin American thinkers out of concepts gained in the fields of the philosophy of history, social theory and epistemology. Modernity cannot be identified exclusively with emancipation, the Renaissance and the Enlightenment, but it is also historically evident that colonialism was another of its central foundations. The conventional conception of modernity needs to be revisited to accommodate the legacy of modern imperialism: the conquest

---

[1] Jill Bennett, *Empathic Vision: Affect, Trauma, and Contemporary Art* (Stanford: Stanford University Press, 2005).

and colonization of the world—a vast enterprise of domination marshaled through wars of aggression, genocides, slavery, plunder and exploitation.[2]

Decolonial Theory has also elaborated a "geopolitics of knowledge", an epistemology that can be characterized as materialist, in contradistinction to the transcendental or idealist dialectics between subject and object in the ambit of the consciousness—as in Descartes, Kant and Hegel's subjectivism. The geopolitics of knowledge is a contextualist epistemology in as much as it finds in politics and history the grounds of knowledge. However, the geopolitics of knowledge does not locate the source of "truth" in a socioeconomic framework with implicit national borders, but in the milieu of the history of the modern world considered as a whole—it departs from the history of world capitalism or, what is the same, modern imperialism, ie the history of the relations between empires and colonies since the late Fifteenth century. In this view, the history of modern ideas— modern rationality itself, conceptions of the state, even Marxist and other critiques of capitalism—runs interrelated to the history of modern imperialism. For a geopolitical analysis of knowledge, the cultural colonization of world civilizations, rationalities and intellectual disciplines ended in the crucial assumption according to which the origin of legitimate thinking is confined to a certain geopolitical location—Europe—excluding the existence of other sites of knowledge generation.[3]

The way human rights are commonly understood is a consequence of this dynamic. Egotism has blinded Europe. Being born out of European events and schools of thinking, the standard theory of human rights ignores or rejects the possibility of non-Eurocentric or Third-World approaches. The decolonization of human rights can be seen as part of the wider task of decolonizing knowledge. The decolonization of the humanities, the social sciences and culture in general is both an intellectual and political project that emerges from the standpoint of the Third World, and aims at opposing colonialism and abuse of power. The quest to decolonize human rights can be summed up in two statements made by Walter Mignolo: "the future demands thinking beyond the

---

[2] Arturo Escobar centers his analysis of the main features of Decolonial Theory in the re-conceptualization of the conventional notion of modernity. See Arturo Escobar, "Worlds and Knowledges Otherwise," *Cultural Studies* 21 (2007).
[3] Walter Mignolo, "The Geopolitics of Knowledge and the Colonial Difference," *The South Atlantic Quarterly* 101 (2002), 59 & 63-74.

Greeks and eurocentrism"[4] and "a radical reconceptualization of the human rights paradigm",[5] so that human rights continue to be a hindrance to imperial projects today and in the future.

The development of the critique of Eurocentrism has antecedents in the five hundred year-long resistance to modern imperialism. From the late Twentieth century onwards it has been renovated and strengthened by a number of schools of thinking, among them Postcolonial Theory and Orientalism, Subaltern Studies, Decolonial Theory, Critical Race Theory, Black Radical Theory, Black Atlantic Studies and Third World Feminism. Within this epochal stream of thinking, some insights developed by the Third World Approach to International Law (TWAIL)[6] are especially relevant for the construction of a Third-World interpretation of human rights. In a fruitful dialogue with a marginal strand of the Western tradition of international law that runs throughout the writings of James Brown-Scott[7], Carl Schmitt[8] and David Kennedy[9], Antony Anghie has shown how the modern tradition of international law was not developed exclusively from the writings of Grotius, Pufendorf and Vattel, and from

---

[4] Walter Mignolo, "Philosophy and the Colonial Difference," in *Latin American Philosophy*, ed. Eduardo Mendieta (Bloomington and Indiana: Indiana University Press, 2003), 85.

[5] Walter Mignolo, "The Many Faces of Cosmo-polis: Border Thinking and Critical Cosmopolitanism," *Public Culture* 12 (2000): 739.

[6] Balakrishnan Rajagopal has examined the capacity of human rights for working as a counter-hegemonic force in world politics. See B. Rajagopal, "Counter-hegemonic International Law: Rethinking Human Rights and Development as a Third World Strategy," *Third World Quarterly* 27 (2006), 767-783. In the same horizon of questioning see U. Baxi, "What may the 'Third World' Expect from International Law?" *Third World Quarterly* 27 (2006), 713-725; O. Chinedu, "Poverty, Agency and Resistance in the Future of International Law: An African Perspective," *Third World Quarterly* 27 (2006), 799-814; I. Mgbeoji, "The Civilised Self and the Barbaric Other: Imperial Delusions of Order and the Challenges of Human Security," *Third World Quarterly* 27 (2006), 855-869; and V. Nesiah, "Resistance in the Age of Empire: Occupied Discourse Pending Investigation," *Third World Quarterly* 27 (2006), 903-922. More recently, Sundhya Pahuja, *Decolonising International Law: Development, Economic Growth and the Politics of Universality* (Cambridge: CUP, 2011).

[7] James Brown-Scott, *The Spanish Origin of International Law: Francisco de Vitoria and His Law of Nations* (Oxford: Clarendon Press, 1934).

[8] Carl Schmitt, *The Nomos of the Earth in the International Law of Jus Publicum Europaeum* (New York: Telos Press, 2006).

[9] David Kennedy, "Primitive Legal Scholarship," *Harvard International Law Journal* 27 (1986), 1-98.

dealing with the problem of regulating relations between European sovereign powers. The modern law of nations also has its origins in the expansion of Europe and the colonization of the world, a theoretical and historical scenario that gave birth to the works of Francisco de Vitoria.[10]

Seeking to combine critical consciousness and moral sensibility, this preface focuses on methods of interpretation or hermeneutical strategies that have already advanced, and can continue to support, the project of decolonizing human rights. In emphasizing new analyses and perspectives that enable us to decipher the deceptions and biases at work in Eurocentric understandings of the subject, this introduction provides a tool-box for creating new decolonial or Third-World discourses. Towards the end of this Introduction, an overview of the topics investigated in this book and how they are organized will be offered.

Critique of Eurocentrism and the Third World Perspective on Human Rights

The labor of constructing a Third World interpretation of human rights entails a departure from Eurocentric theories, i.e. the corpus of today's dominant conceptualizations of rights inspired by different schools of thought, among them modern—Contractarian, Kantian, Hegelian, Marxist—and postmodern theories of human rights. Pointing to the Eurocentric character of a certain body of knowledge is simultaneously an epistemological and a geopolitical issue, as it comprises the unveiling of a genealogical link between knowledge and history. Inasmuch as such a

---

[10] Antony Anghie, 'Colonial Origins of International Law', in E. Darian-Smith and P. Fitzpatrick, eds, Laws of the Postcolonial (Ann Arbor: University of Michigan Press, 1999), 89-90. This debate has been enriched by contributions from scholars such as Fitzpatrick, Kochi and Koskenniemi, who work from the perspective of the European Critical Legal Studies. Peter Fitzpatrick, "Latin Roots: Imperialism and the Making of International Law," in *Law as Resistance: Modernism, Imperialism, Legalism* (London: Ashgate, 2008). Tarik Kochi, The Other's War: Recognition and the Violence of Ethics (London: Birkbeck Law Press, 2009). Martti Koskenniemi, "Colonization of the 'Indies': The Origin of International Law?" in *La idea de América en el Pensamiento Ius Internacionalista del Siglo XXI*, ed. Yolanda Gamarra (Zaragoza: Institución Fernando el Católico, 2010), and "Empire and International Law: The Real Spanish Contribution," *University of Toronto Law Journal* 61 (2011), 1-38. Koskenniemi includes within this tradition the work of Ernest Nys, in particular his *Les Origins Du Droit International* (Charleston: Nabu Press, 2012).

connection is made, it is evident that the hegemonic theory of human rights is the offspring of a particular perspective grounded on a historical and geographical context. As such, modern and postmodern theories of rights that inform today's scholarly debate and orientate activism are to be seen as a few among the various contingent possibilities for understanding rights.[11] These theories conflate a wealth of perspectives on rights, as well as the limitations proper to the space and time coordinates the European epistemic standing point and the European philosophical understanding of history. In consequence, they are biased conceptions and partial accounts of the history of human rights.[12]

However, the Eurocentric theory of human rights presents itself as objective and universal and, while it assumes exclusive authority and legitimacy, it condemns a Third World approach to impossibility or silence.[13] Hiding crucial aspects of their genealogy, the eurocentric theories of rights afford little or no significance to the history of the relations between modern empires and colonies or the Third World. This predisposition is accompanied by a tendency to give a notorious and unfair weight to the events occurring in Europe. This is the case in Hegel's philosophical notion of "universal history", from which Asia, Africa and the Americas are excluded.[14] By framing human rights in conceptions of history based exclusively on European milestones the theory of rights remains within a Eurocentric horizon of understanding. Having been born out of the experience of bourgeois revolutions, European theories of human rights deal mainly with relations between state and society, or between governments and individuals, putting aside the problematic of interactions between empires and colonies.

The critique of Eurocentrism and the challenge to its hegemony do not just thematize the question of the "what"—human rights as the object of reflection; it is also and mainly concerned with interrogations about the

---

[11] Peter Beardsell, *Europe and Latin America: Returning the Gaze* (Manchester: MUP, 2000), 35-37.

[12] The question of Eurocentrism has also been seen as a relevant issue for international law from a European perspective. See Martti Koskenniemi, "Histories of International Law: Dealing with Eurocentrism," *Rechts Geschichte-Zeitschrift des Max-Planck-Instituts für europäische Rechtsgeschichte* 19 (2011), 152-176.

[13] Arturo Escobar, "Imperial Globality and Anti-Globalisation Movements," *Third World Quarterly* 25 (2004): 210.

[14] G.W.F. Hegel, *The Philosophy of History* (Mineola: Dover Publications, 1956), 8-102.

"for whom", "what for" and "from where"—the geopolitical context in which human rights theories are elaborated—and develops a self-understanding of the historical framework in which they are enunciated—Twentieth century, Post-Holocaust or Post-Conquest history. This hermeneutical and geopolitical reflection creates the possibility of thinking of human rights from the "stand point" of those in the South and of setting up decolonial goals. A Third World approach to human rights arises from another geographical space and a different historical horizon of understanding—from the "exteriority" of Europe, an outside that is inextricable from the inside and thus constitutes it.[15]

This distinct historical and geopolitical background can modify the terms, concepts and agenda of the theory and practice of human rights. The interpreter is also conscious of the fact that her perspective—that of the Third World—stands at variance with another perspective—that of Europe. The critique occurs in this shifting of viewpoints, which at the same time creates the conditions for attempting a novel and independent approach to the tradition of natural and human rights, as well as for making possible a dialogue between these two points of view. It encompasses a different interpretation of the philosophy of history in which human rights theory has been customarily or implicitly based on, and gives birth to a new paradigm in which the events of the Conquest of America and the colonization of the world are also recognized as key signposts of modern history. Developing a new version of the history of rights in the context of world history, it brings into consciousness five hundred years of utopian mobilization of natural rights, the Rights of Man and human rights to resist imperialism.

Re-contextualization and Contextualization of Human Rights

The interpretative tool of re-contextualization also can advance the project of decolonizing human rights theory. Drawing from hermeneutics, Rorty adopted a contextualist notion of knowledge, a conception in which 'meaning is a function of context'. In Rorty's Neopragmatic hermeneutics, contextualism is the consequence of abandoning realist and representational notions of truth in which knowledge seeks to grasp the 'real thing', or to

---

[15] Enrique Dussel, "Democracy in the 'Center' and Global Democratic Critique," in *Democracy Unrealized. Documenta 11 Platform 1*, ed. O. Enwezor et al. (Ostfildern-Ruit: Hatje Cantz Publishers, 2002), 274.

produce an adequate representation of objects. As there are no context-independent or pre-contextual ideas, the content of a concept stems from the situation in which it is used. Thus, the meaning of a word is already determined by its context, which most of the time remains latent or implicit. As meaning is a variable of context, the substance of a concept changes if this is located in a different intellectual, cultural or historical framework. If meaning does not follow Saussure's principle of stability and context is contingent, then the search for knowledge can be described with Rorty as the product of the endeavor for re-contextualizing concepts, and not as the result of the search for objectivity, right meaning or 'truth'.[16]

Conventional human rights theory is routinely situated either in the background of European history, or in no context at all. As to the first interpretative practice, single events or series of events can be brought to mind when we think of the historical horizon in which the standard theory of human rights is located. Among the more popular and influential are the Enlightenment, the Hegelian 'world history', the Holocaust,[17] and the sequence constituted by the Renaissance, the Reformation, the English Parliament and the French Revolution, as in Habermas' account of the crucial moments in the formation of modern subjectivity in which history has its beginnings and meaning in Europe and it is realized there, while the events occurring outside are minor episodes or simply are not part of history.[18] This intra-European milieu allows and calls for a re-contextulization of human rights in another historical and geographical

---

[16] Richard Rorty, "Inquiry as Recontextualisation: An Anti-Dualist Account of Interpretation," in *Objectivity, Relativism and Truth. Philosophical Papers I* (Cambridge: CUP, 1991), 99 & 110. See also Richard Rorty, "Is Derrida a Transcendental Philosopher?" in *Essays on Heidegger and Others. Philosophical Papers II* (Cambridge: CUP, 1991), 127.

[17] This is the case with Rorty who states that we live in a Post-Holocaust human rights culture. Richard Rorty, "Human Rights, Rationality and Sentimentality", 115. In a similar sense, Costas Douzinas writes that 'ours is the epoch of massacre, genocide, ethnic cleansing, the age of the Holocaust'. Costas Douzinas, *Human Rights and Empire. The Political Philosophy of Cosmopolitanism* (Abingdon: Routledge-Cavendish, 2007), 71. For a critique of the Post-Holocaust interpretation of human rights see José-Manuel Barreto, "Human Rights and the Buried Crimes of Modernity," in *Critical International Law: Post-Realism, Post-Colonialism, and Transnationalism*, ed. Prabhakar Singh and Vik Kanwar (New Delhi: Oxford University Press, forthcoming 2013).

[18] Jurgen Habermas, *The Philosophical Discourse of Modernity* (Cambridge: MIT, 1990), 17.

landscape that extends beyond the borders of Europe—the backdrop of the globe or the modern world as a whole. This task can be undertaken by thematizing a wider and more comprehensive geopolitical setting, one in which the Conquest of America and the colonization of the world, as well as the movements of resistance against modern imperialism, are at the core of the genealogy of rights.

The standard theory of human rights is sometimes situated in no context at all—it is kept entirely separate from the historical and geographical circumstance in which was constructed. The dominant human rights theory is usually presented as "the" theory of rights as such, or as the "universal" conception of rights. Having roots in Medieval theology and still today significant as a component in the European mindset and theory, the metaphor of universal concepts was developed by the transcendental philosophy of consciousness in its different versions— among others those of Descartes, Kant, Hegel and Husserl. Subjectivism constructed the figure of universal notions such as "pure a priori concepts" and "absolute knowledge" by locating knowledge in an abstract world in which material conditions do not apply, and by getting rid of the human faculties that can take account of it—the senses, the body, intuitions and emotions. Idealist epistemology showed how to avoid of the ways in which the subject spontaneously approaches "material things"—Kant's "ordinary rational knowledge" and "popular moral philosophy"; Hegel's "sensory certainty" and "common sense", and Husserl's "natural attitude" —and sought to reach a point of view from which everything could be seen as it is—the modern version of the scholastic God's eye. Enabling aspirations to universal validity, metaphysical theories of knowledge hide their locus of enunciation by proscribing any reference to the context— epistemic, historical, geographical, political—from which they emerged. European thinking in this stream justifies its claims to objectivity and universal truth by denying that it was born in Europe. Santiago Castro-Gomez describes the grounds and consequences of this variety of epistemology with the metaphor of the "the hubris of the point zero".[19]

It is precisely in this claim to universality made possible by the suppression of its own context that the power of subjectivism resides. The universality of a concept transforms it into the only valid one, and precludes the likelihood of other notions having equal or even some

---

[19] Santiago Castro-Gómez, *La Hybris del Punto Cero. Ciencia, Raza e Ilustración en la Nueva Granada, 1750-1816* (Bogotá: Editorial Universidad Javeriana, 2005).

objectivity. As when engaged with Foucalt's Power/Knowledge, we are here faced with a reflection on what can be called "Power/Epistemology". It is not only knowledge that creates power, or that power resides in knowledge, as in Foucault. As knowledge that "precedes" or justifies knowledge, epistemology always remains in close contact or fused with power. Already in the portrayal of the conditions in which knowledge is possible, epistemology enables domination. In the case of modern subjectivism, it has operated as a metaphysics of colonization when taken across the seas by modern imperialism. The metaphysical epistemology of the West is full of world-political consequences: it has advanced and sustained imperialism by choosing the holders of truth, dictating the colonization of cultures and propelling the West to world hegemony.

Resisting colonization in the field of human rights can proceed by dismantling the notion that knowledge and material conditions are discrete. Contextualizing theories of human rights means showing the genealogical connection that ties the Eurocentric theory of rights to the historical setting in which it was elaborated. Unveiling the linkage to the site of emergence of knowledge weakens or destroys the legitimacy of claims to universality. The dominant theory is no longer "the" theory of human rights, but just a theory born in the background of the history of Europe and, as a consequence, has no claim to be universally compelling. The re-contextualization and contextualization of the hegemonic theory of human rights in the material conditions of modern/colonial geography and history paves the way for re-drawing and re-writing the geography and history of human rights.

Alternative Geographies and Provincializing Human Rights

The introduction of 'alternate geographies' into the human rights field can lead to a substantial transformation of human rights theory. A different mapping of the sources of notions of human rights makes it clear that human rights discourse has *also* been developed in locations outside the borders of Europe—among colonized peoples, or in the Third World. The imperial centers of power—England, France and Germany—have a place in this new map. However, what is a veritable new world atlas also depicts regions that had been kept off limits—neglected, ignored or condescendingly excluded from canonical cartographies. We are presented here with a new topography that enlarges the landscape of rights, one with far reaching consequences for the theory of human rights. This utopian and anti-colonial geography maps new loci of enunciation. Martin Woessner (Chapter 2) describes this political and argumentative strategy as one that attempts to "map out a different conception of human rights altogether, one that looks not just at the clean centers of cosmopolitan power, but at the messier margins of provincial suffering" too. Nevertheless, whereas it establishes ignored regions as valid sources of human rights concepts, it refuses to turn marginal areas into centers. Thus, no center can be found in this new paradigm. This is a truly Borgesian sphere whose "center is everywhere and the circumference nowhere". This awareness is not confined to the past and the present, but it also pinpoints "no-places"—a cartography of utopias indeed—or draws a map of the "futures of human rights", to use Baxi's terms.[20]

Unveiling the extended world of modern human rights does not end here. Areas ripe for a new comprehension of human rights can be found even inside the West—although in the margins of the established tradition. This is the case with Heidegger's critique of Western rationalism and his inheritors. Woessner counts among them Jan Patočka and Václav Havel—leaders of the movements for democracy that put an end to communist totalitarianisms in Eastern Europe. Charles Malik and Dipesh Chakrabarty also make use of Heidegger's concepts, but they do it from the standpoint of the Third World or the subaltern. Heidegger, the Nazi sympathizer, is at odds with human rights projects, but his philosophical critique of modernity and modern thinking has nurtured struggles for rights in all parts of the world.

In addition, inasmuch as human rights—in a Habermasian line of thinking—are a "realistic utopia",[21] or exemplars of the material and world-producing tension between theory and praxis, they are part of the global political landscape. In the words of Woessner, "human rights have become real". When discourses on rights are active forces in political debates, social conflicts, legal decisions and cultural processes, they become a crucial factor in politics and beacons of contemporary world and local cultures. Mapping human rights is synonymous not only with the construction of a "geography of ideas", but also with the elaboration of a topography of "physical accidents of the landscape"—of the geopolitical situation at a given historical moment.

---

[20] Upendra Baxi, *The Future of Human Rights* (Delhi and Oxford: OUP, 2002)
[21] Jurgen Habermas, "The Concept of Human Dignity and the Realistic Utopia of Human Rights," *Metaphilosophy* 41 (2010): 464-80.

In the horizon of these elaborations on human rights the quest to provincialize Europe turns into one of provincializing the mainstream 'universal' conception of rights. Woessner translates Chakrabarty's critique of transcendentalist European thinking[22] into the field of law, and proposes "provincializing human rights". Building on Heidegger's ideas on thought and dwelling, Chakrabarty's work removes the philosophical universalist mask that hides the spatial and historical attachments and limits of European thought by building on Heidegger's ideas on thought and dwelling according to which there is an irresolvable link between ideas and "modes of belonging". The analytical tradition that wipes out the remains of experience and local inheritances in order to arrive at universal concepts is the object of this critical uncovering. For Chakrabarty, the European way of thinking becomes "inadequate" because of its characteristic aspiration to universalism. The consequences for the understanding of human rights are acute. Human rights cannot be based anymore in a priori universal principles detached from geopolitics and history, and Europe—the traditional centre of human rights theory and history—is transformed into one of the provinces in which such histories occur. This is not to dispute that Western thinking remains "indispensable", but rather that as a matter of urgency it needs to be "renewed from and for the margins".[23]

Drawing upon Hollinger's insights, Woessner understands the goal of provincializing human rights as a matter of finding "the field of concrete possibilities that stretches between the abstract notions of provincialism and cosmopolitanism". As every notion of rights comes from provincial loci of enunciation scattered throughout the extended landscape of world geography, the new paradigm of human rights is to be constructed by a conversation between provincialized Europe and notions emerging from those provinces that have been kept marginalized or excluded. The enlarged discussion may be thought of as a multiple exchange between provinces—European and Non-European—a new gestalt or constellation in the making offering enhanced power to speak to all contributors. As geographically grounded interlocutors can however enunciate both locally valid and globally significant[24] theories of rights, provincializing human rights requires a dialogue between provincial and less provincial

---

[22] Dipesh Chakrabarty, *Provincializing Europe: Postcolonial Thought and Historical Difference* (Princeton: Princeton University Press, 2008).
[23] Ibid., 16.
[24] Ibid., x & xi.

views—or between local notions of human rights with both provincial validity and international or worldwide significance.

Deparochializing Legal Theory and the Quest for a Cosmopolitan Jurisprudence

Apparently opposed to the idea of provincializing human rights, the project of deparochializing Western human rights concepts is guided by the same telos. While the former traces so-called universals to their roots in the European local circumstances, the latter is well aware of how Western thinking remains circumscribed to its all too familiar horizon of understanding and needs to see beyond its limits. The placement of European theories in their particular geographical context and the questioning of European claims to universality are complemented here by a certainty about the parochialism of the origins and content of Western jurisprudence. This is the accomplishment of a self-critiquing European consciousness, and it is one of the key tenets of the thinking of William Twining on globalization, law and human rights.[25] Thus, while the provincialization of Europe and human rights are the declared ends of Chakrabarty and Woessner's projects, parochialism is the point of departure for Twining's enterprise.

Twining has developed an internal critique of Western jurisprudence on the basis, or as a consequence, of the experience of living and thinking of law outside Europe—arriving to the conclusion that his own tradition suffers the weakening effects of confinement and myopia. Making use of geographical and mental maps,[26] and through fruitful exchange with Boaventura de Souza Santos' contributions to mapping law and postmodern jurisprudence,[27] Twining (Chapter 9) calls into evidence the blinding effects of the parochialism of Western legal theory, which has been "developed and debated with at most only tangential reference to and in almost complete ignorance of the religious and moral beliefs and traditions of the rest of humankind". Not only mainstream but also critical legal philosophy remains in a veritable soliloquy, ie engaged most of the

---

[25] William Twining, *Globalization and Legal Theory* (London: Butterworth, 2000); William Twining, *General Jurisprudence: Understanding Law from a Global Perspective* (Cambridge: CUP, 2009).
[26] Twining, *Globalization and Legal Theory*, 136-173.
[27] Ibid., 194-244. Boaventura de Sousa Santos, *Towards a New Common Sense* (London: Routledge, 1995).

time only with those who belong to the same theoretical tradition or those living and working in the same Western-wide local parish. Twining not only bears witness to the shortsightedness of Western jurisprudence, but also points to the futility and inconsistency inherent in an insular thinking that claims to be universal:

> Western jurisprudence has a long tradition of universalism in ethics. Natural law, classical utilitarianism, Kantianism and modern theories of human rights have all been universalist in tendency... How can one seriously claim to be a universalist if one is ethnocentrically unaware of the ideas and values of other belief systems and traditions? [28]

The need to deparochialize Western jurisprudence is not only a question of avoiding the cage and boredom of European closed-mindedness. If legal and human rights theory are to engage current processes of globalization they need to start to work in the direction of what Twining calls a "cosmopolitan general jurisprudence". The nature of a cosmopolitan legal theory requires further elaboration here. The term "cosmopolitan" can be related to the scale of the topic under examination, as well as to the characteristics of the perspective from which the analysis is made. In the first case we are speaking about the world or the global political scenario, as when Kant proposes his "Idea for a Universal History with a Cosmopolitan Purpose". The adjective "cosmopolitan" alludes here to the third of the orders into which Kant divides public right—the previous two being political and international right. When we speak of a "cosmopolitan perspective" we are considering something entirely different, ie the standpoint from which a subject approaches law or human rights, or the *world* geographical and historical circumstances in which the modern subject of this enquiry is always already immersed.[29]

---

[28] Twining, Chapter 9. Aníbal Quijano who, together with Enrique Dussel and Walter Mignolo set the foundations of "Decolonial Theory", offers a similar critical insight: "Nothing is less rational... than the pretension that the specific worldview of a particular ethnie should be taken as universal rationality, even if such an ethnie is called Western Europe... [this would be just] to impose a provincialism as universalism." Aníbal Quijano, "Coloniality and Modernity/ Rationality," *Cultural Studies* 21 (2007): 177.

[29] Immanuel Kant, "Idea for a Universal History with a Cosmopolitan Purpose," in *Political Writings* (Cambridge: CUP, 1991). The question of the best translation of the title of this work can further illustrate the difference between the two possible meanings of the words 'cosmopolitan perspective'. There is another popular rendition into English of the same text that can be misguiding: "Idea of a Universal History from a Cosmopolitan Perspective". This title literally suggests that Kant

Twining's proposal of a cosmopolitan jurisprudence is not only an invitation to widen the horizon of Western legal theory—usually national legal orders or Western legal orders—and to look at law as it functions today within the logic of global dynamics on the world stage. The idea of a cosmopolitan jurisprudence entails a further modification of legal theory. Indeed, Twining suggests a double transformation: of both the object and the subject of jurisprudence, enlarging the first and multiplying or globalizing the second. A cosmopolitan jurisprudence requires destabilizing the "mono-logical" or internal conversation in which Western theory has stalled, and recognizing the numerous legal perspectives whose standpoints rest in the vast geography of the world. These other Non-Western legal theories have also developed distinct conceptions of human rights since the beginning of modernity with the Conquest of America.

A truly cosmopolitan theory of human rights can only be constructed through a dialogue between the established Western approach and the other strand of contributions which has itself acquired a tradition in the colonized world since the Sixteenth century. This is precisely the place of encounter and the dialogical dynamics that Twinning has begun to assemble over the past decade, opening up his own Western legal tradition on human rights to contemporary scholarship that has emerged outside the dominant canon (see Critical Dialogue below). After a long period of close intellectual and personal contact with various human rights scholars born in Africa and Asia who have developed insights on human rights from the standpoint of "the South", Twining has elaborated "introductions" to the

---

develops a philosophical reflection on history from a cosmopolitan "point of view". However, if we take into account the ideas presented in this text, the term "perspective" is to be read as a synonym of "context" or "horizon", as it indicates the contours of the object of Kant's investigation—the cosmopolitan order. The first translation appears to be more faithful to Kant's thinking as, in the original title *Idee zu einer allgemeinen Geschichte in weltbürgerlicher absicht*, the last two terms can be more accurately rendered as "cosmopolitan intention". For the second translation see Immanuel Kant, "Idea for a Universal History from a Cosmopolitan Perspective," in *Toward Perpetual Peace and other Writings on Politics, Peace, and History* (New Haven: Yale University Press, 2006). See also Immanuel Kant, "Idea for a Universal History from a Cosmopolitan Point of View," in *On History* (Indianapolis: The Bobbs-Merrill Co., 1963). Above all, the more consistent translation leaves us in front of a paradoxical "non-cosmopolitan" theory of cosmopolitanism, as Kant's reflection is transcendental—that of "metaphysics" and "universal natural laws" —or, what is the same, the European perspective that claims to be universal and valid for all. This Kantian performative contradiction is avoided in Twining's cosmopolitan jurisprudence.

work of Francis Deng, Abdullahi An Na'im, Yash Ghai and Upendra Baxi,[30] and has collected their writings on human rights.[31] The cosmopolitan theory of human rights being elaborated here forgoes the transcendental basis that sustains Kant's cosmopolitanism. It is rather grounded in the critique of Kantian transcendental understanding of natural law and human rights, and in a much wider horizon built through dialogue between the members of an increasingly cosmopolitan constituency situated in the geographical and historical contemporary world landscape.

Universalization and Globalization of Human Rights

H.G. Wells is best known as one of the originators of Science Fiction—that 'literature of ideas' that imagines "possible alternative worlds" or that projects forward past or present tendencies in dystopian futures. Not so well known are his theoretical contributions to human rights. At the start of the Second World War he wrote *The Rights of Man or What We Are Fighting For*, and some years later he presented a draft bill of rights for the consideration of the United Nations when the Universal Declaration was being debated.[32] What is of special interest to us is his insistence upon the "importance of a de-Westernization and true universalization of human rights".[33] This is precisely the direction of decolonization of human rights in the sense of unearthing and recognizing the contribution made by Third World countries and cultures.

---

[30] The studies on the works of Yash Ghai and Upendra Baxi are reproduced in this volume (Twining, Chapter 9), and the collection of all four of them was published in William Twining, "Human Rights: Southern Voices - Francis Deng, Abdullahi An-Na'im, Yash Ghai and Upendra Baxi," *Review of Constitutional Studies* 11 (2006): 203-279.
[31] William Twining, ed., *Human Rights: Southern Voices: Francis Deng, Abdullahi An Na'im, Yash Ghai and Upendra Baxi* (Cambridge: CUP, 2009).
[32] H.G. Wells, *The Rights of Man or What We Are Fighting For* (London: Penguin, 1940). See also Roger Normand and Sarah Zaidi, *Human Rights at the UN. The Political History of Universal Justice* (Bloomington and Indianapolis: Indiana University Press, 2008), 144.
[33] Marina Svensson, *Debating Human Rights in China. A Conceptual and Political History* (Lanham: Rowan & Littlefield, 2002), 26. Wells had a consciousness about the meaning of empire for the history of violence, and some of his most known novels can be read as metaphors for the colonial world and wars, among them *The Time Machine, The Island of Doctor Moreau, The Invisible Man* and *The War of the Worlds*. On the critical import of Wells' work for Victorian imperialism see Sven Lindqvist, *Exterminate all the Brutes* (London: Granta, 1998), 75-81.

What does "universalizing human rights" mean, as Susan Waltz proposes in Chapter 12, when dealing with the Universal Declaration? According to the customary account of the antecedents and sources of the Declaration this document was the result of the unwavering will of the members of an exclusive club of hegemonic powers—chiefly the United States, Great Britain and France. There is also the popular belief that the Universal Declaration was the invention of a handful of European and US authors—René Cassin, Eleanor Roosevelt, John Humphrey and Jacques Maritain. These assumptions are based on the idea that the Universal Declaration is mainly a Western achievement. Dismantling these and other myths requires an interpretative strategy aimed at universalizing the Universal Declaration of Human Rights.[34]

"Universalizing the universal" or globalizing human rights means here, according to Susan Waltz and Zehra Arat (Chapter 13), unveiling and acknowledging the global origins of the Declaration, including the contribution made by Non-Western countries as active participants, advocates and partisans, and as leaders of the political and legislative process that culminated in the adoption of the Declaration. The Human Rights Commission—which debated and wrote a first draft of the Universal Declaration—, and the UN General Assembly—which discussed and approved it—were also composed of Asian, African, Muslim, communist and Latin American countries.[35] Chile, Cuba and Panama presented entire drafts of the Declaration,[36] while the original draft prepared by the Human Rights Commission drew "most heavily" on the one prepared by the Chilean jurist Alejandro Alvarez, as Waltz writes. In this sense, universalizing or globalizing human rights also means retrieving from the archives the contributions made to the edifice of contemporary human rights by individuals who represented Third-World

---

[34] Susan Waltz, "Reclaiming and Rebuilding the History of the Universal Declaration of Human Rights," *Third World Quarterly* 23 (2002), 437-448.

[35] Asian countries: Burma, China, India and the Philippines; African countries: Egypt, Ethiopia, Liberia and South Africa; Muslim countries: Afghanistan, Iran, Iraq, Lebanon, Pakistan, Saudi Arabia, Syria, Turkey and Yemen; communist countries: USSR and Yugoslavia; Latin American countries: Argentina, Bolivia, Brazil, Chile, Colombia, Costa Rica, Cuba, Dominican Republic, Ecuador, El Salvador, Guatemala, Haiti, Honduras, Mexico, Nicaragua, Panama, Paraguay, Peru, Uruguay and Venezuela. Fifty states in total participated in one way or another over a two years period proposing drafts of the Declaration, joining the debates, proposing amendments, wording the articles, voting for and against.

[36] Normand and Zaidi, *Human Rights at the UN*, 144.

countries, as in the cases of Charles Malik from Lebanon, and Carlos Romulo from the Philippines, a task undertaken in this collection by Glenn Mitoma (Chapter 14).

The globalization of human rights can also be accomplished by making more complex the way in which the cultural sources of human rights are described. For a judicious witness to the vicissitudes of the human rights saga they are not simply "a Western concept". As historical evidence shows, the Occident has been also an enemy—the deadliest?—to their existence. As much as the West has produced treatises, manifestos and legal documents that enshrine rights, the Occident has also been the perpetrator of large scale and unspeakable crimes such as that of colonialism—an age long "violation of human rights"—as well as the Nazi atrocities. Towering figures of the European philosophical tradition of rights have also defended or condoned their outright negation, as in the cases of Aquinas, Locke and Mill. Locke, as Arat reminds us, has been uncovered as racist, sexist and classist. He justified slavery theoretically as a 'right of nature' and profited from it by monetary investment.[37]

The project of globalizing human rights can also move ahead by thinking of them not only in legal or philosophical terms but also in connection with the evolution of cultures and civilizations, as well as in relation to the modern anti-colonial tradition of rights. Christianity—a crucial component of Western civilization and a key institution for the preservation and development of the natural law tradition in medieval times—has been at different times a long standing campaigner for love, compassion and mutual respect between human beings, as well as for sexism, intolerance, torture, violence and the Inquisition. The West cannot

---

[37] Other European philosophers can also be found fractured by a twofold engagement with rights. While Kant showed 'enthusiasm' for the French Revolution, he kept silent about the Terror unleashed by Robespierre. Hegel, on his part, denounced the Terror but understood colonialism and colonial genocide as the materialization of the display and advance of the Spirit. A contemporary case in point is that of Zizek, who defended the banner of human rights against the Communist regime in the former Yugoslavia, but declares human rights quasi-bankrupt now when he is living under capitalism, and who criticises neo-colonialism as in Iraq, but salutes and commends the Terror and Robespierre—in a stark inversion of Hegel's position. See Slavoj Zizek, "Against Human Rights," *New Left Review* 34 (2005), 115-131; Slavoj Zizek, The Obscenity of Human Rights: Violence as Symptom, http:// www.lacan.com/zizviol.htm; Slavoj Zizek, *Iraq: The Borrowed Kettle* (London: Verso, 2004) and Slavoj Zizek, Introduction to *Virtue and Terror*, by Maximilien Robespierre (London: Verso, 2007).

claim any sort of identification with, or exclusive parenthood of human rights because it has also been the agent and site of their ruin. In the words of Louis Henkin, quoted by Arat, "the idea of rights... is not more congenial to Western societies than to others". Human rights are not "a Western concept", any more than they are autochthonous for the Eastern or Southern regions of the world. While Non-Western cultures exhibit a record of wilful destruction of human lives, they have also produced concepts and traditions that oppose barbarism on the basis of a certain understanding of 'human nature' and humanity. This allows Arat to maintain that there are Non-Western values that match those impinging on natural law and human rights. In addition, since the very beginning of modernity, at different times and in different places, the ideas of natural rights and human rights have been seized upon by colonized peoples to oppose imperialism and abusive national regimes, a cultural and political endeavor that already constitutes a five centuries long tradition.

Re-writing the History of Human Rights

The rationale of human rights cannot be grasped without considering the ancient European tradition of natural law. A connection between the ideas of *nomos* and *physis* was already present in Greek tragedy and Stoicism. The concept of rational law was central in Roman law and to the philosophy of Cicero. Medieval Europe produced notions of natural law in close association with Christian doctrine as in the case of Aquinas.[38] However, what can be described until the Middle Ages as a unitary tradition, would grew in different directions with similar or opposite rationales. The advent of modernity with the Renaissance and the Conquest of America gave birth to at least two distinct streams within the tradition of natural rights: that elaborated in Europe, and that emerging from the colonies in the wake of resistance to modern imperialism.

While the history of human rights in modernity is manifold, we are usually presented with a single historiography. When genealogical lines are traced in order to pinpoint the vicissitudes of the history and concepts that form the modern philosophy of natural law it is common to find a reiteration of a lineage formed by epoch-making events such as Magna

---

[38] Costas Douzinas, *The End of Human Rights* (Oxford: Hart Publishing, 2000), 23-68.

Carta; the British Revolution and the Bill of Rights[39]; the US Revolution
and the Declaration of Independence; the French Revolution and the
Declaration of the Rights of Man; the Marxist critique[40] and the social
rights proclaimed in the USSR Constitution; the Holocaust and the
Universal Declaration; the emergence of a "genuine" human rights
movement in the 1970s;[41] the end of the Cold War, and September 11 and
the War on Terror. The key events of this history remain concentrated
within the borders of Europe,[42] or are interpreted from the European
horizon of understanding. Not surprisingly, the standard philosophy of
rights continues to be assumed as "the" theory of human rights, as if no
other possibility for thinking human rights would exist outside the history
of ideas represented by names like Hobbes, Locke, Rousseau, Kant, Hegel,
Marx, Habermas, Lyotard, Derrida, Rawls and Rorty.

And yet, there is another canon that remains marginalized or invisible
—that of the theory of human rights that emerged in the context of history
of the modern colonization of the world and the struggle against imperial
violence. One of the key tenets of the historiography of rights in this
horizon of understanding is the idea according to which the history of
human rights in modernity starts with the Conquest of America (Barreto,
Chapter 5). The tradition of natural law was taken to the forefront of the
debate on the legitimacy and consequences of the conquest, for both the

---

[39] Among the more recent accounts see A.C. Grayling, *Towards the Light. The
Story of the Struggles for Liberty and Rights that Made the Modern West* (London:
Bloomsbury, 2007). It should be noted that Grayling dedicates a chapter to the
struggle against slavery.

[40] Louis Henkin describes contemporary human rights as 'a kind of twentieth
century synthesis of an eighteenth century thesis [the US Bill of Rights and the
Rights of Man] and a nineteenth century antithesis [the Marxian critique]. Louis
Henkin, *The Rights of Man Today* (Boulder: Westview Press, 1978), 5.

[41] According to Samuel Moyn, the 'true origins' of human rights are to be located
in the 1970's, and would have been brought about by US President Carter and his
foreign policy, the struggle against communist regimes in Eastern Europe, and the
crisis of both socialism and the newly independent states in the Third World.
Samuel Moyn, *The Last Utopia: Human Rights in History* (Cambridge: Harvard
University Press, 2010), 5-8.

[42] The proper name "Europe" is used here as a shortcut for the philosophical
concept of Europe in a Habermasian sense: not only geographical Europe, but also
the United States, Australia and Japan are part of the world that, because of the
rationalization, democratization and industrialization of their cultures and societies,
has reached an advanced degree of modernization. The term "Europe" also stands
for the "West".

justification of war and plunder—as in the cases of the writings of Vitoria and Sepúlveda—and for opposing violence, genocide and torture—as in the philosophical, legal and theological works and activism of Las Casas, Suárez and Vieira. In the current debate on the history of international law Antony Anghie has pointed to its colonial origins: the question of the relationship between Spain and Portugal, on the European side, and the "New World" on the other side of the Atlantic, created the challenge of imagining a world-encompassing legal system. The philosophical tradition available to answer this need was the doctrine of natural law, as the universality of a metaphysical understanding of natural rights and humanity—of both secular and theological lineage—allowed for the construction of a jurisdiction wide enough to ensure that American aboriginal peoples were placed under the power or protection of "international law".[43]

Above all, this was not only the birth of modern international law. It is precisely the embracing of the theory of natural law by international law that gives sense to the claim that this is also the beginning of modern human rights history, so we can speak of the "colonial origins of human rights". This enable us to claim a genesis of human rights in response to the crisis brought about by colonialism. The foundational stages of human rights theory and history in modern times are to be found not only in the Enlightenment, but even before that, in the resistance to the display of the capacity for destruction of imperialism—the dark side or the other constitutive pillar of modernity. Modernity cannot be indentified exclusively with emancipation; plunder and genocide were prior realities of its formation. The crisis of modernity does not appear with the Holocaust. It was actualized already centuries ago with the Conquest of America.

Such a fruitful dynamic does not consist only in a transfer of concepts and the configuration of two legal spheres. We encounter here a case of reciprocal foundation of intellectual disciplines: while modern international law was constituted by drawing some of its central institutions from natural law theory, human rights in modernity were born in the intellectual and political sphere of international law. This insight is not completely foreign to classic internationalist scholarship about later encounters between international law and human rights. According to Normand and Zaidi, Hersch Lauterpacht suggested that there is a

---

[43] Anghie, *Colonial Origins*, 94.

genealogical link that goes in both directions between international law and human rights:

> Lauterpacht traces the history of the law of nature and its role in the creation of modern international law and the [Rights of Man], noting that 'each of the three has been, in relation to the two others, the recipient and the benefactor, the master and the tool, the originator and the product'.[44]

Acknowledging the origins of modern human rights in the event of the Conquest of America and the colonization of the world is also a question of historical justice. For Paul Gilroy it is essential to make more complex the prevailing "shallow" chronology of human rights, an endeavor that can be pursued by listening to the silences that exist in standard accounts of the trajectory of rights in modern times. Moreover, it is crucial to be more attentive to voices that testified to the struggles against slavery, racial domination and the colonial enterprise. Even though they were articulated in terms of humanity and natural rights, they are usually neglected as valid sources of inspiration for contemporary human rights movements, and for building a comprehensive political and legal theory—among other reasons because of the "myopic Europe-centredness" of human rights scholars.[45] According to Gilroy, it is necessary to construct

> a genealogy for human rights that differs from the usual one. It should begin with the history of conquest and expansion, and must be able to encompass the debates about how colonies and slave plantations were to be administered. At its most basic, this agonistic, cosmopolitan enterprise must incorporate the contending voices of Bartolomé de las Casas and Juan Ginés de Sepúlveda... The counter-narrative of human rights we require is evident in opposition to racial orders, in the struggles of indigenous peoples and in the post- and anti-colonial pursuit of liberation from imperial domination.[46]

This distinct account of human rights in the history of modernity would rest on a different philosophy of history, one in which modernity is

---

[44] Normand and Zaidi, *Human Rights at the UN*, 366-367. Lauterpacht's remarks were originally published in Hersch Lauterpacht, "The Law of Nations, the Law of Nature, and the Rights of Man," *Transactions of the Grotius Society* 29 (1943): 2.
[45] Paul Gilroy, *Darker than Blue. On the Moral Economies of Black Atlantic Culture* (Cambridge: Harvard University Press, 2010), 3 & 55-59.
[46] Ibid., 57 & 71-72.

recognized as co-terminus with coloniality[47], and European civilization is obliged to acknowledge its own barbarism. From this perspective, not only the Renaissance, the Enlightenment and the Holocaust would fulfill the role of historical signposts of modernity and human rights. This path for research is yet to be explored and this book makes a contribution to this endeavor by studying some of the invisible chapters of such a history. The tradition of human rights that emerged in the context of colonialism incorporates events such as the Conquest of America and the wider process of colonization of the world, as well as the movements of resistance to imperialist violence and domination; the anti-slavery movements; the struggles for independence fought from the North to the South of America in the late Eighteenth and early Nineteenth centuries (Barreto, Chapter 5), the singular experience of the Haitian revolution of independence (Bogues, Chapter 7); the Mexican revolution and its land reform; the process of decolonization of Africa, Asia, the Caribbean and the Middle East mainly in the second half of the Twentieth century (Barreto, Chapter 5); the Civil Rights and the Anti-Apartheid Movements; the struggle for human rights alongside the Third World as a reaction to authoritarian regimes; and the contemporary pro-indigenous peoples, anti-globalization, anti-war, environmental and anti-corporations movements. By admitting this alternative narrative of the struggle for natural, civil or human rights we bring out of the shadows significant personalities and thinkers who deserve a place in the lineage of human rights: Vitoria, Las Casas, Sepúlveda, Suárez (Barreto, Chapter 5; Dussel, Chapter 6), Antonio Vieira and Guamán Poma; Jefferson, Toussaint L'Ouverture and Bolívar; Elahuda Equiano, Ottoba Qugoano, Frederick Douglas, Soujurne Truth, W.E.B. du Bois, Martin Luther King (Lloyd, Chapter 8), Malcolm X and Mandela; Gandhi, Fanon, the Dalai Lama and Baxi (Twining, Chapter 9; Baxi, Chapter 10); Ariel Dorfman and Rigoberta Menchu.[48]

---

[47] On the concept of coloniality see Aníbal Quijano, "Coloniality of Power, Eurocentrism, and Latin America," *Nepantla: Views from South* 1 (2000): 3.

[48] There already exists a body of research that starts to bring to light the history of the Third World tradition of human rights –be anti-colonial, liberal, social or democratic. A long-term historical detour that includes Las Casas, Bolívar and the constitutions of independence, the Mexican Revolution and the Latin American contribution to the Universal Declaration can be found in Paolo Carozza, "From Conquest to Constitutions: Retrieving a Latin American Tradition of the Idea of Human Rights," *Human Rights Quarterly* 25 (2003): 2. On Guamán Poma see Fernanda Bragato, "A Contribuisao do Pensamento de Felipe Guaman Poma de Ayala para Repensar o Discurso Hegemonico dos Direitos Humanos," in *A Realizao e a Protecao Internacional dos Direitos Humanos Fundamentais*, eds.

The *Other* Becoming the Self

A critique of the Eurocentric understanding of human rights can also draw upon a heterodox reading of one of the more accomplished elaborations of Emmanuel Levinas' philosophy of otherness, namely Zvetan Todorov's theory of moral history. Todorov's "The Conquest of America. The Question of the Other" takes Levinas' philosophy of alterity to think the history of modern imperialism. In the description given by Todorov of the coming of Columbus to America in terms of the "discovery the self makes of the other", those in America[49]—or outside Europe—are the 'other' for the self that looks at the world from the location of Europe. If the path of reflection that departs from this standpoint is followed, a wealth of insights regarding the constitution of Europe can be gained, showing how the presence of 'the other' is at the core of Europe's political, cultural and historical formation.

Narciso Baez and Douglas Cassel (Joacaba: UNOESC, 2011); on Quobna Qugoano see Anthony Bogues, "The Political Thought of Quobna Qugoano." in *Black Heretics, Black Prophets: Radical Political Intellectuals* (New York: Routledge, 2003). On the Mexican revolution and land rights see Judith Schacherreiter, "Un Mundo donde Quepan Muchos Mundos: A Postcolonial Legal Perspective Inspired by the Zapatistas," *Global Jurist* 11 (2009): 2. On decolonization and the role of Africa and Asia in shaping the international human rights regime, as well as its shorcomings see Roland Burke, *Decolonization and the Evolution of International Human Rights Law* (Philadelphia: University of Pennsylvania Press, 2010); Bonny Ibhawoh, *Imperialism and Human Rights: Colonial Discourses of Rights and Liberties in African History* (Albany: SUNY Press, 2007).

[49] America is not "America". Currently in Europe and the United States it is common—both in day-to-day conversation, the media and in scholarly publications—to refer to the United States of America as "America". This practice is even usual in authors who have presided as the masters of suspicion and critical thinking such as Kafka, Baudrillard, Deleuze and Guattari. Probably adopted just as a helpful and innocuous shortcut or abbreviation, this practice confuses the part with the whole, taking the name of a continent to refer to a single country. What could be pointed to just as a crash example of geographical inaccuracy ends up involving political and philosophical problems. If the United States monopolizes the name America, the countries that stand to the South are dispossessed of their generic name and in this slip of the tongue they disappear from the map and from the notion of America. Mirroring political and economic history, in this appropriation of a word the United States steals something which does not belong to them, dispossessing the American nations of the Caribbean and Central and South America of their "proper name", and of their place in geography and history.

More interestingly, the "conquest of the other by the self" reveals the "other" to be the victim of imperialism.[50] Todorov offers a large-scale picture of the history of modernity that proceeds from its genesis to the current situation laying bare the genocidal consequences for America and the Third World: "What took place in America after 1492, and continues to happen today, is the virtual obliteration of one cultural world by another".[51] Positing the colonized or the Third World subject as a victim in the context of the history of modernity leads to the indictment of Europe as the land of the barbarians, and holds it responsible for the slaughter carried out by centuries of colonialism. Auschwitz is revealed to be nothing new, for in the colonialist depredation of the world since the Fifteenth century Europe has fully deployed its capacity for extermination.

Above all, interpreting Todorov in a Third World key requires a process of de-identification: the reader from the South needs to leave behind the identification with "the other" that has been graciously bestowed upon her, and adopt the role of the "self"—not the mask of the European self, but their own self, ie the self of the colonized. Thus, the subject from the Third World places herself in the role of "the self" that faces the European "self". Todorov refers to this shift when he writes that "others are also 'I's"—subjects just as Europeans are.[52] In addition, the recognition of the Third World subject has to be made not only by the Europeans; more importantly, it needs to be grasped by those in the Third World too—it has to be a process of self-recognition.

When the colonized subject abandons the European self to occupy the place of the Third World self, and recognizes herself us such, the peoples of the Third World embrace the role of agents of self-emancipation and humanization. In the words of Fanon, "the native never ceases to dream of putting himself in the place of the settler—not becoming the settler but of substituting himself for the settler", so that the colonized embodies "history in his own person" and creates "a new humanity".[53] The evidence of such an achievement can be seen throughout the history of the struggles to restrain imperialist violence, and to gain independence and self-determination since the times of the Conquest of America.

---

[50] Zvetan Todorov, *The Conquest of America. The Question of the Other* (Norman: University of Oklahoma Press, 1999).
[51] Ibid., xii.
[52] Ibid., 3.
[53] Frantz Fanon, *The Wretched of the Earth* (London: Penguin, 2001), 28, 31 & 41.

Critique of Critical Theory and Modernity as Crisis

Habermas takes issue with Adorno and Horkheimer's critique of modernity and modern reason because of its supposedly extreme character: the "Dialectic of Enlightenment"[54] would take, he imagines, Critical Theory into the no-go area of nihilism. If the Enlightenment's power for self-destruction outweighs its capacity for emancipation, there would be no reason to believe anymore in the project of modernity.[55] And yet, it is only for a subject that thinks from a Eurocentric point of view—like Habermas—that the "Dialectic of Enlightenment" has gone beyond what is admissible or adequate for a critique of modernity to accomplish.

Nevertheless, for a thinking that stands in the proximity of the history of modern colonialism, Adorno and Horkheimer's critique is not radical enough. This is the path of reflection adopted by Sabine Broeck who, shifted her standpoint—the European horizon of understanding—and opened her thinking to the history of European colonialism. Working in the fields of Black Feminism, African-American and Slavery Studies, Broeck has developed a powerful critique of key tenets of Critical Theory. This "critique of the critique" advanced by Broeck can offer valuable modifications of Critical Theory. More importantly, it strengthens the efforts of the drive to open up the theory of human rights to grasp the weight of the violence generated by imperialism.

According to Broeck (Chapter 3), the incapacity of Critical Theory to fully decipher modern history stems from framing the clash between the dark and the emancipatory sides of modernity as an inner European conflict, so that the climax of modernity's self-destruction and the collapse of civilization are found in the Nazi crimes against humanity. The emphasis placed on this line of interpretation leads Critical Theory to keep modern imperialism out of focus and to "assume modernity innocent of colonialism". The Frankfurt School does not pay due attention to the role played by colonialism and slavery in the constitution of modernity, and it does not recognize that the vast accumulation of capital, political power and knowledge in modern Europe was made possible in a substantial way by the undertakings of imperialism.

---

[54] Max Horkheimer and Theodor Adorno, *Dialectic of Enlightenment. Philosophical Fragments* (Palo Alto: Stanford University Press, 2002).
[55] Jurgen Habermas, *The Philosophical Discourse*, 106-130.

Critical Theory, Broeck states, also fails to realize that "the modern free subject is the result of slave trading and colonialist practices". In this sense, the freedom of the white subject presupposes the non-subjectivity, reification, objectification or abjection of the colonized and the slave. The freedom of the white subject is made possible by the ownership of slaves, which allows for a new definition of "freedom as ownership"—freedom as negation of freedom, or freedom purchased by slavery. Such a deep gash in the hull of Critical Theory comes as no surprise, as it re-enacts a flaw ingrained in the critical tradition—that of thematizing the relationship between the master and the slave without referring to modern capitalist slavery, ie colonial slavery. Hegel preferred to think of the dialectics of master and slave on the basis of the relation between feudal lords and servants, and the transit to the modern subject.[56] Marx, equally blinkered, followed Hegel's dialectics in conceptualizing the class struggle. These immense gaps in Critical Theory's understanding of modern history takes Broeck to conclude that not only the Frankfurt School, but also Foucaultian critique, Psycoanalysis and Feminism, are all characterized by a theoretical "narcissism" that has not allowed them tracing a genealogy of the modern subject that includes colonialism and slavery.

On the basis of this diagnosis, Broeck formulates a number of adjustments that Critical Theory needs to perform in order to gain a more encompassing philosophy of modern history. Critical Theory must adopt a *longue durée* historical approach beyond the consequences for civilization of the Second World War, and widen its field of study as to the defining moments of modernity to include the Fifteenth century and the early modern origins of colonialism and slavery. More radically, Broeck challenges critical scholars to read history from the point of view of the colonized or the slave, and to review the self-understanding of Critical Theory—all within the spirit of one of the archetypal capabilities of Critical Theory, that of self-critique.

Indeed, the Frankfurt School's conceptualization of the crisis of modernity needs to be radicalized. Adorno and Horkheimer's interpretation

---

[56] Susan Buck-Morss' hypothesis according to which Hegel should have, or might have, elaborated his master-slave dialectics taking notice of the Haitian Revolution appears farfetched if we take into account his notion of "world history" from which Hegel excluded the US revolution of independence, as well as the wars of independence fought throughout Central and South America in the early Nineteenth century. See Susan Buck-Morss, "Hegel and Haiti," *Critical Inquiry* 26 (2000): 821-865. G.W.F. Hegel, *The Philosophy of History*, 8-79 & 79-102.

requires a sweeping modification so that our understanding of the history of atrocity and human rights in modernity shows due regard to the victims of colonialism. The schizophrenia of Europe in the Twentieth century, which evinced expressions of high culture and materialistic progress on the surface but concealed the most depraved savagery in extermination camps, ought be understood as present centuries ago. Modern reason and slaughter did not coincide only in Auschwitz. As Europe was giving birth to Humanism and culturally efflorescing, it put millions to death in the Americas. Europe's march of progress from its emergence in the Renaissance has cost an ocean of blood. The first modern genocide already had an extreme anti-moral quality such that, at the very moment the European civilization was blossoming, it had already negated itself, collapsed and disintegrated. Modernity was born already in crisis. Modernity is crisis.[57]

Emotions, the Ethics of Human Rights and Empire/Suffering

The "turn to emotions" or the affective turn, the increasingly pervasive feature of our zeitgeist, is compelling legal theory and, in general, the social sciences and the humanities, to engage with feelings and the 'global sentiment'. This phenomenon entails both an internal, ie European, and a decolonial critique of rationalism. In the field of human rights, the internal shift can be traced back to the 1993 Oxford Amnesty Lecture given by Richard Rorty with the title "Human Rights, Rationality and Sentimentality", in which he distanced himself from Kant's transcendental foundation of ethics and rights, and proposed to understand the culture of human rights as one of sympathy and solidarity.[58] According to Martin Woessner (Chapter 2), Rorty's critique is heir to Heidegger's portrayal of reason "as the most stiff-necked adversary of thought".[59] While Heidegger describes the hardness—the painful tension and the malaise—of rationalism as an enemy of thinking, it is the absence or the repression of emotions that is denounced. We are here in front of another philosophical inversion. The rationalist banishing of emotions and sympathy from truth

---

[57] On the concept of "modernity as crisis" see Barreto, "Human Rights and the Buried Crimes of Modernity."

[58] Richard Rorty, "Human Rights, Rationality and Sentimentality," in *On Human Rights: The Oxford Amnesty Lectures 1993*, eds. Stephen Shute et al. (New York: Basic Books, 1994).

[59] Martin Heidegger, "Nietzsche's Word, 'God is Dead'," in *The Question Concerning Technology and Other Essays* (New York: Harper & Row, 1977), 112.

and ethics is no longer tenable. The opposite is the case: these are times for a "post-rationalist philosophy". And when rationalism is put into question, the modern and dominant rationalist discourse in which human rights are framed becomes the object of suspicion too.

Rorty calls us to abandon a certain kind of human rights discourse—that resting on transcendental foundations—and proposes developing a theory and practice of a cultural politics aimed at strengthening the contemporary human rights tradition. This praxis for human rights is to be carried out by poets, novelists, artists, journalists and all sorts of story tellers who create narratives or chronicles able to elicit identification with strangers or sympathy for the victims of abuse.[60] In the words of Woessner, Rorty's project of the "sentimental education" of the epoch—that of enhancing the capacity of people for moral feeling—can advance human rights "whether human rights were enshrined in local traditions, positivist law, transcendental philosophy, physical science—or not."

In contrast to both Kant's understanding of the Age of Enlightenment as a process of universalization of the use of reason, and Weber's conception of modernization as rationalization of the life world, Rorty poses the idea of the sensibilization of the age. On this basis, we could say that the motto of our times is not the Kantian *sapere aude!*, but the injunction 'dare to feel!'. Postmodernity could be defined in this sense as a process of cultivation of a greater capacity in individuals and collectives—societies and the world community—for moral emotions, or as "the sentimental education of modern culture by the fostering of moral feelings".[61]

Among the host of elaborations on the relationship between emotions and human rights inspired by Heidegger's critique of rationalism we can count also that of Havel and Patočka, as Woessner explores in Chapter 2. Havel and Patočka's reconstruction of human rights out of a capacity for feeling for others was made in the context of the crude and cruel reality of Stalinist totalitarianism, and as a strategy for resisting and overcoming its dogmatic principles of "objectivity, historical necessity, technology, system and the apparat". But the coldness of Leftist totalitarianism is just

---

[60] On Rorty's conception of human rights see José-Manuel Barreto, "Rorty and Human Rights: Contingency, Emotions and how to Defend Human Rights Telling Stories," *Utrecht Law Review* 7 (2011), 93-112. Available at http:// www. utrechtlawreview.org/index.php/ulr/article/viewFile/164/163
[61] Barreto, "Rorty and Human Rights," 106.

an exemplar of the coldness that characterizes modern reason and political culture, the other archetypes being fascism, capitalism and its conjoined twin, modern imperialism. For Woessner we are facing "a new understanding of human rights" based on "irrational ideas" such as empathy, love and "the solidarity of the shaken"—a political culture in which human rights can breed and thrive. This conception of human rights answers to "the suffering of the human person", and emanates "from the heart" and not from the "unflinching, rationalist universalism of previous human rights discourse".

I now turn to another critique of rationalism from the side of authors wrestling with the legacy of colonialism and with the opinion that emotions entail a setback for emancipation. Discussing the sceptical reception in Critical Legal Theory to Harriet Beecher Stowe's *Uncle's Tom Cabin,* Paul Gilroy calls for more nuanced reflection on the process of identification with the suffering of victims:

> The outright dismissal of any useful outcome from the familiarity with the suffering of others should itself be questioned... There are a number of ways in which strategies premised upon emotional communication, psychological identification, and the formation of moral communities might open up possibilities for change achieved through social and political mobilization... What if Stowe's structure of feeling was instrumental in the formation of a moral collectivity and in wining recognition of the suffering humanity of the slave, whom it was no longer possible to dismiss as a brute? [62]

Sharing the concerns of Black Atlantic Theory, Subaltern Studies have elaborated various insights towards establishing a link between colonialism, human rights and feelings. This is the case with Upendra Baxi, whose introduction of "the language of the violated"[63] transforms the nature of human rights discourse. For Baxi, talking about human rights from the perspective of the victim means speaking about abuses in terms of suffering. This narrative opposes and supplements the rationalist mood of established scholarship. Baxi points to the strange discordance experienced in listening to the voices of sorrow and tragedy against the background of the dry and abstract hegemonic discourse on democracy and human rights theory, which remains "sanitized" and purged of references to pain.

---

[62] Gilroy, *Darker than Blue*, 65-66.
[63] Baxi, *The Future of Human Rights*, 126.

Adopting the ethos of the language of the violated, Baxi characterizes the Third World as "the suffering humanity"[64]. In this notion the Third World is defined in terms of the pain it has endured over the centuries as a consequence of imperialism. Suffering becomes in this rights-talk one of the crucial aspects of the history of the Third World, a history of millions of individual lives damaged and destroyed, and a tale of the genocide.[65] This is a suffering that permeates and taints the destiny of continents and our whole era. It is a pain that becomes compounded with the spirit of the times. Speaking about how the 20th century history of the European Jews can be summarized in the word Auschwitz, Lyotard has said that "there is a sort of grief in the Zeitgeist".[66] The agony evoked by the words "a suffering humanity" is of this quality.

Decolonization of human rights can also be pursued by thematizing concepts that offer the possibility of approaching rights from a non-rationalistic point of view, and that are capable of establishing a significant connection between the violence of imperialism and emotions. Such an association can be explored in the concept of "empire/suffering". The exercise of imperial power has resulted in multitudinous individual, and in this sense, unique experiences of pain, despair, anguish and trauma. From a wider perspective this can be described as harm caused to whole peoples, and as social and global suffering. There is an immediate and inexorable link between the power of empire and the suffering of the colonized. The concept of empire/suffering can benefit from revisiting Foucault's dyad "power/knowledge", focusing on its idiosyncratic structure. There exists a causal relation between power and knowledge: "There is no power relation without the correlative constitution of a field of knowledge, nor any knowledge that does not presuppose and constitute at the same time power relations".[67] The counter-intuitive notion according

---

[64] Upendra Baxi, "Global Justice and the Failure of Deliberative Democracy," in *Democracy Unrealised. Documenta 11–Platform 1*, ed. Okwui Enwezor, et.al. (Ostfildern Ruit: Hatje Cantz Publishers, 2002), 113-114.
[65] On the contribution of Baxi and other Third World scholars like Oswald de Andrade and Luis Alberto Warat to the critique of the rational understanding of human rights see Jose-Manuel Barreto, "Human Rights and the Critique of Rationalism: de Andrade, Warat and Baxi", *Revista de Estudos Constitucionais, Hemeneutica e Teoria do Direito* (Forthcoming 2012).
[66] Jean-Francois Lyotard, *The Postmodern Explained: Correspondence, 1982-1985* (Minneapolis: The University of Minnesota Press, 1997), 78.
[67] Michel Foucault, *Discipline and Punish: The Birth of the Prison* (New York: Pantheon, 1979), 27.

to which knowledge is always the product of the operation of power, is "paraphrased" here by the notion of empire/suffering, which encapsulates the all too obvious but neglected historical fact that the deployment of colonial violence was and continues to be followed by pain and anguish in the bodies and minds of the victims of imperialism. In every deployment of imperial power there has been, as an unavoidable consequence, a causation of suffering. Empire and suffering are inextricably and necessarily linked. Empire/suffering does not enshrine another modern binary opposition, but it highlights an amalgam of two inseparable sides: suffering is a potency residing in imperial power, and the consequence of the materialization of power. In the context of modern colonialism this translates into the cruelty of empires which may extend as far as exterminating their victims in masses, and into the suffering of the colonized.

Critical Dialogue

A historiography of human rights that claims to bear witness to the struggles for human rights and to the contributions to human rights theory made by the colonized asserts the existence of a history of human rights in the geography of the colonial world. It also looks for recognition of Third World theory as a valid interlocutor in any conversation about rights— not simply as a listener without a voice, or a ventriloquist's dummy. If human rights are not a 'gift of the West to the rest' it is possible to see that they are an endowment of the Non-West to the world as well. Above all, this is not to suggest that the European legacy should be abandoned or rejected. On the contrary, it calls for the Eurocentric understanding of rights to escape its soliloquy, and to enter into a dialogue with other visions of rights. A Third-World human rights theory operates in a dialogic epistemological ethos that seeks to replace the European monologist and self-centered culture. This is a call for an exchange of ideas in which the status of the interlocutors and the terms of the conversation are transformed by a new geography of knowledge in which all those involved come from different provinces of the world. The hermeneutics of provincializing human rights leads to a dialogue between local conceptions, both those coming from what was the center, as well as those emerging from places that customarily had been reckoned to occupy the margins.

As interpreted by Woessner (Chapter 2), Chakrabarty's and Fanon's idea of an "anti-colonial humanism" is "a new humanism that keeps the universal and the particular always and everywhere in dialogue with each other". The universal mentioned here is rather unique: it is a particular disguised as a universal, or that calls itself universal—the basic epistemological and power-seeking deception of European thinking. Above all, European philosophy and the European conception of human rights form part of the utopian thinking that can contribute both to resisting and reversing the deeds of imperialism, and to creating a new "human being", a "new society" and a "new world".[68] A Third-World theory of human rights—an exemplar of anti-colonial humanism—cannot avoid counting among its sources the European humanist tradition.

Paraphrasing Chakravarty, as quoted by Woessner, Eurocentric human rights theory is 'at once indispensable and inadequate" and it must be "renewed from and for the margins." The European tradition must sacrifice its presumption of centrality and enter into a critical dialogue with those outside Europe in order to rid itself of its destructive core, and to actualize its emancipatory potential for the victims of power both in the centre and in the colonized world. The partiality and bias of Eurocentrism can be left behind by engaging with visions coming from the borders. In this way a cooperative spirit can be mobilized to deal with questions of global justice. In this sense, Woessner puts forward the idea that it is "between the global north and the global south where the utopia—the no-place—of human rights is to be found", and that to provincialize human rights is "to struggle to hold in a permanent state of tension a dialogue between two contradictory points of view".

A similar dialogical stance has been adopted by Decolonial Theory. If, as Quijano maintains, the specific European *weltanschauung* cannot have universal validity, then the only possible way in which universal knowledge can be arrived at is through "epistemological decolonization… to clear the way for new intercultural communication; for interchanging experiences and meaning as a basis of another rationality which may legitimately pretend to some universality".[69] But dialogue is not only the

---

[68] In addition to the possibility of taking the capacity for critique of the Western thinking, including Marxism, to oppose colonialism, there are other thinkers that offer specifically targeted attacks on modern imperialism. On Diderot, Kant and Herder's contribution see Sankar Muthu, *Enlightenment against Empire* (Princeton: PUP, 2003).

[69] Anibal Quijano, quoted in Walter Mignolo, "The Historical Foundation of Modernity/Coloniality and the Emergence of Decolonial Thinking," in *A*

ethos and teleology of the decolonization of knowledge. It is a political quest too: a world-creating hermeneutics and practice, and a path towards a new theory and practice of human rights and global justice. This is evident in the notion of 'transmodernity', an idea formulated by Enrique Dussel in order to go beyond 'postmodern' theory—a critical perspective that aims at transcending modernity from within and that, in doing so, remains a Eurocentric critique of modernity. According to Dussel, in transmodernity:

> both modernity and its negated alterity (the victims) co-realize themselves in a process of mutual creative fertilization. Trans-modernity (as a project of political, economic, ecological, erotic, pedagogical and religious liberation) is the co-realization of that which is impossible for modernity to accomplish by itself: that is of an *incorporative* solidarity that I have called analectic between centre/periphery, man/woman, different races, different ethnic groups, different classes, civilization/nature, Western culture/Third World cultures, et cetera.[70]

A dialogue on human rights can be undertaken between diverse conceptions and from distant geopolitical loci of enunciation, but also between different rationalities. Within the Western philosophical tradition, we can pinpoint the exchange between analytical thinking and hermeneutics as exemplified in the famous Habermas-Gadamer debate, imagine a dialogue between Marx's materialism and Heidegger's ontology as it is suggested by Chakrabarty in "Provincializing Europe". A dialogue can be also enacted between European and decolonial critiques of reason, a conversation that can take us to a new understanding of human rights. In this direction what Woessner asserts (Chapter 2) is germane:

Companion to Latin American Literature and Culture, ed. Sara Castro-Klaren, (Marden & Oxford: Blackwell, 2008), 27.
[70] Enrique Dussel, "Eurocentrism and Modernity," *Boundary 2*, 20 (1993): 76. Dussel himself has been eager to engage in a longstanding philosophical dialogue with Apel, Taylor, Rorty, Vattimo and Ricouer. See Enrique Dussel, *The Underside of Modernity: Apel, Ricoeur, Rorty, Taylor and the Philosophy of Liberation*, trans. and ed. Eduardo Mendieta (New Jersey: Humanities Press, 1993). The inclination for dialogue is not only a Postcolonial and Decolonial enterprise. It is also one of the tenets of the internal critique of European thought. This is the case of Thomas McCarthy who, as quoted by Woessner (Chapter 2), argues that there is no need of abandoning the "universal" discourses of human rights, but that they should enter into a dialogical relation with the "barbarian" voices coming from the borders.

If a connection can be made between the sort of internalist critiques of Western rationalism that we find in Malik, Havel and Rorty, on the one hand, and more recent postcolonial writings from the margins of the West, on the other, perhaps we might be able to hold open, if only temporarily, a fertile space for an alternative conception of human rights, one that fosters empathetic solidarity over and above impersonal, bureaucratic rationalism.

Critiques of rational human rights—of both Western and Non-Western provenance—and rationalist theories of rights can meet in conversations that can create other venues for human rights theory. And yet, a more heterodox path for the dialogical decolonization of rights will be suggested: Can reason and emotion enter into a rational or reasonable dialogue, or can they enter into a—sentimental—relation so that they can feel for each other? This possibility is just to be mentioned; its elaboration and justification will not be undertaken here. In the meantime, let's state that there is a substantial claim in this call for rational and sentimental dialogue, and it has to do again with the decolonial *telos*. Were we to remain within a mere rationalist approach to rights or, taking the opposite stance, restricted to a sentimental comprehension of human rights, we would stick with the modern and colonialist separation of heart and mind. As quoted by Woessner, Chakrabarty has pointed out that the "strong split between emotion and reason" is in itself constitutive of colonialism.

The quest to create conditions for dialogue is another strategy for decolonizing the theory of human rights. It would be fruitful to grasp that even the work of enabling the exchange of ideas and advancing a transition from the habit of monologue to authentic conversation will help us all towards a less ethnocentric view on these matters. The move from soliloquy to dialogue as methodology, hermeneutical process or ethos—the struggle to justify and build spaces for discussion—can take the theory of human rights to a less Eurocentric and provincial outlook. In other words, it can lead to a more universal—based on many perspectives, geographies, histories and rationalities—understanding of human rights, as well as of their consequences for social and global justice.

Overview

This book brings together thinkers who are developing an interpretation of rights from outside Europe, and discourses that develop internal critiques of traditional Eurocentric understandings of human rights. In this sense, this is already a contribution to the decolonization of human rights by fostering dialogue between viewpoints. This collection of articles is also the result of an interdisciplinary approach to human rights. Thus, it puts into conversation important areas of research on human rights, namely philosophy or theory of human rights, history, as well as constitutional and international law, and dedicates one of the three sections in which the book is divided to each one of them. The philosophy of human rights is well established as academic discipline, as well as law—one of the more traditional intellectual niches of human rights. The history of human rights has drawn interest only recently, the declaration of Linda Kerber "we are all historians of human rights"[71] being a telling symptom of this new focus within human rights studies—and of the pulling power of the field of human rights to attract the attention of the Social Sciences and the Humanities. Again, it is in this willingness for exchanging views that this compilation finds a path towards the development of the human rights field, as the theory, history and law of human rights enhance each other's capacity for interpretation. This is also part of the drive for decolonization: the power for critique of the philosophy of rights and the genealogies created by historical analysis make a Third world consciousness aware of the centrality of the European tradition, as well as of the legitimacy of a vision elaborated by the colonized. An exercise of dialogical and interdisciplinary thinking, this collection is organized into three parts:

Part I, "Critique of the Theory of Human Rights" presents some reflections that put into question the standard philosophy of rights. Walter Mignolo (Chapter 1) calls the attention to the deficit of the universality of concepts like "humanity", "reason" and "rights" as created by the Renaissance and the Enlightenment, as well as to the political uses of these concepts in the wide scenario of world colonization. In Chapter 2 Martin Woessner examines heterodox conceptualizations of human rights inspired by Heidegger within and outside the European tradition, including the works of Havel, Patočka and Rorty on the one hand, and the thinking of Charles Malik and the subaltern project of provincializing Europe elaborated by Dipesh Chakrabarty, on the other. Sabine Broeck offers in Chapter 3 an internal critique of Critical Theory as to the limitations of its engagement with imperialism and slavery, and points to the blinds that do not allow White Feminist and Gender Theory to engage with the Non-White woman. On his part, Eduardo Mendieta (Chapter 4) develops a meditation on the implications of art for contemporary political theory, as

---

[71] Linda K. Kerber, "We are All Historians of Human Rights," *Perspectives Online* 44 (2006). Available at http://www.historians.org/ perspectives/issues/ 2006/ 0610/ 0610pre1.cfm

exemplified in the works of Botero and Golup that engage with the violence of empires and dictatorships exercised on the body.

Part II traces the vicissitudes of human rights outside the hegemonic genealogy and opens a wide landscape for the history of human rights in the context of colonialism. Thus, José-Manuel Barreto (Chapter 5) finds in the Conquest and Independence of the Americas, and in the decolonization of Africa and Asia the sites of the struggle for rights. In Chapter 6 Enrique Dussel offers an interpretation of the contributions made to modern political philosophy by Francisco de Vitoria, Bartolomé de las Casas and Francisco Suárez (Chapter 6).

Focusing on the Haitian Revolution Anthony Bogues (Chapter 7) develops a revision of the history of political ideas—which misses the struggle against colonial domination and racial slavery, and for independence and freedom—by looking for new conceptions of freedom elaborated in contexts other than that of the fight against absolutism—the birthplace of conventional modern political and rights theory. To do so, Bogues compares the Code Noir—the catalogue of norms applied to govern and discipline the slaves—with the 1805 Haitian Constitution, which abolished slavery and established rights, equality and independence as the pillars of the new society. Within the turn to emotions in human rights, Vincent Lloyd (Chapter 8) reads Martin Luther King as a thinker that engages "love" as the place to re-imagine human rights. In this interpretation, King is not only a great orator and political leader, but he is also part of the canon of the theory of rights in the context of the struggle against the legacies of colonialism—racism, discrimination, segregation and poverty among them.

Developing his project of deparochializing Western legal theory William Twining (Chapter 9) studies the contribution to human rights made by two contemporary scholars from the Third World. Twining's reading of Yash Ghai focuses on topics such as the role of constitutional frameworks in negotiating conflicting interests in multi-ethnic societies, the "Asian values" debate, and the judicialization of economic, social and cultural rights. The second part of Chapter 9 is dedicated to one of the most important figures in Subaltern Legal Studies and the Third World Approach to International Law (TWAIL). It examines some of the theses developed by Upendra Baxi in his "Futures of Human Rights" and his distinction between the "modern" and the 'contemporary" paradigms of human rights.

Part III studies human rights law, with particular attention given to constitutional and international legal frameworks. Upendra Baxi (Chapter 10) explores the contribution made to the conceptualization of the doctrine of the Rule of law by "non-Western communities of *résistance* and peoples in struggle." In Chapter 11 Nico Horn revisits Australia's Mabo Case—which acknowledged the precolonial rights of the aboriginal peoples to territories their forebears inhabited in the islands of Mer, Dauar and Waier, and rejected previous decisions based on the principle of *terra nullius*. They had lost the ancestral lands to British colonists when they settled in Australia in the Nineteenth century. Horn draws the lessons of this case for urgent land reform in Namibia, examined in the background of the German colonization and the genocide of the Herero, Nama and Darama peoples. Finally, Susan Waltz (Chapter 12), Zehra Arat (Chapter 13) and Glenn Mitoma (Chapter 14) unveil the contribution made by Third World countries to international human rights law, studying particularly the process that led to the adoption of the Universal Declaration of Human Rights.

Bibliography

Barreto, José-Manuel. "Human Rights and the Buried Crimes of Modernity." In *Critical International Law: Post-Realism, Post-Colonialism, and Transnationalism*, edited by Prabhakar Singh and Vik Kanwar. New Delhi: Oxford University Press, forthcoming 2013.

—. "Human Rights and the Critique of Rationalism: de Andrade, Warat and Baxi", *Revista de Estudos Constitucionais, Hemeneutica e Teoria do Direito* (forthcoming 2012).

—. "Rorty and Human Rights: Contingency, Emotions and how to Defend Human Rights Telling Stories." *Utrecht Law Review* 7 (2011). Available online at http://www.utrechtlawreview.org/index.php/ulr/article/viewFile/ 164/163.

Baxi, Upendra. *The Future of Human Rights*. Delhi and Oxford: OUP, 2002.

—. "Global Justice and the Failure of Deliberative Democracy."In *Democracy Unrealised. Documenta 11–Platform 1*, edited by Okwui Enwezor, et.al. Ostfildern Ruit: Hatje Cantz Publishers, 2002.

—. "What may the 'Third World' Expect from International Law?" *Third World Quarterly* 27 (2006).

Beardsell, Peter. *Europe and Latin America: Returning the Gaze.* Manchester: MUP, 2000.

Bennett, Jill. *Empathic Vision: Affect, Trauma, and Contemporary Art.* Stanford: Stanford University Press, 2005.

Bogues, Anthony. "The Political Thought of Quobna Qugoano." In *Black Heretics, Black Prophets: Radical Political Intellectuals* (New York: Routledge, 2003).

Bragato, Fernanda. "A Contribuisao do Pensamento de Felipe Guaman Poma de Ayala para Repensar o Discurso Hegemonico dos Direitos Humanos." In *A Realizao e a Protecao Internacional dos Direitos Humanos Fundamentais*, edited by Narciso Baez and Douglas Cassel. Joacaba: UNOESC, 2011.

Brown-Scott, James. *The Spanish Origin of International Law: Francisco de Vitoria and His Law of Nations.* Oxford: Clarendon Press, 1934.

Buck-Morss, Susan. "Hegel and Haiti." *Critical Inquiry* 26 (2000).

Burke, Roland. *Decolonization and the Evolution of International Human Rights Law.* Philadelphia: University of Pennsylvania Press, 2010.

Carozza, Paolo. "From Conquest to Constitutions: Retrieving a Latin American Tradition of the Idea of Human Rights." *Human Rights Quarterly* 25 (2003).

Castro-Gómez, Santiago. *La Hybris del Punto Cero. Ciencia, Raza e Ilustración en la Nueva Granada, 1750-1816.* Bogotá: Editorial Universidad Javeriana, 2005.

Chakrabarty, Dipesh. *Provincializing Europe: Postcolonial Thought and Historical Difference.* Princeton: Princeton University Press, 2008.

Chinedu, Obiora "Poverty, Agency and Resistance in the Future of International Law: An African Perspective." *Third World Quarterly* 27 (2006).

Douzinas, Costas. *The End of Human Rights.* Oxford: Hart Publishing, 2000.

—. *Human Rights and Empire. The Political Philosophy of Cosmopolitanism.* Abingdon: Routledge-Cavendish, 2007.

Dussel, Enrique. "Eurocentrism and Modernity." *Boundary 2*, 20 (1993).

—. *The Underside of Modernity: Apel, Ricoeur, Rorty, Taylor and the Philosophy of Liberation*, translated and edited by Eduardo Mendieta. New Jersey: Humanities Press, 1993.

—. "Democracy in the 'Center' and Global Democratic Critique". In *Democracy Unrealized. Documenta 11 Platform 1*, edited by O. Enwezor et al. Ostfildern-Ruit: Hatje Cantz Publishers, 2002.

Escobar, Arturo. "Imperial Globality and Anti-Globalisation Movements," *Third World Quarterly* 25 (2004).

—. "Worlds and Knowledges Otherwise." *Cultural Studies* 21 (2007).

Fanon, Frantz. *The Wretched of the Earth.* London: Penguin, 2001.

Fitzpatrick, Peter. "Latin Roots: Imperialism and the Making of International Law." In *Law as Resistance: Modernism, Imperialism, Legalism*. London: Ashgate, 2008.

Foucault, Michel. *Discipline and Punish: The Birth of the Prison*. New York: Pantheon, 1979.

Gilroy, Paul. *Darker than Blue. On the Moral Economies of Black Atlantic Culture*. Cambridge: Harvard University Press, 2010.

Grayling, A.C. *Towards the Light. The Story of the Struggles for Liberty and Rights that Made the Modern West*. London: Bloomsbury, 2007.

Habermas, Jurgen. *The Philosophical Discourse of Modernity*. Cambridge: MIT Press, 1990.

—. "The Concept of Human Dignity and the Realistic Utopia of Human Rights." *Metaphilosophy* 41 (2010).

Hegel, G.W.F. *The Philosophy of History*. Mineola: Dover Publications, 1956.

Heidegger, Martin. "Nietzsche's Word, 'God is Dead'." In *The Question Concerning Technology and Other Essays*. New York: Harper & Row, 1977.

Henkin, Louis. *The Rights of Man Today*. Boulder: Westview Press, 1978.

Horkheimer, Max and Adorno, Theodor. *Dialectic of Enlightenment. Philosophical Fragments*. Palo Alto: Stanford University Press, 2002.

Ibhawoh, Bonny. *Imperialism and Human Rights: Colonial Discourses of Rights and Liberties in African History*. Albany: SUNY Press, 2007.

Kant, Immanuel. "Idea for a Universal History from a Cosmopolitan Point of View." In *On History*. Indianapolis: The Bobbs-Merrill Co., 1963.

—. "Idea for a Universal History with a Cosmopolitan Purpose." In *Political Writings*. Cambridge: CUP, 1991.

—. "Idea for a Universal History from a Cosmopolitan Perspective." In *Toward Perpetual Peace and other Writings on Politics, Peace, and History*. New Haven: Yale University Press, 2006.

Kennedy, David. "Primitive Legal Scholarship." *Harvard International Law Journal* 27 (1986).

Kerber, Linda K. "We are All Historians of Human Rights." *Perspectives Online* 44 (2006). Available at http://www.historians.org/perspectives /issues/2006/0610/0610pre1.cfm

Koskenniemi, Martti. "Colonization of the 'Indies': The Origin of International Law?" In *La idea de América en el Pensamiento Ius Internacionalista del Siglo XXI*, edited by Yolanda Gamarra. Zaragoza: Institución Fernando el Católico, 2010.

—. "Empire and International Law: The Real Spanish Contribution." *University of Toronto Law Journal* 61 (2011).

—. "Histories of International Law: Dealing with Eurocentrism." *Rechts Geschichte-Zeitschrift des Max-Planck-Instituts für europäische Rechtsgeschichte* 19 (2011).

Lauterpacht, Hersch. "The Law of Nations, the Law of Nature, and the Rights of Man." *Transactions of the Grotius Society* 29 (1943).

Lindqvist, Sven. *Exterminate all the Brutes*. London: Granta, 1998.

Lyotard, Jean-Francois. *The Postmodern Explained: Correspondence, 1982-1985*. Minneapolis: The University of Minnesota Press, 1997.

Mgbeoji, I. "The Civilised Self and the Barbaric Other: Imperial Delusions of Order and the Challenges of Human Security." *Third World Quarterly* 27 (2006).

Mignolo, Walter. "The Many Faces of Cosmo-polis: Border Thinking and Critical Cosmopolitanism." *Public Culture* 12 (2000).

—. "The Geopolitics of Knowledge and the Colonial Difference." *The South Atlantic Quarterly* 101 (2002).

—. "Philosophy and the Colonial Difference." In *Latin American Philosophy*, edited by Eduardo Mendieta. Bloomington & Indiana: Indiana University Press, 2003.

—. "The Historical Foundation of Modernity/Coloniality and the Emergence of Decolonial Thinking." In *A Companion to Latin American Literature and Culture*, edited by Sara Castro-Klaren. Marden & Oxford: Blackwell, 2008.

Moyn, Samuel. *The Last Utopia: Human Rights in History*. Cambridge: Harvard University Press, 2010.

Muthu, Sankar. *Enlightenment against Empire*. Princeton: PUP, 2003.

Nesiah, Vasuki. "Resistance in the Age of Empire: Occupied Discourse Pending Investigation." *Third World Quarterly* 27 (2006).

Normand, Roger and Zaidi, Sarah. *Human Rights at the UN. The Political History of Universal Justice*. Bloomington and Indianapolis: Indiana University Press, 2008.

Nys, Ernest. *Les Origins Du Droit International*. Charleston: Nabu Press, 2012.

Quijano, Aníbal. "Coloniality of Power, Eurocentrism, and Latin America." *Nepantla: Views from South* 1 (2000).

—. "Coloniality and Modernity/ Rationality." *Cultural Studies* 21 (2007).

Rajagopal, Balakrishnan. "Counter-hegemonic International Law: Rethinking Human Rights and Development as a Third World Strategy." *Third World Quarterly* 27 (2006).

Rorty, Richard. "Inquiry as Recontextualisation: An Anti-Dualist Account of Interpretation." In *Objectivity, Relativism and Truth. Philosophical Papers I*. Cambridge: CUP, 1991.

—. "Is Derrida a Transcendental Philosopher?" In *Essays on Heidegger and Others. Philosophical Papers II*. Cambridge: CUP, 1991.

—. "Human Rights, Rationality and Sentimentality." In *On Human Rights: The Oxford Amnesty Lectures 1993*, edited by Stephen Shute et al. New York: Basic Books, 1994.

Santos, Boaventura de Sousa. *Towards a New Common Sense*. London: Routledge, 1995.

Schacherreiter, Judith. "Un Mundo donde Quepan Muchos Mundos: A Postcolonial Legal Perspective Inspired by the Zapatistas." *Global Jurist* 11 (2009).

Schmitt, Carl. *The Nomos of the Earth in the International Law of Jus Publicum Europaeum*. New York, Telos Press, 2006.

Svensson, Marina. *Debating Human Rights in China. A Conceptual and Political History*. Lanham: Rowan & Littlefield, 2002.

Todorov, Zvetan. *The Conquest of America. The Question of the Other*. Norman: University of Oklahoma Press, 1999.

Twining, William. *Globalization and Legal Theory*. London: Butterworth, 2000.

—. "Human Rights: Southern Voices - Francis Deng, Abdullahi An-Na'im, Yash Ghai and Upendra Baxi." *Review of Constitutional Studies* 11 (2006).

—. *General Jurisprudence: Understanding Law from a Global Perspective*. Cambridge: CUP, 2009.

—. ed. *Human Rights: Southern Voices: Francis Deng, Abdullahi An Na'im, Yash Ghai and Upendra Baxi*. Cambridge: CUP, 2009.

Waltz, Susan. "Reclaiming and Rebuilding the History of the Universal Declaration of Human Rights." *Third World Quarterly* 23 (2002).

Wells, H.G. *The Rights of Man or What We Are Fighting For*. London: Penguin, 1940.

Zizek, Slavoj. *Iraq: The Borrowed Kettle*. London: Verso, 2004.

—. "Against Human Rights." *New Left Review* 34 (2005).

—. Introduction to *Virtue and Terror*, by Maximilien Robespierre. London: Verso, 2007.

—. The Obscenity of Human Rights: Violence as Symptom. http://www.lacan.com/zizviol.htm

PART I:

CRITIQUE OF THE THEORY OF HUMAN RIGHTS

Chapter One

Who Speaks for the "Human" in Human Rights?

Walter Mignolo

The Issues: Experience and Philosophical Categories

"Human Rights"—as they are conceived in the Universal Declaration of 1948—presupposes that "human" is a universal category accepted by all and that as such the concept of human does justice to everyone. However, the concept of human used in general conversations, by the media, in university seminars and conferences, is a concept that leaves outside of "humanity" a quite large portion of the global population. That men (and women) are all born equal, is a statement that since Eighteenth-century Europe we can find in Bills of Rights and European and American constitutions. The statement has been made under the presupposition that everybody with a basic education, no matter where—in China, in the Middle East, in any region of Africa, Central Asia and South America, in Russia, etc—will agree with such a statement. Indeed, it makes a lot of sense and it can be taken as, if not universal, a global truth. The problem rests there, in the idea of equal status at birth. The problem is that if men —and women—are born equal, they do not remain equal the rest of their lives. The statement that I have never seen written as such but implied in countless places—"men and women are all born equal but they do not remain equal the rest of their lives"—should also be globally, if not universally, accepted. Surely it will be endorsed by the majority of the population of the planet who know by experience that such a statement is true. For all human beings born equal, losing their equality is a humiliating experience.

I will not trace the history of losing equality since the origin of the world—as told in the Bible, the Popol Vuj, or by Big-Bang physical theorists. I will examine how, when, why and which populations of the planet were classified and ranked. The classification and ranking was not a "representation" of a previously existing world already classified and ranked. Someone did the classification. Who did it and how was it legitimized? I will also argue that the concepts of "man" and "human" went hand in hand with the emergence of the concept of "rights." In other words, the idea of human and the idea of rights both separately and in conjunction have been invented by humanists of the European Renaissance. These ideas responded, on the one hand, to the internal history of Western Christians in what would become Europe in their long lasting conflicts with Islam and, on the other hand, to an external history of Christianity. Indeed this was the beginning of a historical process with no precedent. The emergence of the New World and new people forced Renaissance humanists to review their epistemic premises, and forced indigenous intellectuals in Anahuac and Tawantinsuyu,[1] as well as leaders and thinkers of enslaved Africans in the New World, to make sense of a history in which they were the real origin. Cut off from African histories, enslaved Africans had to start anew in the New World. This is the initial moment in which massive number of people began to lose their equality, their humanness and their rights.

Concepts such as "man" and "human" were an invention of European humanists of the fifteenth and Sixteenth centuries, an invention that served them well for several purposes. First, humanists introduced the concept of man to detach themselves (humanists) from the control of the Church. For the Church, being Christian, rather than being man, was what counted. Second, by inventing the idea of man, humanists distinguished themselves from co-existing communities they perceived as a threat, a challenge or as enemies: Saracens or Easterners, and pagans or rustic religions served to establish the difference with man. These two terms are already revealing: He the humanist was the one who placed himself in relation to the Saracens or Easterners, placed himself as Westerner. Westerners then defined the locus of enunciation—not as geo-historically and geo-politically located, but as the enunciation of the universal. Easterners defined instead the enunciated to whom the enunciation was denied: Easterners were defined by Westerners as if Westerners had the universal authority to name without being named in return. He (the humanist) who defined the pagans assumed that his own religion—Christianity in this case—was the point of reference and the most sophisticated religion in

---

[1] "Anahuac" was the name given to ancient Mexico by the Nahualt civilization, and "Tawantinsuyu" the name of the Inca empire.

relation to more rustic religions, the pagans. He (the humanist), who named and described the heathen, anchored his locus of enunciation in Christianity and Judaism, since "heathen" was used to refer and describe all those who were neither Christian nor Jews.

I have no doubt that the ones who were labeled by Christians and humanists did not see themselves as pagans, heathens and Saracens. First of all because the Arab speaking population in the East of Jerusalem and in the South of the Mediterranean, and the Latin and vernacular speaking population in the West of Jerusalem and the North of the Mediterranean, did not share the same history, memories, subjectivities and experiences. What we have here is just half of the story—the regional and provincial history told by Western Christians and Renaissance humanists. However, it was the Latin and Western vernacular categories that have been naturalized in a one-to-one correspondence with the designated entity. I am writing this article inhabiting the Latin and Western vernacular cosmology, not in its uninterrupted form but in its discontinuity: the discontinuity of Western classical tradition disrupted by the emergence of the New World in the consciousness of Western Europeans. Christians repeated with the population of the New World what they had been practicing with their undesirable neighbors and far away co-existing populations. Following Columbus's belief that he had landed in India (guided by Marco Polo's narrative about what is today South-East Asia), the people of Anahuac (today's Mesoamerica) and Tawantinsuyu (today's Andean region) were all named "Indians" and dispossessed of their millenarian identities. In like manner, the diversity of enslaved Africans captured and transported by force were baptized "Blacks", and were also dispossessed of their identities and ancient histories. What prevailed were the memories and identities of Europeans traced back to Greece and Rome.

Being and feeling oneself Western Christian meant also having "dominium" over the enunciation and assuming that whatever was named and conceived according to Greco-Latin principles and categories of knowledge, it would correspond to how the world really was. In the Sixteenth century treatise of historiography it is often stated that history is made of word and things, an assumption that was analyzed by Michel Foucault. Humanists felt authorized to speak for man and the human. The warranty of such belief was religious and epistemological—religious, because it was stated in Biblical narratives and was the dictation of God; and epistemological, because it had been framed by Saint Thomas Aquinas

(1224–1275), who brought together Greek philosophy and Biblical narratives. Needless to say, while Western Christians in the Fifteenth and Sixteenth centuries were demonizing differences that allowed them to create their own identity as Western Christians, Muslims from Africa to Central Asia where living their lives and doing their deeds in the same way as communities and societies in China and India.

It was not quite the same however for the communities and societies of Anahuac and Tawantinsuyu. Since the first half of the Sixteenth century they could no longer continue living their lives as it was before that time. Kingdoms of Africa that were broken by the kidnapping and enslavement of their young population and Black communities in America had to rebuild overcoming the differences of their original Kingdom. It was force and violence from the part of Western Christians and merchants—from Portugal, Spain, Holland, France and England—, but it was mainly the growing power of their own locus of enunciation that allowed them to assume that there was just one God and that they were His representatives on Earth. At the top of the species were Western Christians and placed below the rest: Saracens, Heathens, Pagans, Indians and Blacks. The assumption here is the belief in the absolute possession and control of knowledge and the denial of it to all the people classified outside and below.

Thus, when the idea and the category of man came into the picture, it came already with a privilege: the privilege of being under the framework already created by Western Christians. If then, being Christian was—for Christians themselves—the ultimate point of reference of civility and the correct life, being man was the ultimate point of reference of beauty, morality and knowledge for humanists. Man and Humanities updated the Roman idea of *humanitas* in the sphere of learning. *Humanitas* and *civitas*—close to the modern idea of citizens—presupposed an educated person. During the European Renaissance man was conceived at the intersection of his body and his mind, his body proportion and his intellect. Leonardo da Vinci's *Vitruvian Man* translated into visual language what humanists were portraying in words.[2] Man and *humanitas* became the frame of reference allowing the enunciator inscribed in Greco-Latin genealogy of thoughts to decide who belonged—not just to Christianity—but to humanity. During the European Renaissance He who spoke for the human was the humanist.

---

[2] http://leonardodavinci.stanford.edu/submissions/clabaugh/welcome.html.

He Who Spoke for the Human Spoke Also for Rights

In the European Renaissance the question of rights was not much of a question. The question was of law: divine and natural law. The distinction came from Roman law and the influential works of Cicero. The question of rights is properly a question of the modern/colonial world and not of ancient Rome; and even less ancient Greece. The question of rights was inaugurated by and of the historical foundation of modern colonialism; by the initial moment of imperial/colonial expansion of the Western world and the "spread" of the ideal of being Christian, the ideal man and—by the Eighteenth century—the idea of citizen and of democracy. From the Sixteenth century to the Universal Declaration of Human Rights, He who speaks for the human is an actor embodying the Western ideal of being Christian, being man and being human. In other words, "human" in human rights is an invention of Western imperial knowledge rather than the name of an existing entity to which everyone will have access too. Being an invention of Western knowledge means that the idea of man and human is controlled by certain categories of thoughts entrenched in particular, regional history and experience—for a Jamaican woman like Sylvia Wynter the idea and ideal of what does it mean to be human will certainly differ from the same question asked and responded by Francesco Petrarca, for example.[3]

In this regard, Western imperial knowledge—that is, based on Greek and Latin categories and translated into modern European vernacular languages like Italian, Spanish, Portuguese, German, French and English—controls, i.e. owns, the concept of human. If you want to dispute it from the genealogy of thoughts of Arabic, Urdu, Russian, Aymara, Bambara or any other languages and experiences embedded in non-Western history you would have two options: either to bend and accept what is human according to Western knowledge—grounded in Greek and Latin—or to de-link, to engage in epistemic disobedience denouncing the provincialism of the universal, and to adopt a collective, differential or planetary assumption that being human is not being Vitruvian, Christian or Kantian, but it is instead being able, first, to dispute the imperial definition of humanity. Secondly, it is to engage in building a society in which the human is not defined and rhetorically affirming that we are all equal, but

[3] On Sylvia Wynter's ideas on the subject, and bibliography, see Anthony Bogues, ed., After Man, Towards the Human. Critical Essays on Sylvia Wynter (Kingston: Ian Randle Publishers, 2006).

one in which the human will be what comes of constructing societies on principles that prevent classification and ranking to justify domination and exploitation among people who are supposed to be equal by birth. If you decide for this option, please do not attempt to provide a new truth, a new definition of what does it mean to be human that will correct the mistakes of previous definitions of human. Since there is no such entity, the second option would be de-colonial, that is, to move away—de-link—from the imperial consequences of a standard of the human, humanity and the related ideal of civilization. If you choose this option it doesn't mean that you accept that you are not human and you are also a barbarian. On the contrary, placing yourself in the space that imperial discourse gave to lesser humans, uncivilized and barbarians, you would argue for radical interventions from the perspective of those who have been made barbarians, abnormal and uncivilized. That is, you will argue for justice and equality from the perspective and interests of those who lost their equality and have been subjected to injustices.

Rights then emerged in the process of building what today is conceived as modern/colonial world. In other words, rights is a concept responding to imperial necessity. I will sketch three moments of the trajectory of rights and conclude by showing that human rights today continues to be an imperial tool at the same time that it became a site to fight injustices qualified as violations of human rights. "Humanitarian interventions," which entered the vocabulary of international relations in the past decades, bring back to the present the generally forgotten history of the human and rights.[4]

In the first stage, the question of rights was linked to peoples or nations—communities of birth, *nation*. Theological and legal theorists at the University of Salamanca, in the Sixteenth century, began to address such questions prompted by the "apparition"—much like the apparition of Virgin Mary—on the intellectual horizon of Western Christians, of people who were not accounted for in Biblical narratives. Led by Dominican Francisco de Vitoria, one of the main issues was to solve the problem of *ius gentium*, rights of peoples or of nations. The questions of "natural, divine law and human law" were not new issues; all had a tradition in Christian theology and were laid out by Saint Thomas Aquinas. What is

---

[4] Concurrent arguments can be found in Franz Hinkelammert, "The Hidden Logic of Modernity: Locke and the Inversion of Human Rights." *Worlds & Knowledges Otherwise* Fall (2004): 1–27. Accessible at www.jhfc.duke.edu /wko/ dossiers/ 1.1/ HinkelammertF.pdf.

crucial here is not so much the "novelty" within the same classical
European tradition—that is, the newness within a uni-linear and uni-versal
idea of history—but the *discontinuity*; the moment in which the Western
genealogy that men of the European Renaissance were attempting to build
upon the legacies of Greece and Rome is *dislocated* by the emergence of
people totally outside Greek-Roman—and Jerusalem—legacies. Vitoria
had to deal then with the authority of the Pope and the authority of the
Monarch. Vitoria questioned the authority of the Pope arrogating to
himself the power to "give" half of the New World to the Spaniards and
half to the Portuguese and the Emperor. A second issue Vitoria had to deal
with was the relation between "belief" and "right to property." He argued
that unbelief does not cancel natural law, and since ownership and
dominion are based on natural law, the right to property is not cancelled
either by unbelief. Indians are not believers, but because of natural law
they have, like the Spaniards, property rights. Vitoria's openness and
fairness missed a crucial point: he did not stop to ponder whether Indians
cared about rights and whether Indians relationship to land was a relation
of property, like it was for the Spaniards, and not something else. In other
words, as a good humanist and theologian, Vitoria spoke for humanity and
told half of the story without realizing it; assuming, indeed, that he—and
his colleagues—was dealing with the world as it is, and not as it was for
him/them.

The logic of Vitoria's argument is flawless. The premises are suspect.
Why would Vitoria assume that Aztecs and Incas and other communities
in the New World would have the same "avarice" toward property as
Spanish Christians? Why did he not stop to think for a minute that life and
economy, among the inhabitants of the New World, was organized upon
different principles? He did not. And therefore the next step was to justify
the rights of the Spaniards to dispossess "Indians"—not Aztecs or
Incas—of the "property" that Indians did not conceive as such.
Remember, Indians have property rights. The question was how to find a
way to legitimize Spaniards' appropriation of Indian properties having
acknowledged that Indians had property rights. There were two positions
among Spanish men of letters about the "nature"—humanity—of the
Indians. For the most conservative, Indians were irrational, dirty,
immature, barbarians, etc. For more progressive men of letters like
Dominicans Bartolomé de Las Casas and Francisco de Vitoria himself,
Spaniards and "Indians"—and not for them Náhuatl, Aymara, Quechua,
Tojolabal, etc. speaking people—were rational in their own way.
Spaniards and Indians were both bound by a system of natural law;

therefore, both Spaniards and Indians were subjected to *ius gentium* —natural law of peoples or nations. However, there was something "lacking" among the Indians that placed them in an inferior echelon vis-à-vis Spaniards.

As he was Spaniard and not Aymara or Tojolabal, Vitoria managed to articulate the legal *colonial difference*, based on his control of knowledge —i.e., his assumptions on the principle of argumentations, as well as the belief that whatever questions were relevant for the Spaniards they were also relevant for Indians because their questions were uni-versal.

Here we have in a nutshell the material apparatus of enunciation upon which racial classification will be based from then on, and the concept of man and human that was established in its universality by the regional enunciation of an ethno-class controlling knowledge. Man and human —and not blood of skin color—is the bottom line of racial classification. And racial classification is nothing more than one answer to the question "who speaks for the human?". Classified races do not exist in the world but in the discursive universe of Western theology, philosophy and science. As existing racial classification—since the Renaissance— presupposes a ranking of human beings depending on their approximation to principles of knowledge—belief and rationality, form of life and socio-economic organization—and on ontological approximation to the *Vitruvian Man*—form and social uses of the body such as posture, walking, dance, rituals, and Christian and non-Christian rituals—the actors who perform and maintain racial classification *are the ones who speak for the human*. Theology was the overarching edifice of knowledge in Christian Europe and the New World in the Sixteenth and Seventeenth centuries. Of course Christian theology was not the overarching edifice of knowledge during the Sixteenth and Seventeenth century in China, nor in the Ottoman, Mughal or Safavid sultanates. Neither it was among Incas and Aztecs in the New World. But for European Christian males it was universal knowledge. That is why Vitoria did not stop for a second to ponder whether the concept of "property" as he understood it, was the same among his "Indians."

Siba N'Zatioula Grovogui explored some issues concerning international law and the modern/colonial world as follows:

I seek to demonstrate that the dependence of international politics on the European dominated political economy and its legal apparatus resulted in two of the most significant paradoxes of decolonization: The first is that only the rights sanctioned by the former colonialists were accorded to the colonized, regardless of the needs and demands of the latter [...] The second paradox is that the rules and procedures of decolonization were determined and controlled by the former colonial power to effect specific outcome. This is a paradox because *the right to self-determination* is generally understood to mean *the absolute political authority to create rights and obligations for oneself* [...] The rules and processes of decolonization not only denied African communities the right to the protection of the law, they failed to recognize African's need for such protection.[5]

There is a straight line—to which I will return in the next two sections —in the history interrelating the concept of people, men, citizen, human and rights, which goes from the *colonial revolution* of the Sixteenth century to the *de-colonial revolutions* of the second half of the Twentieth century—starting with India in 1947. Although Grovogui begins his argument with Hugo Grotius—which is a common beginning for scholars of International Law in the English and French speaking worlds—it is obvious for most scholars in the Spanish and Portuguese worlds[6] that his two paradoxes are nothing but the two cases of the constitutive and complementary character of modernity/coloniality. What appears as a paradox is, and has been, the node, the technological key of the simultaneity, always simultaneity, between the rhetoric of modernity announcing salvation, happiness, progress, development, etc., and the necessary logic of coloniality—appropriation of natural resources, exploitation of labor, legal control of undesirables, military enforcements of the law in order to ensure "salvation" through the imposition the interests and a world view inherent to capitalist economy.

The second moment was self-fashioned and enacted between the Glorious Revolution in England (and the Bill of Rights [1689]) at the end of the Seventeenth century, and the American (Declaration of Independence [1776]) and French Revolutions (The Rights of Man and of the Citizen [1791]), at the end of the Eighteenth century. The main difference between the theories of Vitoria (in Spain) and Grotius (in Holland)—which were elaborated around notions of *ius gentium* as

---

[5] Siba N'Zatioula Grovogui, *Sovereigns, Quasi Sovereigns and Africans: Race and Self-Determination in International Law* (Minneapolis: University of Minnesota Press, 1995), 96.
[6] With some exceptions, such as German Catholic Carl Schmitt, for whom the Catholic Spanish intellectual tradition was a necessity, an opinion that also prompted his polemic with Max Weber.

foundations of international law—on the one hand and, on the other, the Bill of Rights and the Rights of Man, was that the latter were no longer operating in the international arena but, instead, were limited to national issues. It was indeed the period in which nation-states were being forged and the advent of the bourgeois ethno-class was being legitimized. Rights were linked to the construction of nation-states and the coming into being and the stabilization of an ethno-class commonly known as the European bourgeoisie. Being human meant to be rational, and rationality was limited to what philosophers and political theorists of the Enlightenment said it was.

By the end of the Seventeenth century, being human became more identified with being secular bourgeois than with being Christian. However, being Christian did not vanish; it remained in the background. Exteriority was no longer a problem. The battle had been already won and the energy was concentrated on an idea of humanity that was re-cast as The Rights of Man and of the Citizen after the French Revolution. "Nations" in the emerging nation-states displaced the idea of "nation" (*gentium*) in Vitoria and Grotius. A new figure of exteriority was necessary when the concept of "citizen" was introduced: the "foreigner" enriched the list of "exterior human," that is, of "defective humans" next to pagan, Saracens, Blacks, Indians, women and those with non-normative sexual preferences. The Enlightenment idea and ideal of man and humanity was adopted and adapted in the colonies. The so-called "American Revolution" was in the hands of white men of British descent. They did not have yet the problem of the "foreigner" as in Europe, but the Founding Fathers had the problem of Indian and Black populations which, of course, Europe did not have. In other words, man and human in the United States were defined at the crossroads of British and European philosophy, and in contradistinction with Indians and Blacks surrounding the Founding Fathers.

In South America—Spanish and Portuguese colonies and ex-colonies —the situation was similar to that of the United States but with significant differences. The similarity was that independence was in the hands of white men from European descent—Spain and Portugal. Leaders of independence movements and nation-state builders of continental South America and Ibero-Caribbean also conceived man and humanity in the European tradition and in contradistinction with Indians—mainly continental Spanish America—and Blacks—mainly Brazil and the Caribbean. However, in the dominant discourse of Northern European ranking of man and human, Spain and Portugal and their nationals, were already considered second class Europeans. Immanuel Kant and G.W.F. Hegel canonized this view. In short, by the Eighteenth century, those who spoke for the human were secular philosophers and political theorists in the heart of Europe—France, Germany and England. That vision was adopted by Creoles from European descent in the United States, South America and the Caribbean. And that vision became constitutive also of the model of man and humanity when England and France began their expansion to Asia and Africa. "The civilizing mission" was nothing else but: a) imposing a model of man and humanity; and b) assuming—after Kant and Hegel's canonization—that not only non-Christian religions were inferior, but that people of color speaking languages non-derived from Greek and Latin were less human. Roman legacy of *humanitas* and *civitas* were rehearsed when European men and citizens appointed themselves to carry civilization to the *anthropos* of the planet.[7]

This view did disappear with the Universal Declaration of Human Rights in 1948. All the talks, problems, and dramas of immigration in the European Union and the United States cannot be properly understood, nor addressed, without asking who speaks for the human in the modern/colonial and casts immigrants in different scales of the sub-human. Old racial categories are being recast when it is no longer the colonist who encounters the *anthropos*, but the *anthropos* who is knocking at the door of the colonist in his imperial home.

"Human" in the Universal Declaration was redefined according to the changing world order and the change of hands in imperial leadership, from England to the United States. Subsuming the nation-state stage of the Bill of Rights and The Rights of Man and of the Citizen, the Universal Declaration returns to the arena of inter-state relations and international law set up by Vitoria and Grotius. In fact, for Grotius, distinct from Vitoria, the problem of international law was twofold: on the one hand, international law meant inter-Europe. He was living and writing in the middle of the Thirty Years Religious War. And indeed he was sitting, literally and metaphorically, in Holland during its short-lasting but quite influential imperial moment. Grotius and Descartes, indeed, were in Amsterdam when Holland was gaining its imperial momentum. Grotius'

---

[7] On the distinction *humanitas*/*anthropos* see Nishitani Osamu, "Anthropos and Humanitas: Two Western Concepts of "Human Being,"" in *Translation, Biopolitics, Colonial Difference*, ed. Naoki Sakai and Jon Solomon. (Hong Kong: Hong Kong University Press, 2006).

Mare Liberum could have been named "universal declaration of rights to the sea in international law." Vitoria did not label the issue he was discussing "universal declaration of rights and international law," but that is what he was doing: defining and profiling the human by tracing the colonial difference, epistemic and ontological.

After the interregnum of nation-state building in Europe and nation-state imperial expansion—mainly England and France—the Universal Declaration was forged with three horizons in mind, under the leadership of the United States: a) the rebuilding of Europe after the Holocaust and the Second World War; b) the "communist menace," which was added to the old list of pagans, Saracens, Indians and Blacks; and c) the uprising in the Third World, of which the independence of India was already a strong sign of alert. United States politics of foreign relations strongly supported self-determination of colonial locales. The motifs were not so much the right to self-determination but, rather, the United States global designs. Very much like the "independence" of South Americans from Spain and Portugal—the building of nation-states that under the fiction of sovereignty depended on France in knowledge, culture and politics, and on England in the economy—decolonized countries in Asia and Africa sooner or later moved under the arm of uncle Sam.

The idea of "human" in the Universal Declaration was taken for granted: it had been already profiled in the Renaissance and rehearsed in the Enlightenment. What else could be said about what being human means? However, a geo-political remapping took place with the same hidden assumptions under which Renaissance humanists were operating. Parallel to the Universal Declaration, a reclassification of the planet was taking place: First, Second and Third World. By the seventies, indigenous people from all the Americas, New Zealand and Australia, made themselves heard: where is our face, they asked, in this world order? A new category was invented to "please them": the Fourth World. Do you think indigenous people of the planet were happy to be a fourth-class global citizen? And who is talking and celebrating, today, global citizenship?

"First World" looked like an objective category, the naming of an existing entity. What was hidden was that the classification was made from the perspective of the First and not from the Second, Third or Fourth World. Five hundred years separated political scientists and economists after Second World War from Renaissance humanists. The logic, however, was exactly the same. Only the content changed. No more pagans, heathens or Saracens, but communists, underdeveloped and—still!— Indians.

The First World was where humanity par excellence dwelled. The rest was inhabited by different kinds of *anthropos*. Liberalism and Christianity set the ideological stage against communism. Humanity par excellence was surrounded by the dangerous Second World, communism, in the Soviet Union, in its colonies at the border of Europe—the Caucasus, Belorussia and Ukraine—, in Central Europe and the Balkans. And then the Third World, the farthest away from the model of humanity par excellence. But, since the Declaration of Human Rights was universal, the entire population of the planet had the right to have rights. This was the First World's gift to the Second and Third Worlds. But it was a gift similar to stating that all men and women are born equal. People of the Second and Third Worlds were told that they have the right to have rights. However, they were also told that they were in the Second and Third World; that the latter were underdeveloped and that the former were under a totalitarian regime. And that it was mainly in the land of the *anthropos* where, it was expected, human rights would be violated. Human rights were not expected to be violated in the First World. The First World was not setting up a Declaration to shoot on their own foot; particularly after Hitler had been already defeated… but Stalin was still alive and well.

In other words, the international order was mapped no longer in terms of *ius gentium* but of human rights. Until 1989 one of the main functions of human rights was to watch closely their violations in communist countries and in countries of the Third World not aligned with the United States. The violators or perpetrators of human rights were denounced, accused and, if possible, penalized. The saviors, in the First World, defended the cause of democracy. It was mainly with Guantánamo and Abu-Ghraib that the First World was caught as violator and perpetrator and no longer as—just—a savior. The difference with the Second and Third World was that the violation did not take place in the First World but in Third World territory. Humanity was not, it is not, a transcendental and neutral essence that just anyone can appropriate and describe. Humanity has been created upon philosophical and anthropological categories of Western thought and based on epistemic and ontological colonial differences. If someone else wants to use human rights they must specify what kind of human he or she is. For example "indigenous rights" are predicated on the assumption of their difference from "universal"—or

White Euro-American—rights. However, by the sheer fact of naming a set of rights "indigenous" it becomes clear that they cannot be universal rights and that what passes as universal is indeed "Euro-American white rights." That is, two "species" of the human, by convention, which is spoken by everybody who want to speak and locate him or himself in a specific community of rights.

When the Cold War ended, human rights took a new impulse and were associated with the second wave of development. The first wave took place between 1950 and 1970 and the labels were "development and modernization of underdeveloped countries." The International Monetary Fund and the World Bank were the two main institutions in charge of advancing the project. After the fall of the Soviet Union, development came back under the label of "globalization and market democracy." Human rights have been recast since the fall of the Soviet Union, with one of its consequences being the Washington Consensus and the neoliberal doctrine. This scenario dominated the 90s and was extended to deal with the consequences of 9/11's aftermath. The question of Islam and human rights then became central.

Basically, the Washington Consensus—a doctrine of about ten points advanced by John Williamson in 1989—was the second wave of "development and modernization" launched in the 1950s and ending around 1970.[8] In the interregnum, Western rhetoric turned to "modernity" and "globalization" and, in the nineties, modernity and globalization were subsumed under the Washington Consensus. What does all of this have to do with human and rights? Quite a bit, indeed.

It has been documented by many that the Washington Consensus doctrine was a road to global disasters. One well informed analysis is the classic book by Joseph Stiglitz *Globalization and its Discontents*[9]. Parallel to the implementation of the Washington Consensus a significant expansion of non-governmental organizations took place. Although a civil society organization to help the needy can be dated back to the mid-Nineteenth century, it was officially established as non-governmental organization in 1945 within the charter of United Nations. As the growing influence of neoliberal doctrine increased, since Ronald Reagan and Margaret

---

[8] Regarding the Washington Consensus, see www.cid.harvard.edu/cidtrade/issues/washington.html.
[9] Joseph Stiglitz, *Globalization and its Discontents* (New York: W.W. Norton, 2003).

Thatcher, so did its devastating consequences. NGOs proliferated. The Washington Consensus operated, at the economic level, in the same frame of mind that missionaries operated at the religious level in the Sixteenth century. Conquering the soul of the Indians by conversion is equivalent to conquering the soul and labor of underdeveloped countries and people. The differences are also important: conversion did not imply exploitation. Exploitation, in the Sixteenth and Seventeenth century, was the job of merchants, plantation owners, *encomenderos* and gold and silver mine owners. However, at that time, they were not attempting to impose their economic behavior; just taking advantage and accumulating wealth.

Thus, parallel to the increase of poverty and widening of the line separating the have from the have-nots, violations of human rights proliferated under damaging conditions. Whether leaders of the Washington Consensus and NGO officers see the connection or not, the fact remains that NGOs have been working to take care of damages inflicted by neoliberalism and the Washington Consensus. Both, the Washington Consensus and NGOs are a Western creation under the global mask of the United Nations. The proliferation of nationally based NGOs still depends on the master plan. In the same vein, the Washington Consensus managed to find and establish their branches in the underdeveloped world, e.g., Menem in Argentina, and Sánchez de Lozada in Bolivia. Consequently, both the Washington Consensus and NGOs were based in the ex-First World and their action directed mainly toward the ex-Second, Third and Fourth Worlds. Or, if you wish, they were both institutions in the *humanitas* geared toward developing and taking care of the *anthropos.* The consequences of the logic of coloniality—disastrous consequences of the Washington Consensus doctrine—were sold and disguised by updating the rhetoric of modernity—development, market, and democracy. With the injuries inflicted by the logic of coloniality in order to advance what the rhetoric of modernity promised, someone has to take care of the damage. And the NGOs were there to help the *anthropos.*

The situation reached a point in which the closed circuit of the rhetoric of modernity, the apparent collateral damages which indeed are the actual consequences of the logic of coloniality, prompted the emergence of a global political society taking destiny in their own hands. In other words, while NGOs operate in the sphere of civil society repairing the damages of neoliberal capitalism, the political society came into being with a different horizon in mind: decoloniality. While NGOs work to help the *anthropos*, the political society is the *anthropos* in arms and thoughts. This very essay is located in the sphere of the *anthropos* and of the political society. Issues of humanity and rights, for the First and Third World, of developed and underdeveloped countries, are called into question. Indeed, what is being called into question is not exactly these categories, but the epistemic locus of enunciation that created them as if they were uni-versal and good for all. What is being called into question is the saying behind the said. That is, it is a call and a process toward de-colonization of knowledge and of being—knowledge and being entrapped by the imperial and modern ideas of man, the human and the Humanities. If then the Humanities—a field of knowledge since the Renaissance—is in part responsible for the creation and maintenance of the concept of human, the first step is to engage in de-colonial Humanities. Or if you wish, de-colonizing the Humanities, tantamount to engaging in practicing de-colonial Humanities.[10]

De-colonial Humanities and the Question of Rights

Contrary to the global order during the European Renaissance and Enlightenment, the control of knowledge and the relative success of Western empires to control and manage discontent, today everyone is speaking. The political society is marching next to—and sometimes in confrontation with—the civil society and NGOs. Muslim and Aymara intellectuals are jumping on the debate about the human, humanity and rights. And scholars in the Humanities and Chinese history are putting in conversation Confucianism and human rights. Afro-Caribbean philosophers are taking front stage. Global projects such as *La via capeskin* is following Monsanto's steps more closely and proposing alternatives for the enhancement and preservation of life rather than initiatives for growth and accumulation and the fertilization of death.

What this means is that human and rights are no longer trusted to Western initiatives and its rhetoric of salvation. Human and rights have been placed in a different universe of discourse, that of the political society and de-colonization. And what all of this amounts to, with pros and cons that should be analyzed in each case, is that everyone is ready to speak for the human and for rights. The premise is *to change the terms and not just the content of the conversation*. To provide a "new"—and satisfy modernity's desire for newness—will be more akin to the task of NGOs than to de-colonial projects. When, for example, Jamaican intellectual and

---

[10] On "de-colonial Humanities" see www.fb10.uni-bremen.de/inputs/tagungen/bericht2006.htm.

activist Sylvia Wynter outlined a horizon "after man, toward the human"—a statement in which the story I told above is implied—we are already in a change of terrain in our conversation about Wynter's question of "what does it mean to be human." Once we have asked this question, the next one follows: how is it that human relations became "enclosed" in relation to rights and not framed in other terms? How a society organized to produce more and to succeed on the basis of domination and exploitation can be the "perpetrator" of rights violations and at the same time the creator of a concept of the human that legitimizes such a community as "savior"? Not long ago I attended a talk by a Danish NGO's representative about violence in Guatemala. The NGO in question was heavily engaged in solving the problem of violence so that a transnational corporation, a chiefly Danish one, could invest and make Guatemala prosper. While it has to be recognized that Guatemalans have the right to live in a consumer society, it is not at all clear if that is what all Guatemalans are looking for. Certainly Danish are looking for that, but Danish and Guatemalan interests could be in conflict. It was in a following talk, by a Guatemalan himself, when I learned that many communities in Guatemala see themselves as poor but not as victims, and as poor they are taking their lives in their own hand and not putting their lives in the hands of Danish NGOs.[11]

The ideas of the human, humanity and rights became a contested arena. The "victims" are not always waiting for the "savior," and the "savior," willingly or not, may work to the benefit of the "perpetrator." Taking their destinies into their own hands, political society's diversity of projects involve actors whose experiences and subjectivities do not match the expectations of NGOs or of peripheral European economic investments. Some actors place themselves in the wide array of imperial interests, now widespread.

At another level, that of the nation-states—instead of the sphere of the civil and political society—current conflicts between the United States and the European Union on the one hand, and Russia, China, Iran, India and Brazil on the other, are conflicts between two types of nation-states: Western nation-states embedded in an imperial history congruent with capitalist economy, and nation-states encountering capitalism. A

---

[11] I am referring to presentations made at the Business School and at the Rehabilitation and Research Center for Torture Victims, Copenhagen.
www.cbs.dk/content/download/81673/1084891/file/PROGRAMMEFINAL%208.5.08.pdf.

polycentric capitalist world is emerging. The principles of a capitalist economy are the same, but national histories, sensibilities, desires, tensions and anger with Western imperial arrogance, places the same economic logic at the service of particular interests, national or regional. The question of human rights emerges here as a place in which the so called "democratic and industrialized" states use the rhetoric of human rights violation to confront their economic rivals. Western expansion and capitalist economy is a terrain of "capitalist contention" today. In that controversy, a polycentric capitalist world order goes hand in hand with a polycentric discourse on human and rights—set in non-Western histories and sensibilities—that cuts across Western history of the idea of the human and of rights from the European Renaissance to the Second World War. The distinction made above between civil society and NGOs, and political society is also valid for the following analysis.[12]

The political society has been and continues to be formed by dissenters and activists whose goal is not to remedy the damages of capitalist economy in order to make its functioning smoother, but to de-link from that system and the belief that the more it is produced the better it is for "the people", and to work toward a society not built on principles of accumulation. There is already enough evidence sustaining and justifying the directions—de-colonial I would say—of the political society.

Let's make clear that the political society cannot be subsumed under de-colonial processes. Many sectors and projects advanced in the political society have a vision and horizon frame which is not de-colonial: theology of liberation, progressive and critical liberalism, Marxism, white feminism and white queer activists. Having said that, it is imperative to remember that the de-colonial option—or de-colonial options if you prefer the plural—is NOT the new and only game in town. It is called "option" precisely because it is an option among others. The purpose of de-colonial thinking is not to debunk concurrent projects neither to capture more converts and became the one and only. Pluriversality, and not universality, is the horizon of de-colonial thinking.

Under the de-colonial processes projects are under way and are emerging and proliferating all over the world and de-linking from the

---

[12] This concept has been introduced by Partha Chaterjee. See, for example, Partha Chaterjee, *The Politics of the Governed. Reflections on Popular Politics in most of the World* (New York: Columbia University Press, 2004). I found it appropriate to refer to a variety of global manifestations such as social movements.

major spheres of dissension in the West. De-colonial projects and the
political society join forces when the horizon and the vision are guided by
the struggle of liberation from the Western control of economy—control
of labor and of natural resources—authority, knowledge, subjectivity,
gender and sexuality.

De-colonial Humanities—or the de-colonial option in the Humanities
—is coming into sight as a consequence born out of the demands of the
de-colonial political society.[13] De-colonial Humanities assume, in the first
place, that the Humanities have been and continue to be a fundamental
dimension of Western scholarship. Secondly, it is assumed that the
Humanities—as a set of disciplinary formations—are bound to the
Renaissance concept of the human and to the Enlightenment concept of
reason. In Western genealogy of thought the Humanities have a double
face: under the name of Humanities, on the one hand, arts, literature,
philosophy, and in certain degree the social sciences, flourished in the
West and enchanted the non-Western world. On the other, the Humanities
were the epistemic site in which it was possible, for social actors, to speak
for the human. The Humanities naturalized, in the modern/colonial world,
the long lasting distinction that has been brilliantly summarized and
argued by Japanese scholar Nishitani Osamu, between *humanitas* and
anthropos.[14]

Osamu's argument can be recast, I hope without making violence to it,
in the language and the purposes of de-colonial Humanities. A de-colonial
Humanities project is not to take in its hands the definition of the human, a
definition that *includes*—inclusion is off de-colonial discourse—
everybody and that presents de-colonial thinking as THE point of arrival.
De-colonial thinking in this sense is naturally non-Hegelian. What the de-
colonial option proposes, and Osamu's article clearly illustrates this, is
that: a) concepts of man, human and humanity are inventions of Western
scholarship since the Renaissance; b) these concepts have links to the
concept of rights, which is also a European Renaissance invention in its
colonial expansion, i.e. its darker side; and c) in a world order of
polycentric capitalist economies, the concepts of man, human and

---

[13] For an example of how de-colonial Humanities are being thought out in Russia
see www.jhfc.duke.edu/globalstudies/currentpartnerships.html, and ww.jhfc.duke.
edu/ globalstudies/Tlostanova_how%20can%20the%20decolonial%20project.pdf
[14] Nishitani Osamu, "Anthropos and Humanitas: Two Western Concepts of
'Human Being'." In *Translation, Biopolitics, Colonial Difference*, edited by Naoki
Sakai and Jon Solomon. Hong Kong: Hong Kong University Press, 2006.

humanity became also a polycentric dispute at the level of states (Jordan, Iran, France) and international institutions. For example, Mohammad Khatami, former President of Iran, launched the project *Dialogue among Civilizations*[15] to counter Samuel Huntington's *Clash of Civilizations*,[16] and UNESCO in 2005 formed a truly international committee, *Alliance of Civilizations*,[17] whose main task has been to work toward peace. UNESCO's project is not the only one. Prince Hassan of Jordan has been leading a similar project under the name of *Dialogue of Civilizations*, which follows Khatami's pronunciation. In the Middle East, Prince Hassan is mainly concerned with dialogue between Muslims, Jews and Christians. All these projects are, I repeat, unfolding at the level of States and institutions of international scope.[18]

De-colonial projects are closer to grass-roots movements than they are to States and institutions in which, directly or indirectly, the question of the human, humanity and rights is being redressed. This of course does not mean that collaboration between de-colonial and institutional is not possible. It only means that these two kinds of projects operate at different levels: one at the level of institutions and the civil society; the other in the sphere of the political society.

In de-colonial thinking, peace, a peaceful world, a peaceful society, requires two main conditions:

1) To de-link from capitalist economy, organized societies, nationally and internationally.
2) To accept—even if for the ruling minority it will be difficult—that indeed the vast majority of marginal human beings are human as the privileged economic and political elites, nationally and internationally.

If these two conditions are fulfilled, no one in particular will speak for the human because the human will just be taken for granted. And in such societies, there will be no need for rights, because there will be no perpetrators violating human and the life rights—in the latter case the

---

[15] www.un.org/Pubs/chronicle/2006/webArticles/102006_Khatami.htm.
[16] Samuel Huntington, *The Clash of Civilizations and the Remaking of World Order* (London: Simon & Schuster, 1997).
[17] www.unaoc.org
[18] On these issues, see: www.qantara.de/webcom/show_article.php/_c-476/_nr-983 /webcom/show_article.php/_c-478/_nr742/i.html?PHPSESSID= ad16a32480e 888 ca549942f86da5191e).

victim being the life of the planet. That is to say, the life of all, including the species described as humanity. The concept of the human, as it has been articulated in Western discourse since the Sixteenth century—from Francisco de Vitoria to John Locke to the Universal Declaration of Human Rights—went hand in hand with Frances Bacon's conceptualization of Nature as something that has to be controlled and dominated by man.

In sum, de-colonial thinking is not arrogating upon itself the right of having the last word about what the human is, but proposing instead that there is no need for someone specific to talk about the human, because the human is what we are talking about. However, what lingers are five hundred years of epistemic and ontological racism constructed by imperial discourses and engrained in the last five hundred years of global history.

Bibliography

Bogues, Anthony, ed. *After Man, Towards the Human. Critical Essays on Sylvia Wynter*. Kingston: Ian Randle Publisher, 2006.

Chatterjee, Partha. *The Politics of the Governed: Reflections on Popular Politics in Most of the World*. New York: Columbia University Press, 2004.

Grovogui, Siba N'Zatioula. *Sovereigns, Quasi Sovereigns and Africans: Race and Self-Determination in International Law*. Minneapolis: University of Minnesota Press, 1995.

Hinkelammert, Franz. "The Hidden Logic of Modernity: Locke and the Inversion of Human Rights." *Worlds & Knowledges Otherwise* Fall (2004):1–27.www.jhfc.duke.edu/wko/dossiers/1.1/HinkelammertF.pdf.

Huntington, Samuel. *The Clash of Civilizations and the Remaking of World Order*. London: Simon & Schuster, 1997.

Osamu, Nishitani. "Anthropos and Humanitas: Two Western Concepts of 'Human Beings'." In *Translation, Biopolitics, Colonial Difference*, edited by Naoki Sakai and Jon Solomon. Hong Kong: Hong Kong University Press, 2006.

Stiglitz, Joseph. *Globalization and its Discontents*. New York: WW. Norton, 2003.

CHAPTER TWO

PROVINCIALIZING HUMAN RIGHTS?
THE HEIDEGGERIAN LEGACY
FROM CHARLES MALIK
TO DIPESH CHAKRABARTY

MARTIN WOESSNER

"Seen in the long perspective of the future, the whole of western European history is a provincial episode."[1]

"So far as human rights are concerned, what matters is what presents itself in our world, now."[2]

Intellectual historian David Hollinger has suggested that one of the most pressing problems of the Twenty-First century "is the problem of

For their comments on various portions and versions of this paper, I thank José-Manuel Barreto, Fred Beuttler, Marlene Clark, Neill Jumonville, Eduardo Mendieta, Samuel Moyn, Alvaro Eduardo de Prat and Roy Scranton. I would also like to thank the participants of both the 11th Annual Comparative Literature Conference at the University of South Carolina on "The Futures of Human Rights", and The Historical Society's 2010 Conference at George Washington University in Washington, DC, where the earliest incarnations of this paper were first presented.

[1] John Dewey, "From Absolutism to Experimentalism" (1930), in *The Essential Dewey, Volume I: Pragmatism, Education, Democracy*, eds. Larry A. Hickman and Thomas M. Alexander (Bloomington: Indiana UP, 1998), 21. I thank....... for calling this quotation to my attention.

[2] Bernard Williams, "Human Rights and Relativism," in *In the Beginning Was the Deed: Realism and Moralism in Political Argument*, ed. Geoffrey Hawthorn (Princeton: Princeton University Press, 2005), 67.

willed affiliation, the problem of solidarity."[3]   It is safe to say that the
topic of human rights, whether conceived in terms of discourse, legacy or
practice, resides at the crux of this problem. Though their exact origins
and their fundamental meaning are still debated, human rights are an
inescapable part of the international community's self-conception in the
age of globalization. Depending on one's perspective, they are either the
last gasp or the final goal of human solidarity. What the proponents and
critics of human rights have in common is the implicit recognition that, in
the early Twenty-first century, human rights cannot be avoided—they can
be supported or suppressed, enshrined or denied, extended or rescinded,
but they cannot be ignored.

Hence the increasingly voluminous literature devoted to the subject,
emerging from almost every corner of the contemporary academy.
Students today can get their human rights lessons not only from faculties
of law and international relations, but also from departments of politics,
philosophy, literature, history and film, as well as the various other
disciplines which comprise the social or human sciences, such as
anthropology, economics and sociology. It goes without saying that this
seemingly universal topical agreement does not immediately translate into
scholarly consensus, but it certainly does reveal the intellectual
preoccupations of the moment. It is significant that even historians, who
are generally slowest to absorb the cutting-edge interests of their
colleagues in other disciplines, are immersing themselves in topics
relevant to the discussion of human rights. "We are all historians of
human rights," declared Linda Kerber, president of the American
Historical Association, in 2006.[4] Whether for good or ill, human rights
really do represent—as one recent study has put it—"the last utopia" of
our age.[5] The possibility of international solidarity seems to rest solely
with them.

No doubt part of the appeal of human rights is that they represent the
age-old desire to actualize normative aspirations, to move from the realm

---

[3] David A. Hollinger, *Cosmopolitanism and Solidarity: Studies in Ethnoracial,
Religious, and Professional Affiliation in the United States* (Madison: University
of Wisconsin Press, 2006), xv.
[4] Linda K. Kerber, "We are All Historians of Human Rights" *Perspectives Online*
44 (2006). Available at http://www.historians.org/ perspectives/issues/ 2006/ 0610/
0610pre1.cfm
[5] See Samuel Moyn, *The Last Utopia: Human Rights in History* (Cambridge:
Harvard University Press, 2010).

of the ought to the domain of the is. In the words of Jürgen Habermas, human rights represent a "realistic utopia."[6] However real human rights have become in the contemporary world, though, their origins nevertheless remain linked to the imaginative, aspirational realm of ideas. Even after they entered into the concrete world of international legal and political discourse with the United Nation Universal Declaration of Human Rights (1948), human rights represented uncharted theoretical and practical territory. In this sense, the many philosophical and ideological debates that took place in the wake of the Universal Declaration were, we might say, struggles over how this new territory should be mapped. They were attempts to forge a new world, or, at the very least, to unveil an old world—as Mary Ann Glendon's influential book has it—"made new."[7]

But what, exactly, is the geography of this new world? And who is responsible for mapping it? If human rights are indeed a constitutive element of the new, contemporary world, it behooves us to inquire into the ways in which they emerged out of the fractured geographies of the old world. Any attempt to outline a geography or even a genealogy of human rights today must not only limn the contours of the future, but also the rough edges of the past.

What we find when we inquire into the contested terrain of human rights in the twentieth century, if not before, is a repeated struggle between those who situate human rights squarely in the intellectual terrain of the Western tradition, and those who do not. Given that so many of the key debates regarding the fate and future of human rights took place against the backdrop of the emerging Cold War, it is not surprising to discover that human rights were a point of contestation between what at the time was seen as the liberal, democratic traditions of the West, and the more communal, if not explicitly Marxist or communist, traditions of the East— of what used to be the Soviet bloc, as well as China and North Korea. But beyond this easy opposition, so famously described by Isaiah Berlin as "Two Concepts of Liberty" in 1958, lays a whole range of debate that sought to use the concept of human rights not to shore up one position or

---

[6] Jürgen Habermas, "The Concept of Human Dignity and the Realistic Utopia of Human Rights," *Metaphilosophy* 41 (2010): 464-80.
[7] Mary Ann Glendon, *A World Made New: Eleanor Roosevelt and the Universal Declaration of Human Rights* (New York: Random House, 2001).

the other, but to call both into question simultaneously.[8] In this sense,
human rights really were a utopia, a no-where place from which critiques
of both the West and the East could be launched.

To speak of the alternate geographies of human rights, then, is not
simply to locate resources situated outside of the West, or even outside of
the West/East standoff. It is also to locate those places situated within
these regions and traditions that fostered suspicion and skepticism
internally. The following account seeks to do just this by tracing the
surprising influence of the work of the German philosopher Martin
Heidegger in the writings of two key figures in the human rights
movement, Charles Malik and Václav Havel, as well as, closer to our own
time, two extremely influential scholars, Richard Rorty and Dipesh
Chakrabarty. Although the title for this work derives from Chakrabarty's
much discussed book, I hope to show that the animating principle of his
attempt to rewrite the history of colonial and postcolonial India, an
animating principle derived fundamentally from Heidegger's longstanding
critique of Western rationalism, can also be found in Malik, Havel and
Rorty. Taken together, this eclectic group of thinkers just might give us
the necessary instruments to map out a different conception of human
rights altogether, one that looks not just to the clean centers of
cosmopolitan power, but to the messier margins of provincial suffering.

Heidegger and Human Rights

In discussions of the philosophical foundations of human rights, the
name of Martin Heidegger rarely comes up, and for good reason we might
think. As a philosopher known to popular culture primarily either for his
hermetic writing or his support for the National Socialist regime in
Germany, Heidegger seems an unlikely source of inspiration for the
current culture of international human rights. In fact, any number of
reasons might cut short an attempt to include him in future discussions of
human rights: he was very much a German nationalist, and consequently
deeply suspicious of liberal internationalism; he was a staunch critic of
philosophical humanism, especially after the Second World War; and his
entire philosophical corpus was predicated upon the rejection of the very
metaphysics that still lingers in the natural law tradition, as well as in so

---

[8] Isaiah Berlin, "Two Concepts of Liberty," in *The Proper Study of Mankind: An
Anthology of Essays*, ed. Henry Hardy and Roger Hausheer (New York: Farrar,
Straus and Giroux, 1998), 191-242.

many other traditions important to the articulation of a coherent intellectual paradigm of human rights today.[9]

Indeed, if we accept the common narrative, which sees the emergence of the United Nations, and the culture of international human rights it supposedly fosters and supports, as the silver lining on the cloud that was the Second World War, then it seems even more improbable that a thinker from the wrong side of that conflict should guide our discussion of the contemporary relevance—if not the future possibilities—of human rights. Whether or not we can truly and honestly see the rise of human rights, via the notion of "crimes against humanity" employed at the Nuremberg Trials, as the glimmering phoenix to emerge from the rubble and ashes of total war, it cannot be denied that the shadows of the war, and more so the Holocaust, loom large over our conceptions of human rights and international justice today.[10] Indeed, some of the arguments made on behalf of the American invasion of Iraq in 2003 were humanitarian arguments that harkened back to this period directly.[11] The war in Iraq was presented as an extension of the liberal fight against totalitarianism—a defense, in the end, of human rights, perhaps proving the point made by composer Arnold Schoenberg in 1947, after the Holocaust, "that most men consider it their human right to dispute, even to overpower, the human rights of their fellows."[12]

Over and against these reasons for keeping Heidegger away from human rights and human rights away from Heidegger, however, it cannot be denied that his work has shaped the human rights discourse we currently employ. Implausibly, surprisingly, Heidegger has been an influence—even if a troubling or problematic one—on intellectuals and activists who played instrumental roles in shaping the human rights legacy

---

[9] The latest book to highlight the more dubious aspects of Heidegger's work is Emmanuel Faye's *Martin Heidegger: The Introduction of Nazism into Philosophy in Light of the Unpublished Seminars of 1933-1935*, trans. Michael B. Smith (New Haven: Yale University Press, 2009).

[10] See, for instance, the documentary film *The Reckoning: The Battle for the International Criminal Court*, 2009, directed by Pamela Yates, which makes this connection explicit.

[11] See, for example, the essays collected in Thomas Cushman, ed., *A Matter of Principle: Humanitarian Arguments for War in Iraq* (Berkeley: University of California Press, 2005).

[12] Arnold Schoenberg, *Style and Idea*, trans. Leo Black (New York: St. Martin's, 1975), 506.

of the later half of the Twentieth century. Because of this, we must confront the topic of Heidegger and human rights, as paradoxical as it might at first glance seem. Even more important than simply setting the intellectual-historical record straight, though, is the task of using the story of Heidegger's influence to reveal some of the longstanding and underappreciated ambiguities that rest within the Western conception of human rights itself, ambiguities that anyone interested in promoting human rights today must eventually come to terms with.

Charles Malik and the "Challenge to the West"

One of the principle drafters of the UN Universal Declaration of Human Rights was the Lebanese philosopher and statesman Charles Malik. As Glendon recounts it in her book on the drafting of the Universal Declaration, Malik played a key role in the process of not only shaping and composing the document, but perhaps even more importantly, of getting it ratified as well. Despite this remarkable achievement—and despite the efforts of his son, the intellectual historian Habib C. Malik, who has begun to oversee the publication of some of his father's more important human rights related papers—Malik père remains shrouded in historical neglect.[13] A fascinating thinker and personality in his own right, he calls out for further study. Too little is known about his philosophical training, and how it may have influenced his later work at the United Nations. Restoring Malik the philosopher, in other words, may very well shed light on Malik the human rights activist.

Charles Malik studied with Heidegger in Freiburg between the First and Second World Wars. Like so many other thinkers who have helped shape our current discourse of rights—figures such as Leo Strauss and Hannah Arendt, for example—Malik's worldview was profoundly shaped by his studies with, and of, Heidegger, though this fact is often overshadowed by his later accomplishments as both an educator and a diplomat.[14] Glendon, for example, hardly discusses Malik's debts to Heidegger. Only in a brief aside, in which she quotes a few cryptic,

---

[13] For his son's efforts to restore his legacy, see Habib C. Malik, ed., *The Challenge of Human Rights: Charles Malik and the Universal Declaration* (Oxford: Centre for Lebanese Studies, 2000).

[14] See Leo Strauss, *Natural Right and History* (Chicago: University of Chicago Press, 1953); and Peg Birmingham, *Hannah Arendt and Human Rights: The Predicament of Common Responsibility* (Bloomington: Indiana University Press, 2006).

though revealing lines from Heidegger found in Malik's notebooks, does she broach the topic. Around the time that the Universal Declaration was presented to the General Assembly, it seems Malik recorded a Heideggerian aphorism, culled from the latter's *Aus der Erfahrung des Denkens*, in his diary. The poetic aphorism, "We are too late for the gods and too/ early for Being," somewhat bleakly suggests that Malik may have had some doubts about his work on behalf of the UN Declaration, but Glendon does not pursue this line of investigation.[15] No explanation for Malik's invocation of Heidegger's portentous remark is given.

If we go beyond the immediate context of the Universal Declaration, though, and examine Malik's earlier philosophical education, we find that the aphorism was not a chance scribbling. It reflects the deep and profound commitment to Heideggerian existentialism that pervaded his earliest writings, including even his doctoral thesis. In his dissertation, which he presented to the "Division of Philosophy and Psychology" on April 3, 1937, Malik undertook a massive project: a lengthy and detailed comparison of the "Metaphysics of Time," in the work of two very important, though almost diametrically opposed, philosophers—Alfred North Whitehead and Martin Heidegger. Malik had the unique experience of studying with both of them. Whitehead and Heidegger, even and especially in 1937, represented two vastly different conceptions of the philosophical persona.[16] The former, a founding figure of process philosophy, was along with his student Bertrand Russell a preeminent example of the philosopher-as-scientist. It was his work in mathematics, logic and what we now call the philosophy of science that formed the foundation of his philosophical worldview. The latter, by contrast, staked his reputation on the rejection of this philosophical trajectory. Indeed, Heidegger's examination of *Existenz* was, as he often admitted, an attempt to get behind or beneath the natural scientific worldview, an aim espoused

---

[15] Glendon, *A World Made New*, 170. The aphorism reads, "*We sind zu spat für die Götter, zu früh für das Sein.*" Heidegger's text was translated into English many years later as "We are too late for the gods and too/ early for Being," under the title "The Thinker as Poet" in *Poetry, Language, Thought*, trans. Albert Hofstadter (New York: Harper Perennial, 1976), 4. Needless to say, as Glendon points out, this is a rather bleak and ominous sentiment for a drafter of one of the most important human-rights documents in history. But perhaps the next line of Heidegger's text puts it into perspective: "Being's poem,/ just begun, is man."

[16] On the importance of the "philosophical persona" in the writing of the history of philosophy, see Ian Hunter, "The History of Philosophy and the Persona of the Philosopher," *Modern Intellectual History* 4 (2007): 571-600.

by his own mentor, Edmund Husserl. Increasingly, this task led him to adopt the persona of the philosopher-as-prophet.

Although he thanks Whitehead profusely in the preface to his dissertation, it is clear that Malik was drawn far more to Heidegger's existential analysis than to the mathematically tinged work of the Harvard philosopher. For the young Malik, philosophy's main purpose was not abstraction, but what we might call instead, after Gilbert Ryle and Clifford Geertz, a "thick description" of the human condition. Heidegger's work, especially his masterpiece *Sein und Zeit* (1927), offered what Malik thought was a "more concrete outlook" than Whitehead's overly abstract and scientific cosmology.[17] The fact that Malik had originally intended to give his dissertation the Heidegger-inspired title "The Nature of the Concrete" reveals the extent to which he fell in line with other young philosophers, like former Heidegger students Günther Anders and Herbert Marcuse, who also sought to follow Heidegger's example in examining the concrete facticity of existence.[18] For these young radicals, philosophy was clearly not to be thought of as a science of the abstract, but as an immersion in the practical.

At the heart of Malik's dissertation, sandwiched between two sober and scholarly philosophical exegeses—one of Whitehead's process philosophy and the other of Heidegger's *Sein und Zeit*—is a very unusual chapter, entitled "From Cosmology to Existenz." It is here that Malik's own voice is most discernible, and this voice is, quite plainly, an existential one. "Philosophers do not take their philosophy seriously," he laments at one point. "It is an exciting game" to them and nothing more.[19] We can detect in these words a not-so-subtle rebuke of mathematical philosophers such as Whitehead who would reduce existential *Sturm und Drang*—the messy and terrifying reality of life—to formulaic propositions and abstractions. Indeed, as Malik points out, "Professor Whitehead's philosophy knows no chasms in existence. It recognizes no absolute,

---

[17] Charles Malik, "The Metaphysics of Time in the Philosophies of A. N. Whitehead and M. Heidegger" (PhD diss., Harvard University, 1937), 241.
[18] Ibid., 240. Interestingly, both Stern and Marcuse—drawn to Heidegger for his seemingly concrete approach—later reproached him for failing to be concrete enough. See Günther Stern-Anders, "On the Pseudo-Concreteness of Heidegger's Philosophy," *Philosophy and Phenomenological Research* 8 (1948): 337-71; and Herbert Marcuse, *Heideggerian Marxism*, ed. Richard Wolin and John Abromeit (Lincoln: University of Nebraska Press, 2005), 34-52.
[19] Ibid., 247.

cataclysmic distinctions. It never quite works up to something like 'radical particularity'."[20]

It is this interest in "radical particularity" that animates Malik the philosopher as well as, later on, Malik the human-rights advocate. His philosophy is a lived philosophy, and it is founded upon the radical particularity of individual, lived experience. As he puts it elsewhere in his dissertation, "it is only when all of you, the whole of you, grasps and flows into what you are that you know what the concrete is."[21] His philosophical thinking, like the work he would put into drafting the Universal Declaration of Human Rights only a decade or so later, was attuned to the concrete and decidedly un-abstract nature of each human life, a core principle of the legacy of human rights—at least in the Western tradition—going all the way back to Thomas Hobbes. But it was also a principle that could be buried all too easily under so many abstractions and rationalizations. To save the individual, Malik, again like Heidegger, sought to translate philosophy into direct practice: "The life of Socrates", he suggests at one point in the dissertation, "was more 'expressive' of his philosophy than his words."[22] Or, as he puts it even more pointedly a page later, "a philosophy that does not express the total man is to me false philosophy."[23]

For the Heidegger of *Sein und Zeit*, the moment of decision is what ensured that each and every individual was responsible for his or her own existence. It was what pulled us out of everyday inauthenticity, and out of false philosophy as well. The moment of decision was a call to action more than reflection and it had more in common with Kierkegaard's leap of faith than it did with Whitehead's philosophical formulae, which translated human existence into so many charts, graphs and numbers. Clearly, Malik not only agreed with this aspect of Heidegger's work, but absorbed it as well. To quote him at length, again from the frank and revealing chapter "From Cosmology to Existenz":

> What is a prophet? A prophet is a person who has handed himself over to God to use him in rousing otherwise descriptively lethargic people to a consciousness of decision. It is the end of the world for him. He offers himself to this demand of decision in other people. His sole concern is to

---

[20] Ibid., 253.
[21] Ibid., 253.
[22] Ibid., 253.
[23] Ibid., 254.

see other people wake up from their descriptive slumber, to an anxious consciousness of decision. This he can do only as his whole being—its total moral worth—is constantly in the balance. He is only striving to impart to other people this sense of being wholly in the balance.[24]

In reading these lines it is difficult not to see a foreshadowing of Malik's own prophetic role in the United Nations Human Rights Commission. But all this points to one of the many paradoxes of Heidegger reception: while Malik was busy translating Heidegger's philosophy of the concrete into a defense of the human person, and later, a foundation for universal human rights, Heidegger was translating it into propaganda for the Nazi revolution, often with the very same kind of language—the language of decision, anxiety and existence. In his infamous 1933 rectorial address, Heidegger asked his university-wide audience what they intended to do "when the spiritual strength of the West fails and the West starts to come apart at the seams, when this moribund pseudo civilization collapses into itself, pulling all forces into confusion and allowing them to suffocate in madness."[25] His answer, as the first Nazi to lead the venerable university at Freiburg: that "our Volk fulfill its historical mission."[26] It is obviously a thin line that separates the prophet of peace in this instance from the prophet of doom.

As was apparent in his doctoral thesis, Malik shared with Heidegger a deep suspicion of Western tendencies towards abstraction and rationalism, which, taken to extremes, threatened to snuff out the vibrancy of individual existences. He may not have accepted Heidegger's famous 1935 suggestion that "the spiritual decline of the earth" could only be halted by the efforts of a new—and newly remilitarized—Germany, but he did accept that the West was indeed in crisis.[27] Malik's defense of human rights was a defense of the West, to be sure, but it also afforded him the opportunity to redefine what the Western tradition should hold most dear. Especially as Cold-War era tensions escalated—as early as 1948 with the Berlin blockade, but also up through the 1960s during the turbulent era of decolonization—Malik was ever ready to stave off the threat of

---

[24] Ibid., 253.
[25] Martin Heidegger, "The Self-Assertion of the German University," in *The Heidegger Controversy: A Critical Reader* ed. Richard Wolin (Cambridge: MIT Press, 1993), 38.
[26] Ibid.
[27] Martin Heidegger, *An Introduction to Metaphysics*, trans. Ralph Manheim (New Haven: Yale, 1959), 38.

communism. His works from this period participated in the ideological struggle of the era not simply by reasserting Western jingoism, but by prophetically appealing to the unfinished spiritual projects of humanism and individualism.

In an address to the Political Committee of the General Assembly delivered on November 23, 1949, Malik defended the "deepest traditions of the West," which, he argued, "conceived of man as the subject of basic and inalienable and universal rights, rights which are based upon his very nature and which are embodied in natural law."[28] For him, human rights were an integral part of the Western tradition. But the Western tradition itself, he went on to explain, was by no means perfect in its defense of these rights. If communism was to be faulted for reducing individuals to merely "the most precious capital" of its international movement, then it also had to be admitted that, increasingly, the West was itself slipping into little more than a "soulless materialism," which, when seen from the perspective of the wider world, hardly differed from the "militant materialism of the East."[29]

These comments come from a section of Malik's presentation entitled, none too subtly, "Critique of the West."[30] For Malik, the gravest danger of the Cold War was not so much the communist threat from without, but rather, the "weakening of the moral fiber" from within.[31] As if harkening back to his Heidegger-inspired critique of the overly abstract and scientific philosophy of Whitehead, Malik dismissed "talk about democracy, freedom, [and] representative government" as "woefully inadequate," as little more than "sheer external machinery," especially if it was not connected to "man's deepest cravings for friendship and understanding and truth and love."[32] Without embedding itself in concrete forms of life, which are based upon much more than the superficial achievements of

---

[28] Charles Malik, *War and Peace: A Statement made before the Political Committee of the General Assembly, November 23, 1949* (Stamford: The Overlook Press, 1950), 23.

[29] Ibid., 25 and 32. As Mary Ann Glendon has put it, "challenged not only the members of the Soviet bloc who wanted to subordinate the person to the state, but also the more individualistic Westerners" in the Human Rights Commission. See Glendon's introduction to Malik, *The Challenge of Human Rights*, 3.

[30] Malik, *War and Peace*, 31.

[31] Ibid., 32.

[32] Ibid., 32.

technocratic rationalism, the tradition of Western individualism, so important for the articulation of human rights, remained hollow:

> It ought to be very bluntly stated that a world that is relatively imperfect from the economic and material point of view, but that retains at its heart the core of love and truth and freedom which has for three thousand years characterized Western civilization at its best, is vastly to be preferred to any world, no matter how absolutely perfect materially and economically, which rejects this creative core of love and truth and freedom. The prefect soul can always correct the imperfect body, but where there is no soul, even the most perfect body is soon but dust and ashes.[33]

As the imagery of souls and ashes makes clear, Malik's defense of the West was rooted in a Christian conception of the dignity of the human person, something that atheistic communism seemed to deny at every turn. Although Malik may have followed a distinctly Heideggerian path in his own thought, he was also a committed Christian. In this sense, he was closer to the Personalism and Neo-Thomism that would later become so important to other human rights thinkers such as Jacques Maritain.[34] We can see as much in Malik's 1963 book *Man in the Struggle for Peace*, which originated in lectures delivered at The Claremont Colleges in California.[35] At least in 1937, however, Malik was more committed to a prophetic, decisionistic philosophical position, one which sought to puncture scientific philosophy's facile attempts to explain away existence and at the same time do justice to the full picture of human experience along the lines of Heidegger's existential analytic—all without necessarily relying upon religion. There is little to distinguish him from Heidegger except for his more humanistic tenor. Perhaps the more explicit dependence upon Christian teaching in later years was an attempt to rein in some of the dangerous tendencies in Heidegger's thought.

In the decades following his work on the United Nations Human Rights Commission, Malik, whether functioning as a diplomat or a

---

[33] Ibid., 43.

[34] For more on Maritain and human rights, see the provocative working paper by Samuel Moyn, "Jacques Maritain, Christian New Order, and the Birth of Human Rights," available online at
http://papers.ssrn.com/sol3/papers.cfm? abstract_id=1134345.

[35] Charles Malik, *Man in the Struggle for Peace* (New York: Harper & Row, 1963). See also the volume of essays edited by Malik, *God and Man in Contemporary Christian Thought* (Beirut: American University of Beirut Centennial Publications, 1970).

philosopher, continued to simultaneously defend and critique the Western tradition, especially as it stood in relation to the concept of human rights. Malik was a "cold warrior" through and through, but his willingness to openly criticize the Western fascination with technical modernization at the expense of spiritual and ethical nourishment set him apart from many of the fervent pro-Western ideologues of his day. "Nothing is more pathetic today"—he declared in a 1951 address—"than the spectacle of man seeking his happiness in the abundance and determination of material things, and forgetting that joy, satisfaction, rest and salvation are all questions of the spirit."[36]   Almost a decade later, in Williamsburg, Virginia, he placed himself "wholly on the side of the West, despite its many imperfections, mistakes, failures, and sins."[37] As he had some nine years earlier, Malik again outlined a great many of these imperfections and mistakes, attributing many of them to a "crisis of faith" in the West's own values.[38] If the Western world could offer anything to the non-Western world, it was its universal spirit, not its technological gadgets or even its material abundance. "Man can live without goods and gadgets," he intoned, "but he cannot live without something human and universal that joins him to his fellow men."[39]

   In the global struggle for the hearts and minds of the so-called Third World during the era of decolonization, Malik made it clear that Western-style "modernization" was not enough. Against the "mandarins of the future"—to borrow the moniker historian Nils Gilman has bestowed upon the various think-tank intellectuals who so fervently shaped American foreign policy during these years—Malik sought to shift the Cold War conversation from matters of modernization and development to issues of spiritual growth.[40] "This is Asia's and Africa's deepest challenge to the West," he suggested, "what have you to give me, not of your trinkets, but

---

[36] Charles Malik, "The Twin Scourges: Materialism and Self-Sufficiency," in Malik, *The Challenge of Human Rights*, 210. The address was originally presented at the Carnegie Endowment for International Peace on September 19, 1951.
[37] Charles Malik, *"Will the Future Redeem the Past?" An Address Delivered at Williamsburg, Virginia, June 11, 1960* (Richmond: Virginia Commission on Constitutional Government, 1960), 4.
[38] Ibid., 16.
[39] Ibid., 17.
[40] Nils Gilman, *Mandarins of the Future: Modernization Theory in Cold War America* (Baltimore: Johns Hopkins University Press, 2003).

of your mind, not of the external husks of your life, but of the substance and marrow of your soul?"[41]

In his keynote address to the Second Corning Conference, held in upstate New York, Malik reiterated this theme. His opening line said it all: "The derivation of man from, and the reduction of man to material, economic, and social conditions is the great heresy of this age."[42] Development was the reigning logic of the day, whether one was an ally of Western, liberal democracy, or Eastern, Soviet communism. For Malik, both had lost sight of the importance of the individual person as a spiritual and ethical being. "The one mortal sin today," he told his audience, "is not atheism, paganism, bigotry, tyranny, cruelty, oppression, immorality, or falsehood: the one mortal sin is to be behind materially, whether as an individual or as a nation."[43] The whole language of development, from which we today get the division of the globe into the First and Third Worlds, stemmed, for Malik, from this fundamental misconception of the nature and purpose of human society.[44] It reduced the complex and plural realities of global societies—conveniently divided up by Malik into seven essential groups, along largely Eurocentric lines—to the level of "sheer economic process."[45] Whitehead had won; process had edged out existence.

Although Malik stressed that "there is no universal modern society and there is no univocal individual in it," he nevertheless believed that the Western concept of the human person, if properly recovered from the oblivion to which modern economic rationalism had sent it, might ensure

---

[41] Malik, "*Will the Future Redeem the Past?*," 18.

[42] Charles Malik, "The Individual in Modern Society," in *The One and the Many: The Individual in the Modern World, The Second Corning Conference*, ed. John Brooks (New York: Harper & Row, 1962), 135.

[43] Ibid., 136.

[44] On the divide between the first and third world in American modernization theory, see Nils Gilman, *Mandarins of the Future*, 72-74. For a slightly different perspective, see Bradley R. Simpson, *Economists with Guns: Authoritarian Development and U.S.-Indonesian Relations, 1960-1968* (Stanford: Stanford University Press, 2008).

[45] Malik, "The Individual in Modern Society," 145 ff. Malik's seven different conceptions of the individual's relationship to society ascend from the tribalism of "African society," through Chinese, Russian, India, Muslim, Latin and Western European models, with the last serving as the ultimate example of a society structured around the freedom of the individual.

freedom and peace for all.[46] The fate of not just the Western individual, but of all individuals everywhere, was at stake. The Cold War, for Malik, was not a battle for military supremacy, economic superiority or even territorial control; it was, first and foremost, a struggle for the hearts and minds of the unaligned states and peoples of the globe. If the West was to win the Cold War, it had to confront its own existence in a way that spoke to the deepest recesses of the human psyche. This much he had already recognized, with the help of Heidegger, in his Harvard dissertation. Like his friend and colleague, the American philosopher John Wild, whose 1955 book *The Challenge of Existentialism* covered similar ground, Malik remained convinced that the Cold War standoff necessitated an internal critique of western superficiality more than the establishment of any external, military posture.[47]

Václav Havel's "Existential Revolution"

With the election of Jimmy Carter as the thirty-ninth President of the United States many years later, the philosophical position that Malik had been long advocating finally seemed to resonate in Washington.[48] Human rights, and not just modernization or development, were made a political priority at long last. But it would be wrong to suggest that Heidegger played much of a role in this context. When it came to matters of concrete policy, Malik's brand of Heideggerian human rights had only limited influence. It was in the East, behind the Iron Curtain, where the Heideggerian strain of human rights thinking really flourished during the 1970s. Czech dissidence proved that, far from being the gift of the United States to the rest of the world, the concept of human rights—whether Heidegger-inspired or not—was mobilized by local communities, pursuing their own concrete and particular interests. It was used, in other words, to stand against both Soviet communism and American liberal democracy.

As historian Aviezer Tucker has shown, Heidegger was a key source of inspiration for two of the most prominent figures in Czech dissidence: philosopher Jan Patočka and man of letters—and later president—Václav

---

[46] Ibid., 152 and 156.
[47] John Wild, *The Challenge of Existentialism* (Bloomington: Indiana University Press, 1955).
[48] On the ambiguities of the Carter administration's record on human rights, see, most recently Iatai Nartzizenfield Sneh's *The Future Almost Arrived: How Jimmy Carter Failed to Change U.S. Foreign Policy* (New York: Peter Lang, 2008).

Havel.[49] Patočka, who had studied with Heidegger and Husserl in Freiburg around the same time that Malik, provided the philosophical foundation for the oppositional Charter 77 movement. His writings addressed truth, authenticity and existence, and became landmarks in the dissident critique of totalitarian rule, which was no doubt why he was imprisoned and interrogated by communist authorities, an ordeal that lead to his premature death on March 13, 1977.

The Charter 77 movement inaugurated Havel's career as a dissident. He was perhaps an unlikely anti-totalitarian figurehead, with thicker ties to music and the arts than to anything overtly political.[50] But his philosophical bent, evident in his writings, set him apart. Havel's most famous essay "The Power of the Powerless," which was dedicated "to the memory of Jan Patočka," was written and distributed underground in 1978.[51] In this essay Havel examined not only the day-to-day workings of communist rule in Czechoslovakia but the possibilities of resistance to it as well. By his lights, communist society was, as Patočka had suggested for some time, inauthentic. It promulgated the very abstractions and evasions that Heidegger—and, like him, Malik—had warned against. What was needed was, in Havel's words, "an existential solution," one that took "individuals back to the solid ground of their own identity."[52] This was the only path back to "authentic existence," to what he calls throughout the essay, in mantra-like, prophetic fashion, "living in truth."[53] Knowing the truth was not enough; one also had to live the truth as well. For Havel, again like Malik before him, human rights were not abstract political or legal concepts, but concrete manifestations of the individual existence.

In his dissertation, Malik wrote of Heidegger's attempt, in *Sein und Zeit*, "to blow away the concealing mists of abstraction, and to just let the

---

[49] "Though the philosophies of Patočka and Havel incorporated distinctly Heideggerian themes, their dissident practice in support of human rights is radically different from Heidegger's practice." Aviezer Tucker, *The Philosophy and Politics of Czech Dissidence from Patočka to Havel* (Pittsburgh: University of Pittsburgh Press, 2000), 12.

[50] Tony Judt, *Postwar: A History of Europe since 1945* (New York: Penguin, 2005), 568 ff.

[51] Václav Havel, "The Power of the Powerless," in *Open Letters: Selected Writings, 1965-1990*, ed. Paul Wilson (New York: Vintage, 1992), 125-214.

[52] Ibid., 152.

[53] Ibid., 148.

honest truth reveal itself in its overpowering clarity."[54]   A similar aim permeates Havel's "The Power of the Powerless," wherein one finds a yearning for the simplicity of individual autonomy, unencumbered by state control or by ideological jargon. In the writings of both Havel and Malik, the simple truth of philosophy is not a grand system, but a humble and authentic existence. Havel calls it "living in truth;" Malik describes it as "you and I living, interacting with our world, enjoying our life, facing it."[55]   For both, the achievements of Western rationalism, of science and industry, are dubious at best, especially insofar as they further alienate the human person from him or herself. For Malik, the scientist does not study human persons, but merely "'living tissue.'"[56]   For Havel, modern, technological society, whether communist or capitalist—his equivalence of the two reveals a certain Heideggerian tendency towards world-historical exaggeration—reduced individuals to "little more than tiny cogs in an enormous mechanism."[57]

Havel's Heideggerian critique of Western science and technology is most apparent in his essay "Politics and Conscience," which Havel wrote in 1984, after having been in and out of prison since 1977 as a result of his dissident activities. In the text he denounces Western science, Western pollution of the environment, and, most of all Western politics, a category that for him subsumed both American liberal democracy and Soviet communism. The blame for these various phenomena, which eviscerated all local cultural and historical ties, is placed squarely upon the tradition of Western "rationalism."[58]   Far from representing a targeted critique of totalitarian rule, "Politics and Conscience" was a wide-ranging indictment of all forms of politics in the modern, industrialized world, especially as they reflect the growth and ever-increasing danger of "impersonal power."[59]   Havel went to great lengths to remind his readers that this looming, bureaucratic, totalitarian threat to human rights originated within—not outside of—the West. For him, there was no East/West divide. "It was precisely Europe, and the European West," he argued,

> that provided and frequently forced on the world all that today has become the basis of such power: natural science, rationalism, scientism, the industrial

---

[54] Ibid., 274.
[55] Malik, "The Metaphysics of Time," 274.
[56] Ibid., 323.
[57] Havel, "The Power of the Powerless," 186.
[58] Havel, "Politics and Conscience," in Havel, *Open Letters*, 260.
[59] Ibid., 263.

revolution, and also revolution as such, as a fanatical abstraction, through the displacement of the natural world to the bathroom down to the cult of consumption, the atomic bomb, and Marxism.[60]

Even if "democratic Western Europe" could not recognize any of itself in the trappings of Soviet totalitarianism, it was undeniable for Havel that Soviet communism was but an "ambiguous export" of Europe itself.[61]

For Malik, communism threatened to throw the Western tradition off course. For Havel, however, the problem went deeper than this. Havel thought that "totalitarian regimes" were a grave danger not because they opposed the West, but because they embodied it: they were "the avant-garde of a global crisis of this civilization, first European, then Euro-American, and ultimately global."[62] Soviet rule was merely the symptom of a much more profound—and far more widespread—peril, namely the detrimental global dissemination of Western rationalism. "No evil has ever been eliminated by suppressing its symptoms," Havel declared. "We need to address the cause itself."[63]

In language reminiscent of Malik's own attacks on the materialism of the modern world, Havel brought "Politics and Conscience" to a close by juxtaposing the "dehumanizing" attempts "to produce better economic functioning" and the far more difficult, but consequently far more necessary, tasks of forging "a new understanding of human rights."[64] While the former were, at bottom, merely "tricks and machinations" of impersonal state bureaucracies, the latter were forays into the realms of "love, friendship, solidarity, sympathy, and tolerance"—all things that, taken together, formed the "genuine starting point of meaningful human community."[65] Havel's politics, which he carefully designated "antipolitical politics," represented a "politics of man, not the apparatus." His politics grew "from the heart, not from a thesis."[66]

At the end of the day, Havel's "antipolitical politics" sought to foster what Patočka had called—in reference to Charter 77—a "solidarity of the

---

[60] Ibid., 258.
[61] Ibid.
[62] Ibid., 260.
[63] Ibid., 261.
[64] Ibid., 268.
[65] Ibid., 267.
[66] Ibid., 269 and 271.

shaken."[67] It sought to pit solidaristic humanity against impersonal inhumanity; individual human beings against abstract legal, political, and/or economic entities. It was a politics from below, rooted in the seemingly backward-looking and irrational idea of "empathy."[68] Although coined in opposition to Soviet totalitarianism, we might find that his assessment applies equally well to the reign of capitalist multinational corporations in the current era of globalization. In both instances, the missing element is, first and foremost, the human person—and more specifically, the suffering of the human person.

It is hard not to hear echoes of Malik's own pleas for recognizing the importance of "friendship and understanding and truth and love" in the impassioned paragraphs of Havel's "Politics and Conscience." But it is important to remember that, despite their affinities, Havel's and Malik's contributions to the discourse of human rights do indeed differ, and sometimes quite significantly. In the name of establishing an authentically philosophical conception of human rights, Charles Malik was more than willing, as we have seen, to subject the West to criticism. But he never entertained the idea that the Western tradition was itself to blame. For him, the descent into the soulless materialism that dominated the exclusively economic-centered paradigm of development and modernization was but a wrong turn for what was otherwise the noble and longstanding journey of the Western idea of the human person, which had traveled from the ancient Greek city-states to the hallways of the United Nations. For Havel, however, it was the Western tradition itself that led to environmental degradation, impersonal bureaucratization, and, worst of all, the threat of nuclear annihilation.

Malik and Havel also developed rather different conceptions of the human person. For the former, the unique dignity of the individual was to be found in his or her soul. This religiously inflected understanding of the person was congenial to a conception of human rights that was timeless and transcendental, beyond and antecedent to any notion of rights in positive law. For the latter, human rights, though they may reflect certain religious tendencies, are more immediately reflective of the relational

---

[67] Ibid., 271.

[68] Ibid., 256: "The phenomenon of empathy, after all, belongs with that abolished realm of personal prejudice which had to yield to science, objectivity, historical necessity, technology, system, and the apparat—and those who, being impersonal, cannot worry. They are abstract and anonymous, ever utilitarian, and thus ever *a priori* innocent."

contexts of the local cultural community, and more widely, the natural environment itself. Malik anchored his notion of human rights in the authority of a transcendent God, whereas Havel attempted to connect the abstract, impersonal individuals of the modern world to their increasingly threatened local communities and regional environments.

In different ways, Heidegger helped Malik and Havel to rescue the human person from the mounting threats of the modern world. But in order to appropriate Heidegger, they had to humanize him. They had to import an ethical worldview into the work of a philosopher who, famously, never wrote an ethics, and who, furthermore, did everything he could to distance himself from philosophical humanism. Malik and Havel thus isolated and adopted aspects of Heidegger's thought that Heidegger himself had put to other uses; preserved, as if in amber, these conceptualizations were holdovers from another Heidegger, maybe even from one who never existed. Malik's talk of the importance of *Existenz* and Havel's talk of an ethically-motivated "existential revolution," were echoes of an imaginary Heidegger, not the real-life Heidegger would go on to declare that he was neither an existentialist nor a moralistic humanist.[69]

Heidegger may have been, as he was for Malik and Havel, a guiding inspiration for prophetic or existential authenticity. But he was also a trenchant critic, as both of them realized, of Western rationalism. It was no coincidence that Malik concluded *Man and the Struggle for Peace* with a chapter entitled "The Need for a Western Revolution."[70] In pointing out the limitations of the West, Malik—and later Havel—was undertaking, perhaps unwittingly, the painstaking process of dismantling the epistemic hubris at work in the Universal Declaration of Human Rights. Though philosophers from around the world weighed in during the initial human rights debates, evidence of which can be found in the 1949 UNESCO symposium devoted to the topic, it was all but taken for granted that human rights, insofar as they were sanctioned and upheld by the United

---

[69] Havel, "The Power of the Powerless," 207 and 209. On Heidegger and existentialism and anti-humanism, see of course his "Letter on Humanism," in Martin Heidegger, *Basic Writings*, ed. David F. Krell (New York, Harper & Row, 1977), 213-266. For more on the context of Heidegger's famous essay, see Anson Rabinbach, *In the Shadow of Catastrophe: German Intellectuals between Apocalypse and Enlightenment* (Berkeley: University of California Press, 2001), 97-128.

[70] Malik, *Man and the Struggle for Peace*, 198-230.

Nations, were the purview of the developed, Western world.[71] And yet, as Malik and Havel demonstrated, though the West may have been the home to great intellectual and spiritual resources, it was also the source of many dangers as well. This was something that the peoples of the rest of the globe already knew.

Richard Rorty's "Sentimental Education"

Nowhere is this tension between Western jingoism and skepticism more evident than in the work of the North-American, neo-pragmatist philosopher Richard Rorty. In a famous essay entitled "Human Rights, Rationality, and Sentimentality," Rorty brought some of the same Heideggerian concerns that can be found in Malik's and Havel's writings forward into the Post-Cold War era. Importantly, though, he did so without committing to any of the larger and more questionable aspects of the Heideggerian "existential revolution."[72] If both Malik and Havel took from Heidegger an over-dependence on the need for existential decisionism and/or revolution, Rorty, by contrast, offered a Heideggerianism that remained more muted and mundane, but one that still reflected the transition from the ideological conflict of the Cold War to that of the current moment of globalization.

In his much discussed 1993 Oxford Amnesty Lecture, Rorty suggested that rather than seeking a rational, transcendental foundation for human rights, activists should instead appeal to the sentiments. In this suggestion, which marks a turn away from the unflinching, rationalist universalism of previous human rights discourse, we can hear reverberations of Havel's talk of empathy and sympathy, as well as Malik's longing for friendship and understanding. More importantly, though, we can also hear echoes of Heidegger's notorious description of reason "as the most stiff-necked adversary of thought." [73]

---

[71] UNESCO, *Human Rights: Comments and Interpretations* (New York: Columbia UP, 1949). Available at
http://unesdoc.unesco.org/images/0015/001550/ 155042eb.pdf
[72] The essay "Human Rights, Rationality, and Sentimentality", was first presented as one of the 1993 Oxford Amnesty Lectures, and has been collected in Richard Rorty, *Truth and Progress: Philosophical Papers, Volume 3* (Cambridge: Cambridge UP, 1998), 167-185
[73] Martin Heidegger, "Nietzsche's Word, 'God is Dead'," in *The Question Concerning Technology and Other Essays*, trans. William Lovitt (New York: Harper & Row, 1977), 112.

Although contemporary commentators often overlook it, the influence of Heidegger's thought on Rorty was profound—so profound, in fact, that at one point in his career Rorty even planned to write a book on Heidegger.[74] As Rorty looked more and more to continental thought for insight and inspiration throughout the 1980s and 1990s, he came to share Heidegger's overarching critique of Western philosophy. Like his predecessor, Rorty thought that excessively rationalist attempts—from Descartes forward—to transform Western philosophy into an ahistorical science were misguided and in some instances even dangerous. But Rorty's proposals for rescuing philosophy from this predicament differed rather drastically from Heidegger's. Insofar as both Rorty and Heidegger insisted on amputating large portions of the philosophical canon, effectively jettisoning all of its residual metaphysical or scientific content, they were both philosophical radicals. But whereas Heidegger put his philosophical radicalism into the practice of a disastrous political radicalism, Rorty instead channeled it into a humble, ameliorative progressivism, one that appealed not to destined epochs in the history of Being—as with Heidegger—, nor to existential revolutions—as with Malik and Havel—, nor even to universal laws of reason—as with somebody like Jürgen Habermas, perhaps—but simply to—as he put it in his lecture on human rights—"sentimental education."[75]

Rorty envisioned a less exalted place for post-rationalist philosophy than did Heidegger. "Because I do not think that philosophy is ever going to be put on the secure path of a science," he admitted in a late essay, "nor that it is a good idea to try to put it there, I am content to see philosophy professors as practicing cultural politics."[76] This is not to suggest that, for Rorty, all politics could be reduced to cultural politics. In fact, he was a rather vocal critic of the professoriate's tendency to mistake cultural

---

[74] I discuss Rorty's relation to Heidegger in my *Heidegger in America* (Cambridge: Cambridge University Press, 2011). For a critique of Rorty's antifoundationalist understanding of human rights see Matthias Kettner, "Rortys Restbegrundung der Menschenrechte. Eine Kritik", in *Hinter den Spiegeln: Beiträge zur Philosophie Richard Rortys mit Erwiderungen von Richard Rorty*, ed. Thomas Schäfer, Udo Tietz, and Rüdiger Zill (Frankfurt am Main: Suhrkamp, 2001), 201-228, as well as Rorty's own response in the same volume, 229-234.

[75] Rorty, "Human Rights, Rationality, and Sentimentality," 176.

[76] Richard Rorty, "Analytic and conversational philosophy," in *Philosophy as Cultural Politics: Philosophical Papers, Volume 4* (Cambridge: Cambridge UP, 2007), 124.

activism for political activism.[77] Nevertheless, Rorty maintained that the political sphere rested upon shared cultural assumptions, and he believed that post-scientific philosophers were particularly well suited for the task of challenging and perhaps even re-imagining these assumptions. Rather than replace the concrete, everyday activities of human rights activists, jurists, or politicians, what proponents of the kind of "sentimental education" Rorty envisaged were to enact what José-Manuel Barreto has called "a long-term strategy" for the promotion and defense of human rights.[78] In helping to establish a human rights culture based on sympathy for the plight of the suffering as well as revulsion toward all instances of cruelty, such "sentimental education" could foster the cause of human rights, whether human rights were enshrined in local traditions, positivist law, transcendental philosophy, physical science—or not. There need not be any waiting, in other words, for the philosophy of human rights to be worked out as if it were some kind of scholastic puzzle. Human rights activism can begin at any moment, provided that our pining for philosophical foundations is left at the door.

While many philosophers have resisted the relegation of their profession to just another voice in the chorus of cultural debate, Rorty maintained that this new calling offered philosophers the opportunity to contribute more positively to the cause of human rights than they had previously. Rather than pushing the human rights conversation towards the shoals of such abstract and intractable notions as universalism, relativism, natural law or human nature, philosophy could simply imagine desirable political utopias, aspirational communities of hope and solidarity. Like novelists and poets, philosophers could inspire and edify, they could impassion and transform. Liberated from its timeless pursuit of transcendental truth and reconceived as a tool of persuasion, philosophy could be used to sway people to the cause of human rights. It no longer had to resort to specious and unconvincing talk of unchanging essences, which might prove contingent and malleable, or historical destinies, which might never come true.

---

[77] Rorty's attacks on what he called the "American cultural Left" are most pointed in his *Achieving Our Country* (Cambridge: Harvard University Press, 1998).

[78] See José-Manuel Barreto, "Rorty and Human Rights: Contingency, Emotions and how to Defend Human Rights Telling Stories," *Utrecht Law Review* 7 (2011), 93-112, which makes a much fuller case for this interpretation of Rorty, but also of wider human rights discourse itself. Available online at http://www.utrecht lawreview.org/index.php/ulr/article/viewFile/164/163

For Rorty, the discourse of human rights was not an expression of the fundamental truth of human existence, as both Malik and Havel, working from Heidegger, would have it. To the contrary, the discourse of human rights was nothing more than a language of sentimental education that could be used to inculcate a sense of "sympathy" for the weak and the oppressed—to get people "to imagine themselves in the shoes of the despised and the oppressed."[79] More important than working for an "increased moral knowledge" was the dissemination of "sad and sentimental stories" that would sway people to the cause of human rights.[80] Just as the later Heidegger turned to the poets for intimations of the "truth of Being," Rorty enlisted the help of novelists to make a better world.[81] In doing so, he abandoned the nostalgia for timeless wisdom that still animated the work of Malik and Havel. Whereas Malik and Havel both held onto Heidegger as somebody who provides insight into the universal human condition, Rorty saw him merely as somebody who calls attention to the limits of rationalism. Rorty's sympathetic solidarity was a chosen affiliation, based not on any common, essential humanity—or even a common theory of humanity—, but on a shared sentimental rejection of acts of inhumanity. His "solidarity of the shaken" jettisoned any and all overarching claims about the existence of "man" or the fate of the West. For him, human rights represented a form of social hope more than it did any preordained outcome of human evolution. There was no essential connection between human rights and the Western tradition, only a contingent one. As a result, the West could not lay claim to human rights discourse.

In an essay from the early nineties that invoked the example of Václav Havel, Rorty lamented that his fellow intellectuals had "grown accustomed to thinking in world-historical, eschatological terms."[82] What Rorty liked most about Havel was that he did not try to translate the messy and unexpected events of the Velvet Revolution into a tidy, predetermined schematic. Communism's collapse in Czechoslovakia was the result of contingent human actions that were rooted in specific human emotions. It

---

[79] Rorty, "Human Rights, Rationality, and Sentimentality," 179-80.
[80] Ibid., 172.
[81] On the later Heidegger, see Joseph J. Kockelmans, *On the Truth of Being: Reflections on Heidegger's Later Philosophy* (Bloomington: Indiana University Press, 1985).
[82] Richard Rorty, "The End of Leninism, Havel, and Social Hope," in *Truth and Progress: Philosophical Papers, Volume 3* (Cambridge: Cambridge University Press, 1998), 238.

was not the outcome of a necessary course of world-historical events. The lesson Rorty drew from Havel was that intellectuals should busy themselves less with the pursuit of ever-elusive transcendental truths and more with the task of influencing human emotion via the production of what he called, after Havel, "a poetry of social hope."[83]

The fundamental question, for Rorty, was the question of solidarity. Throughout the 1980s he continually stressed its importance, even going so far as to argue that our notions of science and objectivity derived from solidarity and not the other way around—as was commonly believed by his more analytically inclined colleagues.[84] In his 1989 book *Contingency, Irony and Solidarity* he was even more forthright: whatever enhanced solidarity, whether it was written by philosophers, poets or novelists, was what truly mattered.[85] Some twenty years later, though, in our current era of globalization, solidarity seems more elusive than ever.[86]

Rorty worried that human rights—like other progressive movements—would shipwreck on doctrinal rocks. He thought that recasting the human rights discussion along the lines of global solidarity might provide safer passage insofar as it would avoid the siren calls of universalism, rationalism and essentialism. But how are we to achieve solidarity in the face of neoliberal globalization, the menace Rorty spent his final years confronting?[87] Widening our field of vision might be a start. If a connection can be made between the sort of internalist critiques of Western rationalism that we find in Malik, Havel and Rorty, on the one hand, and more recent postcolonial writings from the margins of the West, on the other, perhaps we might be able to hold open, if only temporarily, a fertile space for an alternative conception of human rights, one that fosters empathetic solidarity over and above impersonal, bureaucratic rationalism.

---

[83] Ibid., 243.

[84] See, for instance, "Solidarity or Objectivity?" and "Science as Solidarity" in Richard Rorty, *Objectivity, Relativism, and Truth: Philosophical Papers, Volume 1* (Cambridge: Cambridge University Press, 1991).

[85] Richard Rorty, *Contingency, Irony, and Solidarity* (Cambridge: Cambridge University Press, 1989).

[86] For Rorty's optimistic views regarding the prospects of solidarity in the face of globalization, see his "Globalization, the Politics of Identity and Social Hope," in Richard Rorty, *Philosophy and Social Hope* (New York: Penguin, 1999), 229-239.

[87] See, for example, Richard Rorty, *Take Care of Freedom and Truth Will Take Care of Itself: Interviews with Richard Rorty*, ed. Eduardo Mendieta (Stanford: Stanford University Press, 2006).

Following Havel's lead, we might conclude that globalization is indeed the result of the exporting of Western models to the rest of the world. But rather than simply rejecting this historical legacy, however, the task is to reexamine the ways in which it has interacted with local contexts. Only then might we begin to see the outlines of a potential solidarity from below, or rather, from the margins.

Dipesh Chakrabarty and the "Diversity of Human Life-Worlds"

A number of thinkers have helped us to understand the ways in which the so-called First World has come to influence, if not overpower, the peoples of the Third World. The "barbarian words" of figures from the margins of the old empires, to steal a turn of phrase from the Latin American philosopher Enrique Dussel, have revealed the limits of European universalism with both clarity and passion.[88] Their critical writings, especially when placed alongside the more Eurocentric kind of work we have surveyed thus far, serve as testaments, travelogues, topographies even, of the "underside of modernity."[89] Heidegger, who both restores the study of concrete, lived experience and, simultaneously, outlines the limits of modernity's scientific rationalism, serves as a key point of reference, not just for Dussel, but for so many other figures in this tradition as well.[90] Another self-avowed "barbarian," the Caribbean Marxist intellectual C.L.R. James, for instance, went out of his way to

---

[88] See Fernando Gómez, "Ethics is the Original Philosophy; or, The Barbarian Words Coming from the Third World: An Interview with Enrique Dussel," *boundary 2* 28 (2001): 19-73.

[89] See Fred Dallmayr, "The Underside of Modernity: Adorno, Heidegger and Dussel," *Constellations* 11 (2004): 102-120. See also, Linda Martín Alcoff and Eduardo Mendieta, eds., *Thinking from the Underside of History: Enrique Dussel's Philosophy of Liberation* (Lanham: Rowman & Littlefield, 2000). More recently, see also the collected essays in Eduardo Mendieta's *Global Fragments: Globalizations, Latinamericanisms, and Critical Theory* (Albany: SUNY Press, 2007). It is also worth mentioning here Walter D. Mignolo's *Local Histories/ Global Designs: Coloniality, Subaltern Knowledges and Border Thinking* (Princeton: Princeton University Press, 2000) and *The Darker Side of the Renaissance: Literacy, Territoriality, and Colonization* (Ann Arbor: University of Michigan Press, 1995).

[90] On Dussel's connection to Heidegger, see Martín and Mendieta, *Thinking from the Underside of History*, 20.

extol the benefits of Heidegger's concrete approach to philosophy.[91] But he was also quick to point out that Heidegger's existential philosophy, at least as it was expressed in *Being and Time*, which was penned between the catastrophe of the First World War and the even greater calamities of the Second, was basically an account of "the individual in a collapsing society."[92] In short, Heidegger remains the philosopher who both predicts and reflects the collapse of the Western tradition.

For all those who want to disrupt the notion that West is synonymous with the rest, Heidegger is still, it seems, a useful place to start. As he explains in the preface to the new edition of his widely discussed 2000 book *Provincializing Europe: Postcolonial Thought and Historical Difference*, Dipesh Chakrabarty turned to Heidegger precisely because he found in his work a trenchant critique of the West. Given that he was interested in finding out "how thought was related to place," Chakrabarty enlisted the help of hermeneutic thinkers like Heidegger to show that modernization was not a universal process, but a "translational" one.[93] Modernity involved not simply the export of the European or Western tradition to the rest of the world, as Malik and Havel would have it, but the negotiation, on the ground, of local traditions that came into contact with this Western legacy. It also involved the struggle between a singular, universalizing conception of historical progress, which originated in the West—and which Rorty sought to do away with—and the multiple and fragmentary temporalities of cultures that it attempted to subsume.

Chakrabarty's rich and nuanced book explores a number of gaps and oppositions that anybody attempting to write the history of colonialism and anti-colonialism must confront. The most obvious of these is of course the distance between the perspectives of the colonized and the colonizer. But insofar as the modern research university is founded upon Western traditions of social scientific inquiry, any attempt to recount or even revive the perspective of the colonized or the subaltern entails first and foremost an attempt to bracket or question these very traditions themselves.[94] Chakrabarty attempted to do this by placing the universalist

---

[91] C.L.R. James, "Existentialism and Marxism," in *You Don't Play with Revolution: The Montreal Lectures of C.L.R. James*, ed. David Austin (Oakland: AK Press, 2009), 103.
[92] Ibid., 102.
[93] Dipesh Chakrabarty, *Provincializing Europe: Postcolonial Thought and Historical Difference* (Princeton: Princeton University Press, 2008), xiii and xviii.
[94] Ibid., 5.

and transcendentally tinged discourse of Western rationalism back into the
very time and place in which it was constructed—to put abstract concepts
like modernity, reason, capital and rights back into concrete and particular
locales. His aim was "to know how universalistic thought was always and
already modified by particular histories."[95]

Working along what he described as "a fault line central to modern
European social thought," Chakrabarty sketched out a series of concrete
"histories of belonging" that called into question the "abstract figure of the
universal human."[96] Whereas "analytic social science" sought objective
and timeless insights into universal, world-historical phenomena such as
industrial development and political modernity—Marx serves as
Chakrabarty's key figure here—, the "hermeneutic tradition" sought
instead to chronicle "the diversity of human life-worlds" without reducing
them to any overarching, objective schematic. In choosing Heidegger as
his "icon" for this second tradition, Chakrabarty was in many ways
revisiting Malik's own juxtaposition of the philosophies of Whitehead and
Heidegger, the abstracting scientist on the one hand and the concrete
chronicler of *Existenz* on the other.[97] Although Chakrabarty worked from
Marx and not Whitehead, the fundamental opposition he had in mind was
the same as Malik's:

> Marx and Heidegger represent for me two contradictory but profoundly
> connected tendencies that coexist within modern European social thought.
> One is the analytical heritage, the practice of abstraction that helps us to
> universalize. We need universals to produce critical readings of social
> injustices. Yet the universal and the analytical produce forms of thought
> that ultimately evacuate the place of the local. It does not matter if this is
> done in an empirical idiom, for the empirical can often be a result of the
> universal, just as the particular follows from the general. Such thought
> fundamentally tends to sever the relationship between thought and modes
> of human belonging. The other European heritage is the hermeneutic
> tradition that tends to reinstitute within thought itself this relationship
> between thought and dwelling. My attempt in this book has been to write
> some very particular ways of being-in-the-world—I call them Bengali only
> in a provisional manner—into some of the universal, abstract, and
> European categories of capitalist/political modernity.[98]

---

[95] Ibid., xiv.
[96] Ibid., 18-19.
[97] Ibid.
[98] Ibid., 254-255.

As we can see from this quote, Chakrabarty did not seek to abandon the West in *Provincializing Europe*, but only to reframe our view of it—to see it not from the center, but from the outer limits. For him, "European thought is at once both indispensable and inadequate," it must be "renewed from and for the margins."[99]

It is in the provisional spaces between the concrete particularity of the provincial margins and the abstract and cosmopolitan universalism of the metropole, between the developed and underdeveloped worlds, and between the global north and the global south where the utopia—the no-place—of human rights is to be found. As people like Thomas McCarthy have argued, we do not have to abandon entirely the universal heritage of discourses of human rights, progress, or modernity, but we do have to put them into a critical dialogue with the "barbarian" voices from the borders.[100] Or as Chakrabarty put it—in a defense of *Provincializing Europe*—we cannot seek refuge in the comforting embrace of any pre-established "constant" or unchanging conception of "human nature."[101] Whenever we invoke them, we must also question and reassess such concepts as rights, development and modernization.

If human rights are to reestablish solidarity on an international scale, they must reflect the "field of concrete possibilities" that—to use the words of David Hollinger—stretches between the abstract notions of provincialism and cosmopolitanism.[102] Like the effort to provincialize Europe, the idea of provincializing human rights might very well be a matter of "finding the right spot along the spectrum from the local to the universal," recognizing all the while that this spot may be only a temporary resting place, a changing and contested landscape more than any final promised land.[103] These utopian spaces in between might allow for a sentimental solidarity of the shaken to emerge, a solidarity that will probably prove even more compelling and fruitful than the abstract juridico-political pronouncements of nation-states, NGOs or even the

---

[99] Ibid., 16.
[100] See Thomas McCarthy, *Race, Empire, and the Idea of Human Development* (Cambridge: Cambridge University Press, 2009), 190: "There is no easy exit from this predicament."
[101] Dipesh Chakrabarty, "In Defense of *Provincializing Europe*: A Response to Carola Dietze," *History and Theory* 47 (2008), 95.
[102] David Hollinger, *In the American Province: Studies in the History and Historiography of Ideas* (Baltimore: Johns Hopkins University Press, 1989), vii.
[103] Ibid.

bureaucracies of the international community. Borrowing from Chakrabarty, we might say that to provincialize human rights is "to struggle to hold in a permanent state of tension a dialogue between two contradictory points of view"—to recognize, as he has put it elsewhere, that a "strong split between emotion and reason" is in itself constitutive of colonialism.[104]

Conclusion—Provincial Human Rights

If there is any room for Heidegger in the discussion of human rights today it is along these lines. It is Heidegger's critique of Western rationalism that might help proponents of human rights to interrogate and perhaps even overcome the lingering residues of Western imperialism and domination that linger on in the rationalist human rights paradigm[105] —though it behoves all those who adopt this critique to familiarize themselves with the details of Heidegger's own connections to German imperialism. Heidegger does not compel us to reject reason, but he does help us, as Chakrabarty puts it, "to see it as one among many ways of being in the world."[106] If philosophers and theorists are to play a role on the human rights stage, it can only be in this critical, dialogical sense. Malik, who once warned that "too many philosophers could ruin" the United Nations, knew this full well.[107] The grounding of a political organization, let alone a global sentiment, relies as much upon practice as it does abstract philosophy.

If it is paradoxical that a thinker on the wrong side of the Second World War, a thinker for whom only the peoples of the West had history —and among them only the Germans had true philosophy—, should be behind one of the more promising itineraries for human rights these days, it is only because the history of human rights has been a messy and

---

[104] Chakrabarty, *Provincializing Europe*, 254, and "Subaltern Histories and Post-Enlightenment Rationalism," in Dipesh Chakrabarty, *Habitations of Modernity: Essays in the Wake of Subaltern Studies* (Chicago: University of Chicago Press, 2002), 24. On these issues, it is also worth consulting Chakrabarty's correspondence with the novelist Amitav, Ghosh. Amitav Ghosh and Dipesh Chakrabarty, "A Correspondence on *Provincializing Europe*,' *Radical History Review* 83 (2002): 146-172.
[105] Here I am drawing upon José-Manuel Barreto's "The Decolonial Turn and Sympathy: A Critique of the Eurocentric and Rationalist Theories of Human Rights" (PhD diss., Birkbeck College, University of London, 2009).
[106] Chakrabarty, *Provincializing Europe*, 249.
[107] Malik, *Man in the Struggle for Peace*, xxvii.

contingent process.[108]   Far from reflecting the universal march of a triumphant rationality or political modernity, human rights have been forged by the clash of imperial forces and the resulting, all-to-real sufferings they have produced. These sufferings continue to shape the neo-imperial life-worlds of the current moment and belie attempts to think of human rights as a gift of the West to the rest. They also call into question the tendency of the West to impose its will upon the rest of the world, sometimes under the cover of humanitarian interventions such as the Iraq War.[109]

Perhaps it is time we acknowledge this messiness. Perhaps it is time, as Bernard Williams once suggested in relation to human rights, to "give up the universalist belief."[110]   This need not slip into a full-fledged relativism. Rather, what Williams called "the relativism of distance" might allow us to engender good in the world without committing ourselves to the strictures of transcendental talk, demanding of all peoples anywhere and everywhere, anytime and every time, to think like us, to talk like us.[111] For who is this "us" anyhow? Going beyond Williams, perhaps it is time we start listening to "the listeners"—to all those who must endure the theories, policies and practices concocted by governments and non-governmental agencies alike.[112]

Confronting the concrete particularities of human rights today, we might finally admit that, when it comes to human rights, we may not have all the answers, only a hunch of where we should be headed.   The American philosopher J. Glenn Gray—himself a veteran of the Second World War as well as, years later, the primary American translator of Heidegger—once suggested that "difficult as the doctrine of natural rights is to ground philosophically, practically it has been indispensable for every

---

[108] On Heidegger's racism, see Robert Bernasconi, "Heidegger's alleged challenge to the Nazi concepts of Race," in *Appropriating Heidegger*, ed. James E. Faulconer and Mark A. Wrathall (Cambridge: Cambridge University Press, 2000), 50-67.

[109] See, for instance, Costas Douzinas, *Human Rights and Empire: The Political Philosophy of Cosmopolitanism* (New York: Routledge, 2007).

[110] Williams, "Human Rights and Relativism," 67.

[111] Ibid., 68.

[112] According to Geoffrey Hawthorn, Williams divided the audience for political theory into two camps, with "the audience" representing theorists and those with access to power, and "the listeners" representing the supposed recipients of political decisions made on their behalf. See Hawthorn, *In the Beginning Was the Deed*, xv.

age till the present."[113]   Perhaps, listening to him and to Rorty, we should simply abandon the difficult, we might even say impossible, attempt to ground human rights philosophically—that is, abstractly—and focus instead on concrete questions of local practice, the kinds of questions Malik, Havel and Chakrabarty also dare us to ask. We would no longer be interested in how we might legitimize or theorize rights, but rather, how peoples at the margins might themselves secure, foster and protect rights in their own local contexts; best practice, in other words, rather than best theory.   This would be provincial, sentimental education rather than analytical training, and it would rely upon what Chakrabarty has recently called "anti-colonial, utopian humanism," a new humanism that keeps the universal and the particular always and everywhere in dialogue with each other.[114] If human rights represent the new international solidarity, they will have to find a home in the places between the center and the margins, between the geographies of analytical science and hermeneutical empathy, between what seems universal and what seems local. This third way, which Chakrabarty calls, after Heidegger, the path of "dwelling," recognizes and criticizes both the Romantic nostalgia for particular roots, particular histories, as well as the need for universal and abstract aspirations of equality.[115]   In welcoming the "barbarians" from the margins, it might also be worthwhile to remember that, as Hannah Arendt, another Heidegger student, pointed out some time ago, "deadly danger to any civilization is no longer likely to come from without."[116]

---

[113] J. Glenn Gray, *The Promise of Wisdom* (Philadelphia: Lippincott, 1968), 63. For more on Gray and Heidegger, see my "J. Glenn Gray: Philosopher, Translator (of Heidegger), and Warrior," *Transactions of the Charles S. Peirce Society: A Quarterly Journal in American Philosophy* XL (2004): 487-512.

[114] Dipesh Chakrabarty, "Humanism in a Global World," in *Humanism in Intercultural Perspective: Experiences and Expectations*, ed. Jörn Rüsen and Henner Laass (Bielefeld: Transcript Verlag, 2009), 27.

[115] Ibid., 35. Fred Dallmayr has also spoken of the importance of establishing a concept of dwelling that is appropriate for the current historical moment. See, for example, his *Achieving Our World: Toward a Global and Plural Democracy*, (Lanham: Rowman and Littlefield, 2001), and *Peace Talks: Who Will Listen?* (Notre Dame: University of Notre Dame Press, 2004). An older and perhaps even more appropriate discussion of dwelling can be found in the works of one of the first truly global thinkers, Alexander von Humboldt. On his life and legacy, see Laura Dassow Walls, *The Passage to Cosmos: Alexander von Humboldt and the Shaping of America* (Chicago: University of Chicago Press, 2009).

[116] Hannah Arendt, "The Perplexities of the Rights of Man," in *The Portable Hannah Arendt*, ed. Peter Baehr (New York: Penguin, 2000), 44.

Bibliography

Arendt, Hannah. "The Perplexities of the Rights of Man." In *The Portable Hannah Arendt*, edited by Peter Baehr. New York: Penguin, 2000.

Barreto, José-Manuel. "The Decolonial Turn and Sympathy: A Critique of the Eurocentric and Rationalist Theories of Human Rights." PhD diss., Birkbeck College, University of London, 2009.

—. "Rorty and Human Rights: Contingency, Emotions and how to Defend Human Rights Telling Stories." *Utrecht Law Review* 7 (2011): 93-112. Available online at http://www.utrechtlawreview.org/index.php/ulr/ article/ viewFile/ 164/163

Berlin, Isaiah. "Two Concepts of Liberty." In *The Proper Study of Mankind: An Anthology of Essays*, edited by Henry Hardy and Roger Hausheer. New York: Farrar, Straus and Giroux, 1998.

Bernasconi, Robert. "Heidegger's alleged challenge to the Nazi concepts of Race." In *Appropriating Heidegger*, edited by James E. Faulconer and Mark A. Wrathall. Cambridge: Cambridge University Press, 2000.

Birmingham, Peg. *Hannah Arendt and Human Rights: The Predicament of Common Responsibility*. Bloomington: Indiana University Press, 2006.

Chakrabarty, Dipesh. *Habitations of Modernity: Essays in the Wake of Subaltern Studies*. Chicago: University of Chicago Press, 2002.

—.*Provincializing Europe: Postcolonial Thought and Historical Difference*. Princeton: Princeton University Press, 2008.

—. "In Defense of *Provincializing Europe*: A Response to Carola Dietze." *History and Theory* 47 (2008): 95.

—."Humanism in a Global World." In *Humanism in Intercultural Perspective: Experiences and Expectations*, edited by Jörn Rüsen and Henner Laass. Bielefeld: Transcript Verlag, 2009.

Cushman, Thomas. ed. *A Matter of Principle: Humanitarian Arguments for War in Iraq*. Berkeley: University of California Press, 2005.

Dallmayr, Fred. *Achieving Our World: Toward a Global and Plural Democracy*. Lanham: Rowman and Littlefield, 2001.

—. "The Underside of Modernity: Adorno, Heidegger and Dussel." *Constellations* 11 (2004): 102-120.

—. *Peace Talks: Who Will Listen?* Notre Dame: University of Notre Dame Press, 2004.

Dassow Walls, Laura. *The Passage to Cosmos: Alexander von Humboldt and the Shaping of America*. Chicago: University of Chicago Press, 2009.

Dewey, John. "From Absolutism to Experimentalism." In *The Essential Dewey, Volume I: Pragmatism, Education, Democracy*, edited by

Larry Hickman, Alexander A. and Thomas M. Alexander. Bloomington: Indiana UP, 1998.

Douzinas, Costas. *Human Rights and Empire: The Political Philosophy of Cosmopolitanism.* New York: Routledge, 2007.

Faye, Emmanuel. *Martin Heidegger: The Introduction of Nazism into Philosophy in Light of the Unpublished Seminars of 1933-1935*, trans. Michael B. Smith. New Haven: Yale University Press, 2009.

Ghosh, Amitav and Dipesh Chakrabarty. "A Correspondence on *Provincializing Europe.*' *Radical History Review* 83 (2002): 146-172.

Gilman, Nils. *Mandarins of the Future: Modernization Theory in Cold War America.* Baltimore: Johns Hopkins University Press, 2003.

Glendon, Mary Ann. *A World Made New: Eleanor Roosevelt and the Universal Declaration of Human Rights.* New York: Random House, 2001.

Gómez, Fernando. "Ethics is the Original Philosophy; or, The Barbarian Words Coming from the Third World: An Interview with Enrique Dussel." *boundary 2* 28 (2001): 19-73.

Gray, J. Glenn. *The Promise of Wisdom.* Philadelphia: Lippincott, 1968.

Habermas, Jürgen. "The Concept of Human Dignity and the Realistic Utopia of Human Rights." *Metaphilosophy* 41 (2010): 464-80.

Havel, Václav. "The Power of the Powerless." In *Open Letters: Selected Writings, 1965-1990*, edited by Paul Wilson. New York: Vintage, 1992.

Heidegger, Martin. *An Introduction to Metaphysics*, trans. Ralph Manheim. New Haven: Yale, 1959.

—. *Poetry, Language, Thought*, trans. Albert Hofstadter. New York: Harper Perennial, 1976).

—. "Nietzsche's Word, 'God is Dead'." In *The Question Concerning Technology and Other Essays*, trans. William Lovitt. New York: Harper & Row, 1977.

—."The Self-Assertion of the German University." In *The Heidegger Controversy: A Critical Reader, edited by* Richard Wolin. Cambridge: MIT Press, 1993.

—. *Basic Writings*, edited by David F. Krell. New York, Harper & Row, 1977.

Hollinger, David A. *Cosmopolitanism and Solidarity: Studies in Ethnoracial, Religious, and Professional Affiliation in the United States* (Madison: University of Wisconsin Press, 2006).

—. *In the American Province: Studies in the History and Historiography of Ideas* (Baltimore: Johns Hopkins University Press, 1989.

Hunter, Ian. "The History of Philosophy and the Persona of the Philosopher." *Modern Intellectual History* 4 (2007): 571-600.

James, C.L.R. "Existentialism and Marxism." In *You Don't Play with Revolution: The Montreal Lectures of C.L.R. James*, edited David Austin. Oakland: AK Press, 2009.

Judt, Tony. *Postwar: A History of Europe since 1945.* New York: Penguin, 2005.

Kerber, Linda K. "We are All Historians of Human Rights." *Perspectives Online* 44 (2006).

Kettner, Matthias. "Rortys Restbegrundung der Menschenrechte. Eine Kritik." In *Hinter den Spiegeln: Beiträge zur Philosophie Richard Rortys mit Erwiderungen von Richard Rorty*, edited by Thomas Schäfer, Udo Tietz, and Rüdiger Zill. Frankfurt am Main: Suhrkamp, 2001.

Kockelmans, Joseph J. *On the Truth of Being: Reflections on Heidegger's Later Philosophy.* Bloomington: Indiana University Press, 1985.

Malik, Charles. "The Metaphysics of Time in the Philosophies of A. N. Whitehead and M. Heidegger." PhD diss., Harvard University, 1937.

—.*War and Peace: A Statement made before the Political Committee of the General Assembly, November 23, 1949.* Stamford: The Overlook Press, 1950.

—.*"Will the Future Redeem the Past?" An Address Delivered at Williamsburg, Virginia, June 11, 1960.* Richmond: Virginia Commission on Constitutional Government, 1960.

—. "The Individual in Modern Society." In *The One and the Many: The Individual in the Modern World. The Second Corning Conference*, edited by John Brooks. New York: Harper & Row, 1962.

—. *Man in the Struggle for Peace.* New York: Harper & Row, 1963.

—. ed. *God and Man in Contemporary Christian Thought.* Beirut: American University of Beirut Centennial Publications, 1970.

Malik, Habib C. ed., *The Challenge of Human Rights: Charles Malik and the Universal Declaration.* Oxford: Centre for Lebanese Studies, 2000.

Marcuse, Herbert. *Heideggerian Marxism*, edited by Richard Wolin and John Abromeit. Lincoln: University of Nebraska Press, 2005.

Martín Alcoff, Linda and Eduardo Mendieta, eds. *Thinking from the Underside of History: Enrique Dussel's Philosophy of Liberation.* Lanham: Rowman & Littlefield, 2000.

McCarthy, Thomas. *Race, Empire, and the Idea of Human Development.* Cambridge: Cambridge University Press, 2009.

Mendieta, Eduardo. *Global Fragments: Globalizations, Latinamericanisms, and Critical Theory.* Albany: SUNY Press, 2007.

Mignolo, Walter. *The Darker Side of the Renaissance: Literacy, Territoriality, and Colonization.* Ann Arbor: University of Michigan Press, 1995.

—. *Local Histories/Global Designs: Coloniality, Subaltern Knowledges and Border Thinking.* Princeton: Princeton University Press, 2000.

Moyn, Samuel. "Jacques Maritain, Christian New Order, and the Birth of Human Rights." Available online at http://papers.ssrn.com/sol3/papers.cfm? Abstract _id=1134345.

—. *The Last Utopia: Human Rights in History.* Cambridge: Harvard University Press, 2010.

Nartzizenfield Sneh, Iatai. *The Future Almost Arrived: How Jimmy Carter Failed to Change U.S. Foreign Policy.* New York: Peter Lang, 2008.

Rabinbach, Anson. *In the Shadow of Catastrophe: German Intellectuals between Apocalypse and Enlightenment.* Berkeley: University of California Press, 2001.

Rorty, Richard. *Contingency, Irony, and Solidarity.* Cambridge: Cambridge University Press, 1989.

—. *Objectivity, Relativism, and Truth: Philosophical Papers, Volume 1.* Cambridge: Cambridge University Press, 1991.

—. *Truth and Progress: Philosophical Papers, Volume 3.* Cambridge: Cambridge UP, 1998.

—. *Achieving Our Country.* Cambridge: Harvard University Press, 1998.

—. *Philosophy and Social Hope.* New York: Penguin, 1999.

—. *Take Care of Freedom and Truth Will Take Care of Itself: Interviews with Richard Rorty,* edited by Eduardo Mendieta. Stanford: Stanford University Press, 2006.

—. *Philosophy as Cultural Politics: Philosophical Papers, Volume 4.* Cambridge: Cambridge UP, 2007.

Schoenberg, Arnold. *Style and Idea,* trans. Leo Black. New York: St. Martin's, 1975.

Simpson, Bradley R. *Economists with Guns: Authoritarian Development and U.S.-Indonesian Relations, 1960-1968.* Stanford: Stanford University Press, 2008.

Stern-Anders, Günther. "On the Pseudo-Concreteness of Heidegger's Philosophy." *Philosophy and Phenomenological Research* 8 (1948): 337-71.

Strauss, Leo. *Natural Right and History.* Chicago: University of Chicago Press, 1953.

Tucker, Aviezer. *The Philosophy and Politics of Czech Dissidence from Patočka to Havel.* Pittsburgh: University of Pittsburgh Press, 2000.

UNESCO, *Human Rights: Comments and Interpretations*. New York: Columbia University Press, 1949. Available at http://unesdoc.unesco.org/images/0015/ 001550/ 155042eb.pdf

Wild, John. *The Challenge of Existentialism*. Bloomington: Indiana University Press, 1955.

Williams, Bernard. "Human Rights and Relativism." In *In the Beginning Was the Deed: Realism and Moralism in Political Argument*, edited by Geoffrey Hawthorn. Princeton: Princeton University Press, 2005.

Woessner, Martin. "J. Glenn Gray: Philosopher, Translator (of Heidegger), and Warrior." *Transactions of the Charles S. Peirce Society: A Quarterly Journal in American Philosophy* XL (2004): 487-512.

—. *Heidegger in America*. Cambridge: Cambridge University Press, 2011.

CHAPTER THREE

THE LEGACY OF SLAVERY:
WHITE HUMANITIES AND ITS SUBJECT.
A MANIFESTO

SABINE BROECK

The purpose of my project is to connect Critical Theory, including Gender Studies, to the epistemology of the Middle Passage and to Studies of Slavery. The Enlightenment proposal of human freedom strategically splits a certain group of humans—namely enslaved people of African origin—from the constitutive freedom to possess themselves and from any access to subjecthood. Only if critical thinking is able to reflect on its own embeddedness in the Enlightenment, it will be able to overcome its *colonialist and humanist* confines, and to allow for a connection to worlded knowledges of the human being—to follow Sylvia Wynter here.

My project is part of the ongoing revision and critical recapitulation of a new "thick description" of Euro-American modernity, with respect to the productive function that the transatlantic slave trade and the New World slavery had in its constitution, development and in its economic, social, cultural and philosophical (re)articulations—way into postmodernity. This relatively recent critical discourse owes its existence mainly to decades of African-American Studies, as well as to a wider range of historiography, but has only of late slowly trickled into adjacent disciplines and—to a surprisingly hesitant degree—into Western philosophy. Yet, even though slavery as an object of historiography has recently risen to be among the best researched historical phenomenon of the Western world—as various historians have remarked of late—those other disciplines have been largely resistant to even engage with the connection between slavery and modernity's Enlightenment, including its transatlantic history. By way of carefully maintaining disciplinary boundaries, an examination of this connection has hardly reached beyond an admission of modernity's so-called "paradox". An interdisciplinary field able to address the manifold political, cultural and epistemological questions arising from an observation of this intricate interdependency—beyond national canons and boundaries marked by area studies and their linguistic limitations—still awaits its realization. It is within this interdisciplinary field of inquiry that I want to situate my project.

The Subject of Humanism

I want to address critical theory's "deep thinking" about a concept that has become ever more crucial in the recent turn away from "identity" and towards notions of difference, location and agency, namely the post-Enlightenment concept of the subject. The project will assess the degree to which white Western articulation of the free autonomous subject, and its hegemonic capacity to create sociality and resistance, has been itself structurally contingent on discursive premises which hamper a serious and effective reconsideration of critical theory beyond narrowly defined ethnocentric post-modern interests. The subject as *telos* rose to prominence in early modernity as a tool of political and epistemological self-empowerment of Western white men. This process itself was structurally contingent on the slave trade's, slavery and later colonialist practices which, under that very subject's reign, constituted large parts of the world's population as a fundamentally other category of beings without any access to a subject position, neither collectively, nor individually, within the Western modern scheme of things. In the breakthrough of poststructuralist skepticism in academia, and the ensuing academic discourse about the subject as constituted in social practices—as an effect of interpellation and as "always out of step with itself" notwithstanding—the subject's universal reign keeps re-surfacing, e.g., in much of the recent feuilleton and academic discourse about *the West* as a haven for the freedom of subjects and for human rights in general.

White critical theory has not moved far enough beyond an appeal for supplementation within the logic of the Western subject that has screened a vexed problematic: because of the gender-raced location white women and men occupy, their purchase on a subject position comes structurally, not by a fault within the system, but by fault of the very system itself, at the expense of un-subjectifying, and thus *abjecting* what I would like to call *un-whitened* people. White critical theory's *centering of the subject* as its locus of analysis and critique has locked that theory into a paradigm of unacknowledged white discursive hegemony. By way of its reproduction within a genealogy *of the Enlightenment*, even if critically reconsidered, the prevailing theories of subject and subjectivity have envisaged human agency only in *subjects,* paradigmatically white and Western. Critical theory needs to engage this syntax, to re-inscribe the Western white modern subject critically, by way of producing a thick description of how the structural position of the gender-raced white subject evolved as an integral part of Enlightenment's and post-Enlightenment's discursive racist hegemony—over and against the discourses and knowledges of cultures which, for whatever reason, did not share the so-called Enlightenment. Avant-garde theory has not yet taken on the challenge to think about the *epistemological subject* as a contingent *white construction.* European theories of modernism—and postmodernism—in their abstract contemplation of the master-slave dialectic—which has consistently functioned as a mega-metaphor for oppressive relations—could only imagine subjects who were not enslaved, that is, white subjects, because they were free by definition. In reverse, one could say in a rather perverse logic, they decided not to figure the enslaved or colonized as subjects.

Critical theory's affective and epistemological liaison with post-enlightenment theory resulted in an avoidance of a radical historiography of Enlightenment's splitting of the world in slaves and masters, and of their own historical position on the side of the white, within this split. The assumption of freedom, that is, the creation of an individual human subject as the owner of a right to freedom and agency, was the self-authorizing gesture of modernity par excellence, just as it provided the philosophical foundations for emancipatory ethical-political authorities such as critical theory and white feminism. Yet this assumption required a massive break with cultural memory. It required a self-inscription, a collective memory of Western modern subjects as non-enslaved and, at the same time, as opponents to slavery. All of this at a historical juncture in which modernism fostered the slave trade most profitably while, at the same time, modernity was fostered by the latter in surprisingly effective ways.

To come into being the white western subject needed its underside, as it were: the crucially integral but invisible part of the subject has been its *abject*, separated by race: African slaves, i.e. unwhitened humans who were so tied to the emerging subject that—structurally speaking—they could not even occupy the position of the dialectical Hegelian object as "Knecht". Hegel allegorized slavery into a seductive mental model of longue durée acclaim and mental hold over Western cultures. He did so by idealizing the opposition, that is, by severing the signifier from any referent and by creating the modern individual as "former Knecht/slave" that has overtaken his master (feudalism)—that has mastered mastery, as it were. This argument eschews the fact—detectable only from a "black", de-colonial, non-occidental angle—that the previous "Knechte", now the modern free subjects, had enabled themselves to become masters by way of slave trade and colonialism.

As the popular English hymn has it, *Brittania rule the waves, we Englishmen never shall be slaves.* Despite *owning* slaves became an instrumental, useful and productive way of ordering affairs, it did not become a critical issue for European philosophy. The European white identification with the "slave position", which the Hegelian allegory has afforded,[1] has conveniently obscured the fact that, in the global scheme of things, Europeans themselves acted as enslavers. The "Knechte" turned into "Herren", ie. into full subjects, by turning themselves into colonial masters—or at least into potential masters—of humans tied to them as "belongings"; such a chattel was inextricably and quite un-dialectically bound to the master subject by being structurally severed from the race of human subjects.[2] Possession—of self and other—was the sine-qua-non for (white) freedom, which meant that the ones who found themselves possessed could not, by reverse definition, access subjecthood. Thus, the Enlightenment, with its impetus for individual self-ownership, self-responsibility, productive self-realization and subjective and objective rights to freedom, learned to operate within a system of a large-scale racial parasitism.

Seen from a post-Middle Passage perspective, that is, from the position of the enslaved, the modern free subject is the result of slave trading and colonialist practices. This means in turn that the culture of slavery was essential to the formation of modernity—not its somehow paradoxical excess, nor an unwanted, shameful and by now discredited and disowned by-product. In their basic denial of this constitutive role of transatlantic slavery, critical philosophies of modernity have been marked by repetitive configurations of split consciousness and ethical avoidance.

---

[1] See Sabine Broeck, "Never Shall We *Be* Slaves: Locke's Treatises, Slavery and Early American Modernity," in *Blackening Europe: The African American Presence*, ed. Heike Raphael-Hernandez (New York/London: Routledge, 2004).

[2] See Francoise Vergès, *La mémoire enchaînée: Questions sur l'esclavage* (Paris: Michel, 2006); Sylvia Wynter and David Scott, "The Re-Enchantment of Humanism: An Interview with Sylvia Wynter," *Small Axe* 8 (2000): 119-207; Orlando Patterson, *Slavery and Social Death: A Comparative Study* (Cambridge: Cambridge University Press, 1982).

Social critique has used the slave trade and slavery in very creative, but mostly metaphorical ways. Slavery in the abstract provided the modern symbolic with an intricate apparatus for the formulation and critique of mechanisms of social inclusion or exclusion, of privilege and liminality. In Western societies, modernity has constituted itself within a particular logic of the subject. It has done so by creating a philosophically justified freedom of the white subject that presupposes the non-subjectivity of others—a result of the direct or indirect ownership of those others. In the same way, white Western theory has been developed within a framework of a *modernity innocent of slavery* and its emphatic philosophical foundations of the subject and subjectivity. Critical theory has avoided searching for the traces of its own historical rootedness within this philosophical and political *regime of freedom as ownership*. It entered a dialogue almost exclusively with the cultural history of European modernity and postmodernism, rather than with philosophical approaches generated by Black diasporic critical narratives not always posing as "theory"—ranging from 18th century slave narratives to recent postcolonial and African-American interventions—which have questioned the naturalized universality of the free subject's epistemological reign by way of putting enslavement at the center of their investigation of modernity. Neither psychoanalysis, nor Foucaultian theory, nor the Frankfurt School, nor poststructuralist/gender theory have sufficiently dealt with the genealogy of the subject created within social practices of enslavement and colonization. Such practices were characterized by divisions, as well as by convergences, across gender and race constellations marked in turn by the conditions of white ownership—literally, and/or metaphorically—of un-whitened human beings. The aim of such a thick description will be to understand the intricate psychic, social and intellectual mechanics of Western modern culture of control and ownership, and the role the human subject has played in its formulation and (re)production.

Beyond these preliminary theses, an archival textuality of the suppressed and non-remembered controversies around who could emerge as modern human subject will have to be recuperated—controversies of early modern Western societies dating back to the Seventeenth century. This retrieval will be done in order to extend existing protocols in various disciplines about how freedom has been articulated as white self-possession and agency, and in order to position *an ethics of bearing witness* over and against critical theory's narcissism.

One needs to work through the reasons why we need to enter the subject once more, or the motives why we need to look at the Western fascination with the subject in light of what we know about slavery and the European investments—not just financial—in the slave trade. And through the rationale behind why is necessary to look at the gendered/raced subject in the creation of a "master of enslavement"—subjectivity. How to re-think freedom and human articulation in terms other than self-possession —undeservedly read as an opposition to humans beings possessed—is a question that has plagued liberation theory too. This has become urgently important now that the Enlightenment has become militantly vivified within the discourses of European/Western superiority, and in the Western refusal to recognize the problematic of wasted, precarious and unwanted lives. Critical Theory needs to account for its own groundedness in the compromised character of the Enlightenment. Otherwise it will not be productive and useful for reading the post-postmodern global moment. That moment must be de-colonial, which means that Foucault's, Bauman's and Agamben's theory lines—but also advanced gender theory like Butler's or Braidotti's—need to be revised by way of making a historical connection to the early Modern, humanist phase of globalisation: the transatlantic slave trade and New World slavery. Only a thorough and patient re-reading of Western postmodern theory—from Adorno to Bauman and Butler et. al.—from the point of view of Césaire, Spillers or Wynter—to name a small number of black diasporic theorists paradigmatically, whom I offer as witnesses and iconographic markers of my project—can provide the epistemological horizon to re-think global post-postmodernity in ways that go beyond the human subject, as we know it in the West, as motor, agent and guarantor of human history.

Adorno and Horkheimer

As one of the necessary readings in this context I offer here a 'post-middle passage' polemical re-examination, as it were, of Adorno and Horkheimer's *Dialectic of Enlightenment.*[3] I want to engage Adorno/Horkheimer's stringent refusal to look at slavery and colonialism—a refusal which is smoothly but strangely embedded in their radical critique of modernity. Adorno/Horkheimers' focus is on the European modern subject: their post-Hegelian articulation is a recapitulation of the paradigmatic split between, on the one hand, the active and knowing

---

[3] Max Horkheimer and Theodor Adorno. *Dialektik der Aufklaerung* (Frankfurt: Suhrkamp, 2002 [1944]).

human subject of history and, on the other, passive beings clearly distinct from that subject—who figure in the *Dialectic* as creatures who are able to "give themselves to" life.[4] The authors position those beings within a costly logic of teleological development in favor of aggressive instrumental reason, on a scale of before and after—even though for the *Dialectic*, of course, both stages of development have been present in the world at the same time. The text keeps returning to this radical rejection of instrumental reason as a logic of self-extermination of the human subject without, however, acknowledging the divisive and violent historical separation of the modern orbit in its subjects and un-subjects—or abjects, as it were. It refuses to see that those creatures —who in the Enlightenment's logic irrationally surrender to life—by no means predate the modern subject but share the subject's modern orbit in a position of oppressed and abjected *by* this very subject.

Of course, the *raison d'etre* of the *Dialectic* is its epistemological and ethical distance from the Enlightenment as object of their critique. My point here, though, is to argue that the *Dialectic* for all its skepticism is unable to discern the Enlightenment's inherent racism. This is present in its prerogative to point to a division between history and prehistory, or between history and outside-history which, even in the *Dialectic*, figures as a euphemistic and blind abstractum. Thus, the *Dialectic*'s anthropological drive hides the structural split of colonized people—who lived in the same time-space continuum of modern subjectivity—from any access to enlightened rationality. Instead, it dwells on what it sees as an inner-European conflict between the "light" and dark" sides of Enlightenment's subject itself, between instrumental reason and an anarchic natural desire for life, which Adorno and Horkheimer, following Freud, want to rescue. By way of a reversed Hegelian logic, the alleged absence of this paradigmatic conflict in the space of the so-called "primitive"—*die Wilden*—precisely proves the lack of historicity, which in turn may only be guaranteed by the autonomous Western subject. This leaves neither an agent nor an addressee among "the primitives" for enlightened human dialogue. The *Dialectic*, in its abstraction of "natural existence" and its refusal to take modernity's colonial subjection into account, remains bounded by this logic.

By taking recourse to a mythical perennial humanist contrast between "the human" and "nature"—which is being retold paradigmatically as the

---

[4] Ibid., 36.

story of Odysseus' conquests—the *Dialectic* implies an essence of modernity that stands in stark contrast to its actual history; the "essence" of the Enlightenment entailed the categorization of a large part of the world's population as "nature", as an aggressively sought foundation of the Western human subject's free self. The *Dialectics* does not mourn the destruction and annihilation of those "primitives" in the new worlds—which modernity subjected to itself—but contemplates the very Western self subjected to its own instrumental reason. This melancholia reigns the text. Within the mental configurations of the *Dialectic*, early modernity's brute optimism—due to the self-possession that the white subject enjoys in Locke's thinking—appears as *Zurichtung*, as a negative domestication that keeps being haunted by the effects of its violent suppressions. It is the subject's obsessive but disparately impossible fiction of self-possession, then, which culminates in fascist annihilation.

My reading wants to foreground the *Dialectic's* solipsistic blind spot that lies in its missing recognition of the fact—hidden under Adorno/ Horkheimers' metaphorical abstractions—that the white subject accumulated cultural, political and economic gains in the process of this however problematic self-domestication, based as it was on the enslavement and colonization of other human beings. This recognition would entail a surrender of their insistence on fascism as the climax of white modernity's auto-aggression, which finally drowned Europe in an "ocean of violence", as Adorno and Horkheimer call it. They ignore the foundational "ocean of violence"—the Middle Passage here haunting their text rather uncannily— in which the Western subject chose to drown African people. Modernity's entirely rational violence of colonialism and slavery—the annihilation of so many of the world's "possibilities" as Aimé Cesaire called it—only surfaces in the *Dialectic* as a trace of "the primitives", which the text does not want to follow lest it might disturb their theses of the Shoah as the "long-in-coming" collapse of civilization.

Why the *Dialectic* would ground their argument in Odysseus' myth and read, by way of that allegory, the modern subject as gradually overwhelmed by instrumental reason, instead of addressing colonial history as a foundational moment of modernity? That shift in attention might have clearly shown that, always already, and in a manner constitutive of the Western subject's luxury of self-recognition and self-domestication, "the instrumental ratio has come fully into its rights", as the authors phrase it, with slavery and not only in the middle of the Twentieth century with fascism. To forego this context leads the *Dialectic* to rob colonial subjection and abjection of their power to speak of the white subject's split self from the perspective of its outside.

For Adorno and Horkheimer, the Odyssean genealogy of the Enlightenment becomes an object of rhetorical address by which the subjected self figures as the ground of melancholia; the loss of "life" and "nature" are its own loss, and are read as a violation done by the subject to itself—which has to result in fascism—because the subject cannot successfully dominate the monsters which haunt its reason, because the subject, as it were, can never own itself. Horkheimer/Adorno do not acknowledge that modernity's split happened *in history* and that Enlightenment's abject happened to be *world* and *people* which, even in the *Dialectic*, only appear summarily as "primitives"—a rhetorical reminiscence in passing. However, the text cannot evacuate the absent presence of colonialism and slavery. The passages where the Odyssey becomes the story of Robinson contain, even if just a nod, a reference to one of the foundational narratives of early colonial modernity and, within that nod, the trace of a non-mythological genealogy of the white Western subject. Only in one rather short sentence does this aggressive genealogy surface in the *Dialectic*; this sentence rather deconstructs the text's narration in that it ties the oppressive, self-perpetuating logic of the Enlightenment self to slavery. There is an element of radical excess in that sentence, an invitation to rethink the *Dialectic*'s own argument from a different perspective—which Horkheimer and Adorno immediately refuse. This is the stunning passage in question: "The bourgeois, in its successive incarnations of *slave holder*, entrepreneur and administrator is the logical subject of Enlightenment."[5] Thus, Horkheimer and Adorno obviously knew of modernity's foundations; this intervention of historical contingency into their mythologically grounded narrative might have become the germinal moment for an entirely different genealogy of the subject—the *Dialectic*, though, after this fleeting evocation, makes a decision to radically abandon the subject's colonial past. Today's critical re-writing of the European project needs to reckon with this legacy.

With this rather compressed and condensed reading, I want to make the point that even a radically critical self-reflection of modernity, however much shaken to its foundations by fascism, chose to ignore the split subtext of its own history—the access to which was laid open most obviously in the moment of the Haitian revolution. The absence of this

---

[5] Ibid., 90.

moment in Western white self-critical reflection still dominates even postmodern critique, and binds white Western thinking to taking recourse to an *innocent* modernity, as it were. My reflection, then, might best be described as an archeological project: to protocol—Spiller's term—modernity's practices of disappearing its embeddedness in enslavement, which is meant to shift the critical focus very deliberately. In the following I am suggesting what I consider the necessary key moments of this re-focusing.

The Middle Passage as a Point of Departure for Critical Theory

We need to move away from a periodization that—give and take some postmodern misgivings—constructs a "before" and "after" Enlightenment logic of widening emancipation and progress for mankind, towards a reading practice that enables us to understand the *constitutive, pervasive and ongoing* Western trajectory of de-subjectification—of, indeed, abjection of certain human beings that precisely enables the accumulation of rights and agency in the white subject.

We need to engage in some serious transnational theorizing and projecting: the disciplines which have housed us will hardly provide adequate and sustainable frameworks for this kind of inquiry; making connections between American Studies, European Studies, national historiographies, philosophy, Gender Studies and Black Studies falls off the maps we have, in favor of creating mind-lines, as I would call it.

We also—and this is my crucial point—need to reconsider the terms of our debates: if Western critical theory has talked about this modern history at all, it has been in terms of "race", or "the colonial", or even "slavery"—mostly safely relegated to the appropriate disciplines, too! I suggest to move to a discussion of modernity's construction on its own, and by default, White western subject—a construction passing itself as universal, ungendered and unracial of course—which has had to suffer a few dents in its narcissistic picture as a result of ongoing feminist critique and its massive and partly successful claims to enter the logic of the subject. As long as critical thinking continues talking about "race" or "colonialism," the issues implied by these terms will be always somebody else's problem: race, then, remains a problem for black people—so a critique of modernity's racist history belongs to Black Studies, and not to the honor's class of the philosophy department; "colonial" refers us to a history of

Non-Western peoples and their "development", or lack of it—but not to a revision of the parameters of Gender Studies and a compromised history of Western feminism. If we talk about the history of slavery, generally it would end up in African-American, Afro-Brazilian or Caribbean history, but would leave modern sociology of the industrial world untouched. In repeated cycles of negotiation of early modern history by subsequent articulations, slavery became a Negro/Black issue, and the Negro/Black became a slavery issue; thus the subject of investigation and enunciation—in the double sense—remained outside of the prerogative to think about modern enslavement, about what kind of work slavery did for the formation of the white subject and for the European symbolic order.

We need to shift from talking about slavery, and maybe even the slave trade, in its ossified form that has already taken on the "understood-ness" of the term "slave" without retaining the scandal of enslavement—to talking about those white European subject's early modern social, cultural and political practices of *enslavement*. These were the grounds, so to speak, on which the modern "item" *slave* came into being, in the first place, as a movable thing, a monstrous number for cargo, and an object of investigation and metaphor.

We also need to redirect our language with precision: reading up the literature, the evasive prose with which words like "bondage", "serfdom", "servitude", "extreme exploitation of labor", and even "absence of rights" obscure the historically contingent and, at that historical point, *new and creative practice* of enslavement of human beings, and of transforming them into chattel, that is, into movable and hereditary property of the white subject—an interesting construction that partakes both in a logic of early modern capitalist individual possession of things, in Marxian terms "ware", and in an aristocratic logic of bloodlines. How a thing—under conditions of emerging *modern* merchant capitalist economy—can have a status that, with its death, will be passed on through generations, is a question that obviously did not bother early modern slave holding societies. But it should bother us, because, seen in the longue durée, and speaking in broad social terms, modern white hereditary freedom was based on black hereditary absence of it.

We need to link the history of modernity as witnessed by recent slave trade historiography and also by a rich contemporaneous textuality—as available in slave narratives or philosophically neglected texts of early abolitionism—with other disciplines dedicated to the study of modern "humanitas." This is necessary in order not to repeat the epistemology of privilege that allowed generations of post-Enlightenment critical intellectuals to use slavery as a metaphor, while its referent receded to an unrecognized and unrecognizable horizon, on the one hand, and on the other, to restrict their epistemic reference to the Greek, or Roman empires—as, for example, it is visible in Elias and Weber.[6]

We need to bracket poststructuralist insights in the workings of difference between "self" and "other" in subject formations—as it concerns the early modern enslavement of human beings from the African continent, we are not talking about differentiation of humanness and agency. We are talking about the annihilation of human difference by the forceful production of movable thing-ness: as witnesses to the slave trade, we are not primarily talking about conquest of so-called others, or about domination of conquered territory, enforced negotiation and hybridization of human difference. We are talking about the early modern production of something new and not 'other'—in the Hegelian sense—but entirely abject to the categories of emerging subjectivity: a laboring, transportable and linguistically capable self-generative commodity.

We cannot let a debate about enslavement and the white subject's implication in it, be enfolded in debates about "colonialism". Enslavement, which cleared the ground and delivered the economic, political and structural base for later colonialism, both in the metropolises and in the hinterland, transposed the enslaved out of the realm of "difference" and "otherness"—postcolonialism's key signifiers—into *thingness*. This presents a conceptual impasse which needs to be addressed: established colonialism, after the abolition of slavery, was always already a mode of reckoning with human difference, whereas early modern slave trade and enslavement did not figure the to-be-enslaved species and their worlds in the same register.

We need a language anew to talk about material interests of the modern white 'subjected' subject, not to indulge in paradox, inability, melancholia, contradiction, ambivalence, alienation and the like repertoire[7]: responsibility will have to be taken. We need, thus, a new term for the

---

[6] Norbert Elias, *Ueber den Prozess der Zivilisation. Soziogenetische und psychogenetische Untersuchungen* (Frankfurt: Suhrkamp, 1976 [1939]); Max Weber, *Die protestantische Ethik und der Geist des Kapitalismus* (Weinheim: Belz Athenaeum, 2000 [1904/5]).
[7] Sabine Broeck, "Never Shall We *Be* Slaves".

Middle Passage, for the practices and discourses of 300 years of enslavement raids on the African continent, a term that will become recognizable within European annals and philosophies of the subject, and has the capacity to become part of a white archive in ways similar to those in which the Holocaust has become the signifier for absolute evil. At this point, still, the term slavery signifies thingification—*verdinglichung* —only for the slaves themselves and their descendants, the black diaspora. By contrast, popular and even academic wisdom has it that since slavery was abolished long time ago, it does not need any more deliberation, neither within the disciplines of the humanities, nor as a challenge to white collective European memory.

We need to re-write the scholarship of Early Modern Studies, which has exploded in the last 15 years, with black memory, as it were. A range of very erudite, archive-based books[8] that produce knowledge about the period —using a white postcolonial habitus in rather performative terms—only to repeat the early modern subject's gesture of appropriation by way of neglecting the practices of primary enslavement on which the production of those riches and world recognition were based. The word slavery does rarely appear in these books, neither in the index nor in the text, and this is not an oversight. There seems to be a new generation of scholars quite at ease with re-owning the Europe produced for us by the Enlightenment.

Last but not least, white Gender Studies will need to re-write its genealogy with a sharper focus on how white feminisms—after all the grounds on which it stands—has historically occupied a crucially double position: faced with modern patriarchal restrictions of women's humanity, their struggle to gain internal recognition as subjects has been from the beginning implicated in drawing cultural, ideological and political lines against the slave. Early abolitionist resistance against slavery inevitably slid into a conceptualization of women's own subjectivity as "not enslaved". This rhetoric has helped to codify the conceptual category of "the slave" which white woman is not. White feminism has moved to a rhetorizisation of slavery, which made the term lose its power to figure New World enslavement and white women's implications in regimes of enslavement. In this way, feminism and Gender Studies have supported a disarticulation of black male and female agency. The space into which

---

[8] See for just one paradigmatic example: Pamela H. Smith and Paula Findlen, *Merchants & Marvels: Commerce, Science and Art in Early Modern Europe* (New York: Routledge, 2002).

black people would speak publicly, as of abolition, has always already been the space made by that pervasive metaphor—a space furnished by layers of repertoires codified in white female sensibility: restricted to a trope of human dependency within the Hegelian logic—a line that runs from Wollstonecraft all the way to Beauvoir's *The Second Sex* and Marilyn French's *A Woman's Room,*[9] and beyond to the abstractions of the performative subjectivity without history of recent Gender Studies.

This insistence upon the constitutive division between women and slaves is a reflection of the dissection of "flesh" from gender, in the sense that black beings could not have gender. Thus they have not been interpellated by that logic and, ergo, they never have been readable as proper subjects of/in gender[10]—a phenomenon that has gone virtually unnoticed by Gender Studies[11]. Gender theory thus has repeated that practice of splitting, even in its anti-racist benevolent multicultural versions of inclusion of "women in their intersectional diversity". There remains the vexed problematic of to whom gender theory can actually address. If the very category we are using is historically based on a split—in its philosophical and ethical address—between engendered humans who are by default white, on one side, and commodified "black flesh", in Spiller's terms, on the other, that category describes black women, and thus it cannot serve the interests of liberation. Gender as a category needs to be re-engaged by a heuristics of the Middle Passage.

Instead of unwarranted returns to Post-Enlightenment's projections of the innocent subject, I argue for a hermeneutics of *epistemological suspicion* from the point of view of the un-subjectification, or abjection of human beings. To adopt the Middle Passage as a hitherto quite displaced point of departure for postmodern instances of self-reflexivity, within and across disciplines, may open windows to the genealogies of modernity that those disciplines have not yet provided.

---

[9] Simone de Beauvoir, *The Second Sex* (New York: Vintage, 1989 [1949]); Marilyn French, *The Women's Room* (London: Virago, 2007 [1977]).
[10] See Hortense Spillers, *Black, White, and in Color: Essays on American Literature and Culture* (Chicago: University of Chicago Press, 2003), 203-229.
[11] See Sabine Broeck, "Enslavement as Regime of Modernity: Re-reading Gender Studies Epistemology Through Black Feminist Critique," *Gender Forum, Special Issue Black Women's Writing Revisited,* edited by Sabine Broeck, 22 (2008). Available at http://www.genderforum.org/issues/black-womens-writing-revisited/ enslavement-as-regime-of-western-modernity/

Bibliography

Beauvoir, Simone de. *The Second Sex.* New York: Vintage, 1989 [1949].

Broeck, Sabine. "Never Shall We *Be* Slaves: Locke's Treatises, Slavery and Early American Modernity." In *Blackening Europe:The African American Presence,* edited by Heike Raphael-Hernandez. New York/ London: Routledge, 2004.

—. "Enslavement as Regime of Modernity: Re-reading Gender Studies Epistemology through Black Feminist Critique." *Gender Forum, Special Issue: Black Women's Writing Revisited,* edited by Sabine Broeck, 22 (2008). Available at http://www.genderforum.org/issues/black-womens-writing-revisited/ enslavement-as-regime-of-western-modernity/

Césaire, Aime and Joan Pinkham. *Discourse on Colonialism.* New York: Monthly Review Press, 2000 [1950]).

Elias, Norbert. *Ueber den Prozess der Zivilisation. Soziogenetische und psychogenetsche Untersuchungen.* Frankfurt: Suhrkamp, 1976 [1939].

French, Marilyn. *The Women's Room.* London: Virago, 2007 [1977].

Horkheimer, Max and Theodor Adorno. *Dialektik der Aufklaerung.* Frankfurt: Suhrkamp, 2002 [1944].

Smith, Pamela H. and Paula Findlen. *Merchants & Marvels: Commerce, Science and Art in Early Modern Europe.* New York: Routledge, 2002.

Spillers, Hortense. *Black, White, and in Color: Essays on American Literature and Culture.* Chicago: University of Chicago Press, 2003.

Vergès, Francoise. *La mémoire enchaînée: Questions sur l'esclavage.* Paris: Michel, 2006.

Weber, Max. *Die protestantische Ethik und der Geist des Kapitalismus.* Weinheim: Belz Athenaeum, 2000[1904/5].

Wynter, Sylvia and David Scott. "The Re-Enchantment of Humanism: An Interview with Sylvia Wynter". *Small Axe* 8 (2000).

CHAPTER FOUR

'MORAL OPTICS':
BIOPOLITICS, TORTURE AND THE IMPERIAL
GAZE OF WAR PHOTOGRAPHY

EDUARDO MENDIETA

No "we" should be taken for granted when the subject is looking at other people's pain.[1]

The issue is not whether the torture was done by individuals (i.e., "not by everybody") but whether it was systematic. Authorized. Condoned. All acts are done by individuals. The issue is not whether a majority or a minority of Americans performs such acts but whether the nature of the policies prosecuted by this administration and the hierarchies deployed to carry them out makes such acts likely. Considered in this light, the photographs *are* us. That is, they are representative of the fundamental corruptions of any foreign occupation together with the Bush administration's distinctive policies.[2]

The photo cannot restore integrity to the body it registers. The visual trace is surely not the same as the full restitution of the humanity of the victim, however desirable that obviously is. The photograph, shown and circulated, becomes the public condition under which we feel outrage and construct political views to incorporate and articulate that outrage.[3]

...as Botero's Abu Ghraib series reminds us, for the limits of photography are not the limits of art. The mystery of painting, almost forgotten since the

[1] Susan Sontag, *Regarding the Pain of Others* (New York: Farrar, Straus and Giroux, 2003), 7.
[2] Susan Sontag, *At The Same Time: Essays & Speeches* (New York: Farrar, Strauss and Giroux, 2007), 131.
[3] Judith Butler, *Frames of War: When Is Life Grievable?* (London: Verso, 2009), 78.

Counter-Reformation, lies in its power to generate a kind of illusion that has less to do with pictorial perception than it does with feeling.[4]

A life that is in some sense socially dead or already "lost" cannot be grieved when it is actually destroyed. And I think we can see that entire populations are regarded as negligible life by warring powers, and so when they are destroyed, there is no great sense that a heinous act and egregious loss have taken place. My question is: how do we understand this nefarious distinction that gets set up between grievable and ungrievable lives?[5]

There is a long tradition of philosophers using painting as a point of departure for philosophizing. It is a tradition that we can say was inaugurated with Plato. The converse has also been true. There have been painters who have seen their painting as thought captured with paint on canvass. Walter Benjamin found in Klee's angels inspirations for some of his most profound thinking, as Adorno found his in Picasso and Kandinsky. Heidegger found his in Van Gogh, as Sartre found his in Giacometti. Arthur Danto has produced some of the most interesting work, not just in aesthetics, but also in philosophy *tout court*, by engaging over four decades in a most ecumenical and eclectic way with all kinds of works of art and painting. Yet, Foucault is perhaps one of the best examples of a philosopher who philosophized with and through painting. What is interesting is that Foucault's refracted by painting philosophizing influenced one of the twentieth century's most important painters, namely Renè Magritte. In fact, we know that Magritte 'preferred to be considered a thinker who communicated by means of paint.'[6] In turn, we know that Foucault wrote a very incisive and insightful analysis of Magritte's work, articulating the ways in which the latter's work in fact is an exemplification of his work on 'systems of thought.'

The relationship between philosophy and painting is more intimate than we are generally willing to accept. If we take Kant's three questions as guides to what is philosophy, then we can say that painting is also about what can be known, what one ought to do, and what we may hope for. Just as philosophy is not reducible to epistemology, painting is also not reducible to the question of "representational equivalences," to use

---

[4] Arthur C. Danto, "The Body in Pain," *The Nation* November 27 (2006): 24.
[5] Judith Butler, "A Carefully Crafted F**K You: Nathan Schneider interviews Judith Butler" *Guernica*, available at http://www.guernicamag. com/interviews/ 1610/a_carefull_crafted_fk_you/.
[6] Michel Foucault, *This is Not a Pipe* (Berkeley: University of California Press, 1983), 2.

Danto's wonderful phrase. Yet, there is nothing like painting to get us to reflect on the relationship among perception, representation, and cognition. Curiously, a canvass is an epistemological event before it is even an aesthetic one. One may even say that a canvass, a painting can be an aesthetic event only as an event of representation and perception. Benjamin referred to film as a form of surgery of perception, but the fact is that this was already at play in painting. Painting is the archeology of perception that conceals its excavation in its very unconcealment. Thinking with Benjamin, we could advance the idea that photography and film liberated painted from having to dissimulate its own perceptual surgery. Painting turns out to be the ontological proof of Kant's insight into knowledge, namely that it is always a synthesis produced from the interaction of a frame and a naked and blunt perception. As painting was liberated to reflect on its role as an epistemological event, painting gained a license to in turn challenge the givenness and 'objectivity' of what photography and film themselves allege to give us without mediation. Painting has re-claimed its sovereignty over the field of representation and perception. Susan Sontag wrote, "photography is, first of all, a way of seeing. It is not seeing itself."[7] Painting, after the age of the mechanical reproducibility of chemically produced perceptual equivalences, teaches us that seeing itself is a way, a framing. If a picture is a frame, seeing is a way in which we frame the world in accordance with contingent and produced norms of representatibility and cognoscibility. We cannot see if we are not prepared to see –and this is the truth of painting. I think this is what Hans Jonas was trying to say when he wrote in his pioneering *The Phenomenon of Life*: "The artist sees more than the nonartist, not because he has a better vision, but because he does the artist's work, namely, remaking the things he sees: and what one makes he knows."[8] A thought that is aphoristically caught in this other phrase: "Expressing both in one indivisible evidence, *homo pictor* represents the point in which *homo faber* and *homo sapiens* are conjoined—are indeed shown to be one and the same."[9] Painting reveals how *homo sapiens* apprehends not just the world but also itself in acts of representation that unmask the norms of cognoscibility that allow or disallow the seeing of those who are to be acknowledged or not acknowledged.

[7] Sontag, *At the Same Time*, 214.
[8] Hans Jonas, *The Phenomenon of Life: Toward a Philosophical Biology* (Chicago: University of Chicago Press, 1982), 171.
[9] Ibid., 173.

In the following I want to, first, show the ways in which painting stands in an intimate relationship to philosophy by considering Foucault's relationship to Magritte; second, I will argue, in reverse to the prior point, that there are painters who can help us see philosophers in a new light. If you like, if philosophers find painters productive, I want to say that painters in turn can help us re-think, or think at different level, philosophers. I will develop the latter point by discussing Fernando Botero's painting on the Abu Ghraib torture perpetrated by US soldiers. Third, as I discuss the ways in which Botero reveals something new about Foucault, I will bring into discussion Sontag and Butler on the politics and ethics of photographing torture, as I consider Leon Golub's own canvasses of torture, and Arthur C. Danto's own reflections on Golub's provocative elucidation of a 'moral optics.'

I

After the much quoted preface, with its delightful and loud Borgesian laughter, Foucault's *The Order of Things* (1970) opens with a chapter simply titled "Las Meninas." In a way, this famous painting by Velázquez is the visual representation of the very invisibility of the framing of representation. If *Les Mots et les Choses* is about the "positive unconscious of science"[10] that is discerned by Foucault's tracing the map of the "epistemological space" that allows for knowledge to be ordered in a new way, *Las Meninas* offered us a visual feast of that which enables seeing that is itself not seen. Foucault writes in this chapter the following:

> "...the relation of language to painting is an infinite relation. It is not that words are imperfect, or that, when confronted by the visible, they proved insuperably inadequate. Neither can be reduced to the other's terms: it is in vain that we say what we see; *what we see never resides in what we say.* And it is in vain that we attempt to show, by the use of images, metaphors, or similes, what we are saying: the space where they achieve their splendor is not that deployed by our eyes but that defined by the sequential elements of syntax. And the proper name, in this particular context, is merely an artifice" (emphasis added).[11]

The relationship between painting and language is infinite because there is a ceaseless feedback loop in which the named challenges the

---

[10] Foucault, *The Order of Things: An Archeology of the Human Sciences* (New York: Vintage, 1970), xi.
[11] Ibid., 9.

representation and the representation seeks to give us something that is left unsaid in the name. What Velázquez's *Las Meninas* allows us to see is precisely the infinite, inexhaustible, asymptotic relationship between the named and the painted. Velázquez is the painter that paints this abysmal gap that yaws in every painting: it is always at an unbridgeable distance from its subject. What Foucault says here about what is taking place in the grammar of the Velázquez's painting, namely that "what we see never resides in what we say," could be generalized in the following way: "what we see, as being presented, resides neither in what we say we see, nor in what we represent as seen." Magritte, who had read Foucault's *Words and Things*, wrote in a letter to Foucault the following: "There is the thought that sees and can be visibly described. *Las Meninas* is the visible image of Velázquez's invisible thought."[12]   How do you paint what is invisible, especially if it is a thought about that invisibility?

This is one of the questions that Foucault aims to answer in his essay on Magritte, which is titled *This is not a Pipe* (1983), as well as his lecture on Manet (2009), although I will not discuss this here[13]. I think that the heart of this long reflection on Magritte resides in Foucault's affirmation that Magritte's work is the enactment of the dissociation, or uncoupling of similitude and resemblance. For Foucault, resemblance is at the service of representation, while similitude is at the service of repetition. Painting accomplishes its task of constructing a visual field by conjoining resemblance and similitude, without conflating them. Similitude is utilized when resemblance has been exhausted. But what Magritte has done is uncoupling them in order to take similitude to play, rub, question or challenge resemblance. And it is in this playful resistance that painting becomes meta-painting. In fact, it could be claimed that Magritte's work accomplishes this turn to meta-painting that Velázquez had inaugurated with his reflexive painting. What Foucault discerns in Magritte, as well as in Velázquez, is the way in which these two painters unveil the grammar of representation. In Velázquez's case, by the way in which he makes

---

[12] Michel Foucault, *This is Not a Pipe*, 57.
[13] Foucault gave a series of lectures on Manet in the late Sixties, while he was still a professor in Tunis. In fact, according to Nicolas Bourriaud, Foucault drafted a course on the evolution of painting from the Renaissance to the modern period. What is noteworthy is that in his lectures Foucault was also interested in the ways in which Manet made visible the invisibility of both the painter and the viewer by using a visual grammar that directs our gaze without painting the invisible. See Michel Foucault, *Manet and the Object of Painting*, introduction by Nicolas Bourriaud, trans. Matthew Barr (London: Tate Publishing, 2009).

evident the synthesizing role of the absent painter, who is nonetheless the absolute possibility of framing. The artist paints only by framing himself out of the frame. In Magritte's case, by the way in which he provides x-rays, so to say, of how it is that paintings do what they do. Two examples of meta-painting closely discussed by Foucault are *Représentation* (1962) and *Décalcomanie* (1966). In both paintings we have a lateral enactment of similitude. In one case, a bucolic scene is repeated on the left between two incongruous and ornamental pillars (a visual neoplasm, if you will). In the other, the silhouette of a man represented from the back becomes the cut out on a curtain that reveals an empty sky. The relationship is not one of resemblance, which relies on mimesis, neither an approximation of it. What is at work here is similitude dismantling the very act of representation by repeating without reproducing. Similitude militates against symmetric and transparent equivalences that would conceal their artifice behind their naïve mimesis that multiplies objects. Foucault writes:

> ...thanks to *Décalcomanie* the advantage of similitude over resemblance can be grasped. The latter reveals the clearly visible; similitude reveals what recognizable objects, familiar silhouettes hide, preventing from being seen, render invisible... Resemblance makes a unique assertion, always the same. This thing, that thing, yet another thing is something else. Similitude multiplies different affirmations, which dance together, tilting and tumbling over one another.[14]

What takes place, or rather, what is exacted as a drama of representing in Magritte's work, is what Foucault also seeks to stage in his archeology of knowledge. At the heart of Magritte's work is the way in which resemblance and similitude intersect vertically to form a matrix that conditions the space of representability that, at the same time, reveals its constructedness and thus its contingency. Just as Magritte reveals the positive unconscious of painting, Foucault exposes the syntax of what is known through the production of the unknown. We learn to see by learning not to see, to unsee; just as we learn to know by unknowing what we know.

II

The publication of Michel Foucault's Collège de France courses from the seventies through the early part of the eighties is forcing us to reconsider not just the reception of his work, but also where its

---

[14] Foucault, *This is Not a Pipe*, 46.

gravitational core laid. It has become customary to divide the evolution of his thinking into three periods: the archeological, the genealogical and the hermeneutical. Each period is putatively associated with a particular thematic preoccupation. Thus, epistemological questions correspond to the archeological period, while questions of power to the genealogical epoch, and questions of ethics to the hermeneutical phase. Curiously, albeit Foucault's longstanding political activism, some accused Foucault of aestheticism, political nihilism and even of decisionism. Yet, what all the Collège de France courses make evident is the extent to which Foucault was immersed in the production of a historical ontology with a practical or political intent. If these fourteen courses are read in tandem, in sequence, one is left with the indelible and overriding impression that Foucault was a philosopher profoundly in tune with the political situation of his time. No course fails to make reference to a political crisis or debate, and each course's main themes are articulated in terms of a problematic that is more or less made legible in terms of a contemporary political challenge. We cannot, for instance, fail to recognize the crisis of Western liberal democracy as it exploded in the violence of the early seventies, nor the evident critique of racist genocidal policies of certain governments, nor the political-economic challenges of the seventies, in the sometimes explicit, sometimes veiled, references in the courses.

What reading Foucault's Collège de France courses allows us to see is that Foucault's concern with sexuality, the body and psychoanalysis had to do less with a history of sexuality, and more with a history of political agency. In fact, we will have to learn to read Foucault in a new way. We will no longer be able to read Foucault as the archeologist of the abnormal, and the genealogist of perverse desire, but as the philosopher of governmentality. In short, we will have to learn to see Foucault as the political philosopher of the historical production of freedom. Foucault, in fact, was not the philosopher of power, but the philosopher of intractable freedom. We will have to learn to read *The History of Sexuality* (1978), whose introduction is titled *The Will to Know*, as chapters in the history of forms of subjection and subjectification, as chapters in the history of a political anatomopolitics, that is, as chapters in the history of the uses of bodies for political goals. We will have to learn to read Foucault's analyses of sovereignty, discipline, docility, pastoral control and surveillance, as subchapters within a longer history of governmentality.

For the moment, propaedeutically, let me focus on the key last chapter of *La Volonte de savoir*, which is titled "Right of Death and Power over

Life." These few, condensed, but explosive pages, with only two footnotes to the same text, are probably some of the most generative philosophical pages of the second half of the twentieth century. For it is in these pages that in 1976 Foucault announced the project of an analysis of the emergence of a new form of political power, namely biopolitical power. This new form of political power, at least since the seventeenth century, had abrogated for itself the task not of 'putting to death' in the name, in praise, or as exaltation of the might of the sovereign; on the contrary, it had claimed for itself the power over life, to administer life, 'to make live and to let die,' in the name of everyone, not of the sovereign as the king, but of the sovereign as a living body, as a population. This new form of political power, or biopower, has evolved along two axes. Along one axis, it has developed a series of *disciplinary* technologies that come to bear upon the body as a machine. These technologies form an anatomopolitics that aims to optimize the capabilities of the body by rendering it more docile and pliable to be inserted within systems of economic and political control and efficiency. Along the other axes, the body is treated not singularly but as part of a species, a genera, whose basis is entirely biological and organic. Here the body is seen as part of a system of life processes: birth, mortality, health, life expectancy, and anything that increases or decreases these. The body seen as an instance of a species falls under the *regulatory controls* that form a *biopolitics of populations*.[15]

The problematic of sexuality, of the regulation and disciplining of sex, arises precisely because it is the desiring body that mingles to reproduce or not to reproduce, to live out a non-reproductive desire, that allow us to discern the body as both singular and part of a species. It is in sex, in sexuality, where we can see most clearly how the two axes of biopolitical power intersect. As Foucault put it:

> It was at the pivot of the two axes along which developed the entire political technology of life. On the one hand it was tied to the disciplines of the body: the harnessing, intensification, and distribution of forces, the adjustment and economy of energies. On the other hand, it was applied to the regulation of populations, through all the far-reaching effects of its activity.[16]

---

[15] Foucault, *The History of Sexuality. Volume 1. An Introduction* (New York: Pantheon, 1978), 139.
[16] Foucault, *The History of Sexuality*, 145.

The regulation, production and management of sexuality, then, became a biopolitical dispositif that manages the life of a population by regulating the way individual bodies mingle and come together in their desire to consume, to release, to exacerbate their embodied pleasures. Above all, then, under this new form of political power, the management of life, the administration of life is to be dispensed and executed through securing the life of a population whose biological subsistence is to be territorially contained. It is for this reason that we see in the second half of the seventies Foucault's preoccupation with the defense of society and the birth of biopolitics, that is also linked to the clarification of the biopolitical *dispositifs* of territory and population. What we learn from the Collège de France lectures from 1975 through 1978, is that in order to make sense of the emergence of this new form of political power, namely biopolitical power, Foucault had to embark on a history of modalities of government. This is why he undertakes the study of the Christian and Greek pastorates, as well as German and American forms of neoliberalism, which are seen as antecedents of modern biopolitical power.

It is, however, the 1975-6 course *Society Must Be Defended*, that is particularly crucial to our deeper understanding of Foucault's originality, and of how his thinking remains generative and still to be fully exploited. For it is in this course that Foucault offers a fuller analysis of the question that the emergence of biopolitical power immediately provokes, namely: if sovereignty, political power, or governmentality, is now to be understood in terms of the production of life, the administering of life, the making of the live of a population, how is death to be recaptured by the sovereign? According to Foucault, it is racism, as biological racism, enabled by the rise of the biological sciences, which allows now the sovereign to re-store the balance of sovereign power over both life and death. Biopolitical power, and I would say, biopolitical sovereignty, is more encompassing, more absolute, precisely because it is both singularizing and generalizing. It treats the entire body of a population, as it watches over every individual living body through its disciplining technologies. Biopolitical racism intervenes to allow, and to make necessary, the elimination, eradication, extraction and quarantining of that which may be seen as a threat to the life of the population. Society must be defended, always, continuously, vigilantly, resolutely against both extrinsic and intrinsic threats. Society must be defended against itself, principally, because it is its life that is ceaselessly threatened by its own condition of preservation and reproduction. Now we can see why race is like sex. For like sex, race is the pivot where biopolitical discipline and regulations intersect most powerfully. It is for this reason that the simultaneous disciplining and regulation of sex is also the disciplining and regulation of race. Let me here refer you to Ladelle McWhorter's recently published book *Racism and Sexual Oppression in Anglo-America*[17], a brilliant exemplification of this type of biopolitical analytics of both sex and race.

I think that it is Foucault's history of governmentality, with its chapter on the birth of biopolitics, which provides us with some of the most useful analytical means for making sense of what we can call the politics of torture. More specifically, a Foucauldian analytics of biopower allows us to understand how it is that today, in the age of biopolitical power, the politics of torture has become a biopolitics of torture. Yet even more specifically, what a Foucauldian analytics of the biopolitics of torture allows to see all too clearly how the torture of the racialized and sexualized body of so-called "un-lawful" combatants, who are not prisoners, but "detainees," have entered a zone of legal exemption in which they are neither dead nor alive, where they can neither die nor live on their own terms. If biological racism became necessary, that is, indispensable, for modern biopolitical governance, then, biopolitical torture has become also necessary and indispensable for the modern state that must "secure" the nation from "un-lawful" combatants, i.e. terrorists. In other words, terrorists are the racial threats that had to be expunged, excised, or exterminated if society was to be saved and secured from its threats. Another way of saying this is that the biopolitical state has to become a security state, a state that secures the life of the population and administers its life in order to maximize it. For this biopolitical state of security, biological racism (genetic racism, or genetic racialism) was an indispensable dispositif to put to death so as to secure life. By the same token, for this biopolitical state of security, racialized and gendered torture is an indispensable dispositif. A Foucauldian analytics of biopolitical power allows us to understand how torture reenters the staging of state power, even after the Hobbessian sovereign had been forced to abdicate its scaffolding and theater of terror. Now, however, since the biopolitical sovereign is the people, the staging of this power over life and death can only take place within this space of indistinction in which the law is suspended by legal decree. The state of exemption becomes territorialized in the legal "black holes" in which individuals, or enemies of "society," are suspended between life and death. These "non-persons" are the

---

[17] Ladelle McWhorter, *Racism and Sexual Oppression in Anglo-America* (Bloomington: Indiana University Press, 2009).

zombies of the biopolitical state of security that assumed legal status with the Patriot Act.

Fernando Botero, a Colombian artist born in 1932 in Medellín, has been painting already for over five decades. His work is internationally renowned, has been shown in every major museum and gallery across the world, and is also immediately recognizable. Botero's work is so easily identifiable that it is almost iconic. In fact, Botero's unique style has given birth to adjective "Boteresque" or the expression "there goes a Botero" to refer to people with unusual proportions and girth. One way to make sense of Botero's rotund, voluptuous and improbably fat figures is to think that he is surely reflecting and commenting on bourgeois anxieties about the flesh. On the one hand, fatness stands in his paintings for the excesses of the privileged classes, which more often than not are ridiculed, scorned and demoted. The haughty expressions, the ornate dresses, the regal accoutrements, the imperial posturing, are all neutralized and deflated by the heaviness of unbridled and undisciplined bodies. On the other hand, this very same abundant, solid, cherubic and baby-like fatness can be read as a form of humanization. What from an angle can be seen as an anxiety, from another angle—provided within the paintings themselves—allows us to see a vulnerable subject. Against a bourgeois, imperial, sovereign subject—Cartesian, Kantian, but most exactly, against the Cortésian and Pizarronian subject—Botero juxtaposes the corporeality of the flesh that is undisciplined and undisciplinable. We are irreducibly creatures of bodies that hunger and can die both of starvation or gluttony. Our flesh thus is always a source of a profound unease, for it can betray us to the same degree making us vulnerable to another's violence.

Botero's work has also been the target of dismissal and derision, notwithstanding its international recognition. Yet, he is a cross over artist, who has gained acceptance across classes and levels of status alike. His paintings are reproduced for popular consumption and they sell in galleries for exorbitant prizes. Botero's paintings, however, are difficult to characterize, though *prima facie* they seem to repeat the same formal techniques of the venerated masters of painting. While his work has been dismissed as being naïve, folklorist and repetitive, Botero has also produced a vast number of paintings that are overtly political and have gone on to be seen as chronicling the darkest chapters of the last half a century of Latin American history. Notwithstanding all of this, the works that concern me here are his paintings and drawings on Abu Ghraib.

In the spring of 2004, as soon as the US media began to release the pictures of the abuse and torture at Abu Ghraib, Fernando Botero began to make some drawings. As the scandal escalated and more and more photographs were released, Botero undertook to paint an entire series of paintings and drawings. He worked on a total of 86 works on Abu Ghraib. Some of them are based on the released photographs taken by Sabrina Harman and Lyndee England. But some of them are based on Botero's own imaginings and reconstruction of scenes at Abu Ghraib based on the testimony and the reports made public along with the photographs. Some of Botero's paintings about Abu Ghraib were first shown in Europe in the spring of 2005. He offered them to several galleries in the US, which refused them for fear of violence or retaliation, or because showing them would be seen as an act of treason and perfidy. They were finally shown in New York at the Marlborough Gallery. Gallery attendees had to be searched before entering the exhibition, for security reasons. Eventually, in 2007, a traveling exhibition was mounted that went throughout the country, but it was shown only in smaller university based galleries.

The oil paintings are mostly between five by four and seven by five feet. They are life size and occupy easily a wall. The colors are extremely vivid and alive and, given their composition, they evoke the staging of historical events. They monumentalize without celebrating. These paintings have taken the ephemera of war, terror, violence and dehumanization and put them on a historical stage. In this way, Botero has rescued the dignity of those who suffered these acts of terror without condoning or celebrating the violence done unto them. A photograph is a shot. It is a frozen frame. It is the blink of the eye. Yet, a photo shot dissimulates its framing. The evidence of what is seen erases how it is seen, how it has been surrendered to the eye. A photograph is frozen time that dissolves its staging. It is a visual shot captured by a chemical reaction that negates the temporality of all human action. Botero's paintings are an attempt to regain the temporal staging of the acts of torture. Torture is not a moment but a string of actions. It is not an event, or eventuality, but a procedure, a process that goes on over time within certain institutions. Torture is sovereign temporality as it performs its violence within its institutions. Torture is performed within a time frame that is dictated by the sovereign exception.

The acts of torture are not something that a few did, against some unknown "unlawful" combatants. The acts of torture correspond to a frame of action, a policy, an event of force, a staging of military power. By referencing the historically sedimented grammar of Western art—from Caravaggio, through Velázquez, Goya and Rivera to Leon Golub—Botero has rescued from the fleeting and forgetful eventuality of the media frenzy the historical and moral dimension of what took place at Abu Ghraib. These were not acts done by individuals, alone, or simply by individuals. These individuals were caught in the logic of a war. While Botero's paintings put the torture committed at Abu Ghraib on a historical stage, they neither lessen nor detract from the individuality of those tortured. The torturer, however, hardly appears here. The emphasis is on the staging of torture, on the suffering, anguish, and terror of the torture. There is a deliberate asymmetry between the torturer and the tortured in these paintings. The torturers are not individualized. There are only four out of 86 paintings and drawings in which the torturers are represented. There is only one life size oil painting in which the face of a torturer is revealed. In a few occasions a boot is shown. In several cases we see a urine stream falling on the bound bodies. The focus is on the torture and on the suffering flesh of the tortured. The torturer does not need to appear. The torture is the setting itself, what is being done to the bodies, how it is being done. Interestingly, in light of what Judith Butler has written about the Abu Ghraib pictures, the torturer is in most occasions shown stepping from outside the painting into the frame. Torture here is the framing—the stage of pain, the theater of humiliation and mocking.

Even as Botero places on a historical level the torture at Abu Ghraib, echoing Goya's *The Disasters of War*, he also accents, highlights and illuminates that which makes the torture at Abu Ghraib singular. The paintings are persistent on their illustration of the sexual and psychological dimension of torture. Botero has managed to paint shaming and shame. The corpulent and improbably muscular bodies look ridiculous with female lingerie. But this is the point. The panties over the head, the use of police sticks to sodomize, the urinating over prostrated and bound bodies, are shown here on the same level as the staging of the torture: the kicking with boots, the hanging from a limb, the hitting with the police stick. Botero alternates between solid, muscular bodies hanging or tied to a cell grate, and supple, plump bodies in which the pectorals look like female breasts. Some of the figures are ambiguously gendered, or gendered ambiguously—but I don't want to suggest that because they are feminized, they are emasculated. I am not sure every feminization is always an act of emasculation. Or conversely, that every form of emasculation has to be a form of feminization. One can emasculate by comparing to another male, or type of males, or by bestializing, which is why the dogs and the imagery of animalization is also dominant in the Abu Ghraib paintings. In most cases, the male genitalia are shown, but in some cases they are not— perhaps suggesting that these bodies that are being sodomized are being raped—indeed rape can take many forms. Here torture is thoroughly sexualized. Sex was a tool of torture. The massively corporeal bodies of the tortured exude humanity and vulnerable embodiment. At the same time that these tortured bodies are exposed bruised, bloodied, and in some cases covered in filth and feces, they are also shown dripping blood, with their head tilting to one side and the mouth slightly open, as if to suggest that this body has just been hit.

As one gets closer to the paintings, the historical frame recedes, and what comes to the foreground are the details. Botero's Abu Ghraib paintings are full of features that return us to the physicality of torture. As if to underscore this fact, Botero painted two close ups of a hand and a foot bound by a tightly tied rope. The skin is lacerated, mauled, and blood is freshly flowing in droplets. Reduced to anonymity by a military system that racks them in order to extract "vital information," these bodies are shown in their irreducible corporeal injurability. These tortured bodies are human bodies. Human dignity is at base a corporeal dignity. Against the torture of the biopolitical security state, which tortures to save "our" society, Botero juxtaposes the embodied humanity of these tormented bodies. Against the frame of war and official violence, Botero directs us to the detail of the terrorized gape and the bleeding flesh. Abu Ghraib may be "us" as Sontag wrote, and Abu Ghraib may become the visual emblem of the US war against the Iraqi people, but because of Botero, Abu Ghraib has now become part of the archive of human suffering at the hands of the violence of lawless sovereigns.

Perhaps it is not excessive to make clearer the ways in which Botero allows us to see something that Foucault's work theorizes and that has allowed me to make the suggestion that the politics of torture has become the biopolitics of torture in the biopolitical age. In Botero's canvasses we are forced to confront the corporeality of both the tortured and the torturer, and the means by which the absent sovereign is rendered too visible in the useless violence of torture, the alleged acts of securitization—one of the primary aims of the biopolitical state. In this useless violence, the sovereign affirms itself, but as absent. It is a productive absence, and it is neither arbitrary nor accidental that the Abu Ghraib "affair" was produced by the lack of clarity about who was in charge. Biopolitical sovereignty governs through the vacuums it creates. Now, instead of the excessive and flamboyant pageantry of sovereign power, with its guillotine, gallows and hanging platform, we have a power that is dissimulated not just by its semi-clandestine character, but by its performer, who is an average and unimpressive individual. Here torture is performed not by a soldier but by a weekend warrior. Above all, in the intimacy between tortured and torturer—a theme that is also central to Leon Golub's paintings as we will see—the way in which sovereign power retreats to the individual, who are forced to do the utmost in the name of the security of society, is made clear. There is no sovereign, except the individual, who does not have a visible mark of being the agent of the state, except perhaps that they are wearing combat fatigues and boots. Botero's distinct style makes available to him a grammar that always directs us to the mundane and quotidian. It is precisely this grammar what allows Botero to address directly the biopolitics of torture, in as much as he is unmasking the biopolitical sovereign concealed behind our sense of urgency to save ourselves from the so-called terrorists by doing the dirty deeds of a society deliberately rendered anxious about its security.

III

The title of this chapter comes from a wonderful line that is to be found in a short essay by Arthur C. Danto, published in *The Nation*, Nov. 17, 1984. The essay is a review of a retrospective of Leon Golub's work held at the New Museum in New York City, when the museum was still on Broadway. I happen to have seen this exhibition. The canvasses were gigantic. They were probably between 15 and 20 feet high. They hanged from the ceiling, unadorned, unframed, like curtains covering some massive windows. They reminded me of the tapestries depicting wars and animals hunts that adorned the imperial dwellings of medieval royalty. You had to step back, way back to get a sense of the scene. Most of the canvasses depicted scenes of torture, interrogation, and the modus operandi of death squads. Golub was explicit that these were scenes referring to the torture that had taken place during the Contra Wars in Nicaragua and Guatemala, as well as torture scenes in South Africa. The canvass had a photographic framing, or rather they were painted as if taking a picture. They depict staged scenes, as if the torturers had posed for Golub. There is both an intimacy and playfulness that would like to make mundane the violent acts depicted. This makes them even more shocking, for they feign a normality that is belied by what is depicted. One is made to reach for Arendt's wonderful phrase: "the banality of evil." But here, banality is the quotidian and almost pedestrian character of the performance of violence. Soldiers are standing around, smoking, distracted, as if bored, or taking a break, while a tied and hooded figure doubles in pain.

The photographic framing of the canvasses, however, seem to invite our complicity, or at least compliance through our genuflection to photographic evidence. Danto captures this insinuation when he writes "He addresses [Golub, the painter] them [the torturers and death squads] as a photographer who seems to show himself almost as indifferent to the enormities he sees as the agents of those enormities themselves are. It is as though he is there, in the same terrible space as victims and tormentors, asking the latter to stop for a moment and pose for what today is called a 'photo opportunity'."[18] In fact, some of the subjects in Golub's paintings look back directly at you, as if saying "you, there, you see what we have to do to keep you safe, to protect your liberties. This is all part of the work of liberation and democracy." But Golub is in fact challenging us to see past this looking back from the gaze of the torturers. There is a way of gazing that neutralizes our moral response and responsibility, one that sucks us into the quick sands of acceptance, compliance and complicity. This is the imperial gaze that frames out the suffering of the victims and that conceals the very mechanisms that arrange what Judith Butler has called the "domain of representability."[19]

While Golub frames his paintings as photographs, he is actually using the very techniques of painting to unmask the imperial gaze enabled by photography. The size of the canvasses, which in order to be seen require us to step back, force us to take distance from the 'staged scenes,' thus making us pause as they pull us in. But as canvasses that hang and that come across as if crumpled and faded newspaper photographs, they invite us to look closely. Golub used a distinctly painterly technique to give his canvasses that eerily faded and historicized look—scraping the canvass, many times over (think here for a moment of Francis Bacon's own scraped canvases, though I have no knowledge whether there was some influence between these painters). Golub scraped his painted canvasses as if to reduce the image to a diaphanous shimmer, as if to reduce the image to a spectral apparition. The technique is simply unsettling. An image of violence, itself a product of violence, one can almost see Golub angrily

---

[18] Arthur C. Danto, "Leon Golub," in *The State of the Art* (New York: Prentice Hall Press, 1987), 20.
[19] Butler, *Frames of War*, 74.

scrapping at these images as if to perform an exorcism of the violent history of war, torture, human depravity, but above all, human callousness.

Danto comments on this particular aspect of Golub's work in this way: "The power of the works derives from their *moral optics*, from the fact that the artist has entered the world he had previously been separated from by his noisy surfaces" (italics added).[20] Now, I don't have to agree with this entire sentence, especially because Danto already had told us that part of the power of the canvasses resides on the fact that Golub gives us a sense of intimacy by insinuating himself to the torturers—the lets capture this "photo opportunity." What I find incisive and correct is that Danto does capture Golub's moral outrage and how it is manifested in a "moral optics" that Golub wants us, urges us, to adopt. By playing painting with and against photography, Golub is unleashing a visual pedagogy: how to look, how to represent, how to frame, how to ultimately see; in short, how to remain a moral subject through all this making visible the world of human suffering and infliction of this suffering.

In *Camera Lucida*, his wonderful reflection on photography, Roland Barthes wrote:

> I observed that a photograph can be the object of three practices (or of three emotions, or of three intentions): to do, to undergo, to look. The *Operator* is the photographer. The *Spectator* is ourselves, all of us who glance through collections of photographs... And the person or thing photographed is the target, the referent, a kind of little simulacrum, any *eidolon* emitted by the object, which I should like to call the *Spectrum* of the Photograph...[21]

Golub's urging to consider what, how and under what conditions we are witnesses to inflicted and calculative suffering echoes Barthes' reflections on the phenomenology of photography. What are we doing when we gaze at such images, and what do we not see or are not allowed to see precisely in seen through a particular frame? What happens to us, what do we undergo when we submit to such 'optics', such a way of framing the visual field, and what do we look at and thus either admit as seeable or not seeable when we look? These are the kind of questions that Golub unleashes by the photographic framing of his canvasses of torture.

---

[20] Danto, "Leon Golub," 21.
[21] Roland Barthes, *Camera Lucida: Reflections on Photography* (New York: Hill and Wang, 1981), 9.

There has not been a US philosopher who has most consistently, incisively, creatively, urgently and with such a profound sense of moral outrage confronted the US imperial/military/torture machine since 2001 than has Judith Butler. If the history of philosophy is punctuated by war, philosophy pushes back by developing new conceptual tools to challenge the recurrence and endurance of war. Judith Butler has made this amply clear in her work of the last decade, which spans the US wars in the Middle East and the so-called "War on Terror." One of her most recent essays is a critical engagement with Susan Sontag's own meditations on the Abu Ghraib pictures. As against Sontag, who sustained that photographs require captions to provide interpretations and that on their own they are merely selective rather than interpretative, Butler argues that the photograph is itself already an interpretative framing:

> "Indeed, if the notion of 'visual interpretation' is not to become oxymoronic, it seems important to acknowledge that, in framing reality, the photograph has already determined what will count within the frame—and this act of delimitation is surely interpretative, as are, potentially, the various effects of angle, focus, light, etc."[22]

In *Camera Lucida* Barthes argues that photography was not the invention of painters, but of chemists, who gave us the ability to capture light reflected off objects. Photography is a technological dispositif that makes reality available to us in a certain way, as a frame it is already a worlding—the letting the world appear and be perceived in a certain way. Part of the framing effect of photography as it is exhibited in the Abu Ghraib snaps is that all these pictures were digital. Thus, it was part of the photographic framing that a large percentage of soldiers in Iraq had portable digital cameras, and that it was part of the military routine and camaraderie to swap pictures. What is to be noted about the Abu Ghraib pictures is not that they were taken and leaked. This was inevitable and almost necessitated by the logic of digital photography. What would have been utterly amazing is that they had never been leaked. The picture was itself a tool of torture—not simply in that it documented it, but also because the photograph itself became one of the techniques and devices of torture. "We will use these photographs to show your family and friends what depraved person you are"—or something like that went the threat. Barthes again:

---

[22] Butler, *Frames of War*, 67.

"The important thing is that the photograph possesses an evidential force, and that its testimony bears not on the object but on time. From a phenomenological viewpoint, in the photograph, the power of authentication exceeds the power of representation."[23]

By time Barthes means here the trace of a historical event, of what has happened. What is important about the photograph is not so much whether it is accurate and how it delivers the object, but that it framed an event in history. That a photograph was taken is testimony that it happened. This is particularly true of the Abu Ghraib pictures, as Philip Gourevitch and Errol Morris demonstrated in their documentary about the individuals who were involved in the Abu Ghraib scandal.[24] Most of these pictures were taken by US army specialist Sabrina Harman, who was indicted for prisoner abuse and military misconduct. As it emerged from extensive interviews with Morris, Sabrina had been taken pictures to document what the 'army' was doing and letting happen, rather what they themselves were doing, or being forced to do.[25] After Gourevitch and Morris we will have to learn to distinguish between what the Abu Ghraib pictures portrayed, and what they documented; between what was intended with the photographs and what they revealed. Yet, this is one case in which photography's power of framing exceeded its power to reveal and disclose. And this is precisely Butler's point when she writes commenting on the Abu Ghraib pictures:

We do not have to be supplied with a caption or a narrative in order to understand that a political background is being explicitly formulated and renewed through and by the frame, that the frame functions not only as a boundary to the image, but as structuring the image itself. If the image in turn structures how we register reality, then it is bound up with the interpretive scene in which we operate. The question for war photography thus concerns not only what it shows, but *how* it shows what it shows. The "how" not only organizes the image, but work to organize our perception and thinking as well (italics added).[26]

Like a translation is always already an interpretation and not a mere transposition, or a transfer, the photograph is always already an interpretation,

---

[23] Barthes, *Camera Lucida*, 88-9.
[24] Philip Gourevitch and Errol Morris, *Standard Operating Procedure* (New York: Penguin, 2008).
[25] Philip Gourevith and Errol Morris, "Exposure: The woman behind the camera at Abu Ghraib" *The New Yorker*, March 24th, 2008.
[26] Butler, *Frames of War*, 71.

a rendering legible, a granting license to enter the field of representability, and thus a permission to be acknowledged and registered as allowed to command our moral considerability.

I would conclude by noting that just as Botero allows us to read Foucault's biopolitical analytics of torture in new ways, as I hope to have shown above, both Botero and Golub also allow us to counter the mesmerizing and framing power of the imperial gaze that is enabled and commanded by war photography. By playing with and against war photography, Botero and Golub make us see through and around the framing of photography to the corporeal vulnerability and injurability of the tortured. Over against the imperial gaze of war photography, and through the use of the techniques of painting, Botero and Golub juxtapose what we can call along with Jill Bennett "empathic vision,"[27] by which we mean something like a conjunction of affective and critical ways of looking and seeing, framing and gazing, portraying and representing, allowing to be seen and letting see. Using Butler's political ontology of grievable life we can discern more legibly the ways in which Botero and Golub offer us a deconstruction of the phenomenology of the imperial gaze so as to be able to feel morally while seeing the humanity of those who are not allowed to be represented as humans in the imperial field of representability. Being able to see may be a way to feel for those whom we have refused to grieve.

Bibliography

Barthes, Roland. *Camera Lucida*: *Reflections on Photography*. New York: Hill and Wang, 1981.
Bennett, Jill. *Empathic Vision: Affect, Trauma and Contemporary Art*. Stanford: Stanford University Press, 2005.
Botero, Fernando. *Botero: Works 1994-2007*. Milano: Skira Editore, 2007.
—. *Abu Ghraib*. New York: Prestel, 2006.
Butler, Judith. "A Carefully Crafted F**K You: Nathan Schneider interviews Judith Butler". *Guernica*, March, 2010. http://www.guernicamag.com/interviews/1610/a_carefully_crafted_fk_you/
—. *Frames of War: When Is Life Grievable?* London: Verso, 2009.

---

[27] Jill Bennett, *Empathic Vision: Affect, Trauma, and Contemporary Art* (Stanford: Stanford University Press, 2005).

Danto, Arthur C. "Leon Golub." In *The State of the Art*. New York: Prentice Hall Press, 1987.
—. "The Body in Pain" *The Nation*, November 27, 2006. http://www.thenation.com/article/body-pain.
Foucault, Michel. *The Order of Things: An Archeology of the Human Sciences*. New York: Vintage, 1970.
—. *The History of Sexuality. Volume 1. An Introduction*. New York: Pantheon, 1978.
—. *This is not a Pipe*. Berkeley: University of California Press, 1983.
—. *"Society must be Defended" Lectures at the Collège de France 1975-1976*. New York: Picador, 2003.
Gourevitch, Philip and Morris, Errol. "Exposure: The woman behind the camara at Abu Ghraib." *The New Yorker*, March 24, 2008.
Gourevitch, Philip and Morris, Errol. *Standard Operating Procedure*. New York: Penguin, 2008.
Joas, Hans. *The Phenomenon of Life: Toward a Philosophical Biology*. Chicago: University of Chicago Press, 1982.
McWhorter, Ladelle. *Racism and Sexual Oppression in Anglo-America*. Bloomington: Indiana University Press, 2009.
Michaelsen, Scott and Shershow, Scott Cutler. "Does Torture Have a Future?" *boundary 2* 33 (2006): 163-199.
Sillevins, John. *The Baroque World of Fernando Botero*. New Haven: Yale University Press, 2006.
Sontag, Susan. *Regarding the Pain of Others*. New York: Farrar, Strauss and Giroux, 2003.
—. *At The Same Time: Essays & Speeches*. New York: Farrar, Strauss and Giroux, 2007.
Spies, Werner ed. *Botero: Paintings and Drawings*. New York: Prestel, 2007.

PART II:

SIGNPOSTS FOR AN ALTERNATIVE HISTORY OF HUMAN RIGHTS

CHAPTER FIVE

IMPERIALISM AND DECOLONIZATION AS SCENARIOS OF HUMAN RIGHTS HISTORY

JOSE-MANUEL BARRETO

> And this Diego de Landa says that he saw a tree from whose branches a captain hanged many Indian women, and from their feet he also hanged the infant children.
> —Bartolomé de las Casas

The conventional history of human rights counts among its landmarks the Magna Carta, the English and the French Revolutions, the Declaration of the Rights of Man, the Holocaust and the Universal Declaration. Whereas Magna Carta plays the role of a protomodern antecedent, the European anti-absolutist revolutions and the Rights of Man are hailed as the climax or manisfesto of political modernity. The Holocust, on its part, would signal to the collapse of modernity itself, and the Univeral Declaration would be a response or an exit to the crisis. This series of events and interpretation of history are accompanied by the names of Hobbes, Locke, Rousseau, Kant, Hegel, Marx, Habermas, Rawls, Lyotard, Derrida and Agamben, which form the cannon of modern and postmodern theories of human rights.

This chapter contends that such a history and philosophical tradition are the product of a Eurocentric version of the vicissitudes of the natural law theory in modern times. For it is possible to put together another narrative of the fate of human rights from the point of view of the Third World. In this interpretation, events such as the Conquest of America, the independence gained by colonies throughout America in the Eighteenth and Nineteenth centuries, the Mexican Revolution, the decolonisation of Asia, Africa, the Caribbean and the Middle-East in the Twentieth century, the Civil Rights Movement, the Cold War, the Anti-Apartheid Movement and the emergence of indigenous groups, social movements and entire peoples fighting today in the Global South against the policies of contemporary dictators, empires, transnational corporations and international financial institutions also have a place. Outside Europe there exists an intellectual and historical tradition of resistance to imperialism and to the violence of the state—advanced since the very beginning of modernity —in which natural law and human rights are crucial. This alternative canon includes the works of figures such as Bartolomé de las Casas, Antonio Vieira, Guamán Poma, Otobah Qugoano, Olauda Equiano, Toussaint L'Ouverture, Sojourner Truth, W.E.B. du Bois, Gandhi, Martin Luther King, the Dalai Lama, Nelson Mandela, Rigoberta Menchú, Aung San Suu Kyi and Upendra Baxi.

This different history of human rights operates as a critique and a suplemment to the standard narrative, and it is inclined to enter into a dialogue with the Eurocentric point of view—a conversation between diverse modern incarnations of the notions of natural law. The inter-play of different tales about the history of rights can strengthen the human rights movement.

Focusing on three periods of this Third World history of human rights, namely, the Conquest of America in the Fifteenth century, the movement for independence in the Eighteenth and Nineteenth centuries, and the process of decolonisation in the Twentieth century, this chapter presents a critique of the eurocentric history of human rights (1); explores the first modern elaborations of natural law made by Francisco de Vitoria (2), and by Bartolomé de la Casas (3). It then turns to an investigation into the part played by rights in the revolutions of independence in the United States and Latin America (4), and into their role in the more recent process of decolonisation in Asia, Africa, the Middle East and the Caribbean (5). It finally offers some remarks on the consequences of this alternative history for human rights theory (6).

1. Human Rights and the Critique of Eurocentrism

Constructing a history of human rights from the point of view of the Third World sets foot on the contention that the standard history of human rights is Eurocentric. The conventional history is a partial account that presents itself as unbiased and comprehensive, while reclaims exclusive legitimacy and condemns a Third World approach to impossibility or silence.[1] The history of human rights that currently informs the scholarly debate and orientates activism is the offspring of a thinking coming out from a particular geographical context. It conflates a wealth of views on rights, as well as the limitations proper to the space and time coordinates that the European standing point carries as epistemic location. The prevailing account of the saga of human rights is ultimately one among the various contingent possibilities of their historiography.[2] It is also one-sided because it awards a notorious and unfair weight to events occurring within the frontiers of Europe, both in the history of ideas and in the history of the practices of resistance.[3] Thus, by framing human rights in narratives constituted mainly by European signposts, the theory of rights remains within a Eurocentric horizon of understanding.[4] In addition, hiding crucial aspects of their genealogy, the histories of rights elaborated in the West give little or no significance to the relations between the colonized world and modern empires. Being born out of the experience of the bourgeois revolutions, the Eurocentric theories of human rights deal mainly with the relations between the state and society, or between governments and individuals, while putting aside the problematic of the interactions between empires and colonies.

Concealed or suppressed, a Third World approach to human rights emerges from other geography and a different horizon of understanding —from the "exteriority" of Europe, an outside that is inextricable from the

---

[1] Arturo Escobar, "Imperial Globality and Anti-Globalisation Movements," *Third World Quarterly* 25 (2004): 210.

[2] Peter Beardsell, *Europe and Latin America: Returning the Gaze* (Manchester: MUP, 2000), 35-37.

[3] Upendra Baxi, *The Future of Human Rights* (New Delhi and Oxford: OUP, 2002), xi.

[4] This critique of the Eurocentric theory of human rights draws from the "geopolitics of knowledge" and the "decolonial turn" elaborated by the Latin American thinkers Enrique Dussel, Aníbal Quijano and Walter Mignolo, who have drawn close around the Modernity/Coloniality project of investigation. See Enrique Dussel, "Eurocentrism and Modernity", in *The Postmodernism Debate in Latin America*, ed. John Beverly et. al. (Durham and London: Duke University Press, 1995). Aníbal Quijano, "Coloniality of Power, Eurocentrism and Latin America," *Neplanta: Views from the South* 3 (2000): 533-580. Walter Mignolo, "The Geopolitics of Knowledge and the Colonial Difference", *The South Atlantic Quarterly* 101 (2002): 57-96.

inside and constitutes it.[5] In this interpretation the events of the Conquest of America and the colonisation of the world at large are also recognised as milestones of the modern history of human rights. Human rights are thought of in the horizon of the world system and in context of the relationships between modern empires and colonies, placing "the non-Europeans at the core of the human rights discourse".[6] A Non-Eurocentric construction of the genealogy of rights can be framed in a long-term historical horizon. This wider scenario can allow us a glimpse into the tendencies, changes and discontinuities that human rights have undergone, and to contextualise the present situation within the dynamics of the entire history of modernity. From this perspective, the circumstances impinging human rights today go beyond the present and extend to the whole history of the modern world since its begginings.

In this more comprehensive narrative of the moments in which human rights have played a part in the upheavals of modernity, the theories of rights are subjected to a re-contextualisation in a Post-Conquest interpretation of history. A Third World approach to the history of human rights offers a narrative about the role human rights have played in modernity. It brings into consciousness five hundred years of utopian mobilisation of natural law to resist the violence of empires in modern times throughout the vast geography of the globe. The point this chapter wants to make is not only that social movements and peoples in the South have made a significant contribution to the history of human rights. The thesis of this essay is that, for the last five hundred years, a tradition of natural law and human rights have flourished in the colonised world alongside the European tradition, and that these two approaches to rights have run parallel, challenged and enhanced each other. The defence of this claim requires, as Edward Said points out in the context of a similar debate, recovering historical facts neglected by the Eurocentric perspective and justifying their importance for the understanding of rights.[7] In such a project the study of the complexities of the history of practices of the right

---

[5] Enrique Dussel, "Democracy in the 'Center' and Global Democratic Critique," in *Democracy Unrealized. Documenta 11 Platform 1*, ed. Okwui Enwezor et.al. (Osfildern-Ruit: Hatje Cantz Publishers, 2002), 274.

[6] Reza Afshari, "On Historiography of Human Rights. Reflections on Paul Gordon Lauren's The Evolution of International Human Rights: Visions Seen", *Human Rights Quarterly* 29 (2007): 47.

[7] Edward Said, "Foreword," in *Selected Subaltern Studies*, eds. Ranajit Guha and Gayatri Chakravorty Spivak (New York: Oxford University Press, 1988), v.

to self-determination plays a central role.[8] This interpretation put us in a better position to understand the configuration of human rights in the current world situation and to advance once again their emancipatory power.

2. Francisco de Vitoria and the Justification of Conquest and Genocide

The history of modernity starts with the Conquest of America. The arrival of the Europeans to the coasts of America and the circumnavigation of the world destroyed once and for all the ancient popular idea of the flat Earth and confirmed the illustrated theory of the Earth as a globe. The image of the Earth as a globe creates a representation that is able to encompass the material totality of the planet. This is a phenomenon of no small significance, as the formation of the world-system and the world-market is one of the decisive features of the rise of modernity. This is the first and constitutive moment of the process of globalisation, the following steps being stages of further intensification, including the present one.

In the classical history of modern international law it is assumed that the basic problem around which the discipline was built was that of the peace and war between sovereign powers, namely between European monarchies of the Seventeenth century. In this narrative, the works of Grotius and the Peace of Westphalia appear as precursors of the modern tradition of *jus gentium*. However, advancing a Third World approach to international law and building on the works of J. Brown Scott[9] and Carl Schmitt,[10] Antony Anghie has shown that the need for a justification of the occupation of the "New World" was the fundamental topic around which modern international law was constructed.[11] The "emergence" of a whole

---

[8] Upendra Baxi, "Postcolonial Legality," in *A Companion to Postcolonial Studies*, ed. Henry Schwarz et al. (Oxford: Blackwell, 2005), 542.

[9] James Brown Scott, *The Spanish Origin of International Law: Francisco de Vitoria and His Law of Nations* (Oxford: Clarendon Press, 1934).

[10] Carl Schmitt, "The Land Appropriation of a New World," *Telos* 109 (1996); Carl Schmitt, *The Nomos of the Earth in the International Law of the Jus Publicum Europaeum* (New York: Telos Press, 2003).

[11] Antony Anghie, "Colonial Origins of International Law," in *Laws of the Postcolonial*, eds. Eve Darian-Smith and Peter Fitzpatrick (Ann Arbor: University of Michigan Press, 1999), 89-90. See also Antony Anghie, *Imperialism, Sovereignty and the Making of International Law* (Cambridge: Cambridge University Press, 2005). In the same sense see Peter Fitzpatrick, "Latin Roots: Imperialism and the

continent triggered immediately a search for a legal solution to the problem of justifying the conquest of the new territories and their expropriation, as well as their distribution among the Europeans powers. This was the question that set off the endevour of international law in modernity, which initially characterised it and still does. In this sense Schmitt states that this was "the beginning of the epoch of modern international law", and that "for 400 years, from the 16th to the 20th century, the structure of European international law was determined by a fundamental course of events—the conquest of the New World".[12]

The legal tradition used to meet this challenge was the ancient and medieval doctrine of natural law. The need for providing the Conquest with legitimacy led to the deployment of natural law within the field of international law. In this encounter between *lex naturalis* and *jus gentium*, natural rights were first enlisted to validate the crushing of entire cultures and populations. This insight was developed by Francisco de Vitoria in order to justify the rule of the Spanish Empire in the territories of America.[13] This task was accomplished by constructing a universally binding legal framework that was capable of sustaining a jurisdiction within which the Indians were to be held accountable. With this undertaking Vitoria actualised Roman law and natural law in modernity. He defined the relation between *jus gentium* and natural law as one of fatherhood or identity adopting one of the canonical text of the Roman law, the Institutiones Iustinianae I.2.1: "What natural reason has established among all nations is called the law of nations".[14] As the law of nations is dictated by natural reason, the guiding principles of international law that best serve the interest of the just relations between peoples cannot be other than those of natural law. Thus, the modern understanding of international law, one capable of sustaining a worldwide jurisdiction, was created by adopting and incorporating natural law.

The new conception of *jus gentium* understood as a "universal natural law system"[15] was complemented by assigning to the native Americans a status that rendered them capable of making part of it. In order to be a subject under the jurisdiction of natural law it is necessary to be human or,

---

Making of International Law," in *Law as Resistance: Modernism, Imperialism, Legalism* (London: Ashgate, 2008).
[12] Schmitt, "Land Appropriation," 29 & 43.
[13] Francisco de Vitoria, *Political Writings* (Cambridge: CUP, 1991).
[14] Quoted in Vitoria, *Political Writings*, 278.
[15] Anghie, "Colonial Origins," 94.

in the terms of the modern rationalist spirit that pervades the arguments of
Vitoria, to have use of reason. Considering pros and cons Vitoria soon
arrived to the conclusion he needed regarding the status of the Indians. For
him, the justice of the decisions already adopted by Fernando de Aragón,
Isabel de Castilla and Charles V in relation to the invasion and occupation
of America was not in question. As he declares in his introduction, his
lessons are of a demonstrative nature and only pursue to explain truths
already established.[16] In the context of a discussion aimed at establishing
whether or not the "barbarians" had dominion over their possesions and
whether or not they were mad men, Vitoria maintained that they had use
of reason—a conclusion deduced from the evidence of the existence
among them of a political and economic organisation, and of a religion.[17]
However, the impulse behind the recognition of the capacity for reason of
the Indians was not that of the humanistic acknowledgement of the natives
as members of the same species, but rather one of the validation of the
authority of the emperor over his subjects under the principles of natural
law. As Anghie says, "precisely because the Indians possess reason is that
they are bound by *jus gentium*".[18]

This can be an instance of the exercise of "the structured gaze of power
whose objective is authority" in the context of the relationship between
conquistadors and colonised.[19] As reasonable people the native Americans
were equal to the Europeans. However, in an Orwellian-legalistic fashion,
they were less equal anyway. This has been a common feature of the form
in which the European consciousness relates to the colonised throughout
the world, who are considered as similar, and as the same time as alien or
inferiors.[20] The Indians were not as human as the rest of the humans as for
Vitoria they were barbarians and as a consequence, following Aristotle,
slaves. The condition of being barbarians and slaves did not exclude the
Indians from the human race but put them in a lower status. For Vitoria,
such a circumstance was a valid reason to justify the rule over them
because the condition of being slaves implied they were incapable of
governing themselves.[21] And despite Vitoria finds in the Indians the traces

---

[16] Vitoria, *Political Writings*, 234 & 238.
[17] Ibid., 250. In this matter Vitoria takes distance from the more wayward
commentators of the time who, like Juan de Sepúlveda, did not recognise the
humanity of the Indians.
[18] Anghie, "Colonial Origins," 94.
[19] Homi Bhabha, *The Location of Culture* (London: Routledge, 1994), 109.
[20] Ibid., 89-92.
[21] Vitoria, *Political Writings*, 233 & 251.

of reason he still considers they have a "mental incapacity" that puts them very close to those mentally ill and even to animals as:

> there is scant difference between the barbarians and madmen; they are little or no more capable of governing themselves than madmen, or indedd than wild beasts.[22]

So, while Vitoria's interpretation of the condition of the Indians in relation to humanity—as it is for him paradigmatically incarnated in Europeans—has two contrasting faces, it can be said that it comes to a single conclusion. Quoting Aristotle, Vitoria states that the Indians are "insufficiently rational to govern themselves, but are rational enough to take orders".[23] The virtue of reason operates only as a theoretical ploy for both denying Native-Americans political capacity, and for making them skilled enough as to be under submission. In Vitoria's overall understanding of the position of the aborigines in relation to the Europeans, the idea of the Indians as humans only goes until it serves the purpose of locating them within the universal jurisdiction of natural law. This juridical construction permits him to charge the Indians with obligations derived from the rights possessed only by Europeans, always within the rationale of subjecting the aboriginals to the power of the Emperor and the hordes of conquistadors and colonisers. International and natural law operated in this way as a sort of modern criminal law sustaining the status of the natives as subjects under the law, and assigning punishments—war and death—for incurring in certain conducts. The credentials of Vitoria as a true defender of the indigenous peoples of America are doubtful as in his understanding of natural law the Indians were only bound to respect the rights of the Europeans.[24]

---

[22] Ibid., 290-291. In his comtempt for the Indians, comparisson with animals were not uncommon, as Vitoria also contennds that they "appear to be little different from brute animals". Ibid., 239.

[23] Ibidem.

[24] There is controversy about the real stand of Vitoria in relation to the Indians. Acknowledging his at least initial or momentary stance in favour of the rights of the Indians see William Rasch, *Sovereignty and its Discontents. On the Primacy of Conflict and the Structure of the Political* (London: Birkbeck Law Press-Routledge Cavendish, 2004), 140. In some other cases, those who consider him to be on the side of the native Americans have incurred in evident misrepresentations: "The writings of Francisco de Vitoria of the School of Salamanca, defending the claims of the Indians, and asserting only a slender basis for Spanish imposition of colonial authority on the heathen peoples of the Americas, put forward political doctrines which were strikingly liberal in character inasmuch as they asserted the rights of

That Vitoria is to be remembered more as a champion of the Conquest rather than as a defender of the dignity of the Indians can also be supported by an examination of the way he dealt with the news coming from America about the manner in which the Indians were being decimated. Despite the fact he knew about massacres and abuses, and mentioned them disapprovingly,[25] in the end he prefered not to pay attention to the voices of those who were already expressing words of warning about the atrocities commited everywhere the Europeans set foot. Instead he choose to believe a priori, or to suppose in contradiction to the evidence, that the opposite was the case and that conquistadors were just wandering around America:

> Since these travels of the Spaniards are (as we may for the moment assume) neither harmful nor detrimental to the barbarians, they are lawful.[26]

Cynicism allowed Vitoria to say that according to natural law the Indians "should love" the "harmless" Europeans, as the latter would have the status of neighbours and friends, and that it would be "inhumane and unreasonable" for the Indians to ban the Spaniards from travelling across America. His distortion of the events happening in America can also be appreciated when he cites one of Ovid's passages to underpin his modern theory of rights—before Hobbes did and with a wholly different twist. Vitoria illustrates the Indians about the true nature of the conquerors telling them that: "Man is not a wolf to his fellow man, as Ovid says, but a fellow".[27] The logic of fear and self-protection behind the need for a social contract and for limited liberties of the Hobbesian theory of rights, is preceded by Vitoria's "rationale" of deception and wilful misinterpretation of history.

The modern law of nations conceived by Vitoria was capable of upholding a set of rights that were to be respected in America:

---

the individual conscience against the claims of political power". Marc Plattner et.al., *The Liberal Tradition in Focus. Problems and New Perspectives* (Lanham: Lexington Books, 2000), 99.

[25] Vitoria, *Political Writings*, 238 & 333.

[26] Some lines later Vitoria relies again on his flawed presumptions regarding the good behaviour of the conquistadors to draw legal conclusions: "But since the barbarians have no just war against the Spaniards, assuming they are doing no harm, it is not lawful for them to bar them from their homeland". Ibid., 278.

[27] Ibid., 279-280.

> And there are certainly many things which are clearly to be settled on the basis of the law of nations (*jus gentium*), whose derivation from natural law is manifestly sufficient to enable it to enforce binding rights.[28]

The rights emanating from natural law were for Vitoria precisely the just titles by which the Spanish empire ruled over the Indians. These rights, which are possesed only by Europeans, are mainly that "to set forth and travel" and trade, and that of spreading the Christian religion.[29] Any kind of opposition to the exercise of these pristine rights was to be taken as an act of aggression and constituted an act of war. The materialisation of such a hypothesis would provide the Spaniards with the justification to "defend themselves" and to resort to violence and war. For the war of conquest was deemed by Vitoria as a just war. In the circumstances of the Sixteenth century in America this legal framework is to be "inevitably violated by the Indians" as they were always already "in fault".[30] The necessary consequence that follows is that the Spanish were always entitled to fight a just war against the Indians. When the idea of just war became part of the legal title for the conquest, the legal framework for legitimizing the massacre of countless peoples of America was completed. In this way, natural law was transformed into international law of genocide, and human rights into rights of war, no matter if some caveats were made regarding the extent to which violence could be exercised:

> Once the Spaniards have demonstrated diligently both in word and deed that for their own part they have every intention of letting the barbarians carry on in peaceful and undisturbed enjoyment of their property, if the barbarians nevertheless persist in their wickedness and strive to destroy the Spaniards, they may then treat them no longer as innocent enemies, but as treacherous foes against whom all rights of war can be exercised, including plunder, enslavement, deposition of their former masters, and institution of new ones. All this must be done with moderation, in proportion to the

---

[28] Ibid., 280-281.

[29] Vitoria considers other just titles to rule over the "barbarians in the New World, commonly called Indians": the protection of converts, the papal constitution of a Christian prince, the defence of the innocent against tyranny, true and voluntary election, for the sake of allies and friends, and the mental incapacity of the "barbarians". Ibid., 286-291. Vitoria also contends that the Spaniards can declare the war to the "barbarians" because they eat human flesh and practice human sacrifices. He does not consider these practices contrary to natural law, but would be condemnable because they inflict injustice upon other "men". Ibid., 225.

[30] Anghie, "Colonial Origins," 95 & 98.

actual offence. The conclusion is evident enough: it it is lawful to declare war on them, then it is lawful to exercise to the full the rights of war.[31]

It is not uncharacteristic of modernity to simultaneously affirm both butchery and reason. It is neither extraordinary for Vitoria to do the same in the field of international law. In his writings, the theory of natural law, which was based on reason and derived from Roman law, transformed the theological ethos in which it was inmmersed, and set in motion a process of secularisation and rationalisation of medieval *jus gentium*. Adopting natural law and reason as secular basis for international law, Vitoria stated that Christian law and papal decrees did not oblige the Indians, and that only natural law applied to unbelievers due to its inner universality.[32]

Vitoria's theory also was a truly modern understanding of international law because it was centred around the problem of how to create a world order, one of the fundamental features of the emergence of modernity. Thus, Vitoria's theory of natural law of nations and just war can make him the founding father of international law, as Anghie contends.[33] By the same token, Vitoria can be thought of as a precursor of the modern theory of natural law and human rights,[34] a puzzling and even incongruous

---

[31] Ibid., 283.

[32] Ibid., 258-264.

[33] In a similar sense see Fitzpatrick, "Latin Roots". Perhaps the first to assert this opinion was James Brown Scott, who saw Vitoria as the "founder of the modern law of nations". See James Brown Scott, *The Catholic Conception of International Law* (Washington: Georgetown University Press, 1934). Above all, Schmitt negates Vitoria any role as founding father of modern international law, locating his work within the medieval international law, and considering him a theologian who "never became a jurist". However, despite his reservations about Vitoria as a theologian, Schmitt writes of Vitoria's approach to international law: "This allowed theology to become a moral doctrine and in turn (with the aid of an equally generalising *jus gentium*), a "natural" moral doctrine in the modern sense – merely a rational law". Schmitt, "The Land Appropriation," 56-57 & 63. Portraying Vitoria as pre-modern but contending that Nineteenth century international law was a "return to Vitoria" see China Miéville, *Between Equal Rights: A Marxists Theory of International Law* (Chicago: Haymarket Books, 2006), 169-184. See also Martti Koskenniemi, "Empire and International Law: The Real Spanish Contribution," *University of Toronto Law Journal* 61 (2011).

[34] The Spanish theory of international law of the epoch has been seen as a "precursor of currents of thought of natural law in the seventeenth century". See Antonio García y García, "The Spanish School of the Sixteen and Seventeenth Centuries: A Precursor of the Theory of Human Rights," *Ratio Juris* 10 (1997): 25-

construction of natural law in which rights reside first of all in the powerful—the emperor and the hordes of conquistadors—and in which being rational and, therefore, a subject according to natural and international law, becomes the reason for being deprived of every right. For the Native Americans becoming subjects under the jurisdiction of natural law became a trap. Vitoria's law of nations recognised the humanity of the Indians while it also justified the exercise of an entire era of frenetic violence upon them. Being a subject of law is an empty predicate for the aborigines as it does not supposes any entitlement to rights. By contrast, the subjection to law, power and the emperor is total even to the point of anhiliation as subjects and as peoples.[35] Natural law, hypostasised as the new system of international law, was used by Vitoria at the dawn of modernity—the time of the Renaissance and the flourishing of humanism—as a validation of the extermination of those made subjects under the very same system of law.

3. Bartolomé de las Casas and the Natural Rights of Native-Americans

Natural law operated as a safeguard for ensuring respect for the indigenous peoples of America already in the Sixteenth century. The force of the European aggression was answered in the case of Bartolomé de las Casas by his adoption of natural law as a resource for challenging the legitimacy of the violence of the Conquest. In this counter-european variation, the theory of natural law became a shield that was used to protect human beings and peoples being subjected to murder, rape, torture, enslavement and robbery.

Las Casas, a Dominican bishop who lived for years among the Indians in Mexico and witnessed the atrocities committed by the Spaniards, dedicated most of his life to campaign for putting an end to the abuses. After travelling to Mexico and being the owner of an "encomienda"—a large portion of land with dominion and possession over its inhabitants—granted by Columbus to his father, Las Casas became a priest

---

35. See also Peter Fitzpatrick, *Modernism and the Grounds of Law* (Cambridge: CUP, 2001), particularly the chapter "Imperialism", and William Rasch, *Sovereignty and its Discontents*, mainly the section "Human Rights as Geopolitics: From Vitoria to Rawls".

[35] The inner ambiguity of the modern subject of law as *subjectum* and *subjectus* has been extensively elaborated by Costas Douzinas. See Costas Douzinas, *The End of Human Rights* (Oxford: Hart Publishing, 2000), 216-227.

and later a military chaplain. After the horror of witnessing the treatment to which the Indians were subjected, he experienced an "awakening of a dormant sensitivity" and renounced to his own encomienda and slaves.[36] Subsequently, Las Casas denounced the carnage caused by the Spaniards, addressed the Emperor and other authorities, and engaged in public and scholarly debate. He published detailed accounts of the slaughter of the inhabitants of the American continent, from Mexico to what today is Argentina, passing by Cuba and Peru. In some cases he describes what he saw, while in others re-tells what he heard or read in chronicles written by witnesses of the events. A single episode happening in a region that later became Colombia can give us evidence of his engagement with the plight of the indigenous, as well as a glimpse at the type of despicable acts of barbarism about which we are speaking about:

> It was this same brute who was responsible for the deaths of some fifteen to twenty leading citizens in a town called Cota. He had them thrown to wild dogs who ripped them to pieces, and, while there, he also took many prisoners from among the local people, hacking off the noses of several women and children and the hands of many men and women. These (and there must have been some twenty pairs of hands in all) he eventually had strung up on a pole as a grisly warning to the rest of the town.[37]

Although he had a fair knowledge of the extent of the brutalities being perpetrated, Las Casas could not have a full-scale idea of what was going on, nor about what the domination of the Spanish empire came to be during the following centuries. Even the contemporary historical consciousness about this cataclysm appears still to ignore the real extent of the destruction that it caused. Perhaps a cold statistic could provide an idea as to the scope of the events: namely that the devastation caused by the European conquest and colonisation has been found to be responsible for the death of up to 95% of the population of America.[38] The sheer scale of the devastation of millions of lives did not have precedent and has not been matched later, as according to recent historical research "the

---

[36] Silvio Bedini, ed., *Christopher Columbus and the Age of Exploration: An Encyclopaedia* (New York: Da Capo Press, 1992), 408-412.

[37] Bartolomé de las Casas, *A Short Account of the Destruction of the Indies* (London: Penguin, 1992), 122. See also Bartolomé de las Casas, *In Defence of the Indians* (DeKalb: Northern Illinois University Press, 1974).

[38] David Stannard, *American Holocaust: Columbus and the Conquest of the New World* (New York: Oxford University Press, 1992), ix-x.

destruction of the Indians of the Americas was, far and away, the most massive act of genocide in the history of the world".[39]

Drawing from his studies of philosophy, theology and Roman and Canonical law, Las Casas elaborated a theory of natural law and international law with the aim of protecting the Indians from the cruelty of conquistadors. As in the case of Vitoria, Las Casas' work was mainly engaged with the relationship between the Spanish invaders and the peoples of the "New World". Las Casas' preoccupation was again that of creating a base for a universal jurisdiction, an international legal framework able to apply to Indians and Spaniards. However, contrary to Vitoria's interpretation in which the new universal jurisdiction was thought of as a way of proclaiming the rights of the invaders, Las Casas' elaboration of natural rights doctrine sought to counteract the butchery of the war of conquest. Las Casas' arguments were addressed to others representatives of the ideology of the just war, in particular to Juan de Sepúlveda. A cleric and lecturer with whom Las Casas engaged in the "Controversy of Valladolid" in 1550, Sepúlveda wrote:

> The Spaniards rule with perfect right over the barbarians who, in prudence, talent, virtue and humanity are as inferior to the Spaniards as children to adults, women to men, the savage and cruel to the mild and gentle, the grossly intemperate to the continent, I might say as monkeys to men.[40]

Contradicting Sepúlveda, Las Casas contended that the Native Americans were gentle, moderate and as rational as ancient Greeks and Romans. For Las Casas there was no doubt about the humanity of the Indians, nor about the unity of the human race. Drawing from the Stoics' idea of the universal brotherhood and from medieval theories of natural rights,[41] Las Casas wrote:

---

[39] Ibid., ix. The significance of the Conquest for the history of genocide has not been adequately highlighted in the consciousness of our time, and remains hidden or repressed by the modern moral sense, particularly by that of the European "civilization", which continues to profit from it. However, the event of the Conquest still shapes politically, economically and culturally our present condition and worldview, paradoxically blurring our understanding of it.

[40] Juan Ginés de Sepúlveda, *Demócrates Segundo o De las Justas Causas de la Guerra contra los Indios* (Madrid: Instituto Francisco de Vitoria, 1951), 33.

[41] Brian Tierney, *The Idea of Natural Rights: Studies on Natural Rights, Natural Law, and Church Law, 1150-1625* (Michigan: B. Berdmans Publishing, 1997), 273.

> All the peoples of the World are humans and there is only one definition of
> all humans and of each one, that is that they are rational...Thus all the
> races of humankind are one.[42]

If we are all humans the jurisdiction of natural law does not operate
only for Europeans but it also extends to the Indians. Contrary to Vitoria,
to be under the jurisdiction of natural law does not lead to the paradoxical
consequences of not having rights, and of being at all times in fault and
deserving of the punishment of war. While Vitoria's starting point was
that of the right to set forth and travel and trade, Las Casas put emphasis
on the right to liberty to which the Indians would be entitled. At this point,
Las Casas's theory of natural law advances from a defence against the
violence of the conquerors, to become at the same time a foundation of a
right to self-determination of the Indians. Drawing from Aquinas'
elaborations on natural law, Las Casas states that, as all humans are
rational, they are necessarily endowed with a right to liberty:

> As regards humans... they were born free... for liberty is a right (ius)
> necessarily instilled in man from the beginning of rational nature and so
> from natural law (iure).[43]

This right is accompanied or interplays with the right to elect rulers,
from which is derived that authorities could only be instated by voluntary
consent of those under their jurisdiction. Disputing the decision of the
Spanish emperor of granting to Spanish "encomenderos" the possession of
pieces of land in America, which included the property over indians, Las
Casas writes:

> No prince or King, however supreme... may alienate any city, land or
> fortified place however small... unless the citizens or inhabitants... freely
> consent to such alienation.[44]

Notions of self-determination were also advanced by Las Casas in the
wider context of the definition of the relation between the Empire and the
Indians. While Las Casas did not object to the capacity of the Pope to
distribute the New World between the Crowns of Spain and Portugal, he
did not find in the Pope's will enough title for exercising the power on the

---

[42] Bartolomé de las Casas, *Obras Completas, Volume 7. Apologética Historia
Sumaria II* (Madrid: Alianza Editorial, 1992), 536-537.
[43] Quoted in Tierney, *The Idea of Natural Rights*, 279.
[44] Quoted in Tierney, *The Idea of Natural Rights*, 280.

Indians.[45] The Indians, each one of them and their own rulers, should necessarily confirm the jurisdiction handed over to the kings as liberty and consenting on their authorities were rights of the Indians according to natural law. Should the acquiescence of them not be obtained, or their negative not respected, the Indians would lose their liberty.[46]

Las Casas was one of the precursors of modern international law. By advancing a new theory of the law of nations based on the ideas of natural law and natural reason, Las Casas and Vitoria constructed international law as a "system of universal natural law"[47] and set a rich precedent for the international law of human rights. Nevertheless, despite Vitoria advanced a theory of universal law based on the idea of the rationality of all men, he put emphasis on the rights of invaders and conquerors and set the scene for the negation of rights to the Indians. Las Casas, by contrast, elaborated a theory of natural rights able to intervene on behalf of the Indians against the cruelty displayed by the barbarians.[48] In addition, in one of the earliest modern elaborations on the democratic origin of power and the right of self-determination of the peoples, Las Casas created a legal argument that put under question the whole process of conquest and colonisation. In this sense, as Negri and Hardt state, Las Casas' humanitarian ideas and actions constitute a paradigm of utopian counter-empire and counter-globalisation tendencies that accompanied the dawn of European modernity.[49]

4. Rights and the Struggle for Independence in the Americas

The quest for self-government in America has a long history, both in the North and in Latin America. For us, contemporary witnesses of the power of the United States, it can be easy to lose sight of the fact that there was a time in which the US was a colony of the British Empire. A war for independence was fought in North America by the second half of the 18th century, more than a decade before the French Revolution took place. The Declaration of Independence of 1776 sanctioned the end of the rule of the

---

[45] Tierney, *The Idea of Natural Rights*, 280-281.
[46] Ibid., 285.
[47] Anghie, "Colonial Origins," 325.
[48] On the contribution of de las Casas to the creation of a modern theory of universal natural rights see Tierney, *The Idea of Natural Rights*, 273.
[49] Michael Hardt and Antonio Negri, *Empire* (Cambridge: Harvard University Press, 2001), 115-116.

British and proclaimed the rights of the citizens of the former colonies.[50] This veritable bill of rights fulfiled the function of putting into evidence the lack of legitimacy of the subjection of the colonies to imperial rule and, at the same time, it was one of the constitutional pillars for the new republican political organisation.

The Declaration of Independence justifies the struggle for liberation from the British Empire. It responds to a question the Declaration poses to itself about why it is necessary for the colonies to break apart from the British crown. After stating the validity of the universal laws of nature, the Declaration advances according to a clear structure. It enumerates the natural rights to which the inhabitants of the colonies were entitled, then narrates some historical events in which these rights had been violated, and finally reaches the conclusion according to which emancipation from Britain was necessary. The declaration arrives to the same inference later when it considers the right to rebellion against tyranny. Stating the principle according to which governments are established in order to guarantee the principles of natural law, the Declaration points that should they fail to do so, a new right emerges: that of rebelling against the ruler that betrays these principles and of throwing off "such government, and to replace it by a new one". After making a long list of the historical "abuses and usurpations" committed by the King of Great Britain, —whose regime is described as one of "absolute despotism"— emancipation becomes an incontestable duty and a right. In this sense, the abuses committed against the natural rights of the colonies and their inhabitants operate as a justification for the liberation from the empire, while independence itself becomes a right.

The proclamation of rights begins with the motto "all men are created equal", which puts equality as the principle that guides the relation between the British and the inhabitants of the colonies, giving the latter the same status. In this context the term "all" has a meaning that is different to that it usually has in the theory of natural law when thinking about the organisation of society. "All" does not mean here a category encompassing each one of those individuals belonging to a particular state—to a national political organisation. It alludes instead to a world jurisdiction, as equality should be predicated beyond Europe to those who

---

[50] The Declaration of Independence enumerated the rights the British should not have alienated from the inhabitants of the colonies and proclaimed the right to emancipation. A further declaration of rights, the "Bill of Rights", was introduced in 1789 as amendments to the Constitution of 1787.

are not Europeans. The Declaration continues with a reference to "the rights to life, liberty and the pursuit of happiness" in which liberty means the collective right that had been historical eroded in the life of the colonies under tyranny. The right to liberty also carries its long awaited consequences, that is, emancipation and the capacity to freely decide on the destiny of the former colonies.

This reading of the role of the rights proclaimed in the Declaration of Independence has been underestimated in the interpretations made through the prism of the European theory of human rights. From a Eurocentric perspective, rights are mainly understood as paradigms on which the bourgeois society was modelled, and as regulators of the relationship between society and the state. This is the case with Habermas' comparison between the Declaration of Independence and the French Declaration of the Rights of Man. Habermas initially accertains that these two manifestos have different meanings derived from their distinct teleology: while the rights in the Declaration of Independence justify the emancipation from the British empire, in the French Declaration they operate as a legitimisation of the overthrowing of the ancient regime.

Nevertheless, Habermas sidelines a historical approach to these events and ops for an abstract perspective that he calls "immannent". Focused on the role played by natural law in the wake of bourgeois revolutions, Habermas loses sight of the stark difference between the rationale of the US and the French Declarations. In this way, his reflection on the Declaration of Independence remains within the initial and overriding context of his concern for the role natural law in the constitution of the relationships between individuals and the state. Ultimately, for Habermas, the American and the French Declarations are just instances of the same species or "two different constructions of the Natural law of bourgeois society".[51] Althought the War of Independence is a bourgeois revolution by the nature of the new political and economic order it creates, the Revolution of Independence is first of all an anti-imperial enterprise. As Habermas is concerned mainly with the definition of the foundations of the bourgeois society, and with the events that occured within the national borders of the European nation-states, he does not situate his interpretation of the Declaration of Independence in the horizon of understanding of the world system—the modern world at large. Thus, Habermas puts aside the matter of the contribution of natural law to the shaping of the relations

---

[51] Jürgen Habermas, *Theory and Praxis* (Cambridge: Polity Press, 1988), 91.

between Europe and the rest of the world—or what is the same, between empires and colonies.

The dawn of the Nineteenth century also was witness to a surge of struggles for emancipation in Latin America and the Caribbean. From Mexico and Haiti, to the Chilean and Argentinean Patagonia, the "sign of the times" shook most of the colonies of the Spanish, Portuguese and French empires. The philosophy of natural law and the ideals of the US Declaration of Independece and the "Rights of Man" played their part in destroying the legitimacy of 300 years of imperial rule, thus justifying the movement for emancipation, as well as setting the basis for new political institutions. More than 30 years had passed since the United States had declared independence from the British, but the wars being fought to the South of the continent still belonged to the same historical trend. The example set by those who in the North achieved autonomy from the British crown was frequently quoted in support of the struggle against the empires with dominions in the South. The constitutions of the newborn nations were worded in terms similar to those used in the Declaration of Independence, and also gave support to those who believed in a federalist organisation for the new republics.

The inspiration for leaders and intellectuals of the "revolutions of independence" in Latin America also came from another empire, France, and from its Declaration of the Rights of Man. The French variation on the natural law tradition, and the liberal and democratic conception of politics were received with a twist. They provided an updated basis for the political constitution of the new republics, but first of all they acted as the intellectual ammunition for a different type of revolution: a revolution of independence. The Rights of Man put into evidence the existing contrast between the promises of its content and the realities of the day to day rule by European empires. In societies marked by stark hierarchies established between Europeans and Americans—who were assumed to be inferior or less capable because of their place of birth, race or culture—the idea according to which "all men" were equal found a land ripe for becoming history. In the New Granada—today's Colombia, Venezuela, Ecuador and Panamá—for instance, the Declaration of the Rights of Man became essential for those who, like Antonio Nariño, had translated it into Spanish already in 1794 and clandestinely distributed it in the streets of Santa Fe de Bogotá. The 1810 Declaration of Independence welcomed the language of rights and Rousseau's ideas by posing as its pillar "the inalienable right to popular sovereignty". Later the constitutions adopted between 1811 and

1815 by the emancipated federal provinces contained Bills of Rights that included rights that had been proclaimed a few years before in the US and French declarations. This was the case in the Second Section of the Constitution of the Federal State of Antioquia of 1812 on "The Rights of the Man in Society", which began by stating:

> God has equally conceded to men certain natural rights, essential and imprescriptible, like those to defend and keep their lives, acquire, enjoy and protect their properties, seek and obtain their security and happiness. These rights are summarised in four principles, namely: legal freedom and equality, security and property.[52]

In a new series of successful political moves for emancipation in South America, the doctrine of rights proclaimed by the Declaration of Independence and the French Declaration provided a discourse that channeled the popular discontent and contributed to justify the revolutions of independence throughout the continent. At the same time, the doctrine of rights supplied some of the principles that should be abided for the new polities to be feasible and democratic. In these circumstances, again, natural law and rights operated as a utopian force and helped to bring to an end centuries of imperialism. In short, the first developments of the modern theory and praxis of human rights are not to be found in the history of the bourgeois revolutions in European. Rather, they are inscribed within the historical impulse for emancipation and self-determination incarnated by Las Casas, the wars of independence in the United States and throughout America, and in the rights they declared and adopted in their national constitutions.[53]

5. Decolonisation and the Right to Self-Determination

After the Second World War the centuries long resistance against the rule of the European empires in Africa and Asia became an uprising and the liberation struggles led to the political independence of most of the

---

[52] http://www.cervantesvirtual.com/servlet/SirveObras/01338386433137061867680/p0000001.htm#I_3

[53] In addition, it could be said that the conception of human rights developed around the relation between individuals and the state counts among its predecessors and sources a practise and interpretation of human rights rooted in the struggles between the colonies and colonial rule. This is derived from the fact that the US Declaration of Independence influenced the French Assembly of 1791, an historical episode that is well documented but has not been properly thematized.

colonies. Decolonisation then became an unstoppable phenomenon, a process that was peaceful in cases like that led by Gandhi in India and violent, as in Algeria, where it was achieved through a war of national liberation. Nationalism had grown in the colonies since the 1930"s coupled with the crisis of imperialism. They were also accompanied by what Sartre later called a consciousness about the contradiction between the European appeal to humanity as a value—including human rights—and the atrocities committed by the empires and the local authorities on their behalf.[54] Beyond this consciousness about the European betrayal of the ideals of rights, nationalist and anti-colonial struggles like that of Nigeria were accompanied by the formation of human rights movements, and rights operated as a justification for independence.[55] Thus, human rights and natural law were part of the debate of ideas that sustained the drive for liberation, a move that was swiftly counteracted by imperial authorities, accompanying the imposition of harsh measures in some cases with the warning that "no ethical considerations such as the rights of man will be allowed to stand in the way".[56]

The decolonisation process had notable repercussions for the creation of international and regional human rights standards. The landscapes that emerged after the Second World War made evident the outrageous realities of the Holocaust and also those of colonialism and racism.[57] In the wake of the fight for freedom from foreign domination and while liberation was being achieved throughout Africa and Asia, political independence from colonial rule was transformed into a principle of the Charter of United Nations. At the same time the struggle for autonomy from the colonisers and equality between countries in the world order became a human rights issue.[58] As Michael Ignatieff maintains, the principles of self-determination and equality, two of the cornerstones of contemporary international law and human rights, are basically the

---

[54] Jean-Paul Sartre, "Preface," in Franz Fanon, *The Wretched of the Earth* (London: Penguin, 2001), 17.
[55] Bonny Ibhawoh, *Imperialism and Human Rights: Colonial Discourses of Rights and Liberties in African History* (Albany: SUNY, 2007), 2-3 & 6. Ibhawoh's work is one of the first to explore the role rights performed during the process of decolonisation of Africa, a task that is longly overdue.
[56] Cited by Hannah Arendt, *The Origins of Totalitarianism* (San Diego: Harvest Book, 1976), 221.
[57] Afshari, "On Historiography of Human Rights," 46.
[58] Ibid., 48.

consequence of the anti-colonial struggle.[59] In this context, self-determination alludes first of all to political independence, but also to the capacity of all peoples to decide by themselves about their own economic model and cultural development.[60] The right to self-determination is at the basis of the tradition of the peoples" rights and that of the rights of solidarity, which include the rights to development, to control natural resources, to peace and to a clean environment.

When the new independent African and Asian nations were admitted as members of the United Nations in the 1950's and 1960's, the international human rights instruments were enhanced and taken into a different direction. In contrast to classical human rights, the right to self-determination is a right residing in a collective identity, the people. The UN Declaration on Decolonisation adopted in 1960 established that "all peoples have the right of self-determination" and sanctioned that foreign domination of peoples contradicts human rights standards, the UN Charter and world peace. Some years later the 1963 Declaration on the Elimination of All Forms of Racial Discrimination condemned racism as contrary to human dignity and to the principle of equality of all human beings, and reiteratively mentioned apartheid as a practice that should end immediately. The right to self-determination was made the first article of two of the key human rights treaties, the 1966 International Covenants on Civil and Political Rights and on Economic, Social and Cultural Rights. It was also after colonisation faded that the right to self-determination of indigenous and tribal peoples was internationally recognised by the 1989 International Labour Organisation Convention No. 169, and more recently in the 2007 UN Declaration on the Rights of Indigenous Peoples.

The 1966 covenants illustrate in its full extension the principles of interdependence and indivisibility of human rights. The absence of a pre-established hierarchy between sets of rights and the unbreakable bond between them is to be predicated not only of the relationship between civil and political rights on the one hand, and economic, social and cultural ones on the other. By the same token, both generations of rights cannot be separated from the right to self-determination and, while the respect for the first sets of rights rests on the enforcement of the latter, self-determination

---

[59] Quoted in Balakrishnan Rajagopal, "Counter-hegemonic International Law: Rethinking Human Rights and Development as a Third World Strategy," *Third World Quarterly* 27 (2006), 770.
[60] Theo van Boven, *Human Rights from Exclusion to Inclusion: Principles and Practice* (Leiden-Boston: Martinus Nijhoff, 2000), 391.

cannot be thought in the absence of civil, political and economic rights. But decolonisation not only transformed and gave new orientations to the international charter of human rights but also contributed to create a corpus of African human rights instruments. Thus, the concept of the rights of peoples and the right to self-determination became two of the cornerstones and key contributions to the human rights tradition made by the 1981 African Charter on Human and Peoples' Rights.

A caveat is necessary to be made at this point. The paradox between the will of governments and officials to declare rights and the rejection to be subjected to them has accompanied the history of human rights. The French revolutionaries inspired by the likes of Robespierre and Saint Just, recited the Rights of Man and brought about "the Terror". This is the point at which "revolution becomes terror", and the image that operates as a symbol of the event changes from the takeover of the Bastille to the swift guillotine.[61] At the same time, as an imperial power, France enacted the Declaration of the Rights of Man and then negated them to those living in the territories of the French colonies and to the slaves.

By the same token, the emergence of the rights of peoples within the international law of human rights was not free of such ironies. The taxing struggle against colonialism and the quest for stability of the new governments conspired to use the right of self-determination as an ideological pretext to curtail the civil and political rights of the citizens of the new liberated nations, particularly in Africa, the Middle-East and Asia.[62] This phenomenon was accompanied by a lack of interest in human rights other than the right to self-determination in international organisations created by Third World governments to press for a change in the configuration of world power relations and for a new economic order, as in the cases of the Movement of the Non-Aligned Countries and the Group of 77,[63] as well as the Organisation of African Unity (OUA).[64] In

---

[61] David Andress, *French Society in Revolution 1789-1799* (Manchester: MUP, 1999), 1.

[62] In Latin America, where by the mid 1950,s independence was already more than hundred years old, the thread to individual rights and to the international human rights commitments signed by civil governments came instead from right wing elites and military dictatorships which, supported by the US imperialist foreign policy, eroded democracy and systematically violated human rights.

[63] Afshari, "On Historiography of Human Rights," 53-55.

[64] Gino Naldi, "Future Trends in Human Rights in Africa: The Increased Role of the OAU?," in *The African Charter on Human and Peoples' Rights: The System in*

these circumstances a priority was put on the preservation of self-determination, while civil and political rights were abused and neglected, and the principles of indivisibility and interdependency of human rights were not taken into account.

As history gives faith, when a single right or set of rights acquires derogatory status over other rights, human beings are hurt and the cause of human rights damaged.[65] The right to self-determination as such cannot be identified with the privilege of the states to neglect civil, political or economic rights, or with a sort of exclusionary clause that empties international human rights treaties of content. What happened in the newly liberated countries was that nationalism and anti-colonialism became illiberal and non-democratic in their particular historical circumstances.[66] Above all, the appeal to national sovereignty as a way of eschewing international obligations regarding the own nationals has been not exclusive of Third World countries. Since its inception, the leading founding members of the United Nations have been keen to resort to the principle of sovereignty in order to avoid condemnation of abuses committed by their own governments as in the cases of the United States, the United Kingdom and the Soviet Union.[67]

Finally, although tensions are common between generations of rights, this should not take us to think that there is an innate contradiction between the right of self-determination with its call for respect for sovereignty, and the need for international vigilance of the duty of the states to respect and protect the rights of those living under their jurisdiction. Neither the higher standing of self-determination in the realm of human rights after decolonisation should let to a nostalgia of the times of "imperial governance" which, if brought back, would supposedly guarantee greater protection for rights.[68]

Practice, 1988-2000, ed. Rachel Murray and Malcolm Evans (Cambridge: CUP, 2002), 1.
[65] Afshari, "On Historiography of Human Rights," 42-65. On the case of the Middle-East see Reza Afshari, "An Essay on Islamic Cultural Relativism in the Discourse of Human Rights," *Human Rights Quarterly* 16 (1994): 235-236.
[66] Afshari, "On Historiography of Human Rights," 51.
[67] Paul Gordon Lauren, *The Evolution of International Human Rights: Visions Seen* (Philadelphia: University of Pennsylvania Press, 2003), 192.
[68] Niall Fergusson thinks in this direction, quoted in Afshari, "On Historiography of Human Rights," 51.

The idea of self-determination, defended four hundred years before by Las Casas as a principle of natural right, became positive international law when the struggle for decolonisation triumphed in the ambit of international human rights law. In doing so, natural law and human rights were faithful to their emancipatory heritage and actualised one of their primal potentialities, namely that of serving as a shield against the advances and the wrongs of imperialism.

6. Consequences for the Theory of Human Rights

The interpretation of the history of human rights from a Third Word perspective has a number of consequences for the standard theory of rights. Within this distinct vision of the history of rights some of its basic tenets need to be re-thought, including those of the subject of human rights, the historical scenario of its origin, the legal discipline in which it was born, its founding fathers, as well as those of the individual or collective "nature" of rights and the doctrine of the generations of rights.

Human rights need to be thought not only in the framework of the relationship between the state and the individual, but also in the dynamics between empires and colonies.[69] Born in the process of the struggles against absolutism, the Eurocentric theory of rights is of a liberal and democratic inspiration, always dealing with the protection that individuals require for counteracting the power of the state—the freedoms—, and concerned with ensuring individuals have the power to steer the state—the political rights. Once social and economic rights were instituted in the wake of the socialist impulses of the Twentieth century, rights were associated with the issue of how the state could intervene to ensure individuals in general and members of particular groups, have access to basic goods and services. By contrast, from a Third World perspective, the theory of rights was born in the context of the relationship between empires and colonies. In this angle, peoples—the former colonies or current neo-colonies—are entitled, first of all, to the right to political, economic and cultural self-determination, while states—or empire-states—are called upon to respect these rights and are held responsible for their violation.

---

[69] To move from the sphere of the nation-state to the "post-national constellation" is not only the consequence of thinking of human rights from the perspective of the Third World but, as in the case of Habermas, it is also the logical response to the process of globalisation. Lasse Thomassen, "Introduction" in *The Derrida-Habermas Reader*, ed. Lasse Thomassen (Edinburgh: EUP, 2006), 5.

Within the same horizon of understanding, it can be said that the modern struggle for human rights has taken place not only in the ambit of the nation-state, but also in that of the international relations—the world order or the world-system. Human rights are usually thought within the realm of the nation because this was the historical site from which reflections such as those of Hobbes and Locke emerged. That was also the scenario in which the Declaration of the Rights of Man was adopted. But in a reading of human rights as legal and political barriers to the exercise of the power of empires, the sphere in which human rights emerged is that of the modern world as a whole. In this way, after being considered only as a national topic, human rights become a theme to be assessed and decided also in the international or global arena.

By the same token, constitutional law and the theory of the state have been assumed to be the disciplines that functioned as intellectual nests of modern human rights. The debates about the type of political system that should replace the ancient regime after the English and the French revolutions, and about how to organize the new polity through a social contract were made in connection with discussions about bills of rights and their foundations. Nevertheless, it is not sufficiently known that a similar intellectual agitation around natural law took place some centuries before when the Spanish Empire sought to legitimise the Conquest, and when the indigenous peoples of America and their legal and philosophical sympathizers, attempted to organize resistance to the slaughter of millions.[70] Francisco de Vitoria and Bartolomé de las Casas' theories of natural law were made within the field of international law, the realm in which it was possible to set out the norms able to rule the relations between the Emperor and the colonized. These facts allow us to say that human rights are not only the offspring of constitutional law and the theory of state, but also the progeny of Sixteenth century international law.

---

[70] In 1559 Bartolomé de las Casas, together with Domingo de Santo Tomás and Alonso Méndez, were granted legal power from a group of Indians chiefs of Perú to represent them before the Spanish Crown when a decision about "encomiendas"—a system of distribution of land by which the emperor gave complete authority to Spanish colonist over vast portions of land and their inhabitants in exchange of economic compensation—was to be taken. Luciana Pereña and José Manuel Pérez, "Estudio Preliminar," in Bartolomé de las Casas, *De Regia Potestate o Derecho de Autodeterminación* (Madrid: Consejo Superior de Investigaciones Científicas, 1969), ci-cix.

A Third World account of human rights has also ramifications in the debate about the founding fathers of the modern incarnation of the natural law doctrine. After re-writing the history of rights from the perspective of the South it is evident that before Hobbes, Locke, Rousseau, Paine, Kant, Hegel, Grotius, Pufendorf and Vattel elaborated the modern theory of rights and the *jus gentium*, natural law had been already mobilized by Vitoria and Las Casas to put together a modern theory of international law as a response to the challenges posed by the Conquest of America. Although at odds over the purpose of their engagement with rights, both Vitoria and Las Casas constructed international law as a realm of natural law or, conversely, brought natural law into the sphere of international law and, by doing so, they laid the basis of modern human rights and international law already in the Sixteenth century.

Traditionally human rights have been thought of mainly as individual rights—as entitlements of human beings against abuses committed by governments. The classic insight into the character and the holder of rights remains dominant still today after the emergence of social and cultural rights, and even after the rights of peoples appeared in the horizon of the second half of the Twentieth century. But the history of the resistance of peoples to conquest and colonisation through the appeal to the right to self-determination makes also evident that human rights were originally collective rights. It could not be other way if we are to think human rights as to be immersed in the world scene, and within the framework of the relations between empires and colonies, and not only between states and citizens.

This Third World perspective also changes the balance within the standard conception of the so-called "generations of rights". According to the commonly held interpretation, in the Eighteenth century the French Revolution enacted the first generation of rights, that of the civil and political rights. Economic and social rights—the second generation—are associated with early Twentieth century events like those of the Russian Revolution, the implementation of the agenda of the Social Democracy in Europe and the creation of the International Labour Organization. Lastly, the second half of the Twentieth century—in which the process of decolonisation was paramount—would have given birth to a third generation of collective rights, including the right to self-determination, the right to development, environmental rights and the right to peace.

This succession of generations of rights does not only correspond to a historical sequence. It has also been used to draw a hierarchy in which the rights of the first generation hold a principled priority over others sets of rights. Thus, in the theory of classical liberalism, civil liberties, economic freedoms and democratic rules trump social aspirations. A more balanced approach was attempted when welfare policies were adopted in countries in which social democratic visions of the state triumphed. In a similar orientation, a call for the interdependence of civil and political rights and of economic and social rights has been made for the last two decades in the sphere of international human rights law. Nonetheless, after the process of decolonization was substantially completed, solidarity or collective rights have remained relegated to the margins of international law, disregarded by empires and multinational companies and, paradoxically, mainly upheld by dictatorships and states responsible for widespread human rights violations in order to reject foreign criticism and to avoid condemnations by the international community. This is the current situation of the doctrine of generations of rights in a world dominated by capitalism, free market and neo-colonialism.

Within the framework of the understanding of modern human rights elaborated in this chapter not the civil and political rights would be those of the first generation, but that of the right to self-determination. Above all, this is not to say that self-determination should be enthroned on the top of the pecking order of rights. This is rather a call for getting rid of such a hierarchy and for giving the right to self-determination the place it deserves within the horizon of the interdependence of the generations of rights in which all rights hold the same priority and importance. Such a rearrangement would lead to establishing a more comprehensive balance where the different generations of rights get into conflict and conciliation in a field in which they all hold initially equal status.

Concluding remarks

An adequate comprehension of the way in which human rights operate today requires a consideration of their history from the very beginning of modernity. A long-term perspective allows us to see the vicissitudes that human rights have endured and to understand that the current is just the more recent expression of a dynamic extended throughout the entire history of modernity. In order to gain such a broad perspective, an attempt at re-writing the history of human rights has been advanced in this chapter. In this narrative of the moments in which human rights have played a part in the political and social upheavals of modernity, the theories of rights are subjected to a re-contextualisation in a Post-Conquest interpretation of history. In this different framework, human rights are thought of in the horizon of the world system and in context of the relationships between empires and colonies. This alternative history highlights the resistance of the colonised against the violence of the empires in which natural and human rights have been an emancipatory force throughout centuries and alongside the immense geography of the Third World. If this is true, we should relate the history of human rights not only to European thinkers and events, but also to all those who are part of the lineage commenced by Las Casas, whose defence of the rights of the native Americans was "the first counter-discourse of modernity".[71]

While the core of the human rights theory comes from the Greek, Roman and Medieval doctrines of natural law, such an ancient European tradition has a number of modern incarnations, not only in Europe but also in the struggles and theories advanced outside Europe. With the advent of modernity the ancient doctrine of natural law turned into a body of theories that flew in the opposite direction from the colonised peoples towards the European empires. Human rights are not a gift of the West to the rest of the world.[72] The agency and authorship of human rights is also to be found in the peoples resisting colonialism. These peoples have been historical subjects or agents of human rights since the Sixteenth century and will play a similar role in the future. This reframing of the contemporary understanding of human rights can destabilise and supplement the hegemonic Eurocentric history and theory of human rights, which has failed to show their imperial and counter-imperial origins.

Bibliography

Afshari, Reza. "An Essay on Islamic Cultural Relativism in the Discourse of Human Rights." *Human Rights Quarterly* 16 (1994).
—. "On Historiography of Human Rights. Reflections on Paul Gordon Lauren"s The Evolution of International Human Rights: Visions Seen." *Human Rights Quarterly* 29 (2007).

---

[71] Enrique Dussel, "Philosophy in Latin America in the Twentieth Century. Problems and Currents," in *Latin American Philosophy. Currents, Issues, Debates*, ed. Eduardo Mendieta (Bloomington and Indianapolis: Indiana University Press, 2003), 32.
[72] Baxi, *The Future of Human Rights*, vi.

Andress, David. *French Society in Revolution 1789-1799*. Manchester: MUP, 1999.

Anghie, Antony. "Colonial Origins of International Law." In *Laws of the Postcolonial*, edited by Eve Darian-Smith and Peter Fitzpatrick, 1999.

—. *Imperialism, Sovereignty and the Making of International Law*. Cambridge: Cambridge University Press, 2005.

Arendt, Hannah. *The Origins of Totalitarianism*. San Diego: Harvest Book, 1976.

Baxi, Upendra. "Postcolonial Legality." In *A Companion to Postcolonial Studies*, edited by Henry Schwarz et al. Oxford: Blackwell, 2005.

—. *The Future of Human Rights*. New Delhi and Oxford: OUP, 2002.

Beardsell, Peter. *Europe and Latin America: Returning the Gaze*. Manchester: MUP, 2000.

Beldini, Silvio. ed. *Christopher Columbus and the Age of Exploration: An Encyclopaedia*. New York: Da Capo Press, 1992.

Bhabha, Homi. *The Location of Culture*. London: Routledge, 1994.

Brown Scott, James. *The Catholic Conception of International Law*. Washington: Georgetown University Press, 1934.

—. *The Spanish Origin of International Law: Francisco de Vitoria and His Law of Nations*. Oxford: Clarendon Press, 1934.

De las Casas, Bartolomé. *A Short Account of the Destruction of the Indies*. London: Penguin, 1992.

—. *Obras Completas, Volume 7. Apologética Historia Sumaria II*. Madrid: Alianza Editorial, 1992.

—. *In Defence of the Indians*. DeKalb: Northern Illinois University Press, 1974.

De Sepúlveda, Juan Ginés. *Demócrates Segundo o De las Justas Causas de la Guerra contra los Indios*. Madrid: Instituto Francisco de Vitoria, 1951.

De Vitoria, Francisco. *Political Writings*. Cambridge: CUP, 1991.

Douzinas, Costas. *The End of Human Rights*. Oxford: Hart Publishing, 2000.

Dussel, Enrique. "Democracy in the "Center" and Global Democratic Critique." In *Democracy Unrealized. Documenta 11 Platform 1*, edited by Okwui Enwezor et.al. Osfildern-Ruit: Hatje Cantz Publishers, 2002.

—. "Eurocentrism and Modernity." In *The Postmodernism Debate in Latin America*, edited by John Beverly et. al. Durham and London: Duke University Press, 1995.

—. "Philosophy in Latin America in the Twentieth Century. Problems and Currents." In *Latin American Philosophy. Currents, Issues, Debates*, edited by Eduardo Mendieta. Bloomington and Indianapolis: Indiana University Press, 2003.

Escobar, Arturo. "Imperial Globality and Anti-Globalisation Movements." *Third World Quarterly* 25 (2004).

Fitzpatrick, Peter. "Latin Roots: Imperialism and the Making of International Law." In *Law as Resistance: Modernism, Imperialism, Legalism*. London: Ashgate, 2008.

—. *Modernism and the Grounds of Law*. Cambridge: CUP, 2001.

García y García, Antonio. "The Spanish School of the Sixteen and Seventeenth Centuries: A Precursor of the Theory of Human Rights," *Ratio Juris* 10 (1997).

Habermas, Jürgen. *Theory and Praxis*. Cambridge: Polity Press, 1988.

Hart, Michael and Antonio Negri. *Empire*. Cambridge: Harvard University Press, 2001.

Ibhawoh, Bonny. *Imperialism and Human Rights: Colonial Discourses of Rights and Liberties in African History*. Albany: SUNY, 2007.

Koskenniemi, Martti. "Empire and International Law: The Real Spanish Contribution." *University of Toronto Law Journal* 61 (2011).

Lauren, Paul Gordon. *The Evolution of International Human Rights: Visions Seen*. Philadelphia: University of Pennsylvania Press, 2003.

Miéville, China. *Between Equal Rights: A Marxists Theory of International Law*. Chicago: Haymarket Books, 2006.

Mignolo, Walter. "The Geopolitics of Knowledge and the Colonial Difference." *The South Atlantic Quarterly* 101 (2002).

Naldi, Gino. "Future Trends in Human Rights in Africa: The Increased Role of the OAU?" In *The African Charter on Human and Peoples" Rights: The System in Practice, 1988-2000*, edited by Rachel Murray and Malcolm Evans. Cambridge: CUP, 2002.

Pereña, Luciana and José Manuel Pérez. "Estudio Preliminar." In Bartolomé de las Casas, *De Regia Potestate o Derecho de Autodeterminación*. Madrid: Consejo Superior de Investigaciones Científicas, 1969.

Plattner, Marc et.al. *The Liberal Tradition in Focus. Problems and New Perspectives*. Lanham: Lexington Books, 2000.

Quijano, Aníbal. "Coloniality of Power, Eurocentrism and Latin America." *Neplanta: Views from the South* 3 (2000).

Rajagopal, Balakrishnan. "Counter-hegemonic International Law: Rethinking Human Rights and Development as a Third World Strategy." *Third World Quarterly* 27 (2006).

Rasch, William. *Sovereignty and its Discontents. On the Primacy of Conflict and the Structure of the Political.* London: Birkbeck Law Press-Routledge Cavendish, 2004.

Edward. "Foreword." In *Selected Subaltern Studies,* edited by Ranajit Guha and Gayatri Chakravorty Spivak. New York: Oxford University Press, 1988.

Sartre, Jean-Paul. "Preface." In Franz Fanon, *The Wretched of the Earth.* London: Penguin, 2001.

Schmitt, Carl. "The Land Appropriation of a New World." *Telos* 109 (1996).

—. *The Nomos of the Earth in the International Law of the Jus Publicum Europaeum.* New York: Telos Press, 2003.

Stannard, David. *American Holocaust: Columbus and the Conquest of the New World.* New York: Oxford University Press, 1992.

Thomassen, Lasse. "Introduction." In *The Derrida-Habermas Reader,* edited by Lasse Thomassen. Edinburgh: EUP, 2006.

Tierney, Brian. *The Idea of Natural Rights: Studies on Natural Rights, Natural Law, and Church Law, 1150-1625.* Michigan: B. Berdmans Publishing, 1997.

Van Boven, Theo. *Human Rights from Exclusion to Inclusion: Principles and Practice.* Leiden-Boston: Martinus Nijhoff, 2000.

CHAPTER SIX

LAS CASAS, VITORIA AND SUAREZ, 1514-1617

ENRIQUE DUSSEL

Translated by James Terry

Modern political philosophy originated in reflections on the problem of opening the European world to the Atlantic; in other words, it was a Spanish philosophy. As such it is neither Machiavelli nor Hobbes who initiates modern political philosophy, but those thinkers who undertook the expansion of Europe towards a colonial world. The question of the Other and the right of the conquest therefore would be the initial theme of the philosophy of the first Modernity. And the question of the consensus of the people regarding the origin of the legitimate exercise of power would steadily grow from Bartolomé de las Casas to Francisco Suárez, and would remain a critical horizon for later central-European Modernity.

Bartolomé de Las Casas (1484-1566)

Bartolomé de Las Casas is a critic of Modernity whose shadow covers the last five centuries. His is a worldwide critical conscience, one of the greatest magnitude, which extends beyond Europe to encompass even the Indians, the Amerindians. As part of an intercultural dialogue, he very coherently expounds a theory of a *universal claim of truth*—as opposed to the relativism or scepticism of Richard Rorty—for all responsible and honest participants (European or Amerindian, and even African and Arab, as we shall see). It doesn't prevent him, nonetheless, from articulating in a distinguished manner a position not only of tolerance (which is purely negative) but of full responsibility for the Other (which is positive), of a *universal claim of validity*[1] which obligates one ethically and politically to take "seriously" the rights (and for that matter also the inherent obligations of said rights) of the Other, in the manner exemplified up to the twenty-first century[2].

In the biography of Las Casas (1484-1566) we can detect the instances of his ethical-political-philosophical position with respect to the first expansion of Modernity. Initially he is simply one more Andalusian, who departs for the Indies (1502) as a soldier. Afterwards he becomes a Catholic priest. In 1514 his existential orientation changes and he begins his fight against the injustices suffered by the Indians; in 1547 he discovers that the African slaves are suffering the same injustices. He thus experienced a theoretical maturation which we will strive to illustrate.

This first philosophical anti-discourse of Modernity arose in the face of the reality of violence which would later extend to Africa and Asia, in the face of deafness to the cry of the Other. Europe didn't have a completely tranquil conscience; in the beginning at least, criticism was still possible. For this reason we seek to give the explicitly political philosophical thinking of Bartolomé de Las Casas the epistemological importance still not recognized by the history of modern philosophy. He would articulate the first critical discourse of *all* Modernity; a "localized" critical discourse, territorialized in America itself, initially from "the outside" of Europe (in its "exteriority"), continuing the discourse until his death fifty-two years later. Las Casas was an erudite critical observer. Let us consider in the first place a text among many, which operates very well as a "bridge" between two epochs: between the conception of the "ancient world"

---

[1] Our line of argument presupposes a clear difference between "claim (*pretensión, Anspruch*) of truth" and "claim of validity". See Enrique Dussel, *Etica de la liberación en la edad de la globalización y la exclusión* (Madrid: Trotta, 1998), 153; and Enrique Dussel, "Wahrheitsanspruch und Toleranzfähigkeit", in *Zur Logik religiöser Traditionen*, eds. B. Schoppelreich and S. Wiedenhofer (Frankfurt: Verlag für Interkulturelle Kommmunikation, 1998), 267-295. This distinction is impossible in consensualist theories of the truth like those of K.-O. Apel and J. Habermas.

[2] We will demonstrate the way in which Bartolomé de las Casas manages philosophically to articulate a just and universal claim of truth in accordance with the dissidence of the Other, dissidence which the Other has a right to, and as such a just duty (*obligación*) to defend their position even with arms (a "just war" of defense of the Indians against the Spanish Christians) taken as far as the "Final Judgment." As far as I know, there hasn't been a position more coherent and critical.

(which manifests itself vis-à-vis the Muslim world) and the "new world" as a "world system" (manifest vis-à-vis extra-Mediterranean cultures, those of the Atlantic and later the Pacific).

In 1552 Bartolomé writes the *Tratado sobre los indios que se han hecho esclavos,*[3] arguing on the injustice of enslaving the Indians, which would only be justified if there had been cause for a just war, a matter on which Juan Ginés de Sepúlveda would in some ways be in accord:

> That there has not been just cause [... arises] neither because of offences done by the Indians, nor because they persecute, impugn, and torment the Spanish (for the Indians had never seen or encountered them), *as do the Turks and the Moors of Africa*[4]; nor because they possessed lands which in another time had belonged to the Christians (they never did, or at least it has never come to light, *as it did in Africa in the time of Saint Augustine, and the reign of Granada, and as it has in the Empire of Constantinople and the kingdom of Jerusalem*[5]); nor because they are natural adversaries or mortal enemies[6] [...] Well then, solely by the preaching and the dissemination of the faith among the races of heathen lands [...] has there never been divine or human law which consents to and permits war, for it would be totally condemned [...lest] it should be introduced as Mahomet introduced his.[7]

As one can see we are at the "beginning of the beginning" of Modernity. The references are "extra" Latin-European. Nothing is needed to justify the war, the "conquest" of the West Indies, the first European "colonies," on which will be centred the gradual accumulation of riches, of

---

[3] Bartolomé de Las Casas, *Obras escogidas de Fray Bartolomé de las Casas* (Madrid: Real Academia Española, 1957), vol. 1, 258.

[4] "Because they never encountered them" is a reference to the extreme novelty of the occurrence. Furthermore, his suggestions relate to the Mediterranean, to Southern Europe, as is obvious. The most developed countries were in Southern Europe; nothing of geopolitical importance to the "world system" could have come from Northern Europe at that moment.

[5] Again all of his references have to do with southern Christian Europe, with the Mediterranean, from Augustine to Granada, to Constantinople or to the crusaders in Jerusalem. Later, Descartes, Spinoza or Hobbes will no longer refer to the South, the Mediterranean, but to the West, the Atlantic, the "new world." They will be protagonists of a "second" moment of Early Modernity (which passes for being the "absolute beginning" of Modernity for European philosophy even to the present.)

[6] Explicit reference to two kinds of antagonists, already indicating the theme that will occupy C. Schmitt.

[7] Las Casas, *Obras escogidas*, 258-259.

"power," of structures of a still regional hegemony (exercised over the Atlantic Ocean, not over India or China) during almost three centuries, until the industrial revolution, which would eventually allow Europe to "surpass" Hindustan and China economically and technically. It is a criticism argued via a novel strategy in political philosophy; it is the *first* criticism in the very gestation of the "world system" (the origin of the process today termed "globalization"), the first criticism of the violence of the original movement to implant the new system.

In his argumentation Bartolomé de Las Casas decidedly takes the perspective of the dominated indigenous peoples as a point of departure for his critical discourse, organized logically and philosophically from the horizon of the *modern* scholasticism of the School of Salamanca—the most important European academic centre in the sixteenth century, based around the Dominican convent of San Esteban. His advantage over the philosophers of "santiesteban" is that Bartolomé had lengthy military and political experience in the Indies. He arrived, as we have said, on the island of Santo Domingo in the Caribbean on April 15, 1502 (18 years old at the time). In 1514—three years before the beginning of the Lutheran Reformation, and at the moment in which Machiavelli is conceiving *Il Principe*—continuing the *first ethical protest* against the expansion of Modernity, against the conquest, launched by Antón de Montesinos and Pedro de Córdoba in 1511 in Santo Domingo, Bartolomé changes the existential project and the "cura encomendero," transforming him until his death into the "Defender of the Indians"[8]. He immediately discovers in the material negativity of the Other[9]—as Horkheimer would say—the

---

[8] The situation of this ethical change in favor of the liberation of the Indians can be seen very clearly in his autobiographical account: "The priest Bartolomé de Las Casas [...] was going along busily and very carefully in his enterprises [*business* we would say today] like the others, sending the Indians to parcel the mines, to dig out gold and sow the fields, taking advantage of them as much as he could [...But one day] on Pascua de Pentecostés (Whitsuntide) [...] he began to consider [...] Ecclesiastes [*Ben Sira*] chapter 34: *Whomsoever offers something in sacrifice that was stolen is guilty [...] To offer sacrifice with that which belongs to the poor is the same as killing a child in the presence of his father* [...] He began, I say, to consider their misery." Bartolomé de las Casas, *Historia de las Indias* (Caracas: Biblioteca Ayacucho, 1956), Book III, ch.79; Las Casas, *Obras escogidas*, vol.2, 356.
[9] See Dussel, *Etica de la liberación en la edad de la globalización y la exclusión* (Madrid: Trotta, 1998), ch. 4.

misery to which the conquest had reduced the Indian, the "original negativity"[10]:

> From the moment the Spanish laid eyes on them [Bartolomé metaphorically presents the Indians as sheep] they pounced on them like ravenous wolves, or tigers, or lions made cruel from many days of hunger. And they have done nothing else for the past forty years, to the present day, and they do it still, nothing save mangle, kill, terrorize, flog, torture and destroy them with the strangest and most varied means of cruelty, never seen nor read nor heard of before.[11]

Bartolomé is dramatic in his description of the disproportionate violence with which the Europeans treat these first colonial populations. This negative description is dialectically compared with the primitive cultural and ethical positivity of the Indian, before the arrival of the European:

> God made these people, many and varied as they are, the most guileles— without wickedness or duplicity, extremely obedient and faithful to their native masters, without dissension or unrest—of any people in the world. They are likewise the most delicate people, thin and tender in complexion, the least able to endure labors, and who easily die from any infirmity.[12]

The contemptuous judgement of those who deny the dignity of the person and the culture of the Indian is thus false:

> It has been written that they were not rational enough to govern themselves in a humane and orderly fashion [...] I have compiled the data in this book to demonstrate the contrary truth[13]   As far as politics, I say, not only have

---

[10] See the sense of "original negativity" in my work, Dussel, *Etica de la liberación*, 1998, 209.

[11] Las Casas, *Obras escogidas*, vol. 5, 136.

[12] Ibid. The text continues abounding in the qualities of the Indians: "They are also extremely poor people and possess almost nothing, nor do they desire to possess temporal goods [...] They are likewise of pure and free and lively understandings, very receptive and obedient to all good teaching; they are extremely apt at receiving our *sancta fee* [...] These tame sheep, are endowed thus by the Maker and Creator with the above-mentioned qualities [...]". The terms "so meek", "patient", "humble" occur often. Las Casas, *Obras escogidas*, vol. 3, 3.

[13] Here Bartolomé enumerates the territorial organization, the cultural, religious and ethical structure of the American peoples, all of it constituting an immense and authentic *Apología* (hence its name: *Apologética historia*), in two enormous volumes and in two large format columns. Las Casas, *Obras escogidas*, vol. 4, 470

they shown themselves to be very wise and clever and possessed of clear understandings, prudently tending and providing for their republics... and with justice that allows them to prosper [...][14]

The theoretical structure of the Lascasian denunciation begins explicitly with the "dialectic of master and slave" (two and a half centuries before Hegel). Either the Other is murdered, or under the fear of death his life is pardoned but he is condemned to "servitude":

There are two main ways in which those who have travelled to this part of the world who call themselves Christians[15] have uprooted these pitiful peoples and wiped them from the face of the earth. Firstly, by unjust, cruel, and bloody wars.[16] Secondly, they have murdered anyone who might yearn or even think of freedom,[17] or of wishing to escape the torments from which they suffer, as is the case with all the native leaders and the adult males[18] (given that the Spaniards normally spare only women and children in war),[19] crushing them with the harshest, most horrible and brutal servitude [20] that man or beast has ever been subjected to.[21]

& 472. The work culminates with a description of that which is "barbarous," and the four ways of being such, indicating that the unique title of barbarism would be that of "infidel" or one lacking of knowledge of the Christian faith. But this type of barbarism is not culpable nor does it merit any penalty, nor a "just war." Las Casas, *Obras escogidas*, vol. 4, 434.

[14] Las Casas, *Obras escogidas*, vol. 3, 3-4.

[15] Notice how Bartolomé points out how they "call themselves Christians," but in truth they are not. Rather they are the very contradiction of this great critic's understanding of Christianity.

[16] If the "master" kills the Other the dialectic is not initiated, it is the simple annihilation of the exteriority. Thus, the Other is murdered.

[17] For Bartolomé the indigenous rebellions are originated among those who are able "to think freely". Only under the fear of death can they have liberty of thought. Once they are assassinated the "Colonial Order" is inaugurated.

[18] Anticipating by centuries the talk of "*male* mankind" to distinguish from "*female* mankind."

[19] This illustrious text recognizes the economic-political domination of the Indian, the sexual violation of women, and the pedagogy of domination of children. See Enrique Dussel, *Para una ética de la liberación latinoamericana* (Buenos Aires: Siglo XXI, 1973), vol. 2, intro. In effect, Las Casas' text inspired me to develop a political, erotic and pedagogical reading in this work of mine of 1973. Ibid., v. 3, 4 & 5.

[20] He deals explicitly with the "slave" for life.

[21] Las Casas, *Obras escogidas*, vol. 5, 137.

Politically, Bartolomé demonstrates a modern and surprisingly critical position. His argumentative strategy will adhere approximately to the following steps:

a. All human beings, including Christians and Europeans, can (and should) have a reasonable, honest and responsible "universal claim of truth". That is to say, to affirm and believe that one's practical and theoretical position is true for everyone. That which is affirmed to be true (for human beings, period[22]) may be fallible, but it isn't false until the opposite is demonstrable.

b. When two cultures come face to face, as in the case of the invasion of America, it should be recognized that the other culture, its participants and its totality alike, also holds this universal claim of truth. To deny this right to the other is "bad faith." The honest participant of the European or Christian culture may in his internal judgement consider the "claim of truth" of the other culture's participant as an "insurmountable ignorance," by which he cannot be considered culpable.

c. The atmosphere of the discussion emerging thus, it is therefore only possible to demonstrate the falsity of the other culture's position by rational arguments and common sense (the praxis effectively articulated with the theory), and accordingly to cause the will (ethically) and the reason (theoretically) of the Other to accept the reasons, which is called consensus. Accepting the dissent of the Other, in the ambit of validity (simultaneous with granting him the right of his claim of truth) opens a space not only of tolerance (purely negative, as we have said) but of admission of the possibility of not accepting the reasons (consistent with the claim of truth) offered by the European to the Indian. The claim of validity—or of the "acceptability to the Other" of the European's reasons—serves as a limit to the freedom of the Other: the autonomy to not accept the arguments and to persist in dissension. From the non-acceptance of the European's arguments there follows a practical process, which Bartolomé elucidates in a surprisingly modern way.

d. At this point of the argumentation, the Indian not only has the right to still affirm his beliefs as truths (given that they haven't been falsified), but moreover he has the obligation to observe them. Bartolomé goes so far

---

[22] For a believer—Christian, Nahuatl or Muslim—divine revelation can be affirmed as infallible, but its reception, its interpretation, its applications are human, and therefore fallible.

as to demonstrate that the human sacrifices of certain indigenous peoples to their gods not only are not contrary to "natural law", but that it is possible to place them within an infallible rational argument (at least within the argumentative resources of the indigenous cultures before the arrival of the Europeans); for this reason, to not carry out these theoretically rational sacrifices is an ethically culpable act. Furthermore, if the sacrifice is opposed by force of arms (as Ginés as well as Francisco Vitoria affirmed), the Indians' war then becomes a "just war," and they therefore are justified in defending their *duty* to carry out such sacrifices, which to them are obligatory.

e. Bartolomé then departs from the premise by which the Other, the other culture, has the freedom by natural right to accept or not accept arguments. To wage war or violence in order to force acceptance (a matter of consensus or procedural regulations[23]) of the content of the European conqueror's truth (of his "universal claim of truth"), is irrational theoretically and unjust ethically, because nobody can or should "accept" the truth of the other without reasons (by sheer violence, fear, or the timidity to oppose him).

f. The only rational and ethical solution for one who has an honest and responsible universal claim of truth (whose criterion is the production, reproduction and development of a humane way of living[24]) is by argumentation and by giving ethical examples coherent in their praxis. For if one resorts to violence he demonstrates that he doesn't have a "universal claim of validity," because validation is that which is freely accepted by the Other—if the Other's freedom is denied, then a supposed truth, *without validity*, is imposed on him. One's actions thus demonstrate the contradiction of claiming, on the one hand, to have the free and rational consent of the other and, on the other hand, negating that consent. The claim of validity becomes doubtful and the dogmatism, the fanaticism and the confusion of attempting to "make the other accept" one's own truth without persuasion becomes manifest; it becomes, by contradiction, an invalidated truth. For Bartolomé, however, the time period of non-acceptance of the truth is thereby "opened," whereby which one's honest and responsible "claim of validity" knows how *to wait* for the historical maturation of the Other.

---

[23] See Dussel, *Etica de la liberación*, ch.2.
[24] See Enrique Dussel, *Hacia una filosofía política crítica* (Bilbao: Desclèe de Brouwer, 2001).

This argumentation is also valid when taking the Indian as a point of departure (or the slave, the Moor or the Arab, as we shall see). It is the "maximum possible global critical conscience"—not only European but *global*. Let us look at these steps of argumentation in Bartolomé's texts. We'll take an extreme example, the most problematic.

Against Ginés and those who hold that human sacrifices are against natural law, and by extension that there is justification for waging a just war to save the innocents, Bartolomé writes the following. "Men, by natural law, are obligated to honour God by the best means at their disposal, and to offer Him, in sacrifice, the best things."[25] "Now then, it has fallen to the lot of human law and positive legislation to determine what things should be offered to God; the latter is already entrusted to the entire community."[26] "Nature itself suggests and instructs[...] that lacking a positive law prohibiting the contrary, *they should[27] even immolate human victims* as an offering to the true God, or false ones *considered to be true,*[28] so as to offer Him the most precious thing, so that they might appear especially grateful for the benefits received."[29]

That is to say, the offering of sacrifices is not derived from natural law; rather it is a practical decision which the members of a culture are able to make rationally, but it is not contrary to natural law. In other words, "the act of immolating men, although they be innocent, when it is done for the well-being of the republic, is not contrary to natural reason [...] Thus this error may have its origin in natural reason."[30] Accordingly Bartolomé establishes the right to a "lengthy period of dissent":

> They would be acting lightly and would be *deserving of reprimand and punishment* if in so arduous, so important, and so difficult a thing to renounce [...] they were to swear loyalty to those Spanish soldiers, ignoring so many and such grave testimonies, until by the most convincing

---

[25] Las Casas, *Apología* (Alianza, Madrid: 1989), 155-156.

[26] Ibid., 157.

[27] Observe that here he speaks not yet of a "right" but of "obligation" (they should...).

[28] Here Bartolomé concedes the "claim of truth" to the other, as long as it cannot be falsified, as well as the universal "claim of validity" in its respective cultural universe.

[29] Ibid., p.160. If there is no argumentative recourse to disposition in a given culture "we are obliged to offer Him that which seems to us the most important and precious possession, that is, *human life.*" Ibid., p.161.

[30] Ibid., 166.

arguments the Spanish could demonstrate to them that the Christian religion is more worthy than the one they believe in, *which one is not able to do in a short space of time.*[31]

Bartolomé, furthermore, becomes aware of being the first to penetrate the subject with such bold critical judgements, since he writes that when rereading his *Apología* against Sepúlveda, "I asserted and proved many conclusions which no man before me had ever dared to allude to or write about, one of them being that it was not against natural law or reason, *excluding all positive human or divine law*, to offer men to God, false or true (taking the false to be true[32]) in sacrifice."[33] In this Bartolomé would even oppose the best progressive theorists (the likes of Vitoria, Soto and Melchor Cano). And he goes further, to the point of recognizing the right of the Indians to wage a "just war" against the European Christians in defence of their traditions:

> Given that they maintain [...] that in worshipping their idols they are in fact worshipping the true God [...], and in spite of the assumption that they suffer from an erroneous conscience, until we reveal the true God to them, by preaching *with better, more believable and more convincing arguments,*[34] above all by the example of Christian conduct, they are, without a doubt, *obligated to defend the cult of their gods and their religion and to turn their armed forces out* against anyone who intends to deprive them of their cult [...]; they are thus *obligated to fight them, kill them, capture them, and otherwise exercise all the rights commensurate with a just war*, in accordance with the rights of man.[35]

Never before in the history of Europe, and subsequently in the five centuries of Modernity, had this ethical and politically strategic viewpoint been elucidated with such clarity! In the face of "excusable and insurmountable ignorance"[36] one must grant them—using the categories of my *Ethics of Liberation*—the "universal claim of truth", and, from a European "critical universal claim of validity," it is also necessary to

---

[31] Ibid., 154.

[32] If the "false" has not been falsified—by the historical impossibility of available argumentative resources—the "claim of truth" continues being universal, honest and responsible.

[33] Las Casas, *Obras escogidas*, vol. 5, 471.

[34]The position of a critical universalist rationalism remains clearly in evidence. It must be coherent and not hinder (counter to Rorty, *avant la lettre*) recognizing the total liberty of the Other.

[35] Ibid., 168.

[36] Ibid., 166.

honour the total "period of time" required to create the conditions necessary for an honest and responsible acceptance of the rhetoric of the European. The only possible "just war" is that of the Indians against the European Christians in defence of their own customs. The position of Bartolomé de Las Casas is the "maximum possible critical conscience," and he was aware of its originality. Writing a letter to Peru in 1563 he stated: "I read [before the Junta] the *Apología* I made against Sepúlveda [...] in which I asserted and proved many conclusions *which no man before me had ever dared to make, let alone to write*, one of them being that it is not unlawful, nor against natural reason [...] to offer men to God, be He true or false (taking the false for the true [37]), in sacrifice [...]"[38]

In later years Bartolomé delved deeper into the responsibility one should assume vis-á-vis the freedom of the Other, such as the origin of the legitimacy arising from "consensus"—a Latin and Castilian word already in common use in Bartolomé's age—reaching a level of criticism almost unattainable from then on in Modernity. In fact, when in Peru the "encomenderos" (landed conquistadors) propose to the King to buy the encomiendas in perpetuity for a certain price, Bartolomé argues against any act of selling by the Indians. This alignment or sale is criticized in his most important political philosophical works, *De regia potestate*, *De thesauris* and *Doce dudas*, his culminating argumentative moment against the right and legitimacy of the sale on the part of the King, and the

---

[37] Bartolomé always gives the Other, in respect to his Alterity, the right to a "claim of truth," which is the counterpart of the "universal claim of validity," in which he proposes to honestly and responsibly convince the Other with reason (not with violence). If the "claim of truth" is not conceded to the Other, but rather he is posited as a subject of "culpable ignorance," it is possible to impose "the" truth—our "truth," which we "possess" with infallible certainty—on him by violence. In this case the European would not have the "claim of truth" but dogmatic knowledge, and as such, having surpassed the limits of the possibilities of "finite" reason, he would be able to affirm his truth as infallible, as "absolute", thus inevitably containing a completely erroneous position: the incapacity to evolve, to learn the new, to advance historically. It would therefore be unjust with respect to the dignity of the Other as a subject for argumentation to have him placed "asymmetrically". Therefore the "coincidence," not the free and rational "agreement" with the Other, obligated by violence, would not be rational but merely "affirmation" external to the Other in regard to that which is imposed on him with neither conviction nor intersubjective validity. Power and violence do not produce reasons in favor of the truth; they only impose an "untruth" for the Other.

[38] Las Casas, Obras escogidas, vol. 5, 471.

purchase on the part of the encomenderos, by free subjects, arguing from a major premise fundamental to any rational theory of legitimacy: "In the beginning of the human race, all people, all lands, and all things, by laws both natural and derived from man, were free [...] and not the subjects of servitude."[39]   And from this, as a standard universal principle of political validity or legitimacy, he writes: "No king or government, however powerful it may be, may ordain or command anything concerning the republic (*republicam*), in prejudice or to the detriment of the people (*populi*) or the subjects, without having taken the consensus (*consensu*) of the people, in lawful and just form. Any other way would not be valid (*valet*) by law."[40] "No one may legitimately (*legitima*) [...] inflict any kind of harm on the liberty of his people (*libertati populorum suorum*); if anyone should decide to act against the common benefit of the people, without considering the consensus of the people (*consensu populi*), such a decision would be nullified. Liberty (*libertas*) is the most precious and valuable thing a free people can possess."[41]

Bartolomé was not the innovator of all this; rather he applied the ancient tradition of Roman and medieval laws in the defence of a new and modern "political actor", the indigenous Americans, (conditional) citizens on the colonial periphery of a nascent Modernity. Given the illegitimacy, not only of the intended sale of the indigenous lands in the encomiendas of Peru, but of the entire conquest as such, Bartolomé begins a true political campaign for the "restoration of the Empire of the Incas to the Incas"; that is to say, a strategic action to effect the act of restitution demanded by historical justice. Everything was based on the fact that legitimacy requires the "consensus of the governed people," who have full power over their property and their dominions. It is the "first principle" from which the *Tratado de las Doce dudas* (1564) is worked out. He expresses it thus:

> All of the infidels, of whatever sect or religion they may be [...] in regard to natural and divine right, and that which is called the rights of man, justly have dominion over their things [...] And by the same justice they also possess their principalities, kingdoms, states, offices, jurisdictions, and

---

[39] Bartolomé de las Casas, *De Regia Potestate o Derecho a la Autodeterminación* (Madrid: CSIC, 1969), I, §1, 16.
[40] Ibid., § 8, 47.
[41] Ibid., § 8, 49.

domains [... The] regent or governor may not act otherwise save *that the whole society and community has first decided he may* [...]"[42]

The responsibility and obligation of "preaching the Gospels" which the Roman pontiff has given to the Spanish kings grants them the "right over the thing (*jus in re*),"[43] but this right *in potentia* comes into effect only via the consent of the Indians, by the free acceptance of such preaching. Without this consensus the right does not progress to the exercising of it *in actu*, as the "right in relation to the thing (*jus ad rem*)."[44] And as this consensus does not exist on the part of those affected, the conquest is illegitimate. Furthermore, that "the costs and expenses for the attainment of this end were necessary"—contrary to what John Locke would later think—is the Christians' problem, and the Indians have no obligation to pay them, "if of their own volition they have no desire to do so."[45] Bartolomé concludes that "It is therefore obligatory of the King, our master, for the good of his salvation, to restore those kingdoms to King Tito [so this still-living Inca was called], successor and inheritor of Guayna Cápac and the rest of the Incas, and to restore to him all his forces and all his power."[46] Obviously the Europeans would never abandon any colony. But, and here we see the ultimate limitation of Bartolomé's providentialist position, "it would be unlawful of the Spaniards to abandon such regions, and they would be mortally sinning if they were to do so. As such, as has been said, they are obligated, by necessity of salvation, owing to the disappearance of the faith."[47] That is to say, it is illegitimate to impose authority on the Indians against their will, but it is equally unlawful for the Spaniards to renege on their responsibility of saving the Indians by preaching Christianity to them. The only solution, then, is for the Indians to govern themselves regionally while still being under the empire of the King of Spain, having freely and rationally accepted the Christian faith.

Bartolomé de Las Casas will continue to be seen as a political failure in the history of Modernity, but also as the first critic and the most radical sceptic of the civilizing intentions of this Modernity. The "Jesuitical Reductions," like those of Paraguay, in which the indigenous community

---

[42] Las Casas, *Obras escogidas*, vol. 5, 486-487.
[43] Bartolomé de las Casas, *De Thesauris* (Madrid: CSIC, 1958), 101.
[44] Ibid.
[45] Las Casas, *Obras escogidas,* vol. 5, 492.
[46] Las Casas, *De Thesauris*, 218.
[47] Ibid., ch. 36.

governed themselves (mediated of course by the "paternalism" of the priests), without direct contact with Spaniards but under the rule of the King, was historically the most approximate to the Lascasian ideal. But it equally failed in the eighteenth century from the impact of the Bourbon Enlightenment.

Francisco de Vitoria (1483-1546)

None of the "ancient" cultures (from China to Islam) were able to exert hegemony over the world's *transoceanic* cultures. Neither China, Hindustan, nor the Muslim world would ever have the type of dependent subsystems that European Modernity calls "colonies." It is an exclusive particularity of the European economic, political and cultural system which would yield Europe many benefits, but which would also establish a "centre-periphery" asymmetry still in place today. Lacking horses and iron, the Amerindian cultures gave way to this extraordinary kind of relationship between cultural-economic systems. Europe, although it was a secondary and peripheral culture on the Euroasiatic continent until the fifteenth century, would, nonetheless, accumulate territories, populations, wealth, information and geopolitical experience from its American "colonies" (until the eighteenth century, Europe, outside of the American continent, only had a few ports and islands, places that functioned as points of contact for commerce; Latin America was the richest and most significant region of these "colonies").

The existence of this colonial world would generate the same debate in Spain that had already begun in Latin America itself. In its most progressive aspect it had two sides: that of the Dominicans, earlier and more theoretical; and that of the Jesuits, later and more practical.

Influenced by the "Lascasian"[48] political current, initiated in Santo Domingo by Pedro de Córdoba and Antonio de Montesinos in 1511, the Dominican order of Spain became very alarmed over the critical views of the progress of the colonial conquest. Of all the philosophers—or those who argued philosophically—who entered the discussion about the Indians, the most famous was Francisco de Vitoria (1483-1546), famous for having devoted the first university courses in Europe (1539) to the theme of the indigenous American. All, however, were "moderns," in the

---

[48] See Enrique Dussel, *History of the Church in Latin America* (Grand Rapids: Eederman, 1981).

proper sense of the word.[49]   One should still study that which was "modern" in the philosophy of the Second Scholasticism in sixteenth century Europe.   For example, Thomas de Vio Cayetano (1469-1534)[50] was entirely modern in his theory of analogy—he didn't simply repeat the medieval theses.   In politics, he opposed the theocratic conception of Bonifacio VIII in the papal edict *Unam Sanctam* of 1302.   This edict, however, contained nothing new theoretically, since it simply expressed the position of Aegidius Romanus (1316), an Augustinian like Luther, in the tradition of Bernardo de Claraval (1090-1153).   Aegidius wrote *De eclesiastica potestate*, following Agustin de Hipona in the notion that one had to respect the necessary "order" of things, since "if the kings and princes were subject to the Church only in spiritual matters, one sword would not be subordinate to another [...and] there would be no *order* to the powers that be."[51]   From here Aegidius deduces that the Popes have temporal power over the *believing* kings, the Christian kings—the inverse position to that of Thomas Hobbes, for whom the Anglican Church would be entirely subject to the King of England.   Marsilio de Padua (1275-1343),[52] and William of Ockham (1290-1350),[53] who died in Munich

---

[49] Which, evidently, assumes the positive aspect of a great new global development, but, at the same time, according to Heidegger, also that of the post-moderns and anti-Eurocentrics, the negative aspect of the "coloniality of power."

[50] For Cayetano there are three kinds of pagans, infidels, non-Christians or barbarians—terms frequently taken for synonyms: a) the Jews, heretics, and Muslims who are subjects of the Christian princes (as in Castilla); b) those who occupy territories which once were Christian, and who are "enemies" of Christians (i.e. the Turks); and c) those who were never subjects nor occupied Christian territories (like the Tartars).   Regarding the latter, "no king, emperor, nor even the Roman Church should make war against them." (*Commentary on Saint Thomas' Summa Theologiae* (1540), II-II, q. 66, a. 8).   As is evident, the Amerindians would be classified as the third kind.

[51] Aegidius Romanus, *De ecclesiastica potestate* (Weimar: Bölaus, 1929), Book I, ch. 4, 13.

[52] In the *Defensor Pacis*, understanding the elective experience of the "Great Council" with respect to the Venetian *Doge*, he points out that power emanates directly from the people, who is able to choose the king (Marsilio de Padua, *Defensor Pacis*, (Hannover: R. Scholz, 1932), Dictio I, ch.9, § 2, 40),   and therefore no place remains a universal Emperor, and even less for a universal power of the Pope, nor even for power of the other bishops (Dictio III, ch.2, § 17, 606), since, in the latter case, a universal council would have to exercise it (Dictio II, ch.18, § 18, 382).   This nominalist tradition, influenced by the Castilian and Spanish experience in general, would be adopted and developed by Vitoria and Suárez, for example.

under the protection of William of Bavaria, were likewise opposed to the aspirations to political dominion of the Papacy and the Empire. It was not extraordinary, then, that in nominalist Paris, where the brilliant young Vitoria studied—and where he was an alumnus and professor from 1513 to 1522—it was held that the Christians did not have dominion over the Amerindians, for they were never subjects of the Christian kings,[54] let alone believers—nor did the emperor, nor any king, nor the Pope.   In general Vitoria is seen as the founder of international law[55] and a defender of the Indians on the same level as Bartolomé de Las Casas.[56] Both judgements are sustainable. Nevertheless, I would like to comment here on the perspective of this "father" of juridical Modernity regarding the question of European expansion overseas; that is to say, on his justification of the colonial world, the *world system*. I am obligated, therefore, to criticise him in light of our new perspective.

In his *Relecciones* Vitoria deals with exceedingly logical themes[57] revolving around a central conceit: the criticism of the claims of the Papacy and the Empire[58] from the Spanish point of view—one shouldn't forget that in Medina del Campo the *comuneros* were crushed almost to

---

[53] He did not accept the universal power of the emperor, much less the temporal power of the Pope, who ruled only with "spiritual power." William de Ockham, *Dialogus* (Frankfurt: Melchior Goldast, 1614), Pars. III, tr. II, Book. I, ch. 25, 896.

[54] It is well-known that Venice likewise claimed its liberty before the Empire, given its geopolitical position of semi-subordination to the Byzantine Empire, the same as Genoa.

[55] See Juan Botella et al. eds., *El pensamiento político en sus textos. De Platón a Marx* (Madrid: Tecnos, 1998), 143. Alain Guy, *Historia de la Filosofía española*, Barcelona: Anthropos, 1985), 96. Guillermo Fraile, *Historia de la Filosofía* (Madrid: BAC, 1966), 313.   Teófilo Urdanoz, "Introduction to De Indis", in *Obras de Francisco de Vitoria*, Francisco de Vitoria (Madrid: BAC, 1960), 549.

[56] See for example Beuchot: "Bartolomé de Las Casas attempts to follow Vitoria and Soto [...] even seeming to be unworthy in comparison with those two masters." Mauricio Beuchot, *Historia de la Filosofía en el México Colonial* (Barcelona: Herder, 1997), 67. The position of Las Casas ends up being *radically* divergent from those two Spanish thinkers.

[57] In contrast with our opinion, Urdanoz states when considering all the *Relecciones* dictated between 1527 and 1541: "In the face of this union of disparate themes" (Urdanoz, "Introduction", 82).

[58] These are referred to in the following *Relecciones*: *De potestate civili, De potestate Ecclesiae prior* and *posterior*, *De potestate Papae et Concilii*, among the first six.

nonexistence. From the affirmation of "human life,"[59] he proceeds, using the subject of "human sacrifices" as a "bridging" theme, on to the justification of the nascent colonial "order."[60] I will deal only with the essential framework of his argumentation, without dwelling on the reasons he gives to demonstrate the illegitimacy of the conquest,[61] which are well-known; in other words, the determining premises in his justification of the colonial order. Vitoria's critical position is revealed in this conclusion: "Christian princes, even on the authority of the Pope, may not compel the barbarians to give up their sins against the laws of nature, nor punish them for such sins."[62]

But along with many reasons for invalidating the conquest, Vitoria promptly gives other arguments whose "contents" are completely "modern," certainly commercially oriented, which, in my opinion, have been promulgated rather naively, if not cynically. In essence, returning to a principle whose more than four thousand year existence is rooted in the Semite deserts of the Middle East, the argument hinges on the "duty of hospitality" which one is obliged to show to the foreigner, the stranger, the pilgrim—as written, for example, in the "Law of Hammurabi"[63]—but in this case it is subsumed within the horizon of Modernity. "If there are any things among the barbarians which are held in common both by their own people and by their guests (*hospitibus*), it is not lawful for the barbarians to prohibit the Spaniards from sharing and enjoying (*communicatione et*

---

[59] *De homicidio, De matriomonio* (referring to the English problem, in defense of Spain and, finally, the Papacy), *De temperantia*.

[60] *De Indis* y *De iure belli*. The remaining *Relecciones, De augmento caritatis, De eo ad quod tenetur, De simonia* and *De magia*, refer indirectly to some other aspects, but remain outside of our consideration.

[61] In the first part of *De Indis, Relección Primera*, "by what right have the barbarians come under the dominion of the Spanish", one reads that the Indians were "publicly and privately in peaceful possession of things" (Vitoria, *Obras.*, I, 5, 651), and there is no reason in the conquest for the claim of an irrational condition, of heresy, etc. In the "second part", "Unlawful titles...", he rejects as reason for the conquest giving the emperor some privilege (Ibid., II, 667), or the Pope (Ibid., II, 2, 676); by being in a condition of "insurmountable ignorance" (Ibid., 9, 690); because they are "obligated to believe in the faith of Christ" (Ibid., 10, 692); and their not accepting it being a reason to make war on them (Ibid., 11, 693), and still more contradictory reasons for the legitimacy of the war against the Indians are given.

[62] Ibid., II, 16, 698.

[63] "I have done justice to the foreigner". See Dussel, *Etica de la Liberación*, 6.

participatione) them."[64]   In the same sense he says by virtue of "society and natural communication (*societatis et communicationis*)" that "the Spaniards have the right to travel and dwell in those provinces, so long as they do no harm to the barbarians, and cannot be prevented by them from doing so."[65]   "The Spaniards may lawfully trade with the barbarians (*negotiari apudillos*), so long as they do no harm to their homeland, importing the commodities which they lack, and exporting the gold, silver, or other things which they have in abundance."[66]   "If children born in the Indies of a Spanish father wish to become citizens of the country, they cannot be barred from citizenship or from the advantages enjoyed by the native citizens born of parents domiciled in that country."[67]

It might seem that these rights were simply universal, proper and just, but given the situation in the Indies in 1539—the conquest of the Caribbean, Mexico and Peru (by Pizarro and Almagro) had already been realized—such affirmations, as mentioned earlier, are either naive or cynical, given that nobody "passed through" the Indies on pleasure tours, contemplating the beauty of the scenery or bringing about an equitable commercial exchange.   Las Casas described the unjust violence of the colonial situation much more adequately.   With Vitoria, are we actually beholding the discovery of "international rights," on the level of the "public" or "private subjective" among States?   I think, on the contrary, what we see in Vitoria is the *ius gentium* of medieval Christianity (of a secondary and peripheral culture particular to the Muslim world) evolving into the foundation of an *ius gentium europaeum*—as Schmitt explains it in his work *Nomads of the Earth* —the first framework of the law, not "international" in any symmetrical sense, but rather strictly a "metropolitan law", imperial, colonial, Eurocentric.   The rights of those who travel, conduct commerce, or are capable of being transformed into citizens with full rights—according to the *ius solis*—belong only to the Europeans, the metropolitans. These rights are called in name the "rights of all the people," but only the Europeans can avail themselves of them.   Vitoria is not referring to Indians.   It is a euphemism to speak, for example, of "commerce" in the system of the "encomienda," where the Indian had to contribute with *unpaid* labour, receiving nothing in return; and the gold and silver they mined simply became the private property of the metropolitan subject or of the crown, without any kind of interchange with

---

[64] Vitoria, *Obras,* III, 4, 709.

[65] Ibid., 2, 705.

[66] Ibid., 3, 708.

[67] Ibid., 5, 710.

the Indian. The Indians, obligated by the mining system of the "mita" to spend their lives at the bottom of the mines, were considered to be paying the tax of colonial rule, without receiving any salary. Vitoria doesn't recognize the "right" the indigenous people have—which Bartolomé de Las Casas confers on them—to refuse these commercial, travelling and other so-called rights of the citizenry, when the cruel and unjust actions of the Europeans demonstrate that they carry no benefits at all for the invaded peoples, but rather, quite the contrary, produce only death, insults, violations, and domination of every kind. Vitoria denies that the Indians have the right to oppose the violent Spanish presence.

Disgracefully, like Locke in later years, Vitoria will even recognize the Spaniard's right (though not the Indian's) to "indemnify ourselves with the property of the enemy [the Indians] for the expenses of the war and for all the damages unjustly caused by them."[68] In other words, once "victory is achieved, our property recovered, and the peace and tranquillity [of the conquest] secured, we can avenge the injuries received [on the Spanish side] from the enemies [the guilty Indians, and] teach them a lesson, punishing them for the injuries inflicted."[69] Vitoria concludes that "if the barbarians attempt to deny the Spaniards in these rights which I have described as belonging to the law of nations (*a iure gentium*), that is to say from trading and the rest, the Spaniards should (*debent*)[70] [...] give every reason at their disposal, [and] if reasoning fails to win the acquiescence of the barbarians, and they insist on replying with violence, the Spaniards may defend themselves, and do everything necessary for their own safety [...] and exercise the other rights of war."[71] As is evident, Vitoria legitimates the conquest when he takes for his point of departure or his perspective of "observation" the European merchant "in" America.

Francisco Suárez (1548-1617)

The Jesuits arrive in America several decades after the first Orders. There they find a certain already-constituted "colonial order"; they are confronted by an existing state of things. Thus, among those who arrived in Peru, one finds, for example, José de Acosta (1540-1600), who has a

---

[68] Ibid., 18, 827.

[69] Ibid., 19, 829.

[70] Notice that it is a "duty", correlative to the "duty" that Bartolomé confers to the Indians to make sacrifices to their gods and to defend these customs against strangers.

[71] Ibid., III, 6, 711-712.

more conservative, less critical judgement than Bartolomé de Las Casas. His ideas are similar to Vitoria's, since although he doesn't accept the arguments of Ginés de Sepúlveda he nonetheless affirms the legitimacy of the conquest of America, believing he has a fundamental duty to Christianize it. In his work *De procuranda indorum salute*,[72] he suggests that the Indians are called barbarous because "they reject basic reason and man's common mode of life,"[73] without pointing out, as is evident, the Eurocentrism of such a definition, given that he is speaking of the "basic reason" and "common mode of life" of *Europeans* (naively synonymous here with that of all "humans").

For Acosta there are three kinds of "barbarians"—for Bartolomé there were four, without reference, however, to the process of evangelization, and taking into consideration a certain civilizing development. Firstly, there are "those who do not depart too much from basic reason and the common customs of mankind,"[74] and who possess "stable republics, public laws, fortified cities, obedient magistrates, and most importantly, the use and knowledge of letters, for wherever there are books and written documents, the people are more humane." The Chinese, Japanese, and "many provinces of East India" have obtained this stage of development. "In the second class I include those barbarians, who although they haven't reached the level of using writing, nor of philosophical and civil knowledge, nonetheless have a republic and certain kinds of magistrates, as well as stable settlements or populations, guarded by a sort of police and an order of soldiers and captains, and finally a serious form of religious cult. Our Mexicans and Peruvians belong to this class."[75] The "third class of barbarians" are "similar to wild beasts, barely possessing human sentiments"; these are the "infinite herds" of Caribbeans, the Mojos, the Chiriguanos, the people of Brazil, of Florida, *etcetera.* Acosta places himself in opposition to Ginés and, being a humanist, does not admit so easily that the most virtuous and wise should be in command of the most rude and ignorant. "But whoever attempts to deduce from this that it is lawful to seize the power that the barbarians possess would conclude by the same reason that where an adolescent or a woman reigns, it is possible to deprive them of their power by force [...] Taken from the

---

[72] José de Acosta, *Obras del P. José de Acosta* (Madrid: Biblioteca de Autores Españoles, 1954), 391.
[73] Ibid., 392. Evidently they think of "man" as universally European. As always, one is dealing with a decided Eurocentrism.
[74] This and all the following texts are found in Acosta, *Obras*, 392-394.
[75] Ibid., 392.

same philosopher [Aristotle], on the just war against the barbarians who refuse to serve, it is more confusing and instils suspicions that the argument is not derived from *philosophical reason*, but from popular opinion."[76]

It is important to point out that for Acosta, who in the sixteenth century would already have known of the experiences of his Jesuit brothers in the Far East—fully developed civilizations and in many ways superior to Europe—it was necessary to establish differences when comparing China and India with other cultures. "All these nations [China and Hindustan] should be called to the Gospel in a way analogous to when the Apostles preached to the Greeks and Romans [...] Because they are powerful and not lacking in human wisdom, they have to be humbled and subdued by the Gospel, *by its very reason* [...]; if you wanted to subdue them by force of arms, nothing would be gained but to make them avowed enemies of the Christian name."[77]   Alonso Sánchez, a Jesuit missionary in the Philippines who understood the methods of "peaceful cultural adaptation" of the priests Ruggieri, Ricci (in China) and Nobili (in India), would nonetheless be in opposition to Acosta, recommending the use of arms against China and India, as in America. This Eurocentrism, shared by the Roman authorities, would ultimately have terrible consequences.[78]   We have seen that on this point Bartolomé de Las Casas was the most radical, since it was his opinion that not even in America should they have had the right to the violent use of arms.

For his part Francisco Suárez (1548–1617) signified the political-juridical culmination of the philosophy of the "First Modernity," that is the Spanish-Portuguese, fundamental to the development of the new political philosophy of the seventeenth century in France, Flanders, England and Germany. Although implicitly recognized by all, he hasn't been given the place he merits in the history of Modern Political Philosophy.

In fact, Suárez establishes himself in an amazingly creative way to incorporate and surpass the nominalist position (the Ockhamist accepts the knowledge of "particulars," although in a differentiated manner), as well

---

[76] Ibid., book II, ch. V, 437. He then accuses Ginés here of being more of an ideologue than a philosopher.

[77] Ibid., 392.

[78] Acosta wrote his opinion in 1586 in a work untitled *Parecer sobre la guerra de la China*, and in another *Respuesta a los fundamentos que justifican la guerra contra la China*.

as the Scottist (the notion of the "concept"[79]) and the Thomist (the analogy of Being) positions, from the modern experience of subjectivity—in the sense of that which is positive and can be criticized. It is one of the first "modern" syntheses serving as a bridge between the beginning of the sixteenth century, which confronts the problems of the "discovery" of the New World (the absolute alterity of the Indian) and the new experience of the individual subjectivity of European Modernity, the same Jesuitical movement undertaken to develop traditional southern Europe.[80] For this reason, Suárez will be the great master of European rationalism in the seventeenth and eighteenth centuries. There were nineteen editions of his *Disputationes Metaphysicae* printed between 1597 and 1751 (eight in Germany alone). His political writings were praised by Grotius as "without equal"; Descartes, as a Jesuit student in La Fleche, indicated that he had carefully read Suárez ("he is justly the first author who fell into my hands"); Spinoza was inspired by him to read the works of Revius, Franco, Burgersdijk and Heereboord (the latter calls Suárez: "metahpysicorum omnium papam atque principem"); Leibniz meditated on him in his youth; Vico dedicated an entire year to studying him[81]; still more could be said of Christian Wolff[82] or A. G. Baumgarten.[83] Suárez made the philosophical thinking of Northern Europe possible, under the theologizing influence of Lutheranism,[84] giving autonomy to the secular level of

---

[79] See Parthenius Minges, "Suárez und Duns Scotus," *Philosophisches Zeitschrift der Goerres-Gesellschaft* 32 (1919): 334-340.

[80] The "test of conscience" which Suárez experienced each day, would have given him sufficient subject matter for a metaphysic on the conscientiousness of his own subjectivity. It is not extraordinary that Descartes, who likewise effected this daily practice of the "test of conscience," begins his philosophical discourse with a conscientious self-reflection on his own "ego," *ego cogito*, stating: "I am conscientious about being conscientious" while still being somewhat objective. The "individuality" of the subjectivity of the "test of conscience" was the initial ontological philosophical moment. The subject has been amply studied by Etienne Gilson.

[81] See Fraile, *Historia de la Filosofía*, v.3, 468.

[82] It is well-known that his *Philosophia Prima sive Ontologia* of 1729 was structured explicitly on Suárez. See *The Encyclopedia of Philosophy* (New York: Macmillan, 1967), v. 8, 340-341.

[83] His *Metaphysica* of 1739 still shows the Suarezian influence.

[84] On the influence of Spanish philosophy, especially Suarezianism, on Seventeenth century German philosophy see K. Streitcher, "Die Philosophie der Spanischen Spaetscholastiks und den deutschen Universitaeten des siebzehnten Jahrhunderts', in *Gesammelte Aufsaetze zur Kulturgeschichte Spanien* (Münster: Aschendorff Verlag, 1928), and Karl Eschweiler, "Die Philosophie der Spanischens

philosophical reason (which, paradoxically, would be of Catholic, Suarezian inspiration). Repeating in part what has already been mentioned, and adding new examples, Randall Collins writes:

> Suárez's philosophy became the centre of the curriculum in Catholic and many Protestant universities (especially in Germany) for 200 years [...] Wolff takes ontology as purely self-contained argument over first principles, governed by the principle of non-contradiction. From thence he deduces the principle of sufficient reason which governs physical, non-logical necessity [...] This is a touchstone of Leibniz's philosophy as well, and it is implicit in Kant's problematic of pure reason, the justification of the synthetic a priori. When Schopenhauer at the beginning of his career proposed to overthrow constructive idealism and return to Kant, his first statement was *The Four-fold Root of the Principle of Sufficient Reason*, with its explicit admiration of Suárez. Still later, Heidegger—the product of a Catholic seminary education —revived the ontological question [...] This was one more move on the turf delineated by Suárez.[85]

It is in the theory of cognitive subjectivity that Suárez was particularly innovative. He accepts, on the one hand, that "our intellect grasps the material singular by an intentional species"[86]—a nominalist thesis—but at the same time it has the capacity to comprehend universals by an abstract, inductive process[87]—a rationalist thesis. For Suárez, in a much more complex manner, and much closer to Kant than to *The Port-Royal Logic*,[88] the act of knowing (*actus ipse, conceptus formalis, conceptus subjetivum*) is produced when a representation of an object[89]—the representation of a thing found present as an impression of reality on the subjectivity (a

---

Spaetscholastik and den deutschen Universitaeten des siebzehnten Jahrhunderts," in *Spanische Forschungen des Goerres-Gesellschaft I*, (Münster: Aschendorff Verlag, 1928).

[85] Randall Collins, *The Sociology of Philosophies: A Global Theory of Intellectual Change* (Cambridge: Harvard University Press, 2000), 580. Collins points out that from 1550 to 1620 the University of Salamanca had matriculated approximately 6000 students. In view of the population of Spain and the 32 universities that existed on the Peninsula, that amounts to 3% of the juvenile male population. This percentage would be equaled by the United States in 1900, and by the United Kingdom in 1950. Ibid., 581.

[86] Suárez writes: "Intellectus noster cognoscit singulare materiale per propriam ipsius speciem." Francisco Suárez, *Tratado De Anima*, IV, 3, 5.

[87] "Intellectus cognoscit proprio conceptu universalia, abstrahendo a singularibus seu non curando de illis." Ibid., IV, 3, 11.

[88] See Michel Foucault, *Las palabras y las cosas* (México: Siglo XXI, 1996), 67.

[89] And to speak of *objectum* is a "modern" novelty.

species "impressed" by the "active intellect"[90] on the "passive")—is related to the thing (*conceptus objectivum*) in an "express" way: the thing is known *in actu* as an object (as a known thing).[91]

Meanwhile, on the level of politics, the colonial world had already reached a state of "normality", which was essentially the same as slavery; in other words, criticizing this "normality" was given up, and thus it was treated as "a fact."   Suárez, nevertheless, given the geopolitical and historical situation of Spain, proposes certain theses which appear progressive in other parts of Europe, for example in the England of James I.[92] We will briefly observe his most important philosophical-political positions—which will have great relevancy in the process of Latin American emancipation, among other effects, which begins in the nineteenth century.[93]

---

[90] This "active intellect"—of Aristotle and Thomas Aquinas—would remain subsumed in modernity in the productive and creative capacity of human reason in the "constitution" of the "object"—until Husserl or Heidegger.   It would be "subjectivity" as activity. The "passive genesis" of a Husserl would ascertain the "material" assumptions of subjectivity.

[91] Suárez writes: "It is not that in which (*in quo*) knowledge is produced [...], but it is that by which (*id quo*) the object itself (*ipsum objectum*) is known as the formal concept of the known thing (*conceptus formali rei cognitae*), since in order for the thing to be grasped intellectually it is necessary that it be vitally (*vitaliter*) formed in some way in the intellect." Suárez, *De Anima*, IV, 5,11. Unfortunately the thinking of Suárez has been compared with that of Thomas Aquinas, in intra-scholastic transcendental disputes, or it has been used to distinguish him from Kant or Heidegger —by Marechal or Rahner, for example—, but the much more important historical work of explaining the central philosophical themes of the Seventeenth and Eighteenth centuries already intuited and initiated by Suárez has not been done. This is crucial to my attempt to show how philosophical modernity began in Spain in the Sixteenth century, and is formulated at the end of that century by Suárez and many others.

[92] Suárez' *Defensor Fidei*, published in 1613, as we shall see, was a work burned in England and condemned in France, for showing that kings did not receive their power (*potestas*) directly from God.   It also denied, as it was usual in Spanish political philosophy, that the Pope had any temporal power.

[93] In Spanish America, the fact of the imprisonment of the King of Spain, Fernando VII, a Bourbon, at the hands of Napoleon in 1809, unravels the entire process of emancipation deriving from Suarezian juridical rationality—and even from Vitoria—, but not of the enlightened French philosophy. Having the king imprisoned has no effect on the "pact" of the community with the sovereign, and as such the "communities" recover their "principatum" (sovereignty).

The concept of rights—a universal concept inductively[94] abstracted from its singular species—is based on a relation determined by the free subjectivity. In so far as it is free, given that "the rectitude of conscience (*conscientiarum rectitudo*) is based on the observance of the laws [...it is therefore in our interest] to examine the law in its link with the conscience (*conscientiae vinculum*)."[95] Physical law by necessity tends to affect the subject; the law, which constitutes rights, "links," or is related to, or inclines to the subject, intrinsically, as an "obligation" of "conscience."[96] The "obligatoriness" of the law is based ultimately in the will which promulgates it (the legislator). As such, the "obligated" volition indicates a link with the "obliging" volition[97]—the lawmaker—and this obligation is an "imposition to function with moral necessity."[98]

He is articulating, then, a philosophy of rights which already departs from the free individuality of the (modern) subject, without rejecting the community, which is tied to it in an intrinsic, internal or constitutive way, *ex creatione*, and therefore obligated to effect its ethical nature, and moreover to do so affectively.[99] This obligation is not the recommendation

---

[94] "Dicemus enim primo de lege *in communi* et deinde ad singulas species *descendamus.*" Francisco Suárez, *De legibus*, Prologue. It is interesting to note what Marx methodically wrote "from the abstract arises the concrete", but the abstract for Marx was the singular, and the concrete was the universal—the all—from which it subsequently had to "descend" to the singular. Suárez likewise ascends inductively, first, from the singular—conceptual—to the universal—constructed—and from this he then "descends" to the singular—the point from which he inductively began—, in order to verify the universal description in its specific difference.

[95] Suárez, *De legibus*, Prologue.

[96] Kant would comment, in the Suarezian tradition, that in the "factum" of the moral law was included an "obligation." This "obligation" is possible in the ethical subject—not by physical or natural necessity—if he is autonomous, demanding to affirm his "liberty"—which as "noumenon" is empirically unknowable for Kant—by a fundamental, practical postulate, by one of the four "Ideas." All is founded on the "obligatoriness" of the law.

[97] For Suárez, in the final analysis, it was the will of God, and afterwards the will of the human legislator. For us it will be the political community itself, "sovereign" ("*principata*") as such, which, by communal legislative will, gives the law legitimacy, and therefore one ought to obey it, in other words, oblige it.

[98] "Imponendo moralem necessitatem operandi." Ibid., I, 1.

[99] Therefore "law may be called the inclination towards concupiscence (*fomitis propensio*) [...] because law inclines to the moral flaw. Ibid., I, 1, 4.

of "advice," but rather the domain of the *just* "precept."[100] As such one has to distinguish between "common rights" and those that are "individual" or particular, the latter being those which "each person has over that which is his or that which is owed to him,"[101] which in a certain way is anterior to (promulgated) rights, though different from common rights. Let us look at a description of all the types of "differential" rights:

> Once we have spoken of eternal law[102] and of natural, temporal law[103], it is fitting that we should now speak of positive law. This we have divided into divine[104] and human[105] [...] Following Justinian, human law for its part can be divided into common rights[106] and the rights of the self (*proprii*). The first pertains to the rights of the people (*ius gentium*) [...] now we shall treat of the rights of the self within human law, which has been given the name "positive law of the self," of any city, republic (*rei publicae*)[107] or any other similar[108] self-governing community (*perfectae congregationis*).[109]

---

[100] In Latin "necessitudo" indicates a coercive kind of necessity, that of the "debtor" —from *deudo* comes *debitum,* "debtor". In Mexican Náhuatl "mazehual" means, precisely, the "worthy debtor"—debtor of the life worthy of the god.

[101] Ibid., I, 2, 5.

[102] Suárez goes beyond the universal concept of the construct of rights, as such in *De legibus*, Book I, to his "differentia", in the first place as eternal law, in Book II, ch. 1-4.

[103] As natural law. Ibid., II, 5-16.

[104] As positive divine law. Ibid., IX and X.

[105] Ibid., II, 17.

[106] As the rights of man (Book II, ch.17-20), as unwritten or customs (Book VII) or as written.

[107] In Suárez "reipublicae" in general is "the public thing" or "the public" or communal, not the distinct form of government of the monarchy; it is synonymous with community.

[108] Ibid., III, 1, 1-2. The written civil or positive political law would occupy Suárez for all of book III. Furthermore, he would still write on canonical law (Book IV), penal law (Book V) and meritocratic law (Book IX). The work is one of the most systematic ever written on the theme. It is the first in all of Modernity. It is similar, in its logical constitution as a modern "treatise", to his *Disputaciones Metafísicas*. At four moments in his life Suárez was intensively occupied in reflection on the theme of rights and the law: in 1561-1562 as a student in Salamanca; in Rome as a professor between 1582-1584; in Coimbra between 1601-1603, and on his work on *De legibus* around 1612.

[109] Unlike Aristotle, for example, Suárez is thinking about a "community (*comunitas*)" that "can grow until it changes into a kingdom or possesses the *principatum* for the association (*societatem*) of various cities." Ibid., III, 1, 3. Suárez is thinking about Castilla or Aragón, modern nations.

On this point Suárez is the master of modern European political philosophy. With much greater clarity than Hobbes, and later Hume, he expounds a political theory which will be applicable to Spanish America until the nineteenth century, and by which the struggles for anticolonial emancipation will be justified. It will also pave the way for the advances of the current "late Modernity."

In the first place, the power (*potestas*) or "principality (*principatum*)" —the "sovereignty" that had just been defined by Bodin—resides in the people or the community, who receive it from the Creator, not directly in human nature itself[110] or each particular individual, and not even in a community which isn't mature enough to exercise such a mandate, but only when a sufficient civilizing development has been reached. "This power is not to be found in each human in separation,[111] nor in the whole confused, disordered multitude of them, nor in the union of the members of a group [...] because before there is power (*potestas*) the subject of this power (*subiectum potestatis*)[112] has to exist [...]; however, sovereignty is not given in an immutable way but by the consensus (*consensu*)[113] of the community itself [...] although it is the nature of the thing to be free and have power over itself."[114] The position is analytically complex. It doesn't depart from individualism, nor from feudal communitarianism either. One finds the subject already part of a political community, a subject of the existing power, upon whom it is reflected, and having a subsequent, and nonetheless constitutive and permanent, consensus—the subject does not lose power, though it may be transferred, as we shall see.

A first fundamental (*a posteriori*) consensus of ownership, which is not necessarily found written and frequently not even explicit, is therefore given to the political community. "Regarding the human multitude, then,

---

[110] "The domination of one human being over another does not proceed from a fundamental institution of nature" (Ibid., III, 1, 12).

[111] Against metaphysical individualism which was already established in northern European Modernity.

[112] It is interesting to note the present actuality of his terminological expression.

[113] Observe again the almost Habermasian expression. We have already made note of this theory of "consensus" in Bartolomé de Las Casas, as early as 1536 in the *De unico modo*. See Enrique Dussel, *The Invention of the Americas. The Eclipse of "the Other" and the Myth of Modernity* (New York: Continuum, 1995).

[114] Suárez, *De legibus*, III, 3, 6-7. Suárez's position, like that of Las Casas and Vitoria, is clear: "By nature all human beings are born free, and therefore no one has political jurisdiction over another." Ibid., III, 3, 3).

one has to consider it [...] in so far as they are united by a special will (*speciali voluntate*) or common consensus (*communi consensu*) in a body politic (*corpus politicum*) with a link to society"[115]; "[...] not without the intervention of the collective will (*voluntatum et consensuum*) of the human beings by virtue of which the self-governing community was constituted."[116] The human being is not naturally and primarily an individual being. He is always already in a community. Although "by nature the human being is born free,"[117] he is always "subjectibilis": subjectable or capable of being a member of a political body.[118] As in Ch. Peirce or K.-O. Apel, the community is the point of departure, but the particular subject is not dissolved, neither before the original reflexive consensus, nor by a subsequent pact with the governing body, which may be called to account by the community's never-violated freedom and power.

And this is so because the community, in order to be able to exercise power empirically, creates magistrates or kings within its own institutions. Suárez thinks, accordingly, that human beings have the *principatum* —mistranslated by Suárez as "sovereignty"—or the capacity to govern themselves or give themselves institutions in a natural, free and mediated manner: "The civil magistracy [political government: *magistratum civilem*] endowed with temporal power [*potestate temporali*] to rule human beings is just and conforms to human nature."[119] The mode of this delegated exercise of power, in certain cases, is directly reserved by the people or the community, as it was among the Byzantine republics. Speaking of their "legislative power" he writes:

> Having said that, one deduces that the self-governing communities, those not governed by kings but by themselves (*per se ipsa*), also develop this

---

[115] Ibid., III, 2, 4. Like Kant in his *Critique of Pure Reason*—who drew inspiration from Leibniz, who in turn refers to Suárez—Suárez says "they form a mystical body (*corpus mysticum*) which morally (*moraliter*) may be called a body *per se*." For Suárez, however, this "mystical body" is the empirical political body. For Leibniz and Kant the "ethical community"—*moraliter* says Suárez—is transcendental; it is the "Kingdom of the Spirits." Consider moreover that this *a posteriori* ratifying consensus —unlike the *a priori* pact of isolated individuals, as in Hobbes—explicitly constitutes the "link of society" (*societatis vinculo*) as such. Ibid.

[116] Ibid., III, 3, 6.

[117] "Ex natura rei homines nascitur liberi." Ibid., III, 2, 3.

[118] Ibid., III, 1, 11.

[119] Ibid., III, 1, 2.

legislative power (*potestatem legislativam*) in due time, either aristocratically or popularly (*populariter*) [...] like that of Venice, Genova and similar places, which, although they have a *Doge* or principal leader (*principem*), they nevertheless do not transfer (*transferunt*) total power[120] to him; therefore, in these places the régime is mixed. One finds the supreme power (*suprema potestas*) in the entire body, together with the head [...] In this form the power to legislate resides in the whole political community.[121]

The political community, then, being the ultimate repository of political power (*civile potestate*) can transfer it or translate it (*translata potestate*) to a magistrate or king, after making a contract or pact.[122] It is neither a complete nor an irrevocable "alignment (*alienatio*)," but a limited and conditional concession, never the final petition of power. The power, in the final analysis, arises from the people. "Political power (*potestate civile*), when it is found in an institution or a prince by a legitimate title (*legitimo*)[123] [...] is that which has emanated from the people and the community (*ab populo et communitate manasse*), whether immediate or mediated."[124]

Here Suárez arrives at one of the most outstanding expressions in the whole of political philosophy: "Reason [...] is that this power by the nature of the thing (*potestas ex natura rei*) resides immediately in the community; then so that it may begin to justly (*iustem*) reside in some person like a prince, it is essential that the power be imparted to him beginning with the consensus of the community (*ex consensu communitatis*)."[125] Suárez thinks that different types of government derive from "positive institution," although democracy is the only one that

---

[120] This "reserving" of the right of reason or the revocation of the pact rests on the "final petition" of power, which the free subjects of the political community possess. A complex and more interesting solution than many later reductionist positions.

[121] Ibid., III, 9, 6.

[122] There is then a first reflexive consensual moment of wanting to form part of a community—first consensus—, and the second consensual act of transferring the original power, conditionally, to a particular authority—be it the *Doge* or the *King*— the political pact proper. There are not any Levites here.

[123] The concept of "legitimacy" in Suárez has a classically conceptual clarity: it is the power which depends on the consensus of the people, or which adequately fulfills the pact contracted in accord with the conditions of the consensus.

[124] Ibid., III, 4, 2.

[125] Ibid.

doesn't require specific organization, given that it fulfils the requirements of being the "natural establishment or outgrowth, by only abstaining from a new or positive institution."[126] In the case of monarchy this transference is not absolute—as in Hobbes—nor natural, nor of divine establishment —as James I, the Scottish king of England, claimed[127]—but human and conditioned by an agreement or practical covenant.

"That the regime of such a republic (*reipublicae*) or region is a monarchy is a result of a human institution (*ex hominum institutione*) [...], the monarchy itself, then, arises from human beings[128]. A sign of this is that, following the pact or agreement (*pactum vel conventionem*) which creates the kingdom and the king, the power of the latter is greater or lesser."[129] "Once the power is transferred (*translata potestate*) to the person of the king, this same power makes him superior even to the kingdom he was given, for in receiving it he is forced to yield to the people and is deprived of his previous freedom."[130]

In effect, this delegation is an alignment, although a conditional one as we shall see, so as to yield governability through time. "The transference (*translatio*) of this power to the prince at the hands of the republic is not a delegation but rather an alignment (*alientatio*) or complete surrender of all

---

[126] Suárez, *Defensor Fidei*, III, 2, 8-9.

[127] One can understand the anger of the Scottish king when, in *Defensor Fidei*, Suárez writes: "The power of the king comes [...] *by a certain natural consequence* which shows natural reason; by the same token, [political power, even the king's] is *immediately* given by God only to that subject in whom it is found by force of natural reason. Well then, this subject is *the people themselves*, and not some person inside of them." Ibid., III, 3,2.

[128] This gift is effected by election, by the consent of the people, by just war, by legitimate succession, or by some donation. "When the community is self-governing it voluntarily chooses the king, to whom it transfers its power." Suárez, *De legibus*, III, 4, 1.

[129] The communities which effected the pact with the King of Spain were not only in Spain, or Castilla or Aragón, but also in the "Kingdoms of the Indies." When Fernando VII was taken prisoner by Napoleon, the "Kingdoms of the Indies" recovered their power, their autonomy, their liberty equal to that of the other "Kingdoms" on the Spanish Peninsula in 1809. This was rejected by James I of England, by whom Suárez's *Defensor Fidei* was burned in the public square of London. Anglican Christianity was still more royalist, more conservative —Hobbesian— than Spanish Christianity.

[130] Suárez, *De legibus*, III, 3, 6.

the power that was in the community."[131] This "transference" of power
may invalidate it, and the community thus recuperate the exercise of that
power, or part of it, which is conceded to authority "for a certain use," not
as inalienable property. The subject is dealt with in Book III, Chapter 19
of *De legibus*, which we shall discuss shortly. Suárez points out one case
of invalidation in the following example. "The political magistrate
receives its power (*ab populo potestatem*) from the people; as such, the
people could choose not to grant him power if it was not with this
condition, that they were not bound by the laws of the prince if they
themselves did not also consent in accepting the laws."[132]

Even in the case of a "non-democractic (*no democrático*)" regime,
although the "people may have transferred supreme power to the ruler,"
there are many exceptions in which they cannot accept the legitimacy of a
law,[133] especially when "the law is unjust"; is "too oppressive"; when "the
people don't respect the law," and especially in the case of tyranny. "If
the king changes his just power into tyranny, abusing his power for
evident harm to the city, the people may use their natural power to defend
themselves, *because they have never been deprived of it.*"[134] "For which it
is lawful to repel force with force [...] it being necessary for the very
preservation of the republic, [and therefore] it is understood that the first
pact by which the republic transferred its power to the king remains to be
exempted."[135] In other words, when the people reprove the king's exercise
of power, given that they have never been deprived of power, "this power
remains (*permansisse*) in the community" as if "it had not been transferred
to the crown."[136] Furthermore, the Pope does not have the power "to make
civil laws,"[137] nor does the Emperor have "universal power" to control the
whole of Christianity, [138] much less "the entire world (*universum orbem*)."

---

[131] Ibid., III, 3, 11. In the case of the Roman "senate," for example, Suárez
recognizes that the community is of one of those kinds of republics "which are in
fact free since they have reserved for themselves the supreme power" and who are
only "in charge of promulgating the laws to the senate." Ibid., III, 3, 12.

[132] Ibid., III, 19, 2.

[133] Ibid., III, 19, 7-13.

[134] Suárez, *Defensor Fidei*, III, 3, 3.

[135] Ibid., VI, 4, 15.

[136] Suárez, *De legibus*, III, 21, 6.

[137] Ibid.

[138] Ibid., III, 21, 7.

Suárez presciently and explicitly criticizes the loss of normativity of modern political strategic action, as in the case of Machiavelli, by having such a minimalist view of politics:

> *Error de Maquiavelo* [...For Machiavelli] that which secular power (*potestatem laicam*) and civil law directly and chiefly seek is political stability and its preservation [...] the matter (*materiam*) of the laws is whatever serves the cause of political stability and its preservation and progress; to this end laws are made, considering that one finds in them a genuine honesty, even if a feigned and deceiving honesty, going so far as disguising whatever is unjust if it is useful to the republic (*republicae utilia*).[139]

Anticipating Kant, Suárez observes that the law "cannot directly mandate a purely internal act by itself"[140]—in other words, it cannot immediately demand morality—but though it may rule over "exterior acts" it may in consequence "indirectly mandate the internal act"[141]—the legality is necessarily completed by the morality. The real question is "can civil law compel subjects in the court of conscience (*conscientiae foro*)?"[142] He responds with the metaphor of the word *foro* (court). "Initially it was merely the place where trials were held, but later it came to signify judgement itself, and thereby one distinguishes a double jurisdiction, the internal and the external."[143] "Coercion (*coactio*) without the power to compel the conscience is either morally (*moraliter*) impossible, because just coercion supposes guilt [...] or is certainly very insufficient, because in many inevitable cases it wouldn't be possible to sufficiently help the republic by coercion."[144]

---

[139] Ibid., III, 12, 2. It is interesting to note that he has a normative sense of political action, against the simple strategy of modern politics, successful "for a brief time."

[140] Ibid., III, 13, 2.

[141] Ibid., III, 3, 9.

[142] Ibid., III, 21, Title. Note the "modernity" of the terminology. The Jesuits are the masters of the "test of conscience," which Descartes would practice daily in La Fleche, as we have already indicated. Nevertheless, although he defines the legality in the external law-code—like Kant—he shows that civil law has an equally imperative internal capacity, aspiring to a politically strong normativity, greater than the Habermasian—only discursive.

[143] Ibid., III, 21, 2.

[144] Ibid., III, 21, 8. The theme would require an extensive treatment not possible in this brief survey.

We are in the presence of a modern European political philosophy in its most positive sense, without the reductionisms of Hobbesian individualism or, later, Lockean liberalism. This theory of rights will serve, around 1810, as a theoretical-political justification to the communities of Latin American creole and mestizo freedom-fighters. They will use it to recuperate the community's (the "State of the Indies") exercise of power, transferred to the king of Spain or Portugal by an originally implicit agreement—in the case of Portugal the Brazilian community instituted the "new pact" in 1821 with the King of Portugal's son, who would become the Emperor Pedro I of Brazil and Maranao. But the Suarezian ideology would not only motivate the creoles and mestizos—another type of alterity than that of the Indians—but it would also inspire the communal experience of the Jesuitical "reductions," the remotest source and the immediate historical antecedent by which the first European socialists in the Eighteenth century would be inspired, those such as Mably and Morelli, from which would emerge Babeuf's "Conspiracy of the Equals" in 1794, at the height of the French Revolution—the new future revolution in the very heart of the bourgeois revolution.

In fact, the Jesuits of the eighteenth century, who were creoles, would return to their indigenous origins in order to define themselves against the absolutist Bourbon Europeans. It is amazing to discover a great generation, with such eminent intellectual figures as José Gumilla, Vicente Maldonado, Juan de Velasco, Juan Ignacio Molina, Francisco Xavier Clavijero, Francisco Xavier Alegre, Andrés Cavo, Andrés de Guevara, Diego José Abad, Rafael Landívar and so many other Jesuits. Exiled by the Bourbon expulsion of 1767 in Spanish America (and 1759 in Brazil), in a number approximating 2500 priests, they wrote in Europe, in Italy and other countries, not only the colonial history of America, but principally occupying themselves recounting the indigenous life and cultures before the European invasion of the fifteenth century.

Mariano Picón-Salas justly calls it "the literature of the Jesuit emigration,"[145] which gives a philosophical interpretation of the state of

---

[145] Mariano Picón-Salas, *De la Conquista a la Independencia* (México: FCE, 1965), 185. See also Andrés Cavo, *Los tres siglos de Méjico durante el gobierno español* (México: J. R. Navarro, 1852); Gerard Decorme, *La obra de los jesuitas mexicanos durante la época colonial* (México: Porrúa, 1941); Guillermo Furlong, *Los jesuitas y la cultura rioplatense* (Montevideo: Urta y Curbelo, 1933); Francisco Xavier

mind of the creoles—who recall the Indians' most agreeable phase-—against the enlightened Bourbon absolutism—which was unpopular and oppressive for its colonial conception of politics. Andrés Cavo points out that the indigenous Mexicans had a "state of culture which exceeded, in impressive ways, that of the Spanish themselves when they were encountered by the Greeks and the Romans."[146] Clavijero[147] doesn't write a history of the creoles, but of the Aztecs, as a defence against the ignorance of de Pauw[148] on matters concerning the indigenous Americans. Pedro José Márquez, another of them, writes an aesthetic on the Mexican art of the Aztecs, [149] and being in Europe the distance allows him to better appreciate the stature and personality of the indigenous American cultures.

The affirmation which had been nullified since the conquest at the end of the fifteenth century had thus begun in the eighteenth, as a new recognition of Alterity.

Bibliography

Acosta, José de. *Obras del P. José de Acosta*. Madrid: Biblioteca de Autores Españoles, 1954.

Alegre, Francisco Xavier. *Historia de la provincia de la Compañía de Jesús de Nueva España*. Roma: Institum Historioum, 1956.

Beuchot, Mauricio. *Historia de la Filosofía en el México Colonial*. Barcelona: Herder, 1997.

Botella, Juan, Carlos Cañeque and Eduardo Gonzalo, eds. *El pensamiento político en sus textos. De Platón a Marx*. Madrid: Tecnos, 1998.

Cavo, Andrés. *Los tres siglos de Méjico durante el gobierno español*. México: J. R. Navarro, 1852.

Cayetano, Thomas de Vio. *Commentary on Saint Thomas' Summa Theologiae* (1540).

Alegre, *Historia de la provincia de la Compañía de Jesús de Nueva España* (Roma: Institum Historioum, 1956).

[146] Picón-Salas, *De la conquista,* 186.

[147] See Francisco Xavier Clavijero, *Historia Antigua de México* (México: Porrúa, 1945).

[148] See Corneille de Pauw, *Recherches philosophiques sur les Américains, ou Mémoires intéressants pour servir à l' histoire de l' espèce humaine* (Berlin, 1770).

[149] In Italian, *Due Anitchi Monumenti di Architettura Messicana*. In this work he describes the works that were "violently destroyed by the Spanish and which merited comparison with the best works of the Chaldeans, the Assyrians or the Egyptians." Picón-Salas, *De la conquista*, 187.

Clavijero, Francisco Xavier, *Historia Antigua de México*. México: Porrúa, 1945.
Collins, Randall. *The Sociology of Philosophies. A Global Theory of Intellectual Change*. Cambridge: Harvard University Press, 2000.
Decorme, Gerard. *La obra de los jesuitas mexicanos durante la época colonial*. México: Porrúa, 1941.
Dussel, Enrique. *Para una historia de la Iglesia en América Latina*, Barcelona: Estela, 1967. (Later editions with the title *Historia de la Iglesia en América Latina. Coloniaje y Liberación*. Translation into in English *History of the Church in Latin America*. Grand Rapids: Eederman, 1981.
—. *Para una ética de la liberación latinoamericana*. Buenos Aires: Siglo XXI, 1973, vol. 1-2; México: Edicol, 1977, vol. 3; Bogotá: USTA, 1979-1980, vol. 4-5.
—. *The Invention of the Americas. The Eclipse of "the Other" and the Myth of Modernity*. New York: Continuum, 1995.
—. *Etica de la Liberación en la edad de la globalización y la exclusion*. Madrid: Trotta, 1998.
—. "Wahrheitsanspruch und Toleranzfähigkeit." In *Zur Logik religiöser Traditionen*, edited by B. Schoppelreich and S. Wiedenhofer. Frankfurt: Verlag für Interkulturelle Kommmunikation, 1998.
—. *Hacia una Filosofia Política Crítica*. Bilbao: Desclèe de Brouwer, 2001.
The Encyclopedia of Philosophy. New York: Macmillan, 1967.
Eschweiler, Karl. "Die Philosophie der Spanischens Spaetscholastik and den deutschen Universitaeten des siebzehnten Jahrhunderts." In *Spanische Forschungen des Goerres-Gesellschaft I*. Münster: Aschendorff Verlag, 1928.
Fraile, Guillermo. *Historia de la Filosofía*. Madrid: BAC, 1966.
Foucault, Michel. *Las palabras y las cosas*. México: Siglo XXI, 1996.
Furlong, Guillermo, *Los jesuitas y la cultura rioplatense*. Montevideo: Urta y Curbelo, 1933.
Guy, Alain. *Historia de la filosofia española*. Barcelona: Anthropos, 1985.
Las Casas, Bartolomé de. *Obras escogidas de Fray Bartolomé de las Casas*. Madrid: Real Academia Española, 1957.
—. *De Thesauris*. Madrid: CSIC, 1958.
—. *De Regia Potestate o Derecho a la Autodeterminación*. Madrid: CSIC, 1969.
—. *Apología*. Madrid: Alianza, 1989.
Minges, Parthenius "Suárez und Duns Scotus." *Philosophisches Zeitschrift der Goerres-Gesellschaft* 32 (1919): 334-340.

Ockham, William de. *Dialogus*. Frankfurt: Melchior Goldast, 1614.

Padua, Marsilio de. *Defensor Pacis*. Hannover: R. Scholz, 1932.

Pauw, Corneille de. *Recherches philosophiques sur les Américains, ou Mémoires intéressants pour servir à l' histoire de l' espèce humaine.* Berlin, 1770.

Picón-Salas, Mariano. *De la Conquista a la Independencia*. México: FCE, 1965.

Streitcher, K. *Die Philosophie der Spanischen Spaetscholastiks and den deutschen Universitaeten des siebzehnten Jahrhunderts*. In Gesammelte Aufsaetze zur Kulturgeschichte Spanien. Münster: Aschendorff Verlag, 1928.

Suárez, Francisco. *Tratado De Anima*.

—. *Defensor Fidei*.

—. *De legibus*.

Romanus, Aegidius. *De ecclesiastica potestate*. Weimar: Bölaus, 1929.

Vitoria, Francisco de. *Obras de Francisco de Vitoria*. Madrid: BAC, 1960.

CHAPTER SEVEN

THE DUAL HAITIAN REVOLUTION AND THE MAKING OF FREEDOM IN MODERNITY*

ANTHONY BOGUES

Freedom is a must
Babylon try to enslave us…
You know dem have a nerve
Freedom is a ting everyman dem deserve
—*Bounty Killer*

Freedom is how you is from the start
An' when it look different you got to
Move, an' when you movin' say that it a natural
Freedom that make you move.
—*George Lamming, Season of Adventure*

In fact, Sophie my Marie, I who received it know that
Freedom is not given, must not be given.
Liberty awarded does not liberate your soul…
—*Patrick Chamoiseau, Texaco*

Introduction

There are several conventional ways in the history of Western liberal political thought in which the story of freedom is told. However two of these continue to frame the freedom story. The first frame is Isaiah Berlin's famous 1958 lecture, "The Two Concepts of Liberty."[1] In this frame

---

* This essay is a revised version of a paper presented at a conference on slavery held at the University of the West Indies, at Mona, Jamaica, in 2007.
[1] See Isaiah Berlin, *Four Essays on Liberty* (Oxford: Oxford University Press, 1969).

Berlin, drawing from both J. S. Mill and Benjamin Constant, deploys an argument which suggest that there are two versions of freedom, which he calls "positive" and "negative" liberty. Berlin continues Constant's conception of freedom in which there are distinctions between the freedom of the so called "ancients" and that of "moderns." For Constant the main distinction was that, while "the aim of the ancients was the sharing of social power among the citizens of the same fatherland... the aim of the moderns is the enjoyment of security in private pleasures;... individual liberty... is the true modern liberty."[2] It is clear that the overarching definitions of freedom in Constant's conception revolve around questions of the individual's and the community's relationship to political authority. For the "moderns" therefore when freedom becomes "negative"—a freedom from—it primarily resides in non-interference and the creation of a distant space between political authority and the self. In part this distance is rooted in conceptions of a market economy and the private ownership of property and is of course integral to all contemporary forms of liberalism. There are of course many streams of liberal political thought but common to all are the doctrines of natural rights and contract theory.[3]

The second major frame for the discussion about freedom is the rich debate about the shaping influences of Roman conceptions of liberty on 18th century Atlantic political thought.[4] This story proposes that freedom "may be realized through membership of a political community in which those who are mutually vulnerable and share a common fate may jointly be able to exercise some collective direction over their lives... freedom is related to participation in self- government and concern for the common good."[5] This sounds similar in many ways to Constant's freedom of the "ancients." However the matter is complicated by the notion of the "common good," as a primary purpose of political association. It has been successfully argued by J. Pocock that this story of freedom draws from both Roman and Greek political thought and was readapted in the Atlantic world in a form of civic humanism that meshed with Lockean

[2] Benjamin Constant, "The Liberty of the Ancients and the Liberty of the Moderns," in *Political Thought*, ed. Michael Rosen and Jonathan Wolf (Oxford: Oxford University Press, 1999), 123.

[3] For a succinct and able discussion of liberalism as a political philosophy see John Gray, *Liberalism* (Minneapolis: University of Minnesota Press, 1995).

[4] A very good summary of these arguments can be found in Iseult Honohan, *Civic Republicanism* (London: Routledge, 2002.) The key thinkers in this stream are J. Pocock, Phillip Pettit and Quentin Skinner.

[5] Honohan, *Civic Republicanism*, 1.

notions of natural liberty.[6] Quentin Skinner continuing along these lines has suggested that there is another form of liberty other than that contained in liberalism. He calls this a neo-Roman theory of liberty in which civil and political liberties are harmoniously reconciled in the engaged activities of the body politic.[7] What is intriguing about both these stories of freedom is that they miss a fundamental issue which saturated the polity of modernity: the organization of a form of human domination that was embodied in racial slavery and colonial power.

Of course, it could be argued by some that Locke's references to slavery as a feature outside of the compact and Hegel's master/slave model elaborated in his *Phenomenology of Spirit* are recognitions in Western political theory that slavery was a system of human domination that would either hinder our "Self-Consciousness," or could only operate in the Lockean model outside of the contract. But there are two things about this position which we should note. First, that the system of Atlantic slavery was not just rooted in an Aristotle's notion of the "natural slave," but was a system of *racial slavery*. Secondly, as Fanon has pointed out, for the Hegelian model to operate there needs to be a degree of "absolute reciprocity which must be emphasized"[8]—what I have called a "dialectics of recognition." Within the system of Atlantic racial slavery and slave societies such dialectics were not possible as the system rested on other grounds.[9]

In the end therefore I would want to suggest that Western political theory paid little attention to the meanings of Atlantic racial slavery, and therefore not much attention to the ways in which human domination operated in early modernity. Hence questions of freedom became narrowly focused on political authority and the struggles against different forms of European absolutism. One consequence of this is that in our contemporary modernity there would emerge a grammar of freedom which focused on issues of political self-government, defining citizenship as different from subject and then creating classifications of difference that would deny rights. Some theorists have argued that the creation of the

---

[6] See J. G. A. Pocock, *The Machiavellian Moment: Florentine Political Thought and the Atlantic Republican Tradition* (Princeton: Princeton University Press, 1975).
[7] For a discussion of this see Quentin Skinner, *Liberty before Liberalism* (Cambridge: Cambridge University Press, 1998).
[8] Frantz Fanon, *Black Skin White Masks* (New York: Grove Press, 1967), 217.
[9] The story of Frederick Douglass confrontation with his master Covey tells this tale. See Frederick Douglass, *My Bondage and My Freedom* (Penguin: New York, 2003).

above conditions for the denial of rights constituted an exception which is "a kind of exclusion."[10] This exclusion involves processes of suspension thus making the "state of exception... not the chaos that precedes order but rather the situation which results from its suspension."[11] However in the colonial modernity of the Atlantic world both racial slavery and colonial domination were *the* orders; they did not require any suspensions or exceptions. And where they did, these suspensions worked their way back into mainstream political discourse and practices.[12] In such a context, freedom would be circumscribed.

It is therefore clear that the primary focus of the two major narratives of freedom is on the ways in which the individual relates to the political community and its various organs. In the first version, freedom is defined as a freedom from interference, a freedom in which the state and political authority place minimal force upon the individual. In this version it is the individual's private goals and private space which are of primary concern. In the second version freedom is tied to a close affinity with the political community. The model here is Aristotle's dictum that "man is a political animal." The issue which one has to ask about both these versions of freedom is this: why the preoccupation with political authority and the political community? There is as well another issue to which we have already alluded, i.e., what effect did this preoccupation have upon the practices and meanings of freedom? Both questions are central because we know that the study of political thought requires us to think about the meanings of political vocabularies and their contextual surroundings.

The preoccupation with political authority within the dominant narratives of freedom partly derives from the context of their birth. Both arose in the period of colonial modernity. When the political ideas of civic republicanism profoundly shaped the American Revolution, they did not challenge racial slavery in the United States. For many of the key figures in the American Revolution, the definition of slavery revolved around the lack of self-government, and the corruption by the English crown of the

---

[10] The major contemporary theorist of this position is Giorgio Agamben who develops Carl Schmitt's idea about the nature of sovereign power. See Giorgio Agamben, *Homo Sacer: Sovereign Power and Bare Life* (Stanford: Stanford University Press, 1998).

[11] Ibid., 17-18.

[12] For a discussion of this process see Anthony Bogues, *Empire of Liberty: Power, Desire and Freedom* (Lebanon, NH: Dartmouth College Press, 2010).

"rights of English men". Listen to Madison speaking to a crowd in New England:

> The people of Massachusetts uniformly think that the destruction of their charter making the council and judges wholly dependent upon the crown and the people subjected to the unlimited power of parliament as their supreme legislative is *slavery*.[13] (Emphasis added).

From this ground within Western political thought two issues arise in the study of political thought and freedom. The first is: what meanings of freedom emerged from the historic practices of liberalism and from civic republicanism? The second becomes the focus of our essay: what alternative practices and conceptions of freedom emerged from the ideas and actions of those who were, in Fanon's words, "objects amongst objects?" Since this story of freedom is typically ignored in the history of political thought bringing it to the fore may open new vistas about human possibilities, about the ways in which domination and power can be resisted. Importantly the slave and ex-slave freedom story suggest to us that freedom is not a normative ideal but rather that its meanings are embedded within a series of practices and our reflections about these practices. As such a normative political concept of freedom may really be a political grammar which obscures rather than illuminates our social world. So how do we tell the freedom story of the enslaved? In this regard it may be important to pay attention to the historic dual Haitian Revolution of the 18th and early 19th centuries.

So where does the story of the Haitian revolution and in general Caribbean freedom begin? For analytical purposes we may segment our narrative of Caribbean/Haitian freedom into two segments of Atlantic history:

• Conquest, genocide and the fall of "natural man".
• African slavery and colonialism.

These segments should not be understood as calcified typologies of major turning points in Caribbean society which occur in chronological sequence, but rather as porous markers that allow us to grapple with the issues of freedom as they were developed in the political, social and discursive spaces of the region.

---

[13] Cited in Robert H. Webking, *The American Revolution and the Politics of Liberty* (Baton Rouge: Louisiana State University Press, 1989), 116.

Indians, Indies and the Fall of Natural Man

Almost fifty years after Columbus planted the Spanish flag in the Americas, Jose de Acosta published the *Natural and Moral History of the Indies*. During the period of early colonial modernity this text became a major work of reference about the New World.[14] De Acosta's work was a compendium of 16th century European ideas about the so-called New World. His text reviewed biblical arguments about the size and shape of the world, and Aristotle's failure to understand the existence of the New World; examined the possible origins of the indigenous population; mused about the Torrid Zone; speculated on the ecology of the region; and then postulated that the design of Providence was for the Spanish to conquer the region for Christendom. In de Acosta's elaborations about the Indies, the "rights of the indigenous people" could be set aside. This setting aside of rights had already been noted in Francisco de Vitoria's lecture on the native population in which he asked, "by what right were the barbarians subjected to Spanish rule?"[15]

In point of fact the rights of the native population were set aside in concrete practices of brutality during the Spanish conquest, as well as discursively in a series of arguments which relocated the indigenous population in a schema of natural history classification from being a mirror of "natural man"—a state which Europeans thought was then a lower form of human existence in almost Eden-like conditions—to one of natural servitude. In their state of so called naturalness—natural man—the native population could claim some natural rights, since God created them. Certainly when they were Christianized, natural rights might be bestowed since in the early period of colonial modernity humanness was affirmed through Christianity what Sylvia Wynter has called in her schema of Man, "Christian Man." However the dictates of Spanish conquest quickly shifted the parameters of the debate about the rights of the indigenous population. As this occurred, the indigenous population became fallen natural man and, therefore could be conceived of and treated as Aristotle's natural slaves.

This fall made the native population idolaters and subsequently located them outside the pale of Christendom, making them another species life

---

[14] This book was recently translated. See Jose de Acosta, *Natural and Moral History of the Indies* (Durham: Duke University Press, 2002).
[15] Cited in Anthony Pagden, *Lords of all the World* (New Haven: Yale University Press, 1995).

form. It was within this context of conquest, of the setting aside of rights and the fall of natural man, that Bartolomé de Las Casas wrote his defense of the indigenous population, *A Short Account of the Destruction of the Indies*. For Las Casas, the native populations had reason and were therefore creatures of God. The duty of the Spanish imperial power was to Christianize them. Las Casas proclaimed that:

> The people with whom the New World is swarming are not only capable of understanding the Christian religion, but amenable, by reason and persuasion, to the practice of good morals and the highest virtues. Nature made then free... our holy religion adapts itself equally as well to all the nations of the world; it embraces them all and deprives no human being of his natural liberty under pretext or color that he or she is *servus a natura*.[16]

Two things about the Las Casas position should be noted. In the first place he granted the native population natural liberty, thereby making them creatures of God, and secondly he argued that they could be trained into Christian morals. What is also interesting about this position was his understanding that the formal political structure of the native population was one of worth. In his polemic against the brutal treatment of the indigenous population and imperial Spain's organization of native servitude, Las Casas wrote:

> By what authority have you made such detestable wars against these people who lived peacefully... on their own lands? Are these not men? Do they not have rational souls?[17]

This was the crux of the matter and was/is one overarching theme of contestation in the history of Caribbean, and I would argue Atlantic, political thought—the preoccupation with humanity or its lack of for those who were enslaved and placed in bondage in slave and colonial societies. The deliberate setting aside of rights for the indigenous population resulted in the first genocide of colonial modernity. It also shaped the political grammar in which freedom could be constructed alongside various forms of servitude and conquest. The political origins of Caribbean society were therefore in conquest, and more importantly for our essay, its origins were framed by the practice of the setting aside of rights. So when African slavery was introduced into the region the

---

[16] Cited in Gordon Lewis, *Main Currents in Caribbean Thought* (Kingston: Heinemann Educational Books, 1983), 52.

[17] Bartolomé de Las Casas, *A Short Account of the Destruction of the Indies* (London: Penguin Books, 1992), xxi.

discursive ground was already fertile. Indeed, this is one of the grounds on which Caribbean political thought differs significantly from that of conventional Western political thought.

In Western political thought the basis for the examination of rights, political obligation, and the character of freedom proceeds from the stance that the humanity of the subject is already confirmed; indeed it is that humanity which gives natural rights and liberty and therefore citizenship. For the enslaved Caribbean person, on the other hand, it was the purported lack of that humanity which allowed enslavement. From this angle the question of freedom would arise in Caribbean political thought in a different way.

The question of the humanity of the enslaved stands at the heart of the Caribbean slave colonial society. The Caribbean historian Elsa Goveia in her study of Eighteenth century Caribbean slave laws makes the point that the slaves "were a special kind of property—that is property in person."[18] Joan Dayan taking up this argument in the Atlantic world argues that the distinction between civil body and legal slave in Western thought is one where the civil body is "the artificial person who possesses self and property, and the legal slave, the artificial person who exists as both human and property."[19] However to be a "property in person" required making the slave less than human, creating both in legal and social terms a non–person. It is a situation that Orlando Patterson has called "social death."[20]

To accomplish this two moves were required. One was to denaturalize the African slave, making the slave a different species and life form lower than natural man. The second was to develop a series of elaborate conceptions around the meanings of the color of the African slave. These elaborations ranged from climatic, to brain size, to paganism, to biblical stories about Ham, and theories of polygenesis. Once these had been consolidated in Western thought, there could now be constructed a

---

[18] Elsa Goveia, "West Indian Slave laws of the 18th century" in *Chapters in Caribbean History 2*, ed. Douglas Hall, Elsa Goveia, F. Roy Augier (Barbados: Caribbean Universities Press, 1970), 21.
[19] Joan Dayan, "Legal Slaves and Civil Bodies," in *Materializing Democracy: Toward a Revitalized Cultural Politics*, ed. Rus Castronovo and Dana Nelson (Durham: Duke University Press, 2002), 55.
[20] See Orlando Patterson, *Slavery and Social Death: A Comparative Study* (Cambridge: Harvard University Press, 1982).

philosophical anthropology of the human which did not include the
African slave. As a consequence, in the midst of modern racial slavery
rooted in sugar and cotton, the West could debate and practice forms of
"freedom, " without any significant attention to this from of domination ,
Thus these discussions and practices about freedom could not and did not
confront the foundation of modern Atlantic society—racial slavery. We
now turn to the dual Haitian Revolution as an event in which a different
story of freedom unfolds.

Haiti and the making of Caribbean freedom

The dual Haitian Revolution was a cataclysmic event in Caribbean,
Atlantic and world political history. C.L.R. James's *Black Jacobins* (1938)
consolidated its iconic status in Caribbean historiography.[21] Since that
time historical writings on the revolution have largely focused on the
relative roles of the different racial and social groups, the roles of the
different colonial powers, or have been enchanted with the formidable
leadership skills of Toussaint L'Ouverture.[22] Recently Sybille Fisher has
made a compelling argument for the revolution as integral to the meanings
of political modernity, although she does not explicitly attempt to think
about the possible meanings of freedom that emerge from the
revolution.[23] In the literary field, thinking about the revolution has also
produced novels, plays and poems reconfirming its iconic status.[24]

However, much less attention has been paid to the political ideas of the
revolution and when this has occurred it has been done with specific
references to Western political thought. It is as if the activities of the

---

[21] For James's assessment of the book see *Small Axe* 8 2000. For other assessments
see Anthony Bogues, *Black Heretics, Black Prophets: Radical Political
Intellectuals* (New York: Routledge, 2003) Chapter 3, and David Scott, *Conscripts
of Modernity* (Durham: Duke University Press, 2005).
[22] David Patrick Geggus, who has spent a great deal of time examining the
revolution, has made a recent study of the major histories of the revolution. He
argues that for 60 years *The Black Jacobins* dominated the field of study of the
Revolution in English. See David Patrick Geggus, *Haitian Revolutionary Studies*
(Bloomington: Indiana University Press, 2002), especially Chapter 2.
[23] Sybille Fisher, *Modernity Disavowed* (Durham: Duke University Press, 2004).
[24] For a discussion of these literary texts, in particular the plays of Derek Walcott,
see Gordon Collier, "The 'Noble Ruins' of Art and Revolution," in *Fusion of
Cultures?* ed. Peter O. Stummer and Christopher Balme (Amsterdam: Rodopi B.
V.. 1996), 269-328. There is of course Madison Smart Bell impressive three
volume historical novels on the revolution.

enslaved do not merit the status of thought.[25] The Haitian scholar Michel-Rolph Trouillot has made the point that the revolution was "unthinkable." He further states that "by necessity, the Haitian Revolution thought itself out politically and philosophically as it was taking place."[26] Two important texts have made efforts to examine some of the ideas which animated the revolutionary slaves. Carolyn Fisk's *The Making of Haiti* strongly argues that the slaves "agricultural egalitarianism had more to do with their own African origins and the desire to define their lives through their relationship to the land than to French bourgeois revolutionary notions of liberty and equality."[27] For Fick the revolutionary slaves were peasants and their hostility to the labor regime of Toussaint L'Ouverture was one based on the impulse of this social type. Joan Dayan in a remarkable literary and historical study of Haiti asks us to examine Haitian history through grappling with vodou as a "project of thought". She writes:

> The idea of philosophy, of thought thinking itself through history, compelled me. I began to consider not only the historical functions of vodou—its preservation of pieces of history ignored, denigrated, or exoticized by the standard " drum and trumpet" histories of empire—but the project of thought, the intensity of interpretation and dramatization it allowed.[28]

Using the 1805 Haitian Constitution and one period of the revolution I wish to examine the dual Haitian Revolution as a *project of freedom in the Atlantic world that demonstrated practices of freedom different from those of either the American or the French Revolutions.* Importantly, I would suggest that this dual revolution was perhaps the most significant revolution in what has been called by some historians "The Age of Revolution."

---

[25] An example of this is the recent work of Nick Nesbitt. *Universal Emancipation : The Haitian Revolution and the Radical Enlightenment* (Charlotte: University of Virginia Press, 2008)

[26] Michel-Rolph Trouillot, *Silencing the Past: Power and the Production of History* (Boston: Beacon Press, 1995), 89.

[27] Carolyn E. Fick, *The Making of Haiti* (Knoxville: University of Tennessee Press, 1990), 250.

[28] Joan Dayan, *Haiti, History and the Gods* (Berkeley: University of California Press, 1998), xvii.

The Haitian Revolution: Freedom and Independence

The Haitian Revolution was a dual revolution with two impulses. The first impulse was the abolition of racial slavery. The second was the establishment of an independent republic. The revolution did not begin with both of these political objectives. It found its anti-colonial objective in the actual process of the revolution itself. Revolutions are not simply the extraordinary volcanic outburst of the oppressed but, I would suggest, are typically one apex in a series of activities in which oppressed groups engage over many years. In the Haitian case the revolution was the result of a long period of acute resistance and marronage of the slave population.[29] In the orally constructed memory of the revolution, the poisoning campaign of Makandal in 1757 was directly linked to the insurrection that broke out in the north in August 1791.[30] The success of the final insurrection was in great part due to the leadership of the revolutionary army lead in the main by Toussaint L' Ouverture. By 1801, ten years after the insurrection began, Toussaint L'Ouverture had wrested the Spanish section of the colony, rejoined the French side, and finally proclaimed the abolition of the system of the "property of the person."

It is now part of the historical record that Napoleon Bonaparte, who had by then risen to power in colonial France, wanted to restore racial slavery in the colony. To achieve this the French leader engaged in a series of political maneuvers which finally lead to Toussaint's arrest and death in a French prison. In the aftermath, the other generals of the slave revolutionary army lead by Jean Jacques Dessalines, fought a bitter anti-colonial war against the French, finally defeating them and proclaiming the colony's independence on   January 1, 1804. In 1806 Dessalines was assassinated, but before his murder he promulgated the first independent Haitian constitution.

---

[29] This is very ably examined in Jean Fouchard, *The Haitian Maroons: Liberty or Death* (New York: Edward W. Blyden Press, 1981).

[30] The story of Makandal is a heroic one in Haitian history. It is the story of a prophet and tells us about another dimension of Caribbean political thought the role healers/prophets in radical political thinking and action. Alejo Carpentier in his lyrical and evocative *The Kingdom of this World* has imaginatively explored the influence and profound symbolic important of Makandal to the Haitian revolution. Fick does so in Chapter 2 of *The Making of Haiti*. Perhaps the most acute representation of Makandal is the 1991 painting by Wilson Anacreon titled *Makandal the rebel slave with magic powers jumps out of the bonfire.*

Revolutions are swept along by the radical desires of a population. Those desires are typically formulated against a set of conditions which are often codified in a series of laws, customs or conventions. In the case of the American Revolution one element of the political discourse around the revolution was about "the history of the present King of Great Britain," and the "repeated injuries and usurpations, all having in direct object the establishment of an absolute tyranny over these states."[31] Thus in the American Revolution the political objective was to break political bonds and to start anew the search for "free and independent states". In the case of the French Revolution, the political discourse was dominated by what Ellen Meiksins Wood has identified as "two essential historical problems... a divided polity which could not overcome the political 'parcellization' and corporate fragmentation of its feudal past; and a state conceived as a kind of private property, a resource for princes and office–holders..."[32] Thus one major political objective of the French revolution was the creation of structures of rights and sovereignty which would shatter the feudal centralized state. In the Haitian case the conditions of coloniality and racial slave oppression were codified in the Code Noir.

Formulated in 1685, the Code Noir became the slave laws that governed master–slave relationships in the colony. Elsa Goveia argues that the code was not established with metropolitan France in mind but with the conditions of the colonies firmly fixed.[33] The code was a mixture of political control and explicit disciplinary measures for slave control. Precise and concrete, these measures shaped the everyday life of the slaves. For example, the code stated how much food a slave was to get and how many suits of clothes per year s/he was allowed. Although in the code's early years its so-called protective aspects were emphasized, Goveia points out these aspects were increasingly forgotten as the

---

[31] All citations are taken from "American Declaration of Independence" in Michael Rosen and Jonathan Wolff, *Oxford Reader in Political Thought* (Oxford: Oxford University Press, 1999).

[32] Ellen Meiksins Wood, "The State and Popular Sovereignty in French Political Thought: A Genealogy of Rousseau's "General Will," in *History From Below: Studies in Popular Protest and Popular Ideology*, ed. Frederick Krantz (Oxford: Basil Blackwell, 1988), 83-84.

[33] Elsa Goveia extensively reviews the different clauses of the code in "West Indian Slave laws of the 18th century," in *Chapters in Caribbean History 2*, eds. Douglas Hall, Elsa Goveia and F. Roy Augier (Barbados: Caribbean Universities Press, 1970), 35-50.

objective of the control of the slave population came to the fore.[34] The sources for the code were Roman slave law, but also the requirements of slave practices in the New World. Thus its overriding framework was to confirm the inferior status of the slave and to maintain public security under the control of the planter colonial class. By 1771, the French Crown issued the following edict:

> It is only by leaving to the masters a power that is nearly absolute, that it will be possible to keep so large a number of men in that state of submission which is made necessary by their numerical superiority over the whites. If some masters abuse their power, they must be reproved in secret, so that slaves may always be kept in the belief that the master can do no wrong in his dealing with them.[35]

To maintain the system of "the property of person" required political structures and governing rationalities of absolute power. If as Michel Foucault suggests that power is a "complex strategical situation" with a "multiplicity of force relations,"[36] then the condition of absolute power is one in which the disciplinary protocols of "governmentality" aimed at creating of the mental horizons of the subject are replaced with a power directed to the biopolitics of "shaping of bodies,"[37] or what I have called elsewhere, "power in the flesh." Within this frame, absolute power creates the conditions for the capacity to determine who is a human being and who is not, and therefore to dictate who can live and who can die. In this context rights are frozen and negated. Such a condition for the exercise of power is of a different order than those which shaped the American and French revolutions. It is within this context that we should examine the 1805 Haitian constitution, which rejected the form of absolute power practiced in slave societies.

---

[34] For a discussion of the so called protective aspects of the Code see Gwendolyn Midlo Hall, *Slave Control in Slave Plantation Societies* (Baltimore: Johns Hopkins University Press, 1971).

[35] Pierre de Vaissiere, *St Dominique, 1629-1789* (Paris, 1909) cited in Goveia, "The West Indian Slave Laws," 44.

[36] For Foucault's discussion on power see Michel Foucault, *Power: The Essential Works of Foucault 1954-1989 Vol. 3)*, ed. James D. Faubion (New York: The New Press, 2000), especially the essay "The Subject and Power."

[37] This phrase is David Scott's. See David Scott, *Refashioning Futures* (New Jersey: Princeton University Press, 1999), Chapter 3.

The 1805 Constitution

The Constitution was promulgated on May 20th, 1805. It was titled the "Imperial" Constitution of Haiti, and was sanctioned by the "Emperor" Jean Jacques Dessalines. Both the title of the Constitution and that of Dessalines should give us pause. Two ideas seem to be at work here. At first blush it seems that the leadership of the revolutionary slaves was reproducing the common political titles of that period in Europe. Indeed Bonaparte had given himself the title emperor. Secondly, it would seem that the title "imperial" implied continuity with French colonial ambitions. The question however that one has to ask is whether or not the political language of "imperial" and "empire" had the same political meanings in early 19th century Haiti as they did in imperial Europe of the period? There are a couple of things which may help us to answer this question. The first is the argument of John K. Thornton, who states that:

> African soldiers may well have provided the key element of the early success of the revolution. They might have enabled its survival when it was threatened by the reinforced armies from Europe. Looking at the rebel slaves of Haiti as African veterans rather than as Haitian plantation workers may well prove the key that unlocks the mystery of the success of the largest slave revolt in history.[38]

Thornton observes that a significant number of the slaves originated in the lower Guinea coast and the coastal area of Angola, and hence it was quite possible that many of them would have been involved with the civil wars of the period in the vast, politically complex Kongo kingdom.[39] Following the thrust of this perspective would suggest to us that ideas of rulership in the political minds of many of the revolutionary slaves circulated around "kingdoms" and notions of "royalty." The meanings and implications of monarchs and royalty in general were complex in pre-colonial African thought.[40] At the core there seems to be a complicated relationship between kingship, rulership and religious doctrines. Within

---

[38] John K. Thornton, "African Soldiers in the Haitian Revolution," *The Journal of Caribbean History* 25 (1991): 74.

[39] Thornton has further developed these arguments in his "'I am the subject of the King of Congo': African Political Ideology and the Haitian Revolution," *Journal of World History* 4 (1993): 181-214.

[40] The matter is actually even more complex, as the European translation of such words tends to assign the gender male, where the African language often does not. The Kongo and Ngola polities abound in Nzingas, both King and Queen, for example. (I am indebted to Professor Geri Augusto for these observations).

some Bantu languages, the word king comes from *Kani* and is tied to the verb *gan*, which means to tell stories or pronounce judgment. The conception of kings therefore seems to be organized around questions of the origins of "kingdoms," as well as around the performance of the function of a ritual mediator within communities. Of course, all of this is but a small slice of the story, since on the African continent there were myriad forms of political practices. However for the Kongo kingdom, at least, the notion of king as mediator—and one whose powers were mediated by the existence of other aristocrats and a set of indigenous political practices—seems to have been dominant.[41]

These understandings seem to have been influential in Haiti when we observe that during the course of the revolution itself there were vigorous attempts to establish free black communities, and that such communities were politically organized around African conceptions of kingdoms. One important community was the Kingdom of Platons organized in the southern part of the island. Studies on this community show that the ex-slaves developed a civil government and chose a king as formal titular leader.[42] What is important to note about this form of civil government was that it also seemed to contain the tensions present in 18th century Kongolese political thought in which kings could either govern as absolute monarchs, or had to govern by rules within the framework of consensual arrangements with the governed.

The second thing which may help us to grapple with the meanings of the titles has to do with the ways in which many of the revolutionary leaders advocated a political position that would use political power abolish slavery in the Caribbean and Africa. In the 18th and 19th century worlds of racial slavery and colonialism the invasion of an island or colony for the major purpose of the abolishment of slavery was of a different order from the enterprise of colonial conquest, which first established racial slavery and plantation societies in the New World. So, there are other possible meanings to the ways in which "imperial" and "emperor" were generally thought about in the early 19th century.

---

[41] For an examination of this see Christopher Ehret, *The Civilizations of Africa: A History to 1800* (Charlottesville: University Press of Virginia, 2002), as well as John K. Thornton, *The Kingdom of Kongo, Civil War and Transition, 1641-1718* (Madison: University of Wisconsin Press, 1983).

[42] For a discussion of this community see Carolyn E. Fick, "Dilemmas of Emancipation: From Saint Domingue Insurrections of 1791 to the Emerging Haitian State," *History Workshop Journal* 46 (1998), 1-13.

If the titles within the Constitution seem at first glance to be enmeshed in political language which is ambiguous and mimics colonial France, in actuality the preamble of the document is one of the most radical political declarations of the period. After listing the names of the generals who signed the document, the Haitian 1805 Constitution goes on to declare:

> As well in our name as in that of the people of Haiti, who have legally constituted us faithfully as organs and interpreters of their will, in the presence of the Supreme Being, before whom all mankind are equal and who has scattered so many species of creatures on the surface of the earth for the purpose of manifesting his glory and his power by the diversity of his works in the presence of all nature by whom we have been unjustly and for long time considered as outcast children...[43]

There are here of course echoes of the political discourses which were prevalent in the French Revolution. But there are quite a few things as well at work which overturned the foundations of Western political thought of the period. The section that addresses the conception of will was clearly influenced by the political discourse of Jean-Jacques Rousseau and his ideas about contract theory and the "general will."[44]

These ideas were of course popular within French revolutionary circles. For Rousseau the "the general will" was an attempt to resolve the thorny issue of sovereignty, making the state a legitimate public site and allowing natural liberty to be recaptured within what was then called civil society. It was an answer to the problem he himself eloquently posed in his introductory note to *The Social Contract*: "I want to inquire whether, taking man as they are and laws as they can be made to be, it is possible to establish some just and reliable rule of administration in civil affairs."[45] The "general will" therefore had two sides to it. First, it was a foundational

---

[43] Imperial Constitution of Haiti (1805) translated by Jiminie Ha. I wish to thank her for the translation of the entire document.

[44] See for current discussion about Rousseau's political thought, Susan Dunn, ed., *Rethinking the Western Tradition: The Social Contract and the First and Second Discourses, Jean-Jacques Rousseau* (New Haven: Yale University Press, 2002). For a interesting contextual view of Rousseau's genealogy of general will see Ellen Meiksins Wood, "The State and Popular Sovereignty in French Political Thought: A Genealogy of Rousseau's 'General Will'," in *History from Below: Studies in Popular Protest and Popular Ideology*, ed. Frederick Krantz (Oxford: Basil Blackwell, 1988).

[45] Jean-Jacques Rousseau, "The Social Contract," in *Rethinking the Western Tradition*, ed. Susan Dunn, 155.

mechanism for administration. Secondly, it was representative of the deepest political desires of a population. In the Haitian case I would suggest that the expression was primarily used in the second sense. We should also note that when the Haitian Constitution's preamble goes on to speak about the equality of mankind it does so by breaking entirely new ground in this period of colonial modernity simply because it was the most inclusive statement about general human equality of the period.

All the major revolutionary documents of the late 18th and early 19th centuries addressed the issue of the equality of mankind. The American declaration of 1776 stated that "these truths to be self-evident, that all men are created equals..." The French 1789 declaration proclaimed that "Men are born and remain free and equal in rights..." *But we know that neither declaration applied to slaves.* Slavery was not abolished in the United States until 1865 and even though the French National Assembly abolished slavery in 1794, it was reinstated under Napoleon Bonaparte in 1802. On the other hand, the 1805 Haitian Constitution formally confronted the "great chain of being"[46] conceptions of human beings that undergirded Western thought during this period. It did so by arguing that God had scattered human species all over the world to show both his glory and diversity, and that people of African descent had been considered outcast because of slavery. Its explicit opposition to Africans as inferior was the recognition by the revolutionary slaves of one dimension of racial oppression. It was a dimension that was never recognized by any other revolution of the period. The preamble therefore shattered racialized thinking of the period. What is also intriguing is its appeal to a "supreme being." All the revolutionary declarations of the period made the same appeal. However what was different in the Haitian case is how that appeal made God an active being.[47]

Central to all political life are the role of symbols and the naming of entities. The Haitian revolutionary slaves recognized this when in one of their first acts after the war of independence they renamed the previous French colony of St. Domingue as Haiti, its early Amerindian name. Such a symbolic reordering of the island's name was central to the revolutionary

---

[46] For a discussion the this idea and its seminal influences in racist thinking see Winthrop D. Jordan, *White Over Black: American Attitudes Toward the Negro, 1550-1812* (Chapel Hill: University of North Carolina Press, 1969), Chapter 13.

[47] It is interesting to speculate upon the similarities of this conceptualization and some of the views of ancestors and a Supreme Deity in many African indigenous religions, but that is a matter for another paper.

leadership's self–identification with the struggles of the indigenous population against colonial conquest. The Haitian historian Thomas Madiou makes the point that:

> On everyone's lips was the name of "Haiti" a reminder of the island's native inhabitants, who has been wiped out defending their freedom. It received an enthusiastic welcome, and the local people called themselves "Haitians."[48]

From the preamble the Constitution is then constructed into two sections. The first proclaims fifty three articles under seven headings, ranging from a political description of Haiti as "empire," to the establishment of various organs of government. The second section contains another twenty eight articles under the rubric, "general dispositions." In the first section the Constitution affirms the new name of the island, Haiti, and states that "The people... hereby agree to form themselves into a free state, sovereign and independent of any other power in the universe under the name of empire of Haiti." It then goes to proclaim that, "slavery is forever abolished" and that the "citizens of Haiti are brothers at home; equality in the eyes of the law is incontestably acknowledged and there cannot exist any titles, advantages, or privileges, other than those necessarily resulting from the consideration and reward of services rendered to liberty and independence."

There are major political and social ideas embedded in the above statements which suggest a different track than the common revolutionary ideas of the French and American Revolutions. In the first place there is a distinction between liberty and independence. In the Haitian 1805 Constitution, liberty is a clear reference to the condition of the ex-slave, a condition in which they were no longer property. This was different from the liberty of radical Western political thought of the period. In the American declaration liberty was understood as an "unalienable right." This right was one amongst two others, the right to life and the right to pursue happiness. In this sense of right, liberty was tied to conceptions of Lockean natural law and natural liberty. Locke had defined the latter in the following way: "The Natural Liberty of Man is to be free from any Superior Power on earth, and not to be under the Will or Legislative

---

[48] Cited in David Patrick Geggus, *Haitian Revolutionary Studies* (Bloomington: Indiana University Press, 2002), Chapter 13.

Authority of Man, but to have only the Law of Nature for his Rule."[49] This form of natural liberty depended upon issues which revolved around political authority. Its thrust was common to the   political idea of the Free State governed by general public participation. It is accurate to say that for Locke, this "legislative authority" was in his words one that had to be established by consent," again confirming the ground for the definition of liberty as a political one.

In the French case, liberty is listed amongst other rights, "property, security and resistance to oppression." The 1789 declaration attempts to define liberty in a different way than the American declaration. It states in article four:

> Liberty consists in the freedom to do everything, which injures no one
> else; hence the exercise of the natural rights of each man has no limits
> except those, which assure to the other members of the society the
> enjoyment of the same rights. These limits can only be determined by
> law.[50]

It has been argued that it was not possible on the grounds of the French declaration of liberty to have a social system constituted upon the "property of the person." Therefore as Shanti Singham argues this section of the declaration was the cause of conflict amongst the French revolutionaries as it related to black slaves, Jews and women.[51] However it should also be noted that the French National Assembly did not abolish slavery until 1794, when the Haitian Revolution forced the question.[52]

---

[49] John Locke, *Two Treatises of Government* (Cambridge: Cambridge University Press, 1988), 283.

[50] Declaration of the Rights of Man and Citizens (1789) in Michael Rosen and Jonathan Wolff, *Political Thought* (Oxford: Oxford University Press, 1999).

[51] For a good discussion of this see Shanti Marie Singham, "Betwixt Cattle and Men: Jews, Blacks and Women and the Declaration of the Rights of Man," in *The French Idea of Freedom: the Old Regime and the Declaration of Rights of 1789*, ed. Dale Van Kley (Stanford: Stanford University Press, 1999), Chapter 3.

[52] What is also interesting in the general debates in political philosophy about the elements of the declaration is how the discussion ignores racial slavery. See for examples of this Giorgio Agamben, *Homo Sacer: Sovereign Power and Bare Life* (Stanford: Stanford University Press, 1998), Part 3.2, and Etienne Balibar, *Masses, Classes and Ideas: Studies on Politics and Philosophy before and After Marx* (New York: Routledge, 1994), Chapter 2.

It is intriguing as well to note what sections of the French declaration were most cited and used by the French colonial planters in Haiti. Phillip Curtin makes the point that during this period articles 1, 2, 6 and 18 were appropriated by the planters in their struggles for greater autonomy from France.[53] In particular article eighteen, which declared in part that "property being an inviolable and sacred right, no one may be deprived of it...", allowed the planters to argue that since the slaves were property, then the French Revolution in the colony of Saint-Domingue was not about slavery but about the "general will" of the whites and their relationship to France. The French radicals who were sympathetic to the abolition of slavery, and organized in the Society of the Friends of Blacks, themselves were initially timid about abolition. In 1790 in an address to the National Assembly the *Societé des Amis des Noirs* argued for the end of the slave trade calling it despotism. They said:

> we are not asking you to restore to French blacks those political rights which alone, nevertheless, attest to and maintain the dignity of man; we are not even asking for their liberty... we ask only that one cease butchering thousands of blacks regularly every year in order to take hundreds of captives.[54]

Therefore on the question of racial slavery, Western political thought and the revolutionaries during the period of the "The Age of Revolution" were either timid about the matter, or at worst ignored it. Part of the timidity rested in a philosophical anthropology which excluded Africans from the ladder of humanity; another aspect of this reluctance rested in the then-dominant conception of freedom tied to political liberty. The 1805 Haitian Constitution by separating liberty from independence shattered the overarching conceptions of racial slavery. Slavery was no longer the lack of self-government, as in the American case, but instead was both an ideology and a practice of the domination of the "person as property." Haitian liberty by challenging this domination was a different kind of freedom than the practices of natural liberty of the period. It was a freedom which allowed for the creation of a politically independent state

---

[53] Phillip D. Curtin, "The Declaration of the Rights of Man in Saint-Domingue, 1788-1791," *The Hispanic American Historical Review* 30 (1950), 157-175.
[54] Address to the National Assembly in favor of the Abolition of the slave trade, February 5th, 1790, published in Lynn Hunt, *The French Revolution and Human Rights: A Brief Documentary History* (Boston: Bedford/St Martin's, 1996), 107-108.

and created the conditions for human equality of laws, which were unconditional.

Twice the document calls attention to a sovereign state which it refers to as "empire of Haiti". What could this mean? Was it a signal for imperial ambitions? The Constitution spells out the nature of the "empire of Haiti" in articles 15, 16, 17 and 18. These articles proclaim that "the Empire of Haiti is one and indivisible, its territory is distributed into six military divisions." The articles then go on to say that the "generals of the division are independent of each other and shall correspond directly with the Emperor, or with the general in chief appointed by his Majesty." This section of the Constitution is then immediately followed by a section titled "of the Government," suggesting that there was a major distinction in the minds of the framers between military rule and political government. I wish to suggest that military rule in Haiti was conceived of in the classical sense of empire, *imperium*. Pierre Manent in his remarkable essay on the intellectual history of liberalism makes the point that the early ideas of empire did not correspond to what he calls the "conquering zeal of a few individuals." But rather, they corresponded to men's unity, to the universality of human nature, which wants to be recognized and addressed by a unique power".[55] I would suggest that this political usage of the term was   similar to that used in the 1805 Haitian Constitution, because when we further examine the sections of the document dealing with government what is emphasized is the unity of the population under the rulership of the emperor.   We should also note that this emperor is not a hereditary one and can be removed by the state council.[56] As well article thirty-six prohibits the emperor from making any conquest, "nor to disturb the peace and interior administration of foreign colonies."

Within the context of the power of Atlantic plantation slavery and colonialism, the Haitian revolutionaries felt that they had to construct a state in which the military and national unity were the dominant features of national political and social life. The reason for this resided in the fact that the Haitian revolutionaries were never sure when a return to slavery

---

[55] Pierre Manent, *An Intellectual History of Liberalism* (Princeton: Princeton University Press, 1995), 3.
[56] We should recall here the mighty efforts of Napoleon Bonaparte to make his emperorship a hereditary one. For a discussion of this see the magisterial work by Francois Furet, *Revolutionary France, 1770- 1880* (Oxford: Basil Blackwell, 1988). Of course there is no serious mention in this major historical study of the Haitian Revolution.

would be forced upon them by armed invasion, surrounded as they were by slave societies from North America to Brazil. The leadership therefore structured a polity in which over time the military came to play a special and large role. Thus it was not surprising that one article of the Constitution proclaimed "At the first firing of the alarm gun, the cities disappear and the nation rise." Later on, this privileging of the military created enormous difficulties for the development of forms of radical democracy. Thus, two contradictory logics there would emerge within the dual Haitian revolution. One logic circled around practices of freedom of the ex-slave, and the other around the revolutionary army, which becomes a political elite with different conceptions of what the new state should be. This was recognized in the middle of the Nineteenth century with the emergence of subaltern groups who struggled for radical democratic forms of participation asking the question "What kind of free is this?"[57]

Race and Citizenship

Both the American and the French Revolutions established, alongside notions of rights, a conception of the citizen. In these revolutions rights were concretely located in the human who was a citizen, not a subject. To be a subject was to be in servitude but to be a citizen was to be in a position to lay claim to rights. One issue which therefore faced revolutions in this "Age of Revolution" was who should be a citizen? Within the French context the debates about rights and citizenship continued five years after the 1789 declaration and were centered on voting rights and political equality. It was the revolutionary National Convention in 1794 that finally eradicated the property rights for voting while abolishing slavery. In the Haitian Revolution citizenship was linked to two things.

In the first instance, while the French and American revolutions dodged the issue of racial oppression, the Haitian revolutionary Constitution of 1805 proclaimed "the Haitians shall henceforward be known only by the generic appellation of Blacks." This was a profound move on two levels. On the first level it was the reversal of the dominant idea that people of African descent were inferior. By making all Haitians black the Constitution reversed the colonial hierarchical status of human

---

[57] For a very good discussion of this period of Haitian history and the emergence of these groups see, Mimi Sheller, *Democracy after Slavery: Black Publics and Peasant Radicalism in Haiti and Jamaica* (Gainesville: University Press of Florida, 2000).

beings. Secondly, the Constitution stated that white women who "have been naturalized Haytians by the Government... [and] the Germans and Polanders naturalized by government" were Haitians and could also own property. This was central to the conception of Haiti as a black republic, particularly since no "Whiteman of whatever nation he may be shall put his foot on this territory with the title of master or proprietor, neither shall he in future acquire any property therein." For the Haitian revolution therefore citizenship was linked to the capacity to own property, and a positive identification with blackness. This notion of blackness removed its biological basis and made it a political construct.

In terms of rights, all Haitian male citizens were given the same rights and were to be treated with equality under the law. There was masculinity to the Constitution which we should note as article nine declared: "No person is worthy of being a Haitian who is not a good father, a good son, good husband and especially a good soldier." It is once again clear that the military arts were held in high esteem as a central value of citizenship. Again given the context such a value was not surprising. Before leaving the 1805 Constitution we should note that the document allows for the freedom of religion, recognizes the right of every citizen to have a legal defense, and secures the privacy of a citizen's household. Divorce was also permitted.

In what ways can we say that the 1805 Constitution differed from the declarations of the French Revolution? Alexis de Tocqueville makes the point that the achievement of the French Revolution was that it replaced the political institutions of European feudalism "with a new social and political order, based on the equality of all men".[58] This equality was folded into a set of rights both political and civil, and became defined as natural liberty. In the Haitian Revolution the achievement was freedom—the creation of a form of society in which persons were no longer property. Such a dynamic did not negate rights and equality but instead folded them into a notion of freedom larger than that of mere natural liberty. This version of freedom, one in which rights and equality all tumble together, continues to animate radical Caribbean political thought. This is why in the mid-Nineteenth century Haitians could ask "What kind of free is this?"

---

[58]Alexis De Tocqueville, *The Old Regime and the French Revolution* (New York: Anchor Books, 1983), 20.

Before we leave the revolution it may be important to quickly review some of the concrete practices of freedom in which the ex-slaves engaged during its course. These practices can fall under two headings, economic and gender. At the level of the economic, the evidence is clear the in many parts of Haiti, the male ex-slaves formed assemblies on the plantation where they worked and elected management; and that they decided on a five-day work week. They also decided on the prices at which the surpluses of the estate should be sold. Alongside this there were instances in which the male ex-slaves formed brigades which controlled the estates where the planter had abandoned property. All these forms of economic production collided with the revolutionary leadership thrust at the time to develop state-run or planter-run plantations. It was in part the reason for the growing alienation between Toussaint and the ex-slaves. With regard to gender, the most significant thing was the ways which female ex-slaves organized themselves to demand and win equal pay for equal work. This claim was supported by many men in spite of numerous official appeals to the contrary.[59] In all of this we might well understand the lament of one French observer, that the black ex-slave was "unambitious and uncompetitive, the black values his liberty only to the extent that it affords him the possibility of living according to his own philosophy".[60] His was the lamentation of a world turned upside down, of a different conception of freedom.

We can turn now to our final question about the Haitian revolution. In what ways did the Haitian Revolution's abolition of slavery differ from that of other abolition movements of the period, particularly in the French colonies? Here again de Tocqueville might be a useful guide. In a 1843 series of essays on slavery and its abolition he argues that:

> However important the position of the blacks may be, however sanctified their misfortune must be in our eyes, the costs of emancipation are distributed that seems equitable among all those who have interest... complete freedom is to be granted after then years until then, a series of measures [must be undertaken] to morally improve and civilize the Negroes.[61]

---

[59] For an excellent discussion of some of these actions please see Fick, *The Making of Haiti.*
[60] Cited in Fick, *The Making of Haiti*, 179.
[61] Alexis de Tocqueville, *Writings on Empire and Slavery* (Baltimore: John Hopkins University Press, 2001), 221.

This argument was very similar to those of British abolitionism and represented the mid-19th century liberal hostility to slavery, but one shaped by notions of improvement and the civilizing mission of Western civilization.[62] The dual Haitian revolution therefore was the most radical revolution of the period. It enacted a form of abolition in which the enslaved acted and made attempts to create new ways of life through practices of freedom . The dual Haitian revolution posed questions about freedom which are yet to answer in the contemporary world, these would include issues to do with wage labor and the relationship between the social and political as it is worked through a practice of freedom which is not founded primarily on political equality.

Haitian Constitution and Caribbean Freedom

The general discussion about constitutions suggests that they are written in political languages which presuppose forms of critical negotiations in a community held together by agreed conceptions of the common good. The modern constitution is different from the so called "ancient" constitution in that the latter is based upon custom and tradition, while the modern constitution is considered "an act whereby a people frees itself (or themselves) from custom and imposes a new form of association by an act of will, reason and agreement."[63] Certainly, the 1805 Haitian Constitution represented a new type of association between humans in the world of Atlantic slavery and colonial modernity. It did this in two ways. First, it made Haiti the first non-slave society in the Atlantic world. Secondly, it posited a new definition of blackness. These two elements, issues of slavery and identity, would become central in the Caribbean story of freedom. It would make that story of freedom different from those told in civic republicanism or liberalism. If the conventional stories of freedom revolve around the political and issues of sovereignty, then freedom in the Caribbean, and I would argue in the Black Atlantic tradition seeks to grapple not so much with political authority as a special form of domination, but instead focuses on wider forms of human domination. Caribbean freedom (and I would argue freedom in Africa and the general African diaspora) has a preoccupation with values like dignity and respect in ways which the other stories of freedom do not pay

---

[62] For a discussion of this see Anthony Bogues, "J.S. Mill , the Negro Question and the Ladder of Civilization," in *Race and Modern Philosophy*, ed. Andrew Valls (Ithaca: Cornell University Press, 2005).

[63] James Tully, *Strange Multiplicity: Constitutionalism in an Age of Diversity* (Cambridge: Cambridge University Press, 2002), 60.

attention to.   Importantly, both conceptions and practices of freedom within the African diaspora do not separate into distinct realms politics and economics, but rather see economics as central to any program of freedom.[64] To think about the origins of Caribbean freedom therefore is to grapple with another narrative of human effort in colonial modernity. It is to recognize the call of Boukman, the revolutionary slave prophet when, the night before the slave insurrection in Haiti, he asks the revolutionary slaves to listen to the "voice of liberty that speaks in the soul of each of us." That liberty was a quest against human domination. It is a quest we might want to pay attention to.

Bibliography

Acosta, Jose de. *Natural and Moral History of the Indies*, edited by Jane E. Mangan, with commentary by Walter Mignolo, translated by Frances López-Morrillas. Durham: Duke University Press, 2002.

Agamben, Giorgio. *Homo Sacer: Sovereign Power and Bare Life* (Stanford: Stanford University Press, 1998.

Balibar, Etienne. *Masses, Classes and Ideas: Studies on Politics and Philosophy before and After Marx*. New York: Routledge, 1994.

Berlin, Isaiah. *Four Essays on Liberty*. Oxford: Oxford University Press, 1969.

Bogues, Anthony. "J. S. Mill, the Negro Question and the Ladder of Civilization." In *Race and Modern Philosophy*, edited by Andrew Valls. Ithaca: Cornell University Press, 2005.

—. *Black Heretics, Black Prophets: Radical Political Intellectuals*. New York: Routledge, 2003.

—. *Empire of Liberty: Power Desire and Freedom*. Lebanon, NH: Dartmouth College Press, 2010.

Collier, Gordon. "The 'Noble Ruins' of Art and Revolution." *In Fusion of Cultures?*, edited by Peter O. Stummer and Christopher Balme. (Amsterdam: Rodopi B. V. 1996.

Constant, Benjamin. "The Liberty of the Ancients and the Liberty of the Moderns." In *Political Thought*, edited by Michael Rosen and Jonathan Wolf. Oxford: Oxford University Press, 1999.

---

[64] One of the failures of the revolutionary leadership of the Haitian revolution is that it did not grasp the ways in which the revolutionary ex-slaves had a view of freedom, which did not entail wage labor. This is important because it is only in the mid-19th century with the work of Marx that questions of freedom begin to be discussed in relationship to wage labor.

Curtin, Phillip D. "The Declaration of the Rights of Man in Saint-Domingue, 1788-1791." *The Hispanic American Historical Review* 30 (1950): 157-175.

Dayan, Joan. "Legal Slaves and Civil Bodies." In *Materializing Democracy: Toward a Revitalized Cultural Politics*, edited by Rus Castronovo and Dana Nelson. Durham: Duke University Press, 2002.

—. *Haiti, History and the Gods*. Berkeley: University of California Press, 1998.

Douglass, Frederick. *My Bondage and My Freedom*. Penguin: New York, 2003.

Dunn, Susan, ed. *Rethinking the Western Tradition: The Social Contract and the First and Second Discourses, Jean-Jacques Rousseau*. New Haven: Yale University Press, 2002.

Ehret, Christopher. *The Civilizations of Africa: A History to 1800*. Charlottesville: University Press of Virginia, 2002.

Fanon, Frantz. *Black Skin White Masks*. New York: Grove Press, 1967.

Fick, Carolyn E. "Dilemmas of Emancipation: From Saint Domingue Insurrections of 1791 to the Emerging Haitian State." *History Workshop Journal* 46 (1998): 1-13.

Fick, Carolyn. *The Making of Haiti*. Knoxville: University of Tennessee Press, 1990.

Fisher, Sybille. *Modernity Disavowed*. Durham: Duke University Press, 2004.

Foucault, Michel. *Power Essential Works of Foucault 1954-1989 Volume 3*. New York: The New Press, 2000.

Fouchard, Jean. *The Haitian Maroons: Liberty or Death*. New York: Edward W. Blyden Press, 1981.

Furet, Francois. *Revolutionary France, 1770- 1880*. Oxford: Basil Blackwell, 1988.

Geggus, David Patrick. *Haitian Revolutionary Studies*. Bloomington: Indiana University Press, 2002.

Goveia, Elsa. "West Indian Slave laws of the 18th century." In *Chapters in Caribbean History 2*, edited by Douglas Hall, Elsa Goveia and F. Roy Augier. Barbados: Caribbean Universities Press, 1970.

Gray, John. *Liberalism*, Minneapolis: University of Minnesota Press, 1995.

Hall, Gwendolyn Midlo. *Slave Control in Slave Plantation Societies*. Baltimore: Johns Hopkins University Press, 1971.

Honohan, Iseult. *Civic Republicanism*. London: Routledge, 2002.

Hunt, Lynn. *The French Revolution and Human Rights:A Brief Documentary History*. Boston: Bedford/St Martin's, 1996.

Jordan, Winthrop D. *White Over Black: American Attitudes Toward the Negro, 1550-1812.* Chapel Hill: University of North Carolina Press, 1969.

Las Casas, Bartolomé de. *A Short Account of the Destruction of the Indies.* London: Penguin Books, 1992.

Lewis, Gordon. *Main Currents in Caribbean Thought.* Kingston: Heinemann Educational Books, 1983.

Locke, John. *Two Treatises of Government.* Cambridge: Cambridge U Press, 1988.

Manent, Pierre. *An Intellectual History of Liberalism.* New Jersey: Princeton University Press, 1995.

Meiksins Wood, Ellen. "The State and Popular Sovereignty in French Political Thought: A Genealogy of Rousseau's "General Will." In *History From Below: Studies in Popular Protest and Popular Ideology* edited by Frederick Krantz. Oxford: Basil Blackwell, 1988.

Pagden, Anthony. *Lords of all the World.* New Haven: Yale University Press, 1995.

Patterson, Orlando. *Slavery and Social Death: A Comparative Study* Cambridge: Harvard University Press, 1982.

Pocock, J. G. A. *The Machiavellian Moment: Florentine Political Thought and the Atlantic Republican Tradition.* Princeton: Princeton University Press, 1975.

Rosen, Michael and Jonathan Wolff. *Political Thought.* Oxford: Oxford University Press, 1999.

Rosen, Michael and Jonathan Wolff. *Oxford Reader in Political Thought.* Oxford: Oxford University Press, 1999.

Scott, David. *Conscripts of Modernity.* Durham: Duke University Press, 2005.

—. *Refashioning Futures.* Princeton: Princeton University Press, 1999 .

Sheller, Mimi. *Democracy after Slavery: Black Publics and Peasant Radicalism in Haiti and Jamaica.* Gainesville: University Press of Florida, 2000.

Singham, Shanti Marie. "Betwixt Cattle and Men: Jews, Blacks and Women and the Declaration of the Rights of Man." In *The French Idea of Freedom: the Old Regime and the Declaration of Rights of 1789* edited by Dale Van Kley. Stanford: Stanford University Press, 1999.

Skinner, Quentin. *Liberty before Liberalism.* Cambridge: Cambridge U Press, 1998).

Thornton, John K. "African Soldiers in the Haitian Revolution." *The Journal of Caribbean History* 25 (1991): 59-80.

—. "'I am the subject of the King of Congo': African Political Ideology and the Haitian Revolution." *Journal of World History* 4 (1993): 181-214.

—. *The Kingdom of Kongo, Civil War and Transition, 1641-1718.* Madison: University of Wisconsin Press, 1983.

Tocqueville, Alexis de. *The Old Regime and the French Revolution.* New York: Anchor Books, 1983.

—. *Writings on Empire and Slavery.* Baltimore: John Hopkins University Press, 2001.

Trouillot, Michel-Rolph. *Silencing the Past: Power and the Production of History.* Boston: Beacon Press, 1995.

Tully, James. *Strange Multiplicity: Constitutionalism in an Age of Diversity.* Cambridge: Cambridge University Press, 2002.

Vaissiere, Pierre de. *St Dominique, 1629-1789.* Paris, 1909.

Webking, Robert H. *The American Revolution and the Politics of Liberty.* Baton Rouge: Louisiana State University Press, 1989.

CHAPTER EIGHT

LOVE, JUSTICE AND NATURAL LAW: ON MARTIN LUTHER KING, JR. AND HUMAN RIGHTS

VINCENT W. LLOYD

There is no question that Martin Luther King, Jr. has a prominent place in the Twentieth century history of human rights. Not only is he recognized for the role he played as an activist in, and symbol of, the movement that improved the treatment of African Americans, but his work and words also inspired a broad range of what could be called human rights movements, particularly in the global South. Yet the canon in which King is placed is often that of human rights in practice, as opposed to human rights in theory. The implication is that human rights are an assumed end; King mobilizes the means. His oratory receives more attention than his thought. He is taken to be a rhetorician, not a philosopher, and his ideas are of little interest. Those who take the enactment of social justice as primary also are not particularly interested in King's ideas. For them "human rights" sounds like a highfalutin notion, a phrase used to mobilize a certain class—educated white liberals—to support a grassroots social movement. For them, human rights in theory is human rights as ideology, and King is concerned with the only sort of human rights that matters—the practice of protesting injustice.

Perhaps by taking King's ideas seriously the implicit bifurcation of the human rights canon between theory and practice will come into question —and along with it the view of human rights as first world ideology that is supported by and supports that bifurcation. Taking King's ideas seriously is a tricky business, for he was, indeed, a rhetorician. Although he was trained as a theologian—*Doctor* King—his theological views were eclectic. While some scholars and commentators have attempted to systematically interrogate and organize his intellectual influences and affiliations by kneading rhetorical language into theological or philosophical argument, here I will suggest a different approach. My interest is in King's words as rhetoric, but I do not take the label of rhetoric as pejorative. I take it as calling attention to performance, to what King's language *does*. And I will argue that this is where King contributes to discussions of human rights—through his rhetoric of natural law which, in its performative dimension, provides a dynamic, flexible fount from which a human rights imagination—including human rights "theory"— can be renewed.

King's rhetoric of natural law is particularly potent and has often been ignored. The dismissal of natural law language as "mere" rhetoric betrays an allergy to religion, to taking religious language seriously, endemic amongst academics and the cultural elite—at least until recently. Under the ideology of secularism, the only logical possibility is that religious language is "mere" rhetoric: speculation about what it would mean if it were anything more is only suited for seminaries and divinity schools.[1] As the obvious limits of the ideology of secularism have become evident with the increasing in-your-face, in-the-news presence of those who take their religion seriously, this has begun to change. The conservative legal scholar Robert George has suggested that the divorce of human rights and natural law is itself a product of secularist ideology, and that once secularist dogma is abandoned a continuous, the robust tradition in which human rights and natural law are deeply intertwined, will come into view.[2] For George, King is a pillar of this tradition. Tantalizing as this conclusion is, it also elides the all too obvious differences between, say, King and the conservative U.S. Supreme Court Justice Clarence Thomas, whom George also associates with this tradition. An examination of King's views of natural law in a post-secularist context avoids this pitfall.

There is no easy starting point. The very question of what natural law is brings with it so many answers that we are tempted again to throw up our hands and slouch towards an easy dismissal of natural law language as "mere" rhetoric. Contemporary debates in the philosophy of law treat

---

Thanks to Owais Khan and José-Manuel Barreto for helpful comments on this text.
[1] For a criticism of secularist ideology and gestures towards an alternative, see Talal Asad, *Formations of the Secular: Christianity, Islam, Modernity* (Stanford: Stanford University Press, 2003); Dipesh Chakrabarty, *Provincializing Europe: Postcolonial Thought and Historical Difference* (Princeton: Princeton University Press, 2000).
[2] Robert P. George, *The Clash of Orthodoxies: Law, Religion, and Morality in Crisis* (Wilmington: ISI Books, 2001), Chapter 9.

natural law simply as the opposite of positive law. Philosophers committed to a positive law position hold that there is no necessary connection between law and morals; those committed to a natural law position hold that there is. In other words, natural law jurisprudence holds that our view of the law can be colored by our moral beliefs, our beliefs about right and wrong. To this one might respond: Isn't the claim of natural law trivially true? Isn't law obviously connected with our beliefs about right and wrong? Proponents of positive law would note that what matters, to judges and lawyers and citizens, is just that a law exists; it is a separate question altogether, a question for a separate, political process, to create *good* or *just* laws. That moral question is bracketed when we think about jurisprudence, claim positive law theorists say: a law is a law, with all what entails—for example, an obligation to obey. Not so, say natural law theorists: an unjust law is no law at all; citizens have no obligation to obey unjust laws. Note how natural law in this context is about neither of the topics with which it is most often associated in the popular imagination: religion or nature.

Stepping from contemporary philosophy of law to the historical tradition of religious and secular reflection on natural law, the meaning of natural law is rather different. In this tradition there is not just a generic moral domain that influences our view of the law—that is necessarily connected with what the law is. There is a specific, alternative law, a law that is in some sense "higher." It is this higher law that colors our view of actually existing law, of worldly law. If worldly law is in conflict with this higher law, worldly law is no law at all. The crudest form of this higher law, the form that has a tendency to capture—perhaps to titillate—the public imagination is a higher law derived from facts about nature, or human nature, or about what is right and wrong from God's perspective. A more sophisticated form of this higher law combines these: through human nature certain portions of God's law, the eternal law, can be known, and it is these—along with certain extra portions ascertained through revelation —that are to influence how we view worldly law. Human nature here is not some set of characteristics shared by all humans—it is not that they are featherless bipeds. Rather, it is a capacity that all humans share: a capacity to reason. It is through humans' capacity to reason that we are capable of ascertaining what the higher law is. Once again, natural law is quite different than its caricature's association with religion or nature. Now it is much more about reason: reason that is characteristic of human nature, and reason as the means by which a portion of God's law, the eternal law, can be known.

Yet these two senses of natural law do not seem to provide an especially helpful framework to approach what Martin Luther King, Jr. might mean by natural law. Certainly, he is appealing to a higher law, but never does King suggest that it is through some process of deep thought, of rational reflection, that this higher law is ascertained. Perhaps we should turn to another tradition of reflection on "higher law," a tradition particular to the United States. The first sentence of the U.S. Declaration of Independence refers to "the Laws of Nature and of Nature's God" to defend the "equal station" of the colonists and the English. There is a strand of political thought, and jurisprudence, which understands these words to place God's law at the heart of the law of the United States.[3] The "higher" law against which actually existing law can be checked is two things at once: the Declaration of Independence and the law of God—they are one and the same. In this tradition, labeled by Daniel Elazar the American Covenant Tradition, the Declaration of Independence provides the spirit of the law and the Constitution—with its references to slavery, *inter alia*—provides the letter of the law; the letter must be interpreted in light of the spirit. As a consequence, rulings of the Supreme Court remain subject to critique, on this view, for the Supreme Court interprets the letter of the Constitution and often forgets the spirit animating that letter of the law—the God-given spirit.

King has been read as part of the American Covenant Tradition, as a political theorist who privileges the Declaration of Independence.[4] On this reading, King's religious language, his talk of God's law, is not dismissed, but it is subsumed through its association with the higher law of the Declaration of Independence. It is not "mere" rhetoric, but it is a rhetoric that locates King in a tradition of the United States patriots, focusing on his aspiration to make a better nation rather than to make a holy nation, whatever that might mean—Frederick Douglass's occasionally patriotic language has sealed him to a similar fate in the hands of recent interpreters. Yet is this not just another byproduct of secularist ideology, of the need to understand religious language through some other, non-religious framework?

During his first civil rights campaign, the Montgomery bus boycott, King would employ the language of natural law in a call for social justice.

---

[3] Daniel J. Elazar, *Covenant & Constitutionalism: The Great Frontier and the Matrix of Federal Democracy* (New Brunswick: Transaction Publishers, 1998).
[4] Barbara Allen, "Martin Luther King's Civil Disobedience and the American Covenant Tradition," *Publius* 30 (2000): 71-113.

Through this campaign he would achieve international recognition; at the time it began, he was a 26 year old junior minister who had just finished his academic studies. Born in Atlanta to an earthy minister in 1929, King started his studies at the historically black Morehouse College when he was 15. He continued his studies at Crozer Theological Seminary and Boston University, where he wrote a dissertation titled "A Comparison of God in the Thinking of Paul Tillich and Henry Wiseman." During these years, King was exposed to, and sought out, a wide array of intellectual influences. He read Marx, Gandhi and Thoreau. He was influenced by the socially engaged Christianity of Walter Rauschenbusch and Reinhold Niebuhr, as well as the lively debates between liberal and neo-orthodox strands of Protestantism represented by Paul Tillich and Karl Barth, respectively. Of course, King also took courses in the history of Christian thought; his papers from this time show that he studied heresies and orthodoxies from the first centuries onwards. He wrestled with perennial theological questions, and he had a particular interest in understanding humanity's fallen condition.[5]

King read widely, and he was no one's disciple. His own views were decidedly eclectic, so much so that the distinctiveness of King's own theological voice has become a matter of scholarly debate—the discovery of widespread plagiarism in his dissertation made this question all the more troublesome.[6] While some scholars have attempted to discern a system in King's thought—to claim a place for him amongst U.S. Twentieth century systematic theologians—this effort seems to rest on a certain forgetfulness of King's vocation.[7] He was first and foremost a preacher, and a persuader. He knew his audiences: what they believed, what would affect them, and what would move them, whether his audience

---

[5] Martin Luther King Jr., *The Papers of Martin Luther King, Jr.*, ed. Clayborne Carson, Ralph Luker and Penny A. Russell (Berkeley: University of California Press, 1992-). For a recent assessment of King's theological influences, see Richard W. Wills, *Martin Luther King Jr. and the Image of God* (Oxford: Oxford University Press, 2009).

[6] Martin Luther King, Jr., Papers Project, "The Student Papers of Martin Luther King, Jr.: A Summary Statement on Research," *The Journal of American History* 78 (1991): 23-31.

[7] In contrast to Richard W. Wills, Timothy Jackson begins with the premise that King is not a systematic theologian. Timothy Jackson, "Martin Luther King, Jr. (1929-1968)," in *The Teachings of Modern Christianity on Law, Politics, and Human Nature, Vol. 1*, ed. John Witte, Jr. and Frank S. Alexander (New York: Columbia University Press, 2006).

was his theology school professors, his black congregants, or white liberal supporters.

The speeches and texts of King's career employ a whirlwind of references that authorize and position King and his political work. Reference to natural law is sometimes caught up in this whirlwind, one of many intellectual affiliations that come fast and furious. In his "Letter from Birmingham City Jail," King provides a textbook account of Aquinas's natural law theory: "How does one determine when a law is just or unjust? A just law is a man-made code that squares with the moral law or the law of God. An unjust law is a code that is out of harmony with the moral law. To put it in the terms of St. Thomas Aquinas, an unjust law is a human law that is not rooted in eternal and natural law".[8] But then King quickly moves on, in the next sentence gesturing towards the Personalist theology King encountered at Boston University and associating it with natural law theory. He writes, "Any law that uplifts human personality is just. Any law that degrades human personality is unjust". A couple sentences later, King is on to another intellectual influence: "To use the words of Martin Buber, the great Jewish philosopher, segregation substitutes an 'I-it' relationship for the 'I-thou' relationship, and ends up relegating persons to the status of things. So segregation is not only politically, economically and sociologically unsound, but it is morally wrong and sinful". And then, to conclude the paragraph, King is on to yet another profound influence: "Paul Tillich has said that sin is separation. Isn't segregation an existential expression of man's tragic separation, an expression of his awful estrangement, his terrible sinfulness?".

In the face of such eclecticism, where King seems to be weaving together all the religious reflection that he can get his hands on into an incontrovertible brief against segregation, the dual temptations to dismiss each of King's references or to organize them into a logical system grow all the stronger. But King's famous "Letter" was written in 1963, and the circumstances of its composition—and its authorship—limit its helpfulness in understanding King's thought on natural law, beyond the reminder that the language of natural law remained an important part of King's

---

[8] Martin Luther King Jr., *A Testament of Hope: The Essential Writings and Speeches of Martin Luther King, Jr.*, edited by James M. Washington (San Francisco: HaperSanFrancisco, 1986), 293.

vocabulary throughout his career as an organizer, agitator and minister.[9] Let us return to that first moment when King stepped into the spotlight, that first campaign in Montgomery, Alabama, to improve the treatment of black people on the public buses. It was not King who chose the moment. But, soon after the respectable Rosa Parks was arrested for failing to give up her seat on a public bus to white passengers, topping off a pattern of ill treatment by the bus company, the African American ministers of Montgomery took the lead in organizing a response. As a new preacher in town, King stood apart from the divisions and grudges of other old time ministers who might have been chosen to lead the protest movement. And, of course, King could preach.

In his account of the Montgomery protest movement, King describes how he was used to spending many hours in preparation before his Sunday sermons; before his first speech to the nascent bus boycott movement, he had but a few minutes to prepare.[10] He would speak the words that came to him, and he did so with tremendous success. "We will be guided by the highest principles of law and order," he intoned.[11] A wonderfully ambiguous statement, King was at once differentiating the boycott movement from vigilante whites and associating it with the Kingdom of God. The former task required special delicacy, as organizations such as White Citizens Councils and the Ku Klux Klan themselves claimed the moral high road. When the Supreme Court forced school integration, these organizations could appeal to a "higher" law, beyond the law of worldly Courts. The challenge of distancing the tactics of the civil rights movement from that of its staunchest opponents would dog King and other leaders, and would contribute to the evolution of natural law language that King employed. However, in 1955, in Montgomery, Alabama, King began by separating the just cause of the boycott organizers from the injustice advocated by their opponents, focusing on the means by which each side sought to implement its higher law. Even if each side was willing to set aside the law on the statute books in favor of a higher law, the bus boycotters—or so King extolled—would not employ any violence in doing so. The methods of the partisans of segregation "lead to violence and lawlessness," kidnappings and lynch mobs. The methods of the boycotters, while not

---

[9] See S. Jonathan Bass, *Blessed Are the Peacemakers: Martin Luther King, Jr., Eight White Religious Leaders, and the "Letter from Birmingham Jail* (Baton Rouge: Louisiana State University Press, 2001).
[10] Martin Luther King, Jr., *Stride towards Freedom: The Montgomery Story* (Boston: Beacon Press, 2010).
[11] Ibid., 51.

necessarily following the letter of the law, would be peaceful and would not undermine the rule of law in general.

The other associations conjured by King with his invocation of "the highest principles of law and order" were theological. He proceeded to assert, "[O]ur actions must be guided by the deepest principles of our Christian faith. Love must be our regulating ideal".[12] Whatever else, the blacks of Montgomery must not hate their enemies. The "law and order" that King envisioned was the law and order characteristic of a world animated by love, and that world was accessible through Christian faith. Jesus Christ provided a model of perfect loving, the model that was to be imitated in the present, in the face of the bleak circumstances faced by the African American community of Montgomery. The boycott they were about to undertake did not have only a pragmatic purpose—to make the lives of a few people in one corner of the world better. It had a divine purpose, and that vision of a community with love as its regulating ideal was to animate—in a strong sense, more than motivate—the boycott movement throughout its duration. Indeed, King argues in retrospect, it would be impossible to explain the origins of the Montgomery bus boycott without attributing agency to the divine.

At that first meeting of the black protesters, the idea of the boycott was still inchoate. The grand ideals of faith and love did not immediately translate into a call for equality, or even an awareness that the higher law to which the protesters were committed might be in conflict with the law of the land. Three demands were put forward at that first meeting, and they were far from revolutionary. The protesters would end their boycott when they were assured of "courteous treatment", when the bus company employed black bus drivers, and when "passengers were seated on a first-come, first-served basis—Negroes seating from the back of the bus towards the front while whites seated from the front towards the back."[13] In other words, there was no initial demand for desegregation, just a demand for gentler segregation. Moreover, the boycotters at first argued that they were demanding nothing more than compliance with existing law; the bus drivers had been going beyond the law by not only segregating buses, but allowing whites to sit in seats that should have gone to blacks if segregationist law was implemented correctly.

---

[12] Ibid.
[13] Ibid., 97.

However, these moderate demands soon grew into a demand for fully desegregated buses. The tension between the "highest principles of law and order" invoked by King and the actually existing laws, manipulated by the white-dominated city government to criminalize the boycott, became too great. Further, the boycotters learned the degree to which the meaning of the law of the land would be manipulated by its authorized interpreters in order to justify the status quo. In early negotiations to conclude the boycott, King and his associates presented their argument that the boycott's demands required no change in the law. While one city official agreed with the boycotter's interpretation of the law, another dissented, offering not a legal basis for his dissent but a political one. "If we granted the Negroes these demands," the bus company's attorney argued, "they would go about boasting of a victory that they had won over the white people"[14]. From this the protesters discovered that injustice and law could be entangled much more thoroughly than they had imagined—and the higher law to which they appealed seemed all the more distant. Those "highest principles" were not to be found in Montgomery, at least not until the intervention of the United States Supreme Court.

In the years following the Montgomery bus boycott, King appealed to a higher law, or to God's law, in his political speeches and sermons. In one sermon, drawing on the thought of the modernist minister Harry Emerson Fosdick, King speaks of the obligation to love as different in kind from the obligation to obey worldly laws. It is "a higher law" that produces love, he argues, and so matters of love are outside the jurisdiction of worldly courts. Here King equivocates, noting the possibility of ending segregation "by the force of law," even if it would be impossible for the federal courts to force southern whites to love blacks.[15] There is a tension in King's remarks—or perhaps a rhetorically forceful elision—in that the strict division he ostensibly imagines between "higher law" and worldly law cannot hold. He imagines worldly law as pragmatically useful, forcing integration of public institutions even if it does not end irrational fears and resentments. Such feelings as these are "dark and demonic responses" to the changing worldly law; such feelings would change when "the invisible, inner law which etches on their hearts the conviction that all men are brothers" takes effect.[16] Yet it is just this disposition to love, alternately labeled by King here "higher law" and "inner law," that is also

---

[14] Ibid., 100.

[15] Martin Luther King, Jr., *Strength to Love* (Philadelphia: Fortress Press, 1981), 37.

[16] Ibid., 38.

"mankind's most potent weapon for personal and social transformation".[17] So potent is this higher or inner law that it motivates the pragmatic use of worldly law in the interest of creating a more loving world. And so we are back to the conventional conceptual arrangement of natural law theory: a higher law against which the legitimacy of worldly laws can be judged. That higher law is determined by something that human beings share, the capacity to love—but note the distinctiveness of this position, as opposed to other natural law theories that focus on a shared human capacity to reason as the means to access that higher law, a point that will be discussed more extensively below.

Elsewhere in his sermons, King abandons the pretense of confining "higher law" to the "inner" world of individuals. Writing of world history and the connection between struggles against colonialism and against segregation, King writes: "There is a law in the moral world—silent, invisible imperative, akin to the laws in the physical world—which reminds us that life will work only in a certain way. The Hitlers and the Mussolinis have their day, and for a period they may wield great power, spreading themselves like a green bay tree, but soon they are cut down like the grass and wither as the green herb".[18] While it seems sensible, at first, to distinguish this sort of "law in the moral world" from the "higher law" or "inner law" about which King elsewhere writes, King forces the distinction to be blurred. In the next paragraphs, he writes of segregation, now moribund, as a system that went against this same moral law; its fate inevitable because of its injustice. The civil rights movement is "God working through history"—necessarily so, because the laws of segregation were "not in harmony with the moral laws of the universe" and so God was acting in the world through the efforts of those who would oppose such an abomination.[19] The connection between God's agency and the moral law is tighter still: it is God, King preaches, who put in place those "absolute moral laws" in the first place. The "forces of evil" tempt us to disobey these laws; it is up to us to resist.

Where do King's natural law ideas come from? The distinctiveness of his views is easy to overlook when we forget the degree to which natural law has been associated with Catholicism, and the more-than-arm's length distance that many mid-century Protestant theologians kept from all things Catholic. Those theological sources with whom King is most often

---

[17] Ibid.

[18] Martin Luther King, Jr., *Stride towards Freedom*, 110.

[19] Ibid., 111.

associated had little to say about natural law, and what they did say was often derogatory. Paul Ramsey, an influential Protestant ethicist, dismisses natural law together with the law codes of the Old Testament in a section of his *Basic Christian Ethics* entitled "What the Christian does without a Code"—the answer, in short, is *love*.[20] Paul Tillich, a towering figure of mid-century U.S. theology and a subject of King's dissertation, associated natural law theory with the Roman Catholic Church's legalistic explication of the Ten Commandments and the Sermon on the Mount. While he affirms the values of equality and freedom he finds in natural law theory, Tillich argues that these concepts, when applied to the existing world "become indefinite, changing, [and] relative," with the result that "natural law theory cannot answer the questions of the contents of justice" —Tillich finds the answers to those questions in love, and power.[21] Reinhold Niebuhr, a renowned public intellectual and theological proponent of "Christian realism," pointedly writes of "the perils of moralism and self-righteousness in the rigidities of the natural law."[22]

If not from the theological giants of his day, where was it that King picked up the idiom of natural law? It is tempting to speculate that haunting the caesura in the evidence is a vernacular African American idiom of God's law and a higher law. It is tempting to imagine that this is a vocabulary that King picked up, say, from the country preaching of his father, or from other black churches he visited as a child in Georgia. And it is tempting to build this idiom into a tradition, stretching to other civil rights activists, such as those students arrested in Lynchburg, Virginia, who stated that their actions were in accordance with "a Higher Law than the law of governments"; to stretch this tradition forwards to Clarence Thomas who writes of picking up the idiom of higher law in his childhood in rural Georgia; and to stretch the tradition backwards, to Frederick Douglass, whose speech opposing the Dred Scott decision appeals to a heavenly court of justice higher than the Supreme Court.[23] Even W. E. B.

---

[20] Paul Ramsey, *Basic Christian Ethics* (New York: Charles Scribner's Sons, 1950).
[21] Paul Tillich, *Love, Power, and Justice: Ontological Analyses and Ethical Applications* (London: Oxford University Press, 1954), 82.
[22] Reinhold Niebuhr, *The Nature and Destiny of Man: A Christian Interpretation, Vol. 1* (Louisville: Westminster John Knox Press, 1996 [1941]), 221.
[23] Davis W. Houck and David E. Dixon, eds. *Religion, Rhetoric, and the Civil Rights Movement* (Waco: Baylor University Press, 2006), 426; Clarence Thomas, *My Grandfather's Son: A Memoir* (New York: Harper, 2007); Frederick Douglass, "Speech on the Dred Scott Decision," in *African-American Social and Political*

Du Bois, religious skeptic that he was, at one point describes his sociological studies of the black community as discerning the "natural law."[24] But the tantalizing possibility that such a vernacular idiom exists must wait for future research to be confirmed or disputed.

However, there is archival evidence that suggests that King's natural law language was shaped by at least one specific, surprising individual, a correspondent who wrote to King in 1960.[25] In November of that year, King participated in a televised debate about "The Nation's Future." His opponent, James Kilpatrick, associated law-abiding behavior with moral behavior, law-breaking behavior with chaos and riots. What civil rights activists were doing, Kilpatrick charged, was breaking the law, and breaking the law leads you down the slippery slope towards violent anarchy. King's too quick response was that an unjust law was no law at all, and should be resisted; Kilpatrick just as quickly pointed out that Southern whites resisting the integration of schools brought about by *Brown v. Board of Education* would readily agree with King. Indeed, some southern whites were proclaiming loudly that integration should be resisted by any means necessary. In the debate, King appeared hesitant and came off as unconvincing—the debate format, limiting the usefulness of King's oratorical gifts, certainly did not help. John H. Herriford, a political science student at the University of Minnesota, watched the debate on NBC and sent King a letter suggesting possible criteria King might use to distinguish just laws from unjust laws, and so to make his argument more compelling. King responded gratefully and requested additional clarification and suggestions. He incorporated Herriford's ideas into his future presentations of natural law theory as a justification for the civil rights movement. Among the ideas that Herriford suggested was the criterion that an unjust law be "tyrannous," and the celebrated phrase "difference made legal."

Thought, 1850-1920, ed. Howard Brotz (New Brunswick: Transaction Publishers, 1992), 247-262.

[24] Cited in Adolph L. Reed, *W. E. B. Du Bois and American Political Thought: Fabianism and the Color Line* (Oxford: Oxford University Press, 1999), 201 n.6; cf. Dwight Hopkins, "W. E. B. Du Bois on God and Jesus," in *The Souls of W. E. B. Du Bois: New Essays and Reflections*, ed. Edward J. Blum and Jason R. Young (Macon: Mercer University Press, 2009), 18-40.

[25] This paragraph draws on Allen, "Martin Luther King's Civil Disobedience," and on archival research at the Dr. Martin Luther King, Jr. Archive housed in the Howard Gotlieb Archival Research Center at Boston University.

In "Love, Law, and Civil Disobedience," a November 1961 address to an interracial audience, the seemingly *ad hoc* manner in which King made use of natural law is brought together and distilled—and secularized. King begins by asserting that an unjust law is one "which does not square with the moral law of the universe."[26] He then imagines a skeptic who is suspicious of "these abstract things" that King is talking about, or suspicious that God has a law at all. King responds by explaining that a law is unjust when it "is a code that the majority inflicts on the minority that is not binding on itself. So that this becomes difference made legal".[27] Further, the minority does not craft this alternative law; it is *inflicted* on the minority. The civil disobedience of the civil rights movement does not lead to anarchy because it affirms that some laws, most laws, are perfectly legitimate and must be followed, just so long as they are not tyrannous, imposed by the majority on the minority. King employs the secular idiom that Herriford suggests with this interracial audience in a way that allows King to hold on to the "higher law" language to which he is committed, but also allows him to translate it for a broader audience by focusing on one specific, purely rational means of accessing that higher law—indeed, King embraces the language of rationality here, describing "just law" as "saneness made legal".[28]

King's natural law language congealed, and took on added importance, for another reason as well. In the mid-century Cold War atmosphere, natural law provided a way for King to differentiate his civil rights work from Communism. Describing his own intellectual development, King recalls reading *Das Kapital* and *The Communist Manifesto* while an undergraduate student at Morehouse College, during the Christmas holiday.[29] After several paragraphs of objections to Communist ideology, and a description of Communism as "basically evil," King finally describes Communism as having "laid hold of certain truths which are essential parts of the Christian view of things." Communism, King suggests, should pose a challenge to every Christian. It is a challenge that can be met by appeal to natural law: "for the Communist there is no divine government, no absolute moral order, there are no fixed, immutable principles; consequently almost anything—force, violence, murder, lying—is a justifiable means to the 'millennial' end." In other words, what Communism is lacking is commitment to a higher law. Even if the *telos* of

---

[26] King, *Testament of Hope*, 49.
[27] Ibid.
[28] Ibid.
[29] King, *Stride towards Freedom*, 92-95.

the Communist is something quite near the beloved community of the Christian, the Communist will strive to reach that *telos* by any means, will break any law, will overturn all laws. The Christian, in contrast, is subject to "fixed, immutable principles" by which she must live even in the pre-millennial world—the distinction is not quite so clear-cut; the laws that civil rights protesters disobeyed were not necessarily the unjust ones: King at Birmingham was in jail for violating a permit law.

While King's natural law language changed over time, and depending on which sort of audience he was speaking to, it never vanished. In his final book *Where Do We Go From Here?*, published in 1967, King brings together the topics for which he is best known, love and justice, on the one hand, and natural law, on the other. Dramatically, King suggests that even more troublesome than the white supremacists of the Ku Klux Klan is the "white liberal who is more devoted to 'order' than to justice, who prefers tranquility to equality."[30] If the crux of natural law for King is an opposition between law and justice, here it seems as though "order" is a proxy for law, and the great shortcoming of the white liberal is that he refuses to acknowledge natural law. In other words, the white liberal knows only worldly law, shutting himself off the higher law, God's law. King no longer writes of justice as defined merely by the absence of tyrannous law, by the absence of "difference made legal." Instead, King writes, "justice at its best is love correcting everything that stands against love".[31] The higher law is the law of love. It is not a law at all in the sense that it does not inflict punishments; it corrects through love. Worldly laws that stand against this higher law are to be corrected in this very way: through love. This is the story of the civil rights movement from King's perspective: unjust worldly laws being disobeyed not out of malice or hate or violence but out of love. And, if we are to allow for God's agency in history, as King would have us do, the disobedience of civil rights movement protesters clearly shows God's workings in the world—because *God is love.*

In *Where Do We Go From Here?* King seems to offer an alternative account of how social justice could be achieved in the United States, an account that focuses on the much more worldly-sounding concept of empathy instead of love or justice. King writes: "Empathy is fellow feeling for the person in need—his pain, agony and burdens. I doubt if the

---

[30] Martin Luther King, Jr., *Where Do We Go From Here: Chaos or Community?* (Boston: Beacon Press, 2010), 93.
[31] Ibid., 38.

problems of our teeming ghettos will have a great chance to be solved until the white majority, through genuine empathy, comes to feel the ache and anguish of the Negroes' daily suffering".[32] Where King earlier in his life, and earlier in this text, spoke of such changes as achievable only through a conversion of individuals' "inner law" to the "law of love," here it seems as though the transformation can take place in this much less mysterious manner, simply through empathy. Perhaps there is a way to close this apparent gap: to read King's discussion of empathy together with his discussion of love, and together with his discussion of law. In this passage, perhaps we can read King as suggesting that empathy is a way through which higher law can be recognized. Through empathy—which any human being, even a white liberal!, can partake in—an individual can be converted to the law of love.

A fundamental, though easily misunderstood, tenet of natural law theory is that higher law is "self-evident." This does not mean that the higher law is obvious, nor does it mean that the higher law is constructed from ethical intuitions. Rather, the higher law is self-evident if it is perceived rightly, but perceiving it rightly can take a good deal of work, and continuing investigation. The dominant group of contemporary natural law theorists, most prominently John Finnis and Robert George, consider reason to be the means by which self-evident precepts are perceived. Indeed, George has taken an emphasis on reason—characteristic of human "nature"—to be the definitive feature of the natural law tradition from Cicero to the medievals to Locke to Jefferson... to King.[33] The inclusion of King in this tradition is perplexing, as King never writes about access to higher law—or God's law—through reason. King writes about access to higher law through empathy, and through love. With the recent surge of interest in affect, restoring affect to full partnership with reason as components of human nature, perhaps King's view of natural law offers a way of re-imagining the natural law tradition itself.[34]

---

[32] Ibid., 107.

[33] George, *Clash of Orthodoxies*.

[34] A recent example in political theory is Sharon R. Krause, *Civil Passions: Moral Sentiment and Democratic Deliberation* (Princeton: Princeton University Press, 2008), but the work of, for example, Eve Sedgewick, Martha Nussbaum, and Simon Blackburn are also relevant. For an interesting attempt to link human rights and affect, see José-Manuel Barreto, "Ethics of Emotions as Ethics of Human Rights: A Jurisprudence of Sympathy in Adorno, Horkheimer and Rorty," *Law and Critique* 17 (2006): 73-106.

Such a grand undertaking is well beyond the scope of this chapter. Let us return to Montgomery, to that first meeting to discuss the bus boycott. In his unscripted speech to the packed church, King followed his appeal to "the highest principles of law and order" with a call to be guided by love as a "regulating ideal." In between, he told his listeners: "Our method will be that of persuasion, not coercion. We will only say to the people, 'Let your conscience be your guide'."[35] The phrase at first seems trite, but perhaps it grows profound when its juxtaposition with love and law is taken seriously. King was extolling his audience not to *think* but to *feel*—to feel the love of God—and to feel love for those who would mistreat them. It is through this feeling of love that they could access the "highest principles of law." And this feeling of love would be contagious: that their position was just would be evident to everyone allowing themselves to feel rightly, to love, to empathize. This is what would stir in the conscience of those they sought to persuade, near and far: right feeling, no longer clouded by the impurities sedimented by years of segregation. And it was this right feeling that King himself transmitted so effectively, so powerfully, to those in the church that evening, and to many others, near and far. Perhaps the example of King suggests that the ancient division between rhetoricians and philosophers must be transformed. A rhetorician is said to persuade that an arbitrary position is correct, and one technique of persuasion is arousing the emotions of his listeners. A philosopher is said to reason, arguing logically to a conclusion that is good and true. Might it be that what King does is to arouse the emotions of his listeners in such a way that the result is not some arbitrary position but what is necessarily good and true? If the higher law, the law within, may be accessed through affect, might it also be contagious—the empathizing, loving soul spontaneously becoming silver-tongued, radiating the goodness, the truth, and the beauty of his conscience?

No doubt this line of questioning pushes much too far. But the direction that it pushes is one that becomes possible when the assumptions of secularist ideology are set aside, when we take seriously religious language, and religious ideas, and religious practice. In this direction may be other resources for reflection on human rights that refuse the comforts of secularism, so central to the self-identity of the West. Also in this direction, when human rights and natural law have ended their forced estrangement, we may find human rights to be more than an empty

---

[35] King, *Stride Towards Freedom*, 62.

signifier—we may find a tradition which is a fount of critical inquiry inextricably linked with movements for social justice.[36]

What of the politically conservative heritage of the natural law tradition, what of Clarence Thomas's uncomfortable association with Martin Luther King? Do they not drink from the same fount? One response would be to associate Thomas with the tradition of natural law inquiry limiting access to natural law to the mechanism of practical reason, distancing him from a vernacular African American natural law tradition that accesses natural law through affect. This is not a satisfactory response because, independent of Thomas's own jurisprudential persuasion, it is clear that affect is not pure, that affect is no guarantor of access to a natural law that furthers a conventional social justice agenda. Indeed, it could not be: the promise of natural law is that its normative consequences are unknown; it is a process of reflection that can and does take a critical stance towards the taken-for-granted politics of the day. And, as an engine for such reflection, there can be as many pathologies of affect as there can be pathologies of reason. Just as the mainstream natural law tradition commends reflection on reason, the natural law tradition of which King is a part must commend reflection on affect, or, as Michel Henry has termed it, auto-affection—affect not tainted by the conventions of the day but given, to return to King's wonderfully uncomfortable language, from God.[37]

Bibliography

Allen, Barbara. "Martin Luther King's Civil Disobedience and the American Covenant Tradition." *Publius* 30 (2000): 71-113.

Asad, Talal. *Formations of the Secular: Christianity, Islam, Modernity.* Stanford: Stanford University Press, 2003.

Barreto, José-Manuel. "Ethics of Emotions as Ethics of Human Rights: A Jurisprudence of Sympathy in Adorno, Horkheimer and Rorty." *Law and Critique* 17 (2006): 73-106.

---

[36] Cf. Costas Douzinas, *The End of Human Rights: Critical Legal Thought at the Turn of the Century* (Oxford: Hart Publishing, 2000).

[37] This, as it happens, is a language to which Henry would assent. See Michel Henry, *I am the Truth: Toward a Philosophy of Christianity*, trans. Susan Emanuel (Stanford: Stanford University Press, 2003), which offers rich resources for reflection on affect, religion, ethics and politics.

Bass, S. Jonathan. *Blessed are the Peacemakers: Martin Luther King, Jr., Eight White Religious Leaders, and the "Letter from Birmingham Jail.* Baton Rouge: Louisiana State University Press, 2001.

Chakrabarty, Dipesh. *Provincializing Europe: Postcolonial Thought and Historical Difference.* Princeton: Princeton University Press, 2000.

Douglass, Frederick. "Speech on the Dred Scott Decision." In *African-American Social and Political Thought, 1850-1920*, edited by Howard Brotz. New Brunswick: Transaction Publishers, 1992.

Douzinas, Costas. *The End of Human Rights: Critical Legal Thought at the Turn of the Century.* Oxford: Hart Publishing, 2000.

Elazar, Daniel J. *Covenant & Constitutionalism: The Great Frontier and the Matrix of Federal Democracy.* New Brunswick: Transaction Publishers, 1998.

George, Robert P. *The Clash of Orthodoxies: Law, Religion, and Morality in Crisis.* Wilmington: ISI Books, 2001.

Henry, Michel. *I am the Truth: Toward a Philosophy of Christianity*, trans. Susan Emanuel. Stanford: Stanford University Press, 2003.

Hopkins, Dwight. "W. E. B. Du Bois on God and Jesus." In *The Souls of W. E. B. Du Bois: New Essays and Reflections*, edited by Edward J. Blum and Jason R. Young. Macon: Mercer University Press, 2009.

Houck, Davis W. and David E. Dixon, eds. *Religion, Rhetoric, and the Civil Rights Movement.* Waco: Baylor University Press, 2006.

Jackson, Timothy. "Martin Luther King, Jr. (1929-1968)." In *The Teachings of Modern Christianity on Law, Politics, and Human Nature, Vol. 1*, edited by John Witte, Jr. and Frank S. Alexander. New York: Columbia University Press, 2006.

King, Jr., Martin Luther. *Strength to Love.* Philadelphia: Fortress Press, 1981.

—. *A Testament of Hope: The Essential Writings and Speeches of Martin Luther King, Jr.*, edited by James M. Washington. San Francisco: HarperSanFrancisco, 1986.

—. *The Papers of Martin Luther King, Jr.*, edited by Clayborne Carson, Ralph Luker and Penny A. Russell. Berkeley: University of California Press, 1992.

—. *Stride towards Freedom: The Montgomery Story.* Boston: Beacon Press, 2010.

—. *Where Do We Go from Here: Chaos or Community?* Boston: Beacon Press, 2010.

Krause, Sharon R. *Civil Passions: Moral Sentiment and Democratic Deliberation.* Princeton: Princeton University Press, 2008.

—. Papers Project. "The Student Papers of Martin Luther King, Jr.: A Summary Statement on Research." *The Journal of American History* 78 (1991): 23-31.

Niebuhr, Reinhold. *The Nature and Destiny of Man: A Christian Interpretation, Vol. 1.* Louisville: Westminster John Knox Press, 1996 [1941].

Ramsey, Paul. *Basic Christian Ethics.* New York: Charles Scribner's Sons, 1950.

Reed, Adolph L. *W.E.B. Du Bois and American Political Thought: Fabianism and the Color Line.* Oxford: Oxford University Press, 1999.

Thomas, Clarence. *My Grandfather's Son: A Memoir.* New York: Harper, 2007.

Tillich, Paul. *Love, Power, and Justice: Ontological Analyses and Ethical Applications.* London: Oxford University Press, 1954.

Wills, Richard W. *Martin Luther King Jr. and the Image of God.* Oxford: Oxford University Press, 2009.

CHAPTER NINE

HUMAN RIGHTS, SOUTHERN VOICES:
YASH GHAI AND UPENDRA BAXI[*]

WILLIAM TWINING

In Ahdaf Soueif's novel, *The Map of Love*, an Egyptian woman, Amal, is expecting an American visitor: "Wary and weary in advance: an American woman -a journalist, she had said on the phone. But she said Amal's brother had told her to call and so Amal agreed to see her. And braced herself: the fundamentalists, the veil, the cold peace, polygamy, women's status in Islam, female genital mutilation—which would it be?"[1]

---

[*] This is a shortened version of the published text of the Annual MacDonald Lecture, delivered at the University of Alberta on March 31st, 2005 and published in *Review of Constitutional Studies* 11 (2006): 203-279. The substance of this article is reproduced here, with minor changes, by kind permission of the copyright holders. The original text also included discussions of the work of Dr Francis Deng and Professor Abdullahi An-Na'im. A reader containing selections of the writings of all four jurists has now been produced as William Twinning, ed., *Human Rights: Southern Voices: Francis Deng, Abdullahi An Na'im, Yash Ghai and Upendra Baxi* (Cambridge: Cambridge University Press, 2009). In addition to being an anthology of the works in the authors' own words, this book contains comparisons of their lives and works and a discussion of a number of issues, such as the meanings of "Southern" and "voice" in this context, unheard voices, and who else might be included in future volumes of this kind. The text of this chapter was completed in 2005; since then all four authors have continued to write with their usual ebullience—a few of their more recent publications are referred to in the footnotes.

[1] Ahdaf Soueif, *The Map of Love* (London: Bloomsbury, 1999), 6.

Amal is a cosmopolitan scholar, who moves easily between the worlds of Cairo, New York and Europe. She is weary of the simplistic repetitious stereotyping of Egypt, Arab culture and Islam by Westerners. Western normative jurisprudence faces similar charges of parochialism about its agenda and about the bearing of other traditions on normative questions.

Western jurisprudence has a long tradition of universalism in ethics. Natural law, classical utilitarianism, Kantianism and modern theories of human rights have all been universalist in tendency. But nearly all such theories have been developed and debated with at most only tangential reference to and in almost complete ignorance of the religious and moral beliefs and traditions of the rest of humankind. When differing cultural values are discussed, even the agenda of issues has a stereotypically Western bias. How can one seriously claim to be a universalist if one is ethnocentrically unaware of the ideas and values of other belief systems and traditions?

As the discipline of law becomes more cosmopolitan it needs to be backed by a genuinely cosmopolitan general jurisprudence.[2] This chapter is part of a project to make the ideas of some individual "Southern" thinkers more accessible to English-speaking audiences. This is part of the larger enterprise of de-parochialising our own traditions of jurisprudence at a time when we need to take seriously the implications of the complex processes of globalization for our understanding of law. The immediate purpose is to provide a clear and fair exposition of their ideas about human rights, based on a finite number of accessible texts, set in the context of their lives and concerns.

Yash Ghai and Upendra Baxi have both been prominent as activists as well as scholars. Ghai has played a major role in post-independence constitution-making and reform, especially in the South Pacific and Kenya. Baxi has been an influential publicist and campaigner in India and on the international stage, as well as serving as Vice-Chancellor of two Indian universities. For the last twenty years he has campaigned and litigated on behalf of the victims of the Bhopal disaster. As theorists they have related, but contrasting perspectives. Both were born in 1938, they were educated in English, studied law in the common law tradition, and

---

[2] William Twining, *Globalization and Legal Theory* (London: Butterworth, 2000); William Twining, *General Jurisprudence: Understanding Law from a Global Perspective* (Cambridge: Cambridge University Press, 2009).

started their careers in the immediate post-Independence period, Baxi in India, Ghai in East Africa. Both have been deeply concerned with problems of racism, colonialism, post-Independence politics, poverty and injustice in the South. Each had a Marxian period, but neither has ever been a doctrinaire Marxist. Each has written extensively about many topics.

Here we are concerned only with their views on human rights. Ghai is skeptical of most claims to universality that are made for human rights; however, adopting a pragmatic materialist stance, he reports that he has found through practical experience of post-colonial constitution-making that human rights discourse provides a workable framework for negotiating political and constitutional settlements among politicians and leaders claiming to represent different majority, minority, and ethnic interests in multi-ethnic societies. It also facilitates popular participation in constitutive processes. Baxi argues that as human rights discourse becomes commodified, professionalized by technocrats, and sometimes hijacked by powerful groups, it is in grave danger of losing touch with the experience of suffering and the needs of those who should be the main beneficiaries—the poor and the oppressed. They are the main authors of human rights. To take human rights seriously, is to take suffering seriously. Ghai and Baxi make a fascinating study in contrasts. Although they differ, they probably do not disagree on most fundamentals. How far they complement each other is for the reader to judge.

Yash Ghai: A Realist and Materialist Interpretation[3]

Yash Pal Ghai, a Kenyan citizen, born in Nairobi in 1938. He went to school there and then studied law in Oxford and Harvard and was called to the English Bar. He started teaching law as a lecturer in Dar-es-Salaam in 1963, eventually becoming Professor and Dean, before leaving in 1971. Since then he has held academic posts in Yale, Warwick and Hong Kong. In addition to numerous visiting appointments, he was Research Director of the International Legal Center in New York 1972 to 1973, and a Research Fellow at Uppsala University from 1973 to 1978. He has written or edited nearly 20 books, mainly about public law and constitutionalism,

---

[3] Yash Ghai's writings on human rights are only one part of his very extensive list of publications. The biographical section draws on publicly available sources, personal knowledge, and (i) "Legal Radicalism, Professionalism and Social Action: Reflections on Teaching Law in Dar-es-Salaam" in *The Limits of Legal Radicalism,* ed. Issa Shivji (University of Dar-es-Salaam, 1986), 26. The section on negotiating claims in multi-ethnic societies draws heavily on two of his publications: (ii) "Universalism and Relativism: Human Rights as a Framework for Negotiating Interethnic Claims", *Cardozo Law Review* 21 (2000): 1095, and (iii) Yash Ghai, ed., *Autonomy and Ethnicity: Negotiating Competing Claims in Multi-Ethnic States* (Cambridge: Cambridge University Press, 2000). The section on the Asian Values debate is based mainly on (iv) "Human Rights and Asian Values", *Public Law Review* 9 (1998): 168, and (v) "The Politics of Human Rights in Asia" in *Frontiers of Legal Scholarship*, ed., Geoffrey Wilson (Chichester: Wiley, 1995); (vi) "Asian Perspectives on Human Rights" *Hong Kong Law Journal* 23 (1993): 342-57; (vii) "Rights, Duties and Responsibilities" in *Asian Values: Encounter with Diversity*, eds. J. Caughelin, P. Lim and B. Mayer-Konig (London: Curzon Press, 1998); (viii) *Asian Human Rights Charter: A People's Charter* (Asian Human Rights Commission, 1998); (ix) "Rights, Social Justice and Globalization in East Asia" in *The East Asian Challenge to Human Rights*, eds. Joanne R. Bauer and Daniel A. Bell (Cambridge: Cambridge University Press, 1999). The section on the role of judges in implementing rights is mainly based on Yash Ghai and Jill Cottrell, eds., *Economic, Social and Cultural Rights in Practice: The Role of Judges in Implementing Economic, Social and Cultural Rights* (London: Interights, 2004). Ghai's views are further developed in recent papers on the right to development, constitutionalism and reflections on constitution-making: "A Journey Around Constitutions," *South African Law Journal* 122 (2005): 804; "Redesigning the State for Right Development" in *Development as a Human Right: Legal, Political and Economic Dimensions*, eds. B-A Andreassen and Susan Marks (Cambridge: Harvard University Press, 2006); "Understanding Human Rights in Asia" in *International Protection of Human Rights: A Textbook*, eds. Catarina Krause and Martin Scheinin (Turku: Institute for Human Rights, 2008) . On his bleak assessment of the state of human rights in Asia see Twining, *Human Rights: Southern Voices*, 120-50. Other writings are cited as they arise.

covering several states and regions, but particularly in Commonwealth countries.

Ghai is highly respected as a scholar, but he is even better known as a legal adviser to governments and agencies, especially in Asia, the South Pacific and East Africa. He has been highly influential on post-independence constitutional development in the South Pacific, serving as constitutional adviser in Papua New Guinea, Vanuatu, Fiji, Western Samoa and the Solomon Islands, among others. He has also been involved in a variety of peace-keeping and trouble-shooting activities in Bouganville, Sri Lanka, Afghanistan, East Timor and Nepal. He has been prominent in debates about public law in Hong Kong and China. In 2005 he was appointed the Special Representative of the UN Secretary-General on human rights in Cambodia. Over the years he has received numerous honors, including election as a Corresponding Fellow of the British Academy in 2005.

From November 2000 to July 2004 he was full-time Chair of the Constitution of Kenya Review Commission, on leave from Hong Kong. Despite enormous difficulties, the Commission produced a draft Constitution in December, 2002, not long before the ouster of President Moi and the ruling party, KANU, in an election that was accepted by foreign observers as being generally "free and fair". Unfortunately, once in power the new leaders were less keen on reform than they had been when in opposition. However, after long delays and a referendum, a watered-down version of the Commission's draft was ratified in August 2010. The killings and displacement of over half a million people that followed the elections of December 2007 were widely attributed by Kenyans and external mediators to the failure to implement the draft Constitution that had been adopted by the Kenya National Conference (serving as a constitutional assembly), which had been chaired by Yash Ghai.

Ghai has unrivalled experience of constitution-making in post-colonial states. Besides his unquestioned academic and practical expertise, he has succeeded in winning the trust of many rival political leaders of different persuasions, often in tense situations, not least because of the obvious sincerity of his commitment to opposing all forms of colonialism and racism. He has shown great courage in standing up to domineering Heads of Government, such as President Moi of Kenya and Prime Minister Hun Sen of Cambodia. His courage and negotiating skills are legendary.

Almost all of the constitutions that Yash Ghai has helped to design and introduce have included a Bill of Rights.[4] They have generally fitted broadly liberal ideals of parliamentary democracy, judicial independence, and the Rule of Law. He has been an outspoken critic of governmental repression, especially detention without trial and torture; but there is a discernible ambivalence in his attitude to human rights. For example, he was editor and principal draftsman of an important report by the Commonwealth Human Rights Initiative, entitled *Put Our World to Rights*,[5] published in 1991. Yet in 1987 he was co-editor (with Robin Luckham and Francis Snyder) of *The Political Economy of Law: A Third World Reader* which presented a distinctly Marxian perspective and which contains no mention of rights, human rights, or constitutional rights in the index, except a few references to habeas corpus.

After the "collapse of communism", symbolized by the fall of the Berlin Wall, some former Marxist intellectuals adopted the discourse of human rights.[6] However, Ghai's ambivalence has deeper roots. Perhaps the key is to be found in the essay "Legal Radicalism, Professionalism and Social Action: Reflections on Teaching Law in Dar-es-Salaam", his own account of his intellectual development. In a refreshingly frank memoir, he tells how he moved from orthodox legal positivism—Oxford and the English Bar—, through a phase of liberal reformism—Harvard and the early years in Dar-es-Salaam—to accepting the basics of Marxist critiques of neo-colonialism and of Julius Nyerere's African Socialism from about 1967.[7] He acknowledges that his acceptance of Marxism was not whole-

---

[4] The most influential model has been the Nigerian Bill of Rights (1959/60), which in turn was heavily influenced by the European Convention on Human Rights. The Independence Constitution of Nigeria represented a change of attitude by the Colonial Office in London, who until then had been lukewarm about bills of rights. Thereafter the Nigerian Bill of Rights became a model for many Commonwealth countries in the period of decolonization. The story is told in A.W.B. Simpson, *Human Rights and the End of Empire* (Oxford: Oxford University Press, 2001), 862-73. However the constitutions with which Ghai has been associated generally involved extensive participatory constitutive processes and are to some extent "home grown".

[5] Ghai was the main author *of Put Our World to Rights* (London: Commonwealth Human Rights Initiative, 1991).

[6] e.g. Issa Shivji, *The Concept of Human Rights in Africa* (London: Codesria, 1989).

[7] This essay appears in a volume commemorating the twenty-fifth anniversary of the Law Faculty of Dar-es-Salaam University: Issa Shivji, ed., *The Limits of Legal Radicalism* (Dar-es-Salam: University of Dar-es-Salaam, 1986).

hearted. He recognized the value of Marxian structural analysis of political economy. But this was tempered by three concerns: first, as an East African Asian he was especially sensitive to racist attitudes that he discerned among locals as well as expatriates: "What passed in general for radicalism in those days included a large amount of racism and xenophobia." [8] Secondly, he had a "predilection for free debate", which was beginning to be stifled by a local form of political correctness; and, thirdly, while his academic colleagues were academically stimulating, most lacked any sense of the importance of legal technicality and practical sense. They taught their students to despise the law, but not how to use it:

> "My experience seemed to point to the problems when fidelity to the law weakens—the arrogance of power, the corruption of public life, the insecurity of the disadvantaged. I was not unaware, of course, of other purposes of the law which served the interests of the rich and the powerful. But the fact was that it did increasingly less and less so; a whole body of statutory law since TANU (the ruling party) came to power had begun to tip the scales the other way. I retained my ambivalence about the legal system, and was not attracted to the attitudes of many private practitioners I met (or the interests they served). At the same time I knew the evasion of the law or the dilution of its safeguards harmed many of the people the radical lawyers were championing." [9]

Ghai's experiences in Dar-es-Salaam were formative in important respects. In nearly of his work since then three tensions are apparent: a strong commitment to certain basic values, tempered by a pragmatic willingness to settle for what is politically feasible in the circumstances; a genuine interest in theory, especially political economy, and a determination to be effective in the role of a good hard-nosed practical lawyer;[10] and a materialist, Marxian perspective on political economy sometimes in tension with a sincere belief in liberal values embodied in the Rule of Law, an independent judiciary, and human rights. For more than thirty years he has also had to balance the demands of teaching, research, and writing with practical involvement in high-level decision-making in a continually expanding range of countries. As a consultant he has also had to reconcile his belief in the importance of local context—historical, political and economic—with a general approach to constitutionalism and constitution-making. He is a rare example of a foreign consultant who genuinely rejects the idea that "one size fits all"

---

[8] Ibid., 27.
[9] Ibid., 29-30.
[10] Ibid., 31.

and he has very extensive practical experience of the tensions between universalism and relativism on the ground.[11]

In the early years of his career, Ghai wrote about many topics mainly from a public law perspective. He joined in East African debates about the arguments for and against Bills of Rights[12] and he addressed particular topics, such as habeas corpus, racial discrimination and the position of ethnic minorities.[13] However, it was not until about 1990 that he focused his attention regularly on human rights as such. This is perhaps due to "the increased salience" that human rights discourse achieved during this period.[14] Even then, he has consistently viewed Bills of Rights and the international human rights regime as one kind of means among many that

---

[11] Ghai's evaluation of this paradox ends with a lament: "Comparative constitutional law has been mired in formalism and pseudo-universalism and the wonderful multiplicity of the constitution has been lost." Ghai, "A Journey around Constitutions", 831.

[12] Yash Ghai and Patrick McAuslan, *Public Law and Political Change in Kenya* (Nairobi and London: Oxford University Press, 1970), at c. XI & XIII. At Independence Kenya opted for a weak bill of rights, while Tanganyika—later Tanzania—decided against one at this stage of development and nation-building. See Julius Nyerere, *Freedom and Unity (Uhuru na Umoja): A Selection from Writings and Speeches 1952-65* (Dar-es-Salam: Oxford University Press, 1966) *passim*, esp. c. 62. Ghai and McAuslan argued that even a limited Bill of Rights is one way of making a government publicly accountable, but after the disillusioning experience of the Kenya Bill of Rights in the immediate post-Independence period, they reluctantly concluded that "an ineffective Bill is worse than no Bill at all, as it raises false hopes... [t]he total effect of the Bill of Rights in practice is occasionally to require Government to do indirectly what it cannot do directly—a strange mutation of its normal role." Ibid., 455-56. This theme is echoed in his more recent writings, for example Yash Ghai, "Sentinels of Liberty or Sheep in Woolf's Clothing? Judicial Politics and the Hong Kong Bill of Rights", *Modern Law Review* 60 (1997): 459. For a subsequent assessment of the Kenyan Bill of Rights, see Yash Ghai, *"Creating a New Constitutional Order: Kenya's Predicament,"* in *Governance, Institutions and the Human Condition*, ed. Elizabeth Gachenga, et al. (Nairobi: LawAfrica & Strathmore University Press, 2009), 13-30. On the post-Independence history of human rights in Tanzania, see Jennifer A. Widner, *Building the Rule of Law: Francis Nyalali and the Road to Judicial Independence in Africa* (New York: Norton, 2001).

[13] See especially Yash Ghai, "Independence and Safeguards in Kenya", *East African Law Journal* 3 (1967): 177; Yash Ghai and D.P. Ghai, eds., *Asians in East and Central Africa* (London: Minority Rights Group, 1971), and Ghai and McAuslan, *Public Law*.

[14] See especially Ghai, "Universalism and Relativism", 1095.

may serve to protect the interests of the poor and the vulnerable as well as satisfying majority and minority interests.[15] As we shall see, his approach has generally been more pragmatic than idealistic and it is only quite recently that he has devoted much space to writing about human rights theory. Rather than try to attempt to trace his intellectual development or summarize his general constitutional theory, I shall here focus on three papers which illustrate more general aspects of his approach to human rights: the role of human rights discourse in reaching constitutional settlements in multi-ethnic societies; his critique of the Asian values" debate of the early 1990s; and his exchange with Abdullahi An-Na'im about the justiciability of economic and social rights. In considering these particular pieces it is important to bear in mind that Yash Ghai is primarily a public lawyer for whom Bills of Rights are only one aspect of constitutionalism and human rights discourse is but one aspect of constitutional and political theory.

Negotiating competing claims in multi-ethnic societies[16]

Yash Ghai, as a Kenyan Asian, comes from an embattled minority. One of his first monographs, written with his brother, an economist, was entitled *Asians in East and Central Africa*.[17] In nearly all of the countries where he has served as a constitutional adviser, protecting the interests of significant ethnic or religious minorities has presented a major problem. And, of course, multiculturalism is a pervasive phenomenon in most societies today. So it is hardly surprising that this theme has been in the foreground of his more general writings on human rights.

In a symposium published in the *Cardozo Law Review* in February 2000,[18] Ghai drew on his experiences of constitution-making to make what is perhaps his fullest statement of a general position on human rights. His central thesis is that both debates about universalism and relativism and about 'Asian Values' obscure the political realities and the potential

---

[15] For example, in discussing issues and prospects for constitution-making in post-war Iraq, "full respect for the principles of universal human rights" is only one of nine principles to be accommodated in a settlement likely to be acceptable to the Shia and other groups." Yash Ghai, "Constitution-making in a new Iraq" in *Building Democracy in Iraq*, eds. Yash Ghai, Mark Lattimer and Yahia Said (London: Minority Rights, 2003), 27.

[16] For the main sources of this section, see *supra* note 3.

[17] Ghai and Ghai, *Asians in East and Central Africa*.

[18] Ghai, "Universalism and Relativism."

practical uses of human rights discourse as a flexible framework for negotiating acceptable compromises between conflicting interests and groups.

Ghai warns against interpreting human rights discourse too literally or solely in ideological terms. Rather, he adopts "a more pragmatic and historical, and less ideological, approach."[19]. In his experience, concerns about "culture" have in practice been less important than the balance of power and competition for resources. Human rights rhetoric may be used —sometimes cynically manipulated—to further particular interests or, as in the 'Asian values' debate to give legitimacy to repressive regimes by emphasizing the right to self-determination of sovereign states—but not necessarily of peoples or minorities within those states.

Nevertheless, in his view, human rights discourse has provided a useful framework for mediating between competing ethnic and cultural claims, and in combating repressive regimes, just because it is flexible and vague and not rigidly monolithic.[20] In domestic constitutive processes and constitutional law the international human rights regime has provided a crucial reference point for local debates. In a study of constitution-making in four quite different countries—India, Fiji, Canada, and South Africa—he found that the relevance of rights was widely acknowledged, much of the content and orientation of competing viewpoints was drawn from foreign precedents and international discourse, and groups presented their claims in terms of different paradigms of rights, drawn largely from transnational sources. In short, international norms and debates were used as resources for local arguments and negotiations in the process of achieving a constitutional settlement:

---

[19] Ibid., 1099.

[20] "By the 'framework of rights' I mean the standards and norms of human rights reflected in international instruments and the institutions for the interpretation and enforcement of rights. This means that no permissible policies are arbitrary. Instead, they must be justified by reference to a recognized right, the qualifications that may be lawfully imposed on the right, or a balance between rights. The procedures and guidelines for the balance and tradeoffs must be included within the regime of rights. The notion of framework also refers to the process of negotiations or adjudication which must be conducted fairly within certain core values of rights. There must also be the acceptance of the ultimate authority of the judiciary to settle competing claims by reference to human rights norms." Ibid., 1103-04.

"For multicultural states, human rights as a negotiated understanding of the acceptable framework for coexistence and the respect for each culture are more important than for mono-cultural or mono-ethnic societies, where other forms of solidarity and identity can be invoked to minimize or cope with conflicts. In other words, it is precisely where the concept or conceptions of rights are most difficult that they are most needed. The task is difficult, but possible, even if it may not always be completely successful. And most states today in fact are multicultural, whether as a result of immigration or because their peoples are finding new identities."[21]

Ghai uses his four case studies to explode a number of myths: First, he challenges the assumption that culture is the salient element in determining attitudes to rights, a matter of significance when "cultural relativism" is invoked to undermine the case for human rights.[22] "Culture" is not irrelevant, but it operates in complex ways. Culture is not monolithic, but protean; no community has a static culture;[23] cultures change and intermix; homogeneity of culture within a nation state is nowadays exceptional, and indeed much state effort is devoted to artificially creating a common culture as a prop for national unity. Questions of the relation of rights to culture arise *within* communities, as when women or minorities have invoked rights to challenge or interrogate "tradition". As Santos and others have suggested, cross-cultural discourse can generate new forms and enrich the culture of rights.[24] Perhaps, most

---

[21] Ibid., 1102.

[22] In respect of the four case studies he concluded: " 'Culture' has nowhere been a salient element determining attitudes to rights. It has been important in Fiji, Canada, and South Africa, but it has been important in different ways... With the exception of the Canadian first nations ['the Aborigines'], the proponents of the cultural approach to rights were not necessarily concerned about the general welfare of their community's cultural traditions. They were more concerned with the power they obtain from espousing those traditions... The manipulation of 'tradition' by Inkatha is well documented. Fijian military personnel and politicians who justified the coup were accused of similar manipulation by a variety of respectable commentators." Ibid., 1135-36.

[23] cf. Fishbayn's insightful paper on judicial interpretations of "culture" in family cases in South Africa: Lisa Fishbayn, "Litigating the Right to Culture: Family Law in the New South Africa," *International Journal of Law, Policy and the Family* 13 (1999): 147.

[24] Ghai, "Universalism and Relativism," 1098, citing Boaventura de Sousa Santos, *Towards a New Common Sense* (London: Routledge, 1995). See Jeremy Webber's thesis that aboriginal rights in Canada are best understood to be the product of cross-cultural interaction rather than as the result of some antecedent body of law. Jeremy Webber, "Relations of Force and Relations of Justice: The Emergence of

important, Ghai emphasizes that "the material bases of 'rights' are stronger than cultural."[25]

Second, Ghai attacks as a myth the idea that the origins and current support for universal rights are solely Western. Historically, the sources of the international regime are quite diverse, with different "generations" having different supporters.[26] During the colonial period, for example, the British were among the strongest opponents of rights talk, especially in relation to self-determination or local Bills of Rights. At that time, nationalist leaders were strong supporters of human rights, especially the right to self-determination, but that enthusiasm did not always survive beyond Independence. Bentham, Burke, and Marx were among the critics of rights within the Western tradition. During the Cold War the Eastern bloc generally championed social and economic rights, the Western powers individual civil and political rights. In South Africa it was the whites, who historically opposed universal human rights, and, after the end of apartheid, it was the black majority who were the most committed to them.[27] In modern times political leaders have invoked "the right to self-determination" as a defense against external criticism of internally repressive regimes and at the same time dismiss "rights discourse" as a form of Western neo-colonialism—as in "the Asian values" debate.

It is no doubt true that the current international regime of rights derives largely from western intellectual traditions, but Ghai points out that today "there is very considerable support for rights in Asia, among parliamentarians, judges, academics, trade unionists, women's groups, and other non-governmental organizations."[28] When Western-dominated organizations, such as the World Bank, International Monetary Fund and state foreign aid agencies, promote "human rights and good governance and democracy" they tend to emphasize a narrow band of individual and property rights rather than the whole spectrum that were included in the

---

Normative Community between Colonists and Aboriginal Peoples", *Osgoode Hall Law Journal* 33 (1995): 624.

[25] Ghai, "Universalism and Relativism," 1100 and 1136.

[26] Compare Upendra Baxi's account of alternative human rights histories, *infra* 'Two Paradigms of Human Rights in History: "The Modern" and "The Contemporary".'

[27] Ghai, "Universalism and Relativism", 1137-38.

[28] Ghai, "Human Rights and Asian Values", 169.

original Universal Declaration of Human Rights.[29] Such selectivity illustrates the flexibility, and possibly the incoherence, of the general framework of rights discourse. Whatever the origin, the general framework and current support are not specifically Northern or Western.

Third, Ghai strongly challenges the use of sharp dichotomies in this context. For example, he identifies at least five types of relativist positions that need to be distinguished:[30] (i) strong cultural relativism, viz. that rights depend upon culture rather than universal norms; (ii) that cultural differences do indeed exist, but only the Western concept of human rights is acceptable as a basis for universal norms. Conversely, some Asian politicians argue that their societies are superior to the West because their cultures emphasize duty and harmony rather than individual rights and conflict; (iii) moderate cultural relativism—i.e. that a common core of human rights can be extracted from overlapping values of different cultures;[31] (iv) that cultural pluralism can be harmonized with international standards by largely internal re-interpretation of cultural tradition—this is

---

[29] The Universal Declaration of Human Rights includes social, economic and cultural rights as well as civil and political rights, and recognized the importance of duties. Ibid, 170.

[30] Ghai, "Universalism and Relativism", 1095-99. The formulation in the text is mine. Ghai's categories are recognizable, but some writers distinguish between many more positions. On the ambiguities of "relativism" see Susan Haack, *Manifesto of a Passionate Moderate* (Chicago: University of Chicago Press, 1998), c. 9.

[31] A prominent modern example is Alison Dundas Renteln, *Relativism and the Search for Human Rights* (London: Sage, 1990). See also Alison Dundas Renteln, "Relativism and the Search for Human Rights", *American Anthropologist* 90 (1988): 64. This continues a tradition that can be traced back to the search for cultural universals by George P. Murdock and the attempts by Father Thomas Davitt SJ. to find empirical support for natural law in universal values and norms in preliterate societies e.g. Thomas Davitt SJ., "Basic Value Judgments in Preliterate Custom and Law", Council for the Study of Mankind, Conference on Law and the Idea of Mankind (Chicago, 1963/4) (unpublished paper). Apart from problems of the "naturalistic fallacy"—deriving 'ought' propositions from 'is' premises—, such efforts tend to encounter two main lines of objection: (i) that general prescriptions of the kind "killing is condemned in all known societies" are so hedged with exceptions and qualifications as to have virtually no content and (ii) such accounts tend to play down or pass over in silence unattractive near-universals such as aggression and the subordination of women. Ghai cites Charles Taylor arguing that, although human nature is socially constructed there is often sufficient overlap to ground a workable common core of human rights. Ghai, "Rights, Social Justice and Globalization", 241.

the basic approach of Abdullahi An Na'im.[32] (v) That an enriched version of rights can be developed by inter-cultural discourse, which can lead towards a new form of universalism. Ghai concludes:

> "On the more general question of universalism and relativism, it is not easy to generalize. It cannot be said that bills of rights have a universalizing or homogenizing tendency, because by recognizing languages and religions, and by affirmative policies a bill of rights may in fact solidify separate identities. Nevertheless, a measure of universalism of rights may be necessary to transcend sectional claims for national cohesion. Simple polarities, universalism/particularism, secular/religious, tradition/modernity do not explain the complexity; a large measure of flexibility is necessary to accommodate competing interests. Consequently most bills of rights are Janus-faced (looking towards both liberalism and collective identities). What is involved in these arrangements is not an outright rejection of either universalism or relativism; but rather an acknowledgement of the importance of each, and a search for a suitable balance, by employing, for the most part, the language and parameters of rights."[33]

On the basis of these four case studies, backed by his wide practical experience, Ghai suggests some further general conclusions: First, rights provide a framework not only for cross-cultural discourse and negotiation, but also "to interrogate culture" within a given community, as when women have used them to challenge traditionalists in Canada, India, and South Africa.[34]   Second, "in no case are rights seen merely as protections against the state. They are instruments for the distribution of resources, a basis for identity, a tool of hegemony, and they offer a social vision of society. Rights are not necessarily deeply held values, but rather a mode of discourse for advancing and justifying claims."[35]   Third, in multicultural societies, balancing of interests requires recognition of collective as well as individual rights, including rights connected with being a member of a group, as with affirmative action in India.[36] Fourth, where rights are used for balancing interests, there is no room for absolutism of rights. They have to be qualified, balanced against each other, or re-conceptualized.[37] Fifth, a stable settlement in a multi-ethnic society often involves

---

[32] See Twining , "Human Rights, Southern Voices", c. 3.4.
[33] Ghai, "Universalism and Relativism", 1139-40.
[34] Ibid., 1137.
[35] Ibid.
[36] Ibid., 1138.
[37] Ibid.

recognition and appropriate formulation of social, economic, and cultural rights. This in turn requires an activist state.[38] Sixth, "since interethnic relations are so crucial to an enduring settlement , and past history may have been marked by discrimination or exploitation, a substantial part of the regime of rights has to be made binding on private parties".[39] Finally, the requirements of balancing conflicting interests within a framework of rights, gives a major role to the judiciary in interpreting, applying, and reinterpreting the constitutional settlement in a reasoned and principled way.[40]

Ghai's approach is illustrated by his treatment of the so-called "Asian Values debate". This is widely perceived as a concerted attack on human rights by spokesmen for what is wrongly regarded as representing some kind of Asian consensus. Ghai argues that the debate has obscured both the complexity and the richness of debates about rights within Asia.

The "Asian Values" debate(s)[41]

"The authoritarian readings of Asian values that are increasingly championed in some quarters do not survive scrutiny. And the grand dichotomy between Asian values and European values adds little to our understanding, and much to confounding of the normative basis of freedom and democracy." Amartya Sen [42]

"The Asian Values debate" refers to a controversy that flared up in the run- up to the Vienna World Conference on Human Rights in 1993. After the collapse of communism, increased attention to human rights issues had led to growing criticism of human rights violations in China and also in countries that had been allies in the Cold War. This was also the period of increased conditionalities being imposed by international financial institutions and Western aid agencies in the name of "human rights, good governance and democracy". In a regional meeting preparatory to the Vienna Conference, many Asian Governments signed "The Bangkok Declaration", which was widely interpreted as an attempt to present a

---

[38] Ibid.
[39] Ibid.
[40] Ibid. 1138-39. See, however, his caveats about the role of the judiciary in relation to economic and social rights, discussed below.
[41] For sources of this section see *supra* note 3.
[42] Amartya Sen, "Human Rights and Asian Values: What Lee Kuan Yew and I Peng don't understand about Asia", *The New Republic*, July 14, 1997, 40.

united front against growing Western hegemony. Lee Kuan Yew (and the Government of Singapore) and Muhathir Mohamed (and the Government of Malaysia), who could hardly be considered representative of the whole of Asia, framed this North-South confrontation in terms of a fundamental conflict between "human rights and Asian values".[43]

The Asian values debate has rumbled on for over a decade and has surfaced in a number of different contexts, of which one of the most interesting and important is the positions taken by China both internally and externally in response to western criticism.[44] Yash Ghai was one of a number of "Southern" intellectuals who jumped to the defense of ideas about human rights and democracy as not being peculiarly Western. In a series of papers published between 1993 and 1999, he sharply criticized the arguments and positions adopted by the leaders of Singapore and Malaysia and in the process developed his own general position on human rights.[45]

We need not enter into the details of Ghai's criticisms of the Singapore and Malaysian versions of the "Asian values" position, which he treats as

---

[43] Accessible documents include The Bangkok Governmental Declaration (1993), online: www.unhchr.ch/html/menu5/wcbangk; Government of Singapore, *Shared Values* (Singapore: Government Printers, 1991), and a useful symposium in *Foreign Affairs* 73 (1994): 109-26, including an interview of Lee Kuan Yew by Fareed Zakaria, and the response by Kim Dae Jung, "Is Culture Destiny?". See also Bauer and Bell, *The East Asian Challenge.*

[44] See, e.g., Ann Kent, *China, the United Nations and Human Rights: The Limits of Compliance* (Philadelphia: University of Pennsylvania Press, 1999) and Rosemary Foot, *Rights Beyond Borders* (Oxford: Oxford University Press, 2000). .

[45] In the version of "the Asian values position" advanced by Lee Kuan Yew and the Government of Singapore the core of the argument is summarized by Ghai as follows: (1) The West is decadent—lawless, amoral, and in economic decline. This decadence is due to its emphasis on democracy and human rights based on extreme individualism. "Rights consciousness has made people selfish and irresponsible and promoted confrontation and litigiousness." (2) Asian societies have maintained social stability, economic progress, and a sense of moral purpose on the basis of a culture and ethos that emphasizes duties and subordinates individual interests to the welfare of the community. (3) There is a Western conspiracy to subvert Asian political independence and economic success by imposing decadent alien values on Asian culture. Ghai challenges all of these positions. Ghai, "Human Rights and Asian Values", 176-77; cf. the more detailed critique in Ghai, "The Politics of Human Rights in Asia".

both insincere and confused.[46] He suggests that the true motive for their campaign was to justify authoritarian regimes at a time when they were being subjected to criticism both internally and internationally for repression of dissent and civil liberties. However, participating in the debates sharpened Ghai's focus on the connections between culture, the market, and human rights. Here it is sufficient to quote his own summary of his treatment of one phase of the debate as it surfaced before and during the Bangkok meeting in March-April 1993 in the run up to the Vienna World Conference on Human Rights:

"Asian perceptions of human rights have been much discussed, particularly outside Asia, stimulated by the challenge to the international regime of rights by a few Asian governments in the name of Asian values. Placing the debate in the context of international developments since the Universal Declaration of Human Rights 50 years ago, [the author] argues that international discussions on human rights in Asia are sterile and misleading, obsessed as they are with Asian values. On the other hand, the debate within Asia is much richer, reflecting a variety of views, depending to a significant extent on the class, economic or political location of the proponents. Most governments have a statist view of rights, concerned to prevent the use of rights discourse to mobilize disadvantaged or marginal groups, such as workers, peasants, or ethnic groups, or stifle criticisms and interventions from the international community.[47] However, few of them [i.e. governments] subscribe to the crude versions of Asian values, which are often taken abroad as representing some kind of Asian consensus. [The author] contrasts the views of governments with those of the non-governmental organizations (NGOs) who have provided a more coherent framework for the analysis of rights in the Asian context. They see rights as promoting international solidarity rather than divisions. Domestically,

---

[46] Ghai tended to dismiss the Bangkok Declaration as an incoherent and self-contradictory document, a political compromise that was hardly worth deconstruction (e.g. Ghai, "The Politics of Human Rights in Asia", 209, and Ghai, "Human Rights and Asian Values", 174) and to concentrate on the arguments of Lee and Muhathir, about whom he was equally scathing: "To draw from their pretentious and mostly inconsistent statements a general philosophy of Asian values is like trying to understand Western philosophy of rights and justice from statements of Reagan and Thatcher." Ibid.

[47] Ghai points to the highly selective presentation of Asian values by some protagonists, glossing over the hierarchical structures of relationships, subordination of women, the exploitation of children and workers, nepotism and corruption based on family ties, and the oppression of minorities. Ghai, "Human Rights and Asian Values", 177.

they see rights as means of empowerment and central to the establishment of fair and just political, economic and social orders." [48]

To start with Ghai was quite dismissive of arguments that human rights represent a form of cultural imperialism—the imposition of values that are atomistic, confrontational and self-seeking on a culture that emphasizes harmony, consensus, hard work, and solidarity. This argument, in his view, exaggerated the homogeneity of "Asian" cultures, distorted the nature of human rights, and over-emphasized the place of culture in economic success. However, in a later paper on "Rights, Duties and Responsibilities" he decided to take more seriously the argument that some Asian traditions, notably Hinduism and Confucianism, emphasize duties rather than rights and that this is a superior way to organize society.[49] "Duty" in this context is more abstract than the Hohfeldian idea of duty; it refers to obligations or responsibilities attached to office or status or class, rather than merely being the correlative of claim rights. Such responsibilities prescribe right and proper conduct in respect of a given role or relationship, like father-son, husband-wife, friend-friend, and most important, ruler-subjects. On one interpretation of Confucianism such duties could be said to be less self-regarding than rights, more communitarian, oriented to harmony rather than conflict, more informal, emphasizing honor, peace and stability. "The key duties are loyalty, obedience, filial piety, respect, and protection."[50] Ghai acknowledges that in some societies this version of Confucianism can be attractive:

"I do not wish to oppose a broader notion of duty in the sense of responsibilities or civic virtue. There is clearly much that is attractive in persons who are mindful of the concerns of others, who wish to contribute to the welfare of the community, who place society above their own personal interests. No civilized society is possible without such persons. There is also much that is attractive in societies that seek a balance between rights and responsibilities and emphasize harmony. Nor do I wish to underestimate the potential of duty as a safeguard against abuse of power and office. I am much attracted to the notion of the withdrawal of the Mandate of Heaven from rulers who transgress upon duties of rulers (although I am aware that this was largely impotent as a device of responsiveness or accountability or discipline of rulers)." [51]

---

[48] This is based on the Abstract of Ghai, "Human Rights and Asian Values".
[49] Ghai, "Rights, Duties and Responsibilities".
[50] Ibid., 29.
[51] Ibid., 37-38.

However, these virtues mainly concern social relations of human beings within civil society rather than relations between citizens and the state, which is the primary sphere of human rights. Moreover, as modern Confucian scholarship suggests, there is a down side to such a philosophy: a duty-based society tends to be status oriented and hierarchical; in some societies Confucian duties rarely extended beyond family and clan, promoting corruption rather than a genuine civic sense.[52] Confucius himself emphasized the moral responsibilities of the ruler, was contemptuous of merchants and profits, and was against strong laws and tough punishments—for authoritarian, market-oriented and often corrupt governments to invoke Confucius is hypocritical. By conflating the ideas of state and community, the official protagonists of "Asian values" obscure the role of the regime of rights to mediate between state and community:

> "That the contemporary celebration of duty has little to do with culture and much to do with politics is evident from the various contradictions of policies and practices of governments heavily engaged in its exhortation."[53]

In the present context, perhaps the important point is a warning against taking any debates and discourse about human rights too literally. The context is typically political and the same discourse can be used or abused for a wide range of different political ends. Above all, such discourse is historically contingent:

> "I believe that rights are historically determined and are generally the result of social struggles. They are significantly influenced by material and economic conditions of human existence. It is for that reason unjustified to talk of uniform attitudes and practices in such a diverse region as Asia. Rights become important, both as political principles and instruments, with the emergence of capitalist markets and the strong states associated with the development of national markets. Markets and states subordinated

---

[52] Ibid., 38, citing W.T. de Barry, *The Trouble with Confucianism* (Cambridge: Harvard University Press, 1991). Ghai also points out that traditional Confucianism placed more emphasis on the individual than has generally been recognized, citing Yu-Wei Hsieh, "The Status of the Individual in Chinese Ethics," in *The Chinese Mind: Essentials of Chinese Philosophy and Culture*, ed. Charles Moore (Honolulu: University of Hawaii Press, 1967), and Tu Wei-Ming, *Confucian Thought: Self-hood as Creative Transformation* (Albany: State University of New York Press, 1989).

[53] Ghai, "Rights, Duties and Responsibilities", 34.

communities and families under which duties and responsibilities were deemed more important than entitlements. Rights regulate the relationship of individuals and corporations to the state. Despite the lip service paid to the community and the family by certain Asian governments, the reality is that the State has effectively displaced the community, and increasingly the family, as the framework within which an individual or group's life chances and expectations are decided. The survival of community itself now depends on rights of association and assembly."[54]

The Role of Judges in Implementing Economic, Social and Cultural Rights

The UN Declaration covered both civil and political rights (CPR) and economic, social and cultural rights (ESCR). It made no formal distinction between the two classes. However, during the Cold War the distinction became significant and was sharpened in the ideological battles between the Western powers and the Eastern bloc, the former prioritising CPR, the latter ESCR. This distinction became further entrenched both in international covenants and through the influence of the colonial powers and the Soviet Union on subordinated countries. Thus the European Convention on Human Rights is restricted to civil and political rights and this has spread to many Commonwealth countries.[55] The distinction still lives on, for example in the domestic and foreign policies of the United States and the People's Republic of China. However, the constitutions of India (1949) and South Africa (1994) are significant exceptions to this.

The validity of the distinction has long been a matter of contention and the claim that "human rights are interdependent and indivisible" is widely supported by the human rights community.[56]   At the start of the Millennium the debate became sharply focused within Interights, an influential London-based NGO, by the responses to a memorandum prepared by Yash Ghai that was intended to focus the program of Interights on ESCR:

---

[54] Ghai, "Human Rights and Asian Values," 169. Pressure of space precludes my doing justice to Ghai's analysis of the complex relationship between economic globalization and human rights in Asia, on which see Ghai, "Rights, Social Justice and Globalization in East Asia," and Twining, "Human Rights: Southern Voices," 131-48.

[55] Convention for the Protection of Human Rights and Fundamental Freedoms, 4 November 1950, 213 U.N.T.S. 222 (entered into force 3 September 1953).

[56] On Baxi's criticism of this "mantra", see Baxi, *The Future of Human Rights* (Delhi: Oxford University Press, 2002).

"It was not my intention to expound a theory of ESCR, but to suggest a focus for work. I acknowledged the importance of ESCR as rights, but cautioned against over-concentration on litigation strategies and pointed to limitations of the judicial process in view of the nature of ESCR. The memo implied the need to avoid polarities or dichotomies (such as justiciability and non-justiciability and civil and political/economic and social rights). In this as other instances of enforcement of the law, there was a division of labor between court-oriented strategies and other modes of enforcement. It was important, in discussions of the enforceability of ESCR, to pay attention to the relationship between judicial enforcement and the supporting framework that other institutions could provide, as well as to the effects of litigation on wider participation in the movements, and lobbying, for human rights." [57]

The memorandum provoked mixed reactions. The ensuing debate culminated in a valuable collection of essays, edited by Yash Ghai and Jill Cottrell.[58] This throws light not only on issues such as justiciability but also on the specific nature of ESCR, different methods of implementation, and the experience of the courts in several countries in dealing with them. The final chapter by the editors represents a significant development of Ghai's views.

In this volume the debate was initially framed by contrasting positions asserted by Abdullahi An Na'im[59] and Lord (Anthony) Lester.[60] An Na'im objected in principle to the classification of human rights into two broad classes. He argued that this distinction leads to the perception that ESCR are inferior;[61] it denies the claim that human rights are indivisible and

---

[57] Jill Cottrell and Yash Ghai, "The Role of the Courts in the Protection of Economic, Social and Cultural Rights," in Yash Ghai and Jill Cottrell, eds., *Economic, Social and Cultural Rights in Practice: The Role of Judges in Implementing Economic, Social and Cultural Rights* (London: Interights, 2004). Part of this argument is transcribed in Twining, *Human Rights: Southern Voices*, 152-54.

[58] Ibid.

[59] Abdullahi An-Na'im, "To Affirm the Full Human Rights Standing of Economic, Social and Cultural Rights," in Ghai and Cottrell, eds., *Economic, Social and Cultural Rights in Practice,* 7.

[60] Lord Lester of Herne Hill and Colm O'Cinneide, "The Effective Protection of Socio-Economic Rights" in Ghai and Cottrell, eds., *Economic, Social and Cultural Rights in Practice,* 16-22.

[61] For example, "within the European system, ESCR has been relegated to non-binding charters and optional protocols." An-Na'im, "To Affirm the Full Human Rights Standing," 11.

interdependent;[62] it is not based on any consistent or coherent criteria of classification; and it undermines "the universality and practical implementation *of all human rights*".[63] In particular, An Na'im attacked the idea that no ESCR should be enforced by the judiciary. All human rights need to be supported by a variety of mechanisms, and the role of each mechanism should be assessed and developed in relation to each right. But it is not appropriate to leave promotion and enforcement to national governments, for the fundamental aim of protecting human rights "is to *safeguard them from the contingencies of the national political and administrative processes*." [64] The judiciary has a vital role to play in this. An-Na'im placed great emphasis on the importance of human rights as universal standards incorporated in the international regime and backed by international co-operation in their implementation. The framework of international standards is crucial for the recognition of ESCR as *human rights*.

Lord Lester and Colm O'Cinneide developed a familiar response: while acknowledging that ESCR are indeed human rights and the poor and the vulnerable need protection from violations of both classes of rights, they argued that ESCR are best protected by non-judicial mechanisms. For reasons of democratic legitimacy and practical expertise, the judiciary should have a very limited role in those aspects of governance that involve allocation of resources, setting priorities, and developing policies.

In the ensuing debate it became clear that the range of disagreement was quite narrow. This is hardly surprising within a group of human rights experts (mainly lawyers) arguing in the context of an NGO that is committed to promoting ESCR. There appears to have been a consensus on a number of points: that ESCR should be treated as *rights*; that their effective enforcement and development was a matter of concern; that this requires a variety of mechanisms; that the idea of the interdependence of rights is of genuine practical importance; and that the concept of "justiciability" is too abstract and too fluid to provide much help in delineating an appropriate role for the judiciary in respect of ESCR.

---

[62] For example, a right to freedom of expression is not much use to the vulnerable without a right to education; conversely implementation of a right to education is dependent on freedom to research and communicate freely. Ibid.

[63] Ibid. [emphasis added].

[64] Ibid., 8.

Ghai took issue with An-Na'im on two main grounds: An-Na'im placed too much emphasis on the international regime as the foundation for national policies on rights;[65] and he was wrong in suggesting that those who want a restricted role for the judiciary are necessarily opposed to ESCR as rights.   Nevertheless, Ghai suggested that the differences between An- Na'im and the proponents of judicial restraint can easily be exaggerated—they are mainly differences of emphasis about a role that is contingent on local historical and material conditions. Several of the commentators made the point that courts have taken ESCR into account when interpreting CPR provisions.

One senses that Ghai may have been somewhat impatient with a debate, which seems to have been based largely on mutual misunderstandings of the seemingly conflicting viewpoints. No one denied that courts had some role to play in this area, while An-Na'im was not asking that they should be seen as the only relevant mechanism. However, the debate stimulated Ghai to develop his own ideas about the nature of ESCR and the role of human rights discourse in framing state policies. Without claiming to do justice to a rich and detailed analysis, one can perhaps pinpoint three key ideas underlying his position.

First, he was stimulated to articulate his view of the role of courts in relation to EHCR. This should not be static but generally speaking should be less prominent than their role in relation to CPR. After a survey of the case law developed so far, especially in India and South Africa, including cases in which courts had been felt by critics to have become too involved, Ghai concluded:

"Courts can play an important role in 'mainstreaming' ESCR by (a) elaborating the contents of rights; (b) indicating the responsibilities of the state; (c) identifying ways in which the rights have been violated by the state; (d) suggesting the frameworks within which policy has to be made, (to some extent the South African courts have done this, by pointing to the need to make policies about the enforcement of rights, and the Indian courts by highlighting the failure of government to fulfil [Directive Principles of State Policy] so many years after independence). There is a

---

[65] "Reliance on international norms brings in all of the difficulties of hegemony and alleged imposition; and it ignores the national character of the constitution as a charter of the people themselves to bind their rulers … and it ignores the critical importance of local action, democracy, etc." Yash Ghai, introduction to Ghai and Cottrell, eds., *Economic, Social and Cultural Rights in Practice,* 2. Interestingly, Baxi makes a similar criticism of Ghai in a different context. See *below* n. 97.

fine balance here, for there is always a risk that courts may cross the line between indicating failures of policy and priorities and indicating so clearly what these priorities ought to be that they are actually making policy." [66]

"The primary decision-making framework must be the political process". [67] The main contribution of courts in Ghai's view should be "in developing core or minimum entitlements". [68] However, once policies have been formulated by government or other agencies, backed by standards and benchmarks, courts may also have a role in implementing such standards.

Second, Ghai and Cottrell point out that issues about justiciability cannot turn on the difference between CPR and ESCR, nor on some untenable distinction between negative and positive rights. [69] They distinguish between two aspects of justiciability that are often confused: [70] (a) *explicit non-justiciability* when a constitution or law explicitly excludes the jurisdiction of the courts, for example the Directive Principles of State Policy in the Indian Constitution; and (b) *non-justiciability as a matter of appropriateness*, a more delicate and complex matter. This may be based on arguments about separation of powers, or legitimacy, or the competence of courts, or some concept of what is a "political" question or a combination of them. These are contested matters in which no clear consensus has emerged in the case law, except a tendency to reject sharp distinctions. [71]

---

[66] Cottrell and Ghai, "The Role of the Courts", 86. They cite with approval dicta in the South African case of *Government of the Republic of South Africa v Grootboom and Others* [2000] ICHRL 72 (4 October 2000), 2000 (11) BCLR 1169 (CCSA) (QL), and of Canadian Justice Louise Arbour—as she then was—dissenting in *Gosselin v Québec (Attorney-General)* [2002] 4 S.C.R. 429, 2002 SCC 84, where she draws a distinction between recognition of the kinds of claims individuals may assert against the state, and questions of how much the state should spend and in what manner: "One can in principle answer the question whether a Charter right exists—in this case, to a level of welfare sufficient to meet one's basic needs—without addressing how much expenditure by the state is necessary in order to secure that right. It is only the latter question that is, properly speaking, non-justiciable" (at *para.* 332).

[67] Ibid., 89.

[68] Ibid., 87.

[69] Ibid., 70-71.

[70] Ibid., 66-70.

[71] "Courts are considered an unsuitable forum where there may be no clear standards or rules by which to resolve a dispute or where the court may not be able

Third, the discussion of the role of the courts throws light on the nature of ESCR. Ghai rejects any sharp distinction between ESCR and CPR, but nevertheless argues that there are certain tendencies that characterize ESCR and suggest a more limited role for the courts in relation to many, but not all of them.[72] For example, in many domestic and international instruments there is a tendency for ESCR provisions to be drafted in terms that allow considerable discretion in respect of standards, timing, and methods of enforcement.[73] Such notions as "progressive realization", "margin of appreciation", and "to the extent of its available resources" further limit the role of courts. No human rights are costless, but all implementation of all human rights depends on "a complex interaction of policies in numerous sectors, institutions, and entitlements."[74] However, as the Indian and South African cases have shown, there is scope for courts to define what is the minimum core of any given right (a notoriously difficult and contentious matter), to sanction state violation of established rights, and to point out that "progressive realization" implies that the state has a constitutional duty to start implementation and a further duty to ensure that there is no deterioration of standards. Ghai's essentially evolutionary and pragmatic argument is consistent with An-Na'im's insistence that what are appropriate mechanisms of implementation should be decided on the merits in respect of each right in particular contexts rather than by reference to abstract categories. But in light of the experience of the case law, there may be a considerably more significant role for courts in the long run than An-Na'im suggests.

---

to supervise the enforcement of its decision or the highly technical nature of the questions, or the large questions of policy involved may be thought to present insuperable obstacles to the useful involvement of courts". Ibid., 69. The case of *Upendra Baxi v State of Uttar Pradesh* (1986) 4 SCC 106 is cited as an example of the courts getting involved in an unsuitable activity—here the court supervised a home for women for five years.

[72] See the excellent discussion by Ghai and Cottrell of the way these considerations affect rights to education, medical treatment, housing, environment and social security. Cottrell and Ghai, "The Role of the Courts", 76-82.

[73] But there are exceptions: for example, the right to free and compulsory primary education. Ibid., 61.

[74] Ibid., 62.

Fourth, and more important, Ghai's main concern was to focus attention on other means of implementing and developing ESCR and to make a general case for the idea that human rights discourse can provide a broad over-arching framework for constructing state policies and priorities.[75] One trouble with the debates about "justiciability" has been that "human rights" has tended to be treated as doctrine (often legal doctrine) rather than as discourse and that it focuses attention on litigation (usually a last resort) and away from the range of other possible mechanisms and resources that need to be employed in the realization of all human rights, including ESCR.

One senses that Ghai is sometimes impatient with theoretical debates about rights and prefers to work at less general levels. Like many others he rejects strong versions of both universalism and relativism; he criticizes a tendency to over-emphasize "culture" rather than material interests; he argues that the debate on "Asian values" greatly exaggerated the uniformities of "East Asian culture" and was used to divert attention away from the failings of repressive regimes and human rights violations; the result was to obfuscate genuine issues about human rights in different contexts in East Asia. Similarly the debate about the justiciability of ESCR amounted to little more than differences of emphasis among lawyers about the proper role of courts—a role that should depend on timing and context in any given country. Most of the protagonists have been lawyers who have tended to argue on the basis of human rights as legal doctrine rather as a discourse that provides a workable framework for mediating conflicting interests and providing a basis for settlements that are accepted by local people as legitimate.

Many of these themes are illustrated in specific ways in Ghai's writings about Hong Kong, in which the same dichotomies between theory and practice, socialism and liberalism, and idealism and pragmatism are discernible in creative tension. After a generally pessimistic diagnosis of the situation he ends on a pragmatic note of hope about the future by appealing to enlightened self-interest:

---

[75] Ibid., 61.

"It is easy for the Central Authorities, if they were so minded, to bypass or undermine the Basic Law, and they would presumably always find people who are willing to collaborate with them in this enterprise. However, China stands to gain more from a faithful adherence to the Basic Law, to keep promises of autonomy, to permit people of all persuasions to participate in public affairs, to respect rights and freedoms, and to let an independent judiciary enforce the Basic Laws and other laws. This is a more effective way to win the loyalty of Hong Kong people. An adherence to legal norms and consultative and democratic procedures would ultimately benefit the Central Authorities as they grapple with the difficult task of managing affairs on the mainland as economic reforms and the movement for democracy generate new tensions." [76]

Yash Ghai advances a pragmatic materialist interpretation that is broadly supportive of the current international human rights regime. He emphasises the uses and limitations of Bills of Rights as devices for limiting governmental power and increasing accountability. He focuses on the use and abuse of human rights discourse in real-life political contexts, especially by governments that invoke the right to self-determination against external critics of their treatment of their own citizens. His views are not surprisingly controversial.[77] But he provides a uniquely realistic perspective on the practical operation of human rights discourse, especially in the context of constitutional negotiation and settlement.

---

[76] Yash Ghai, *Hong Kong's New Constitutional Order* (Hong Kong: Hong Kong University Press), 500.

[77] For example, "naturalists" believe that human rights embody universal values; and cultural relativists might argue that he is too dismissive of the core of truth in the idea that there are strong communitarian traditions in Asia that are far less individualistic than Western ideologies of individual rights; and his views are likely to be anathema to free-market "liberals". He has also been attacked from the left by Upendra Baxi for too readily taking the international regime of human rights as the starting-point for constitutionalism and for failing to emphasize how human rights discourse can obfuscate "the real historical struggles" of "subaltern" peoples. (See further below n. 97).

Upendra Baxi [78]

For hundreds of millions of "the wretched of the earth", human rights enunciations matter, if at all, only if they provide shields against torture and tyranny, deprivation and destitution, pauperization and powerlessness, desexualization and degradation.[79]

[T]he task of human rights, in terms of making the state ethical, governance just, and power accountable, are tasks that ought to continue to define the agendum of activism.[80]

Human rights languages are perhaps all we have to interrogate the barbarism of power, even when these remain inadequate to humanize fully the barbaric practices of politics.[81]

---

[78] This section is based mainly on Upendra Baxi: (i) *The Future of Human Rights* (2002a) (hereafter FHR I); a second edition (FHR II) was published in 2006, but as the first edition is more readily available references to it have been retained, except where there is a significant change; (ii) an article, 'Voices of Suffering, Fragmented Universality and the Future of Human Rights," *Transnational Law and Contemporary Problems* 8 (1998): 125 (hereafter VS 1998); (iii) 'Voices of Suffering, Fragmented Universality and the Future of Human Rights' in Burns H. Weston and Stephen P. Marks, eds. *The Future of International Human Rights* (Ardsley: Transnational, 1999) (hereafter VS 1999). This 1999 version contains a succinct restatement of Baxi's basic ideas. For many it is probably the best place to start, even though there are many more recent writings. It is reproduced in full in Twining, *Human Rights: Southern Voices*, c. 5.2); and (iv) a draft introduction to Upendra Baxi & Shulamith Koenig, *The People's Report on Human Rights Education* (New York: The People's Movement for Human Rights Education, 2002) (hereafter HRE). A revised version was published years later as Upendra Baxi, The Human Right to Human Rights Education? *Some Critical Perspectives* (New Delhi: Universal Law Book Co, 2006). Reference will also be made to a number of articles and to three books published in 1994: *Inhuman Wrongs and Human Rights: Some Unconventional Essays* (New Delhi: Har Anand); *Mambrino's Helmet: Human Rights for a Changing World* (New Delhi: Har Anand) and, with O. Mendelsohn, *The Rights of Subordinated Peoples* (New Delhi: Oxford University Press). Some of Baxi's later writings are collected in *Human Rights in an Inhuman World* (New Delhi: Oxford University Press, 2007). The biographical information is based in part on an interview and correspondence with Professor Baxi.

[79] Baxi, "Voices of Suffering," 103.

[80] Baxi, *The Future of Human Rights*, xii.

[81] Baxi, "Voices of Suffering," 102.

Upendra Baxi was born in Rajkot, Gujerat in 1938.   His father,
Vishnuprasad Baxi, was a senior civil servant and a noted scholar of
Sanskrit. Upendra was brought up in a large household, which sometimes
numbered as many as seventy people under one roof, excluding servants.
He remembers his childhood environment as a mix of perpetual
pregnancies, relentless micro-politics and a complete lack of privacy. His
view of the extended communal family has remained decidedly unromantic.
In his words "I declared UDI [Unilateral Declaration of Independence] at
the first opportunity" and he reacted against this aspect of Hindu culture.
He went to university, did well and soon embarked on a career as an
academic, public intellectual and legal activist.

After graduating in law from the University of Bombay (LLM, 1963),
he taught at the University of Sydney (1968-73). There he worked closely
with Julius Stone, the well-known legal theorist and public international
lawyer.   During this period he spent two years at Berkeley, where he
obtained the degrees of LLM (1966) and JSD (1972), having written a
thesis on private international law under the supervision of Professor
Albert Ehrenzweig. On his return to India he held the post of Professor of
Law at the University of Delhi from 1973 until 1996. During this period
he also served as Vice-Chancellor of South Gujerat (1982-85), Director of
Research at the Indian Law institute (1985-88) and Vice-Chancellor of the
University of Delhi (1990-94). From 1996 to 2010 he has been Professor
of Law and Development at the University of Warwick. He has also held
visiting appointments in several American law schools.

Baxi has been a prolific writer. In addition to producing over twenty
books and many scholarly articles, he has between a frequent broadcaster
and contributor to the Indian press. His early work was largely concerned
with public law and law and society in India and he consciously addressed
mainly Indian audiences. As an activist he has been very influential both
in India and South Asia. He contributed much to legal education; he was a
leading commentator and critic of the Indian Supreme Court and a pioneer
in the development of social action litigation and "the epistolary
jurisdiction" that gave disadvantaged people direct access to appellate
courts. He was also extensively involved in legal action and law reform
concerning violence against women and opposition to major dam
projects.[82] For over twenty years he has campaigned and litigated on

---

[82] Upendra Baxi, "What Happens Next is Up to You: Human Rights at Risk in
Dams and Development", *American University International Law Review* 16
(2001): 1507.

behalf of the victims of the Bhopal catastrophe.[83] Over time Baxi's interests and audiences expanded geographically, but he has maintained his concern and involvement with Indian affairs. His more recent interests have included comparative constitutional law, the legal implications of science and technology, law and development, responses to terrorism, and above all the strategic uses of law for ameliorating the situation of the worst off.[84]

Baxi's describes his perspective on human rights as that of a comparative sociologist of law. Julius Stone, his main academic mentor, was a student of the sociological jurist, Roscoe Pound. Baxi embraced the sociological perspective, but as a follower of Gandhi and Marx (later Gramsci), and as an active participant in protests at Berkeley in 1964 to 1967,[85] he gave the ideas of Pound and Stone a distinctly radical twist. Stone called him a "Marxist natural lawyer";[86] others have pointed to his lengthy engagement with post-modernism. But such labels do not fit him. Marxism proved too rigid and doctrinaire,[87] and post-modernism too

---

[83] Upendra Baxi, *Mass Torts, Multinational Enterprise Liability and Private international Law* (The Hague: Martinus Nijhoff, 2000).

[84] Baxi has written a great deal about the uses and limitations of law in furthering the interests of the worst off, but his views on human rights extend beyond law to include ideas, discourse and praxis.

[85] "It was 'heaven to be alive' those days! To go to the Greek Amphitheater adjoining the International Student House and to hear Joan Baez stringing protest melodies. To read the classic text *Soul on Ice*, the first to utter the now heavily jargonized phrase: 'When confronted with a logical impossibility, you have the choice to be part of the problem or part of the solution' Before Berkeley, I never marched with the processions carrying placards. 'Radicalization' occurred on a wholly different learning curve as well as when I attended... Professor David Daube's seminars on the notion of impossibility in Roman and Greek law! Professor Daube's charismatic problematic of course was the situation when a horse was sworn as a Roman Senator!... David taught me memorably—long before the Derridean/ postmodernist vogue—the ways in which the law makes the impossible possible." (Communication to the author).

[86] Upendra Baxi, "From Human Rights to Human Flourishing: Julius Stone, Amartya Sen and Beyond?" (The Julius Stone Lecture 2001, University of Sydney), in Baxi, *Human Rights in a Posthuman World*.

[87] While there is a distinct Marxian strain in Baxi's thought, especially through Gramsci, he has been as critical of Soviet ideology and praxis as of free market capitalism: "Both the triumphal eras of bourgeois human rights formations and of revolutionary socialism of Marxian imagination marshaled this narrative hegemony for remarkably sustained practices of the politics of cruelty." Baxi, *The*

irresponsible to be of much use to a practical political agenda.[88] Neither quite fits his not uncritical sympathy for the ideas of Amartya Sen and Martha Nussbaum.[89] Above all Baxi's concern has been for those whom, following Gramsci, he calls "subaltern peoples". Perhaps more than any other scholarly writer on human rights he consistently adopts the point of view of the poor and the oppressed.

Since the early 1990s most of Baxi's work has concerned human rights. Much of what he writes is critical of discourses of human rights, the complexities and compromises involved, and the misuses to which the discourses have been put. The tone is passionate, polemical and radical, but the style is learned, allusive and quite abstract.[90] Some of the distinctions that he emphasizes have occasioned puzzlement: for example, the distinction between the politics *of* human rights and politics *for* human rights,[91] between human rights movements, human rights markets, and market-friendly human rights,[92] between justified and unjustifiable human suffering,[93] and between "modern" and "contemporary" human rights[94]— all of which need explication. While much of his argument is complex, dialectical, and often ironic, one clear message rings out: taking human rights seriously must involve taking human suffering seriously.

At first sight, Baxi seems deeply ambivalent about rights: he is a fervent supporter of universal human rights, yet he is sharply critical of much of the talk and practice associated with it and he emphasizes many of the obstacles and threats to the realization of their potential. Much of

---

Future of Human Rights, xiv, 35 and 137-38. Anyway, Baxi is far too eclectic intellectually to be categorized as a Marxist.

[88] Ibid. 78-80 and 97-100.

[89] Baxi, "From Human Rights to Human Flourishing"; cf. Baxi and Koenig, *The People's Report on Human Rights Education,* 50.

[90] He moves smoothly from his Indian intellectual heritage (Gandhi, Ambedkar, the Supreme Court of India) to Western, especially Anglo-American, jurisprudence (he has written about Bentham, Kelsen, Rawls, Dworkin and Stone) through Marxian theory (Marx, Gramsci, Benjamin) and Natural law (Aquinas, Gewirth), drawing on contemporary sociology (e.g. Beck, Bourdieu, and Castells) and Continental European philosophy (Foucault, Derrida, Laclau, Levinas), engaging with but distancing himself from post-modernism (especially Rorty) and Critical Legal Studies, and dealing more sympathetically with Nussbaum and Sen.

[91] E.g. *The Future of Human Rights*, x-xi, 13-14, 42-44 *et passim*.

[92] Ibid., vi, 121-31

[93] Ibid., 17-18.

[94] Ibid., 27-28.

his account relates "to the narratives of unrealized and even unattainable human rights".[95] Rather than accept this as ambivalence, he recalls Gramsci's distinction between pessimism of the intellect and optimism of the will.[96] Although he writes about human rights futures, Baxi is more concerned with struggle than with prediction.

In their writings, Yash Ghai and other "Southern" jurists, such as Francis Deng and Abdullahi An-Na'im, use the international human rights regime as their starting-point. As lawyers, they are aware that this regime is changing, dynamic, complex, and open to competing interpretations. However, they treat it, and especially the Universal Declaration of Human Rights as being sufficiently stable and clear to provide standards for appraising and giving direction to other normative orders.[97] Like them Upendra Baxi opposes all forms of imperialism, colonialism, racism and patriarchy. He steers a subtle path between universalism and relativism.[98] He agrees that humankind as a whole should be the subject of our moral concern. He treats the Universal Declaration as one high point of the development of the current human rights regime. But he sees that regime as being inherently fragile and problematic. And his general tone and positions are more radical than the other three.

Like Ghai, Baxi's initial attitude to human rights is pragmatic: we need to work within human rights discourse not because it clearly embodies

---

[95] Ibid., xii.

[96] In writing about attempts to develop "enlightened" policies for the construction of major dams, rather than ceasing their construction as inevitably involving major human rights violations, Baxi comments: "Human rights violations urge us, however, to profess pessimism of will and the optimism of intellect. We need to hunt and haunt all erudite discourses that seek to over-rationalize development. We need to defend and protect people suffering everywhere who refuse to accept that the power of a few should become the destiny of millions." Baxi, "What Happens Next is up to You", 1529.

[97] Baxi criticizes Ghai for taking the international regime of human rights as his starting-point for comparing four constitutional narratives, without mentioning that the Indian Constitution preceded and went further than the Declaration, and without emphasizing sufficiently the extent to which human rights are the product of struggles rather than benign "top down" problem solving.   Upendra Baxi, "Constitutionalism as a Site of State Formative Practices," *Cardozo Law Review* 21 (2002): 1183.

[98] Chapter 6 of *"The Future of Human Rights"* is entitled "What is Living and Dead in Relativism?"

universal moral principles,[99] but because in the second half of the twentieth century it became the dominant mode of moral discourse in international relations, edging out other moral tropes such as distributive justice or "solidarity".[100] Just because they have become so dominant the discourses of human rights have been used to support a wide variety of often incompatible interests and this in turn has led to complexity, compromise, contradiction, and obfuscation in both the discourse and the practices of human rights. More than Ghai, Baxi consistently adopts the standpoint of the worst off.[101]

Baxi presents the international human rights scene as fragile, contradictory, riddled with myths, false histories and ambiguities. It is marked by frenetic activity, explosive articulation of human rights standards and norms, and varied critiques and skepticisms about this dominant discourse. Global capitalism, new technologies, and both global terrorism and post-9/11 responses to "terrorism" ("terrorism wars")[102]

---

[99] Baxi makes interesting points that I cannot pursue here about the intellectual history of who counts as "human", Baxi, *The Future of Human Rights*, 28-29; the Hegelian idea of concrete universality—what it is to be fully human, Ibid., 92-97; and the implications of biotechnology for ideas of "human dignity", Ibid., 161-63. Baxi distances himself from strong relativist positions, while acknowledging that post-modernists and anti-foundationalists have usefully problematized ideas of universality, Ibid., 97-118. cf. Ghai, "Universalism and Relativism". Baxi concludes: "The universality of human rights symbolizes *the universality of the collective human aspiration to make power increasingly accountable, governance progressively just, and the state incrementally more ethical.*" Baxi, *The Future of Human Rights*, 105.

[100] Like me, Baxi does not think that human rights discourse can adequately capture the concerns of distributive justice; unlike me he is surprisingly kind to John Rawls' much-criticized *The Law of Peoples* (Cambridge: Harvard University Press, 1999); cf. Twining, *Globalisation and Legal Theory*, 69-75; Twining, *General Jurisprudence*, 153-72.

[101] Baxi criticizes Ghai from a "subaltern perspective on constitutionalism" for masking the suffering involved in human rights struggles, for "a wholly utilitarian construction of rights", and for accepting too readily the views of political elites at the expense of ordinary people. Baxi, "Constitutionalism as a Site", 1191. Some of this criticism is, in my view, unduly harsh. The sharp tone may have spilled over from his criticism of Kenneth Karst in the same symposium for painting an idealized picture of American constitutional history without even mentioning slavery.

[102] This theme is developed at length in Upendra Baxi, "The War *on* Terror and the War *of* Terror: Nomadic Multitudes, Aggressive Incumbents, and the 'New'

further threaten the fragile, contingent advances made by human rights movements. Small wonder then that there is a crisis of confidence even among the most committed and "progressive" activists and NGOs:

> "The astonishing quantity of human rights production generates various expressions of skepticism and faith. Some complain of exhaustion (what I call "rights weariness"). Some suspect sinister imperialism in diplomatic maneuvers animating each and every human rights enunciation (what I call "rights-wariness"). Some celebrate human rights as a new global civic religion which, given a community of faith, will address and solve all major human problems (what I call "human rights evangelism"). Their fervor is often matched by those NGOs that tirelessly pursue the removal of brackets in pre-final diplomatic negotiating texts of various United Nations' summits as triumphs in human solidarity (what I call "human rights romanticism"). Some other activists believe that viable human rights standards can best be produced by exploring contingencies of international diplomacy (what I call "bureaucratization of human rights"). And still others (like me) insist that the real birthplaces of human rights are far removed from the ornate rooms of diplomatic conferences and are found, rather, in the actual sites (acts and feats) of resistance and struggle (what I call "critical human rights realism")."[103]

International Law. Prefatory Remarks on Two 'Wars'," *Osgoode Hall Law Journal* 43 (2005): 7.

[103] Baxi, "Voices of Suffering," 116. A longer version adds "Some activists celebrate virtues of dialogue among the communities of perpetrators and those violated (what I term human rights *dialogism*)." Baxi, *The Future of Human Rights*, 51. Baxi is sympathetic to "moderate forms of dialogism", exemplified by Truth and Reconciliation Commissions and the writings of Abdullahi An Na'im, Ibid, 58-59, but warns that dialogue with the worst kinds of perpetrators of violations may delegitimize the idea of human rights in the eyes of the violated, Ibid. 60. For example: "The idea that a handful of NGOs can dialogue with a handful of CEOs of multinationals to produce implementation of human rights is simply Quixotic". Ibid, 58. Cf. Baxi's more pragmatic approach to the UN's proposed Norms on Human Rights Responsibilities of Transnationals and other Business Corporations, arguing for a pragmatic negotiated compromise between the competing ideologies of business and international regulation. Upendra Baxi, "Market Fundamentalisms: Business Ethics at the Altar of Rights," *Human Rights Law Review* 5 (2005): 3.

The Future(s) of Human Rights

The Future of Human Rights contains the most comprehensive statement of Baxi's views on human rights.[104] Since 1990 Baxi has published several books and many articles on the subject. More are in the pipeline. Nevertheless, the core of his thinking is quite stable. Perhaps it can be rendered in four parts: first, the starting-point is a concern for and a quite complex idea of human suffering as it is actually experienced anywhere, but especially in the South; second, a comprehensive assessment, often sharply critical, of the past history and current state of human rights discourse, theory and praxis; third, an aspirational vision of a just world in which all human beings know and genuinely own human rights as resources which can empower vulnerable communities and individuals to interpret their own situations, to resist human rights violations, and to participate in genuine dialogues about alternate and competing visions for a better future in a world that will continue to be pluralistic, ever changing, and possessed of finite resources to meet infinite human wants;[105] and, finally, pragmatic suggestions about possible strategies and tactics in the perpetual struggle to move realistically towards realizing this vision (the politics *for* human rights).

Baxi's aim in *The Future of Human Rights* is: "to decipher the future of protean forms of social action assembled by convention, under a portal named 'human rights'. It problematizes the very notion of 'human rights', the standard narratives of their origins, the ensemble of ideologies animating their modes of production, and the wayward circumstances of their enunciation".[106]

---

[104] Baxi, *Future of Human Rights*. These ideas are developed at greater length, often more concretely, in lectures, speeches, articles, and pamphlets scattered around websites, learned journals, and activist magazines that are spread widely both geographically and intellectually. Some take the form of detailed commentaries on particular reports or draft texts. Among the most substantial of these are: Upendra Baxi, "'A Work in Progress?': The United Nations Report to the United Nations Human Rights Committee," *Indian Journal of International Law* 38 (1996): 34; Upendra Baxi, "'Global Neighbourhood' and the 'Universal Otherhood': Notes on the Report of the Commission on Global Governance," *Alternatives* 22 (1996): 525; and Baxi, "Market Fundamentalisms." Short extracts from these are reproduced in Twining, *Human Rights: Southern Voices*, 204-09.

[105] This formulation is constructed from several passages in Baxi and Koenig, *Human Rights Education*.

[106] Baxi, *The Future of Human Rights*, v.

In short, his objective is to mount a sustained and complex critique of much of the discourse and many of the practices that surround human rights at the start of the twentieth century and to present a vision, rooted in experiences of suffering that can serve as a secular equivalent of liberation theology.[107] For Baxi such a vision—"critical human rights realism"— should become part of the symbolic capital of the poor and the dispossessed to be used as a resource in their struggles for a decent life.

Baxi claims that *The Future of Human Rights* advances a distinctive "subaltern" activist perspective on human rights futures.[108] His central theme is that human rights discourse only has value if it fulfills the axiom "that the historic mission of contemporary human rights is to give voice to human suffering, to make it visible and to ameliorate it."

Baxi considers this task to be formidable. The second half of the twentieth century has been called "the Age of Rights"[109] and discourses of human rights have been said to be "the common language of humanity",[110] yet what difference in fact have human rights made to human suffering? [111] "The number of rightless people grows even as human rights norms and standards proliferate."[112]

The Future of Human Rights is diffuse, polemical and difficult to summarize. Perhaps the main themes can be succinctly stated largely in his own words as follows:[113]

- Human rights discourse is fraught with haunting ambiguities, complexity, and contradiction.[114] It is intensely partisan and cannot be reduced to a single coherent set of ideas. A crucial distinction is

---

[107] Baxi and Koenig, *Human Rights Education*.

[108] Baxi, *The Future of Human Rights*, xiii.

[109] Ibid., c.1.

[110] Boutros Boutros Ghali, "Human Rights. The Common Language of Humanity" (1993) cited in Baxi, "Voices of Suffering," 101.

[111] Cf. "But politics of cruelty continue even as sonorous declarations of human rights proliferate". Baxi, "Voices of Suffering," 102.

[112] Baxi, *The Future of Human Rights*, viii.

[113] This outline is based on Baxi, *The Future of Human Rights*, Baxi, "Voices of Suffering," and a talk given by Baxi at the University of Essex in May, 2003.

[114] Baxi focuses mainly on human rights discourses, but he insists that "the non-discursive order of reality, the materiality of human violation, is just as important, if not more so, from the standpoint of the violated." Baxi, *The Future of Human Rights*, 14.

between the statist discourses of the powerful and educated
(*illustrado*) and the subversive discourses of the violated
(indigenous/*indio*).[115]

- Taking rights seriously must involve *taking human suffering
  seriously.*
- *Suffering is ubiquitous*; it can be both creative and destructive of
  human potential. It is not confined to poor or undemocratic countries.
- *How suffering is justified* must be a central concern of human rights
  discourse. Historically, human rights discourse has been used to
  legitimate state power, colonialism, imperialism, and patriarchy in
  various forms, and to exclude large sectors of humanity from moral
  concern.[116] Conversely, successful human rights movements create
  new forms of justifiable suffering.[117]
- *The true authors of rights* are communities in struggle, not Western
  thinkers or modern states.[118] Linking human rights to experienced
  human suffering is the best hope of ensuring that human rights
  discourse (i) is not hijacked by a trade-related, market-friendly
  paradigm of human rights;[119] (ii) is not obfuscated by the politics *of*
  human rights (e.g competition between NGOs) rather than political
  struggles *for* human rights;[120] (iii) is not dominated by the complacent
  discourse of the powerful.[121]

---

[115] Ibid.

[116] See notes 142-144.

[117] "Gender equality makes patriarchs suffer. The overthrow of apartheid in the
United States made many a white supremacist suffer… People in high places suffer
when movements against corruption gain a modicum of success". Baxi, *The Future
of Human Rights*, 17.

[118] A vivid example of this thesis is Peter Linebaugh and Marcus Rediker, *The
Many–Headed Hydra: Sailors, Slaves, Commoners and the Hidden History of the
Revolutionary Atlantic* (London: Verso, 2000), which argues that freed slaves
were among the main originators of Western human rights ideas.

[119] Baxi, *The Future of Human Rights*, c. 8. Cf. Baxi's satirical "Draft Charter of
the Human Rights of Global Capital". Ibid., 149-51. Compare the more pragmatic
tone of Baxi, "The War *on* Terror and the War *of* Terror."

[120] The former serves the ends of *Realpolitik*, with "the latter seeking to combat
modes of governance (national, regional, or global) that command the power to
cause unjustifiable human suffering and impose orders of radical evil." Baxi, *The
Future of Human Rights*, ix, 40-41.

[121] To the powerful the World Food Summit goal of halving the number of starving
people by 2015 appears ambitious, even unrealistic; to the poor it appears remote
and "rather callous". Baxi, *The Future of Human Rights*, vii. Baxi regularly

- Modern human rights discourse is secular. It has severed the connection between human rights discourses and religious cosmologies.[122] This involves a radical acceptance of human finitude (no life after life/death); justifications are only of this world; it problematises custom and tradition; and creates a secular civic religion, a community of faith.[123]
- The contemporary production of human rights is exuberant (even "carnivalistic") producing a riot of perceptions. Clearly there are too many "soft" human rights enunciations, but very few "hard" enforceable rights.[124] To some human rights inflation is a threat; others point to the glacial progress made in the direction of "hard", enforceable human rights norms; yet others read the uncontrolled production of human rights as, perhaps, the best hope for a participative creation of human futures; attempts by the UN or other agencies to control the rate of production are likely to favor the rights of global capital.
- Increasingly human rights movements and NGOs "organize themselves in the image of markets",[125] competing with each other (in fund-raising, advertising, building capital) like entrepreneurs in a spirit of nervous "investor rationality"[126] and being forced into the trap of commodifying human rights.[127]
- Economic "globalization" threatens to supplant the ideals of the Universal Declaration of Human Rights with a trade-related, market-friendly paradigm, which emphasizes the right to property, the rights of investors, and even the rights of corporations (side-lining the poor

---

contrasts the glacial pace of response to the *misfortune* of poverty and hunger with the urgency for pursuing the war on terrorism after the *injustice* of 9/11.

[122] "Human rights education symbolizes a secular, or multi-religious equivalent of 'liberation theology'". Baxi, *Human Rights Education*, 18.

[123] Baxi, *The Future of Human Rights*, 14.

[124] Ibid., 71.

[125] Ibid., 121; Baxi, "Voices of Suffering," 144.

[126] Ibid., 145.

[127] Baxi, *The Future of Human Rights*, c. 8 and 125-29. Committed supporters of human rights have objected to this economic analogy. Baxi concedes that non-governmental human rights praxis can be interpreted analytically in terms both of social movements and "quasi markets", but he maintains that the comfortable language of "networks" and "associational governance" glosses over the contradictions and complexity of human rights movements. Ibid., 121.

to feed off the drips from the alleged trickle down effects of capitalist prosperity).[128]

- Post-modernism, ethical and cultural relativism, and skeptical critiques of rights discourse draw attention to some genuine difficulties, but they fail to provide constructive strategies for action to alleviate suffering and, however well-intentioned, they make possible toleration of vast stretches of human suffering.[129]
- The politics of difference and identity views human rights as having not just an emancipative potential but also a repressive one.[130]
- Globalization and the development of techno-scientific modes of production threaten to make contemporary human rights discourse obsolescent.[131]
- Rights have several different uses as symbolic resources in politics *for* human rights: (i) as markers of policies—testing whether policy enunciations recognize, respect, or affirm human rights); (ii) as constraints on policy implementation (self-conscious restraint and positive disincentives); (iii) as resources for policy—processes and structures of policy implementation legitimated by reference to specific human rights regimes; (iv) as providing access to effective legal redress; (v) as resources for collective action—e.g. to mobilize (discontent with policy or its implementation).[132]

---

[128] Ibid, c. 8.

[129] See note 90.

[130] Baxi, "Voices of Suffering," 103. This is the converse of Santos' argument that, even though law is often repressive, it has the potential to be emancipator. Santos, *Toward a New Common Sense*, c. 9. The difference is mainly one of emphasis.

[131] Baxi, *The Future of Human Rights*, 156. This means that the increasing dominance of science and technology, as a mode of production and as an ideology that presents itself as progressive, "threatens us all with the prospect of rendering human rights language *obsolescent*", e.g. in civilian use of nuclear energy, expanding information technology and development of new biotechnologies. Ibid. See Upendra Baxi, *Human Rights in a Posthuman World* (New Delhi: Oxford University Press, 2007.

[132] This formulation is a paraphrase of a passage on "the place of rights" in policy making and implementation. Although written specifically in the context of a discussion of population policies in India, it has a broader significance. Upendra Baxi, "Sense and Sensibility," *India Seminar 511*: March, 2002. http://www.India-seminar.com/semsearch.htm. In respect of international law Baxi emphasizes that the strategic aims should include enforcing positive law, expanding the range and refining the content of *ius cogens*, and moving beyond positive law to address the processes of norm formulation and using the discourse of rights to "write against

Each of these themes is developed in *The Future of Human Rights*, some of them at greater length and more concretely in other works. Rather than attempt a comprehensive exposition, I shall focus on a topic that is pivotal in Baxi's argument and among his more original contributions: different conceptions of the history of human rights.

Two paradigms of human rights in history: "the modern" and "the contemporary"

A standard account of the history of human rights is presented in terms of "generations": the first phase in response to the Holocaust and the horrors of World War II was marked by a pre-occupation with civil and political rights. The second generation was represented by the International Covenant on Economic, Social and Cultural Rights (ICESCR). The third phase marked a move from emphasis on individual rights to recognition of collective rights, including concern for the environment—"green rights"—in tension with "the right to development". A fourth phase involved a progressive recognition of the rights of peoples.[133] While talk of "generations" of international human rights has sometimes been a convenient simplifying device, most commentators distance themselves from this taxonomy. At best it can describe one phase of international law. It is generally accepted such "history" is too crude. For example, the Universal Declaration of Human Rights, which is the starting-point of modern development, covered economic and social rights as well as civil and political—but these became split in the period of the Cold War. Today, most orthodox commentators at least pay lip-service to the claim that human rights are universal, interdependent, and indivisible.[134]

---

the law" ("that is [using] subversive forms of story-telling against totalizing narratives of human rights"). Baxi and Koening, *Human Rights Education*, 15-18.

[133] E.g. Ghai, *Put Our World to Rights*, 9-11. Ghai would clearly agree that it is a simplification. Ibid. 34-35.

[134] See, for example, the skilful way in which Henry Steiner and Philip Alston, in *International Human Rights in Context: Law, Politics, Morals* (Oxford: Clarendon Press, 2008)—the leading student course book on international human rights—bring out the complexity of the story, first by acknowledging that most development of human rights issues has been local (at 24-5), and second by identifying the different sources out of which the current international regime developed: "It would be possible to study human rights issues not at the international level but in the detailed contexts of different states' histories, socio-economic and political structures, legal systems, cultures, religions and so on." (Ibid., 24). Baxi might criticize this as too top down or state centric, underplaying

Upendra Baxi advances a more fundamental critique of such "history". In his view, it represents a complacent, patronizing, Euro-centric or rather "Northern-centric", top-down view of the sources of human rights, suggesting that rights are "the gifts of the West to the Rest".[135] It entirely overlooks the contribution of struggles of the poor and the oppressed to the slow recognition of human rights as universal.[136]

To make sense of human rights, Baxi argues, one must see the basic ideas not as emanating from Christian natural law nor the liberal Enlightenment nor the reactions of Western Governments to the horrors of World War II. The main context of the production of human rights has been local communities in struggle against the diverse sources of suffering; the main impetus has been direct experience of suffering; the main authors have been those involved in grass-roots struggles[137]—some have become well-known, the great majority have been unsung:

"After all it was a man called Lokmanya Tilak who in the second decade of this century gave a call to India: *swaraj (independence) is my birthright and I shall have it*, long before international human rights proclaimed a right to self-determination. It was a man called Gandhi who challenged early this century racial discrimination in South Africa, which laid several decades later the foundation for international treaties and declarations on the elimination of all forms of racial discrimination and apartheid. Compared to these male figures, generations of legendary women martyred themselves in prolonged struggles against patriarchy and gender inequality. The current campaign based on the motto "Women's Rights *Are* Human Rights" is inspired by a massive history of local struggles all around."[138]

Even within the Eurocentric perspective, narratives articulated in terms of "generations" of rights radically foreshorten history in ways that hide the fragmented ideas that preceded the Universal Declaration. For

---

the significance of social movements, but he would no doubt concede that the state would still be a major player in any history written from below.

[135] Baxi, *The Future of Human Rights*, vi.

[136] See Linebaugh and Rediker, *The Many–Headed Hydra*.

[137] "Almost every global institutionalisation of human rights has been preceded by grassroots activism." Baxi, "Voices of Suffering," 124.

[138] Baxi, "The Reason of Human Rights and the Unreason of Globalization" (A. R. Desai Memorial Lecture, Bombay, 1996), cited in Baxi, "Voices of Suffering," 124-5 n. 76. See also Baxi, *Human Rights in a Posthuman World*, 97-103.

example, human rights doctrine *preceded* the abolition and often condoned slavery. The right to property and the right to govern were used to justify various forms of colonialism and imperialism. Only very recently in the long history of rights talk has there been reason to celebrate the maxim that "Women's Rights are Human Rights", but this does not mark the beginning or the end of women's struggle for equality.[139]

Instead, of a linear history, Baxi substitutes two contrasting "paradigms" (or ideal types) of conceptions of human rights both of which mask the continuities in the historiography of these two forms: the modern (or modernist) paradigm[140] and the "contemporary" paradigm:

> "The distinction between "modern" and "contemporary" forms of human rights is focused on *taking suffering seriously*. In the 'modern' human rights paradigm it was thought possible to take human rights seriously without taking human suffering seriously. Outside the domain of the laws of war among and between "civilized" nations, 'modern' human rights regarded large-scale imposition of human suffering as *just* and *right* in pursuit of a Eurocentric notion of *human 'progress'*. That discourse silenced human suffering. In contrast, the "contemporary" human rights paradigm is animated by a politics of activist desire to render problematic the very *notion of politics of cruelty*". [141]

---

[139] Like other 'Southern' jurists like Francis Deng, Abdullahi An Na'im and Yash Ghai himself, Baxi is unequivocal in his assertions that women's rights are human rights. He sees the phrase "the rights of man" as an example of the logic of exclusion in human rights discourse; and he is cautious of the rhetoric of some claims about progress: e.g. "The near-universality of ratification of the CEDAW, for example, betokens no human liberation of women; it only endows the state with the power to tell more Nietszchean lies." Baxi, *The Future of Human Rights*, 87. He is a friendly critic of the feminist movement in India. Upendra Baxi, *Memory and Rightlessness* (Delhi: Centre for Women's Development Studies, 2003). See also "Gender and Reproductive Rights in India: Problems and Prospects for the New Millenium" (Lecture Delivered for the UN Population Fund, New Delhi, 2000).

[140] Baxi, *The Future of Human Rights*, 27-28. Baxi's labels can be confusing. "Modern" here refers to modernity with its associations with the Enlightenment, liberalism, and rationality; "contemporary" is associated with, but deliberately distanced from, post-modernism. This distinction seems to me to be quite close to Boaventura de Sousa Santos' contrast between "regulatory" (modern) and "emancipatory" forms of law. Santos, *Toward a New Common Sense*, c 1, 2 & 9.

[141] Baxi, *The Future of Human Rights*, 34-35; Baxi, "Voices of Suffering," 114.

This passage needs some unpacking. Baxi presents the two paradigms in terms of four main contrasts:

Modern	Contemporary
1. Logics of exclusion	1. Inclusiveness
2. Right to govern	2. Radical self-determination
3. Ascetic (a thin conception of rights)	3. Exuberant (proliferation of rights)
4. Rhetoric of "progress"	4. Voices of suffering

First, while the "contemporary" paradigm is inclusive, the "modern" paradigm for most of its history interpreted "human" to exclude all those who were not to be regarded as human by virtue of having the capacity to reason and an autonomous moral will:

> "In its major phases of development, 'slaves', 'heathens', 'barbarians', colonized peoples, indigenous populations, women, children, the impoverished, and the 'insane' have been, at various times and in various ways, thought unworthy of being bearers of human rights... These discursive devices of Enlightenment rationality were devices of *exclusion*. The 'Rights of Man' were human rights of all men capable of autonomous reason and will."[142]

Baxi is cautious about universalism in relation to claims that there are moral principles that are valid for all times and all places, but he emphasizes the enormous normative significance of the inclusive claim that human rights apply to all human beings by virtue of their humanity.[143]

Second, the logic of exclusion led to the justification of colonialism. The language of 'modern' human rights was often used to justify colonialism, imperialism and patriarchy through the right of property (especially occupation of "terra nullius"—ignoring the presence of indigenous people) and "a natural collective human right of the superior races to rule the inferior ones."[144] In contrast, the contemporary human

---

[142] Ibid., 109-110; Baxi, *The Future of Human Rights*, 29.

[143] All human beings are included, but it is "an anthropomorphic illusion that the range of human rights is limited to human beings; the new rights to a clean and healthy environment... take us far beyond such a narrow notion". Baxi, "Voices of Suffering," 104-5.

[144] Ibid., 110. Cf. Baxi, *The Future of Human Rights*, 29-30. "The construction of a collective right to colonial/ imperial governance is made sensible by the co-

rights paradigm is based on the premise of radical self-determination, insisting that every human person "has a right to a voice, a right to bear witness to violation, a right to immunity from disarticulation by concentrations of economic, social, and political formations. Rights languages, no longer so exclusively at the service of the ends of governance, open up sites of resistance." [145]

Third, "modern" human rights are state-centric and ascetic, treating the state as the only legitimate source of rights and limiting their scope.[146] The sources of "contemporary" human rights are ebullient, leading to "a carnival of production", though this in turn creates problems. They extend not only to discrete minorities but also to "wholly new, hitherto unthought-of, justice constituencies":[147]

"Contemporary enunciations thus embrace, to mention very different orders of example, the rights of the girl child, migrant labor, indigenous peoples, gays and lesbians (the emerging human right to sexual orientation), prisoners and those in custodial institutional regimes, refugees and asylum seekers, and children." [148]

Fourth, the "modern" human rights cultures traced their pedigree to ideas of progress, social Darwinism, racism, and patriarchy. They used these ideas to justify "global imposition of cruelty as 'natural', 'ethical', and 'just'."[149] Because of the exclusionary logic the suffering of large

---

optation of languages of human rights into those of *racist* governance abroad and *class* and *patriarchal* domination at home." Ibid., 31.

[145] Ibid.

[146] e.g. in the conventional discourse torture, cruel inhuman and degrading treatment are classified as violations of human rights, but starvation and domestic violence are not. Ibid., 13 n. 21.

[147] Ibid., 32.

[148] Ibid.; Baxi, "Voices of Suffering", 112.

[149] Baxi, *The Future of Human Rights*, 32. Baxi also uses this idea to attack technocratic   justifications of dams and population control in the name of "progress". For example: "Policy-makers as well as human science specialists are not persuaded, on available evidence, by the rights approach. The reasons for this 'benign neglect' of rights vary. Malthusians and neo-Malthusians are wary of a rights approach, in general, because they perceive 'over-population' as a social scandal and menace; the hard core among them are not perturbed by excesses in 'family planning' programs and measures implementing these. In their view, 'man'-made policy disasters are as welcome as 'natural' disasters that in net effect

numbers of "sub-human" peoples were rendered invisible. By contrast, especially in the wake of the revulsion occasioned by the Holocaust and Hiroshima/Nagasaki, "'contemporary' human rights discursivity is rooted in the illegitimacy of all forms of politics of cruelty."[150] The ensuing regime of international human rights and humanitarian law outlawed some barbaric practices of state power and "this was no small gain" from the standpoint of those violated.[151]

Baxi presents the "modern" as state-centric, top-down, technocratic, exclusionary, lean and mean, used by those in power to legitimate their position and their actions; he presents the "contemporary" as bottom up, rooted in experience of suffering, ebullient, involving radical self-determination, with human rights serving as weapon of protest and empowerment of the dispossessed These two paradigms are not meant to represent successive stages in history; rather they are two ideal types of conceptions of human rights that have been used discursively, sometimes concurrently and sometimes sequentially, mainly in connection with state-oriented Western discourses.

Baxi suggests that an adequate account of the future(s) of human rights requires a developed social theory of human rights, as well as a re-imagined history. At present we lack both. Baxi has been a leading pioneer of socio-legal studies in India, but it is fair to say that he has no more than hinted at what such a social theory might be like.[152] But he has sketched a

---

reduce population levels." Some argue that reduction in population levels may serve better futures for human rights. Baxi, "Sense and Sensibility".
[150] Baxi, *The Future of Human Rights*, 33.
[151] Ibid., 34.
[152] "By a social theory of human rights I wish to designate bodies of knowledge that address (a) genealogies of human rights in "pre-modern", "modern" and "contemporary" human rights discursive formations; (b) contemporary dominant and subaltern images of human rights; (c) tasks confronting projects of engendering human rights; (d) exploration of human rights movements as social movements; (e) impact of science and high-tech. on the theory and practice of human rights; (f) the problematic of the marketization of human rights; (g) the economics of human rights." Ibid., 32 n. 18. The whole of FHR could be said to be a contribution to such a social theory in that it comments briefly on most aspects of this agenda, but mainly in a preliminary and very general way, with very little empirical basis or relationship to mainstream social theory. Baxi cites a number of general books by Santos, Unger, Shivji and others that mark "beginnings" of such an enterprise, but he acknowledges that we are a long way from achieving the kind of "grand theory" that he thinks is needed. Ibid.

general approach to the kind of history needed to underpin his vision of a healthy future for human rights. Clearly such history would need to be based on the kind of detailed "history from below" exemplified by Edward Thompson, Peter Linebaugh, or George Rudé,[153] as well as the kind of sardonic work on official archives of a Brian Simpson.[154] But it would also need the grand sweep of world history that one associates with Eric Hobsbawm, Immanuel Wallerstein or Patrick Glenn.[155] Baxi does not claim to have written a history of human rights, but he has made a devastating critique of the predominant mode of complacent, self-congratulatory narratives that dominate much human rights literature.

Baxi characterizes human rights discourse as ebullient, even carnivalistic. These adjectives might be applied to his own writings on human rights. Since 1990 he has published several books, a revised edition of *The Future of Human Rights* and many articles on the subject. More are in the pipeline. He has written specifically on population control, bio-technology, international business ethics, environmental issues, globalization, terrorism and responses to terrorism, and good governance all in relation to human rights. In short he is a prolific writer who presents a continuously moving target. Some of his most colorful passages are found in quite particular studies. Nevertheless, they are given coherence by a single theme:

---

[153] E. P Thompson, *Whigs and Hunters* (Harmondsworth: Peregrine, 1977), and *The Making of the English Working Class* (Harmondsworth: Peregrine, 1963); Linebaugh and Rediker, *Many–Headed Hydra*, and George Rudé, *The Crowd in the French Revolution* (Oxford: Clarendon Press, 1959). See also Balakrishnan Rajagopal, *International Law from Below* (Cambridge: Cambridge University Press, 2003), c. 1 & 2. Like Baxi, Rajagopal locates much of the history of human rights in resistance to colonialism.

[154] A.W. Brian Simpson, *Human Rights and the End of Empire: Britain and the Genesis of the European Convention* (Oxford: Oxford University Press, 2001).

[155] E.g. Eric Hobsbawm, *Age of Capital 1848-1875* (New York: Vintage Books, 1996), *The Age of Empire 1875-1914* (London: Abacus, 1994), *The Age of Extremes 1914-1991* (London: Abacus, 1995); Immanuel Wallerstein, *The Capitalist World Economy* (Cambridge: Cambridge University Press, 1979); and Patrick Glenn, *Legal Traditions of the World* (Oxford: Oxford University Press, 2004); cf. Lauren Benton, *Law and Colonial Cultures: Legal Regimes in World History 1400-1900* (Cambridge: Cambridge University Press, 2002).

"Human rights futures, dependent as they are upon imparting an authentic voice to human suffering, must engage in a discourse of suffering that moves the world." [156]

Conclusion

A just international order and a healthy cosmopolitan discipline of law need to include perspectives that take account of the standpoints, interests, concerns and beliefs of non-Western peoples and traditions. The dominant scholarly and activist discourses about human rights have developed largely without reference to these other perspectives. Claims about universality sit uneasily with ignorance of other traditions and parochial or ethnocentric tendencies.

As was indicated above, this chapter is part of a larger project to make writings about human rights from non-Western perspectives more accessible in the West. The two individuals whose more general ideas on human rights are presented here cannot be considered to be a representative sample of "Southern" viewpoints on human rights; nor can they claim to be spokespersons for any group or people any more than can other public intellectuals. It is hoped that the ideas of many more legal writers, not only those occupied with human rights, can be made similarly accessible.

Even if one restricts oneself to writings in English, there are many candidates. For instance, two Nobel Prize winners, Shirin Ebadi and Aung San Suu Kyi might right the gender balance. There are other contemporary scholars from outside Europe who have written about human rights. Some like Amartya Sen, Nelson Mandela and Justice Christie Weeramantry are world famous, as are successive Secretary-Generals of the United Nations. Others, such as Issa Shivji of Tanzania, several Latin America jurists, or the late Neelan Tiruchelvan of Sri Lanka are well-known in their own regions and in specialist circles. There is a younger generation of scholars who are coming into prominence, some of whom are quite skeptical about human rights.[157] And there is an extensive literature on Islam, human rights and law reform. If the project is extended to include writings in other languages, writings about other areas of law, writings in other media and so on, the possibilities are endless. I have selected these examples solely because I am familiar with their work, know them personally and

---

[156] Baxi, "Voices of Suffering", 156.
[157] E.g. Makau Mutua, Mahmood Mamdani and Balakrishnan Rajagopal.

believe that their ideas need to be better known. So the case studies in this chapter are part of a quite narrow project intended to illustrate one potential route to a broader perspective on human rights discourse and action.

Bibliography

Andreassen, B-A and Susan Marks, eds. *Development as a Human Right: Legal, Political and Economic Dimensions.* Cambridge: Harvard University Press, 2006.

An-Na'im, Abdullahi. *Toward an Islamic Reformation: Civil Liberties, Human Rights and International Law.* Syracuse: Syracuse University Press, 1990.

—. *Human Rights in Cross-cultural Perspectives: Quest for Consensus.* Philadelphia: Pennsylvania University Press, 1992.

—. "To Affirm the Full Human Rights Standing of Economic, Social and Cultural Rights". In *Economic Social and Cultural Rights in Practice: The Role of Judges in Implementing Economic, Social and Cultural Rights*, edited by Yash Ghai and Jill Cottrell. London: Interights, 2004.

Barry, W. T. de. *The Trouble with Confucianism.* Cambridge: Harvard University Press, 1991.

Bauer, Joanne and Daniel A. Bell, eds. *The East Asian Challenge to Human Rights.* Cambridge: Cambridge University Press, 1999.

Baxi, Upendra. *Courage, Craft and Contention: The Indian Supreme Court in the Eighties.* Bombay: Tripathi, 1985.

—. *Inhuman Wrongs and Human Rights: Some Unconventional Essays.* New Delhi: Har Anand, 1994.

—. *Mambrino's Helmet?: Human Rights for a Changing World.* Delhi: Har Anand, 1994.

—. " 'A Work in Progress?': The United Nations Report to the United Nations Human Rights Committee". *Indian Journal of International Law* 38 (1996).

—. " 'Global Neighbourhood' and the 'Universal Otherhood': Notes on the Report of the Commission on Global Governance". *Alternatives* 21, 1996: 525-549.

—. "The Unreason of Globalization and the Reason of Human Rights". A.K. Desai Memorial Lecture, University of Bombay, 1996.

—. "Voices of Suffering, Fragmented Universality, and the Future of Human Rights". In *The Future of International Human Rights*, edited by Burns H. Weston and Stephen P. Marks. Ardsley: Transnational Publishers, 1999.

—. "Mass Torts, Multinational Enterprise Liability and Private international Law" In *Recueil des Cours 276*, Hague Academy of International Law. The Hague: Martinus Nijhoff, 2000.

—. "Constitutionalism as a Site of State Formative Practices." *Cardozo Law Review* 21 (2000).

—. "What Happens Next is Up to You: Human Rights at Risk in Dams and Development." *American University International Law Review* 16 (2001).

—. "Too many, or too few, human rights?" *Human Rights Law Review* 1 (2001).

—. *The Future of Human Rights*. Delhi: Oxford University Press, 2002.

—. *Memory and Rightlessness*. New Delhi, Centre for Women's Development Studies, 2002.

—. "Sense and Sensibility" *India Seminar 511*: March, 2002. www.India-seminar.com/semsearch.htm.

—. "Market Fundamentalisms: Business Ethics at the Altar of Rights" *Human Rights Law Review* 5 (2005).

—. "The War *ON* Terror and the War *OF* Terror: Nomadic Multititudes, Aggressive Incumbents, and the 'New' International Law: Prefatory Remarks on Two 'Wars'." *Osgoode Hall Law Journal* 43 (2005).

—. *The Future of Human Rights*. New Delhi: Oxford University Press, 2006.

—. *The Human Right to Human Rights Education? Some Critical Perspectives*. New Delhi: Universal Law Book Co, 2006.

—. "Development as a Human Right or as Political Largesse? Does it make any difference?" (Founder' Day Lecture) Madras: Madras Institute of Development Studies, 2006.

—. *Human Rights in a Posthuman World*. New Delhi: Oxford University Press, 2007.

Baxi, Upendra and A. Dhandha eds. *Valiant Victims and Lethal Litigation: The Bhopal Case*. Bombay: Tripathi, 1990.

Baxi, Upendra and Shulamith Koenig. *The People's Report on Human Rights Education*. New York: The People's Movement for Human Rights Education, 2002.

Benton, Lauren. *Law and Colonial Cultures: Legal Regimes in World History 1400-1900*. Cambridge: Cambridge University Press, 2002.

Davitt SJ. Father "Basic Value Judgments in Preliterate Custom and Law", Chicago: Council for the Study of Mankind-Conference on Law and the Idea of Mankind, 1963/4 (unpublished paper).

Dembour, Marie. *Who Believes in Human Rights? The European Convention in Question.* Cambridge: Cambridge University Press, 2006.

Fishbayn, Lisa. "Litigating the Right to Culture: Family Law in the New South Africa". *International Journal of Law, Policy and the Family* 13 (1999): 147.

Foot, Rosemary. *Rights Beyond Borders.* Oxford: Oxford University Press, 2000.

Ghai, Dharam and Yash Ghai. *Asians in East and Central Africa.* London: Minority Rights Group, 1971. (Reprinted in Whitaker, Ben ed. *The Fourth World Victims of Group Oppression.* New York: Schoken, 1973).

Ghai, Yash. "Independence and Safeguards in Kenya." *East African Law Journal* 3 (1967): 177.

—. "The Asian Minorities of East and Central Africa." In *The Fourth World Victims of Group Oppression,* edited by Ben Whitaker. New York: Schoken, 1973.

—. "Legal Radicalism, Professionalism and Social Action: Reflections on Teaching Law in Dar-es-Salaam." In *The Limits of Legal Radicalism,* edited by Issa Shivji. Dar-es-Salaam: University of Dar-es-Salaam, 1986.

—. "Law, Development and African Scholarship." *The Modern Law Review* 50 (1987): 750.

—. ed. *Put Our World to Rights.* London: Commonwealth Human Rights Initiative, 1991.

—. "Asian Perspectives on Human Rights." *Hong Kong Law Journal* 23 (1993): 342.

—. "The Politics of Human Rights in Asia." In *Frontiers of Legal Scholarship,* edited by Geoffrey Wilson. Chichester: Wiley, 1995.

—. "Sentinels of Liberty or Sheep in Woolf's Clothing? Judicial Politics and the Hong Kong Bill of Rights." *Modern Law Review* 60 (1997): 459.

—. "The Rule of Law and Capitalism: Reflections on the Basic Law." In *Hong Kong, China and 1997: Essays in Legal Theory*, edited by Raymond Wacks. Hong Kong: Hong Kong University, 1993.

—. "Rights, Duties and Responsibilities." In *Asian Values: Encounters with Diversity*, edited by J. Caughelin, P. Lim, and B. Mayer-Konig. London: Curzon Press, 1998.

—. "Human Rights and Asian Values." *Public Law Review* 9 (1998): 168.

—. *Asian Human Rights Charter: A People's Charter.* Hong Kong: Asian Human Rights Commission, 1998.

—. *Hong Kong's New Constitutional Order*. Hong Kong: Hong Kong University Press, 1999.

—. "Rights, Social Justice and Globalization in East Asia." In *The East Asian Challenge to Human Rights*, edited by Joanne Bauer and Daniel A. Bell. Cambridge: Cambridge University Press, 1999.

—. ed. *Autonomy and Ethnicity: Negotiating Competing Claims in Multiethnic States*. Cambridge: Cambridge University Press, 2000.

—. "Universalism and Relativism: Human Rights as a Framework for Negotiating Interethnic Claims." *Cardozo Law Review* 21 (2000): 1095.

—. *Public Participation and Minorities*. London: Minority Rights Group International, 2003.

—. "Constitution-making in a new Iraq." In *Building Democracy in Iraq*, edited by Yash Ghai, M. Lattimer and Y. Said. London: Minority Rights Group International, 2003.

—. "A Journey around Constitutions" (Beinart Lecture, University of Capetown, 2002) *South African Law Journal* 122 (2005): 804.

—. "Redesigning the State for Right Development." In *Development as a Human Right: Legal, Political and Economic Dimensions,* edited by B-A Andreassen and Susan Marks. Cambridge: Harvard University Press, 2006.

—. "Understanding Human Rights in Asia." In *International Protection of Human Rights: A Textbook*, edited by Catarina Krause and Martin Scheinin. Turku: Institute for Human Rights, 2008. (Reprinted in *Human Rights: Southern Voices*, edited by Twinning, William. Cambridge: Cambridge University Press, 2009).

Ghai, Yash and Patrick McAuslan. *Public Law and Political Change in Kenya*. Nairobi and London: Oxford University Press, 1970.

Ghai, Yash, Mark Lattimer and Yahai Said. *Building Democracy in Ira.* London: Minority Rights Group International, 2003.

Ghai, Yash and Jill Cottrell eds. *Economic, Social and Cultural Rights in Practice: The Role of Judges in Implementing Economic, Social and Cultural Rights*. London: Interights, 2004.

Ghali, Boutros Boutros. "Human Rights. The Common Language of Humanity." In *The Vienna Declaration and the Programme for Action*. UN World Conference on Human Rights, 1993.

Glenn, Patrick. *Legal Traditions of the World.* Oxford: Oxford University Press, 2004.

Government of Singapore. *Shared Values*. Singapore: Government Printers, 1991

Haack, Susan. *Manifesto of a Passionate Moderate*. Chicago: University of Chicago Press, 1998.

Hobsbawm, Eric. *The Age of Capital 1848-1875*. New York: Vintage Books, 1996.

—. *The Age of Empire 1875-1914*. London: Abacus, 1994.

—. *The Age of Extremes: The Short Twentieth Century, 1914-1991*. London: Abacus, 1995

Hsieh, Yu-Wei. "The status of the individual in Chinese ethics." In *The Status of the Individual in East and West*, edited by Charles Moore. Honolulu: University of Hawaii Press, 1968.

Jung, Kim Dae. "Is Culture Destiny?" *Foreign Affairs* 73 (1994): 189.

Karst, Kenneth. "The Bonds of American Nationhood." *Cardozo Law Review* 21 (2000): 1095.

Kent, Ann. *China, the United Nations and Human Rights: The Limits of Compliance*. Philadelphia: University of Pennsylvania Press, 1999.

Krause, Catarina and Martin Scheinin eds. *International Protection of Human Rights: A Textbook*. Turku: Institute for Human Rights, 2008.

Lester, Lord of Herne Hill and Colm O'Cinneide, "The Effective Protection of Socio-economic Rights." In *Economic, Social and Cultural Rights in Practice: The Role of Judges in Implementing Economic, Social and Cultural Rights*, edited by Yash Ghai and Jill Cottrell. London: Interights, 2004.

Linebaugh, Peter and Marcus Rediker. *The Many–Headed Hydra: Sailors, Slaves, Commoners and the Hidden History of the Revolutionary Atlantic.* London: Verso, 2000.

Mamdani, Mahmood. *Beyond Rights Talk and Culture Talk: Comparative Essays on the Politics and Rights of Culture.* New York: St Martin's Press, 2000.

Mendhelson, Oliver and Upendra Baxi eds. *The Rights of Subordinated Peoples.* Delhi: Oxford University Press, 1994.

Nyerere, Julius. *Freedom and Unity (Uhuru na Umoja): A Selection from Writings and Speeches 1952-65.* Dar-es-Salam: Oxford University Press, 1966.

Rajagopal, Balakrishnan. *International Law from Below: Development, Social Movements and Third World Resistance.* Cambridge: Cambridge University Press, 2003.

Rawls, John. *The Law of Peoples.* Cambridge: Harvard University Press, 1999.

Renteln, Alison Dundas. *Relativism and the Search for Human Rights.* London: Sage, 1990.

Rudé, George. *The Crowd in the French Revolution.* Oxford: Clarendon Press, 1959.

Santos, Boaventura de Sousa. *Towards a New Common Sense* London: Routledge, 1995.

Sen, Amartya. "Human Rights and Asian Values: What Lee Kuan Yew and I Peng don't Understand about Asia." *The New Republic* July 14 (1997): 21, 33 & 40.

Shivji, Issa ed. *The Limits of Legal Radicalism.* Dar-es-Salam, University of Dar-es-Salam, 1986.

—. *The Concept of Human Rights in Africa.* London: Codesria, 1989.

Siddiqi, Muhammad Nejatullah. *Banking Without Interest.* Leicester: The Islamic Foundation, 1997.

Simpson, A. W. Brian. *Human Rights and the End of Empire: Britain and the Genesis of the European Convention.* Oxford: Oxford University Press, 2001.

Soueif, Ahdaf. *The Map of Love.* London: Bloomsbury, 1999.

Steiner, Henry and Philip Alston. *International Human Rights in Context: Law, Politics, Morals.* Oxford: Clarendon Press, 2008.

Taylor, Charles. "Conditions of an Unenforced Consensus on Human Rights." In *The East Asian Challenge to Human Rights, edited by* oanne Bauer and Daniel Bell. Cambridge: Cambridge University Press, 1999.

Thompson, Edward P. *The Making of the English Working Class.* Harmondsworth: Peregrine, 1963.

Thompson, Edward P. *Whigs and Hunters.* Harmondsworth: Peregrine, 1977.

Twining, William. *Globalisation and Legal Theory*. London: Butterworth, 2000.

—. "Human Rights: Southern Voices" (MacDonald Lecture, University of Alberta). *Review of Constitutional Studies* 11 (2005): 203.

—. "General Jurisprudence." University of Miami International and Comparative Law Review 15 (2007).

—. *General Jurisprudence: Understanding Law from a Global Perspective.* Cambridge: Cambridge University Press, 2009.

—. ed. *Human Rights: Southern Voices. Francis Deng, Abdullahi An-Na'im, Yash Ghai and Upendra Baxi.* Cambridge: Cambridge University Press, 2009.

Wallerstein, Immanuel. *The Capitalist World-Economy.* Paris & Cambridge: Editions de la Maison des Sciences de l'Homme & Cambridge University Press, 1979.

Webber, Jeremy. "Relations of Force and Relations of Justice: The Emergence of Normative Community Between Colonists and Aboriginal Peoples." *Osgoode Hall Law Journal* 33 (1995): 624.

Wei-Ming, Tu *Confucian Thought: Self-Hood as Creative Transformation.* Albany: State University of New York Press, 1985.

Widner, Jennifer A. *Building the Rule of Law: Francis Nyalali and the Road to Judicial Independence in Africa.* New York: Norton, 2001.

Wilson, Geoffrey ed. *Frontiers of Legal Scholarship.* Chichester: Wiley, 1995.

Zakaria, Fareed. "A Conversation with Lee Kuan Yew." *Foreign Affairs* 73 (1994): 109.

PART III:

DECOLONIZING CONSTITUTIONAL AND INTERNATIONAL HUMAN RIGHTS LAW

CHAPTER TEN

THE RULE OF LAW IN INDIA

UPENDRA BAXI

A New Discourse?

The Rule of Law (as a set of principles and doctrines -hereafter ROL) has a long normative history that privileges it as an inaugural contribution of the Euro American liberal political theory. ROL emerges variously, as a "thin" notion entailing procedural restraints on forms of sovereign power and governmental conduct, which may also authorize Holocaustian practices of politics[1] and as a "thick" conception involving the theories about the "good", "right", and "just".[2]

---

[1] G. Agamben, *Homo Sacer: Sovereign Power and Bare Life* (Stanford: Stanford University Press, 1995). See also G. Aderni, "Legal Intimations: Michael Oakeshott and the Rule of Law" *Wisconsin Law Review* (1993): 838; U. Baxi, "The Gujarat Catastrophe: Notes on Reading Politics as Democidal Rape Culture" in *The Violence of Normal Times: Essays on Women's Lived Realities*, ed., K. Kababiran (New Delhi: Women Unlimited and Kali for Women, 2005), 332-384; U. Baxi "Postcolonial Legality", in *A Companion to Postcolonial Studies*, eds., H. Schwartz and S. Roy, (Oxford: Blackwell, 2001) 540-555; B. Fine, *Democracy and the Rule of Law: Liberal Ideals and Marxist Critiques* (London: Pluto Press, 1984); M. Galanter, *Competing Equalities* (Delhi: Oxford University Press, 1984); M. Hidyatuallah, *The Fifth and Sixth Schedules of the Constitution of India* (Gauhati: Ashok Publishing House, 1979); C. Schmitt, *Political Theology: Four Chapters on the Concept of Sovereignty* (Cambridge: The MIT Press, 1985); A. Sen, *Development as Freedom* (Oxford: Oxford University Press, 1999) and J. Stone, *The Social Dimensions of Law and Justice* (Sydney: Maitland, 1966), 797-799.
[2] See, for this distinction variously elaborated, L. Fuller, *Morality of Law* (New Haven: Yale University Press, 1964); N. McCormick, "Natural Law and the Separation of Law and Morals" in *Natural Law Theory: Contemporary Essays*, ed., R. P. George (Oxford: Clarendon Press, 1992), 105- 133; J. Finnis, *Natural Law and Natural Rights* (Oxford: Oxford Clarendon Press,1980) and G. Q.

The patrimonial liberal ROL discourse organizes amnesia of alternative traditions. It allows not even a meagre reflection on the normative socialist ROL conceptions. It disregards the possibility that other ROL traditions of thought ever existed: for example, the pre-colonial, those shaped by the revolt against the Old Empire, or the non-mimetic contributions by the proud judiciaries in some "developing societies".[3]

Likewise, a community of critical historians has demonstrated that in the countries of origin, both the "thin" and "thick" versions for long stretches of history remained consistent with violent social exclusion; the institutional histories of ROL in the metropolis for a long while remained signatures of domination by men over women, by the owners of means of production over the possessors of labour-power, and by persecution of religious, cultural and civilizational minorities. Students of colonialism/ imperialism have stressed that the ROL values remained wholly a "whites-only" affair.[4] The triumphalist celebration of ROL as an "unqualified human good" even goes so far as to reduce struggles against colonialism/ imperialism as an ultimate unfolding in human history of the liberal values coded by the ROL.[5] Even the insurgent histories that generate a universal recognition of human right to self determination and further the itineraries of contemporary human rights stand misrecognized as the miming of the Euroamerican ROL world-historic imagination! The historic fact that non-Western communities of *résistance* and peoples in struggle have enriched 'thick' ROL conceptions is simply glossed over by the persistent myths of the "western" origins;[6] the promotion of ROL as prize cultural export continues old contamination in even more aggressive forms in this era of contemporary globalization.

Walker, *The Rule of Law: Foundation of Constitutional Democracy* (Carlton: Melbourne University Press, 1988).

[3] A valuable comparative beginning is made by a group of scholars: see, R. Peernbohm, *Asian Discourses on the Rule of Law: Theories and Implementation of Rule of Law in Twelve Asian Countries, France and U.S.* (London: Routledge, 2004). The present essay substantially extends and revises my contribution to the volume.

[4] See R. Young, *Postcolonialism: An Introduction* (Oxford: Blackwell, 2001) and U. Baxi, "The Colonialist Heritage" in *Comparative Legal Studies: Traditions and Transitions*, eds., P. Legrand and R. Munday (Cambridge: Cambridge University Press, 2003), 6-58. See also the materials therein cited.

[5] E. P. Thompson, *Whigs and Hunters: The Origins of the Black Act* (London: Allen Lane, 1975).

[6] U. Baxi, *The Future of Human Rights* (New Delhi: Oxford University Press, 2006).

The "New-ness" of Contemporary ROL Talk

In contemporary talk, however, ROL goes transnational or global. It is no longer a bounded conception but is now presented as a universalizing/ globalizing notion. In part, the new "global rule of law" relates to the emerging notions of global social policy and regulation.[7]

More specifically, the networks of international trade and investment regimes promote a view that national constitutions are obstacles that need "elimination" via the newly-fangled discourses of global economic constitutionalism.[8] The war *on* "terror" now altogether redefines even the "thin" ROL notions.[9] The paradigm of Universal Declaration of Human Rights stands now confronted by a new paradigm of trade-related, market-friendly human rights.[10] The inherently undemocratic international financial institutions (IFIs), notably the World Bank, not the elected officials in "developing" societies, now present themselves as a new global sovereign who decides how the "poor" may be defined, poverty measured, the "voices of the poor" may be globally archived, and how poverty alleviation and sustainable development conditionalities may expediently redefine "good governance". The precious and manifold diverse civil society and new social movement actors do not quite escape

---

[7] Differently presented, for example in J. Braithwaite and P. Drahos, *Global Bussines Regulation* (Cambridge: Cambridge Univeristy Press, 2000), M. Chibundo "Globalizing the Rule of Law: Some Thoughts at and on the Priphery," *Indiana Journal of Global Legal Studies* (1999): 79-116 and B. S. Chimni, "Co-option and Resistance: Two Faces of Global Administrative Law," *New York Journal of International Law and Politics* 4/5 (2005): 799-827.

[8] See S. Gill, "Toward a Post-Modern Prince? The Battle in Seattle as a Moment in the New Politics of Globalization," *Millenium* 1 (2000): 131-141, and D. Schneiderman, "Constitutional Approches to Privatization: An Inquiry into the Magnitude of Neo-Liberal Constitutionalism", *Law and Contemporary Problems* 4 (2000): 83-109.

[9] See U. Baxi, "'The War on Terror' and the 'War of Terror': Nomadic Multitudes, Aggressive Incumbents and the 'New International Law'", *Osgoode Hall Law Journal* 1/ 2 (2005): 1-36. See also M.L. Satterthwaite, "Rendered Meaningless: Extraordinary Rendition and the Rule of Law", *New York University Public Law and Legal Theory Working Papers*, 43 (2006), and Asociation of the Bar of the City of New York and Centre for Human Rights and Global Justice, *Torture by Proxy: International and Domestic Law Applicable to "Extraordinary Rendition"* (New York: ABCNY and NYU School of Law, 2004).

[10] Baxi, *Future*.

the Master/Slave dialectic; even when they otherwise contest wholesale, they accept in retail the new globalizing ROL notions and platforms.

Space constraints forbid a fully detailed analysis of the newness of ROL; however, it remains appropriate to point at least to some crucial factors. First, the current extension of ROL to the realms of international development, economic, strategic and even military international orders is discontinuous with the Cold War, which marked at least two violently competing paradigms of ROL: the bourgeois and the socialist. Today, the socialist ROL, a form in which private ownership of means of production was not considered the foundation of a "good" society and human freedom, has almost disappeared from view.[11] Second, increasingly now it becomes difficult to keep apart the ROL from the new human rights and global social policy languages; I may rather refer here for example, to voluminous ongoing work of the United Nations human rights treaty bodies, the effort to develop the right to development, the Millennial Development Goals and Targets, which develop rather different kinds of globalizing ROL-oriented normativity. Third, the merger between these human rights and global social policy carries some costs. The so-called universal human rights become eminently negotiable instruments in the pursuit of diverse global policies. Fourth, even as the so called "judicial globalization" promotes an unprecedented salience of judicial actors, their modes of activist justicing, at national, regional and supranational levels introduces new ways of articulation of ROL values and standards, it also, at the same moment, promotes, the structural adjustment of judicial activism.

Fifth, human rights and social activism practices contribute more than ever before to a multitudinous re-articulation of the rolled-up ROL notions. Human and social rights activism needs to contest the hyper-globalizing ROL talk, promoting the reach of the communities of direct foreign investors, often personified by the new sovereign estates of multinational corporations (MNCs), and more generally by their normative cohorts, principally international financial institutions, and development assistance regimes. At the same time historically situated activist agencies also remain confronted with the need to reinvigorate some proceduralist and some "thick" ROL conceptions.

---

[11] But see R. Peernbohm, "Let One Hundred Flowers Bloom, One Hundred School Contend:
Debating Rule of Law in China," *Michigan Journal of International Law* 23 (2002): 471.

Sixth, the new ROL discursivity/idolatry presenting it as a new form of global public good remains unmarked and untroubled by the bounded ROL conceptions, which had as its cornerstone the doctrine of separation of powers, or differentiation of governance functions, that fosters the belief in limited governance, an antidote to tyranny, signified by concentration of powers. True, as Louis Althusser[12] reminded us, the doctrine also masks the "centralized unity of state power". The bounded ROL talk at least provided platforms of critique; the globalizing ROL knowing no such conception that may limit "global good governance" further undermines the "rationality" of the bounded ROL conceptions.[13]

At stake then remains in the new ROL discourse a deep contradiction between ROL as a globalizing discourse that celebrates various forms of "free" market fundamentalisms and some new forms that seek "radically" to universalize human rights fundamentalisms. This incommensurability defines both the space for interpretive diversity and also a growing progress in measurement that standardize, via human rights and development indicators/benchmarks, new core meanings of the ROL.

Government of Laws and Men

ROL notions have suffered much by two popularizing aphorisms: ROL signifies "government of laws, not of men"; "Rule of Law is both, and at once, government of law and of men". If "men" is used inclusively as signifying all human beings, the slogans may signify secularity: not Divine authority but human power makes both government and law. This however poses the question whether constitutions and laws based on religion disqualify at the threshold from being ROL societies. On a different plane, in the feminist practices of thought that inclusiveness remains always suspect. It identifies literally both these slogans as representing the government of, by, and for men. This raises the question concerning feminization of state and law in a post-patriarchal society.

---

[12] Ben Brewster, trans., *Althusser, Montesquieu, Rousseau, Marx: Politics and History* (London: Verso, 1982).

[13] Indeed, the separation of powers invests the executive with sovereign discretion in the realms of macro and micro development planning, arms production (inclusive of weapons of mass destruction), decisions to wage many types of (covert as well as overt) war, or management of insurgent violence. Our ROL talk unsurprisingly, but still unhappily, more or less, ends where the militarized state begins-the "secret" state-to evoke E. P. Thompson. See E.P. Thompson, *Writing by the Candlelight* (London: The Merlin Press, 1989).

Likewise, the emerging critique on the platform of rights of peoples living with disability translates both "government" and "men" as affairs of dominance by all those temporarily able-ed. This raises the question of indifference to difference. I may not here pursue these, and related, questions for reasons of space save to say that all ROL notions that ignore them remain ethically fractured.

The ROL message that those in power should somehow construct and respect constraints on their own power is surely an important one. But the importance of this sensible requirement is not clear enough. To be sure, rulers as well as ruled ought to remain bound by the law (conceived here as a going legal order, an order of legality) regardless of the privilege of power. But it is never clear enough whether they ought to do so instrumentally (that is in Max Weber's terms "purpose rational", even expedient rule following conduct) or intrinsically (legality as an ethical value and virtue.) Instrumentalist compliance negotiates ROL languages in ways that perfect pathways of many a hegemonic and rank tyrannical credential. To follow ROL values because they define the "good", the right, and the "just" law and state conduct is to develop a governance ethic. It is at this stage that massive difficulties begin even when we may want to consider the ROL tasks as those defining the "rule of *good law*".

Elucidating "good" law entails "a complete social philosophy" which deprives the notion of "any useful function". As Joseph Raz[14] acutely reminds us: "We have no need to be converted to rule of law in order to discover that to believe in it is also to believe that good should triumph". But the "good" that triumphs, as a "complete social philosophy", may be, and indeed has often been, defined in ways that perpetuate states of Radical Evil— complete social philosophies have justified, and remain capable of justifying, varieties of violent social exclusion. Is this the reason why contemporary postmetaphysical approaches invite us to tasks of envisioning justice–qualities of the basic structure of society, economy, and polity, in ways that render otiose the Rule of Law languages?[15]

---

[14] J. Raz, "The Rule of Law and its Virtue", *Law Quarterly Review* 93 (1977): 208.
[15] See J. Rawls, *The Law of Peoples* (Cambridge: Harvard University Press, 1999) and *Political Liberalism* (New York: Columbia University Press, 1993). See also J. Habermas, *Between Facts and Norms: Contributions to a Discourse Theory of Law and Democracy* (Cambridge: The MIT Press,1996).

What ROL Addresses and Doesn't?

In any response to this question, it may be useful to make a distinction between ROL as providing constraint-languages and facilitative languages. As constraint–languages, fully informed by the logics and languages of contemporary human rights, ROL speaks to what sovereign power and state conduct may not, after all, *do*. It is now normatively well accepted that state actors may not as ways of governance practice genocide, ethnic cleansing, institutionalized apartheid, slavery/slave-like practices, and rape and other forms of abuse of women. Outside this, the ROL constraint languages stipulate/legislate the following general notions:

1. State powers ought to be differentiated; no single public authority ought to combine the roles of the judge, jury and executioner.
2. Laws/decrees ought to remain in the public domain; that is, laws ought to be general, public, and ought to remain contestable political decisions.
3. Governance via undeclared emergencies remains violative of ROL values and illegitimate.
4. Constitutionally declared states of emergency may not constitute indefinite practices of governance and adjudicative power ought not to authorize gross, flagrant, ongoing, and massive violation of human rights and fundamental freedoms during the states of emergency.
5. The delegation of legislative powers to the executive ought always   to respect some limits to arbitrary sovereign discretion.
6. Governance at all moments ought to remain limited by regard for human rights and fundamental freedoms.
7. Governance powers may be exercised only within the ambit of legislatively defined intent and purpose.
8. Towards these ends, the State and law ought not to resist, or to repeal powers of judicial review or engage in practices that adversely affect the independence of the legal profession.

These "oughts", far from constituting any fantastic wish-list, define the terrain of ongoing contests directed to inhibit unbridled state power and governance conduct. The question is not whether these "oughts" are necessary but whether they are *sufficient*. It is here that we enter the realms of the ROL facilitative languages which leave open a vast array of choices for the design and detail of governance structures and processes. These choices concern the processes of composing legitimate political authority, forms of political rule, obligations of those governed and of those who govern.

Constitution of legitimate authority

The ROL does not quite address this dimension. Assuming, however, that universal adult franchise constitutes a core ROL value, the ROL seems equally well served by both the "first past the post" or "proportional" and "preferential" voting systems and related variants. Neither the thin nor the thick ROL versions offer any precise norms and standards for the delimitation of constituencies in ways that avoid gerrymandering representation.[16] Further, ROL remains rather indifferent to the question of state funding of elections; nor does it engage corporate campaign funding. Elections cost big money for political leaders and parties at fray; what "regulation" may violate the liberal ROL freedom of speech and association values remains an open question. So do appeals to forms of "hate speech" in the competitive campaign politics. The dominant ROL discourse moreover remains indifferent to the question of affirmative programs of legislative representation, which modify the right to contest elections for cultural and civilizational minority groups and coequal gender representation. The ROL languages, for weal or woe, insufficiently address the notion of participation, do not extend so far as to prescribe means of constitutional change such as referenda, or the right to recall of errant or corrupt legislators.

Forms of political rule

As concerns structures of governance, ROL remains rather indifferent to choices amongst *federalism* over *unitary*, *republican* over *monarchical*, *secular* over *theocratic*, *flexible* over *rigid*, constitutional formats. Nor do these foreclose choices concerning the scope and method for amending constitutions. The composition, of judicial power and of the administration of justice (methods of judicial appointment, tenure, and removal of judges, constructions of judicial hierarchies, etc.) remain infinitely open within the ROL languages.

---

[16] See J. Morgan Kouseer, *Colorblind Injustice: Minority Voting Rights and the Undoing of the Second Reconstruction* (Chapel Hill: University of North Carolina Press, 1999).

Obligations of governed and of governors

The celebrated constraints upon lawmaking (legislative) power do *not* entail any ethical *obligation* to make laws for instance, a public 'right' to have a law made for disadvantaged, dispossessed, and deprived peoples; these remorseless non-decisions impact upon many a human, and human rights, future. Niklas Luhman reminded us poignantly that political decision concerning the making/unmaking/remaking of laws remains nothing but the *positivization of arbitrariness*. However, this arbitrariness is overridden by the disciplinary globalization where the South States have mandatory obligations to make law favouring the communities of direct foreign investors over those of their own citizens; these obligations stand fostered by transnational corporations and international financial institutions which themselves owe very little democratic accountability and human rights responsibilities.

Finally, without being exhaustive, how may ROL address its Other? A multitude of mass illegalities often historically generate forms of citizen understandings that eventually redefine interpretations of the ROL. Inflected by indeterminate notions of popular "sovereignty", these divergent insurgencies signify terrains of struggle of the Multitudes against the Rule of the Minuscule.[17] What space may we, and how, may "we", (the ROL "symbol traders") provide for these militant particularisms in our narratives?

This summary checklist of anxieties is *not* intended to suggest that we dispense altogether with the ROL languages and logics. Rather, it invites sustained labours that subject the normative and ideological histories and frontiers of ROL with very great care and strict scrutiny.

---

[17] I invite your attention to such diverse phenomena as May 1968, the campus protest in the
United States against the Vietnam War, massive peoples demonstrations against the Uruguay
round and the WTO, the Tiananmen Square, the struggles against apartheid regimes in the United States and South Africa, against perversions of the East and Central European socialist legality and more recently the protests against the invasion of Iraq and the various 'velvet' and 'orange' revolutions. For befittingly amorphous notions of 'multitudes' see, A. Negri, *Insurgencies: Constituent Power and the Modern State* (Minnesota: University of Minnesota Press, 1999); A. Negri and M. Hardt, *Empire* (Cambridge: Harvard University Press, 2000); and in a rather dissimilar genre see P. Virno, *A Grammar of the Multitude. For an Analysis of Contemporary Forms of Life* (Los Angeles and New York: Semiotext(E), 2004).

Towards this end, I reiterate my one sentence summation: ROL is always and everywhere a terrain of peoples' struggle incrementally to make power *accountable*, governance *just*, and state *ethical*. Undoubtedly, each romantic/radical term used here (accountability, justice and ethics) needs deciphering and in what follows I seek to do so by reflecting on the Indian ROL theory and practice.

Originality and Mimesis-Postcolonial Indian ROL

Of necessity, many a colonially induced historic continuity[18] marks the Indian Constitution. But the colonial inheritance relates more to the apparatuses and institutions of governance than to conceptions of justice, rights, and development. These in turn affect continuities with the colonial past. The distinctiveness of the Indian ROL lies in providing space for a continuing conversation among four core notions: "rights", "development", "governance" and "justice".[19] Thus it also offers revisions of the liberal conceptions of rights, which affect distinctive forms of constitutional life of the South.[20]

The hegemonic ROL talk underestimates the world historic pertinence of the Indian constitutionalism ROL conceptions. In the scramble for a New Empire, the constituent imagination of the so-called "transitional societies" remains tethered primarily to what these former socialist societies may learn from the American constitutional experience. Thus stand monumentally sequestered some considerable opportunities for comparable learning from the Indian ROL experience and imagination. Postsocialist constitution-making has much to learn from the originality of

---

[18] G. Austin, *The Indian Constitution: The Cornerstone of Nation* (Delhi: Oxford University
Press, 1964); G. Austin, *Working a Democratic Constitution —The Indian Experience* (Delhi: Oxford University Press, 1999), 540-555. U. Baxi, "The Colonialist Heritage" in *Comparative Legal Studies: Traditions and Transitions*, eds., P. Legrand and R. Munday (Cambridge: Cambridge University Press, 2003), 6-58.
[19] Jawaharlal Nehru captured this relationship by insisting that the "rule of law" must not be divorced from the "rule of life".
[20] The Indian constitutionalism makes normative impact on postcolonial constitutionalism, illustrated most remarkably and recently by the post-apartheid South African Constitution. So inveterate, however, are Euroamerican habits of heart that the dominant, even comparative, discourse represents the Indian and related Southern forms of constitutionalism as merely mimetic.

the postcolonial form; however, and despite renewed interest in comparative constitutional studies, it seems that the "New" Europe has very little to learn from the old Global South. For the moment, I briefly consider below the relatedness of these four key notions: governance, rights, justice, and development.

Governance

The Holocaust of the Partition of India furnishes the histrionic moment in which the Indian constitution stands composed. The establishment of frameworks for collective human security and order was considered as a crucial ROL resource in the same way that today the making of a new global ROL remains affected by the two "terror" wars. The notion that the radical reach of self-determination ought to be confined merely to the end of the colonial occupation furnishes a new leitmotif for Indian governance; integrity and unity of the new nation redefines Indian ROL to authorize vast and ever proliferating powers of preventive detention and eternal continuation of many colonial security legislations as laws in force.[21] Since its birthing moment, the Indian ROL itineraries are shaped by both the doctrine of the reason of the state and the accentuated practices of militarized governance. No ROL value consideration in general, overall, is allowed to intrude upon state combat against armed rebellion aimed at secession from the Indian Union. In this the Indian experience is scarcely unique.

What is distinctive, however, is the governance/management of the politics of autonomy.[22] In theory, Parliament has the power of redrawing the federal map, creating new states, diminishing or enlarging their boundaries, and even the names of states without any democratic deliberation. Yet the almost constant creation of new states within the Indian federation, along linguistic/cultural/identity axes, entails multitudinous people's movements, considerable insurgent and state violence. The politics of autonomy requires Indian understanding of the federal *principle* and *detail*.

---

[21] The Indian Supreme Court has thus constructed a magnificent edifice of preventive detention jurisprudence subjecting acts of detention to strict scrutiny, while sustaining legislative constitutionality of such measures. But see U. K. Singh, *The State, Democracy, and Anti-terror Laws in India* (New Delhi: Sage, 2007).

[22] See, for more recent perspectives, R. Samaddar, *The Politics of Autonomy* (New Delhi: Sage, 2005).

If the federal principle privileges the *local* within the *national*, respecting the geography of difference in ways that authorize local knowledges, cultures, powers, and voices to inform and shape governance, the federal detail—mainly the distribution of legislative, executive, and administrative powers—seeks to negate this. True, this distribution of powers can only be changed by constitutional amendments and these remain difficult of negotiation and achievement in the current era of coalitional politics. However, the Indian Parliament retains a generous residuary authority that empowers it to legislate on matters not specified in the state and concurrent list; further, the laws it may make often have an overriding national authority. Additionally, Article 35 specifically gives Parliament overriding powers to make laws that outlaw millennially imposed disabilities and discriminations on India's untouchables (Article 17) and slavery and slave-like practices (Articles 23-24.) And, drawing heavily from the "experience" of comparative Commonwealth federalism, especially Canada and Australia, the Indian Supreme Court innovates constantly in its interpretive provenance to further hegemonic national role for the Union government.

India's distinctive cooperative federalism remains defined and developed by many institutional networks. The constitutionally ordained National Finance Commission constructs human rights normativity in allocation of federal resources to states. The constitution and the law create India-wide national agencies[23] entrusted with the tasks of protection and promotion of the human rights of "discrete and insular" minorities. The Comptroller and Auditor General of India, assisted by the Central Vigilance Commission, at least help fashion the discourse concerning corruption in high places. And, overall, the Indian Election Commission has incrementally pursued the heroic tasks of attainment of a modicum of integrity in the electoral process. The ways in which these and related agencies actually perform their tasks is a subject of lively political discourse, within the practices of investigative journalism, and social movement and human rights activism made constitutionally secure by the exertions of State High Courts and the Supreme Court of India.

All this enables continual re-articulation of people's power confronted by a heavily militarized polity and state formation, which put together and

---

[23] Such as, for example, the Inter-State Development Council, the Planning Commission, Human Rights Commission, the Minorities and Women Commissions, the Scheduled Castes and Tribes Commission, the Central Vigilance Commission, The Indian Law Commission.

often inflict heavy democratic deficit on the processes, institutions, and networks of governmentability. Thus, increasingly civil society interventions activating high judicial power have led to some softening of the anti-democratic aspects of the Indian Constitution at work.[24]

Overall, it seems to be the case that the federal principle holds within normative restraints of the federal detail. Put another way, Indian federalism contributes to the ROL discourse not just as facilitating governance but also as empowering participatory forms of citizen resilience and self–reliance. This experience needs to be accorded a measure of dignity of discourse in our "comparative" constitutionalism conversations.

Rights

The Indian ROL notions remain deeply bound to the ways in which fundamental rights stand conceived. Far from reiterating either the liberal or libertarian theologies of rights as corpus of limitation on state sovereignty and governmental conduct, the Indian ROL conceptions also empower progressive state action. Thus, for example, the following constitutional rights enunciations authorize legislative and policy action manifestly violative of some liberal conceptions of rights:

- Article 17 outlaws social practices of discrimination on the ground of "untouchability".
- Articles 23-24, enshrining "rights against exploitation", outlaws the practices of agrestic serfdom (bonded and other forms of un-free labour) and related historic practices of violent social exclusion.
- Articles 14-15 authorize, under the banner of fundamental rights, state combat against vicious forms of patriarchy.
- Articles 25-26 so configure Indian constitutional secularism as to empower state to fully combat human rights offensive practices of the dominant "Hindu" religious tradition.

---

[24] For example, the extraordinary power to impose the President's Rule, suspending or dismissing state governments/legislatures once liberally exercised has now been attenuated to a vanishing point by various decisions of the Supreme Court. The power to declare and administer the states of constitutional emergency in situations of armed rebellion and of external aggression that result in wide-ranging suspension of human rights under Part 111 of the Constitution, have been steadily brought under judicial scrutiny and human rights-friendly constitutional amendments.

• Articles 27-30 provide a panoply of fecund protection of the rights of religious, cultural, and linguistic minorities.

The Indian ROL stands here normatively conceived not just as a *sword* against state domination and violation and historic civil society norms and practices but also as a *shield* empowering an encyclopaedic regime of "progressive" state intervention in the life of civil society. In so doing, it engages in simultaneous disempowerment and re-empowerment of the Indian State in ways that makes more complicated governance, politics, and constitutional development. In terms of social psychology of the yesteryear, the Constitution thus inaugurates "cognitive dissonance" in ways that necessarily marks its rather schizoid course of development.

The rights texts, enunciated in a coequal world-historic time of the Universal Declaration of Human Rights, further impact on the development of international human rights norms, standards, and even values. I have here in view Part IV of the Constitution which enacts the distinction between regimes of civil and political rights and social and economic rights, which subsequently dominate the global human rights forms of talk.

The Directive Principles of State Policy declared as paramount as fashioning the ways of governance – acts of making law and policy – thus incarnate the previously unheard code of state constitutional obligations. Many actually installed at the time of origin, and subsequent governance mechanisms and arrangements, articulate institutional ways of moving ahead with this mission. I do not burden this text with any detailed enumeration.[25]

---

[25] The reference here is to a variety of Directives reinforcing structures of governance –structures such as the Commission for the Scheduled Castes and Tribes, the Planning Commission, the Finance Commission, the Election Commission, and some recent national human rights institutions such as the National Human Rights Commission and the National Commission for Women, some also replicated in state governance. Although explicitly declared non-justiciable, the Directives cast a "paramount" duty of observance in the making of law and policy. Because of this, Indian courts have deployed the Directives as a technology of constitutional interpretation: they have favoured interpretation that fos ters , rather than frustrates , the Directives. This "indirect" justiciability has contributed a good deal towards fructification of the substantive/"thick" versions of the Indian ROL.

The Indian ROL conceptions further fashion an extraordinary scope for judicial review powers – a new jewel in the postcolonial Indian crown, as it were. The extraordinary powers to redress violation of fundamental rights have achieved, here summarily put, the following results. First, a stunning achievement which refers to administrative law jurisprudence directed to combat and control uses of discretionary powers; second, wide adjudicatory surveillance over legislations accused of violating fundamental rights or the principle and detail of Indian federalism; third, the enormous achievement fashioned by the Supreme Court of India giving its inaugural, and awesome powers of invigilation over the exercise of plenary amendatory powers via the doctrine of the basic structure and the essential features of the Constitution. These powers now stand further routinized to bring home micro-accountability for the exercise of everyday legislative, executive, and administrative exercises of power under adjudicatory surveillance.[26]

The exercise of judicial midwifery to deliver human rights and limited governance is not uniquely Indian; what is distinctive of the Indian story is that justices increasingly believe, and act on the belief, that basic human rights are safer in their interpretative custody than with representative institutions. This belief and practice combine to produce a distinctive type of "constitutional faith" (to borrow a fecund expression of Sanford Levinson, 1988) which further enduringly renders legitimate expansive judicial review.

Justice/Development

An extraordinary feature of the constitutionalism that informs Indian ROL is posed by the question of *justice of rights*. I have recently elaborated this in some anxious detail[27] suggesting further that the problematic of justice of rights may not be grasped by conceptions of Indian development, or the constitutionally imagined/desired social order. In the moment of making the constitution at least three salient justice- of-rights type questions stood posed. First, if promotion and protection of

---

[26] I do not burden this article with references and sources that testify to this achievement. Interested readers may find it useful to consult treatises on Indian constitutional and administrative law, notably by D. Das Basu, H. M. Seervai, M.P. Jain, S.N. Jain, S.P. Sathe, I.P. Massey, R. Dhavan, among eminent others.

[27] U. Baxi, "Justice of Human Rights in Indian Constitutionalism: Preliminary Notes" in *Modern Indian Political Thought*, eds., T. Pantham and V. R. Mehta, (New Delhi: Sage, 2006), 263-284.

human rights and fundamental freedoms entailed maximal deference to full ownership over the means of production as the very foundation of freedom, how may "just" social redistribution *ever* occur? Second, how may fullest deference to communitarian rights be reconciled with the individual rights of persons who wish to belong to a community and yet also protest against individual rights violation within privileged acts of group membership? Third, how far should go group differentiated rights that privilege programmes of affirmative action, not just extending to educational and employment quotas, but also to legislative reservations for the scheduled castes and tribes, as ways of righting past and millennial wrongs?

These three interlocutions also define the constitutional conceptions of "development". If one were to take the Preamble and the Directive Principles of State Policy at all seriously, development signifies the *disproportionate* flow of state and societal resources that enhance real-life benefits for the Indian impoverished masses that Babasaheb Ambedkar luminously and poignantly described as India's *atisudras*, the social and economic proletariat. Much before the right to development-based notions of governance and development arrived on the scene of global ROL, the Indian constitution had already codified this understanding. In any event, the "justice of rights" problem has been variously recurrent in the Indian experience and I offer to view below some vignettes.

ROL as unfolded by the Indian Judiciary

The Indian Supreme Court is a forum with unparalleled vast general jurisdiction. It is not a constitutional court, though much of its business relates to issues concerning the enforcement of fundamental rights. The law laid down by the Court is declared to be binding on all courts throughout the territory of India and by necessary implication upon citizens and state actors. Further, not merely all authorities of the state are obligated to aid the enforcement of the apex judicial decisions but also the Court is empowered to do "complete justice", an incredible reservoir of plenary judicial power, which it has used amply in the past two decades. Legislative overruling of apex judicial decisions occurs but infrequently; however, an extraordinary device called the 9th Schedule has been invoked since the adoption of the Constitution to immunize statutes placed in it from the virus of judicial review, even when ex facie the legislations inscribed therein remain fundamental rights violative. In a recent decision, the Supreme Court has assumed powers of constitutional superintendence over the validity of laws thus immunized.

In the early years, the Court took the view that although the Directives cast a "paramount" duty of observance in the making of law and policy, their explicit non- justiciability meant that the rights provisions overrode the Directives. This generated high –intensity conflict between Parliament and the Court, resulting in a spate of constitutional amendments. In the process, much constitutional heat and dust has also been generated, in the main over a "conservative" judiciary that seemed to frustrate a "progressive" Parliament committed to agrarian reforms and redistribution leading to Court "packing" Indian – style.[28]

Over time, two kinds of adjudicative responses developed. First, the Supreme Courts began to deploy the Directives as a technology of constitutional interpretation, favouring an interpretative style that *fostered*, rather than *frustrated*, the Directives. This "indirect" justiciability has contributed a good deal towards fructification of the substantive/ "thick" versions of the Indian ROL. Second, in its more activist incarnation since the eighties, the Court has begun to *translate* some Directives into rights. Perhaps, a most crucial example of this is the judicial insistence that the Directive prescribing free and compulsory education for young persons in the age group 6-14 is a fundamental right.[29] The Court here generated a constitutional amendment enshrining this right as an integral aspect of Article 21 rights, to life and liberty.

Simultaneously with the adoption of the Constitution, Indian Justices strove to erect fences and boundaries to the power of delegated legislation (processes by which the executive power actually legislates.) They conceded this power but with a significant accompanying caveat: the rule-making power of the administration ought not to usurp the legislative function of enunciation of policy, accompanied by prescriptive sanctions. Thus came into being the "administrative law explosion", where Justices did not so much invalidate delegated legislation but vigorously policed its

---

[28] See S. P. Sathe, *Judicial Activism in India* (New Delhi: Oxford University Press, 2002). Also U. Baxi, *The Indian Supreme Court and Politics* (Lucknow: Eastern Book, 1980) and *Courage, Craft and Contention: The Indian Supreme Court in the Eighties* (Bombay: N.M. Tripathi, 1985).

[29] C. Raj Kumar, "International Human Rights Perspectives on the Right to Education: Integration of Human Rights and Human Development in the Indian Constitution" *Tulane International and Comparative Law* 12 (2004): 237.

performance. The executive may make rules that bind; but courts made it their business to interrogate, and even invalidate, specific exercises of administrative rule-making. A stunning array of judicial techniques over the review of administrative action has been evolved.

Justices asserted judicial review power over the constitutionality of legislative performances. Laws that transgressed fundamental rights or the federal principle and detail activated the "essence" of judicial review power. Whenever possible the Supreme Court sought to avoid invalidation of laws; it adopted the (standard repertoire of "reading down the statutory scope and intendments so as to avoid conflict and by recourse to the peculiar judicial doctrine of 'harmonious construction"'). But when necessary, enacted laws were declared constitutionally null and void. And even when resuscitated by legislative reaffirmation, they were re-subjected to the judicial gauntlet of strict scrutiny. The instances of judicial invalidation of statutes far exceed in number and range the experience of judicial review in the Global North.

Going beyond this, Indian Justices have assumed awesome power to submit constitutional amendments to strict judicial scrutiny and review. They performed this audacious innovation through the judicially crafted doctrine of the Basic Structure of the Constitution, which stood, in judicial, and juridical discourse, as definitive of the "personality" defined, from time to time, as the "essential features" of the Constitution. They proclaimed the "Rule of Law", "Equality", "Fundamental Rights", "Secularism", "Federalism", "Democracy" and "Judicial Review" as essential features of the Basic Structure, which amendatory power may not ever lawfully transgress.

Initially articulated as a judicial doctrine crafting the limits of amendatory power, the regime of the Basic Structure limitation has spread to other forms of exercise of constitutional, and even legislative, powers. The ineffable adjudicatory modes also mark a new and a bold conception: "constituent power" (the power to remake and unmake the Constitution) stands conjointly shared with the Indian Supreme Court to a point of its declaring certain amendments as constitutionally *invalid*.

This judicial, and juridical, production then momentously (because justices undertook the task of protecting the constitution against itself!) traversed constitutional jurisprudence of Pakistan, Bangla Desh, and

Nepal. The "comparative" ROL discourse so far wholly passes by this diffusion.

To conclude this narrative, the appellate courts under the leadership of the Supreme Court had devised an extraordinary form of jurisdiction under the rubric of social action litigation (SAL) still miscalled "public interest litigation". Here summarily put, the SAL has accomplished the following astonishing results:

- a radical democratization of the doctrine of *locus standi*; every citizen may now approach courts for vindicating the violation of human rights of co-citizens.
- the "de-lawyering" of constitutional litigation in the sense that petitioners-in-person with all their chaotic forensic styles of argumentation are being admitted.
- the establishment of new styles of fact-finding via socio-legal commissions of enquiry to assist adjudicatory resolution.
- the generation of a new adjudicatory culture; the SAL jurisdiction is conceived not as adversarial but as a collaborative venture between citizens, courts, and a recalcitrant executive.
- the invention of continuing jurisdiction through which courts continue to bring about some minimal restoration of human rights in governance practices.
- the fashioning of new ways of judicial enunciation of human rights, a complex affair in which the Supreme Court especially brings back to life rights deliberatively excluded by the constitution makers (such as the right to speedy trial), creates some component rights to those enunciated by the constitutional text (such as the right to livelihood, privacy, education and literacy, health and environment), re-writing the constitution by way of invention of new rights (such as right to information, immunity from practices of corrupt governance, rights to constitutional secularism, the right to compensation, rehabilitation, and resettlement for violated populations).

This new judicial disposition, or *Dispositif*, had its share of acclaim as well as criticism. The acclaim registers the emergence of the Supreme Court itself as an integral part of the new social movement aspiring to re-democratize the Indian state and governance. The criticism takes in the main two principal forms. First, the agents and mangers of governance cry "judicial usurpation". This outcry has a hollow ring indeed because in reality SAL assumes many labours and functions that increasingly coalitional regime political actors simply can no longer manage; put another way, the Supreme Court assumes the tasks of national governance, otherwise appropriately assigned to democratic governance. Second, the frequently disappointed SAL litigants cry foul when the SAL fails to deliver its promises. The expectational overload here remains diverse and staggering, respecting no limits of the capacity, opportunity, and potential of judicial power as an arm of national governance. Thus, the apex Court often falters and fails in addressing, let alone redressing, contentious politics concerning ways in which the Judiciary may:

- fully declare mega-irrigation projects constitutionally human rights offensive.
- deprive constitutional legitimating of the current policies of privatisation/ deregulation as being anti-developmental and human rights violative/ offensive.
- translate, with full constitutional sincerity, the current motto: women's rights are human rights, with due deference to religious and social pluralisms.
- the adjudicatory voice promote "the composite culture" of India (Article 51-A) in fashioning ROL conceptions of rights, justice, development and governance.
- foster and further participation in governance as the leitmotiv of the constitutional conception of the Indian ROL. How may they "best" meet the   argument against achieving equality of opportunity and access for the millennially deprived peoples via educational/ employment quotas in state administered/aided educational institutions and state and federal employment.[30]

Some Conclusionary Remarks

It is beyond the bounds of this essay to provide even a meagre sense of violence and violation embedded in the histories of rule of law in India. Not merely have the impoverished been forced to cheat their ways into meagre survival, "jurispathic" (to evoke Robert Cover's phrase) dimensions of the extant Indian ROL have continually worked new ways

---

[30] The various constitutional amendment bills providing reservation for women in national and state legislatures have yet to materialize. Their chequered contemporary legislative histories remain mired, in socially significant ways, over the issue of "reservations within reservations". That is the issue whether this device should be stratified so as to enable/ empower women doubly/multiply oppressed by state and civil society, through provisions for a representational quota for women belonging to "underclasses".

of their disenfranchisement. These stories of violent social exclusion may be told variously. I have recently narrated the institutionalisation of the "rape culture" in the context of Gujarat 2002 violence and violation.[31]

But it is to literature rather than to law that we must turn to realize the full horror of the betrayal of the Indian "Rule of Law". Mahasweta Devi's *Bashai Tudu* speaks to us about the constitutive ambiguities of the practices of militarized 'rule of law' governance and resistance in contemporary India. Rohintoon Mistry's *A Fine Balance* educates us in the constitutional misery of untouchables caught in the ever-escalating web of "constitutional" governance. These two paradigmatic literary classics abundantly invite us to pursue a distinctively Indian law and literature genre of study, outside which it remains almost impossible to grasp the lived atrocities of Indian ROL in practice.

These also make the vital point (with the remarkable Indian *Subaltern Studies* series) that the pathologies of governance are indeed normalizing modes of governance as a means of controlling (to evoke Hannah Arendt's favourite phrase) "rightless" peoples. The jurispathic attributes of the Indian Rule of Law at work can be described best in terms of social reproduction of rightlessness. Indian judicial activism begins to make and mark a modest reversal.

The Indian story at least situates the significance of the forms of creationist South narratives for contemporary Rule of Law theory and practice. Time is surely at hand for constructions of multicultural (despite justified reservation that this term evokes) narratives of the Rule of Law precisely because it is being loudly said that "history" has now ended, and there remain on horizons *no* meaningful "alternatives" to global capitalism.

The authentic quest for renaissance of the Rule of Law has just begun its world historic career. ROL epistemic communities have choices to make. Our ways of ROL talk may either wholly abort or aid to a full birth some new ROL conceptions now struggling to find a voice through multitudinous spaces of people's struggles against global capitalism that presage alternatives to it.

---

[31] Baxi, "The War on Terror".

We need after all, I believe, to place ourselves all over again under the tutelage of Michael Oakeshott.[32] He reminds us, preciously, that far from being a "finished product" of humankind history, the Rule of Law discourse "remains an individual composition, a unity of particularity and generality, in which each component is what it is in virtue of what it contributes to the delineation of the whole". That virtue of the "whole" may not any longer legitimate Euro American narratology. Rather the task remains re-privileging other ways of telling ROL stories as a form of participative enterprise of myriad "subaltern" voices.

Bibliography

Aderni, G. "Legal Intimations: Michael Oakeshott and the Rule of Law." *Wisconsin Law Review* 4 (1993): 838.

Agamben, G. *Homo Sacer: Sovereign Power and Bare Life*. Stanford: Stanford University Press, 1995.

Association of the Bar of the City of New York and Centre for Human Rights and Global Justice. *Torture by Proxy: International and Domestic Law Applicable to "Extraordinary Rendition."* New York: ABCNY and NYU School of Law, 2004.

Austin, G. *The Indian Constitution: The Cornerstone of Nation*. Delhi: Oxford University Press, 1964.

—. *Working a Democratic Constitution—The Indian Experience*. Delhi: Oxford University Press, 1999.

Baxi, U. *Courage, Craft and Contention: The Indian Supreme Court in the Eighties*. Bombay: N.M. Tripathi, 1985.

—. *The Indian Supreme Court and Politics*. Lucknow: Eastern Book, 1980.

—. "Postcolonial Legality." In *A Companion to Postcolonial Studies*, edited by H. Schwartz and S. Roy. Oxford: Blackwell, 2001.

—. "'The War on Terror' and the 'War of Terror': Nomadic Multitudes, Aggressive Incumbents and the 'New International Law'." *Osgoode Hall Law Journal* 1/ 2 (2005): 1-36.

—. "Justice of Human Rights in Indian Constitutionalism: Preliminary Notes." In *Modern Indian Political Thought*, edited by T. Pantham and V. R. Mehta. New Delhi: Sage, 2006.

---

[32] M. Oakeshott, *On Human Conduct* (Oxford: Oxford University Press, 1975), 1-31.

—. "The Colonialist Heritage." In *Comparative Legal Studies: Traditions and Transitions*, edited by P. Legrand and R. Munday. Cambridge: Cambridge University Press, 2003.

—. "The Gujarat Catastrophe: Notes on Reading Politics as Democidal Rape Culture." In *The Violence of Normal Times: Essays on Women's Lived Realities*, edited by K. Kababiran. New Delhi: Women Unlimited and Kali for Women, 2005.

—. *The Future of Human Rights*. New Delhi: Oxford University Press, 2006.

Braithwaite, J. and P. Drahos. *Global Bussines Regulation*. Cambridge: Cambridge Univeristy Press, 2000.

Brewster, B. trans. *Althusser, Montesquieu, Rousseau, Marx: Politics and History*. London: Verso, 1982.

Chibundo, M. "Globalizing the Rule of Law: Some Thoughts at and on the Periphery." *Indiana Journal of Global Legal Studies* 6 (1999): 79-116.

Chimni, B.S."Co-option and Resistance: Two Faces of Global Administrative Law." *New York Journal of International Law and Politics* 4/5 (2005): 799-827.

Fine, B. *Democracy and the Rule of Law: Liberal Ideals and Marxist Critiques*. London: Pluto Press, 1984.

Finnis, J. *Natural Law and Natural Rights*. Oxford: Oxford Clarendon Press, 1980.

Fuller, L. *Morality of Law*. New Haven: Yale University Press, 1964.

Galanter, M. *Competing Equalities*. Delhi: Oxford University Press, 1984.

Gill, S. "Toward a Post-Modern Prince? The Battle in Seattle as a Moment in the New Politics of Globalization" *Millenium. Journal of International Studies* 1 (2000): 131-141.

Habermas, J. *Between Facts and Norms: Contributions to a Discourse Theory of Law and Democracy*. Cambridge: The MIT Press, 1996.

Hidyatuallah, M. *The Fifth and Sixth Schedules of the Constitution of India* Gauhati: Ashok Publishing House, 1979.

McCormick, N. "Natural Law and the Separation of Law and Morals" in *Natural Law Theory: Contemporary Essays*, ed., R. P. George (Oxford: Clarendon Press, 1992), 105- 133.

Morgan Kouseer, J. *Colorblind Injustice: Minority Voting Rights and the Undoing of the Second Reconstruction*. Chapel Hill: University of North Carolina Press, 1999.

Negri, A. *Insurgencies: Constituent Power and the Modern State*. Minneapolis: University of Minnesota Press, 1999.

Negri, A. and M. Hardt. *Empire*. Cambridge: Harvard University Press, 2000.

Oakeshott, M. *On Human Conduct*. Oxford: Oxford University Press, 1975.

Peernbohm, R. "Let One Hundred Flowers Bloom, One Hundred School Contend: Debating Rule of Law in China." *Michigan Journal of International Law* 23 (2002): 471.

—. *Asian Discourses on the Rule of Law: Theories and Implementation of Rule of Law in Twelve Asian Countries, France and U.S.* London: Routledge, 2004.

Raj Kumar, C. "International Human Rights Perspectives on the Right to Education: Integration of Human Rights and Human Development in the Indian Constitution" *Tulane International and Comparative Law* 12 (2004): 237.

Rawls, J. *Political Liberalism*. New York: Columbia University Press, 1993.

—. *The Law of Peoples*. Cambridge: Harvard University Press, 1999.

Raz, J. "The Rule of Law and its Virtue", *Law Quarterly Review* 93 (1977): 208.

Samaddar, R. *The Politics of Autonomy*. New Delhi: Sage, 2005.

Sathe, S.P. *Judicial Activism in India*. New Delhi: Oxford University Press, 2002.

Satterthwaite, M.L. "Rendered Meaningless: Extraordinary Rendition and the Rule of Law", *New York University Public Law and Legal Theory Working Papers*, 43 (2006).

Schmitt, C. *Political Theology: Four Chapters on the Concept of Sovereignty* Cambridge: The MIT Press, 1985.

Schneiderman, D. "Constitutional Approches to Privatization: An Inquiry into the Magnitude of Neo-Liberal Constitutionalism." *Law and Contemporary Problems* 4 (2000): 83-109.

Sen, A. *Development as Freedom*. Oxford: Oxford University Press, 1999.

Singh, U.K. *The State, Democracy, and Anti-terror Laws in India*. New Delhi: Sage, 2007.

Stone, J. *The Social Dimensions of Law and Justice*. Sydney: Maitland, 1966.

Thompson, E. P. *Whigs and Hunters: The Origins of the Black Act*. London: Allen Lane, 1975.

—. *Writing by the Candlelight*. London: The Merlin Press, 1989.

Virno, P. *A Grammar of the Multitude. For an Analysis of Contemporary Forms of Life*. Los Angeles and New York: Semiotext(E), 2004.

Walker, G.Q. *The Rule of Law: Foundation of Constitutional Democracy* Carlton: Melbourne University Press, 1988.

Young, R. *Postcolonialism: An Introduction*. Oxford: Blackwell, 2001.

CHAPTER ELEVEN

EDDIE MABO AND NAMIBIA LAND REFORM AND PRE-COLONIAL LAND RIGHTS

NICO HORN

The acts and events by which that dispossession in legal theory was carried into practical effect constitute the darkest aspect of the history of this nation. The nation as a whole must remain diminished unless and until there is an acknowledgment of, and retreat from, those past injustices. In these circumstances, the Court is under a clear duty to re-examine the two propositions. For the reasons which we have explained, that re-examination compels their rejection. The lands of this continent were not terra nullius or "practically unoccupied" in 1788. The Crown's property in the lands of the Colony of New South Wales was, under the common law which became applicable upon the establishment of the Colony in 1788, reduced or qualified by the burden of the common law native title of the Aboriginal tribes and clans to the particular areas of land on which they lived or which they used for traditional purposes.[1]

What does the small Murray Islands—Mer, for the natives—in the Torres Strait off the Queensland coast of Australia, with a total land area of hardly nine square kilometers, have in common with Namibia? Surely not geography, neither their history of occupation. Unlike the bloody German/Herero and Nama wars, no shot was fired when Her Majesty's administration in Queensland declared the Murray Islands a Crown colony of the British Empire. The governor of Queenstown exercised some power over the islands since 1870, although they were not part of the colony. In 1878 Queen Victoria signed Letters Patent to include the Murray Islands —with others in the Torres Straight—in the colony of Queenstown. The

---

[1] High Court of Australia, Eddie Mabo and Others v. The State of Queensland (No. 2), [1992] HCA 23 (1992) 175 CRL 1, F.C. 92/014, Judges Deane and Gaudron' Declaration, point 56.

inhabitants were informed of their new status as British subjects in September 1879.

In terms of the understanding of colonial law of that time, when a territory became part of the Crown's dominions, the law of England—so far as applicable to colonial conditions—became the law of the Murray Islands and its inhabitants, the Merian people. Her Majesty acquired absolute ownership of all land in the islands. Neither the Merian people nor the individuals on the islands had any right or interest to any land in the territory. Only the Crown could thereafter grant possession or ownership to anyone.[2]

For the Namibian people occupation was a bloody affair. The boundaries of Namibia were, like most African countries, drawn by the European colonial powers at the end of the Nineteenth century. Before the arrival of the German occupation forces, Namibia was populated by some twelve tribes with very different customs, and vaguely demarcated areas over which the tribal kings had jurisdiction. Between 1884 and 1890 Namibia stretched from the Orange River at the southern border with South Africa, to the Kunene and Okavango Rivers in the north, and from the Atlantic Ocean in the West to the 21st parallel in the East. The German colonial authorities later obtained a finger of land next to the Zambezi River. Walvis Bay was not included in Namibia, since it was occupied by Britain. European mission societies started working in Namibia in the 1840's. In 1890 the German forces in Namibia started a vigorous crusade to subject the native tribes. This resulted in the extermination of 75% of the Herero population, and 50% of the Nama and Damara populations.

Yet, the two peoples had a common history of submission to a colonial power. The Merian people to a British authority in Queensland, who allowed them to remain on the ancestral land—but never informed them that they were colonized—and who pretended that they were there to advance the Merian people.[3] The Namibians to a German colonial authority

---

[2] This principle was confirmed by the Crown courts for more than hundred years, beginning with the case of Attorney-General v. Brown (1847) 1 Legge 312. See R. v. Kidman (1915) 20 CLR 425; Liquidators of Maritime Bank of Canada v. Receiver-General (New Brunswick) (1892) AC 437; The Commonwealth v. New South Wales (1923) 33 CLR 1.

[3] See Judges Masson and McHugh's Declaration, in High Court of Australia, Mabo and Others, point 20: "Without pausing to enquire into the legal support for the 'system of self-government' instituted by Douglas or for the jurisdiction of the

determined to drive the Herero people out of their motherland, or kill them.[4]

The two peoples also shared the effects of a common interpretation of Western law that denied their rights to their ancestral land. And it did not really matter if the land was occupied, ceded or conquered.[5] According to Nineteenth and early Twentieth century colonial legal thought all "undiscovered land", that is to say land where no Europeans had settled, was considered as *res nullius*. It was immaterial whether or not the natives had previously occupied the land. While one may resent the arrogance of Nineteenth century colonial mentality, it nevertheless makes sense to classify uninhabited land as *res nullius*, at least in legal terms. However, to categorize land that has been inhabited for centuries as *res nullius*, had no logical sense. To make sense of this nonsense, jurists had to give the term a definition other than its clear, logical meaning. Initially the term was widened to include land not cultivated by native inhabitants.[6] But even this definition did not fit the Namibian or the Marian people, as in both cases the land had been cultivated.[7]

Island Court, it appears that the Meriam people came peacefully to accept a large measure of control by Queensland authorities and that officials of the Queensland Government became accustomed to exercise administrative authority over the Murray Islands. Formal annexation had been followed by an effective exercise of administrative power by the Government of Queensland."

[4] The decree of General Lothar von Trotha is well-known: "The Herero people will have to leave the country. Otherwise I shall force them to do so by means of guns. Within German boundaries, every Herero, whether found armed or unarmed, with or without cattle, will be shot. I shall not accept any more women or children. I shall drive them back to their people – otherwise I shall order them to be shot. Signed: the Great General of the Mighty Kaiser, von Trotha."

[5] Elizabeth Evatt, "The Acquisition of Territory in Australia and New Zealand," in *Studies in the History of the Law of Nations*, ed. Charles H. Alexandrowicz (The Hague: Martinus Nijhoff, 1968), 16.

[6] Emer de Vattel, *The Law of Nations, Or, Principles of the Law of Nature, Applied to the Conduct and Affairs of Nations and Sovereigns Book I* (1797), 100-101. See also Alex C. Castles, *An Australian Legal History* (Sydney: Law Book Co., 1982), 16-17, quoted in High Court of Australia, Mabo and Others, Judges Masson and McHugh's Declaration, point 33.

[7] This argument is often raised in Namibia. See Nico Horn, "Land Claims and History" (paper presented before the Seis Farmers Community, March 2003). However, while the land was not developed in a Western sense of the word, the Herero and Nama people were known to be cattle farmers, an activity in which they were extremely successful.

Other philosophers worked within a theory of supremacy of the European nations over the territories of backward nations.[8] This theory was clothed in morality by legal scholars who pointed out the benefits that Christianity, and the European culture and civilization would bring to the backward people.[9] Above all, already in the first half of the Nineteenth century legal philosophers questioned the morality of killing, massacring and destroying local communities, and then classifying the land as *res nullius*. It was not possible to reconcile the moral ideals of Christianizing and civilizing the backward people of Africa, with the vicious, sadistic edict of General von Trotha. Among the scholars who pointed to such incongruity was William Blackstone, who remarked:

> ...so long as it was confined to the stocking and cultivation of desert uninhabited countries, it kept strictly within the limits of the law of nature. But how far the seizing on countries already peopled, and driving out or massacring the innocent and defenceless natives, merely because they differed from their invaders in language, in religion, in customs, in government, or in colour; how far such a conduct was consonant to nature, to reason, or to Christianity, deserved well to be considered by those, who have rendered their names immortal by thus civilizing mankind.[10]

However, no matter how illogical the theory may sound, it gave rise to another legal fiction in British colonial law: all the colonial land acquired by subjects of colonial powers in Europe belonged to the sovereign or Crown of the colonial power. This possession, the courts further ruled, included both land title and sovereign government. In other words, after colonization, in whatever form, the European sovereign became the political sovereign and the *de facto* owner of all the land of the country. It further meant that the representative of the sovereign started with a clean slate, as if the land he had taken over was indeed *res nullius*. Consequently, only the property rights acknowledged by him were valid.

---

[8] See Mark F. Lindley, *The Acquisition and Government of Backward Territory in International Law* (London: Longmans-Green, 1926), c III and IV, quoted in High Court of Australia, Mabo and Others, Justice Brennan's Declaration, points 33 and 39.

[9] Johnson v. McIntosh (1823) 8 Wheat 543, at 573 (21 US 240, at 253).

[10] William Blackstone, *Commentaries on the Laws of England Book II* (London: Sweet & Maxwell, 1830), 7.

As a rule, the representatives of the sovereign gave title only to European settlers.[11]

British and colonial courts followed the fiction of the supreme power and title over property in colonized countries for more than hundred years.[12] Although England occupied Walvis Bay and administered it as part of the South African colonies, no indigenous land claims by Namibians were ever made against England in Southern African courts.[13] The closest case to Namibia was possibly the Rhodesian case of 1919.[14] In this case the court, not unlike the courts in other parts of the Commonwealth, worked from the premise of the irreconcilability between the tribal and colonial systems:

> The estimation of the rights of aboriginal tribes is always inherently difficult. Some tribes are so low in the scale of social organization that their usages and conceptions of rights and duties are not to be reconciled with the institutions or the legal ideas of civilized society. Such a gulf cannot be bridged. It would be idle to impute to such people some shadow of the rights known to our law and then to transmute it into the substance of transferable rights of property as we know them.[15]

Consequently, the issue was not so much if the indigenous people had land rights, but if those rights were close to the British legal understanding of land and possession. If the indigenous people failed the second part of the test for whatever reason, they have no entitlement to land. The Lords judges rejected the claim of the applicants that they "were the owners of the unalienated lands long before either the Company or the Crown

---

[11] See Attorney-General v. Brown (1847) 1 Legge 312, for an example of how the British controlled courts dealt with challenges to the Crown's authority over land in the colonies.

[12] See New South Wales v. The Commonwealth (1975) 135 CLR 337; Wade v. New South Wales Rutile Mining Co.Pty. Ltd. (1969) 121 CLR 177; and Randwick Corporation v. Rutledge (1959) 102 CLR 54, for judgments appreciative of Attorney-General versus Brown (1847), more than a hundred years later.

[13] Jeremy Sarkin points out that only in 2001, eleven years after Namibia's independence, the Herero People's Corporation filed the first case relating back to colonial days, against Deutsche Bank, Terex Corporation and Woermann Line for the atrocities suffered under colonial rule. Jeremy Sarkin, "The Coming of Age of Claims for Reparation for Human Rights Abuses Committed in the South," *SUR International Journal on Human Rights* 1 (2004): 88-89.

[14] *In re* Southern Rhodesia (1919) AC 211.

[15] Ibid., 233-234.

became concerned with them and from time immemorial... and that the unalienated lands belonged to them still" because the maintenance of those rights was inconsistent with the white settlement of the country and the system that caused the development in the country.[16] As a result, another system replaced the aboriginal one. The irreconcilability of native rights with Western legal understanding of title remained the standard for more than a hundred years, especially in British common law and the laws of the colonies.

Forerunners of Mabo

While the Commonwealth courts virtually ignored the radical changes in the international community that started with the formation of the United Nations after the Second World War, and gained momentum with the independence of the colonies of Africa and Asia in the 1950's and 1960's, international law took the first steps to evaluate the meaning of decolonisation. With this panorama in the background, the High Court of Australia took cognizance of the advances in international law, especially of the advisory opinion of the International Court of Justice on Western Sahara.[17] There the majority judgment defined *terra nullius* as a territory not belonging to anyone.[18] The court stated that only then a legal occupation can take place, other than by cession or succession.[19] The judges were unanimous in their ruling that Western Sahara was not *res nullius* when it was occupied by Spain in 1884.[20] Judge Brennan in the Mabo case summarizes the Western Sahara opinion as follows:

> Whatever differences of opinion there may have been among jurists, the State practice of the relevant period indicates that territories inhabited by tribes or peoples having a social and political organization were not regarded as *terrae nullius*. It shows that in the case of such territories the acquisition of sovereignty was not generally considered as effected unilaterally through   'occupation' of *terra nullius* by original title but through agreements concluded with local rulers. On occasion, it is true, the word 'occupation' was used in a non-technical sense denoting simply acquisition of sovereignty; but that did not signify that the acquisition of sovereignty through such agreements with authorities of the country was

---

16 Ibid., 234.

[17] Western Sahara, Advisory Opinions, I.C.J Reports, 1975.

[18] See also Legal Status of Eastern Greenland (Den. v. Nor.), 1933 P.C.I.J. (ser. A/B) No. 53., 44f and 63f.

[19] Western Sahara, Advisory Opinions, I.C.J Reports, 1975, 39.

[20] Ibid., 86.

regarded as an 'occupation' of a "terra nullius" in the proper sense of these terms. On the contrary, such agreements with local rulers, whether or not considered as an actual 'cession' of the territory, were regarded as derivative roots of title, and not original titles obtained by occupation of *terrae nullius*.[21]

The Judgment in the Mabo Case

The High Court bench of seven ruled in favor of the plaintiffs with one dissenting voice. Eddie Mabo had passed away before the judgment, but as part of the Meriam people the other two plaintiffs were granted a right to the Murray Islands, while their specific entitlements were to be determined by reference to traditional law or custom.[22] It is not important for the purpose of this paper to go into all the detail of the judgment. The essence of the judgment entails the acknowledgement of the High Court of Australia that pre-colonial land rights of the aboriginal people not only survived colonialism, but that those rights are enforceable by law. And while judge Brennan—who wrote the majority decision—relied strongly on developments in international law, the judgment made clear that these rights are enforceable in the municipal courts of Australia.

As already stated, the Advisory Opinion of the International Court of Justice in the Western Sahara case played a decisive role in the argument of the court. More interesting is the fact that two judges took cognizance of the separate opinion of ICJ Vice-President Ammoun.[23] Ammoun

---

[21] High Court of Australia, Mabo and Others, Justice Brennan's Declaration, point 40.

[22] The text of the judgment reads as follows:
(1) that the land in the Murray Islands is not Crown land within the meaning of that term in s.5 of the Land Act 1962-1988 (Q.);
(2) that the Meriam people are entitled as against the whole world to possession, occupation, use and enjoyment of the island of Mer except for that parcel of land leased to the Trustees of the Australian Board of Missions and those parcels of land (if any) which have been validly appropriated for use for administrative purposes the use of which is inconsistent with the continued enjoyment of the rights and privileges of Meriam people under native title;
(3) that the title of the Meriam people is subject to the power of the Parliament of Queensland and the power of the Governor in Council of Queensland to extinguish that title by valid exercise of their respective powers, provided any exercise of those powers is not inconsistent with the laws of the Commonwealth.

[23] High Court of Australia, Mabo and Others, Justice Brennan's Declaration, Points 40 and 41, and Judge Toohey's Declaration, point 19.

affirmatively referred to one of the parties' submission that the essence of the rights of indigenous people to the land lies in the spiritual and "ancestral ties between the land, or 'mother nature', and the man who was born therefrom, remains attached thereto, and must one day return thither to be united with his ancestors."[24] The Vice-President went on to say:

> This amounts to a denial of the very concept of terra nullius in the sense of a land which is capable of being appropriated by someone who is not born therefrom. It is a condemnation of the modern concept, as defined by Pasquale Fiore, which regards as terrae nullius territories inhabited by populations whose civilization, in the sense of the public law of Europe, is backward, and whose political organization is not conceived according to Western norms.[25]

The importance of the Western Sahara case is that it excludes the possibility of considering inhabitant land as *terra nullius* based on technical terms or some test of civilization. Judge Brennan observed that if the concept of *terra nullius* or inhabited lands is no longer supported in international law, the doctrines developed by the court to defend it must also be rejected. The position of the Rhodesian case—that native peoples may be "so low in the scale of social organization" that it is impossible to grant them land title in terms of Western law[26]—is obviously out of line with international law. And since common law is not static, and it has been kept in step with international law in the past, there is no reason why it cannot correct the illogical thinking of the past.[27]

Judges Deane and Gaudron pointed to the fact that even in conservative Commonwealth jurisprudence there are indications that at least some property rights of the native people were not only recognized, but also protected by the new colonial powers:

> Thus, in In re Southern Rhodesia, (170) (1919) AC, at p 233 the Privy Council expressly affirmed that there are "rights of private property", such as a proprietary interest in land, of a category "such that upon a conquest it is to be presumed, in the absence of express confiscation or of subsequent expropriatory legislation, that the conqueror has respected them and forborne to diminish or modify them". Similarly, in Amodu Tijani v.

---

[24] Western Sahara, Advisory Opinions, I.C.J Reports, 1975, 85-86.
[25] Ibid.
[26] *In re* Southern Rhodesia (1919) AC 211, 233-234.
[27] High Court of Australia, Mabo and Others, Justice Brennan's Declaration, point 41.

Secretary, Southern Nigeria ("Amodu Tijani") (171) (1921) 2 AC 399, at p 407, the Privy Council affirmed and applied the "usual" principle "under British... law" that when territory is occupied by cession, "the rights of property of the inhabitants (are) to be fully respected".[28]

While these were never a full acknowledgement of the right to title, and often in the form of usufructuary occupation, the Crown nevertheless respected them. In Adeyinka Oyekan v. Musendiku Adele[29] the Privy Council stated that the courts in the colonies operate with the assumption that the Crown will respect indigenous property rights and pay compensation for land expropriated. However, these rights vested in the indigenous people of British colonies meant little since it was practically impossible for them to defend their rights in courts of law.[30] The judges nevertheless did not see these rights as totally unimportant:

> The practical inability of the native inhabitants of a British Colony to vindicate any common law title by legal action in the event of threatened or actual wrongful conduct on the part of the Crown or its agents did not, however, mean that the common law's recognition of that title was unimportant from the practical point of view. The personal rights under the title were not illusory: they could, for example, be asserted by way of defense in both criminal and civil proceedings (e.g. alleged larceny of produce or trespass after a purported termination of the title by the Crown by mere notice as distinct from inconsistent grant or other dealing). More important, if the domestic law of a British Colony recognized and protected the legitimate claims of the native inhabitants to their traditional lands, that fact itself imposed some restraint upon the actions of the Crown and its agents even if the native inhabitants were essentially helpless if their title was wrongfully extinguished or their possession or use was forcibly terminated.[31]

Deane and Gaudon evaluated what they called the "Dispossession of the Original Inhabitants."[32] After looking at the historical dispossession of the aborigines and their exclusion from the Commonwealth Parliament, their judgment was based on the theory that legally New South Wales was *terra nullius* when occupied in 1788, and was unaffected by native title.

---

[28] High Court of Australia, Eddie Mabo and Others, Judges Deane and Gaudron' Declaration, point 10.
[29] (1957) 1 WLR 876, 880
[30] High Court of Australia, Eddie Mabo and Others, Judges Deane and Gaudron' Declaration, point 4.
[31] Ibid., point 30.
[32] Ibid., point 48f.

The Mabo case is an important judgment for dispossessed native inhabitants of former European colonies all over the world. For one thing, the High Court of Australia not only acknowledged the important leaps in favour of justice taken by international law; it actually changed Australian common law to bring it in line with international principles of justice. In the process one of the oldest justifications for the occupation of inhabited land, the so-called *terra nullius* rule, was abandoned. Further, it not only recognized the existence of pre-colonial land rights, but made it possible for the dispossessed to defend their rights in courts of law. Consequently, the racist theories that had introduced Western legal questions like the category of "rights of private property"; or that natives "are so low in the scale of social organization that their usages and conceptions of rights and duties are not to be reconciled with the institutions or the legal ideas of civilized society"[33] can no longer be justifications for not recognizing pre-colonial rights.

Criticism of the Mabo Judgment

The Mabo judgment was not left unchallenged, and the challenges are not unfamiliar to Namibian observers. Cooray complains that the constitutional approach gives the judges a political rather than a judicial function, and calls the judgment an edict rather than a judicial decision,[34] as envisaged by Judge Brennan.[35] Cooray also compares the results of the Mabo case with apartheid:

> This will be analogous to the notorious South African homelands. But it will be different from the South African experience, in that the inhabitants of territories in Australia will sit on vast mining and economic resources. The productive agricultural land and the rich mining areas were outside the South African homelands. The beneficiaries in Australia will be a tiny minority and the deprived will constitute the vast majority of the people. In

---

[33] *In re* Southern Rhodesia (1919) AC 211, 233-234.
[34] Mark Cooray, "The High Court In Mabo—*Legalist* or *L'egotiste*", accessed June 29, 2011, http://www.ourcivilisation.com/cooray/mabo/ index.htm.
[35] The judge allegedly stated that a Bill of Rights would bring the courts into the political process as a new and dominant force: "Once the right is defined, the Court must weigh the collective interest against the right of the individual. This is the stuff of politics, but a Bill of Rights purports to convert political into legal debate, and to judicialise questions of politics and morality." Justice Brennan, quoted in Mark Cooray, "The High Court In Mabo."

South Africa under apartheid the beneficiaries were a tiny majority and the deprived constituted the vast majority.[36]

Galligan accuses the High Court of making law, but adds that it has always done so.[37] Marchant criticizes the judges and accuses them of being dishonest with history.[38] His main concern is that a decision on a group of farmers in the Murray Islands was made applicable to the Aborigine people of the Australian mainland. It is Cooray, again, who echoes the typical paternalistic view that the indigenous people should be thankful for their dispossession, since the conquerors brought with them the advantages of Western civilization:

> How would Aborigines live if Australia had not been conquered? Would their economic standards of living be any better? Would their tribal law and customs be superior to the Common Law and statutory mix which prevail today? Would they have developed the land, in the way it has been developed? A negative answer to the latter three questions spring to my mind from common sense and logic.[39]

From the criticism it seems as if the opponents of the Mabo decision were concerned that the rights of the present title holders—eventually all whites—will be affected by the decision, and that they will eventually be dispossessed. While the Aborigines are a poor minority in Australia the fears seems unfounded, and almost impossible to an observer in Namibia. However, if the Namibian Supreme Court receives a similar application, the fears of an indiscrete land grab will undoubtedly grip the sons and daughters of the European colonists.

---

[36] Mark Cooray, "The High Court In Mabo."

[37] B. Galligan, "The Power of Seven," *The Weekend Australian*, July 17-18, 1993.

[38] Marchant quoted in Galligan, "The Power of Seven."

[39] Mark Cooray, "The High Court In Mabo."

Namibia and Eddie Mabo

The Namibian Constitution guarantees private property rights,[40] and the government has always vowed to abide by the Constitution in any land reform programme. However, the debate has not always been conducted on a level of mutual acceptance of *bona fides*. One of the main reasons for this is possibly the fact that the government works from a very specific premise that land reform should be aimed at returning land presently in the hands of whites to the original inhabitants of the land. A case in point is the President Sam Nujoma's interview with Baffour Ankomah, editor of the magazine *New African*. Nujoma states that the Constitutional Principles were introduced by the US and Britain "to favor the interests of individual white settlers who had, 'by hook or by crook" acquired and occupied Namibian land during the colonial era. The President went on to make it clear that the willing seller-willing buyer clause in the Constitution was never in line with SWAPO's policy plan to address the land issue.[41]

On the other side of the issue, the white farmers have emphasized its Constitutional rights in terms of Article 16. However, none of the parties have thus far attempted to place their points of departure in a historical context. For the government, the original inhabitants of the land are synonymous with the previously disadvantages. The white farmers, on the other hand, have thus far not made an effort to consider the possibility of the other rights that may exist on their farms. The idea that more than one right can exist over a farm is not unknown to both common law and statutory law in Namibia. For example, the rights of a farmer on his or her land can be restricted by a lease contract that is in place at the time of the

---

[40] Article 16. The text reads:
(1) All persons shall have the right in any part on Namibia to acquire, own and dispose of all forms of immovable and movable property individually or in association with others and to bequeath their property to their heirs or legatees: provided that Parliament may be legislation prohibit or regulate as it deems expedient the right to acquire property by persons who are not Namibian citizens
(2) The State or a competent body or organ authorized by law may expropriate property in the public interest subject to the payment of just compensation, in accordance with requirements and procedures to be determined by Act of Parliament.
[41] Ibid. The South Western African People's Organization, SWAPO, was the political party of Sam Nujoma, who was the first President of Namibia after independence from South Africa. He was sworn in 1990 and remained in office until 2005, after being re-elected for a third term.

purchase,[42] and mining rights are not included in the rights of an agricultural landowner.

The example of the Mabo case provides an opportunity to approach the land reform program from a different perspective at least in the central and southern regions of the country. I shall not deal with the question of whether the German/Herero war constituted an act of genocide.[43] For the purposes of this chapter it is adequate to accept that Namibia, like Western Sahara, did not constitute *terra nullius* at the time of the German occupation. I shall further accept at this stage *prima facie* evidence that confirm the property rights of the Herero and Nama people at the time of the German occupation.[44]

If the rights of the Herero and Nama people can be substantiated at least for certain parts of the land, the debate can be lifted to a new level. And those people who suffered under colonial rule can then be identified. They can become known to both the white farmers presently owning the land and the government, which will ultimately decide the future of the land. A tribunal can be set up to hear the claims of people or peoples to specific land claims. The Land Reform Act already provides for a tribunal. Small amendments to the Act will make it possible for the tribunal to deal with claims emanating from the 1904 wars. The South African Lands Claim Court has been in operation for several years and can also serve as a helpful example.

Once a claim has been proved, the government can take the process over and deal with it in terms of a pre-determined program, while

---

[42] The common law dictum huur gaat voor koop—lease takes preference to purchase—is enforced by the Namibian courts on a regular basis.

[43] I generally agree with Jeremy Sarkin and Carly Fowler that although the term genocide was not known in 1904, it is possible to evaluate the acts of the German forces and the communications of their commander, General Lothar von Trotha, with the definition than became part of international law. Jeremy Sarkin and Carly Fowler, "Reparations for Historical Human Rights Violations: The International and Historical Dimensions of the Alien Torts Claims Act Genocide Case of the Herero of Namibia," *Human Rights Review* 9 (2008): 3f. See also Jeremy Sarkin, "The Coming of Age" and Manfred Hinz, "One Hundred Years Later: Germany on Trial in the USA—The Herero Reparations Claim for Genocide", *Namibian Human Rights Online Journal* 1 (2003).

[44] The presumptions are based on preliminary discussions with traditional authorities from the Nama and Herero people at workshops in Windhoek and Keetmanshoop held in 2004.

simultaneously acknowledging the Constitutional rights of the present owners. It must be emphasized that pre-colonial rights, while surviving colonialism, can nevertheless not destroy the present property rights guaranteed by the Constitution, just as colonization could not destroy the property rights of the indigenous peoples. However, the proof of indigenous land rights is not without meaning. Government, or even the tribunal, can begin to negotiate with the present owner on the basis of willing buyer-willing seller.

If government and the present owner can reach an agreement, the only issue will be the money to pay for the farm. Since the claims will be of an individual or sometimes tribal nature, they will possibly fall outside the present budget provisions of government. However, several donor countries and even the European Union can be requested to assist in the financing of this part of the process. Both the European Union and Germany have in the past expressed its willingness to assist Namibia with the financing of the programmed land reform.

It is granted that the process may not go as smooth as it may look on paper. What if the present owner is no longer a white person, but someone from a previously disadvantaged group? What will the government do if the present owner refuses to negotiate, or if after negotiations refuses to sell his or her farm? What will the consequences be when more than one group lays claim to the same land? It is not possible to go into detailed discussions on each of the above questions. Suffice to say that under certain circumstances the government may be convinced that expropriation is in the best national interest, while aggrieved parties will always have the right to take the matter to a court of law. The legislator may want to establish an appeal or higher tribunal, or simply determine the High or Supreme Court as the body to hear appeals. If no donor can be found, government may decide to divert some of the money budgeted for land reform to this project.

Conclusion

The principles of the Mabo case are surely not the only ones that will take land reform forward, but the acknowledgement of pre-colonial rights will have several advantages. It will create a mechanism to deal with one of the saddest pages in the history of Namibia. It will also bring justice to peoples who almost suffered extinction at the hands of European colonialism.

And it will restore the land rights of second and third generation descendants of the pre-colonial owners of the land.

Obviously, no program can restore all the injustices of the past. Opponents of the restoration of pre-colonial land rights may object to the fact that it will not treat equally all the people of the country who have suffered under South African occupation and apartheid.[45] Unfortunately, this program does not deal with the second big injustice committed against the people of Namibia. But it does not negate the fact that it can deal with the injustice of 1904 in an effective manner. Others will complain that it does not deal with the injustices of the pre-colonial wars between the different groups in the southern and central parts of the country. Yet others would want to know how a tribunal could deal with the injustices committed against the nomadic groups such as the San and the Himbas before, during and after colonization.

But it is not the intention of this paper to recommend the restoration of pre-colonial rights as the best or only possible option for land reform in Namibia. I would rather propose a process in which several strategies are used to achieve the final goal: A just distribution of land to all the peoples of Namibia in such a way that it contributes to peace, prosperity and stability. Consequently, the willing buyer-willing seller program can go on, while the government simultaneously proceeds with its programs to expropriate the farms of foreign absentee farmers and other farms in the national interest.[46] But a land tribunal on rights lost through the German colonization can assist in bringing a new dimension to land reform.

Bibliography

Blackstone, William. *Commentaries on the Laws of England Book II.* London: Sweet & Maxwell, 1830.

Castles, Alex. *An Australian Legal History.* Sydney: Law Book Co., 1982.

Cooray, Mark. "The High Court In Mabo—*Legalist* or *L'egotiste*." Accessed June 29, 2011. http://www.ourcivilisation.com/cooray/mabo/index.htm.

---

[45] See Jeremy Sarkin, "The Coming of Age," 92-93.

[46] Since the programme is still in a planning stage, one will have to wait until government has either defined national interest or start with the process before commenting on the pros and cons thereof.

Evatt, Elizabeth. "The Acquisition of Territory in Australia and New Zealand." In *Studies in the History of the Law of Nations*, edited by Charles H. Alexandrowicz. The Hague: Martinus Nijhoff, 1968.

Galligan, B. "The Power of Seven." *The Weekend Australian*, July 17-18, 1993.

Hinz, Manfred. "One Hundred Years Later: Germany on Trial in the USA—The Herero Reparations Claim for Genocide." *Namibian Human Rights Online Journal* 1 (2003).

Horn, Nico. "Land Claims and History." Paper presented before the Seis Farmers Community, March 2003.

Lindley, Mark F. *The Acquisition and Government of Backward Territory in International Law*. London: Longmans-Green, 1926.

Sarkin, Jeremy. "The Coming of Age of Claims for Reparation for Human Rights Abuses Committed in the South," *SUR International Journal on Human Rights* 1 (2004): 67-125.

Jeremy Sarkin and Carly Fowler. "Reparations for Historical Human Rights Violations: The International and Historical Dimensions of the Alien Torts Claims Act Genocide Case of the Herero of Namibia," *Human Rights Review* 9 (2008): 331-360.

Vattel, Emer de. *The Law of Nations, Or, Principles of the Law of Nature, Applied to the Conduct and Affairs of Nations and Sovereigns Book I*. 1797.

Commonwealth Cases

Adeyinka Oyekan v. Musendiku Adele (1921) 2 AC 399.

Amodu Tijani v. Secretary, Southern Nigeria (1957) 1 WLR 876.

Attorney-General v. Brown (1847) 1 Legge 312.

The Commonwealth, versus New South Wales (1923) 33 CLR 1.

In re Southern Rhodesia (1919) AC 211.

Johnson v. McIntosh (1823) 8 Wheat 543.

Liquidators of Maritime Bank of Canada v. Receiver-General (New Brunswick) (1892) AC 437.

Eddie Mabo and Others v. The State of Queensland (No. 2), [1992] HCA 23 (1992) 175 CRL 1, F.C. 92/014.

New South Wales v. The Commonwealth (1975) 135 CLR 337.

R. v. Kidman, (1915) 20 CLR 425.

Randwick Corporation v. Rutledge (1959) 102 CLR 54.

Wade v. New South Wales Rutile Mining Co. Pty. Ltd. (1969) 121 CLR 177.

Judgments of the International Court of Justice

Western Sahara, Advisory Opinions, I.C.J Reports, 1975.
Legal Status of Eastern Greenland (Den. v. Nor.), 1933 P.C.I.J. (ser. A/B) No. 53.

CHAPTER TWELVE

UNIVERSALIZING HUMAN RIGHTS:
THE ROLE OF SMALL STATES
IN THE CONSTRUCTION OF THE UNIVERSAL
DECLARATION OF HUMAN RIGHTS

SUSAN WALTZ

In the fifty years that have passed since the United Nations General
Assembly approved the Universal Declaration of Human Rights (UDHR),[1]
literally hundreds of books on the subject of human rights have come to
fill the shelves of major university libraries in the United States and
around the world. Human rights has claimed the attention of scholars in
several disciplines, and the notion is alternatively approached as a
philosophical idea, a legal concept, or a political project. Human rights
readily finds a home in Western political philosophy, where theories of
natural rights and social contract are well-anchored and help elaborate the
modern concept of human rights. Human rights has also been discussed in
comparative philosophical frameworks.[2] Human rights as a legal concept
is part of the bedrock of contemporary international law, and neither legal
scholarship nor discussion of the international implementation mechanisms
(and their flaws) is wanting. The study of international human rights as a
political project, however, has been relatively neglected. A political
project refers to concerted efforts to build a public and worldwide

---

[1] Universal Declaration of Human Rights, *Adopted* 10 Dec. 1948, G.A. Res. 217A
(III) U. N. GAOR, 3d Sess. (Resolutions, Pt. 1) At 71, U.N. Doc A/810 (1948).
[2] Jack Donnelly, *Universal Human Rights in Theory and Practice* (Ithaca: Cornell
University Press, 1989); Johan Galtung, *Human Rights in a Different Key*
(Cambridge: Polity Press, 1994); Ann Mayer, *Islam and Human Rights: Tradition
and Politics* (Boulder: Westview Press, 1995); Abdullahi Ahmed An-Na'im, ed.,
Human Rights in Cross-Cultural Perspectives: A Quest for Consensus (Philadelphia:
University of Pennsylvania Press, 1991) and Michael Freeman, "The Philosophical
Foundations of Human Rights" *Human Rights Quarterly* 16 (1994): 491.

consensus around the idea of human rights, including political strategies, diplomatic initiatives, agreement of explicit principles, and conclusion of an international accord.[3] The field of international relations is the most natural disciplinary home for such inquiry, but until the 1970s, the paradigmatic attachment to the notion of sovereignty excluded virtually all treatment of human rights. Scholars in international relations tended to view concern with human rights as a matter of domestic governance, and thus out of their domain. It was only with discussions of transnationalism, international regimes, and the limits to political realism that human rights began its slow creep into that literature.[4] Political analyses of international human rights began to appear in the late 1980s, and today they are complemented by a growing body of writings about the construction of international human rights as a political project.[5]

As this chapter will demonstrate, recent scholarship on the political origins of the UDHR has proved enlightening. Efforts to account for both inspiration and political motivation have taken several scholars deep into archives, and in the process several forgotten or obscured facts have been unearthed. As the erstwhile unproblematic history of the UDHR has been reconstructed, it has become more complex, and more nuanced. One of the subtle but powerful truths to emerge is that no single, straightforward story about the origins and content of the International Bill of Rights can be told.[6]

---

[3] I have borrowed this term from Tony Evans, whose usage is similar. Tony Evans, *US Hegemony and the Project of Universal Human Rights* (New York: St. Martin's Press, 1996).

[4] The evolution of this literature can be traced over several decades through publications in journals such as International Organization, World Politics, International Studies Quarterly and Millennium-Journal of International Studies.

[5] Donnelly, *Universal Human Rights*; R. J. Vincent, *Human Rights and International Relations* (Cambridge: Cambridge University Press, 1986) and David C. Forsythe, *The Internationalization of Human Rights* (Lexington: Lexington Books, 1991). Also see Henry Shue, *Basic Rights: Subsistence, Affluence, and U. S. Foreign Policy* (Princeton: Princeton University Press, 1980); Lars Schoultz, *Human Rights and US Foreign Policy toward Latin America* (Princeton: Princeton University Press, 1981) and David C. Forsythe, *Human Rights and US Foreign Policy: Congress Reconsidered* (Gainesville: University of Florida Press,1988).

[6] The Universal Declaration of Human Rights together with the International Covenant on Civil and Political Rights and the International Covenant on Social, Economic and Cultural Rights comprise the "International Bill of Rights." For many months between 1946 and 1948 there was active debate about whether or not to have a single document and the exact form any document(s) should take. After

Familiar Accounts and Less Familiar Scholarship:
A Review

The historical account of the UDHR best known in the United States begins with the Roosevelts.[7] In his 1941 State of the Union address to Congress, Franklin Delano Roosevelt delivered the well-known Four Freedoms speech,[8] providing a rhetorical touchstone for many who subsequently took up the cause. So influential was the notion of "fundamental freedoms" that the 1941 speech is considered by many as the seminal contribution. However important was Franklin Roosevelt's contribution, though, his widow's role was more celebrated: from January 1947 to June 1948 she chaired the UN Human Rights Commission that produced the draft Declaration.[9] In her own time, Eleanor Roosevelt was famous—or infamous—as an advocate of social justice. In the years after her death, however, a number of film documentaries have popularized an understanding of her leadership role in promoting international human rights.[10]

---

the declaration was acclaimed in 1948, debate continued as to whether there should one or two main treaties. Largely due to pressures from the United States–whose own internal political landscape had changed dramatically from 1945 to 1952–the covenants were split. See Evans, *US Hegemony*, 89-92. In this chapter, the term "International Bill Of Rights" has two meanings: (1) When capitalized this term refers to the three documents, namely the UDHR, ICCPR and ICESCR; and (2) when not capitalized, it refers to the entire political project before it was known that there would be three, not one, document.

[7] M. Glen Johnson, "The Contributions of Eleanor and Franklin Roosevelt to the Development of International Protection for Human Rights," *Human Rights Quarterly* 9 (1987): 19.

[8] Roosevelt's speech proclaimed freedom of speech, freedom of religion, freedom from fear and freedom from want.

[9] For additional insights into Eleanor Roosevelt's role, see Tony Evans, *US Hegemony*; A. Glen Johnson, *The Contributions*; John P. Humphrey, *Human Rights and the United Nations: A Great Adventure* (New York: Transnational Publishers, 1984); David Gurewitsch, *Eleanor Roosevelt: Her Day* (New York: Interchange Foundation, 1973). As the chair of the Commission of Human Rights, Eleanor Roosevelt was invited to introduce the draft UDHR to the Third Committee for formal debate. See U.N. GAOR, 3d Sess., 3d Comm., Pt. 1, At 32-33 (1948) [Hereinafter Third Committee Records].

[10] See, e.g., *The Eleanor Roosevelt Story* (Richard Kaplan, 1966); *Eleanor Roosevelt: A Restless Spirit* (A&E Home Video, 1994); *The American Experience: Eleanor Roosevelt* (PBS, 1999).

From this side of the Atlantic there are few challenges to a view that the Roosevelts shaped and molded the human rights story, and indeed, many consider the human rights project was no more and no less than an American project.[11] Alternative views persist, however, and there are variations to challenge even this most basic story. The fact that the UDHR was finalized under the shadow of the Eiffel Tower allows France to call itself the birthplace of universal human rights. The version of the story commonly told in France puts renowned legal scholar Rene Cassin at center stage. Cassin had great influence over the final draft text and was awarded the Nobel Peace Prize for his role in fostering the UDHR. As part of their own political legacy, the French recall that the Rights of Man manifesto arose from the French Revolution. When the freshly created United Nations Economic, Social and Cultural Organization (UNESCO) decided in 1946 to conduct an international survey on the multicultural basis of the philosophical idea of human rights, French philosopher Jacques Maritain was among those chosen to participate in the study. That UNESCO investigation had no appreciable impact on the political project of human rights (which was carried out by the Commission on Human Rights, under the aegis of the Economic and Social Council, ECOSOC), but Maritain's active participation nevertheless buttresses the French claim to sponsorship of the human rights project.[12]

In recent years, scholars have had opportunity to peruse many contemporaneous documents and retrospective accounts. Eleanor Roosevelt's rather circumspect views were published concurrently with her own participation in the process, as installments in the news column Her Day.[13] Her autobiography contains additional notes, as do some of her private papers and US State Department documents.[14] John Humphrey, the United Nation's first Director of the Division on Human Rights, published his own memoir in 1984, presenting the account of another player central to the political process of constructing the UDHR.[15] More recently, in 1996,

---

[11] Evans, *US Hegemony.*

[12] Jacques Maritain, "On the Philosophy of Human Rights," in *Human Rights: Comments and Interpretation: A Symposium,* ed. UNESCO, (London-New York: A. Wingate, 1949), 72.

[13] Gurewitsch, *Eleanor Roosevelt.*

[14] Eleanor Roosevelt, *The Autobiography of Eleanor Roosevelt* (Cambridge: Da Capo Press, 1992). For an account based in part on a review of Eleanor Roosevelt's private papers, see Tony Evans, *US Hegemony.*

[15] Humphrey, *Human Rights.*

British political scientist Tony Evans developed an account of the international human rights project that privileges hegemonic interests. Grounding his carefully researched and well-documented study in the dominant theory of international relations, he argues that the UDHR was an American project that rose, and fell, with the tide of US interest.[16] Studies of US domestic politics during the Truman-Eisenhower transition also help explain the waning of US interests in a project initially championed by a US president.[17]

An alternative perspective on political dynamics is offered by William Korey, whose richly anecdotal version of the story emphasizes the arguably crucial role of nongovernmental organizations.[18] Representatives of some forty-two US-based and international nongovernmental organizations were invited to the April 1945 San Francisco conference that created the United Nations. Although formally they served in an advisory capacity to the US delegation, they contributed to debates and influenced delegates from their position offstage, in the corridors and private meeting rooms. It was thanks to their lobbying efforts that a Human Rights Commission was created, and of course it was that body which was charged to draft the Universal Declaration.[19] Jan Burgers' investigation of political developments during the interwar period also emphasizes the role of non-state actors in promoting the human rights idea. Archival research led Burgers to uncover evidence that a groundswell of support for creating international human rights standards was growing among civic groups in Europe and the US well before the worst Nazi atrocities were known.[20] His work has been expanded by Paul Lauren, who traces the international human rights movement back to the late nineteenth century.[21]

Finally, there has also been scholarly scrutiny of the drafting process

---

[16] Evans, *US Hegemony.*

[17] Richard Davies, *Defender of the Old Guard: John Bricker and American Politics* (Columbus: Ohio State University Press, 1993) and Duane Tananbaum, *The Bricker Amendment Controversy: A Test of Eisenhower's Political Leadership* (Ithaca: Cornell University Press, 1988).

[18] William C. Korey, *NGO's and the Universal Declaration of Human Rights* (New York: St. Martin's Press, 1998).

[19] Korey, *NGO's,* 36.

[20] J. Herman Burgers, The Road to San Francisco," *Human Rights Quarterly* 14 (1992): 465.

[21] Paul Gordon Lauren, *The Evolution of International Human Rights: Visions Seen* (Philadelphia: University of Pennsylvania Press, 1998), 72-138.

itself. A group of Scandinavian scholars published an article-by-article examination of the origins of the Universal Declaration in 1992, and their work supplements accounts published several decades ago.[22] More recently, Johannes Morsink has opened UN archives to consider both the process and the politics of the initial drafting phases. His book *The Universal Declaration: Origins, Drafting, and Intent* is by far the most comprehensive and authoritative work on the authorship of the Universal Declaration.[23]

Small States and the UDHR

Despite the rich historical resources now at our disposal, at least one version of the story remains untold as an account unto itself. Some 250 delegates and advisors from fifty-six countries were accredited to participate in the construction of the Universal Declaration, but most scholarly attention has been directed to the role of a few delegations. The story of the majority remains enshadowed. It is that story, and most particularly the role and contribution of states that would come to be known as the Third World, which is most intriguing. Parts of their story, of course, have appeared in other versions, often as interesting sidelines or incidental elements. This chapter is intended to present a systematic review that allows readers to understand the contributions and appreciate the commitment of participants from these small states. Similarly, the author hopes that this presentation will inspire researchers from countries that played significant roles in the historical process to extend this investigation to the debates and positions developed within their countries' delegations.

In reassembling this account of the UDHR's birth, the author makes no claim to present the main version of the story, much less the "true" version of events that unfolded from 1946 through the early 1950s. To

---

[22] Asbjorn Eide, Gudmujndur Alfredsson, Goran Melander, Lars Adam Rehof and Allan Rosas, eds., *The Universal Declaration of Human Rights: A Commentary* (Oslo: Scandinavian University Press, 1992). See also Nehemiah Robinson, *The Universal Declaration of Human Rights: Its Origins, Significance, Application and Interpretation* (New York: Institute of Jewish Affairs, Louvain-Paris: Editorial Nauwelaerts, 1958), and Albert Verdoodt, *Naissance et Signification de la Declaration Universelle des Droits de l'Homme* (1963).
[23] Johannes Morsink, *The Universal Declaration Of Human Rights: Origins, Drafting and Intent* (Philadelphia: University of Pennsylvania Press, 1999).

the best of my knowledge, the material presented below is truthful and represents *one* accurate version of events that transpired, and this version is an important one. Novelists, filmmakers, and literary critics have helped us appreciate the value of considering a story from alternative perspectives, both to capture complexity and to query a given account that might otherwise go unexamined. At very least, the story of Third World contributions and contributors enriches our understanding of the range of political dynamics and concerns that were brought to the table as the International Bill of Rights was being negotiated. It also sheds light on the knotty question of the universality of human rights.

Unfortunately, a coherent story that accents the role and contributions of small states is not easily told. The narrative assembled is complex and interwoven. Elements that in more familiar versions of the story commonly figure in the foreground must recede here, and more obscure events, prominent in an account that privileges the smaller states, require additional explanation. Except to those intimately familiar with historical events of the post-war era, there is risk that the sheer detail of the story, organized as a narrative, would overwhelm and bore even the most tolerant. The account that follows is thus organized to preserve the goodwill of readers, Rather than recount a chronologically ordered narrative, I have identified four principal roles that Third World participants played. In the pages that follow I offer anecdotes to illustrate and substantiate the claim.

To engage directly with the material that follows, some familiarity with the most basic sequence of events in the UDHR story is required. The UDHR went through several distinct phases, and the anecdotes that will be recounted come from various phases. It will also be useful to consider that the argument presented is not that small state participants dominated the debate over the UDHR. The argument here is more modest, and the threshold of proof accordingly lower. The claim made here is a simple but important one: a wide range of participants outside the Western bloc made significant contributions to the construction of the most elemental international standard of human rights, and they were aware at the time of the significance of their words and deeds.

Well before the opening of the San Francisco conference that was to create a United Nations, the idea of establishing an international human rights standard was in the air. The concept of a worldwide declaration of human rights can be traced back at least as far as the 1920's, soon after the non-governmental Federation Internationale des Droits de l'Homme (FIDH) was created in Paris.[24] Later, in 1939, aging science fiction writer H. G. Wells published an impassioned plea for a mid-century declaration that set humanitarian standards for future generations.[25] His own version of such a declaration was disseminated in many languages.[26] The 1941 Atlantic Charter signed by Roosevelt and Churchill, and subsequently endorsed by forty-four additional countries, referred to human rights and fundamental freedoms.[27] It galvanized popular support and raised many hopes around the world for social justice in the areas of race relations, women's rights, and colonial rule. US Undersecretary of State Sumner Welles was a strong advocate of human rights, and under his guidance, a working group at the State Department made some initial efforts at drafting their own international bill of rights.[28]

It seemed natural that the idea of a human rights declaration would find its way into proposals for a new worldwide organization of United Nations. It did, but barely. Papers prepared by the US in preparation for meetings at Dumbarton Oaks referenced human rights, but support was at best lukewarm. Though it will seem ironic today, of the four Sponsoring Powers, it was China that was most supportive of the idea.[29] The Chinese argued that a central purpose of the UN should be to enforce justice for the world. To that end they were prepared "to cede as much...sovereign power

---

[24] *FIDH Homepage* (2010), http://www.fidh.org

[25] H. G. Wells, "War Aims: The Rights of Man," *The Times* October 25, 1939. For the original draft of his Declaration Of Rights and additional commentary on human rights see H. G. Wells, *The Rights of Man or What Are We Fighting for?* (Harmondsworth-New York: Penguin, 1940).

[26] For a discussion of Wells' work, see Burgers, *Road*, 465-468, and Lauren, *Evolution*, 152-153 and 329. Lauren notes that Wells' declaration was translated into Chinese, Japanese, Arabic, Urdu, Hindi, Bengali, Guajarati, Hausa, Swahili, Yoruba, Zulu and Esperanto. Wells also circulated his declaration among European and North-American intellectuals. For the broad range of Well's political concerns during this period, see Michael Foot, *The History of Mr. Wells* (London: Doubleday, 1995), 253-307.

[27] The document commonly known as the Atlantic Charter was initially released as the "Declaration of Principles Issued by the President of the United States and the Prime Minister of the United Kingdom" on 14 August 1941.

[28] Lauren, *Evolution*, 161-162.

[29] Ibid., 166. The four sponsoring powers were the United States, Great Britain, the USSR and China. These were the four states that met at Dumbarton Oaks, producing the proposal for the United Nations, which was then discussed in San Francisco.

as may be required." [30] Neither Churchill nor Stalin, however, recognized China's status as a great power, and China's views did not carry substantial weight.[31] For their part, both the USSR and the United Kingdom resisted the idea of human rights.[32] So did US Secretary of State Cordell Hull, who in the meantime had forced the resignation of Sumner Welles. Hull regarded human rights chiefly as a useful wartime propaganda tool, otherwise antithetical to the interests of a sovereign nation, and his views prevailed.[33] The Dumbarton Oaks proposals ultimately contained only one small reference to human rights.[34]

As the curtain rises on our story, there was no reason at all to expect that the nascent United Nations would focus rhetorical attention on human rights. There was nothing inevitable about the Universal Declaration, much less the human rights treaties that followed. Certainly, the Great Powers did not advance the idea. Once it was loose, their concern was to manage the process and ensure at least that the results did not run counter to their interests. They quickly seized leadership roles in the crafting of the human rights project, but the smaller powers also participated actively. In many regards the story of the UDHR belongs to them. Some of the ideas advanced by smaller powers were incorporated into the final product. Some were not. Sometimes they supported the larger powers; sometimes they did not. Sometimes they were divided among themselves. In several instances, their concerted efforts prevented the larger powers from having their way.

From a review of relatively accessible documents and secondary texts, four distinct roles played by small states can be identified. First, the smaller powers were witnesses and accessories to the creation of the International Bill of Rights. They were included in a process that extended over a period of eighteen months. Second, these nations were active participants. Third, they provided leadership from their own ranks. Fourth, Third World delegates were also ardent advocates and partisans, advancing agendas of their own. There is little doubt that without their efforts that the International Bill of Rights would have looked rather different, if indeed it had finally been agreed at all. Each of these four

---

[30] Ibid.

[31] Ibid., 148-149,166-171 and 331-332.

[32] Farrokh Jhabvala, "The Drafting of the Human Rights Provisions of the UN Charter," *Netherlands International Law Review* 64 (1997).

[33] Lauren, *Evolution*, 165.

[34] Jhabvala, *Drafting*, 32.

roles is elaborated and illustrated in turn.

The Small Powers as Witness

Contrary to what is often imagined, the negotiations over the UDHR were a very public affair. There were no doubt important conversations that took place off the record, but for a variety of reasons, the debates were protracted and to a significant degree open to all. Official records were kept during the debates of both the Commission and the Third Committee proceedings (Phases II and III, Figure I). Whether or not they actively participated in the debate, every delegate who attended the Third Committee debates of autumn 1948 at minimum heard, and witnessed, discussion of the meaning of human rights. Sometimes that discussion strayed into the abstractly philosophical. More often, comments were pedantic; the official record is replete with suggestions for amending the text.[35] As the following pages show, there is ample evidence, though, that delegates also wrestled in a basic way with the substance of human rights problems. They understood that their debate was helping to define rights as well as create standards. Regular reference to poignant and concrete problems of the day kept the purpose of the debate in clear focus.

Not surprisingly, Nazi atrocities and fascist brutalities were frequently evoked. Delegates referred to Nazi practices during the drafting and discussion of more than half of the Declaration's thirty articles. Sometimes anecdotal references to Nazi practices were adduced to buoy political arguments and sway opinions. In other places, profound reactions to Nazi practices in the concentration camps appear to have shaped the very essence of the moral code being drafted. Articles 3, 4, and 5 (establishing the general right to life, liberty and security of

> person and prohibiting practices of slavery and torture) in particular were deeply influenced by the Holocaust experience, and not simply by Enlightenment thought enshrined in many existing national constitutions.[36]

The Nazi holocaust was frequently evoked, but it was not by any means the only point of reference for participants in the Third Committee debates. During these debates, Soviet bloc delegates regularly pointed out the human rights shortcomings of their Western counterparts. They noted

---

[35] See *Third Committee Records, passim.*
[36] Morsink, *Universal,* 38-43.

the Swiss denial of the political franchise to women,[37] and the British empire's denial of the franchise to the vast majority of its subjects worldwide.[38] They noted the US Congress' ignominious failure to approve a proposed federal law against lynching.[39] Delegates were witness to many attacks on South Africa, where the Afrikaner Nationalist Party had just come to power on a platform of racist and segregationist promises they intended to keep.[40]

Some of the issues hit very close to home. An emergency report from UN envoy Ralph Bunche on the crisis of Palestinian refugees was the only issue allowed to interrupt the concentrated focus on the UDHR during the two-month session of the Third Committee in 1948.[41] Delegates from Egypt and Iraq seized the opportunity to point out that there was nothing abstract about that particular human rights crisis. Less far-reaching, but with its own measure of drama, the Chilean delegation brought its grievance about the Soviet Union's restrictions on emigration to the deliberating body.[42] Just as the Third Committee debates were opening in Paris in September 1948, the USSR had denied an exit visa to a Soviet member of the Chilean ambassador's family. In the resulting imbroglio, Chile broke off diplomatic relations with the USSR, and for several tense days each country held the other's ambassador in custody.[43]

The UDHR was constructed with great deliberation. At all stages of the drafting, delegates understood what they were about, even if they could only imagine the ultimate significance of their work. No participating delegation could reasonably claim to have been unaware of its content, or its relevance.

---

[37] Swiss women received the right to vote only in 1971. See *Third Committee Records*, 461.

[38] Ibid

[39] Ibid., 142.

[40] Ibid., 57, 92 and 131.

[41] Bunche was replacing Count Folke Bernadotte of Sweden, who served in 1948 as the Security Council's mediator in Palestine. Count Bernadotte had been negotiating a ceasefire between Arab and Jewish leaders in Palestine when he was assassinated by Zionist extremists, less than two weeks before the Third Committee convened in Paris. See Ralph Hewins, *Count Folke Bernadotte: His Life and Work* (London: Hutchison & Co, 1950).

[42] *Third Committee Records*, 316.

[43] "Human Rights Questions at the Third Regular Session of the General Assembly: The United States Position", *Foreign Relations of the United States 1948* 1, (1975): 289, 293-299. [hereinafter Human Rights Questions.]

The Small Powers as Active Participants

Representatives of the small powers were not passive participants in any stage of the international human rights project. From the moment that the Dumbarton Oaks proposals were distributed, Latin American participants began to discuss a common approach to the question of human rights. Along with other small states in the West, they helped bring the Commission into being. Once the Commission was appointed, the UDHR project moved to the drafting phase, and some eighteen states were formally represented in the drafting committee. Included in this number were Chile, China, Egypt, India, Iran, Lebanon, Panama, Philippines, and Uruguay.[44] Delegates from fourteen other small non-western powers served in a second tier of drafters. Representatives of the small powers actively contributed to discussions on the full gamut of rights under consideration. They proposed additions and changes to the initial draft prepared by the UN Secretariat; they queried and challenged proposed changes suggested by others.[45]

Small states remained vocal during the proceedings of the General Assembly's Third Committee, convened in September 1948. Out of the 166 written proposals to amend the declaration as drafted by the Commission on Human Rights, twenty-eight were forwarded by the Cuban delegation.[46] The Soviet Union, Panama, Lebanon, France, and Egypt each offered at least ten written amendments.[47]

Whether or not they tried to shape or re-shape the draft document through written amendments, nearly every delegation participated in the oral debate at some juncture. Whether the contributions represented a formal government position or not depended largely on the delegation–and on the matter at hand. US State Department records show that the US delegation agreed positions in advance, but so, for example, did Pakistan.[48] Then as now, many other delegates from a wide variety of nations were allowed considerable latitude in shaping their interventions. As a random

---

[44] Morsink, *Universal*, 32-33. Morsink identifies by name approximately forty "second-tier" delegates who in his estimation made significant contribution during the drafting phase.

[45] *Third Committee Records*, Annexes, 9-58.

[46] Ibid., Appendix.

[47] Ibid.

[48] Shaista Ikramullah, *From Purdah to Parliament* (Karachi-Oxford: Oxford University Press, 1998), 182-192 and 202-208.

example of the oral exchange, on the text that eventually became Article 21, some twenty-eight voices joined the debate, including delegates from Belgium, Uruguay, the United States, Greece, Brazil, Venezuela, Iraq, China, Haiti, Cuba, Sweden, the former Soviet Union, Lebanon, Philippines, and Saudi Arabia.[49] In their interventions, small powers engaged substantive issues, and they engaged each other. During the debate on what would become Article 5 (prohibiting torture), for example, the Philippine Republic objected to a proposal by Cuba to insert provisions for cultural differences. The Philippine delegate argued that with such a provision in place, Nazis might have claimed that their torture chambers were customary and therefore legal in Nazi Germany.[50] In the debate on what would become Article 16, the Pakistan delegation resisted efforts by Saudi Arabia to change the provisions for marriageable age from "full age" to "legal marriageable age." Mrs. Shaista lkramullah argued that the original draft language more clearly conveyed the intent to prevent child marriages, and non-consensual marriages.[51] Emile Saint Lot of Haiti voiced reservations about voting by secret ballot–where citizens were predominantly illiterate.[52] The Mexican delegation paid homage to Thomas Jefferson but went on to argue for inclusion of socio-economic rights, compatible with the ideals of the Mexican Revolution. And as Morsink has documented, throughout the entire two-year process of constructing the Declaration, the oft-repeated debate over natural rights was of great concern to delegates from a wide range of countries, and not least of them Lebanon, Brazil, Uruguay, Chile, Cuba, and China.[53]

Small states were active and engaged participants in the process that produced the UDHR. Some Western powers, in fact, might have preferred less participation on their part. Minutes from meetings of the US delegation to the Third Committee indicate that the United States was committed to moving the draft UDHR through the General Assembly as quickly as possible, initially hoping that debates could be finished within a few days.[54] They were soon brought to realize not only the futility, but the political inadvisability, of attempting to limit debate. Charles Malik, who chaired the Third Committee sessions, informed the US delegation that

---

[49] *Third Committee Records*, 448-473.

[50] Ibid., 214.

[51] Ibid., 374.

[52] Ibid., 466.

[53] Johannes Morsink, "The Philosophy of the Universal Declaration," *Human Rights Quarterly* 6 (1984): 310-316.

[54] "Human Rights Questions," 289-291.

many states were attached to the idea of examining the draft text in detail, and some of the smaller US allies argued that states that had not participated in the drafting phase should have opportunity to express their views on the draft Declaration.[55]

The breadth of the eventual participation testifies to interest in the document's content, and the feeling of joint ownership. At the opening session of the Third Committee hearings on 30 September 1948, Costa Rica's delegate had warned of the dangers that lurked when a state put its own interests over those of individual citizens; the Lebanese delegate had heralded lessons that could be learned from both the East and the West; the Pakistani delegate had suggested the UDHR could mark a turning point in human history.[56] Some two months later, in the final plenary session convened on 9 December 1948, Charles Malik noted that the UN Third Committee had devoted eighty-five sessions to the discussion of the draft Declaration; eighteen of the twenty-nine articles in the draft text had been adopted without opposition; and throughout the debate nearly 90 percent of the votes had been taken in the affirmative.[57] More than fifty states had taken part in discussions on the Universal Declaration that had spanned more than two years.[58] Not until the establishment of the United Nations had small states been afforded such opportunity to participate in the construction of international norms.

Small Power Leadership

Leadership is an elusive quality that comes in many forms. Several individuals substantially contributed not only to the shape of the UDHR, but to the process of seeing it through. Eleanor Roosevelt is often singled out as the heroine of the UDHR, but her role is both overstated and under-appreciated. Eleanor Roosevelt's genius was a political one: during the critical early phases of the UDHR project, she steered the debate and moved it along. The modesty she projected was both charming and disarming, and her seemingly effortless exercise of political savvy–hosting quiet conversations, diplomatically limiting

---

[55] Ibid., 290-291.

[56] *Third Committee Records*, 37-51.

[57] U. N. GAOR, 3d Sess., Pt. 1, 180th Plenary Meeting., (1948), 860 [Hereinafter U.N. GAOR, 180th Plenary Meeting.]

[58] Forty-eight states voted for the UDHR in the General Assembly plenary convened on 10 December 1948; eight states abstained. A handful of those states did not participate in the Third Committee Debates. See Ibid., 934.

debate–provided necessary lubrication for the wheels and cogs of a newly invented international mechanism, the UN Commission on Human Rights. Without Eleanor Roosevelt's effort and attention, the UDHR project might not have come to fruition, and the ovation she received from the UN General Assembly was well-deserved. Eleanor Roosevelt, however, did not write any version of the UDHR.

Rene Cassin is often credited with authoring the UDHR, but that acclaim also appears to be misplaced. With the status of chief legal adviser to Charles de Gaulle during the war and with experience drafting the constitution of the Free French, Cassin was indeed an active, vital, and respected participant in all stages of the discussion and debate.[59] As to the question of authorship, however, Morsink has established that Cassin "did not enter the room until the baby was born." [60] Cassin did edit an initial draft of the UDHR which had been prepared by the UN Secretariat, but careful comparison of the two documents shows that at least three-quarters of Cassin's text flowed directly from the UN draft.[61] His most brilliant contribution to the political project of international human rights arguably came after 1948. According to Morsink, "more than any other drafter, Cassin spent the post-adoption years interpreting the Declaration to the larger world." [62] Cassin developed and promoted an elaborate and inspiring presentation of the architecture of the UDHR, a portico leading to a world where human rights are respected.[63]

The task of assembling an initial draft declaration actually fell to the United Nation's first Human Rights Director, Canadian law professor and committed socialist, John Humphrey. There appears to have been an intent, in 1946, to have the appointed officers of the new Human Rights Commission prepare some draft, but a first assay resulted only in a heated philosophical argument between Vice Chair Zhang Pengjun (also known as Peng Chen Chang) and Rapporteur Charles Malik. Humphrey's

---

[59] In retrospect, it is difficult to assess Cassin's precise contribution to the process. He clearly annoyed Humphrey, who claimed that few were persuaded by Cassin's arguments (See Humphrey, *Human Rights*, 24). Eleanor Roosevelt does not mention Cassin's contribution–though she mentions many others.

[60] Morsink, *The Universal*, 29.

[61] Ibid., at 8.

[62] Ibid., at 29.

[63] Mary Ann Glendon, "Knowing the Universal Declaration of Human Rights," *Notre Dame Law Review* 73 (1998): 1163, citing Marc Agi and Rene Cassin, *Fantassin des Droits de l'Homme* (Paris: Plon, 1979): 317.

memoir relates in some detail his efforts to assemble a draft out of numerous documents that had been submitted to the UN office. His claim that he relied most heavily on a draft prepared by the American Law Institute and heavily influenced by the respected Chilean jurist Alvaro Alvarez—and presented by Panama at the 1945 conference convening the United Nations--is substantiated by Morsink's research, which included a review of the Humphrey papers at McGill University.[64] Early in Phase II the draft provided by Humphrey was annotated by some 400 pages matching the articles in the draft Declaration to articles in existing constitutions from around the world.[65]

History has been somewhat less kind to John Humphrey than to Eleanor Roosevelt and Rene Cassin, but each of these three figures has received a measure of recognition. The efforts of Soviet delegate Alexei Pavlov and the leadership roles of Charles Malik (Lebanon), Hernan Santa Cruz (Chile) and Zhang Pengjun (China) have been much less appreciated.

Charles Malik held two positions of substantial responsibility: he first served as rapporteur of the Human Rights Commission and subsequently was elected Chair of the 1948 UNGA Third Committee proceedings. As Rapporteur, Malik compiled the records that permitted Commission members to discuss and debate substantive issues. His records helped frame the issues. As chair of the Third Committee, he was responsible for moving debate forward, much as Eleanor Roosevelt had done in the Commission. Malik chaired every one of the Third Committee's daily sessions from late September to early December 1948. A stickler for procedure, he recognized the importance of allowing all delegates to have their say on the draft Declaration. Though many participants no doubt regretted his decision to scrutinize the draft Declaration article by article, it is largely due to his leadership that we have a record of debates that reflect concerns raised by various countries in both the Commission and the Third Committee.[66]

---

[64] Humphrey, *Human Rights*, 32. Also see comments by Charles Malik before the UN General Assembly session on 9 December 1948, in *Third Committee Records*, 858. Morsink's Findings are reported in Morsink, *Universal*, 6. The American Law Institute was composed of jurists from all over the Western hemisphere, and was heavily influenced by Latin jurists. Lauren, *Evolution*, 158.
[65] Morsink, *Universal*, 7.
[66] *1947-1948 United Nations Year Book*, 1075.

Malik was forty years old when he took up work with the Human Rights Commission. He was teaching philosophy in Beirut when he was asked to join Lebanon's delegation to the UN. Biographic sketches emphasize his career as a diplomat, but he preferred to think of himself as a philosopher and a scholar. Humphrey identified him, along with Zhang, as one of the two most gifted intellects on the Commission.[67] Some delegates–most notably the British Lord Dukeston–found his attachment to Thomist legal doctrine[68] too dogmatic, and on several occasions his proposals were defeated. Malik was educated at the American University of Beirut and at Harvard, but he was widely recognized and respected as a product of his Mediterranean and Middle Eastern culture.

Zhang Pengjun served as Vice Chair of the Human Rights Commission. Zhang received a doctorate from Columbia Teachers' College[69] and was well acquainted with Western philosophic traditions. He spoke admiringly of Western philosophy from time to time, but he was also firmly implanted in his own culture. The record reflects his deep concern that the UDHR not be "too" Western. In an incident recounted by both Eleanor Roosevelt and John Humphrey, Zhang took early opportunity to establish that the Universal Declaration could not be a simple reflection of Western philosophy–and to that end, he advised UN staff to embark on a study of Confucian thought.[70] Zhang was remembered and

---

[67] Humphrey, *Human Rights*, 23.

[68] Ibid., 25. Thomas Aquinas (1226-1274) posited and differentiated four kinds of law, including natural law and positive law. Attachment to natural law, of which Malik was a proponent, presumes that rational beings can recognize and will obey certain principles "by nature." Aquinas suggested that positive law could be derived from natural law, and it is just this argument that led Malik into deep debate with his colleagues in the Human Rights Commission. See Ibid., 23. As an aside, it is perhaps interesting to note that Thomist doctrine provided a Christian medieval synthesis of contending traditions then represented as Christian (drawing on Augustine and Plato) and Muslim (Aristotle by way of Averroes). See Norman F. Cantor, *Western Civilization: Its Genesis and Destiny* (Gleenview: Scott & Foresman, 1969), 351 and 463.

[69] Zhang was born in Tientsin in 1892 and was educated at Nankai Middle School. After earning a doctorate in education he returned to China and became dean of Tsing Hua College. Zhang was a member of the Peoples' Political Council of China under Chiang Kai-shek. He served as minister to Turkey and to Chile before becoming representative to the UNGA in 1946. See *1947-1948 United Nations Year Book*, 1055.

[70] Humphrey, *Human Rights*, 29, and Roosevelt, *Autobiography*, 316-317.

appreciated for two kinds of contributions. On one hand, he regularly caught the attention of other delegates by referring to Chinese practice or quoting a pertinent Chinese proverb. Official records reflect some of these contributions, and in some instances they appear to have had the effect of helping delegates appreciate an alternative perspective and move beyond an impasse. Third Committee records note his advice to sweep the snow in front on one's own doors and overlook the frost on others' roof tiles.[71]

Zhang's second contribution was at least as far-reaching, and may have been an extension of culture as well as a gift of personal intellect. More than any other delegate in the drafting or debate stages, Zhang attended to the logical structure of the Declaration. According to John Humphrey, it was Zhang who first envisaged three instruments: a declaration, a treaty, and measures of implementation.[72] He regularly offered diplomatic editorial resolutions to problems in which the debates were mired. On numerous occasions he suggested altering the order of articles, or re-ordering clauses within articles. He appears to be the first to have appreciated the internal logic of the Declaration, and Cassin may well have used Zhang's initial analysis to elaborate his own colorful metaphor of the portico.[73]

Unlike Zhang and Malik, Hernan Santa Cruz held no position of responsibility within the Commission or the Third Committee, but his political and substantive contributions were such that both Humphrey in his memoir and Morsink through his review of documents single out the important role he played.[74] Before joining Chile's UN delegation, Santa Cruz served as a judge on Chile's Superior Military Court. Prior to that, he had taught criminal procedure and military procedure at various military

---

[71] *Third Committee Records*, 177.

[72] Humphrey, *Human Rights*, 40

[73] Not all of Zhang's suggestions have been applauded. Morsink holds Zhang responsible for "damage" to the UDHR that resulted when in the final days of the Commission's work, Zhang successfully advocated moving the article on duties to the end of the Declaration, far away from its early position as the second article. Morsink speculates as to whether this late suggestion from Zhang was colored by his preoccupation with events in China. On the day the change was made, the New York Times carried two stories about China on its front page—one concerning delays in a US-China aid bill and one about Mao's drive to Shanghai and Nanking. See Morsink, *Universal*, 246.

[74] Humphrey, *Human Rights*, 40.

academies. Santa Cruz had supplied one of the initial drafts with which Humphrey worked, and he was particularly attached to provisions about socioeconomic rights. Particularly in the drafting stages, Santa Cruz was vigilant in his defense of these rights and stepped in with persuasive arguments when North Atlantic nations sought to trim them back. Morsink credits Santa Cruz' intellectual attachment to socioeconomic rights as one of the important reasons why the 1948 Declaration ultimately transcended eighteenth century Enlightenment philosophy.[75]

A note on Alexei P. Pavlov is in order, simply to complete the record of exceptional individual contributions. Although his proposals were rarely accepted either in the Commission or by the Third Committee and though he frequently irritated other delegates, Pavlov was tireless in his efforts to promote certain causes. He did not often use diplomatic niceties to couch his criticisms of Western powers, but because many of his comments were meticulously researched,[76] they found their targets. The Declaration's final clear statement on nondiscrimination is attributed to Pavlov's persistence, and advocates of non-sexist language and certain social and economic rights found him in a steadfast ally.[77] Like counterparts from other countries and other traditions, Pavlov was deeply engaged in the process of constructing the Universal Declaration.

The different styles and perspectives of this small group of leaders were often a source of conflict in the drafting and debate stages of the UDHR. The fact that several strong personalities were involved in the process, however, increased the level of engagement and scrutiny of a wide range of participants. No less than key delegates representing large states, leaders from the small states ensured that issues they viewed as important were brought to the table and inserted into the record. Each in

---

[75] Morsink, *Universal*, 30. Santa Cruz would later lead the fight for a single human rights covenant to enact the Declaration and in so doing would earn the label of "mischief-maker" from Mrs. Lord, who replaced Eleanor Roosevelt as the US representative on the Commission on Human Rights. See "United States Policy Regarding the Draft United Nations Covenants on Human Rights: The 1953 Change", *Foreign Relations of the United States*, 3 (1979): 1952-1954, 1536 and 1579.

[76] Eleanor Roosevelt recounts one speech by Pavlov that referred to a Mississippi statute regarding the length of an ax handle that a man could use to beat his wife. She had an advisor telephone Washington for advice and was chagrined to learn that, indeed, such legislation remained on record. Roosevelt, *Autobiography*, 311-312.

[77] Morsink, *Universal*, 30-31.

various ways helped lend form and substance to the UDHR.

Advocates and Partisans

Small powers were not latecomers to the discussion of international human rights. As early as 1933, American states had convened to discuss issues of rights and duties–of states. They met again in February 1945 at Chapultepec, Mexico, to examine the Dumbarton Oaks proposals to create a global organization, scrutinizing the proposals for ways to check big power dominance of the new world organization.[78] Many Latin American states chafed under US domination, and within the region there was strong interest in twin legal notions of rights and duties. No state was more concerned about its own rights than was Panama, and perhaps this explains how the Panamanian delegation came to arrive in San Francisco for the first meeting of the forty-six United Nations with a human rights manifesto that it hoped to see incorporated into the UN Charter.[79]

Several small states participating in the San Francisco conference hoped that human rights would become a more central concern of the new United Nations. Thanks to their efforts, seven references to human rights were incorporated into the text of the UN Charter (Phase I). Some states–including Cuba, New Zealand and Norway–went on record with views that any bill of rights should be made binding on all states.[80] Four separate proposals–from Uruguay, Panama, France, and jointly from Brazil, Dominican Republic and Mexico-- would have given the new United Nations the explicit purpose of *ensuring* respect for human rights.[81] Three small states–Cuba, India, and Panama–went on to propose a treaty against genocide.[82] Cuba defended (unsuccessfully) the right to resist tyranny and

---

[78] Lawrence O. Ealy, *The Republic of Panama in World Affairs: 1903-1950* (Philadelphia: University of Pennsylvania Press, 1951), 125.
[79] Less than two years later a Panama-US dispute over the Panama Canal would be referred to the UN Trusteeship Council. Along with Chilean jurist Alejandro Alvarez, Panama's Foreign Minister (and former President) Ricardo Alfaro had participated in the elaboration of the American Law Institute's Draft Bill of Human Rights, upon which Humphrey based his own first draft. See Ibid., 154-157 and Humphrey, *Human Rights*, 32.
[80] Lauren, *Evolution*, 188.
[81] Jhabvala, *Drafting*, 9.
[82] In November 1946 Cuba, India and Panama asked the UN Secretary General to include this item in the UNGA agenda, but it was instead referred to the UNGA Sixth Committee. "The United Nations Convention on the Prevention and Punishment of the Crime of Genocide," *Foreign Relations of the United States*

oppression.[83]

It is neither surprising nor unnatural that historians and other analysts should focus attention on the dominant events of an epoch, and so it has been with the Cold War. Cold War tensions gave texture to the UDHR discussions as soon as they opened, and the impact of those tensions on both the UDHR itself and the subsequent development of the multilateral human rights regime have been subject to many analyses.[84] However, more than one political agenda claimed global attention in 1948. The secondary agendas have received far less attention from scholars, but remembering the concerns they reflect helps explain the interest of many small states in the UDHR project, and it re-establishes the record of their active engagement. Often the interests of these states coincided with Soviet bloc positions, but when small states offered passionate defense of an issue, it generally emanated from their own direct experience. Several of their concerns extended from the ignominies of colonial rule and racism prevalent in a world dominated by Western powers.

In the shadow of Cold War debates, various small states delegates–singly or in formal representation of their delegations–advocated and defended five particular issues. First, small states defended the place of socioeconomic rights in the UDHR, and this is no doubt their most significant contribution to the UDHR. Personally committed to the ideals of socialism, Humphrey on his own had inserted ten separate articles elaborating such rights into his initial draft.[85] Morsink has traced the origins of Humphrey's text back through several sources, including drafts presented to the UN by Latin American states, the 1948 Bogota Declaration, and some Latin American national constitutions.[86] The Soviet bloc, naturally, defended the "new rights," but so did delegates from Latin

---

1949, 2 (1975): 386.

[83] Cuba presented this proposal at the end of the 1948 session of the Third Committee, after that body had completed its debate on the Commission's draft text and shortly before the freshly debated draft UDHR was to be reported out to the plenary session of the General Assembly. The debate is recorded in *Third Committee Records*, 748-753, and is summarized by Morsink, *Universal*, 307-312.

[84] Forsythe, *Internationalization*; Evans, *US Hegemony*; Humphrey, *Human Rights*; David P. Forsythe, "Socioeconomic Human Rights: The United Nations, the United States and Beyond," *Human Rights Quarterly* 4 (1982): 433; Tom Farer, "The United Nations and Human Rights: More than a Whimper, Less than a Roar," *Human Rights Quarterly* 9 (1987): 550.

[85] Humphrey, *Human Rights*, 31-32.

[86] Morsink, *Universal*, at 132.

America, Asia, and the Middle East. Early in the work of the Commission (Phase II) many of the provisions were collapsed or diluted, and it was only through concerted efforts of nongovernmental organizations, small states, and the Soviet bloc that most were restored. Extending provisions of several Latin American constitutions that set out social and economic rights, Article 25 of the UDHR establishes that a decent standard of living depends upon adequate food, clothing, housing, and medical care. The inclusion of clothing in that list is a direct result of comments, and arguments, by the Philippine and Chinese participants in the Commission's work (Phase II).[87] In the Third Committee debates (Phase III), such voices were joined by the Saudi delegate, who reminded other participants of the Muslim tenet of *zakat* (regular alms-giving) and by the Syrian delegation, which argued —unsuccessfully —for a broader language of "social justice."[88] Thanks to such efforts, the UDHR establishes the right to food, clothing, shelter, and medical care as well as social security, education, and decent working conditions.

Small state delegates were also outspoken in defense of women's rights. Most prominent in this regard were Hansa Mehta (India, Phase II), Minerva Bernardino (Dominican Republic, Phase Ill) Shaista Ikramullah (Pakistan, Phase II), and Lakhsmi Menon (India, Phase III), along with Bodil Begtrup from Denmark. Hansa Mehta appears to have irritated Humphrey, who described her as a "determined woman."[89] In the Commission, she objected to Humphrey's initial, gendered phrase that "all men are created equal." Eleanor Roosevelt apparently found the wording unobjectionable,[90] and the Commission initially agreed that the term "men" was generic. Mehta and the UN Commission on the Status of Women continued to pursue the issue, and the efforts to find a felicitous phrase continued. Ultimately, through what appears to have been a clerical error, the text transmitted to the Third Committee (Phase III) contained a phrase that had never formally been voted by the Commission—but which was never subsequently disputed.[91] In some sense all the same, it is thanks to Mehta's persistence that the text of the UDHR reads "All human beings are born free and equal..." [92]

---

[87] Ibid., 192-199.
[88] *Third Committee Records*, 504 and 515.
[89] Humphrey, *Human Rights*, 24.
[90] Gurewitsch, *Roosevelt*, 22.
[91] Morsink, *Universal*, 119-120.
[92] UDHR, Art. 1.

Thirdly, many of the small states were very sensitive to discrimination of any kind. Although the Soviet bloc used the question of discrimination to badger the US delegation, the practice of discrimination was hardly limited to the treatment of racial minorities in the United States. After all, discriminatory legislation had laid a foundation for the Nazis' genocidal policy and practice. In addition, many different cultures chafed under racist attitudes and policies of imperial powers in the first half of the twentieth century. At the close of World War 1, Japan had argued for the basic human right of racial equality,[93] and at the end of World War II, China took up the refrain. China, in fact, proposed inserting reference to racial equality in the Dumbarton Oaks documents.[94] The South Asian delegates also expressed deep concerns about discriminatory practices, particularly in South Africa. They pursued their concerns with vigor over several years, at one point provoking a rupture within the US delegation to the United Nations.[95] As communist ideology also eschewed racial discrimination, the Soviet bloc countries persistently raised the issue. They usually found themselves in large company.

---

[93] Lauren, *Evolution*, 91; Humphrey, *Human Rights*, 32 (noting his regret that the UNGA decided to remove reference to minorities from his earliest draft). On several occasions, Eleanor Roosevelt reminded delegates that issues of discrimination would be taken up with a separate protocol on minorities, no doubt a political concession in which the United States and the United Kingdom had equal interest.

[94] Lauren, *Evolution*, 169-170.

[95] "The United Nations, V 'The Question of the Treatment of the People of Indian Origin in South Africa'," *Foreign Relations of the United States 1950*, 11 (1976), 559-575 (document originally classified "secret"). In 1950 South Asian states took the question of the treatment of Indians in South Africa to the General Assembly. Over several months, the US delegation analyzed the situation as "a case of discord among two non-Communist governments" and in efforts to avoid exacerbating the conflict and thereby provide opportunities for the Soviets to exploit, they discouraged the initiative. Ibid., 561. The delegation was sent into a tailspin when Senator Henry Cabot lodge briefly joined the delegation and forcefully disagreed with the position. As the delegate responsible for the item "he was surprised at the innocuous Indian resolution, and he thought the United States should vote for it... To him this item provided a great opportunity for the United States to build strength to overcome some of the grave disadvantages under which our country labored because of the civil rights question." Ibid., 565. Following extended discussion, Lodge did make a statement before the UN's Ad Hoc Political Committee, but the US position remained an equivocal one, ultimately settled by Secretary of State Dean Acheson. Ibid., 575.

Fourth, as a general point, many of the small states were committed to carving out a role for themselves as full partners in the international system. To this end, the Cuban delegation continuously argued in Third Committee debates that articles of the draft UDHR should be recast to conform with the American Declaration of the Rights and Duties of Man that had been proclaimed in Bogota by the Organization of American States (OAS) just five months before the UNGA committee began its formal consideration of the draft UDHR.[96] Their insistence on this careful consideration of the text no doubt tried the patience of many delegates, but it also had the effect of ensuring that every single article of the UDHR was scrutinized by the UNGA Third Committee.

Last, but far from least, many small state delegations sought an end to colonial rule. Just as the great powers deployed human rights as a rhetorical weapon in the Cold War, many small states saw and seized opportunity to use the human rights projects to advance the cause of independence and self-determination. They argued pointedly that human rights should apply to all people everywhere–irrespective of the political status of their country. As with many other issues that rankled the colonial powers, this issue was pursued most cleverly and most relentlessly by Soviet bloc delegates.[97] The charge was readily joined by states with clear and poignant memories of colonial tutelage, including Syria, Haiti, and Pakistan. Omar Loufti of Egypt, for example, supplied the phrase that eventually found its way into the opening paragraph of the UDHR Preamble, mandating that rights were to be upheld "both among the peoples of the Members States themselves and among the peoples of *territories under their jurisdiction.*" [98]

A number of parliamentary maneuvers within the Third Committee, a drafting subcommittee, and again before the final UNGA Plenary (all within Phase III) played themselves out before the UDHR text was finalized. Very late in the debate, Yugoslavia–by that time diplomatically distanced from the USSR–proposed a new and separate article making explicit the universal applicability of the nearly completed UDHR. The colonial powers resisted, masking their objections with lofty rhetoric extolling textual integrity and sage cautions against unnecessary clauses. In the end, the Yugoslav-led efforts to have a separate article failed.[99]

---

[96] See generally, *Third Committee Reports.*
[97] Ibid.
[98] Morsink, *Universal*, 98 (emphasis added by author).
[99] *Third Committee Records*, 740-746, 853-863; U.N. GAOR, 180th Plenary

Nevertheless, even without a separate article, the language now included in Article 2 reflects the clearest statement of the principle of universality within the body of the Declaration's thirty articles:

> "Everyone is entitled to all the rights and freedoms set forth in this Declaration, without distinction of any kind, such as race, color, sex, language, religion, political or other opinion, national or social origin, property, birth, or other status.
> Furthermore, no distinction shall be made on the basis of the political, jurisdictional or international status of the country or territory to which a person belongs, whether it be independent, trust, non-self-governing or under any other limitation of sovereignty.[100]

The debate on Article 2 also had the impact of advancing discussion on the right to self-determination. In the heat of that debate, Pakistani delegate Mr. Shari gave strong support to the universal applicability of the Declaration. He argued "that the greatest deprivation a people could suffer was to be denied its political independence" and asserted an "intellectual conviction that freedom [is] indivisible."[101] Over the next several years, the notion that fundamental freedoms must include the right to political independence was cultured among the states of South Asia and the Middle East. In debates over the Covenant on Civil and Political Rights (Phase IV), the twelve states of Afghanistan, Burma, Egypt, India, Iran, Iraq, Lebanon, Pakistan, Philippines, Saudi Arabia, Syria, and Lebanon proposed to include the right to self-determination and to register the obligation of those responsible for non-self-governing states.[102] Their efforts were resisted at every turn by colonial powers not yet persuaded that de-colonization was an idea whose time had arrived. For much of the 1949-1952 period, western powers fretted about how to counter the growing sympathy for what the US State Department called "the Muslim resolution."[103] The twelve-country coalition eventually won their fight for

---

Meeting., 932.

[100] UDHR, Art. 2.

[101] *Third Committee Records*, 745.

[102] "The United Nations, II. 'Proposals for the Right of Peoples and Nations to Self-Determination'," *Foreign Relations of the United States 1951*, 2 (1976), 775.

[103] Declassified documents reveal a discourse that was largely disingenuous, turning on procedural questions and oblique concerns. Ibid. At one point an apparently bemused Assistant Secretary of State with regional responsibilities queried how the US had come to stand in "opposition to a resolution relating to a peculiarly American concept [self-determination]." Ibid, 784. Previous passages make clear that the underlying concern was how to avoid alienating the French delegation,

a legal right to self-determination, and when the International Covenant on Civil and Political Rights entered force in 1976, that right became a provision of international law.

Reflections on the Complex History of the Universal Declaration

In laying out the evidence of active participation by non-Western states in the political construction of the UDHR, I hope to have presented a persuasive rebuttal to claims that the international human rights project was an extension of US and Western hegemony–or more precisely, a rebuttal to claims that it was *only* designed and promoted to serve such purpose. When a story is told from several perspectives, each re-telling helps the listener appreciate its inherent complexities. Each re-telling also serves as an invitation to return, more critically, to initial versions. Alternative accounts inevitably privilege different contributions, and different contributors. In regards to the story (stories) of the UDHR, a number of observations can be made.

First, the UDHR never had a single author–at any stage. This observation is most significant for those who, fifty years later, either claim or question ownership of the document. Over the years numerous sources have credited Cassin with authorship, but with benefit of archival materials and close scrutiny of contemporaneous documents, it is now clear that while this noted legal scholar participated actively in the debates, his main contribution toward "authoring" the declaration was to copy it, by hand, and make minor adjustments to the text.[104] In a fundamental sense, the UDHR is a composite and negotiated text.

Second, it is apparent that in privileging one set of actors, there is risk that some important contributions will be overlooked or discounted. In an otherwise important and insightful book highlighting the contributions of nongovernmental organizations, William Korey unfortunately falls into this trap, writing: "Far more consequential than the efforts of the *tiny group of small Latin American powers* [my emphasis] was the lobbying of

---

which was "very much worried about the inclusion of any kind of article on self-determination, no matter how carefully drafted the language might be." Ibid., 787.

[104] In a footnote, Morsink traces some of the events and publicity that led to a widespread belief that Cassin provided the initial draft. See Morsink, *Universal*, 343 n. 59.

important American nongovernmental groups."[105] Likewise, in this chapter I have been aware that some of my own efforts to highlight contributions of small states have given short shrift to other actors who at various points were actively engaged in a shared endeavor. If we are committed to acknowledging the validity of different stories, there is no easy solution to this problem. At minimum, it is important to acknowledge that there are multiple stories, and thus multiple truths. It may be tempting to view the UDHR saga as an account of hegemonic maneuvers pure and simple, but such a reductionist approach involves risk for the analyst. Some ideas included in the UDHR–most notably the concern for socioeconomic rights, but equally as we have seen the expression of gender equality–were actually opposed (or disregarded) by the hegemon. Some of these ideas are reflected in the UDHR and other human rights instruments because small states argued for them, and won.

Third, it is worth considering the extent to which hegemonic approaches in and of themselves contribute to the mystique of hegemonic dominance. What is the effect of assuming that the United States, and its allies, were the promoters of the UDHR? It is my conclusion that hegemonic approaches to the analysis of the political project of human rights have tended to exaggerate the US commitment to the human rights project, even in the early stages. In the field of international relations, hegemonic approaches come in two varieties. Realist approaches emphasize the overt moral authority of a powerful state and frequently attribute all positive outcomes to its efforts.[106] Alternatively, Gramscian

---

[105] Korey, *NGOs*, 39 (emphasis added by author.)

[106] Defending hegemonic stability theory, Robert Gilpin writes: "[a]n international system is established for the same reason that any political system is created; actors enter social relations and create social structures in order to advance particular sets of political, economic, or other interests. Because the interests of some of the actors may conflict with those of other actors, the particular interests that are most favored by the social arrangements tend to reflect the relative powers of the actors involved." Robert Gilpin, *War and Change in World Politics* (Cambridge: Cambridge University Press, 1981), 9. In a pertinent discussion of these matters as they pertain to human rights, several years ago David Forsythe challenged Jack Donnelly's assertion that dynamics within the American regional human rights regime, centered around the Organization of American States, could be attributed to the dominant power of the United States. While acknowledging the importance of Donnelly's contribution, Forsythe's examination of dynamics within the OAS regime suggests that US influence can be overestimated, and that a number of regime developments came about despite US opposition or passivity. See Jack Donnelly, "International Human Rights: A Regime Analysis," *International*

approaches emphasize the subtle influence of social and political forces in producing and reproducing structures that maintain dominance by those already in power.[107] In rather crude terms, both paths lead to the same conclusion, namely that the interests of power are always served. With regard to human rights, hegemonic approaches attribute the political project of international human rights to the United States (or the West) and ascribe as its purpose the service of hegemonic interests.

Hegemonic approaches offer important insights and their value should not be disregarded.[108] At the same time, it is important to understand and appreciate the limitations of approaches that privilege the role of power. Just as they tend to exaggerate the role and interests of the hegemon, hegemonic approaches discount other confluent interests. In the case of the UDHR, attention to Cold War dynamics has tended not simply to dominate the literature, but to obfuscate understanding of the full range of relevant political dynamics. Although it was sometimes difficult for the US delegation to appreciate and accept,[109] small non-European states tended to identify and pursue human rights issues that were relevant to their own global political concerns. In addition, Burgers has shown that in the interwar period, many nongovernment organizations were pressing for political action on human rights.[110] The FIDH launched the first call for a worldwide declaration of human rights in the late 1920's. Latin Americans were shocked by European and American impassiveness in the face of

---

Organization 40 (1986): 625. And Forsythe, *Internationalization*, 92-94.

[107] Robert W. Cox, "Gramsci, Hegemony and International Relations: An Essay in Method", *Millennium. Journal of International Studies* 2 (1983): 162-175; David Forgacs and Eric Hobsbaum, eds., *The Antonio Gramsci Reader: Selected Writings 1916-1935* (New York: New York University Press, 2000).

[108] Evans, for example, has used hegemonic analysis to explain how, without the support of the United States, the multilateral human rights regime was weakened from the start. Evans, *US Hegemony*.

[109] An internal memorandum of the 1950 US delegation to the General Assembly notes: "Many members of the Third Committee seemed to me to be motivated by deep emotional convictions rather than by the political considerations which are in evidence elsewhere in the Assembly. They take very seriously the fact that the Third Committee deals with social, cultural, and humanitarian problems, and they take pride in discussing these problems on their own merits without regard to political considerations... [i]n the Third Committee they take pleasure in voicing their independence and in functioning almost as though the "Cold War" did not exist." "The United Nations, V 'Post-Mortem on the Third Committee'," *Foreign Relations of the United States 1950*, 11 (1976).

[110] Burgers, *Road*, 450-454.

brutal attacks on civilians during the Spanish Civil War; American Southerners organized to stop lynchings in the United States; and the plight of Jewish refugees won the sympathy of political activists well before the worst atrocities were known. Many felt Franklin Roosevelt was slow to act, and his 1941 four freedoms speech, when it came, is better described as a catalytic agent that gathered sentiments others had put in circulation, than as a seminal event that inspired the entire project.

Even Gramscian approaches tend to exaggerate hegemonic powers. Eleanor Roosevelt was popularly acclaimed as "First Lady of the World," but many fail to recognize that she was not at all popular in some influential circles. De-classified State Department records reveal some important rifts between her own views and those advanced by senior advisors within the State Department.[111] If put to popular referendum in the US in 1948, it is doubtful that the UDHR would have been endorsed by the electorate. Among the leading opponents of the international human rights project was Frank Holman, President of the American Bar Association. Along with other opponents of "treaty law" he launched a crusade against the international bill of rights, shamelessly pandering to racists as he decried any initiative that might limit states' rights.[112] By 1953, in fact, the US had abandoned the international human rights project it helped inaugurate.[113] It took nearly thirty years for the United States to ratify the ICCPR, and in the interim, the United States was completely

---

[111] "The United Nations, I. 'The Draft International Covenant on Human Rights'," *Foreign Relations of the United States 1951*, 2 (1976): 740-742 [Hereinafter The Draft International Covenant on Human Rights.]

[112] For additional information about Holman's role in this era, see Davies, *Defender*, 145-191.

[113] As suggested in note 104, realist approaches do help explain the United States' abrupt -but little remembered- change of heart about international human rights. Cold War concerns abroad and the defense of states' rights at home easily eclipsed the Second World War rhetoric of human rights and fundamental freedoms. Almost immediately following Roosevelt's death–and just two weeks before the opening of the meeting in San Francisco that chartered the United Nations–the US began to backpedal on its commitment to human rights. Korey is correct to claim that nongovernmental organizations played a heroic role at San Francisco. Their intensive lobbying of the US delegation was instrumental in persuading the United States to maintain its initial commitment (Korey, *NGOs*, 35; Lauren, *Evolution*, 246-248). Eleanor Roosevelt, once appointed to the Commission, did become an ardent and formidable champion of human rights, but she had her own battles to fight with the US State Department. Roosevelt, *Autobiography*. See also *The Draft International Covenant on Human Rights.*

removed from processes that institutionalized the work of the ICCPR's Human Rights Committee.[114]

As a final observation, in the area of human rights at least, there is inherent risk in conflating ideas of US perspectives with those of the "West." (Likewise, there is risk inherent in stereotypic thinking about the Soviet bloc, Third World, or "small states" as I have called them here, but in this passage I wish to call particular attention to divisions within what might appear a cohesive "western" bloc.) While Franklin Roosevelt promoted the idea of human rights at Dumbarton Oaks, Great Britain resisted the idea. France was one of the strongest initial supporters of the international human rights project, but soon after the Universal Declaration was finalized, its worries about the dismantling of an empire–in North Africa and beyond–eclipsed its initial enthusiasm. Throughout the entire process of negotiating components of what is now known as the International Bill of Rights, US delegations were edgy about the issue of racial discrimination, and perhaps more so about the elaboration of socioeconomic rights. Australia, New Zealand, Netherlands, Sweden, and Norway frequently voted opposite their European and North American colleagues.

The problems with counterfactual analysis are well recognized,[115] but by way of conclusion, it is useful to speculate about what might have been the eventual form and content of the UDHR had small states not been present, and active, in its construction. The UDHR might have been a shorter, more inspirational document, as the US wanted–though the United Kingdom initially (in Phase II) pressed for a fully justiciable declaration.[116] Almost certainly, the content would have been more limited. Without the arguments and votes of the small states, the UDHR would probably not have included socio-economic rights or consistent condemnation of discrimination. The rights of women might also have been downplayed. Without the insistence of small states on the applicability of human rights even in the shadow of colonial tutelage, the Declaration might not have

---

[114] Dominic McGoldrick, *The Human Rights Committee: Its Role in the Development of the International Covenant on Civil and Political Rights* (Oxford: Clarendon Press, 1991), 16-18.

[115] For an approach to evaluating counterfactuals see Philip E. Tetlock and Aaron Belkin, eds, *Counterfactual Thought Experiments in World Politics: Logical, Methodological and Psychological Perspectives* (Princeton: Princeton University Press, 1996).

[116] Morsink, *Universal*, 8, and Humphrey, *Human Rights*, 39.

included explicit provisions of universality and its name might in fact have remained the *International* Declaration rather than the *Universal* Declaration of Human Rights. The Soviet bloc, or even certain Western delegations, would in any event have pressed some of these issues, but the critical votes were delivered by small states subsequently recognized as the "Third World." Their contributions are among the features of the UDHR that permit people from all sorts of backgrounds to embrace the Declaration "out of their own normative heartland."[117]

In the history of the modern state, the drafting and ratifying of treaties has rarely been subject to public scrutiny, in any country. Approval processes for the UDHR and human rights treaties over the second half of the twentieth century have generally conformed to the historical practice. At the end of the twentieth century, and into the twenty-first, new sensibilities about "democratic deficits" are challenging that established practice, and it may change someday.[118] This chapter is not intended to defend a reification of the Declaration approved in 1948. Like most foundational texts of its kind, the Universal Declaration is a living document, subject to interpretation and elaboration. As new understandings of human rights problems and challenges develop, the need may arise to amend or supplement the document that for several decades has benchmarked the practice of good governance.

It is right and good that discussions about the ownership of human rights and the international documents that undergird them take place. Without such discussions, the document cannot find local anchor. As these discussions progress, though, it is important that proponents of universality

---

[117] Morsink, *Universal*, 96.

[118] That prospect, however, should give some pause to human rights activists, for it was concern about just such a democratic deficit—expressed in the language of the day as "states rights"—that fed the most serious domestic challenge to US participation in the international human rights regime. The proliferation of foreign agreements during the Roosevelt administrations inspired Senator John Bricker and his cohorts to propose a constitutional amendment to prohibit a president from entering treaties and agreements without express consent from the federated states. Bricker's initiative failed by only one vote in the US Senate. Conceding defeat after a decade of ardent campaigning, American Bar Association President Frank Holman wrote to console Bricker: "[a]lthough a constitutional amendment was not achieved, the fight for it exposed and stopped the attempt by Mrs. Roosevelt and her do-gooders to superimpose upon our own Bill of Rights so called 'human rights' covenants, pacts, conventions and treaties." Davies, *Defender*, 191.

develop a more robust appreciation of the document's origin. Contrary to a belief that--ironically--has served hegemonic interests, the UDHR was not the brainchild of the great powers. At best it was their stepchild. As Syrian delegate Abdul Rahma Kayala put it during the UNGA plenary session that approved the UDHR,

> Civilization [has] progressed slowly through centuries of oppression and tyranny, until finally the present declaration [has] been drawn up. It was not the work of a few representatives in the Assembly or in the Economic and Social Council; it was the achievement of generations of human beings who [have] worked towards that end. Now at last the peoples of the world [will] hear it proclaimed that their aim had been reached by the United Nations.[119]

The birth of the UDHR was nothing less than a political event, and its legitimacy as a standard for good behavior by states derives not so much from its intellectual lineage as from the political recognition of its birth. As the more obscure parts of the UDHR history are reclaimed, perhaps disputes over parentage can be set aside. Whatever the future holds for the elaboration of human rights standards, the UDHR is a legacy that all of us can rightfully claim.

Bibliography

Agi, Marc and Cassin, Rene. *Fantassin des Droits de l'Homme.* Paris: Plon, 1979.

An-Na'im, Abdullahi Ahmed, ed. *Human Rights in Cross-Cultural Perspectives: A Quest for Consensus.* Philadelphia: University of Pennsylvania Press, 1991.

Burgers, J. Herman. "The Road to San Francisco." *Human Rights Quarterly* 14 (1992).

Cantor, Norman F. *Western Civilization: Its Genesis and Destiny.* Gleenview: Scott & Foresman, 1969.

Cox, Robert W. "Gramsci, Hegemony and International Relations: An Essay in Method." *Millennium. Journal of International Studies* 2 (1983).

Davies, Richard. *Defender of the Old Guard: John Bricker and American Politics.* Columbus: Ohio State University Press, 1993.

Donnelly, Jack. "International Human Rights: A Regime Analysis." *International Organization* 40 (1986).

---

[119] U. N. GAOR, 180th Plenary Meeting, 922.

Donnelly, Jack. *Universal Human Rights in Theory and Practice.* Ithaca: Cornell University Press, 1989.

Ealy, Lawrence. *The Republic of Panama in World Affairs: 1903-1950.* Philadelphia: University of Pennsylvania Press, 1951.

Eide, Asbjorn, Gudmujndur Alfredsson, Goran Melander, Lars Adam Rehof and Allan Rosas, eds. *The Universal Declaration of Human Rights: A Commentary.* Oslo: Scandinavian University Press, 1992.

Evans, Tony. *US Hegemony and the Project of Universal Human Rights.* New York: St. Martin's Press, 1996.

Farer, Tom. "The United Nations and Human Rights: More than a Whimper, Less than a Roar." *Human Rights Quarterly* 9 (1987).

Foot, Michael. *The History of Mr. Wells.* London: Doubleday, 1995.

Forgacs, David, and Hobsbawn, Eric, eds. *The Antonio Gramsci Reader: Selected Writings 1916-1935.* New York: New York University Press, 2000.

Forsythe, David C. *Human Rights and US Foreign Policy: Congress Reconsidered.* Gainesville: University of Florida Press, 1988.

—. *The Internationalization of Human Rights.* Lexington: Lexington Books, 1991.

Forsythe, David P. "Socioeconomic Human Rights: The United Nations, the United States and Beyond." *Human Rights Quarterly* 4 (1982).

Freeman, Michael. "The Philosophical Foundations of Human Rights." *Human Rights Quarterly* 16 (1994).

Galtung, Johan. *Human Rights in a Different Key.* Cambridge: Polity Press, 1994.

Gilpin, Robert. *War and Change in World Politics.* Cambridge: Cambridge University Press, 1981.

Glen Johnson, M. "The Contributions of Eleanor and Franklin Roosevelt to the Development of International Protection for Human Rights." *Human Rights Quarterly* 9 (1987).

Glendon, Mary Ann. "Knowing the Universal Declaration of Human Rights." *Notre Dame Law Review* 73 (1998).

Gurewitsch, David. *Eleanor Roosevelt: Her Day.* New York: Interchange Foundation, 1973.

Hewins, Ralph. *Count Folke Bernadotte: His Life and Work.* London: Hutchison & Co, 1950.

Humphrey, John P. *Human Rights and the United Nations: A Great Adventure.* New York: Transnational Publishers, 1984.

Ikramullah, Shaista. *From Purdah to Parliament.* Karachi-Oxford: Oxford University Press, 1998.

Jhabvala, Farrokh. "The Drafting of the Human Rights Provisions of the

UN Charter." *Netherlands International Law Review* 64 (1997).

Korey, William C. *NGO's and the Universal Declaration of Human Rights.* New York: St. Martin's Press, 1998.

Lauren, Paul Gordon. *The Evolution of International Human Rights: Visions Seen.* Philadelphia: University of Pennsylvania Press, 1998.

Maritain, Jacques. "On the Philosophy of Human Rights." In *Human Rights: Comments and Interpretation: A Symposium,* edited by UNESCO. London-New York: A. Wingate, 1949.

Mayer, Ann Elizabeth. *Islam and Human Rights: Tradition and Politics.* Boulder: Westview Press, 1995.

McGoldrick, Dominic. *The Human Rights Committee: Its Role in the Development of the International Covenant on Civil and Political Rights.* Oxford: Clarendon Press, 1991.

Morsink, Johannes. "The Philosophy of the Universal Declaration." *Human Rights Quarterly* 6 (1984).

—. *The Universal Declaration Of Human Rights: Origins, Drafting and Intent.* Philadelphia: University of Pennsylvania Press, 1999.

Robinson, Nehemiah. *The Universal Declaration Of Human Rights: Its Origins, Significance, Application and Interpretation.* New York: Institute of Jewish Affairs, 1958.

Roosevelt, Eleanor. *The Autobiography of Eleanor Roosevelt.* Cambridge: Da Capo Press, 1992.

Schoultz, Lars. *Human Rights and US Foreign Policy toward Latin America.* Princeton: Princeton University Press, 1981.

Shue, Henry. *Basic Rights: Subsistence, Affluence, and U. S. Foreign Policy.* Princeton: Princeton University Press, 1980.

Tananbaum, Duane. *The Bricker Amendment Controversy: A Test of Eisenhower's Political Leadership.* Ithaca: Cornell University Press, 1988.

Tetlock, Philip E. and Belkin, Aaron, eds. *Counterfactual Thought Experiments in World Politics: Logical, Methodological and Psychological Perspectives.* Princeton: Princeton University Press, 1996.

UNGA Sixth Committee. "The United Nations Convention on the Prevention and Punishment of the Crime of Genocide," *Foreign Relations of the United States 1949,* 2 (1975).

United Nations, "I. The Draft International Covenant on Human Rights." *Foreign Relations of the United States 1951,* 2 (1976).

—. "II. Proposals for the Right of Peoples and Nations to Self-Determination. " *Foreign Relations of the United States 1951,* 2 (1976).

—. "Human Rights Questions at the Third Regular Session of the General Assembly: The United States Position", *Foreign Relations of the United States 1948* 1, (1975).

—. "V. Post-Mortem on the Third Committee." *Foreign Relations of the United States 1950*, 11 (1976).

—. "V. The Question of the Treatment of the People of Indian Origin in South Africa" *Foreign Relations of The United States 1950*, 11 (1976).

United Nations. GAOR, 3d Sess., 3d Comm., Pt. 1, At 32-33 (1948) (Third Committee Records)

Verdoodt, Albert. *Naissance et Signification de la Déclaration Universelle des Droits de l'Homme.* Louvain-Paris: Editorial Nauwelaerts, 1963.

Vincent, J.R. *Human Rights and International Relations* Cambridge: Cambridge University Press, 1986.

Wells, H.G. "War Aims: The Rights of Man." *The Times* October 25, 1939.

—. *The Rights of Man or What Are We Fighting for?* Harmondsworth-New York: Penguin, 1940.

CHAPTER THIRTEEN

FORGING A GLOBAL CULTURE
OF HUMAN RIGHTS:
ORIGINS AND PROSPECTS
OF THE INTERNATIONAL BILL OF RIGHTS

ZEHRA F. KABASAKAL ARAT

Starting with its charter, the United Nations initiated a movement toward a political system that redefined not only the interstate relationship, but also the relationship between states and individuals. The UN Charter[1] placed the promotion of human rights among the purposes of the United Nations, on the same footing as the maintenance of international peace and security;[2] assigned its members the responsibility of promoting "universal respect for, and observance of, human rights and fundamental freedoms for all without distinction as to race, sex, language or religion;"[3] and explicated that "[a]ll members pledge themselves to take joint and separate action in co-operation with the Organization for the achievement of the purposes set forth in Article 55."[4] What was initiated by the Charter was later reinforced by the Universal Declaration of Human Rights (the Universal Declaration), which defined the content of human rights and allowed the UN to introduce changes to the normative foundations of international politics.[5] The International Covenant on Economic, Social,

---

[1] U.N. Charter, signed 26 June 1945, 59 Stat. 1031, T.S. No. 993, 3 Bevans 1153 (entered into force 24 Oct. 1945).

[2] Ibid. art. 1.

[3] Ibid. art. 55.

[4] Ibid. art. 56. It would not be wrong to claim that despite the wording of Article 1 of the UN Charter, the member states have treated human rights as inferior to the goals of maintaining peace and security. The recognition of human rights as a goal and normative framework for international affairs gained a momentum later and largely as a result of the dedicated work of individuals and non-state actors.

[5] Universal Declaration of Human Rights, adopted 10 Dec. 1948, G.A. Res. 217A

and Cultural Rights (ICESCR) and the International Covenant on Civil and Political Rights (ICCPR) devised in 1966, as well as subsequent human rights treaties and treaty bodies, further expanded the human rights obligations of states and created an international human rights regime.[6]

The post-Second World War period observed the proliferation of human rights treaties and the advancement of the concept of human rights as a diplomatic and political currency, largely due to its function as a legitimizing device. The regime's performance in improving people's human rights conditions, however, has been far from impressive. The ineffectiveness of the regime has been explained by various factors, including the lack of commitment by states parties, the lack of enforcement mechanisms, a partial endorsement of rights with preferences assigned to different kinds, the persistent emphasis on state sovereignty, the prevalence of "realism" in international politics, the global power structure, the inconsistent policies of hegemonic states, the economic or political weakness of the state in developing countries, and the resistance of the privileged and powerful groups.[7] Despite the universal appeal of the concept, the universality of rights articulated in the Universal Declaration and the two Covenants, together known as the International Bill of Rights,

---

(III), U.N. GAOR, 3d Sess. (Resolutions, pt. 1), at 71, U.N. Doc. A/810 (1948).

[6] International Covenant on Economic, Social and Cultural Rights, adopted 19 Dec. 1966, G.A. Res. 2200 (XXI), U.N. GAOR, 21st Sess., Supp. No. 16, U.N. Doc. A/6316 (1966), 993 U.N.T.S. 3 (entered into force 3 Jan. 1976); International Covenant on Civil and Political Rights, adopted 19 Dec. 1966, G.A. Res. 2200 (XXI), U.N. GAOR, 21st Sess., Supp. No. 16, U.N. Doc. A/6316 (1966), 999 U.N.T.S. 171 (entered into force 23 Mar. 1976).

[7] Robert F. Drinan, *The Mobilization of Shame: A World View of Human Rights* (New Heaven: Yale University Press, 2001); Richard Falk, *Human Rights Horizons: The Pursuit of Justice in a Globalizing World* (New York & London: Routledge, 2000); David P. Forsythe, *Human Rights in International Relations* (New York: Cambridge University Press, 2000); David P. Forsythe, *American Exceptionalism and Global Human Rights* (Lincoln: University of Nebraska Press, 1998); Adamantia Pollis & Peter Schwab eds., *Human Rights: New Perspectives, New Realities* (Boulder & London: Lynne Rienner Publishers, 2000); Tim Dunne and Nicholas J. Wheeler eds., *Human Rights in Global Politics* (Cambridge: CUP, 1999); Jack Donnelly, *International Human Rights* (Boulder: Westview Press, 1998); Tony Evans, "Introduction: Power, Hegemony and the Universalization of Human Rights," in *Human Rights Fifty Years On: A Reappraisal*, ed. Tony Evans (Manchester: MUP, 1998); David Gillies, *Between Principle and Practice: Human Rights in North-South Relations* (Montreal & Kingston: McGill-Queen's University Press, 1996); Michael H. Hunt, *Ideology and the U.S. Foreign Policy* (New Heaven: Yale University Press, 2009).

has been contested. A significant challenge to the universal applicability of human rights is posed by cultural relativists, who criticize the philosophical and cultural origins of the International Bill of Rights and who view the current conceptualization of human rights in international documents as an outgrowth of Western thought, a tool used by Western powers to interfere into the affairs of other states, or as a design of Western cultural imperialism.

This chapter contests the argument that the International Bill of Rights is grounded in Western culture but carries the debate beyond the well-known arguments of the universalism-relativism controversy. Employing historicism, it shows that: (1) the Universal Declaration and the subsequent international human rights treaties have been issued as responses to violations and constructed through negotiations by state representatives who had different cultural backgrounds and philosophical dispositions; (2) as critics of human rights violations, which have been allowed within all prevailing cultures, the international human rights instruments attempt to change local cultures and replace them, at least partially, with one that upholds equality and human dignity; and (3) although the Universal Declaration ushered in a new international culture, this new cosmopolitan subculture is still evolving and struggling against other dominant cultures--national and international.

The International Human Rights Regime and Culture

Norberto Bobbio aptly asserts that "human rights however fundamental are historical rights and therefore arise from specific conditions characterized by the embattled defense of new freedoms against old powers. They are established gradually, not all at the same time, and not for ever [sic]."[8] The Universal Declaration was a big leap for the advancement of human rights. It has proclaimed "universal" human rights that apply to the entire humanity and should be respected by all states, persons, and social organizations; the UN-led international human rights regime, based on the principles of universality, indivisibility, and solidarity, has introduced further norms and procedures that serve as a prelude to the development of an international culture of human rights. This international culture challenges the prevalent national, regional, or local cultures and attempts to curb their discriminatory practices and impacts.

---

[8] Norberto Bobbio, *The Age of Rights* (Cambridge: Polity Press, 1996), xi.

The transformative mission of the regime and its overarching culture naturally raise questions about the origin of international human rights and the ultimate purpose of their promotion. The Universal Declaration is often viewed as an instrument that was based on Western philosophy and understanding of human rights, both by the supporters and critics of human rights.[9] Consequently, countries that have experienced different forms of Western imperialism, which was often justified as an altruistic and civilizing mission, tend to be particularly skeptical.

Although the current vocabulary of human rights has more easily detectable references in Western philosophical writings, this does not mean that the notion of human rights was alien to other cultures or that the Western cultures and societies have been pro-human rights. Now there is a burgeoning literature that identifies various concepts, norms and practices that have prevailed in non-Western societies and that correspond to some rights articulated in the Universal Declaration and other UN instruments.[10] It is true that these rights often have no "universal" claims. As stratified societies that followed various forms and degrees of authoritarian rules, they have been repressive and discriminatory. But, despite their pro-right philosophical assertions, Western societies, too, have demonstrated the very same characteristics. Even the natural rights philosophers, who are applauded for their universalism, recognized only few rights, which

---

[9] The American Anthropological Association (AAA) argued against the possibility of universal human rights and warned the drafting UN Committee about the futility of its efforts. For a brief review of challengers who have considered the notion of human rights or the Universal Declaration as based on Western culture see the Introduction to Johannes Morsink, *The Universal Declaration of Human Rights: Origins, Drafting, and Intent* (Philadelphia: University of Pennsylvania Press, 1999). It should be noted that the AAA has later changed its position in favor of universalism; its 1999 declaration defines the Universal Declaration of Human Rights and related international law as the baseline of human rights, which are evolving. See AAA, "Declaration on Anthropology and Human Rights." Committee for Human Rights, American Anthropological Association. June 1999. http://www.aaanet.org/stmts/humanrts.htm (accessed September 10, 2011).

[10] Micheline R. Ishay, *The History of Human Rights: From Ancient Times to the Globalization Era* (Berkeley: University of California Press, 2004); Paul Gordon Lauren, *The Evolution of International Human Rights: Visions Seen* (Philadelphia: University of Pennsylvania Press 1998); Micheline R. Ishay ed., *Human Rights Reader: Major Political Essays, Speeches, and Documents from the Bible to the Present* (New York & London: Routledge, 1997); Abdullahi An-Na'im ed., *Human Rights in Cross-Cultural Perspectives: A Quest for Consensus* (Philadelphia: University of Pennsylvania Press, 1992).

comprise a far shorter list than that of the Universal Declaration, and they treated some "humans" as not full adults who can claim and exercise these rights. John Locke's conceptualization was not only sexist and classist, but also justified slavery:

> [T]here is another sort of servants which by a peculiar name we call slaves, who, being captives taken in a just war, are by the right of nature subjected to the absolute dominion and arbitrary power of their masters. These men . . . forfeited their lives and with it their liberties, and lost their estates, and being in the state of slavery not capable of any property, cannot in that state be considered as any part of civil society, the chief end whereof is the preservation of property.[11]

More than a century later, John Stuart Mill presented a more egalitarian theory of natural rights, but his inclusive approach fell short of universalism and took some exceptions that could be characterized as nothing but racist:

> It is, perhaps, hardly necessary to say that this doctrine is meant to apply only to human beings in the maturity of their faculties. We are not speaking of children, or of young persons below the age which the law may fix as that of manhood or womanhood. Those who are still in a state to require being taken care of by others, must be protected against their own actions as well as against external injury. For the same reason, we may leave out of consideration those backward states of society in which the race itself may be considered as in its nonage.[12]

The Medieval Church, which revived the Stoic notion of natural rights, was not only notorious for repressing religious freedom but justified hierarchal systems and various forms of discrimination. St. Thomas Aquinas wondered why God would even create a "misbegotten or defective" creature like woman in the first production of things,[13] and others questioned if women had souls (if they were fully human). In the early modern era, when Western imperialist expansion was on the rise, such "soul searching" was extended to the aboriginals.[14] Colonialism, with

---

[11] John Locke, *The Second Treatise of Government* (New York: The Liberal Arts Press, 1952), 47-48 & 85.

[12] John Stuart Mill, *On Liberty* (London: Penguin Books, 1975), 69.

[13] Thomas Aquinas, *Summa Theologicae*, Question XCII, art. 1, Whether Woman Should Have Been Made in the First Production of Things, available at http://www.newadvent.org/summa/109201.htm.

[14] See Lauren, *The Evolution*, 1-36. On the continuation of the dehumanization of "the other" in our age of human rights (e.g., the Serbian treatment of Muslims in

its policies of exploitation, economic oppression, and political repression, was a violation of human rights and the principle of universalism, no matter what the colonists preached about their enlightening and civilizing missions.

The practice of human rights in the West lagged far behind the theory, and all forms of abuse, ranging from torture to starvation, were common, even during the "Age of Enlightenment." The subsequent centuries witnessed a gradual expansion of some rights to some members of nations, but discrimination on the basis of sex, race, ethnicity, and sexuality largely prevailed. Even in the mid-twentieth century, when the drafting of the Universal Declaration was in process, all participating states could be charged with state-sanctioned violation of human rights, which were to be included in the Universal Declaration. The Western philosophy and history, when examined critically, provides no support for the argument that the member states of the UN were trying to produce a document that would be modeled after the Western culture and practices. Moreover, the entire project was largely facilitated by the atrocities of the Nazi Germany, a Western society; it can be viewed as an attempt to prevent the similar atrocities in the future, as well as other violations.[15] Even Louis Henkin, a famous student of international human rights law who sees the origin of human rights in Western philosophy, takes an exception:

> The idea of rights as a political principle in a political theory prescribing relations between individual and society may have been articulated by some Western philosophers, but is not more congenial to Western societies than to others.[16]

---

the 1990s) and its philosophical implications, see Richard Rorty, "Human Rights, Rationality, and Sentimentality," in *On Human Rights*, eds. Stephen Shute and Susan Hurley (New York, Basic Books, 1993).

[15] John P. Humphrey, *Human Rights and the United Nations: A Great Adventure* (Dobbs Ferry: Transnational Publishers, 1984); Morsink, *The Universal Declaration*, ch. 1. Susan Waltz accepts the Nazi Holocaust played a role but, by pointing out that there were various episodes of international human rights discussions that predated the Second World War, she objects to the notion that the Universal Declaration was a response to the Holocaust and calls this prevailing notion "a myth." Susan Waltz, "Reclaiming and Rebuilding the History of the Universal Declaration of Human Rights," *Third World Quarterly* 23 (2002): 437- 440.

[16] Louis Henkin, *The Age of Rights* (New York: Columbia University Press, 1990), 27-18.

The Universal Declaration was formulated through debates that involved participants from different cultures. Although representation in the UN Human Rights Commission, which drafted the Universal Declaration, was not global, it was not limited to the Western states either.[17] Two of three main intellectual forces in the drafting subcommittee, Charles Malik from Lebanon, and Peng-chun (P.C.) Chang from China, had their roots in the Middle-Eastern and Asian cultures.[18] Also, both the United Nations Secretariat and the United Nations Educational Scientific and Cultural Organization (UNESCO) tried to compile information about the conceptualization and formulation of human rights in different societies and philosophical traditions,[19] although the actual influence of the UNESCO data is dubious.[20] Moreover, once the Commission submitted its draft to the "Third Committee" of the General Assembly, Charles Malik, who became the elected chair of the Committee, allowed painstakingly long arguments and discussions on every article of the document, to ensure the emergence of a consensus and the development of a sense of ownership among the member states.[21]

It is true that a good portion of the world population was still subject to colonial rule and had no voice in these debates, but the presence of a significant number of non-Western states, whose representatives made their views known,[22] should suffice to discredit at least the claims about

---

[17] The eighteen-member Commission would include five Great Powers (USA, USSR, UK, France and China) and thirteen other UN members that would rotate at three-year intervals. The first Commission, which was established in 1946, included delegates from Australia, Belgium, Byelorussia, Chile, China, Egypt, France, India, Iran, Lebanon, Panama, Philippines, Ukraine, USSR, UK, USA, Uruguay, and Yugoslavia. Mary Ann Glendon, *A World Made New* (New York: Random House, 2001), 32.

[18] The third influential person was René Cassin from France. The core of the drafting group included also Eleanor Roosevelt (the chair of the Committee), John Humphrey (the appointee from the UN Secretariat), and the delegates of Australia, Chile, UK and USSR.

[19] Glendon, *A World Made New*, 17; Morsink, *The Universal Declaration*; Humphrey, *Human Rights*.

[20] Susan Waltz, "Universalizing Human Rights: The Role of Small States in the Construction of Universal Declaration of Human Rights," *Human Rights Quarterly* 23 (2001): 44, 47. Reprinted in this volume.

[21] Glendon, *A World Made New*, 143-144.

[22] The fifty-eight members of the UN at the time were Afghanistan, Argentina, Australia, Belgium, Bolivia, Brazil, Burma, Byelorussia, Canada, Chile, China, Colombia, Costa Rica, Cuba, Czechoslovakia, Denmark, Dominican Republic,

the Universal Declaration being solely based on Western philosophy and its individualistic perception of human nature. In fact, the recent analyses of the transcripts of the UN discussions by Morsink and Waltz show that the representatives of several non-Western states, including those from the Muslim populated states, participated in discussions and shaped the content and wording of the document.[23] Moreover, the Western intellectual heritage overlaps with the Middle-Eastern and Mediterranean cultures from which it borrowed, and it is far from yielding a single, uniform perception of rights or human nature.

Although the colonized peoples had no representatives in negotiating the content of the Universal Declaration, the decolonization process that gained momentum in the post-Second World War era expanded the membership of the United Nations and allowed more diverse views to be expressed during the drafting of the two Covenants.[24] Finally, the member states, including the Western states, were not willing to accept the full scope of the International Bill of Rights (the resistance has been evident in the ratification process, and various justifications of selectivity will be discussed in the later sections of this chapter), and they were all anxious about the restrictive impact of human rights commitments on their sovereignty.[25]

Examining debates within their historical contexts confirms that the international human rights instruments and the international human rights regime are products of political negotiations among states, which were lobbied by civil society groups, and that human rights are constructed amidst power struggles.[26] The influence of the political atmosphere on the construction of rights is best demonstrated when the bipolar world structure of the Cold War era bifurcated the human rights efforts as well and

---

Ecuador, Egypt, El Salvador, Ethiopia, France, Greece, Guatemala, Haiti, Honduras, Iceland, India, Iran, Iraq, Lebanon, Liberia, Luxemburg, Mexico, Netherlands, New Zealand, Nicaragua, Norway, Pakistan, Panama, Paraguay, Peru, Philippines, Poland, Saudi Arabia, Siam, Sweden, Syria, Turkey, Ukraine, Union of South Africa, the USSR, United Kingdom, the USA, Uruguay, Venezuela, Yemen, and Yugoslavia.

[23] Morsink, *The Universal Declaration*; Waltz, *Universalizing Human Rights*; Waltz, "Reclaiming and Rebuilding"; Susan Waltz, "Universal Human Rights: The Contribution of Muslim States," *Human Rights Quarterly* 26 (2004): 799.

[24] Humphrey, *Human Rights and the United Nations.*

[25] Morsink, *The Universal Declaration*; Glendon, *A World Made New.*

[26] Glendon, *A World Made New*; Morsink, *The Universal Declaration*; Humphrey, *Human Rights and the United Nations.*

crowned the Universal Declaration with two Covenants, instead of one.

Historical analyses of human rights discourses show that the changing social conditions present new needs and awareness about the actual violations of human dignity, and that the power structures, struggles, and negotiations offer specific formulations of rights.[27] In other words, the construction of rights is grounded empirically, not theoretically. The representatives of states and groups, who are engaged in negotiations, of course, may be inspired or influenced by different theories and schools of thought, but whatever theoretical foundations they may rely upon, the right recognized at the end of the negotiations would be based on an amalgamation or an unspecific, yet complex, theoretical heritage, if any.

In fact, when the draft Universal Declaration was debated at the Third Committee, some delegates expressed interest in specifying the spiritual or theoretical foundations of the rights, but others, including P.C. Chang (China), Mrs. Lakshmi Menon (India), and Salomon Grumbach (France), argued against such an effort. It is reported that Grumbach "reminded the group of Jacques Maritain's conclusion (in the UNESCO philosophers' committee) that the nations should and could reach practical agreement on basic principles of human rights without achieving a consensus on their foundations."[28]

In light of these debates, this chapter contends that the current international human rights regime is an improvised and negotiated design, which was developed as *a* reaction to the atrocities, and it maintains a reactive pattern. Moreover, because each violation is allowed, if not sanctioned, by the prevailing cultures, the recognition of each right emerges as critical of some aspects of each culture, at least implicitly. The empirical foundation and the critical charge of human rights were both acknowledged by Charles Malik, when he introduced the Universal Declaration to the UN General Assembly on 9 December 1948. After identifying the "negative roots" of the document in the atrocities of the Second World War, he proclaimed that the Declaration would "serve as a potent critic of existing practice" and would "help to transform reality."[29]

---

[27] Bobbio, *The Age of Rights*; T. H. Marshall, *Class, Citizenship and Social Development* (New York: Doubleday, 1964); Seymour M. Lipset, "Some Social Requisites of Democracy: Economic Development and Political Legitimacy," *American Political Science Review* 53 (1959): 69.
[28] Glendon, *A World Made New*, 147.
[29] Ibid., 165.

Thus, the advocacy of each additional right has meant acknowledging new offenses, demanding cultural changes, and taking steps toward transforming societies. For the advocate of human rights, all values, norms, and practices that sanction or reinforce discrimination and violation of human dignity, become targets of criticism and change.

Therefore, constructing universal human rights means constructing norms for a global culture. Culture is a system of symbols and meanings that human beings create and then use to organize their lives. Clifford Geertz notes that "[b]elieving, with Max Weber, that man is an animal suspended in webs of significance he himself has spun, I take culture to be those webs."[30] Those webs include sets of learned ideas and behaviors that individuals acquire as members of society but also continue to interpret, modify, and subvert them. The human agency yields cultural traditions that are dynamic and open to change, and also prevent cultures from being monolithic or internally harmonious.

In the construction of a global human rights culture, individuals with different cultural backgrounds, who often act on behalf of an organization or state, which in turn has its own culture and goals, engage in a deliberate act of construction and an attempt of reaching a consensus. They create "formal" procedures and processes that constitute part of the international culture, and what is produced through these processes includes new value systems that would resonate and trigger change, as well as resistance, in all local cultures. With its treaties and negotiation procedures, the international human rights regime may appear to be requiring participation in a limited political or legal program, but the compliance with its norms demands a moral change and political commitment. That commitment, expressed through the ratification process, requires the states parties not only to respect the rights but also to promote and protect them by eliminating the obstacles, which may find their expression in their local cultural norms and values. Moreover, the expansion, full recognition, and protection of rights would demand the transformation of not only cultural norms but also their material foundations. This comprehensive feature of the International Bill of Rights, which would mean ethical, social, and economic transformation, is what makes it attractive to the disadvantaged, on the one hand, but leads to resistance and selective treatment by the states, on the other.[31]

---

[30] Clifford Geertz, *The Interpretation of Cultures* (New York: Basic Books, 2000), 5.
[31] I will address the selective treatment issue in the next section of the chapter. However, I would like to briefly address a neglected, or deliberately ignored,

Presenting international human rights culture as a critique of prevailing local cultures points to an ironic situation in the universalist position. Most universalists attempt to advance their arguments against relativist claims by pointing out that several rights embodied in the International Bill of Rights have existed and have been respected in the cultural and religious traditions of most societies. Further, universalists argue that their position enjoys empirical support; as noted earlier in this chapter, the recognition and respect for some rights articulated in the International Bill of Rights can be found in cultural references and religious texts of many communities, usually as duties. At the same time, however, the traditional cultural norms and practices include numerous discriminatory stipulations. Historical records tend to confirm that more rights have been violated than those that have been protected, practically in all societies. Violations often occur as a result of fulfilling some cultural requirements (e.g., female circumcision), due to the profit and prestige related to the practice (e.g., slave ownership), or because the cultures lack protective norms and permits discrimination and indignity (e.g., domestic violence). It can be argued that the novelty of the International Bill of Rights is not reasserting the rights recognized but enumerating the rights violated within prevailing cultures.

Of course, establishing cultural bridges to the international human rights, by highlighting the pro-rights aspects of local cultures, can help promote rights, but doing so should not lead to turning a blind eye to the discriminatory practices, let alone maintaining them in the name of cultural preservation. The advocacy of universal human rights calls for scrutinizing cultural norms and practices for their inconsistencies.

---

aspect of the International Bill of Rights. The equality and anti-discrimination principles, when applied to all aspects of life, make certain economic and political organizations incompatible and directly in conflict with the advancement of human rights. While the authoritarian politics is often addressed as inappropriate for or source of violations of civil and political rights, capitalist, or more benignly defined market economy, is seldom identified as an obstacle for the realization of human rights or as a target of change for the human rights project. Noticing the same void in human rights debates, Michael Freedman points out that there has been no "political economy of human rights." Michael Freeman, *Human Rights: An Interdisciplinary Approach* (Cambridge: Polity Press, 2002), 173. We may argue that the implementation of full spectrum of human rights call for a social democratic model, if not a substantial democracy (as opposed to procedural) that can be actualized only in a socialist economy. The radicalism embedded in such an argument, however, makes human rights less palatable to some people. This may explain why the study of human rights has been short on political economy and why many advocates of human rights advocates strategically avoid controversy.

Competing Cultures and the Resistance to the International Bill of Rights

Two overlapping grounds of resistance to the recognition and implementation of the International Bill of Rights may be identified: (1) state sovereignty, and (2) communitarian claims/exceptionalism. While the claims of state sovereignty are clearly about political power, the communitarian arguments also attempt to preserve the prevailing power relations. Although the latter group of claims may have resonance in cultural relativist arguments that are often raised by non-Western states, this chapter contends that Western states, too, employ a selective approach to the International Bill of Rights and consequently contribute to the ineffectiveness of the international human rights regime.

1. State Sovereignty and Statist Arguments

For a long time, starting with the Treaty of Westphalia in 1648, which ended the Thirty Years' War in Europe, the prominent legal actors in international politics were sovereign states, and the state sovereignty served as the principle on which international relations have been patterned. State sovereignty was the primary normative value around which institutions and decision-making processes were formulated. Students of international politics and human rights agree that the establishment of the United Nations and its human rights instruments imposed a constraint on the sovereignty principle. Although the international human rights culture competes against this still strong international culture that cherishes state sovereignty, contrary to the common expectation, state sovereignty cannot be absolute as long as there is an international system. As convincingly argued by Stephen Krasner, claims of unconditional sovereignty have always been exaggerated.[32] Despite the emphasis placed upon sovereignty, even the Westphalian model actually has failed to uphold this principle for several reasons.

First, although the Westphalian world was based on the assumption that sovereign states were equals, that notion of equality remained conjectural. The variation in the economic and military capabilities of states yielded an international system of unequal states, with different political capabilities. These differentiations led to the emergence of hegemonic states and spheres of influences that undermined the

---

[32] Stephen Krasner, *Sovereignty: Organized Hypocrisy* (Princeton: PUP, 1999).

sovereignty of smaller or weaker states.

Second, while nonintervention was the correlative duty of the right to sovereignty, the hierarchal international power structure allowed some states to interfere with the affairs of the weaker or clientele states, either through unilateral action or through the use of international organizations. While the conduct of the League of Nations immediately after the First World War demonstrated multilateral interference, the prominence of the British, French, and Russian states in the internal affairs of the Ottoman Empire since the late eighteenth century illustrates the unilateral efforts that undermined state sovereignty. These two examples can be highlighted, because both cases involved human rights pretexts. In the case of the Ottoman Empire, the Western powers presented themselves as the protectors of the rights of the non-Muslim populations of the Empire and manipulated their nationalist aspirations.[33] Similarly, the League of Nations assigned the Arab populated provinces of the Ottoman Empire to the control of the British or French governments, as mandates and protectorates, which would presumably "assist" the Arabs in asserting their right to "self-determination" and exercising "self-rule."[34]

Third, the very existence of the international treaty bodies or international law contradicts the notion of absolute sovereignty, because treaties impose restrictions upon the policies and actions of the states parties. Even a bilateral nonaggression pact or a trade agreement would create obligations for the signatory states, and international treaties construct norms and procedures that would affect even those states that are not parties to the conventions. The fulfillment of treaty obligations often requires adjustments in domestic policies and affairs of the state and ultimately limits the state sovereignty. In this sense, international human rights treaties and laws are not much different from other international treaties and laws; they set international standards to be carried out by the state parties through legal and political adjustments within their domestic order.

---

[33] Kemal Karpat, "The Ottoman Rule in Europe From the Perspective of 1994," in *Turkey Between East and West: New Challenges for a Rising Regional Power*, eds. Vojtech Mastny and Craig Nation (Boulder: Westview Press, 1996), 1; Benjamin Braude and Bernard Lewis, eds., *Christians and Jews in the Ottoman Empire* (Teaneck: Holmes & Meier Publishers, 1982); Roderic Davison, *Reform in the Ottoman Empire, 1856-1876* (Princeton: PUP, 1973); Arnold Toynbee and Kenneth P. Kirkwood, *Turkey* (London: Ernest Benn, 1926).

[34] Reeva Spector Simon and Eleanor H. Tejirian, *Creation of Iraq, 1914-1921* (New York: Columbia University Press, 2004).

Finally, as elaborated in the bourgeoning literature on the recent phase of globalization,[35] state sovereignty is highly limited by a global complex of transnational corporations and agencies. Through their effective control over production, finance and consumption, they change the role of the state from initiating policies to responding to the corporate action and demands and to reacting to the impact of global social forces.[36]

Therefore, the international human rights declarations and treaties are not unique in their attempt to constrain the state sovereignty. Their distinct feature lies in creating obligations for the state parties that are held not only toward other states parties but also toward their own residents. In other words, different than other international laws, human rights laws, by recognizing individual rights rather than state rights, shifts the emphasis from state sovereignty to individual sovereignty.[37] Consequently, the international human rights regime pressures the already shaky grounds of state sovereignty two ways: (1) by restricting the state's behavior toward its own citizens and residents, and (2) by obliging the states parties to uphold and protect universal rights of all persons, including those living within the borders of other states. The latter one promotes interventionism and introduces a different notion of international legitimacy.[38] In sum, the impact of international human rights treaties on state sovereignty is different from a disarmament or trade treaty not because they impose restrictions but because they do so at a higher degree.

2. Selectivity and Communitarian Arguments

The Universal Declaration embodies a long list of rights, and the subsequent declarations, covenants, and protocols developed within the

---

[35] The current treatment of globalization as an economic phenomenon is both narrow and a-historical. Globalization entails the development of common norms, as well as integrated markets, and it has been an ongoing process that peaked at certain junctures as a result of technological advancements in transportation and communication, as well as socio-political developments such as colonialism or the end of the Cold War. See Zehra F. Kabasakal Arat, "Human Rights and Globalization: Is the Shrinking World Expanding Rights?" *Human Rights & Human Welfare* 5 (2005): 137.

[36] Evans, "Introduction"; R.W. Cox, "The Crisis in World Order and the Challenge of International Organization," *Cooperation & Conflict* 29 (1994): 99.

[37] Michael W. Doyle and Anne-Marie Gardner, "Introduction: Human Rights and International Order," in *The Globalization of Human Rights*, eds. Jean-Marc Coicaud, et al., (Tokyo: United Nations University Press, 2003), 1 and 9.

[38] Donnelly, *International Human Rights*.

United Nations and by various regional organizations expanded the scope of rights. The equality and interdependency of rights were affirmed in documents produced by the international Human Rights Conferences. In addition to the Proclamation of Teheran, issued in 1968, the Vienna Declaration and Programme of Action of 1993 stresses that human rights are not only universal but also "indivisible and interdependent and interrelated," and of equal importance for human dignity.[39] However, there has been resistance to this declaration, and human rights have been disconnected and subjected to prioritization by states and private groups. The resistance to the International Bill of Rights and the selective treatment of rights can be discussed within four thematic arguments that have been raised by different states and groups.

a. Positive versus negative rights and the tradeoff between liberty and equality

Those who subscribe to natural rights theories define human rights as the rights that individuals enjoyed in their natural state (at a pre-society and pre-state stage). Therefore, when they enter the state of society, these rights should be protected against the state. Specified as the right to life, liberty, and estate in the Lockean tradition, these rights are presumably enjoyed only if the state does not interfere but constrains its domain and power. They are referred to as "negative rights," the rights that are enjoyed as a result of non-action by the state. Some other rights, such as the right to education, employment, and health care, on the other hand, are treated as rights that can be realized only through a positive action by the state and society.[40] Thus, the latter group of rights, typically what falls within the International Covenant of Economic, Social and Cultural Rights, is placed in a different and secondary category; they are treated as "aspirations" that do not quite fit the notions of natural rights.

The false assumptions behind these arguments, the interdependency of rights, and the fact that the enjoyment of civil and political rights would

---

[39] Vienna Declaration and Programme of Action, U.N. Doc. A/CONF. 157/23, 12 July 1993.
[40] Bernard Mayo, "What are Human Rights?," in *Political Theory and the Rights of Man*, ed. D.D. Raphael (Bloomington: University of Indiana Press, 1967), 68; Maurice Cranston, "Human Rights, Real and Supposed: A Reply to Professor Raphael," in *Political Theory*, ed. D.D. Raphael, 43, 95; R.S. Downie, "Social Equality," in *The Philosophy of Human Rights: International Perspectives*, ed. A.S. Rosenbaum (Westport: Greenwood Press, 1980), 127.

also require positive action have been already expounded by many philosophers, legal scholars, and political scientists.[41] Nevertheless, in some states' approach, there still exists a stronger commitment to the property rights and civil liberties and a dismissal of social, economic, and cultural rights. The most powerful liberal democracy of the West, the United States, has been vehement in its libertarian approach. As noted by Philip Alston, "the United States has, [especially] since 1981, frequently sought to characterize these rights as 'goals', or 'aspirations' but certainly not 'human rights'."[42] Even the Carter administration was ambivalent and negligent about social and economic rights; although the State Department included the assessment of these rights in its annual "Country Reports," they were assigned no value or weight in foreign policy formulations,[43] or they were not a part of the language used in domestic policy debates.

Tony Evans, who aptly insists that the assessment of human rights should involve the analysis of interests and power, points out that the United States not only formulated "an American conception of rights," which is based on ideas of individualism, freedom and *laissez-faire* economics, but also used human rights as a justification of projecting this particular conception of rights across the globe to assert its hegemony and gain access to world markets.[44] He notes that the concerns over preserving its hegemonic status and self-interest led the United States to take a status

---

[41] D.D. Raphael, "The Rights of Man and the Rights of the Citizens," in *Political Theory*, ed. D.D. Raphael, 101; D.D. Raphael, "Human Rights, Old and New," in *Political Theory*, ed. D.D. Raphael, 54; Peter Schneider, "Social Rights and the Concept of Human Rights," in *Political Theory*, ed. D.D. Raphael, 81; Henry Shue, *Basic Rights: Subsistence, Affluence, and U.S. Foreign Policy* (Princeton: PUP, 1980); John Charvet, "A Critique of Human Rights," in *Human Rights: Nomos XXIII*, eds. J.R. Pennock and J.W. Chapman (New York: NYUP, 1981), 31; Frithjof Bergmann, "Two Critiques of the Traditional Theory of Human Rights," in *Human Rights*, eds. J. R. Pennock & J.W. Chapman, 52; Susan Moller Okin, *Is Multiculturalism Bad for Women?* (Princeton: PUP, 1999); Michael C. MacMillan, "Social Versus Political Rights," *Canadian Journal of Political Science* 283 (1986): 19; Ruth Gavison, "On the Relationship between Civil and Political Rights, and Social and Economic Rights," in *The Globalization*, eds. Jean-Marc Coicaud, et. al., 23.

[42] Philip Alston, "The Importance of the Inter-play between Economic, Social and Cultural Rights, and Civil and Political Rights," in *Human Rights at the Dawn of the 21st Century* (Strasburg: Council of Europe, 1993), 59 and 61.

[43] Zehra F. Kabasakal Arat, "Human Rights and Democracy: Expanding or Contracting," *Polity* 32 (1999): 119.

[44] Evans, "Introduction," 6-7.

quo oriented position vis-à-vis human rights:

> There is obvious tension between promoting universal values and the
> exercise of state hegemony. Constraints on state power designed to protect
> universal human rights are constraints on all states, even the hegemon. To
> avoid this difficulty, the hegemon must sustain a view of human rights that
> demands little change to the existing social practices.[45]

Unlike the United States, other Western states do not flatly reject social
and economic rights. Most Western European countries have developed
comprehensive welfare programs that are partially based on a
philosophical acceptance of social and economic rights. Moreover, the
European Human Rights regime includes a Social Charter that recognizes
a set of social and economic rights, along with the European Convention
for the Protection of Human Rights and Fundamental Freedoms, which
embodies mainly civil and political rights. Nevertheless, the separation of
rights into two different contracts and the time lapse between the
Convention, which was opened for signatures by the Council of Europe in
1950, and the Social Charter, started to be signed in 1961, illustrates the
differential treatment of the two sets of rights by the European states.
Furthermore, including a procedure of filing complaints about the
violation of the provisions of the Convention and creating the European
Court of Human Rights to enforce the implementation of the Convention,
the Convention enjoys the support of a judicial system that the Social
Charter lacks.

Civil and political rights or social and economic rights have been also
subject to preferential treatment by those who considered liberty and
equality as essentially irreconcilable values that can be achieved only at
each other's expense. By associating civil and political rights with liberty,
and social and economic rights with equality, the inevitability of a tradeoff
between the two sets of rights is defended both by the followers of liberal
schools and those who try to justify the need for authoritarian rule, at least
during the period of transition to a society of equals. These two positions
were demonstrated clearly by the super powers during the Cold War years,
both in their domestic and foreign policy formulations. Now, in the post-
Cold War era, the United States, as the only super power, has been able to
exercise an unusual influence and help neo-liberalism to triumph in
international finance and politics. Thus, social and economic rights will
continue to be placed on the back burner. Nevertheless, the close

---

[45] Ibid., 7.

connection between liberty and equality, as well as the indivisibility and interdependency of human rights, have been argued and illustrated both by scholars and various UN agencies.[46]

b. Individual Rights versus Collective Good: Asian Values

Subject to criticisms about the state repression of civil liberties and use of corporal punishment, the authoritarian leaders of some East Asian countries have presented a certain conceptualization of Asian values in their defense. They argue that Asian values are incompatible with some aspects of the International Bill of Rights, which were shaped by Western values; and as the leaders of Asian societies that favor community welfare and order over the individual's rights, they would emphasize economic development and political stability.[47]

Although peace, order, and economic development are important to the protection of human rights, maintaining them at the expense of individual freedom and personal integrity would violate the essence of human rights. By defining the "right to development" as a communal right and "order" as a social good that can override individual liberty, the Asian values argument takes a utilitarian approach, which has been problematic for the promotion of human rights. Morton E. Winston reminds that, "[r]ights exist precisely to protect individuals from being used indiscriminately as means to achieve general social or political ends..."[48] Ronald Dworkin acknowledges that "[c]itizens have personal rights to the State's protection as well as personal rights to be free from the State's interference, and it may be necessary for the Government to choose between these two sorts

---

[46] See, e.g., Gavison, "On the Relationship"; Amartya Sen, *Development as Freedom* (Oxford: OUP, 1999); Amartya Sen, *Inequality Reexamined* (Cambridge: Harvard University Press, 1992); Susan Moller Okin, "Liberty and Welfare: Some Issues in Human Rights Theory," in *Human Rights*, eds. J.R. Pennock and J.W. Chapman, 230. United Nations Development Programme, Human Development Report (2002); United Nations Development Programme, Human Development Report (2000).

[47] Lynda S. Bell, et al. eds., *Negotiating Culture and Human Rights* (New York: Columbia University Press, 2001); Joanne R. Bauer and Daniel A. Bell eds., *The East Asian Challenge for Human Rights* (Cambridge: CUP, 1999); William Korey, *NGOs and the Universal Declaration of Human Rights: "A Curious Grapevine"*, (New York: Palgrave: 1998).

[48] Morton E. Winston, "Introduction: Understanding Human Rights," in *The Philosophy of Human Rights*, ed. Morton E. Winston (Belmont: Wadsworth, 1989), 1 and 15.

of rights."[49] However, he notes that in an effort to balance the rights of the individual and the demands of society at large, the government cannot and should not infringe on individual rights under a pretext of maintaining security and order that fails to make a distinction between "what may happen" and "what will happen."[50]

Finally, it should be noted that arguments that define Asian values as different from or incompatible with the international human rights values are rejected by some Asian political leaders and philosopers.[51] They resist establishing a sharp division between individualism and communitarianism and argue that Asian traditions neither establish a hierarchy between the two nor assign absolute authority to the state to protect community interests.[52] It is further noted that "the tension between individualism and communitarianism runs not between the West and Asia but through both of them."[53]

c. The separation of equality from dignity

While the international human rights instruments are based on the principle of equality in maintaining human dignity, which is reiterated in their nondiscrimination clauses, some states resist the notions of equality and equal treatment of individuals by assigning separate notions of dignity to different persons. This form of resistance is most common among some Muslim clergy and state officials who reject the equality of sexes and devise alternative human rights instruments that undermine women's equality with men.

---

[49] Ronald Dworkin, "Taking Rights Seriously," in *The Philosophy of Human Rights*, ed. Winston, 104.

[50] Ibid., 105.

[51] While government officials in Singapore, Malaysia, China, and Indonesia tend to adhere to the cultural relativist position, the leaders of Taiwan subscribe to universalism. See e.g., Lee Teng-hui, "Chinese Culture and Political Renewal," in *Consolidating the Third Wave Democracies: Regional Challenges*, eds. Larry Diamond, et. al. (Baltimore: The Johns Hopkins University Press, 1997), 192.

[52] Bell et al., *Negotiating Culture*; Bauer and Bell, eds., *The East Asian Challenge*; Diamond, et al., eds., *Consolidating*, ch. 2 and 3.

[53] Tatsuo Inoue, "Human Rights and Asian Values," in *The Globalization*, Coicaud, et al., eds. For a discussion of individualism within Islamic religion —which is also often treated as a communitarian tradition that rejects individualism—see Zehra F. Kabasakal Arat, "Women's Rights in Islam: Revisiting Qur'anic Rights," in *Human Rights: New Perspectives,* eds. Pollis and Schwab, 69.

Typically justified as measures that would protect women's dignity and well-being, several articles of the Cairo Declaration on Human Rights in Islam, which was adopted by the Foreign Ministers of the members of the Organization of Islamic Conference at its Cairo meeting on 5 August 1990, contain various discriminatory clauses and display substantial deficiencies with regard to women's rights and equality.[54] Article 6 of the Cairo Declaration starts with a promising statement that "[w]oman is equal to man in human dignity, and has rights to enjoy as well as duties to perform…"[55] However, in stipulating her rights, it only mentions that "she has her own civil entity and financial independence, and the right to retain her name and lineage."[56] On the other hand, by specifying that "the husband is responsible for the support and welfare of the family," it rejects the principle of equality between husband and wife in the union of marriage.[57] Some other articles of the Cairo Declaration also explicitly state that some rights and freedoms are recognized for men only. Article 12, for example, explicitly states that the freedoms of movement, selecting residence, and seeking asylum are reserved only for men.[58]

The Cairo Declaration is not only presented as an Islamic human rights framework, but it also specifies its religious foundation in several articles including Article 24, which states that "[a]ll the rights and freedoms stipulated in this Declaration are subject to the Islamic Shari'ah," and Article 25, which reaffirms that "[t]he Islamic Shari'ah is the only source of reference for the explanation or clarification of any of the articles of this Declaration."[59] Similarly, several Muslim states that are parties to the United Nations Convention on the Elimination of All Forms of Discrimination Against Women placed reservations on several articles of the Convention on the grounds that they would be incompatible with the Islamic Shari'ah or reserved the right to uphold the provisions of the

---

[54] For a methodological analysis of this document and its comparison to the UN approach, see Ann Elizabeth Mayer, "Universal Versus Islamic Human Rights: A Clash of Cultures or a Clash with a Construct?," *Michigan Journal of International Law* 15 (1994): 307; Ann Elizabeth Mayer, *Islam and Human Rights: Tradition and Politics* (Boulder: Westview Press, 1999).

[55] Cairo Declaration of Human Rights, adopted 5 Aug. 1990, Islamic Conference, 19th sess., art. 6.

[56] Ibid.

[57] Ibid.

[58] Ibid. art. 12.

[59] Ibid. art. 25.

Convention only if they are consistent with the Islamic Shari'ah.[60]

The codification of the spiritual and moral guidelines provided in the Qur'an, Hadith, and Sunna, however, involves a process of interpretation, and interpretations can vary.[61] In fact, the traditional method of interpretation is challenged by some Muslim jurists, and the validity of the sexually discriminatory interpretations has been disputed by several theologians and scholars.[62]

---

[60] Convention on the Elimination of All Forms of Discrimination Against Women, adopted 18 Dec. 1979, G.A. Res. 34/180, U.N. GAOR, 34th Sess., Supp. No. 46, U.N. Doc. A/34/46 (1980) (entered into force 3 Sept. 1981), 1249 U.N.T.S. 13; Zehra F. Kabasakal Arat, "Promoting Women's Rights against Patriarchal Cultural Claims: The Women's Convention and Reservations by Muslim States," in *Global Human Rights and Diversity: Area Studies Revisited*, eds. David Forsythe and Patrice McMahon (Lincoln: Nebraska University Press, 2003), 231.

[61] The diversity in interpretation and the different applications of religious beliefs to human rights surfaced when the draft Declaration was debated by the Third Committee of the UN General Assembly in 1948. It should be noted that representatives from different Muslim countries took positions that were different from each other's on the articles that maintained the equality of sexes in family relations and the freedom to change one's religion. Glendon, *A World Made New*, 153-55, 168; Waltz, *Universal Human Rights*, 813-819.

[62] Sheikh Rached Al-Ghannouchi, "Panel Discussion," in *Islam and Justice: Debating the Future of Human Rights in the Middle East and North Africa*, eds. Lawyers Committee for Human Rights (US) (New York: 1997); Abdullahi An-Na'im, *Toward an Islamic Reformation: Civil Liberties, Human Rights, and International Law* (Syracuse: SUP, 1990); Mahmud Muhammed Taha, *The Second Message of Islam* (Syracuse: SUP, 1987); Amina Wadud, *Qur'an and Woman: Rereading the Sacred Text from a Woman's Perspective* (Oxford: OUP, 1999); Anne Sofie Roald, "Feminist Reinterpretation of Islamic Sources: Muslim Feminist Theology in the Light of the Christian Tradition of Feminist Thought," in *Women and Islamization: Contemporary Dimensions of Discourse on Gender Relations*, eds. Karin Ask and Marit Tjomsland (Oxford: Berg, 1998); Barbara Stowasser, "Gender Issues and Contemporary Quran Interpretation," in *Islam, Gender, and Social Change*, eds. Yvonne Yazbeck Haddad and John Esposito (Oxford: OUP, 1998), 30; Nimat Hafez Barazangi, "Muslim Women's Islamic Higher Learning as a Human Right," in *Muslim Women and the Politics of Participation: Implementing the Beijing Platform*, eds. Mahnaz Afkhami and Erika Friedle (Syracuse: SUP, 1997), 43; Reza Afshari, "An Essay on Islamic Cultural Relativism in the Discourse of Human Rights," *Human Rights Quarterly* 16 (1994), 235; Asghar Ali Engineer, *The Rights of Women in Islam* (New Delhi: Sterling Publishers, 1992).

d. Indigenous populations/pre-modern claims

As stated earlier, the concept of human rights has developed gradually in different parts of the world and the scope of rights has been expanded as a response to the social and technological changes.[63] As a product of the twentieth century, the International Bill of Rights responds to the violations of human dignity that have become evident in modern and industrial societies. The rights to employment, fair wages, and equal remuneration for work of equal value, for example, are clearly relevant only to those societies that have economies organized around wage-labor, which has been a modern phenomenon. Thus, the applicability of some rights to pre-modern societies, as well as what constitutes a violation of human dignity, is questioned by some indigenous groups that have been largely left out of the negotiation process in the formulation of human rights declarations and treaties.

Richard Falk notes that "[w]hat human rights and self-determination mean to various indigenous peoples was not at all reflected in the Universal Declaration or the Covenants, which are drafted on the assumption of protecting individuals living in modern societies."[64] Although the International Labour Organization (ILO) attempted to address indigenous populations' concerns by drafting a convention in 1957 (Convention No. 107), the measures in this convention followed the nondiscrimination principle and attempted to increase indigenous peoples' access and integration into the larger society.[65] Discontent with the prevailing conventions led to the development of a global network of indigenous peoples who started to prepare a declaration that would emphasize the indigenous populations' distinct culture and status and their right to self-determination in 1977.[66] In 1982, a Sub-Commission on the Prevention of Discrimination and Protection of Minorities of the UN Human Rights Commission formed the Informal Working Group of Indigenous Populations. The working group started to draft a declaration

---

[63] Bobbio, *The Age of Rights*; Marshall, *Class*; Lipset, "Some Social Requisites".

[64] Falk, *Human Rights Horizons*, 62-63.

[65] Convention concerning the Protection and Integration of Indigenous and Other Tribal and Semi-Tribal Populations in Independent Countries (ILO No. 107), adopted 26 June 1957 (entered into force 6 February 1959). This convention was revised in 1989 by the Convention concerning Indigenous and Tribal Peoples in Independent Countries (ILO No. 169), adopted 27 June 1989, (entered into force 5 September 1991).

[66] Falk, *Human Rights Horizons*.

in 1985 and produced the UN Draft Declaration on the Rights of
Indigenous Peoples in 1994.[67]

Indigenous peoples challenge the current understanding of the rights
that are articulated in the international documents and consider some
definitions as inconsistent with their values, practices, and structures. For
example, while corporal punishment is deemed to be a violation of
personal integrity and treated as a form of torture within the current
international regime of human rights, some indigenous populations claim
that in their cultures, imprisonment as a punishment is more torturous than
inflicting shame and physical pain by whipping.[68]

While some of these alternative conceptualizations and the indigenous
populations' demand for dignity as peoples have many sympathizers
within the international human rights community, the states often resist the
indigenous claims with a concern over the fragmentation of rights and
with the fear that the self-determination claims may be pretexts for
secessionist movements. These claims that are based on cultural
distinctiveness, however, constitute a problem for the advocates of human
rights as well. The right to self-determination and preservation of cultures
would undermine the egalitarian aspects of human rights especially if the
culture in question embodies hierarchal and discriminatory structures and
values. The emancipatory aspects of the international human rights
regime, especially in regard to gender equality, can be undermined and
jeopardized in the name of cultural preservation.[69]

In assessing the validity of communitarian and cultural claims that
attempt to redefine the content of human rights or to selectively apply
certain rights, attention must be given to who makes the claims and which
aspects of the culture are emphasized. Cultures, of course, are neither
monolithic nor static, but within each culture there are people who would
benefit from making it monolithic and keeping it static. Cultures are not
only based on power structures, but through their value systems they also

---

[67] UN Draft Declaration on the Rights of Indigenous Peoples, U.N. Doc. No.
E/CN.4/Sub.2/1994/2/Add.1, 20 Apr. 1994.
[68] Russell Barsh, "The Fortunate Unmeasurability of Human Rights" (paper
presented at the Conference Towards an Indicators System in Human Rights,
International Institute for the Sociology of Law, Oñati, Spain, September 16-17,
1999).
[69] For a variety of arguments on this last point, see Moller, *Is Multiculturalism Bad
for Women?*

maintain them. Culturally (and officially) promoted values privilege some members of the society and disadvantage others, and the privileged ones would tend to use their power to perpetuate those values that would justify and sustain their privileged positions.

Peoples' right to self-determination is one of the earliest group rights recognized in the International Bill of Rights. It has been explicitly stated in the first articles of both of the International Covenants. However, the ambiguities around the peoples' right to self-determination raise several questions: What comprises people? How would the will of the people be determined? Who speaks on behalf of the people? Or, who interprets the meaning of culture?[70] More importantly, what happens to human rights, if this collective right is exercised by an exclusive group, especially if the exclusiveness is condoned by the culture? In other words, how can we resolve the conflict if the cultural rights and goals of a group are predisposed to violate some individual rights or other groups' rights?

Today, the independent states embrace the peoples' right to self-determination as an anti-colonial principle and as another assertion of the principle of state sovereignty. Minority groups and indigenous populations within a state claim self-determination in an effort to maintain their cultural identity and to resist assimilation. Their authoritarian structures and monopoly over interpretation, however, may prevent people from exercising sovereignty. Thus, invoking cultural relativism and the right to self-determination, in contexts where people are not allowed to interpret the cultural sources and determine their own lives, may end up serving only as shields of protection for the privileged. Without any democratization of the interpretation and decision-making processes, people cannot exercise their right to self-determination.

Conclusion

Despite the rhetorical triumph of human rights during the last sixty years, people's ability to enjoy them has been disheartening, and the situation may change for the worse. The current trend of corporate-led globalization, concentration of power and wealth,[71] and the hegemony of

---

[70] Karen Engle, "From Skepticism to Embrace: Human Rights and the American Anthropological Association from 1947-1999," *Human Rights Quarterly* 23 (2001): 536.

[71] United Nations Development Programme, Human Development Report 6 (2000) reports that "the distance between the incomes of the richest and poorest country

the United States, which has constantly refused to recognize social and economic rights, are likely to increase the number of people struggling against the misery of poverty and for their dignity. After 11 September 2001, the US government has shown that it has been willing to undermine civil and political rights as well, in the name of security and war on terrorism.

Moreover, since human rights are about power (they reject discrimination, promote equal treatment and involve capacity building), and power is distributed and maintained by cultural traditions, in each society, those who are in privileged positions will continue to resist the use of human rights treaties by their disenfranchised and marginalized citizens. The noble notions of cultural autonomy and national sovereignty can be also used as convenient tools of manipulation. In other words, while the international human rights culture attempts to influence and change the state and individual behavior in favor of recognizing and respecting human rights, the states (more accurately, people in power), which approach the international relations from their own cultural perspectives, attempt to curb the content and reach of universal human rights.[72]

Under these dire circumstances, arguments against the universal relevance of rights are detrimental to human rights struggles. Framing the Universal Declaration, the two Covenants and other instruments of the global human rights regime as products of specific cultures or tools of Western imperialism would only help strengthening those who attempt to preserve their hegemony and discriminatory cultural practices. Only by reiterating that human rights treaties are constructed outcomes of negotiations that demand change in all discriminatory and repressive cultures, can we stop the selective adoption of human rights and challenge all states that give lip service to human rights but continue to violate the rights of their citizens, support repressive regimes, or uphold corporate interests over human rights and dignity.

---

was about 3 to 1 in 1820, 35 to 1 in 1950, 44 to 1 in 1973 and 72 to 1 in 1992" and that "gaps between rich and poor are widening in many countries," industrial and developing.

[72] Jacinta O'Hagan, "Conflict, Convergence, or Coexistence? The Relevance of Culture in Reframing World Order," in *Reframing the International: Law, Culture, Politics*, eds. Richard Falk et al., (2002), 187.

Bibliography

AAA, "Declaration on Anthropology and Human Rights." Committee for Human Rights, American Anthropological Association. June 1999. http://www.aaanet.org/stmts/humanrts.htm (accessed September 10, 2011).

Afshari, Reza. "An Essay on Islamic Cultural Relativism in the Discourse of Human Rights," *Human Rights Quarterly* 16 (1994).

Al-Ghannouchi, Sheikh Rached, "Panel Discussion." In *Islam and Justice: Debating the Future of Human Rights in the Middle East and North Africa*, edited by Lawyers Committee for Human Rights (US). New York: 1997.

Alston, Philip. "The Importance of the Inter-play between Economic, Social and Cultural Rights, and Civil and Political Rights." In *Human Rights at the Dawn of the 21st Century*. Strasburg: Council of Europe, 1993.

An-Na'im, Abdullahi ed. *Human Rights in Cross-Cultural Perspectives: A Quest for Consensus*. Philadelphia: University of Pennsylvania Press, 1992.

An-Na'im, Abdullahi. *Toward an Islamic Reformation: Civil Liberties, Human Rights, and International Law*. Syracuse: SUP, 1990.

Aquinas, Thomas. *Summa Theologicae*, Question XCII, art. 1, Whether Woman Should Have Been Made in the First Production of Things, available at http://www.newadvent.org/summa/109201.htm.

Barazangi, Nimat Hafez. "Muslim Women's Islamic Higher Learning as a Human Right." In *Muslim Women and the Politics of Participation: Implementing the Beijing Platform*, edited by Mahnaz Afkhami and Erika Friedle. Syracuse: SUP, 1997.

Barsh, Russell. "The Fortunate Unmeasurability of Human Rights." (paper presented at the Conference Towards an Indicators System in Human Rights, International Institute for the Sociology of Law, Oñati, Spain, September 16-17, 1999).

Bauer, Joanne R. and Daniel A. Bell eds. *The East Asian Challenge for Human Rights*. Cambridge: CUP, 1999.

Bell, Lynda S. et al. eds. *Negotiating Culture and Human Rights*. New York: Columbia University Press, 2001.

Bergmann, Frithjof. "Two Critiques of the Traditional Theory of Human Rights." In *Human Rights: Nomos XXIII*, edited by J. R. Pennock and J.W. Chapman. New York: NYUP, 1981.

Bobbio, Norberto. *The Age of Rights*. Cambridge: Polity Press, 1996.

Braude, Benjamin and Bernard Lewis, eds. *Christians and Jews in the*

Ottoman Empire. Teaneck: Holmes & Meier Publishers, 1982.

Charvet, John. "A Critique of Human Rights." In *Human Rights: Nomos XXIII*, edited by J.R. Pennock and J.W. Chapman. New York: NYUP, 1981.

Cox, R.W. "The Crisis in World Order and the Challenge of International Organization," *Cooperation & Conflict* 29 (1994).

Cranston, Maurice. "Human Rights, Real and Supposed: A Reply to Professor Raphael." In *Political Theory*, edited by D.D. Raphael. Bloomington: University of Indiana Press, 1967.

Davison, Roderic. *Reform in the Ottoman Empire, 1856-1876*. Princeton: PUP, 1973.

Donnelly, Jack. *International Human Rights*. Boulder: Westview Press, 1998.

Downie, R.S. "Social Equality." In *The Philosophy of Human Rights: International Perspectives*, edited by A.S. Rosenbaum. Westport: Greenwood Press, 1980.

Doyle, Michael W. and Anne-Marie Gardner. "Introduction: Human Rights and International Order." In *The Globalization of Human Rights*, edited by Jean-Marc Coicaud, et al. Tokyo: United Nations University Press, 2003.

Drinan, Robert F. *The Mobilization of Shame: A World View of Human Rights*. New Heaven: Yale University Press, 2001.

Dunne, Tim and Nicholas J. Wheeler eds. *Human Rights in Global Politics*. Cambridge: CUP, 1999.

Dworkin, Ronald. "Taking Rights Seriously." In *The Philosophy of Human Rights*, edited by Morton E. Winston. Belmont: Wadsworth, 1989.

Engineer, Asghar Ali. *The Rights of Women in Islam*. New Delhi: Sterling Publishers, 1992.

Engle, Karen. "From Skepticism to Embrace: Human Rights and the American Anthropological Association from 1947-1999." *Human Rights Quarterly* 23 (2001).

Evans, Tony. "Introduction: Power, Hegemony and the Universalization of Human Rights." In *Human Rights Fifty Years On: A Reappraisal*, edited by Tony Evans. Manchester: MUP, 1998.

Falk, Richard. *Human Rights Horizons: The Pursuit of Justice in a Globalizing World*. New York & London: Routledge, 2000.

Forsythe, David P. *American Exceptionalism and Global Human Rights*. Lincoln: University of Nebraska Press, 1998.

—. *Human Rights in International Relations*. New York: Cambridge University Press, 2000.

Freeman, Michael. *Human Rights: An Interdisciplinary Approach.* Cambridge: Polity Press, 2002.

Gavison, Ruth. "On the Relationship between Civil and Political Rights, and Social and Economic Rights." In *The Globalization*, edited by Jean-Marc Coicaud, et al. Tokyo: United Nations University Press, 2003.

Geertz, Clifford. *The Interpretation of Cultures.* New York: Basic Books, 2000.

Gillies, David. *Between Principle and Practice: Human Rights in North-South Relations.* Montreal & Kingston: McGill-Queen's University Press, 1996.

Glendon, Mary Ann. *A World Made New.* New York: Random House, 2001.

Henkin, Louis. *The Age of Rights.* New York: Columbia University Press, 1990.

Humphrey, John P. *Human Rights and the United Nations: A Great Adventure.* Dobbs Ferry: Transnational Publishers, 1984.

Hunt, Michael H. *Ideology and the U.S. Foreign Policy.* New Heaven: Yale University Press, 2009.

Inoue, Tatsuo. "Human Rights and Asian Values." In *The Globalization of Human Rights*, edited by Jean-Marc Coicaud, et al., Tokyo: United Nations University Press, 2003.

Ishay, Micheline R. ed. *Human Rights Reader: Major Political Essays, Speeches, and Documents from the Bible to the Present.* New York & London: Routledge, 1997.

Ishay, Micheline R. *The History of Human Rights: From Ancient Times to the Globalization Era.* Berkeley: University of California Press, 2004.

John Locke, *The Second Treatise of Government.* New York: The Liberal Arts Press, 1952.

Kabasakal Arat, Zehra F. "Human Rights and Democracy: Expanding or Contracting," *Polity* 32 (1999).

—. "Human Rights and Globalization: Is the Shrinking World Expanding Rights?" *Human Rights & Human Welfare* 5 (2005).

—. "Promoting Women's Rights against Patriarchal Cultural Claims: The Women's Convention and Reservations by Muslim States." In *Global Human Rights and Diversity: Area Studies Revisited*, edited by David Forsythe and Patrice McMahon. Lincoln: Nebraska University Press, 2003.

—. "Women's Rights in Islam: Revisiting Qur'anic Rights." In *Human Rights: New Perspectives, New Realities*, edited by Adamantia Pollis and Peter Schwab. Boulder & London: Lynne Rienner Publishers,

2000.

Karpat, Kemal. "The Ottoman Rule in Europe from the Perspective of 1994." In *Turkey Between East and West: New Challenges for a Rising Regional Power*, edited by Vojtech Mastny and Craig Nation. Boulder: Westview Press, 1996.

Korey, William. *NGOs and the Universal Declaration of Human Rights: "A Curious Grapevine."* New York: Palgrave: 1998.

Krasner, Stephen. *Sovereignty: Organized Hypocrisy* (Princeton: PUP, 1999).

Lauren, Paul Gordon, *The Evolution of International Human Rights: Visions Seen*. Philadelphia: University of Pennsylvania Press, 1998.

Lipset, Seymour M. "Some Social Requisites of Democracy: Economic Development and Political Legitimacy." *American Political Science Review* 53 (1959).

MacMillan, Michael C. "Social Versus Political Rights," *Canadian Journal of Political Science* 283 (1986).

Marshall, T. H. *Class, Citizenship and Social Development*. New York: Doubleday, 1964.

Mayer, Ann Elizabeth. "Universal Versus Islamic Human Rights: A Clash of Cultures or a Clash with a Construct?," *Michigan Journal of International Law* 15 (1994).

—. *Islam and Human Rights: Tradition and Politics*. Boulder: Westview Press, 1999.

Mayo, Bernard. "What are Human Rights?" In *Political Theory and the Rights of Man*, edited by D.D. Raphael. Bloomington: University of Indiana Press, 1967.

Mill, John Stuart. *On Liberty*. London: Penguin Books, 1975.

Moller Okin, Susan. "Liberty and Welfare: Some Issues in Human Rights Theory." In *Human Rights: Nomos XXIII*, edited by J.R. Pennock and J.W. Chapman. New York: NYUP, 1981.

—. *Is Multiculturalism Bad for Women?* Princeton: PUP, 1999.

Morsink, Johannes. *The Universal Declaration of Human Rights: Origins, Drafting, and Intent.* Philadelphia: University of Pennsylvania Press, 1999. ///

O'Hagan, Jacinta. "Conflict, Convergence, or Coexistence? The Relevance of Culture in Reframing World Order." in *Reframing the International: Law, Culture, Politics*, eds. Richard Falk et al., (2002).

Pollis, Adamantia and Peter Schwab eds. *Human Rights: New Perspectives, New Realities.* Boulder & London: Lynne Rienner Publishers, 2000.

Raphael, D.D. "Human Rights, Old and New." in *Political Theory*, ed. D.D. Raphael. Bloomington: University of Indiana Press, 1967.

—. "The Rights of Man and the Rights of the Citizens." in *Political Theory*, ed. D.D. Raphael. Bloomington: University of Indiana Press, 1967.

Roald, Anne Sofie. "Feminist Reinterpretation of Islamic Sources: Muslim Feminist Theology in the Light of the Christian Tradition of Feminist Thought." in *Women and Islamization: Contemporary Dimensions of Discourse on Gender Relations*, eds. Karin Ask and Marit Tjomsland. Oxford: Berg, 1998.

Rorty, Richard. "Human Rights, Rationality, and Sentimentality," in *On Human Rights*, eds. Stephen Shute and Susan Hurley. New York, Basic Books, 1993.

Schneider, Peter. "Social Rights and the Concept of Human Rights," in *Political Theory*, ed. D.D. Raphael. Bloomington: University of Indiana Press, 1967.

Sen, Amartya. *Development as Freedom*. Oxford: OUP, 1999.

—. *Inequality Reexamined*. Cambridge: Harvard University Press, 1992.

Shue, Henry. *Basic Rights: Subsistence, Affluence, and U.S. Foreign Policy.* Princeton: PUP, 1980.

Simon, Reeva S. and Eleanor H. Tejirian, *Creation of Iraq, 1914-1921.* New York: Columbia University Press, 2004.

Stowasser, Barbara. "Gender Issues and Contemporary Quran Interpretation." in *Islam, Gender, and Social Change*, eds. Yvonne Yazbeck Haddad and John Esposito. Oxford: OUP, 1998.

Taha, Mahmud Muhammed. *The Second Message of Islam*. Syracuse: SUP, 1987.

Teng-Hui, Lee. "Chinese Culture and Political Renewal." in *Consolidating the Third Wave Democracies: Regional Challenges*, eds. Larry Diamond, et. al. Baltimore: The Johns Hopkins University Press, 1997.

Toynbee, Arnold and Kenneth P. Kirkwood. *Turkey.* London: Ernest Benn, 1926.

United Nations Development Programme. Human Development Report. 2002.

—. Human Development Report. 2000.

Wadud, Amina. *Qur'an and Woman: Rereading the Sacred Text from a Woman's Perspective*. Oxford: OUP, 1999.

Waltz, Susan. "Reclaiming and Rebuilding the History of the Universal Declaration of Human Rights." *Third World Quarterly* 23 (2002).

—. "Universal Human Rights: The Contribution of Muslim States." *Human Rights Quarterly* 26 (2004).

—. "Universalizing Human Rights: The Role of Small States in the Construction of Universal Declaration of Human Rights." *Human*

Rights Quarterly 23 (2001).

Winston, Morton E. "Introduction: Understanding Human Rights." in *The Philosophy of Human Rights*, ed. Morton E. Winston. Belmont: Wadsworth, 1989.

CHAPTER FOURTEEN

MODE D'ASSUJETTISSEMENT: CHARLES MALIK, CARLOS ROMULO AND THE EMERGENCE OF THE UNITED NATIONS HUMAN RIGHTS REGIME

GLENN MITOMA

Although frequently overlooked, the contemporary human rights movement and the Third World emerged at the same historical moment. Amidst the realignment of global order that followed the Second World War, the discourse of universal human rights that had emerged among the Allies was taken up at the United Nations as the new lingua franca of global morality, and codified in the 1948 Universal Declaration of Human Rights (UDHR) as the standard for the protection of human dignity worldwide. As the UN Human Rights Commission struggled to draft the covenants that would give the principles of the UDHR the force of international law, the French economist Alfred Sauvy first dubbed the emerging nations of Asia and Africa "the Third World" in a 1952 article for *L'Observateur*. "We speak freely of two existing worlds," he wrote, "of their possible confrontation, of their coexistence, etc., forgetting all too often that a third one exists, the most important and indeed the first in chronological order… For this Third World, ignored, exploited, scorned, like the Third Estate, also wants to be something." The idea of the Third World depended, of course, on the existence of a geopolitical order already polarized between Western First World and Eastern Second World, but to the extent that the Third World lives on after the Cold War, it is perhaps useful to recall that aspect of Sauvy's original metaphor that reached beyond the horizon of the 1950s to the historical legacy of an earlier rights revolution. For here the *Tiers Monde* is the modern heir of the *Tiers Etat*, the "ignored, exploited, scorned" class of eighteenth century France in whose name the Declaration of the Rights of Man and of the Citizen was composed and proclaimed. Thus, while the contemporary

tendency has been to eschew as an anachronism the trope of the Third
World in favor of the term "Global South," re-membering the Third World
reminds us of the entwined genealogies of these two figures.[1]

Approaching the discourse, structures and practices of human rights
from a Third World perspective requires a number of components and
gestures in a variety of scholarly directions. An historical recovery of the
contributions of non-Western individuals to the broad constellation of laws
and institutions that make up the contemporary international human rights
regime has begun, and constitutes a much needed corrective to the
tendency to view global human rights as an exclusively Western initiative.
There have been and continue to be elaborations of distinctive theories of
human rights grounded in the specific historical experience of the peoples
of the Third World which pluralize the philosophical foundations of rights.
Increasingly as well, sociologists, anthropologists and others have
documented and analyzed the particular practices performed under the
rubric of human rights activism that have proliferated in recent years in the
Third World, demonstrating the flexibility and efficacy—or lack thereof—
of human rights at the local level.[2]

If such an intellectual project is possible, it is in part because
inhabitants of the Third World, like the members of the Third Estate,
have—at different times, in different ways and to different extents—come
to recognize themselves as subjects of something called 'human rights.'
In his multi-part history of sexuality, Michel Foucault termed the process
by which this recognition is achieved the *mode d'assujettissement* (mode
of subjection/subjectification), defining it as "the way in which the
individual establishes his relation to the rule and recognizes himself as
obliged to put it into practice." This notion of "the rule" and the deeply
felt obligation to uphold it was critical to Foucault's understanding of the
way in which the modern ethic of desire—as opposed to the classical ethic
of pleasure—constituted a privileged site for the penetration of bio-power
into the human body. But it is also true that the *mode d'assujettissement* is

---

[1] Alfred Sauvy, "The Third Worldist Movement," *Current History* 98 (1999): 360.
Sauvey comments appear in their original French in Alfred Sauvy, "Trois Mondes,
Une Planète," *L'Observateur*, August 14, 1952, 14.
[2] See, for example Susan Waltz, "Reclaiming and Rebuilding the History of the
Universal Declaration of Human Rights," *Third World Quarterly* 23 (2002);
Upendra Baxi, *The Future of Human Rights* (Oxford: Oxford University Press,
2002), and Mark Goodale, *Surrendering to Utopia: An Anthropology of Human
Rights* (Stanford: Stanford University Press, 2009).

a way of understanding the subject as such. Ethical formulae are not simply guides for proper action, but the constituent conditions for the formation of agents capable of taking action. As a version of Althusserian interpellation, the Foucaultian *mode d'assujettissement* emphasizes the significance of ethics as the most important field of subject formation. Human rights, which stand astride the interface between ethics, politics and law, can be understood in precisely these terms: technologies for the incorporation of particular kinds of subjects.[3]

If this is true, and there are reasons to think that it may be, then the project of understanding human rights from a Third World perspective must include an excavation of the historical processes by which individuals in the Third World have constituted themselves as ethical subjects under the authority of human rights. The methodology for such an excavation would be necessarily biographical, approaching the history of "how we constitute ourselves as moral agents" through a close reading of the specific lives of actually existing historical figures. I return briefly to some of the methodological assumptions and implications of this approach in the conclusion, but undoubtedly part of what this focus on human rights as a *mode d'assujettissement* means is an analytic frame open not only to the impersonal functions of structures and the determinative power of discourse, but also to the intervention of human actors.[4]

What follows, therefore, is a sketch of this kind of analysis, which, while partial and limited, suggests some of the benefits and limitations of approaching the history of human rights as a question of subjectification— as an ethical project. This essay examines the post Second World War efforts of two unlikely diplomats, Charles Malik of Lebanon and Carlos Romulo of the Philippines, on behalf of human rights at the United Nations in light of their experiences in American educational institutions.

---

[3] Michel Foucault, *The Use of Pleasure: The History of Sexuality Volume 2*, trans. Robert Hurley (New York: Vintage Books, 1990), 27; Michel Foucault, "On the Genealogy of Ethics: Overview of Work in Progress" in *The Foucault Reader*, ed. Paul Rabinow (New York: Pantheon Books, 1984), 351.

[4] This approach is particularly important, I think, for a genealogy from a Third World perspective because too much has been made of the "Muslim" or "Asian" or "African" perspective on human rights as if there were no internal diversity or dissent, or as if the "Asian" or "African" perspective emerged like mangroves from the tropical saline swamps rather than through the concrete, lived, historical experiences of particular human beings.

These two were among the most prominent Asian advocates for a robust
UN human rights program, and their work was historically influential and
conceptually significant to the development of human rights from a Third
World perspective. This work, however, must be understood in relation to
an educational experience in which particular aspects of their subjectivities
emerged in relation to a set of material and intellectual practices rooted in
different colonial circumstances. Thus while their educations cannot and
should not be understood as indoctrination—whether into a human rights
ideology or any other—the negotiated development that took place under
American sponsorship was the essential component in their subjectification
to human rights.

Two Asian Advocates of Human Rights

Charles Habib Malik and Carlos Peña Romulo were two of the most
prominent diplomats in the West during the 1940s and 1950s.
Representatives of small, newly independent nations on the edges of Asia,
their reputations were built through eloquence—or at least loquaciousness
—in English, anti-communist partisanship in the Cold War, and early
effort on behalf of the UN human rights program. Each was closely
associated both at home and abroad with the United Nations. Romulo
served as ambassador to the UN from 1945 to 1954, where he was elected
President of the General Assembly in 1949, and came within a few votes
of succeeding Trygve Lie as Secretary General in 1953. Malik led the
Lebanese delegation to the UN from 1946 to 1954 as well, serving as
President of the Economic and Social Council in 1948-49, and as
Chairman of the Human Rights Commission from 1951 to 1953. He too
was elected President of the General Assembly, his term coming in 1958-
59 and marking the tenth anniversary of the UDHR. The early and
important engagement with the concept of human rights by Malik and
Romulo—and their work to institutionalize human rights law through the
United Nations—has been noted by a number of observers, both then and
now, and confirms, as Susan Waltz and Zehra F. Kabasakal Arat have long
argued, that much of the impetus for the UN human rights regime came
from outside the West.[5]

---

[5] Waltz, "Reclaiming and Rebuilding", passim; Zehra F. Kabasakal Arat, "Forging
a Global Culture of Human Rights: Origins and Prospects of the International Bill
of Rights," *Human Rights Quarterly* 28 (2006): passim. (Included in this collection
as Chapter Thirteen).

This work began as early as the 1945 founding of the UN, where Malik and Romulo, along with a coalition of other "small powers" delegates and US civil society organizations, worked to ensure the UN Charter contained a broad mandate to protect and promote human rights internationally. Charles Malik, who only weeks before had been teaching philosophy at the American University of Beirut, arrived at the San Francisco Conference convinced of the necessity of the international protection, at the very minimum, of universal rights to freedom of conscience and thought. Delivering his country's opening address, he called for the "military and political aspects" of the new international organization to be balanced by a robust commitment to "international justice" as a condition of world peace. Once the work of drafting the Charter began, Malik helped to ensure such a balance by supporting both the inclusion of the promotion of "human rights and fundamental freedoms" as an express purpose of the UN under Article 1, and the creation of a Human Rights Commission—the only such commission specifically authorized by the Charter—under the auspices of the Economic and Social Council. For Malik and many other delegates, particularly a number from Latin America and the British Commonwealth, these amendments were essential for the pursuit of a "dynamic and positive conception" of peace.[6]

Malik was atypical in his adamancy about the absolute priority of freedom of conscience and thought, but he joined with a majority of other delegates in supporting the expansion of the UN human rights mandate. Even before the San Francisco conference, Chinese representatives had stressed the importance of "justice" and the rule of international law in talks with the US and United Kingdom. Not long after, Latin American nations reiterated and reasserted the importance of human rights in particular to the postwar order at a conference of American states held in Mexico City. Cuba and Panama brought drafts of an international bill of rights to San Francisco, including one drafted under the auspices of the hemispheric American Law Institute. While none of these were included in the Charter, the presentation of these documents helped to ensure that the first task taken up by the UN Human Rights Commission (HRC) would be the drafting of an international human rights instrument. The US, UK and Soviet Union—the so-called "Big Three"—were all more reluctant to expand the human rights commitments of the UN, and outright opposed to the negotiation and adoption of a bill of rights at San

---

[6] *The United Nations Conference on International Organization, San Francisco, California, April 25 to June 26, 1945, Selected Documents Vol. 1* [hereafter *UNCIO*], (United States Government Printing Office, Washington, 1946), 251-53.

Francisco. Owing to pressure from domestic civil society organizations, such as the Carnegie Endowment for Peace, the American Jewish Committee and the National Association for the Advancement of Colored People, the US eventually agreed to propose and support much of the human rights language of the Charter as it was adopted, but it is clear that the real enthusiasm lay elsewhere than in Washington.[7]

Carlos Romulo, of course, also supported expanding the mandate of the United Nations to include an express commitment to human rights. His emphasis at the San Francisco conference, however, was not simply to enhance a general commitment to universal rights, but to shape the UN into an advocate for decolonization and the rights of colonial peoples. Thus he proposed a new Charter chapter on the status of colonial territories that set "independence" as the political telos of all colonial administrations. Unsurprisingly, he met with rigid opposition from the colonial powers, of whom the United Kingdom and France were the most significant. But through careful lobbying of the US delegation and with the support of both the Chinese and Soviet delegations, Romulo managed to secure inclusion of what became Chapter 11 of the Charter: "Declaration Concerning Non-Self-Governing Territories." While the term "independence" was assiduously avoided, colonial governments nonetheless pledged to "develop self-government" and "free political institutions" within the territories under their authority. Whether or not, as Romulo supposed, this formula represented the "spirit" of independence, the inclusion of a reference to colonial territories in general—as opposed to just those that would become part of the UN's Trusteeship program— was a singular achievement.[8]

Although Romulo was not alone in seeing the problem of colonialism as the most important postwar issue—W.E.B. Du Bois, Jawarhalal Nehru and Léopold Sédar Senghor all agreed on this—he was more precocious than most in articulating anti-colonialism in the discourse of human rights. Strategically, framing colonialism as a violation of human rights allowed

[7] Robert C. Hilderbrand, *Dumbarton Oaks: The Origins of the United Nations and the Search for Postwar Security* (Chapel Hill: University of North Carolina Press, 1990), 58-59; Glenn Mitoma, "Civil Society and International Human Rights: The Commission to Study the Organization of Peace and the Origins of the UN Human Rights Regime," *Human Rights Quarterly* 30 (2008): 607-30.

[8] *UNCIO*, Vol. 1, 292-293; Vol. 8, 138; Carlos Romulo to Sergio Osmena, 14 June 1945, Box 1.1, Folder 15, Papers of Carlos P. Romulo, Manuscript Collection, University of the Philippines, Diliman, Manila.

Romulo and other anti-colonial advocates to align their cause with the Allied war aims and the emerging postwar US ascendancy. It also ensured that the effort to specify and institutionalize the general commitments to human rights in the UN Charter would be divided not only along the border between First and Second Worlds, but between First and Third Worlds as well. This latter fault line became apparent in one the first attempts to define and protect a specific set of human rights, an effort Romulo initiated. During the first session of the UN General Assembly, Romulo proposed a conference with the aim of drafting an international convention on freedom of information. Arguing that "the voice that is raised in the name of freedom [i.e. colonial liberation] must be free," Romulo pressed for the international protection of free speech and the "unimpeded transmission" of news and information as a way of ensuring the international visibility of colonial peoples, as well as a more open global public sphere.[9]

But if the anti-colonial thrust was apparent in this part of Romulo's effort, a post-colonial edge was also visible. In addition to considering ways of guaranteeing "the right to gather, transmit and publish new anywhere and everywhere without fetters"—a globalization of US principles of free speech and media capitalism—Romulo sought a convention that acknowledged that such freedom implied both rights and responsibilities, including "the moral obligation to seek the facts without prejudice and to spread knowledge without malicious intent." By the time Romulo opened the Geneva conference on freedom of information in March of 1948, tension over these two aspects of freedom of information had created a novel political division: delegations from Asia, Africa and Latin America came together to support a notion of press responsibility that authorized governments to regulate and respond to press coverage they deemed detrimental to their national image and prestige, while representatives from Western Europe, North America, Australia and New Zealand opposed such a formula. In the months after the conference, Raul Noriega of Mexico, Renuka Rey of India and Jamil Baroody representing Saudi Arabia, all pressed for a strong freedom of information convention, but one that emphasized governments' "right of reply" to "insulting" or "slanderous" press coverage, protection against "monopolistic" media

---

[9] Carlos Romulo, "Human Rights as a Condition of Peace in the Far East," *Annals of the American Academy of Political and Social Sciences* 243 (1946): 9-10; United Nations, *Plenary Meetings of the General Assembly, Verbatim Record, 23 October – 16 December 1946* (Flushing Meadow: United Nations, 1948), 820-21; United Nations Document *A/C.3/76* (1946).

practices, and the positive duties of journalists to facilitate peace and goodwill among nations. Ultimately, these divisions meant that a broad freedom of information convention eluded the UN, but what was found through this debate was a consolidation of a "Third World" perspective on human rights. It was, as the late historian Ken Cmiel has written, the "crucial moment where the self-consciousness of the Third-World countries" coalesced around an idea of human rights that included both rights and duties. For Romulo, such self-consciousness did not imply anti-Westernism so much as an increased assertiveness on the part of the Third World in shaping global governance.[10]

The failure to adopt a convention on freedom of information has been, perhaps properly, overshadowed by the successful drafting and adoption of the Universal Declaration and the subsequent human rights Covenants, a process to which both Romulo and Malik contributed as inaugural members of the HRC. Indeed, at the opening meeting Romulo nominated Malik to the position of Rapporteur, and in general both men shared a similar vision of what the UN human rights program could and should do. Malik, however, was much more deeply involved in the drafting process and would eventually succeed Eleanor Roosevelt as Chair of the HRC in 1951. John Humphrey, the long-time director of the Secretariat's Human Rights Division, thought Malik one of the two dominant intellectual forces on the Commission—the other being Chinese representative Peng Chun Chang—, and Johannes Morsink places him among the "inner circle" of most influential UDHR drafters. Thus, while much of the import of Romulo's contributions lay in his articulation of anti-colonialism in the discourse of human rights, and the subsequent emergence of a distinct Third World perspective on human rights, Malik's imprint can be seen more clearly in the text of the UDHR and the passage of the Covenants.[11]

Broadly speaking, Malik's contributions can be summarized as centering on the following themes: creating a robust, legally binding international

---

[10] Ibid.; Kenneth Cmiel, "Human Rights, Freedom of Information, and the Origins of Third-World Solidarity," in *Truth Claims: Representation and Human Rights*, eds. Mark Bradley and Patrice Petro (Piscataway: Rutgers University Press, 2002), 108.

[11] United Nations Document *E/CN.4/SR.1* (1947); John P. Humphrey, *Human Rights and The United Nations: A Great Adventure* (Dobbs Ferry: Transnational Publishers, 1984), 23; Johannes Morsink, *The Universal Declaration of Human Rights: Origins, Drafting and Intent* (Philadelphia: University of Pennsylvania Press, 1999), 30.

human rights instrument; protecting the autonomy of individuals and "intermediate" institutions against encroachment by the state; establishing a coherent intellectual foundation for the UN human rights program, and defending intellectual and spiritual freedoms with a particular emphasis on the right of each individual to develop and change his or her deepest held beliefs. From the first HRC meeting, Malik was among the most adamant supporters of ensuring that the international protection of human rights had the force of international law. He was author of a critical revision to the UDHR preamble intended to give the Declaration some standing in international law—positioning it as an amendment to the Charter and a clarification of the commitments made therein to protect and promote human rights. Malik was also central to the development of the human rights Covenants, having worked on the Covenant sub-committee beginning in 1947. In fact, it was Malik who ensured that the term "Covenant" was used—in place of the more typical and perhaps accurate "Convention"—as a way of expressing the gravity and priority of what became the International Covenant on Civil and Political Rights (ICCPR) and the International Covenant on Economic, Social, and Cultural Rights (ICESCR). In the early 1950s, Malik was instrumental in maintaining what little momentum there was for completing the Covenants after taking over as Chair of the HCR from Eleanor Roosevelt. By then, both the US and USSR support for the Covenants had all but vanished and Malik, in conjunction with allies outside the Cold War dyad, had to press hard to keep the drafting process moving forward.[12]

Often labeled an individualist, Malik is perhaps more accurately described as an anti-statist, and many of his most memorable interventions were intended to position human rights as restraints on state power. He was particularly concerned by the HRC's willingness to subordinate individual rights to "those of the national community." Given his reputation, it is ironic that Malik was also the originator of the only right in the Declaration that specifically devolves to a group rather than an individual. Article 16, Paragraph 3, reads: "The family is the natural and fundamental group unit of society and is entitled to protection by society and the state." Special recognition and protection of the family, however,

---

[12] United Nations Document *E/CN.4/SR.37* (1948); Mary Ann Glendon, *A World Made New: Eleanor Roosevelt and the Universal Declaration of Human Rights* (New York: Random House, 2001), 117-18; Morsink, *The Universal Declaration*, 281, 294-95; United Nations Document *E/CN.4/SR.42* (1948); Charles Malik, *The Challenge of Human Rights: Charles Malik and the Universal Declaration*, ed. Habib C. Malik (Oxford: The Charles Malik Foundation, 2000), 149 and 223-25.

was fully in keeping with his anti-statism, as it represents one of many "intermediate groups" that Malik believed were essential buffers between the individual and the state.[13]

Concern with intermediate organizations also reflects the fact that Malik did not consider himself a politician, but rather an educator and scholar with loyalties to the academy as an independent force for good in society. Trained as a philosopher, Malik was also more interested than most with outlining a solid intellectual foundation for the entire UN human rights effort. Thus he badgered the HRC members to deal with the "ultimate" questions about the nature of the human being and the fundamental basis of truth, which, for the most part they ducked in the interest of avoiding schisms among the ideologically diverse Commissioners. Nevertheless, Malik's foundational efforts are evident in the form of Article 1 of the Declaration. The article, originally drafted by Carlos Romulo and Rene Cassin from France, reads: "All human beings are born free and equal in dignity and rights. They are endowed with reason and conscience and should act towards one another in a spirit of brotherhood." During the drafting process most members of the HRC favored deleting the references to reason and conscience. There was—and remains— dispute as to whether it was a necessary statement, whether and how this clause related to the first, and fear that it set a threshold for membership in the human family that excluded the mentally or morally deficient—i.e. children, the developmentally disabled and the mentally ill. At the time Malik took a Kantian stance, arguing that the endowment of reason and conscience was not a criteria for the possession of fundamental rights, but rather the metaphysical ground on which humanity as a whole could recognize and seek to protect and promote rights for all. It was, according to Malik, the capacity of moral reflection and rational deliberation that distinguished human beings from animals—what Johannes Morsink calls the "ontological reading"—and that allows for the possibility of human solidarity—what Morsink calls the "epistemological reading". For many delegates, the clause remained problematic, but votes to delete it failed apparently out of respect for the strength of Malik's convictions and his essential roll in the drafting process, as well as out of a sense that the passage was too vague and abstract to have any real impact on interpretation of the Declaration. Thus, the biggest, and perhaps only,

---

[13] United Nations Document *E/CN.4/AC.1/SR.38* (1948); United Nations Document *E/CN.4/SR.14* (1947); Morsink, *The Universal Declaration*, 123; Malik, *The Challenge of Human Rights*, 95.

crack in the UDHR's anti-foundationalism was included in the final draft.[14]

Finally, Malik's interest in the possibilities of the UN human rights regime originated in an absolute commitment to the principle of freedom of thought and of conscience, and in a conviction that these were dynamic and progressive rights that implied development and change. He was critical in the development of Article 18 of the UDHR, which guarantees the right to "change religion or belief," and Article 18 of the ICCPR, which explicitly prohibits "coercion" in matters of faith and belief. During the General Assembly debate of the UDHR, these provisions drew opposition from the Saudi representative Jamil Baroody—who was, ironically, a Lebanese Christian acquaintance of Malik's—as they would be in conflict with the apostasy injunction common to the Wahabi interpretation of Islam. Although it caused Saudi Arabia to abstain from supporting the UDHR in 1948, the freedom of conscience clauses represented Malik's proudest contribution to the substance of the UN human rights documents.[15]

Mode d'Assujettissement

This aggressive advocacy on behalf of human rights by Charles Malik and Carlos Romulo was rooted not only in the postwar political dynamic that saw small and medium powers pursue international law as a way of constraining the great powers, but also in the biographical experiences they brought to the UN. Indeed, both men regarded their human rights efforts as personal crusades, and each was given wide latitude by their respective governments in determining and pursuing policies in this area. Of course, this was not true of the majority of their diplomatic work, and it was certainly not typical of many individuals involved in the construction of the UN human rights regime. Nevertheless, these exceptional cases provide an opportunity to analyze what, given the rapid and expanding diffusion of human rights discourse over the past six decades, is undoubtedly a broader phenomenon: the recognition, on the part of a

---

[14] United Nations Document *E/CN.4/AC.2/SR.9* (1947); United Nations Document *E/CN.4/SR.50* (1948); Malik, *The Challenge of Human Rights*, 108; Morsink, *The Universal Declaration*, 297.

[15] Morsink, *The Universal Declaration*, 24; Glendon, *A World Made New*, 153-55; Vratislav Pechota, "The Development of the Covenant on Civil and Political Rights," in *The International Bill of Rights: The Covenant on Civil and Political Rights*, ed. Louis Henkin (New York: Columbia University Press, 1981), 48-49.

diverse range of individuals, of the self in the human rights subject. Thus, it is of critical import to examine the way in which these two individuals came to inhabit this political-ethical discourse, and to consider the ways in which it relates to their development as particular subjects.

Of the same generation, Romulo was born in 1899 and Malik in 1906, both men shared a similar background and set of experiences despite being from the opposite ends of Asia. Both were eldest sons of Christian, provincial, agrarian families of some local prominence. Romulo's family was the more prosperous, controlling a number of tenant farms in the rice growing area of central Luzon, where they exercised a degree of political influence—his father eventually became governor of Tarlac province—that granted the young Carlos a variety of privileges. Malik's family was professional, but economically vulnerable. His father, Habib Malik, was a physician, but not a particularly successful one who had to sell much of the family land by the time Malik entered college. Habib Malik was, however, convinced of the importance of modern education and made sure all of his children—two daughters and three sons—went to university. For their part, both Malik and Romulo were precocious and gifted students, and most importantly, both pursued educations under the auspices of colonial or para-colonial American systems—Romulo in the broad system of public education established in the wake of the US annexation of the Philippines, and Malik in the more limited, although older, system of Protestant missionary schools in the Near East.[16]

Both systems taught the two boys to read, write and speak English at an early age, and both gave them frequent access and exposure to sympathetic and earnest Americans, who, for the most part, were genuinely committed to the education and welfare of their charges. But there are a number of critical differences. The system into which Romulo entered in 1906 had been established in 1901 and was part of a larger effort on the part of the US colonial administration first to complete "pacification" of rebel areas, and later to transform Filipino society root and branch. As such, the system was far broader, enrolling some 610,493 students during the 1910-11 school year, and more integrated with the other structures of the colonial administration. By contrast, a 1924 report listed the number of students in all the schools administered by the Syrian

---

[16] Carlos Romulo, *I Walked with Heroes* (New York: Holt, Rinehart, Winston, 1961), 12-13, 70-71; Diary [of Habib Malik], 7 July 1914, Folder 5, Box 278, Papers of Charles H. Malik, Manuscript Division, Library of Congress, Washington, DC [hereafter: Malik Papers].

Mission of the Board of Foreign Missions of the Presbyterian Church in the USA, which included almost all American-run schools in Lebanon and Syria, at 3095. Many of these schools, however, had been established for almost a century and, while they had variable and at times contentious relations with state authorities in the region, were far more integrated into the local communities than those of the Philippines. Emblematic of this integration was the high ratio of local instructors, which in 1924 stood at 253, as compared with 43 "foreign" staff members. In the Philippines substantial numbers of Filipino teachers would not become predominate until the eve of the Second World War.[17]

Neither education system operated, however, as an engine of "Americanization," even if this was the express aim of the officials and administrators in charge. Indeed, while "social engineering" may have been the goal of reformers such as General Superintendent of Public Instruction in the Philippines David Prescott Burrows, the actual experience and effects of schooling were far more complex and reflect, as the historian Benjamin C. Fortna has argued, "a still wider range of unforeclosed individual trajectories and cumulative societal outcomes." Such trajectories and outcomes are evident in the educations of Carlos Romulo and Charles Malik, which were not simply experiences of transition or translation between East and West, but characteristic of a specific kind of colonial social space. The particular configuration of cultural, social and intellectual opportunities and limitations cannot be understood under the rubric of "engineering" or "Westernization," but was nonetheless transformative, and the subjectivities and the rights ethics the two men devised were both provoked and enabled in large part through their engagement with these American institutions.[18]

As was common to many top students within imperial education system, both Malik and Romulo experienced their schooling as a series of displacements, moving them from their natal villages through the colonial capital and onto the metropolitan center—in these instances, two Ivy

---

[17] About Filipino numbers see Glenn Anthony May, *Social Engineering in the Philippines* (Westport, Greenwood Press, 1980), 121; For Lebanese numbers see "Institutions Under Care of the Syria Mission of the Board of the Foreign Mission of the Presbyterian Church in the U.S.A." 30 January 1924, Box 8, Folder 11, RG 115, United Presbyterian Church in the U.S.A. Syria Mission, Records, 1808-1967 (Bulk 1823-1959), Presbyterian Historical Society, Philadelphia, PA.
[18] May, *Social Engineering,* 104; Benjamin Fortna, "Education and Autobiography at the End of the Ottoman Empire," *Die Welt des Islams* 41(2001): 3.

League universities—before returning to the periphery with advanced degrees but limited horizons. Such educational routes served to distance them from their less mobile peers and home cultures, yet failed—for reasons including the racist logic of the colonial order, as well as a sense of national solidarity and political opportunity—to integrate them into an "American" identity. Beginning primary school in his hometown of Camiling, Romulo completed secondary school in Manila before enrolling at the University of the Philippines where he earned a bachelor's degree in 1920. His matriculation at Columbia University was made possible by a scholarship from the Bureau of Commerce and Industry. This served the broader policy of "Filipinization" by which the colonial authorities sought to replace American functionaries with properly trained Filipinos. After arriving in New York, however, Romulo completed one semester of the foreign trade services courses the Bureau had sent him to study, before switching to the English department where he completed his Master's degree in literature under the tutelage Carl Van Doren. This skillful exploitation of the opportunities presented by the colonial system—an example of the complex strategies of resistance available to colonial subjects—distinguished Romulo as one of a class of intellectual elites and allowed him to literally master the language of the colonizer, but for his own ends. Indeed, he regarded his study of English as a form of personal empowerment. "With word," he later wrote, "I could move men and mountains, I could carve into any design I wished my future and my world. With words I could develop my personality to its fullest and help to bring recognition to the Philippines."[19]

With equal skill, Malik exploited the opportunities offered to him, although the more complex and shifting nature of Lebanese politics—during Malik's time in school the territory would go from Ottoman province to French Mandate to quasi-independent republic—meant that the political significance was less overt. He attended primary school in the villages, moving on to board and study at the Tripoli Boys School in 1920. From there, he enrolled at the American University of Beirut, where he graduated in 1924 with a degree in math and physics. Unlike Romulo, Malik struggled for several years after to assemble a patchwork of funds in order to come to the US for graduate school, eventually enrolling in the Philosophy Department at Harvard University where he studied under John Wild, George Sarton, and Alfred North Whitehead. He received his Ph.D. in 1937, after having spent a year abroad in Germany where he

---

[19] Romulo, *I Walked with Heroes*, 44-50, 72-73, 125-29, 140.

studied at the University of Freiburg with Martin Heidegger. His years in missionary institutions failed to produce a convert, however, as Malik remained devoutly Greek Orthodox throughout his life. Similarly, as a philosophy student he remained impressed, but unconvinced by either the process theology of Whitehead or the phenomenology of Heidegger— even going so far as to react with abhorrence to the dire political implications of the latter, repercussions he saw firsthand in Nazi Germany. Rather, the specific curriculum mattered less than the pedagogic model of his early teachers, which, modeled on the progressive and pragmatic ideas of John Dewey, emphasized independent thinking and creative, individual expression. Combined with the advanced training and exposure to intellectual life he received at Harvard and Freiburg, Malik returned convinced of his exceptional status. "I have," he wrote to a friend on the eve of his return to Beirut, "absorbed of Western thought and philosophy more I think than anybody in the East has done (or, as I personally and perhaps foolishly think, is likely to do in this generation)."[20]

The individuated subjectivity with which Malik and Romulo emerged from their American educations was also one infused with a sense of responsibility that was critical to their human rights agency. Indeed, their sense of themselves as exceptional individuals was in part premised on their recognition of the disadvantages, discriminations and desperate circumstances faced many of their fellow countrymen. Malik's escape to Tripoli Boys School occurred in the aftermath of the horrific deprivations of wartime rural Lebanon, and his progressive education at the AUB included participation in a novel village welfare program that highlighted the economic and social marginalization of the Lebanese hinterland. Further, the global economic depression of the 1930s was experienced with particular acuteness in the Malik family which, despite having achieved high levels of education—his father was a medical doctor, his elder sister was a college graduate, remained economically vulnerable until well after the Second World War. For his part, Romulo experienced less economic insecurity, but found that class and education failed to protect either him personally, or Filipinos generally, from the racist biases as assumptions of colonial authorities. Further, his commitment to Filipino nationalism—a commitment he regarded as his birthright given the participation of his father and grandfather in the original anti-Spanish

---

[20] Charles Malik, "A Near East Witness to Christian Missions," *Today* 5 (1949): 527-28; Charles Malik to Asadollah [?], 26 May 1931, Folder 7, Box 53, Malik Papers; Charles Malik to James K. Quay, 14 Apr. 1937, Folder 9, Box 38, Malik Papers.

and then anti-American insurgency—provided a political locus to his personal journey of educational development. "I am a nationalist," he wrote prior to independence, "because I was educated in America and have absorbed the principles of democracy and liberty that are so thoroughly a part of America."[21]

Critically, what emerged through this double gesture of individualism and responsibility was a personal and political identity that sought to activate the experience of colonial education through the reconciliation of East and West. Upon returning to their respective countries, both self-consciously adopted the mantle of the translator or mediator, Romulo as journalist and newspaper editor intending on presenting and explaining Filipino nationalism in the language of American democracy, and Malik as an educator and philosopher dedicated to disseminating what he considered the true heritage of the West to the Arab world. Romulo, working for the most prominent Filipino politician of the period, Manuel Quezón, advocated for Filipino independence on the basis of the American principles, which he claimed were instilled in him by his education, of freedom, equality and self-determination. Once a commitment to independence was secured with the 1934 Tydings-McDuffie Act, Romulo transcribed this language to the global stage by linking the emerging discourse of universal human rights to the project of decolonization generally. Malik's efforts leading up to his UN appointment consisted in attempting, as the head of the AUB's philosophy department, to reorganize and rededicate the University to a new spiritual mission: "...to liberate the souls of men and women, and to set their minds on the secure path of freedom." At the core of this project was an absolute commitment to freedom of thought and conscience, which would foster the development of "liberal, humane" values within the Near East and provide an ethical core to the economic and political transformations the region was undergoing.[22]

---

[21] The village welfare program is described by Malik's childhood friend and classmate Afif Tannous in his memoir, *Village Roots and Beyond* (Beirut, Dar Nelson, 2004), 116-20. Tannous would go on to do rural development work for the US State Department. Carlos Romulo, *I Saw the Philippines Fall* (New York: Doubleday, Doran & Co., 1943), 19.

[22] . Carlos Romulo, *Mother America* (New York: Doubleday, Doran & Co., 1943), 78-79; Charles Malik, "Freedom of Thought," 1944, Folder 4, Box 208, Malik Papers; Charles Malik, "The Idea of the School of Arts and Sciences of the AUB," 1942, Folder 4, Box 124, Malik Papers.

As they journeyed from Asia to San Francisco—one travelling east the other travelling west—both Charles Malik and Carlos Romulo found in the emergent discourse of human rights an ideal international and diplomatic medium for their colonial humanist form of political agency. Indeed, both Malik and Romulo saw the possibility of an international human rights law as a potential resource for the creation of a post-colonial world order in which individuals and nations long excluded from the opportunity of full development—both in its economic and subjective sense—might have that opportunity. Understanding themselves as having developed personally by exploiting to the fullest a series of educational advantages that were presented to them by privilege or by chance, they sought to make such opportunities a matter of right for all people. But if, therefore, the UN human rights regime took shape in part from a colonial subjectivity striving for a post-colonial one, it was a striving through progressive continuity rather than a revolutionary rupture. Human rights, at least as articulated by Malik and Romulo, buried the colonial world even as it kept alive, in its globalization, the legacy of the colonial dynamic.

Biography and Human Rights

The biographical sketches above suggest that the emergence of human rights discourse during the 1940s was bound up not only with the human catastrophe of the Second World War, but also with the transition from a colonial to a post-colonial world order. In the cases of Carlos Romulo and Charles Malik, the effort to create an international human rights regime provided a political and ethical program through which they could activate their experience of colonial education in a way that pointed toward a future beyond empire. The language of rights was one that came easily to these two individuals, not only because it reflected an American political discourse they had learned as students of American teachers, but because it described a subject position—autonomous, cosmopolitan and modern—to which they could aspire and from which they could pursue their political and personal agendas. As a *mode d'assujettissment*, Malik and Romulo's engagement with human rights was undoubtedly a process by which the two came to see themselves as bearers of rights—i.e., as human beings— but also as bearers of a responsibility to extend and defend the rights of other human beings. Thus human rights not only interpellated them into particular identities, but also structured and enabled a schema for agency in which action was both normatively understandable and practically possible. In 'subjecting' themselves to the rule and rules of human rights,

Malik and Romulo achieved not only a 'subjectivity' capable of moral and political action, but also the kind of 'personality' implied by Articles 22, 26 and 29 of the UDHR, which call for an international order dedicated to the "free and full development" of the "human personality."

But if human rights were an ethical code to which individuals in the Third World and beyond could subject themselves, in the immediate aftermath of the Second World War it was a sufficiently inchoate and plastic code to ensure that the kinds of subjectivization that it authorized were hardly mere duplicates of an ideal type struck from the mould of the West. If Foucault's concept of the *mode d'assujettissement* is to be useful here, it will have to be reconfigured to accommodate this fact that ethical codes—most especially human rights—are not static, and that the process of subjectivization proceeds as negotiation rather than as fiat. Malik and Romulo's active attempts to shape the scope and content of the nascent UN human rights regime is indicative of precisely this dynamic, and to the extent that the human rights framework continues to operate as a *mode d'assujettissment* in the Third World, it is not simply because of ongoing Western or US global hegemony, but because human rights remains amenable to a relatively wide range of practices and re-articulations. This hospitality of the human rights ethic, allows for an as yet unexhausted range of possible configurations of both personal subjectivity and social justice, and continues to be a powerful force for imagining and pursuing novel relations between and within the First, Second and Third Worlds.

Mapping these worlds—and the opportunities for justice they open up and foreclose—will require a scholarly ecumenism that extends and deepens the interdisciplinary trends described at the outset of this essay. And while the legacy of post-structuralism and the linguistic turn within the humanities and social sciences includes an increased awareness of the autonomy of discourses and their importance for the re-creation, transformation and perpetuation of structures of authority and power, the disappearance of the subject has left a lacuna in the literature that needs to be filled if we are to understand how human rights work as a set of manifold discourses, structures and practices. Exploring the intersections of ethics, politics and subjectivities may well require a more rigorous engagement with the methodologies of biography, not necessarily to reinstate the universal man of the Enlightenment to the center of history, but in order to scrutinize the ways in which subjectivities constitute and are constituted by their encounter with ethics—and its reformulation. A human rights biography would re-ground the study of human rights in the analysis of individual human lives as they are and have been lived. And while reconstructing these lives may require a return to a more empirical and narrative form of history, it will also of necessity engage a broad range of theories that provide insight into the opacities of global systems and structures, cultural patterns and politics, and individual agency and interiority. A tall order, to be sure, but one that offers the possibility, particularly important for considerations of human rights and the Third World, of productively disengaging from the perennial impasse between universalism and cultural relativism by eschewing the abstract essentialisms of "culture" and "humanity," in favor of the contextualizing contingencies of specific lives lived as particular bodies, in particular places, at particular times.

Bibliography

Baxi, Upendra. *The Future of Human Rights.* Oxford: Oxford University Press, 2002.

Cmiel, Kenneth. "Human Rights, Freedom of Information, and the Origins of Third-World Solidarity." In *Truth Claims: Representation and Human Rights*, edited by Mark Bradley and Patrice Petro. Piscataway: Rutgers University Press, 2002.

Fortna, Benjamin. "Education and Autobiography at the End of the Ottoman Empire." *Die Welt des Islams* 41(2001): 1-31.

Foucault, Michel. "On the Genealogy of Ethics: Overview of Work in Progress." In *The Foucault Reader*, edited by Paul Rabinow. New York: Pantheon Books, 1984.

—. *The Use of Pleasure: The History of Sexuality Volume 2*, trans. Robert Hurley. New York: Vintage Books, 1990.

Glendon, Mary Ann. *A World Made New: Eleanor Roosevelt and the Universal Declaration of Human Rights*. New York: Random House, 2001.

Goodale, Mark. *Surrendering to Utopia: An Anthropology of Human Rights*. Stanford: Stanford University Press, 2009.

Hilderbrand, Robert C. *Dumbarton Oaks: The Origins of the United Nations and the Search for Postwar Security*. Chapel Hill: University of North Carolina Press, 1990.

Humphrey, John P. *Human Rights and the United Nations: A Great Adventure*. Dobbs Ferry: Transnational Publishers, 1984.

Kabasakal Arat, Zehra F. "Forging a Global Culture of Human Rights: Origins and Prospects of the International Bill of Rights." *Human Rights Quarterly* 28 (2006): 416-437.

Malik, Charles. Charles Malik to Asadollah [?]. 26 May 1931, Folder 7, Box 53, Malik Papers.

—. Charles Malik to James K. Quay. 14 Apr. 1937, Folder 9, Box 38, Malik Papers.

—. "A Near East Witness to Christian Missions," *Theology Today* 5 (1949): 527-28.

—. "Freedom of Thought," 1944, Folder 4, Box 208, Malik Papers;

—. "The Idea of the School of Arts and Sciences of the AUB," 1942, Folder 4, Box 124, Malik Papers.

—. Papers of Charles H. Malik, Manuscript Division, Library of Congress, Washington, DC.

—. *The Challenge of Human Rights: Charles Malik and the Universal Declaration*, edited by Habib C. Malik. Oxford: The Charles Malik Foundation, 2000.

May, Glenn Anthony. *Social Engineering in the Philippines*. Westport, Greenwood Press, 1980.

Mitoma, Glenn. "Civil Society and International Human Rights: The Commission to Study the Organization of Peace and the Origins of the UN Human Rights Regime" *Human Rights Quarterly* 30 (2008), 607-30.

Morsink, Johannes. *The Universal Declaration of Human Rights: Origins, Drafting and Intent.* Philadelphia: University of Pennsylvania Press, 1999.

Pechota, Vratislav. "The Development of the Covenant on Civil and Political Rights." In *The International Bill of Rights: The Covenant on Civil and Political Rights*, edited by Louis Henkin. New York: Columbia University Press, 1981.

Presbyterian Historical Society. "Institutions under Care of the Syria Mission of the Board of the Foreign Mission of the Presbyterian Church in the U.S.A." 30 January 1924, Box 8, Folder 11, RG 115, United Presbyterian Church in the U.S.A. Syria Mission, Records, 1808-1967 (Bulk 1823-1959), Philadelphia.

Romulo, Carlos. *I Saw the Philippines Fall* (New York: Doubleday, Doran & Co., 1943.

—. *Mother America.* New York: Doubleday, Doran & Co., 1943.

—. "Human Rights as a Condition of Peace in the Far East," *Annals of the American Academy of Political and Social Sciences* 243 (1946): 9-10.

—. *I Walked with Heroes.* New York: Holt, Rinehart, Winston, 1961.

—. Papers of Carlos P. Romulo, Manuscript Collection, University of the Philippines, Diliman, Manila.

Sauvy, Alfred. "The Third Worldist Movement." *Current History* 98 (1999): 360. Originally published as Alfred Sauvy. "Trois Mondes, Une Planète." *L'Observateur*, August 14, 1952, 14.

Tannous, Afif. *Village Roots and Beyond.* Beirut, Dar Nelson, 2004.

United Nations Conference on International Organization, San Francisco, California, April 25 to June 26, 1945, Selected Documents. Vol. 1. Washington: United States Government Printing Office, 1946.

United Nations Document *A/C.3/76* (1946).

—. *E/CN.4/AC.2/SR.9* (1947).

—. *E/CN.4/SR.1* (1947).

—. *E/CN.4/SR.14* (1947).

—. *E/CN.4/AC.1/SR.38* (1948).

—. *E/CN.4/SR.37* (1948).

—. *E/CN.4/SR.42* (1948).

—. *E/CN.4/SR.50* (1948).

United Nations, *Plenary Meetings of the General Assembly, Verbatim Record, 23 October – 16 December 1946.* Flushing Meadow: United Nations, 1948.

Waltz, Susan. "Reclaiming and Rebuilding the History of the Universal Declaration of Human Rights." *Third World Quarterly* 23 (2002): 437-48.

POSTFACE

I confess, it was whispered to me, that I was bound in Duty as a Subject of *England*, to have given in a Memorial to a Secretary of State, at my first coming over; because, whatever Lands are discovered by a Subject, belong to the Crown... But I had another Reason which made me less forward to enlarge his Majesty's Dominions by my Discoveries: To say the Truth, I had conceived a few Scruples with relation to the distributive Justice of Princes upon those Occasions. For Instance, A Crew of Pyrates are driven by a Storm they know not whither; at length a Boy discovers Land from the Top-mast; then go on Shore to rob and plunder; they see an harmless People, are entertained with Kindness, they give the Country a new Name, they take formal Possession of it for the King, they set up a rotten Plank or a Stone for a Memorial, they murder two or three Dozen of the Natives, bring away a Couple more by Force for Sample, return home, and get their Pardon. Here commences a new Dominion acquired with a Title by *Divine Right*. Ships are sent with the first Opportunity; the Natives driven out or destroyed, their Princes tortured to discover their Gold; a free Licence given to all Acts of Inhumanity and Lust; the Earth reeking with Blood of its Inhabitants: And this execrable Crew of Butchers employed in so pious an Expedition, is a *modern Colony* sent to convert and civilize an idolatrous and barbarous People.

But this Description, I confess, doth by no means affect the *British* Nation, who may be an Example to the whole World for their Wisdom, Care, and Justice in planting Colonies; their liberal Endowments for the Advancement of Religion and Learning; their Choice of devout and able Pastors to propagate *Christianity*; their Caution in sticking their Provinces with Peoples of sober Lives and Conversations from this the Mother Kingdom; their strict Regard to the Distribution of Justice, in supplying the Civil Administration through all their Colonies with Officers of the greatest Abilities, utter strangers to Corruption: And to crown all, by sending the most vigilant and virtuous Governors, who have no other Views than the Happiness of the People over whom they preside, and the Honour of the King their Master.

—Jonathan Swift, *Gulliver's Travels*.

CONTRIBUTORS

Zehra F. Kabasakal Arat is Juanita and Joseph Leff Professor of Political Science at Purchase College, State University of New York. Her books include *Democracy and Human Rights in Developing Countries* (iUniverse, 2003), *Human Rights Worldwide: A Reference Handbook* (ABC-CLIO, 2006) and *Human Rights in Turkey* (University of Pennsylvania Press, 2007).

José-Manuel Barreto is Research Fellow, Goldsmiths College, University of London. He is the author of *De los Derechos, las Garantías y los Deberes* (with Libardo Sarmiento, Comisión Colombiana de Juristas, 1998). His works have appeared in collections such as *Critical Legal Theory* (Routledge, 2011) and *Critical International Law: Post-Realism, Post-Colonialism, and Transnationalism* (Oxford University Press, forthcoming 2013).

Upendra Baxi held the position of Professor of Law at the University of Delhi and served as Professor of Law in Development, University of Warwick. His publications include *The Future of Human Rights* (Oxford University Press, 2012) and *Human Rights in a Posthuman World: Critical Essays* (Oxford University Press, 2007).

Anthony Bogues is Harmon Family Professor of Africana Studies and Director of the Center for the Study of Slavery and Justice, Brown University . He is the author of *Caliban's Freedom: The Early Political Thought of C.L.R. James* (Pluto, 1997), *Black Heretics and Black Prophets: Radical Political Intellectuals* (Routledge, 2003) and *Empire of Liberty: Power, Freedom, and Desire* (University Press of New England, 2010).

Sabine Broeck is Professor of American Studies at the University of Bremen. She is the author of *White Amnesia - Black Memory? Women's Writing and History* (Peter Lang, 1999) and *Der entkolonisierte Koerper. Die Protagonistin in der afro-amerikanischen weiblichen Erzähltradition der 30er bis 80er Jahre* (Campus, 1988). She is currently President of the International Collegium for African-American Research (CAAR).

Enrique Dussel is Professor in the Department of Philosophy at the Autonomous Metropolitan University, Mexico. His publications include *Ethics of Liberation in the age of Globalization and Exclusion* (Duke University Press, 2012), *Twenty Theses on Politics* (Duke University Press, 2008) and *The Invention of the Americas. Eclipse of "the Other" and the Myth of Modernity* (Continuum, 1995).

Nico Horn is Professor in the Faculty of Law, University of Namibia. He is the author of *Human Rights and the Rule of Law in Namibia* (with A Bösl, MacMillan 2008) and *The Human Face in the Globalizing World, Ten Years of Human Rights Education* (with M.O. Hinz and C. Mchombu, University of Namibia, 2002).

Vincent Lloyd is Assistant Professor of Religion, Syracuse University. He is the author of *The Problem with Grace: Reconfiguring Political Theology* (Stanford University Press, 2011) and *Law and Transcendence: On the Unfinished Project of Gillian Rose* (Palgrave Macmillan, 2009).

Eduardo Mendieta is Professor of Philosophy at the State University of New York. He is the author of *Global Fragments: Latinamericanism, Globalizations, and Critical Theory* (SUNY Press, 2007) and *Adventures of Transcendental Philosophy: Karl-Otto Apel's Semiotics and Discourse Ethics* (Rowman and Littlefield, 2002).

Walter Mignolo is William Wannamaker Professor of Literature, Duke University. His publications include *The Darker Side of Western Modernity: Global Futures, Decolonial Options* (Duke University Press, 2012), *The Idea of Latin America* (Blackwell, 2005) and *Local Histories/Global Designs* (Princeton University Press, 2000).

Glenn Mitoma is Assistant Professor, Human Rights Institute, University of Connecticut. His research interests include the history and contemporary working of universal human rights as discourse, structure, and practices, and is currently focused on developing a "human rights biography" of Charles H. Malik.

William Twinning is Emeritus Quain Professor of Jurisprudence, University College London. His publications include *General Jurisprudence: Understanding Law from a Global Perspective*, (Cambridge University Press, 2009) and *How to Do Things With Rules* (with David Miers, CUP, 2010). He is the editor of *Human Rights: Southern Voices* (CUP, 2009).

Susan Waltz is Professor of International Relations and Public Policy, University of Michigan. She has written "Universal Human Rights: The Contribution of Muslim States." (*Human Rights Quarterly*, 2004) and "Reclaiming and Rebuilding the History of the Universal Declaration of Human Rights," *Third World Quarterly*, 2002. She currently sits on the Board of Amnesty International-USA.

Martin Woessner is Assistant Professor of History & Society, The City College of New York's Center for Worker Education (CUNY). He is the author of *Heidegger in America* (Cambridge University Press, 2011).

INDEX OF NAMES

Clavijero, 204, 205, 206
Cmiel, 426, 437
Coicaud, 401, 403, 406, 414, 415
Collier, 216, 233
Collins, 194, 206
Columbus, 24, 46, 151, 152, 169, 171,
    213, 357, 384
Constant, 209, 233
Cooray, 345, 346, 350
Córdoba, 175, 185
Cottrell, 259, 276, 278, 279, 280, 303,
    306, 307
Cover, 331
Cox, 380, 384, 401, 414
Cranston, 402, 414
Curtin, 227, 234
Cushman, 69, 97
Dae Jung, 271
Dalai Lama, 23, 141
Dallmayr, 90, 96, 97
Danto, 118, 119, 120, 131, 132, 133,
    137
Darian-Smith, 5, 144, 169
Das Basu, 326
Dassow Walls, 96, 97
Daube, 285
Davies, 357, 381, 383, 384
Davison, 400
Davitt, 268, 304
Dayan, 215, 217, 234
De Andrade, 31, 38
De Gaulle, 367
De Padua, 186, 207
De Pauw, 205, 207
De Santo Tomás, 165
De Tocqueville, 230, 231, 236
De Vaissiere, 220
Deane, 336, 343, 344
Decorme, 204, 206
Deleuze, 24
Dembour, 305
Deng, 16, 42, 256, 287, 297, 308
Derrida, 8, 20, 42, 140, 164, 171, 286
Descartes, 3, 9, 54, 86, 174, 193, 203
Dessalines, 218, 221
Devi, 332

Dewey, 65, 97, 433
Dhandha, 304
Dhavan, 326
Diamond, 406, 417
Diderot, 33
Dietze, 93, 97
Donnelly, 353, 354, 379, 384, 385,
    389, 401, 414
Dorfman, 23
Douglas, 23, 24, 39
Douglass, 210, 234, 240, 247, 254
Douzinas, 8, 19, 39, 95, 98, 151, 169,
    253, 254
Downie, 402, 414
Doyle, 401, 414
Drahos, 314, 334
Drinan, 389, 414
Du Bois, 23, 141, 248, 254, 255, 424
Dukeston, 369
Dundas Renteln, 268
Dunn, 223, 234
Dunne, 389, 414
Dussel, 7, 14, 23, 34, 37, 39, 90, 97,
    98, 99, 142, 143, 168, 169, 172,
    173, 175, 176, 177, 179, 185, 188,
    198, 206
Dworkin, 286, 405, 406, 414
Ealy, 372, 385
Ebadi, 302
Ehrenzweig, 284
Ehret, 222, 234
Eide, 358, 385
Eisenhower, 357, 386
Elazar, 240, 254
Elias, 113, 116
Engineer, 408, 414
England, 128
Engle, 411, 414
Enwezor, 7, 31, 38, 39, 143, 169
Equiano, 23, 141
Eschweiler, 193, 206
Escobar, 3, 6, 39, 142, 170
Esposito, 408, 417
Evans, 163, 170, 354, 355, 356, 357,
    373, 380, 385, 389, 401, 403, 414
Evatt, 338, 351